Richard 👉 C0-AUT-725

WOODWORKING TECHNOLOGY

HAMMOND / DONNELLY / HARROD / RAYNER

Excerpts from:

The Deacon's Masterpiece

Or, The Wonderful "One-Hoss Shay"

So the Deacon inquired of the village folk
Where he could find the strongest oak,
That couldn't be split nor bent nor broke, —
    That was for spokes and floor and sills;
    He sent for lancewood to make the thills;

The crossbars were ash, from the straightest trees,
The panels of white-wood, that cuts like cheese,
But lasts like iron for things like these;
    The hubs of logs from the "Settler's ellum," —
    Last of its timber, — they couldn't sell 'em,

Never an axe had seen their chips,
And the wedges flew from between their lips,
Their blunt ends frizzled like celery-tips;
    Step and prop-iron, bolt and screw,
    Spring, tire, axle, and litchpin too,
    Steel of the finest, bright and blue;

Thoroughbrace bison-skin, thick and wide;
Boot, top, dasher, from tough old hide
Found in the pit when the tanner died.
    That was the way he "put her through."
    "There!" said the Deacon, "naow she'll dew!"

Oliver Wendell Holmes

WOODWORKING TECHNOLOGY

HAMMOND / DONNELLY / HARROD / RAYNER

James J. Hammond
Chancellor
Massachusetts State College System
Boston, Massachusetts

Edward T. Donnelley
Formerly Professor and Director
  of Industrial Arts
Fitchburg State College
Fitchburg, Massachusetts

Walter F. Harrod
Formerly Associate Professor
  of Industrial Arts
Fitchburg State College
Fitchburg, Massachusetts

Norman A. Rayner
Formerly Head of Industrial Arts Department
Wachusett Regional High School
Holden, Massachusetts

McKNIGHT Publishing Company

FOURTH EDITION

Copyright 1980, 1972, 1966, 1961

by McKnight Publishing Company

Lithographed in U.S.A.

Library of Congress
Catalog Card Number: 79-66294

SBN: 87345-893-1

Robert W. Todd
Editor

Production: Deborah Nelson
Layout: Elizabeth Purcell
Copy Editing: Joan Dunbar
Design: Jim Coventry
Art: Howard Davis

FOREWORD

Woodworking Technology *is designed to provide complete and easily accessed information related to the area of woodworking. Wood materials, processes, tools, and machinery are presented in a straightforward, topical orgnization that complements instructional procedures and is suitable for quick, easy reference.*

Many topics contain clear, step-by-step procedures for specific operations. Topics also contain relevant background information on tools, machines, materials, and career opportunities. The topics are grouped into 19 sections according to process or subject. These topics need not be read in sequence; students may concentrate their learning on information or procedures of immediate interest.

Woodworking Technology *covers virtually all types of woodworking tools. Hand tools, portable power tools, and stationary power tools are discussed in detail, giving the reader important knowledge and the confidence needed to operate each tool safely and effectively. A sharpening section describes methods and techniques of keeping these tools in good condition.*

The processing of wood is also given detailed attention. Methods of cutting, shaping, forming, and finishing wood are explained in terms of theory and procedure. The easy-to-follow instructions are well illustrated. Many unique operations, such as carving a decorative sunburst or shell, making a cabriole leg, hand cutting dovetails, and applying inlay and insets, are included in addition to the basic processing operations.

Safety is emphasized throughout Woodworking Technology. *Safety considerations are included with information on each potentially dangerous process or machine. OSHA regulations for woodworking tools and machinery are also included, as a guide for proper machine setup, operation, and maintenance. In addition to the safety factors and OSHA regulations that punctuate the text, a separate section has been devoted to general safety in order to prepare students for safe activity in the shop or laboratory.*

The metric system is incorporated in Woodworking Technology *in a manner consistent with industrial practices. For the most part the lumber and construction industries have been slow in adopting the metric system of measurement. For this reason, and in order to avoid confusion associated with determining equivalents, the use of metrics in this text is limited.*

A wood species section is included, providing students with photographs and up-to-date information about 69 wood species. The wood samples are presented in full color and represent the common and many of the not-so-common woods. Each wood species is paired with a description about its use, workability, and source. Photographs of many unique and skillfully made wood products are also included to provide students with examples of quality workmanship and wood selection.

In addition to providing motivating examples for making wood products, Woodworking Technology *also encourages student activity in the shop or laboratory through its presentation and design. Quick, easy referencing of tools, materials, and processes, as well as clear illustrations and procedures, make it an invaluable companion during the actual building of projects or during other hands-on experiences.*

Woodworking Technology *contains comprehensive instructional material appropriate for courses on the senior high, junior college, and college levels. This text is also appropriate for vocational woodworking classes or may be used for reference purposes.*

The authors are extremely appreciative of the assistance received during the development of this text. Special thanks are extended to Dr. Bruce Hoadley of the University of Massachusetts, Brad Brakke and Michael Morrilly of Lilly Chemical Products, Nathan Pickel of Bostich Division of Textron, John Greenland, John Lucchini, and Walter Pollard.

Thanks are also extended to Dr. Wayne Andrews of Illinois State University and Cory Bloom of Olympia High School, Stanford, Illinois, for their help with photographs, and to Dr. Everett Israel, Chairman of the Department of Industrial Technology, Illinois State University, for his generous support and cooperation.

The Authors

v

TABLE OF CONTENTS

TABLE OF CONTENTS

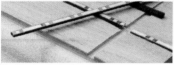

TABLE OF CONTENTS

SECTION ONE.

Wood and Wood Materials

Topic 1.

Wood, Trees, and Lumber

The Nature of Wood

Wood is made up of long cells growing close together, forming a material that is both porous and compact. Wood has been referred to as an elastic, plastic honeycomb. The relatively light weight of most wood is explained by the fact that approximately half its volume is made up of these hollow cells. If wood were dried and crushed into a solid material, it would weigh approximately one-and-a-half times as much as an equal volume of water and consequently would sink. It is because of this hollow cell structure that most woods are buoyant, can take finishing materials, and can hold nails, screws, glue, and other fasteners.

Though most wood is readily recognized as wood, every piece is different from every other. This is because each piece comes from a living plant that differs from other plants in species or in growing conditions. Trees belong

Fine Hardwoods/American Walnut Association

Fig. 1-2.   Small-scale logging operation.

to botanical families, and lumber from each family has its own identifying characteristics. Each tree is different from other trees of the same family. Pieces of wood cut from the same section of a tree will often differ in color, grain, and figure.

Wood is named and classified according to the species of tree from which it is cut. **Hardwood** comes from **deciduous** (broad-leaved) trees, and **softwood** comes from **coniferous** (needle-bearing) trees. This classification is a botanical one and does not indicate the degree of hardness of the wood. Some of those listed as hardwood are actually softer than some of those listed as softwood. Pines, firs, and other evergreens are softwood trees. Maples, oaks, elms, poplars, and other shade and fruit trees are hardwood trees.

Wood is also classified as **close-** or **open-grain.** This classification refers to the cell structure of the wood. Softwoods are termed close-grain because they have a very close-knit and nonporous cell structure. Hardwoods, on the other hand, are generally termed open-

Fig. 1-1.   Coniferous forest.

Western Wood Products Association.

grain woods because of their porous cell structure. Oak and mahogany are easily identified as being open-grain because of visible, open pores on the surface of these woods. Cherry and maple, however, have such small cell structures that they are considered close-grain even though they are from the hardwood family.

It is impossible to identify woods by chemical analysis. Woods may be identified only by physical characteristics such as cell structure and cell pattern, color, grain, figure, and sometimes by odor or taste. Shakes, stains, sap streaks, pitch pockets, knots, cross grain, bird pecks, and other blemishes are frequently present. These characteristics either improve the quality of the lumber or are considered defects.

Wood does not decay naturally through age, nor will it decay if it is constantly kept dry or is continuously submerged in water. The principal conditions affecting the rate of decay are **moisture, temperature,** and **air supply.** Damp or wet wood is likely to become a nest for wood ants, termites, and other insects. Such wood is subject to the action of fungi, which cause it to become spongy and decomposed (dry rot).

Wood is tested for various types of strength and is rated according to physical, mechanical, and chemical properties. In general, wood is very strong and durable. It can be worked with tools and with machines, and can be compressed,

Fig. 1-4. Seedlings growing in a forest-regeneration greenhouse.

bent, and joined. Wood is also graded in terms of its fabricating properties. Authorities have established data on the degree of success with which nails, screws, glue, paint, and other materials can be applied to specific woods. Data is also available on the insulation and fire-resistant qualities of wood. The commercial users of wood utilize available scientific data to select lumber that will provide them with the best working material for their purpose.

Tree Growth

Most species of trees grow from seeds. These seeds must be deposited and exposed to suitable environmental conditions before germination and continued growth can occur. Most species of trees find certain conditions more favorable for growth than other conditions. Those which are favored thrive and become dominant. This may result in predominance of only one or a few species of trees in any given location. This accounts for the difference in plant species from one region to another both within the United States and throughout the world.

The growth of the tree takes place at the tips of the tree's branches, its roots, and around its circumference. The tree becomes taller and fuller as new buds produce growth at the tip of the branches, and thicker as layers of wood are added to the perimeter of the tree. This type of growth also accounts for expansion of the tree's root system.

Fig. 1-3. The strength and versatility of wood make it a primary construction material.

How the log is used

Debarking the log is essential to its full utilization because bark cannot be used for paper-making, and therefore any piece dropped in the chipper has to be free of bark. But the bark can be used for fuel and soil mulch.

The rounded sides of the log, called "slabs," are the first pieces sent to the chipper as the log goes through the saw-mill. This idealized picture shows the entire log being used for lumber, except for the slabs. Actually, as cutting continues, other pieces go to the chipper, including edgings, trim ends, and other parts of the log not usable as lumber. Each log presents different problems and can be handled differently.

The outer portions of the log have the fewest knots. This "clear" lumber is usually made into boards or planks varying in thickness from one to three inches.

Toward the center of the log, knots increase and the wood is less suitable for boards. Heavier planks, and square or rectangular beams are normally sawed from this section. The center of the log is used primarily for structural beams strong enough so that they are not weakened by knots. Knots are most frequent here because this is the oldest section of the tree. Branches that were removed during the early years of the tree's life left knots that were covered over as the tree grew outward.

Plywood is, in effect, a sandwich of thin wooden veneers. Veneer is made by "peeling," that is, holding a long blade against a rotating log. The wood is continuously peeled off, down to an eight-inch core. The core is then treated as though it were a small log. It can be made into lumber and, of course, the rounded portions go to the chipper.

St. Regis Paper Company

Fig. 1-5.   Example of cutting method that best utilizes the trunk portion of the tree.

Trees do not become taller by elongation of the tree trunk. This is best demonstrated by observing a fence wire that has been attached to a tree. Over a period of years, the position of the wire will not change in its relationship to the undisturbed ground beneath it. Observing the same wire over a period of years will reveal something else about the growth of the tree. As the trunk of the tree becomes thicker it may slowly surround the wire. Therefore, part of a tree may become larger at the location it was produced but will not move higher on the tree.

The Structure of Wood

A tree is composed of many parts. Figure 1-6 provides a detailed look at the woody portion of the tree. It is from the tree trunk that we obtain construction lumber, material for veneer and plywood, and pulpwood used in the production of paper products.

A major portion of the woody structure of the tree is composed of lifeless **heartwood.** The heartwood is the oldest part of the tree and provides structural support. Surrounding the heartwood is an area of wood called **sapwood.** This is newly produced wood. It will become heartwood as the tree grows older. Sandwiched between the sapwood and the protective bark of the tree is a layer of specialized cells known as the **cambium.** This cambium layer completely envelops the tree.

Two major cell groups are produced in the cambium. **Phloem** cells are produced toward the outside of the cambium and are responsible for conducting food, produced by the leaves, to needed areas throughout the plant. As these cells are replaced, the old phloem cells become part of the bark.

Xylem cells are produced toward the inside of the cambium layer. These cells are responsible for transporting water and minerals up through the tree from the root system. As new xylem cells are produced in the cambium, old xylem cells die and become sapwood.

Newly produced xylem cells are quite large during the tree's peak growing period. This layer of large cells is known as **springwood.** See Fig. 1-7. As conditions become less favorable for growth, the xylem cells being produced become smaller. These cells form what is known as **summerwood.** A cross section of a tree trunk will reveal a series of rings, the result of this difference in growth rate. The unique growth pattern of springwood and summerwood makes it possible to distinguish one growing season from another. When the tree is cut, these annual rings may be counted. The number of rings a tree has tells the age of the tree. Forest managers can determine the age of a living tree by taking a small boring from the center of the tree and counting the growth divisions, Fig. 1-8.

St. Regis Paper Company

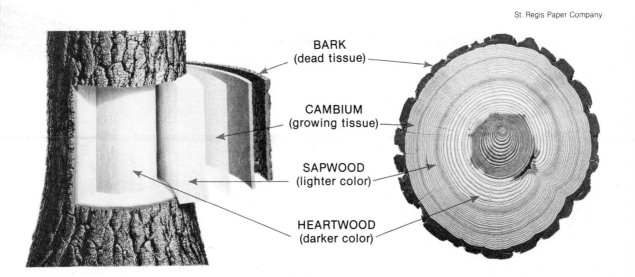

BARK
(dead tissue)

CAMBIUM
(growing tissue)

SAPWOOD
(lighter color)

HEARTWOOD
(darker color)

Fig. 1-6.   Cutaway view (left) and cross section (right) of tree trunk.

The growth pattern of springwood and summerwood also determines the relative porosity of the wood. Hardwood is classified under one of the following groups:

Ring-porous wood has pores that are very large in spring growth and very small in summer growth. There is an abrupt transition between these growth patterns. This type of wood (oak and ash, for example) has very pronounced grain pattern.

Semi ring-porous wood has pores that are large in spring growth and become gradually smaller until, in late summer growth, they are very small. This type of wood includes mahogany and walnut.

Diffuse-porous wood has pores that are fairly uniform within spring and summer growth. This type of wood has a less conspicuous grain pattern and includes such woods as birch, basswood, and maple.

Softwood is considered nonporous because of its small, uniform cell structure.

The width of the annual growth rings may vary from year to year, depending on the growing conditions. Trees of the same species may show wide variation throughout the growing range, also as a result of different growing conditions. Periodic sampling by a forest manager will allow some estimation as to the production level of the forest.

Western Wood Products Association

Fig. 1-8.   A forester uses an increment borer to take a core sample of a tree. This is done to determine the current growth pattern and the age of the tree.

Forest Products Laboratory

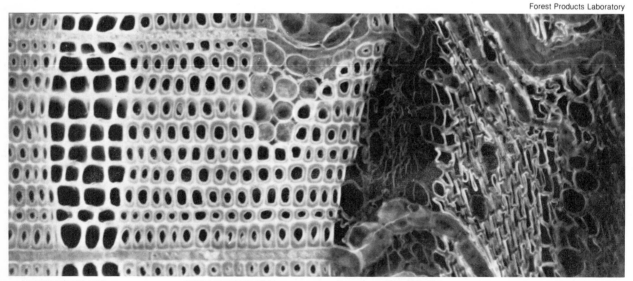

SPRINGWOOD   SUMMERWOOD   CAMBIUM   BARK

Fig. 1-7.   Magnified section through an annual ring.

Fig. 1-9. A gas analyzer system measures photo-synthetic activity of seedlings to determine how heat, cold, and drought affect growth.

Fig. 1-10. A helicopter fertilizing forestland in western Washington.

Research and Management of Forests

The management of our forests becomes increasingly important as the human need for wood products continues to expand. Product research now makes it practical to utilize a greater portion of the tree than was possible in previous years. In the days of the early pioneer, it took an average of 70 trees to build a 320-square-foot cabin. The same number of trees today supply enough wood to build a 3500-square-foot home and enough wood materials to supply a family with paper products for 30 years. In the past these wood by-products were simply burned.

Further research and management has led to the concentrated reestablishment of once-prime forest areas. This research has resulted in the development of faster-growing, disease-resistant species. The use of insecticides and fertilizers has also contributed to this increased growth rate. Advanced logging techniques and improved fire-prevention and fire-control procedures have reduced damage to the forest areas. All of these factors, combined, have resulted in more efficient tree production.

Log Measure

To find the number of feet (board measure) in a log of a given size, measure its diameter at the small end. Subtract 4″ from this amount and square the remainder. Multiply the result by the length of the log. Divide by 16. The result will be the board-measure content of the log. The diameter of logs over 24′ in length is usually measured at the center.

Sawing Considerations

Trees are cut into logs. These logs are usually 8′ or more in length. The size depends largely on the relative straightness of the tree and on the ease with which it can be handled. The individual logs are either squared by slabbing, or the log is first split through the center and squared into a **cant.** In most cases, the cant is then sawed into timbers, planks, and boards. Sometimes logs are selected for special purposes and are cut accordingly. Some logs, for example, are sawed radially into clapboards.

In some cases, figure (the wood's appearance) is the factor that determines whether a log will be plain- or quartersawed. In other cases, an effort must be made to minimize warping. Slash-, radial-, and quartersawed boards each have distinctive qualities.

Lumber is graded for market according to the natural condition of the wood and the method by which it was sawed and milled. In

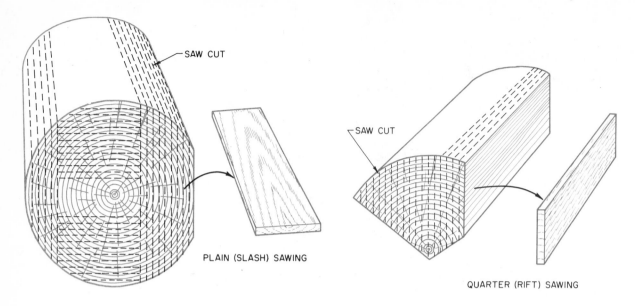

SAW CUT

PLAIN (SLASH) SAWING

SAW CUT

QUARTER (RIFT) SAWING

Fig. 1-11. Sawing methods.

In plain sawing, the boards are cut tangent to the annular growth rings. Lumber cut in this way generally has more attractive grain figure but a greater tendency to warp than quartersawed lumber. Warpage is usually opposite the annular rings.

Quartersawed lumber is cut perpendicular to the perimeter of the log. Lumber cut in this manner tends to shrink less and is stiffer than plain-sawed wood.

Western Wood Products Association

Western Wood Products Association

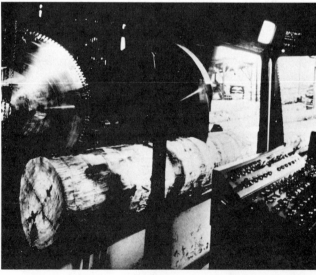

Fig. 1-12. A mechanical debarking machine removes the bark from logs before they are sawed into lumber.

Fig. 1-13. Before logs are cut into lumber, they are first cut into shorter lengths. This is called bucking.

Fig. 1-14. A high-speed band saw or head rig cuts the log into lumber. It is at this point that the sawyer decides, with the aid of an electric scanner, where to make the first and subsequent cuts.

Fig. 1-15. A sawyer controlling the cutting of lumber from an automated console. Television monitors keep the sawyer informed of related operations.

Fig. 1-17. Chipper-edger machines true up the rough edges of freshly sawed lumber.

Fig. 1-18. Multiple overhead automatic trimmer. The left-end saw cuts one end of every board while the other end is cut to standard length as determined by the operator. The saws not selected are lifted out of cutting position by the wheels riding over the face of the lumber.

Fig. 1-16. Colonial log saw. This vertical, upright log saw was powered by a waterwheel.

their cutting, sawyers take into account the properties of lumber and the probable use to be made of it. Thus, each log is cut with regard to maximum yield, grain pattern, strength, minimum warpage, or in accordance with some other purpose. See Fig. 1-11.

Seasoning of Lumber

The wood cells of a tree contain water in both the cell cavity and the cell walls. When the tree is cut down, the water remains, and the moisture content of the wood may be well over 100%. Such a tree is said to be **dead green**. The evaporation of this moisture must be controlled if good lumber is to be obtained, as rapid drying causes checking and cracks. To help prevent this rapid drying, freshly cut logs are commonly submerged in water until they are to be cut into lumber dimensions. During this time, the green log absorbs additional moisture.

After the log has been cut into lumber, the boards are piled horizontally and placed in vertical storage racks. (See "Air-Drying," this topic.) Here, the water in the cell cavity evaporates. During this process of evaporation, the lumber is dimensionally stable (does not change in size). The only change is in the decrease in moisture content and weight. When the cell cavity is dry and the cell walls still contain all the molecular water they can hold, it is said to have reached its **fiber saturation point** (f.s.p.). At this point, the moisture content will be between 25% and 28%, depending on the species.

As the lumber continues to dry, the molecular water leaves the cell walls, and the stock will decrease in width, thickness, and weight. Stock that has been **slash sawed** (cut tangent to the annual rings) will shrink in width approximately 8% from the f.s.p. to ovendry. This is due to the fact that the **medullary rays,** which radiate out from the center of the tree, do not shrink lengthwise. Hence, there is decreased width shrinkage in quartersawed lumber. The shrinkage in thickness, however, is likely to be double that of slash-sawed lumber.

In the early stages of the drying process, the outside of the lumber first dries and then shrinks, producing a state of tension on the surface. The center remains wet and does not shrink, which results in a state of internal compression. As the drying process continues, the center dries and shrinks, producing a state of internal tension. The outside, which is already

Fig. 1-19. Test samples.
Examples of case hardening and reverse case hardening, resulting from internal stresses of compression and tension set up by adverse drying conditions.

dry, does not shrink, and a state of compression results. This condition is called **case hardening,** Fig. 1-19.

Controlled drying conditions (regulation of temperature and humidity) reduce the intensity of these forces. Continued adverse drying conditions may cause the pressure to push beyond the elastic limits of the wood fibers, resulting in surface checking and internal collapse. (This is called **honeycombing**).

The drying may be done by air-seasoning or by the modern, faster, and more expensive kiln-drying process. (Air-dried lumber is better for outside work and kiln-dried for inside work.) The drying of wood is a methodical, scientific process.

> *INTERESTING FACT: While the effects of daily temperature changes must be considered in the construction of such structures as metal bridges, it is not necessary to allow for such factors in wood construction, as wood is not subject to these conditions. Temperature changes have no significant effect on wood. In terms of its length, wood is quite stable, even when subjected to high humidity. Because of this constancy of length, wood was the material chosen for the rod in the highly accurate pendulum clocks that were once common.*

Air-Drying

Air-seasoning reduces moisture content to 12% to 18%, depending upon the climatic conditions. This method consists of piling the

Fig. 1-20. Splits and checks.
Open wood cells in end grain dry rapidly, resulting in frequent splits and checks. To prevent this, the ends of green lumber are painted or sealed.

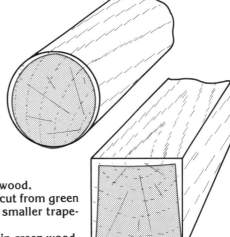

Fig. 1-21. Effects of cutting green wood.
If a true square were cut from green wood, it would become a smaller trapezoid when seasoned.
If a cylinder were cut in green wood, it would become an oval when seasoned.

Fig. 1-22. Vertical storage racks.
Mahagony is being air-dried prior to being put into kilns. Boards range from 14′ to 20′ in length. Lengthwise slope of the boards should be about one inch per foot length. Therefore, the slope measured at the base is 14″ to 20″.

Fig. 1-23. Careful piling and sticking of boards for gradual air-drying.
Piling sticks are placed close to the end of each board, for it is claimed that checks normally will run only as far as the first stick.
Pile bottoms and covering boards are very carefully arranged to provide adequate air circulation. Efficient piling makes for straight lumber, since the weight of the pile tends to keep lumber from warping during drying. Covering boards prevent the top layers of lumber from becoming spoiled as a result of water penetration.
Some piles are stacked with the rear lower than the front to make drainage easier.

lumber outside, either vertically or horizontally. If lumber is dried in vertical storage racks, the lengthwise slope should be about one inch per foot length. See Fig. 1-22. If lumber is stacked horizontally, the first layer of boards is supported about twelve inches above the ground. The boards are laid flat with a space of about 1-1/2″ between each edge. Each layer of boards is separated by wooden strips called **stickers,** about 1-1/2″ × 2″, which are laid at right angles to the length of the rows. See Fig. 1-23. This provides an air space around each board and in between the layers of boards, hastening the drying process and helping to prevent warpage. Coverings are placed over the top of each pile in order to protect the wood from the sun and rain. Air-drying may also be done in a well-ventilated building. Care must be taken that the piles of green lumber are properly spaced and stuck.

This method of drying takes from one to five years. A general rule is to allow a year for each inch of thickness. The longer the drying period, the more even the moisture content.

Forced-Air Drying

Forced-air drying (or fan-drying) is the process of accelerating seasoning or achieving faster and more uniform predrying prior to kiln-drying. In this method, fans are used to boost and to equalize the circulation of air around each board. The boards are either piled in tiers inside a building or are arranged in parallel rows outside. If they are placed outside, they must be covered for protection from rain and from the direct rays of the sun. In either case, fans approximately 48″ in diameter are arranged in such a way that the air is controlled at desirable temperatures and is thoroughly circulated. In some cases, automatic humidity controls add to the effectiveness of this method. Some authorities claim that this rapid drying is made possible by the continuous rapid movement of the air film surrounding the surface of the lumber. In still air, this film becomes saturated with moisture from the lumber. This causes it to act as an insulator, slowing the rate of evaporation. The quicker air movement hastens the drying process.

Temperature is an important factor in the drying of lumber. The greatest use of forced-air drying in the United States is in the South and Southwest. This method is most effective when the temperature is between 21°C and 35°C (70°F and 95°F). Below this temperature, this method of drying is not economical to use. Within this temperature range, forced-air drying can reduce the moisture content of stock from 40% to 15% in a matter of weeks.

Kiln-Drying

Kiln-drying begins with forced-air or fan-drying. This process is done in a specially built room or chamber. It differs from air-drying in that the process is sped up through control of the temperature, the humidity, and the air circulation. Partially dried lumber (lumber that has been air-dried for four to six weeks) is piled on racks, as in air-drying. This is done so that the air may circulate around each piece. These racks are moved into the rooms where the controlled drying process takes place. First, the lumber is heated by steam so that all pieces are the same temperature and have a uniform moisture content. Then, while air is being circulated to carry off the excess humidity, the heat is gradually decreased. See Fig. 1-24.

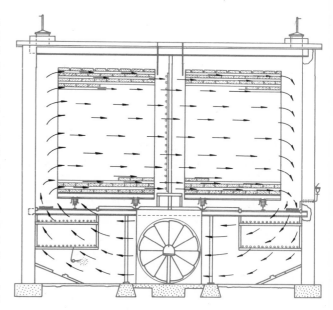

Fig. 1-24. Schematic of kiln.

To be suitable for furniture, lumber must be dried to between 5% and 8% moisture content. The kiln mechanically blows dry air back and forth and around the stuck lumber. The air's heat and humidity are controlled automatically.

Another method of kiln-drying is to pass the racks of lumber through a series of chambers. These chambers have regulated temperature and moisture conditions.

Kiln-drying reduces the moisture content of lumber to between 5% and 8% within a period of three to four weeks. (These are the figures for 1″ lumber. Thicker dimensions take proportionately longer periods.)

Radio-Frequency Dielectric Drying

The use of radio-frequency dielectric heating for drying wood has made many improvements in the quality of wood. For example, this method has improved the shear strength of wood, its impact resistance, its resistance to checking, and its surface finish. One manufacturer has dried as many as 3,500 board feet of turning squares in 24 hours, bringing the moisture content (M.C.) down from 30% to 6%. The same manufacturer has dried 6,000 board feet within 24 hours, starting with stock at 20% M.C.

When the electronic disturbance occurs, the innermost molecules begin moving. Because the heat is generated uniformly throughout, the normal problems of case hardening and checking are eliminated. Steam merely continues to push out through the pores until the piece is dry.

With uniform shrinkage and no distortion from internal stress, dry dimensions for rough (green) blocks can be computed quite accurately. By reducing the need for a large allowance in making final cuts, a greater quantity of usable wood can be produced. This decrease in waste results in a cost reduction.

This method of drying reduces end checking, eliminates staining, and improves the natural color and other physical properties of the wood.

The drying heaters are about 36″ square and stand 6′ high. The end opening is 6″ × 12″. It will accept stock up to 5″ × 10″ in cross section. The maximum practical stock length has not been established, but lengths of 5′ and 6′ have been dried.

Any wood that can easily be filled with preservatives is more tolerant to electronic drying. Therefore, open-pored woods are ideal. Softwood species present a problem with regard to electronic drying, as the pores are more closely spaced.

Moisture Content of Lumber

The approximate moisture content of lumber can be easily determined in the laboratory. Sections from three or four samples are used as test pieces. The samples are taken, across the width of the board, at least two feet from the end. Each sample should be weighed before and after it is heated. The samples should be maintained at 100° C (212° F) until the stock

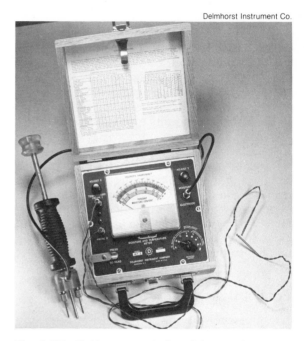

Delmhorst Instrument Co.

Fig. 1-25. Battery-operated moisture meter.

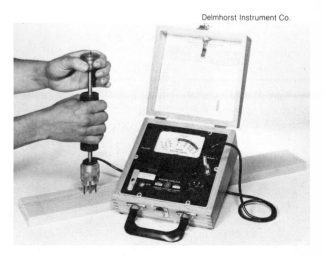

Delmhorst Instrument Co.

Fig. 1-26. Driving prongs into a board.

stops decreasing in weight. The loss in weight divided by the dry weight equals the percentage of the lumber's moisture content.

Battery-operated **moisture meters,** Figs. 1-25 and 1-26, give reasonably accurate readings of the amount of moisture in a piece of stock. The electrical resistance of wood depends on the amount of moisture in the wood. The higher the moisture content, the greater the conductivity. Hence, the moisture meter is basically an ohmmeter. (An ohmmeter measures resistance to current flow.) The two outer prongs of the moisture meter are driven into the wood to determine the moisture content below the surface. The center pin determines the moisture content on the surface. The needle indicates the average of the two.

Wood is an **anisotropic** material. That is, it does not have the same properties in every direction. This accounts for the uneven shrinkage in different dimensions.

Experiments at the Forest Products Laboratories have produced the following statistics concerning the shrinkage of green wood to its ovendry condition: Across-the-grain shrinkage of a flat-sawed board is about 8%. For a quartersawed board, shrinkage is about 4-1/2%. Most species exhibit essentially no shrinkage parallel to the grain.

Equilibrium Moisture Content

Whatever drying process is used, the lumber should be conditioned to its place of use by further storage. Wood is a **hygroscopic** material. That is, it absorbs and holds moisture from the air. Wood also tends to adapt to its surroundings. Thus, if the air surrounding a piece of wood is drier than the wood itself, the wood will release molecules of water. If the air contains more moisture than the wood, the wood will absorb moisture. This equalizing process is called **equilibrium moisture content** (E.M.C.). Because of its structure, wood absorbs and releases moisture 12 to 15 times faster on the end grain than it does on the side grain.

Wood Stabilization

Recent technical developments enable wood processors to stabilize the dimensions of wood. Polyethelene glycol 1000 serves an an

excellent agent in improving the dimensional stability of the cellulose in wood. It helps to stabilize the dimensions of the wood, even over a wide range of relative-humidity conditions. When stock is submerged in this agent, the solution saturates the wood fibers, thus replacing most of the moisture. This reduces the shrinkage that would otherwise occur when evaporation took place inside the cell walls. This treatment is most effective on green wood, but can also be used on dry wood. When used on dry wood, it reduces both swelling and shrinkage.

Palmer & Parker Lumber Co.

Fig. 1-27. These logs are part of 9,500-ton consignment of 2,000 large mahogany logs from the Ivory Coast of French West Africa. Some individual logs are 27' or 28' long and over 6' in diameter, weighing as much as 15 tons each. This shipment could provide 75,000,000 square feet of 1/28" veneer. Actually, only 25% of the wood will be suitable for veneer. Hence, 18,000,000' of veneer will be cut and the remainder will be manufactured into lumber.

Palmer & Parker Lumber Co.

Fig. 1-28. Logs soaking in a log pond prior to sawing.

Both air- and kiln-dried lumber should be stored (for air circulation) for a period of three to six months. This lumber should be stored in the same type of environment as that in which it is to be processed, so that minimal dimensional change will occur.

Dimensional change takes place as a result of the wood's continual release and absorption of moisture. It is an important factor to consider in the selection of lumber for a given job. Even after boards have been used in a piece of furniture, those which have been slash- or plain-sawed will have a tendency to cup. This is evidence of dimensional change. Quartersawed boards, however, are less prone to dimensional change and are less likely to warp. See Fig. 1-11.

Dimensional change continues as the humidity of the surrounding atmosphere changes. It cannot be completely controlled, but it can be minimized. This is done through adaptation of the structure of the article. It can also be done through the use of sealers, finishes, and laminates.

Lumber Terms, Defects, and Grading	Topic 2.

Terms Applied to Lumber

Lumber is the term applied to wood that has been sawed or split into timbers, planks, and boards. It is classified according to its degree of manufacture. The following are the classifications of lumber as it exists in various states of manufacture.

1. **Rough lumber** is lumber as it comes from the saw.
2. **Surfaced** or **dressed lumber** is lumber as it comes from the planer. It has at least one smooth side.
3. **Worked lumber** is milled on the molder to a specified edge.
4. **Shop lumber** is usually better-grade lumber, which is to undergo further cutting and manufacture.
5. **Yard lumber** is less than 5″ in thickness. Yard lumber includes strips, boards, and framing members. (Framing members are studs, joists, and rafters.) Yard lumber is graded by length and the condition of that length.
6. **Dimensioned lumber** is yard lumber that is between 2″ and 5″ thick.
7. **Structural lumber** is similar to yard lumber but is over 5″ in thickness and in width. The grading of structural lumber is based on the strength of the entire piece.
8. A **slab** is a piece of lumber cut tangent to the annual rings, running the full length of the log and containing one flat surface.
9. A **timber** is a piece of lumber 5″ or larger in its smallest dimension.
10. A **plank** is a wide piece of lumber with a thickness of between 1-1/2″ and 5″.
11. A **board** is a piece of lumber less than 1-1/2″ thick and 4″ or more in width.

12. A **sheet** is a term applied to a piece of veneer, plywood, or other manufactured board.
13. A **flitch** is a log or a thick piece of lumber that is to be cut into veneer. It may also refer to the pile of veneer cut from one log.

Terms Applied to Shaped Stock

1. A **billet** is a piece of stock cut to rough dimensions, which will later be machined to final form.
2. A **blank** is a piece of precut or partially formed stock, selected for properties such as appropriate grain structure. Blanks are used in the construction of such items as gunstocks, water skis, and tabletops.
3. A **cant** is a log that has been slabbed or a longitudinal section taken from a log.
4. A **shook** is a bundle of wooden strips ready for use in the construction of objects such as barrels, casks, and boxes.
5. A **stave** is a prepared strip that is grouped with other staves to form rounded containers such as pails, tubs, and barrels. The term "stave" also refers to the blanks or billets used for bows and skis.
6. A **square** is a bundle of similarly shaped wood forms, sufficient to cover an area of 100 square feet.
7. A **turning square** is a precut and dimensioned square form used in turning legs, pedestals, or spindles.
8. A **withe** is a tough, flexible, ribbonlike strip of wood, split from ash, willow, or dogwood.

Surface Characteristics of Lumber

When lumber is sawed, surfaces that formerly were hidden become exposed. These new surfaces have characteristics that are generally classified as either figure or defects or as a combination of these.
1. **Figure** is the overall appearance of a wood face. This category includes the grain, blemishes, and texture of the wood, with regard to the way each of these characteristics is affected by the particular method of sawing.
2. **Grain** is the direction, arrangement, and appearance of the fiber growth of wood. It does not include texture. Grain patterns

produced by plain or slash sawing and by rotary cutting usually appear as wavy lines. These lines are commonly referred to as **flame** or **leaf grain.** This effect is the result of cutting the stock tangent to, and severing, the annual rings. **Straight grain** patterns are produced by cutting at right angles to the annual rings. This is called **quartersawing.**
3. A **blemish** is a discoloration or imperfection caused by foreign matter or by injury to the tree during growth. When boards have been sawed, the damage to the wood will appear as an unusual marking of the wood face.
4. The **texture** is the character of the surface, determined by the size and degree of uniformity of cells. The cells range in size from fine to coarse, and in uniformity from even to uneven. Softwood is generally fine textured, while hardwood varies from fine to coarse, as illustrated by the extremes represented in basswood and oak.

Defects

Defects are irregularities in wood. Some common defects are checks, knots, pitch pockets, holes, shakes, pith, wane, and bird pecks. All these tend to lower the strength, durability, and utility value of the piece. The standard defects are as follows:
1. A **check** is a long, narrow crack (called a **fissure**) in the wood. It usually extends across the growth rings. Checks are caused by internal stress during drying.
2. A **knot** is a mass of compact, hard cross-grained fibers at the starting point of a limb or branch.
3. A **pitch pocket** is an internal cavity that contains, or has contained, pitch and/or bark in varying quantities.
4. **Holes:**
   a. **Pinworm holes** — not over 1/16" in diameter.
   b. **Spot wormholes** — over 1/16" in diameter, but not over 1/8" in diameter.
   c. **Shot wormholes** — over 1/8" in diameter, but less than 1/4" in diameter.
   d. **Grub holes** — 1/4" in diameter or larger.
   e. **Rafting-pin holes** — caused by peavies and cant hooks during the processes of rolling logs and turning stock on the saw.

5. A **shake** can be either of these types:
   a. **Ring shake** — a separation between the annual rings, which becomes more pronounced during seasoning.
   b. **Wind shake** — a break across the annual rings produced, during growth, by excessive bending caused by wind.
6. The **pith** is the small, soft core in the structural center of a log. This is considered a defect when it is visible on the lumber's surface.
7. A **wane** is the natural bevel formed on the edge of a board cut from a log that had not been completely squared.
8. **Bird pecks** are seen on the lumber as a patch of distorted grain. They are the result of birds pecking through the tree's growing cells. Bird pecks sometimes contain a hole or ingrown bark.

While **crook, bow, wind,** and **cup** are not considered "standard defects," these characteristics may affect the suitability of a piece of stock for a particular purpose. (See Topic 16, "Getting Out Stock.")

Standards for Grading Defects

Defects in lumber are graded according to the following standards, established by the lumber manufacturers' associations:

1. One knot or hole 1-1/4″ in diameter is considered **one standard defect.**
2. When located away from edges and ends, where they cannot be considered equivalent to wane defects, each of the following shall be regarded as **one defect.**
   a. Four pinworm holes or their equivalent.
   b. Three spot wormholes or their equivalent.
   c. Two knots or other defects, the diameter of which, when added together, does not exceed 1-1/4″.
   Not more than two standard defects of the above types can be admitted to the piece. Each additional pinworm hole, spot wormhole, knot, or hole 5/8″ or less shall be considered one additional standard defect.
3. Except for wane and split, defects larger than one standard defect shall be considered in the following diameter measure:
   a. 2-1/2″ knots or their equivalent shall be considered **two defects.**

   b. 3-3/4″ knots or their equivalent shall be considered **three defects.**
   c. 5″ knots or their equivalent shall be considered **four defects.**
4. One split equal in length (in inches) to the surface measure of the piece (in feet), and averaging not more than one inch to the foot in length, is regarded as **one defect.**
5. Wane (or its equivalent in other defects) that is 1″ wide and one-sixth the length of the piece along the edges, or the equivalent of this at one or both ends, is **one defect.**
6. Wormholes, grub holes, knotholes and rafting-pin holes not exceeding 1-1/4″ in diameter are considered **one defect.**

Grading of Hardwood Lumber

Hardwood lumber is inspected and graded according to the rules and regulations established by the National Hardwood Lumber Association. For specific grading rules, the Association's publications must be consulted. The grade to which a particular board is assigned is based on its usable content (excluding defects) in relation to the **surface measure** of the board (in square feet). This usable content is expressed in the total number of **cutting units** that the board contains. A cutting unit is 1″ wide and 1′ long. Thus, the number of cutting units in each clear cutting is determined by multiplying the width of the clear stock (in inches and fractions) by the length of the clear stock (in feet and fractions). Repeat for each clear cutting and total the number of cutting units in the board.

The grading rules also specify the maximum or minimum width, the length, the number of clear cuttings, and the cutting units for various grades. The grades are as follows:

First Grade refers to pieces in which 91-2/3% of the surface measure is clear face material.

Second Grade includes pieces in which 83-1/3% of the surface measure is clear face material.

First and Second Grades are usually combined into one classification called **FAS.** This classification admits boards not less than 6″ wide and not less than 8′ long. FAS requires that the number of cutting units be ten times the surface measure of the piece. The smallest-size clear face cuttings permitted for FAS are 4″×5′ and 3″×7′. See Fig. 1-29A.

For a board to be classified as a **Select,** the face side must be equal to that of a Second, the board must be a minimum size of 4″ wide and 6′ long, and the yield in cutting units must be ten times the surface measure. On the reverse side, the board must be as sound and as good as #1 Common and must yield cutting units equal to eight times the surface measure.

See Figs. 1-29 B and 1-29 C. The smallest-size clear face cuttings permitted for classification as Selects are those 4″×5′, 2″×7′ on the better face.

Number 1 Common grade boards should be at least 3″ wide and 4′ long and should yield cutting units equal to eight times the surface measure. See Fig. 1-29 D.

$$\text{Surface measure of board} \quad \frac{12' \times 12''}{12''} = 12'$$

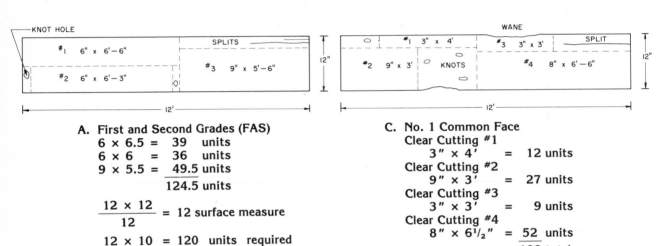

A. **First and Second Grades (FAS)**

    6 × 6.5 = 39   units
    6 × 6   = 36   units
    9 × 5.5 = 49.5 units
           ─────────────
            124.5 units

$$\frac{12 \times 12}{12} = 12 \text{ surface measure}$$

    12 × 10 = 120 units required
              for FAS hence the piece
              is FAS

C. **No. 1 Common Face**

    Clear Cutting #1
        3″ × 4′   = 12 units
    Clear Cutting #2
        9″ × 3′   = 27 units
    Clear Cutting #3
        3″ × 3′   =   9 units
    Clear Cutting #4
        8″ × 6½″   = 52 units
                   ─────────────
                     100 total
                         units

Since this face has 100 units, it meets the specifications for #1 Common Face.

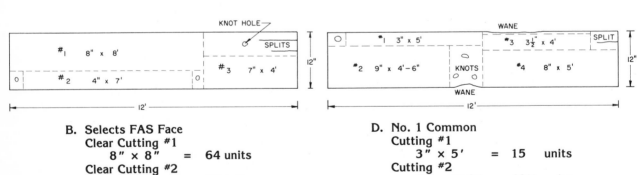

B. **Selects FAS Face**

    Clear Cutting #1
        8″ × 8″   = 64 units
    Clear Cutting #2
        4″ × 7′   = 28 units
    Clear Cutting #3
        7″ × 4′   = 28 units
                   ─────────────
                     120 total
                         units

Since this face has 120 units, it meets FAS specifications.

D. **No. 1 Common**

    Cutting #1
        3″ × 5′   = 15   units
    Cutting #2
        9″ × 4′6″ = 40½ units
    Cutting #3
        3½ × 4′   = 14   units
    Cutting #4
        8″ × 5′   = 40   units
                   ─────────────
                     109½ total
                          units

This board meets the requirements for #1 Common.

Fig. 1-29. Grading of hardwood lumber.

For #1 Common, four clear cuttings are required. The minimum size of these clear cuttings is 4″ × 2′ or 3″ × 3′. The clear face cutting units for #1 Common is eight times the surface measure (12) or 8 × 12 = 96.

For **#2 Common,** the minimum size for clear cuttings is 3″ wide and 2′ long. Number 2 Common should yield cutting units equal to six times the surface measure.

Sound Wormy includes lumber that is as good as #1 Common or better. The difference is that wormholes, bird pecks, stain, and small, sound knots are admitted in clear cuttings. The cutting units must equal eight times the surface measure.

In **#3A Common,** the minimum size for clear cuttings is 3″ wide and 2′ long. The grade of the better face must be as good as #2 Common, and the reverse face must be sound. There is no limit to the number of cuttings of clear stock, but cutting units must be equal to four times the surface measure.

In **#3B Common,** the minimum size permitted for clear face cuttings is 1-1/2″ wide or wider. This grade must contain a minimum of 36 square inches of surface area.

Below-Grade lumber includes all hardwood lumber of poorer quality than #3B Common grade.

Normally, orders placed for use in school shops do not specify grades below #1 Common. This ensures the availability of required lengths and widths for use in school shop projects. Lumber that is to be used for architectural woodwork requires higher-quality stock than any of the standard grades listed above. Even FAS permits defects not acceptable for architectural woodwork.

Computers are now used in grading hardwood lumber. This method may be faster than traditional grading methods. Also, computer grading does a better job of getting the best-quality and maximum-quantity lumber from each log. However, grading for color and for percentage of heartwood and sapwood still requires visual inspection.

The computerized grading program was developed for hardwood standard grades of the National Hardwood Lumber Association. These grades can be adapted for expression in the mathematical language required for computer programming.

The information that is fed into the computer is a mathematical description of the board and its defects. This is done by first finding the graphical location of defects on a vertical scale. This scale is divided in 1/4″ units along the length and width of each board. Using this graph, a given knot is located so many quarter inches from the lower lefthand corner of the board. Similarly, the size of the board is designated by the lower lefthand and upper righthand corners of a rectangle enclosing it. Irregular defects (such as wane and checks) are described by a series of such rectangles. The computer analyzes each piece and determines the best placement for and the sizes of the cuttings it will yield.

Scientists are experimenting with a scanning instrument able to read the size and location of defects by shooting sound pulses through a log at various angles. Variations are interpreted by the computer, which, it is hoped, can specify the best way to edge trim, to crosscut, and to rip the log to get the maximum grade and size of hardwood lumber. If this system works satisfactorily, experimentation will begin in the attempt to develop a new type of log-scanning device. This device would give adequate information to control the head rig of a sawmill to produce the best possible yield of high-quality flitches.

Grading of Softwood Lumber

There is no single procedure for grading softwood. All softwood has the same grade, but the standard varies with each particular kind. The rules governing the grading of softwood are as follows:

The best grade is called **#1 and 2 Clear** (B grade and better). This grade consists of all the better cuttings of the stock and must be at least 4″ wide. Much of the stock is clear, but a typical piece might have one or two minor blemishes, slight enough that they do not detract from the appearance or high quality of the stock.

C-Select is the next best grade. Like #1 and 2 Clear, this grade must be at least 4″ wide. The characteristics are the same as those of #1 and 2, except that the blemishes are larger and more numerous. Providing there are no other marked defects on the stock, it is acceptable to have either a medium stain covering one third of the face or a lighter stain covering a greater area.

D-Select stock must also be 4″ or more in width. This grade is between the higher-finish lumber and the common grades. Many pieces have a finish appearance on one side, while the reverse side may show numerous or serious defects. A piece in this grade may have a defect. This defect must be cut before the piece can be used in finish work. It is permissible in this grade to have medium stain over the entire face of the wood.

Common lumber is distinguished from the finish grades by its generally coarse appearance. This appearance is caused by various combinations of defects. In Common lumber, a check (or group of checks) within a tightened knot is not considered to be a defect unless the opening is so pronounced as to impair the lumber's use.

Number 1 Common grade includes all sound, tight knots, the size of the knot being the determining factor in the grade. Very small pitch pockets, light stains, season checks, or equivalent characteristics are permitted. The character of this grade makes it suitable for shelving, for cornices, and for all work requiring Common lumber of the best quality and appearance.

Number 2 Common grade permits larger and more pronounced defects.

Number 3 Common includes part of the lower cutting of the log. The characteristics permitted are more pronounced than those admitted in #2 Common.

Number 4 Common is much the same as #3 Common, but the defects are greater or more pronounced.

Number 5 Common is the lowest recognized grade. Any defect or combination of defects is admissible in this grade, provided the piece is of usable quality.

Topic 3.

Practices of Lumber Computation

Classification

Methods of computing lumber quantity

Procedure

1. The common unit of measure for lumber is the **board foot,** a standard unit of 144 cubic inches. This measurement is equivalent to the volume of a piece of wood 1″ thick, 12″ wide, and 12″ long. It is also the measure of any piece of an equivalent volume, such as a board 1″ thick, 2″ wide, and 72″ long.

   For purposes of computation, any board under 1″ in thickness is considered a 1″ board. Commercially, lumber is sawed to a standard thickness of 3/8″, 1/2″, 5/8″, or 1″, and is surfaced on two sides to 1/4″, 3/8″, 1/2″, or 13/16″. Stock sawed to dimension and not surfaced is scaled in price according to thickness.

   When, in order to meet the buyer's specifications, it is necessary to machine a board to thickness, the board footage is computed on the thickness of the presurfaced board. The customer pays according to the number of board feet contained in the rough stock. Thus, it could be said that the buyer pays for the waste as well as for the lumber.

2. When figuring the number of board feet in softwood, remember that, except for those 3″ and 5″ wide, boards that are less than an even number of inches in width are counted as the next-higher, even width. Softwood is sawed to 3″, 4″, 5″, 6″, 8″, 10″, and 12″ widths. Thus, a 3″ board is computed as 3″ in width, while a 3-1/2″ board is figured as being 4″ in width, and a 5-1/4″ board is figured as being 6″ in width.

3. For hardwood lumber between 1″ and 2″ thick, thickness is figured by quarters. For lumber between 2″ and 3″ thick, thickness is figured by halves. For lumber 3″ or more, thickness is calculated in full inches. In the case of stock 1″ to 2″ thick, a piece that is

between quarters is figured as the next-higher quarter. For stock 2″ to 3″ thick, a piece that is between halves is figured as the next-higher half. For example, 1-1/8″ stock is figured as 1-1/4″ or 5/4 (five quarters), 2-1/8″ stock is figured as 2-1/2″ or 10/4 (ten quarters), while 3-1/8″ is considered as 4″ or 16/4 (sixteen quarters).

4. A board of uneven width is figured by its average width.

5. When all the dimensions are in inches, the following formula should be used to determine board feet:

T = thickness, W = width, L = length

$$\frac{T'' \times W'' \times L''}{144} = \text{Board Feet}$$

If the length is in feet, use this formula:

$$\frac{T'' \times W'' \times L'}{12} = \text{Board Feet}$$

6. Strip lumber (moldings, trim, furring, and grounds) is sold by the lineal foot.
7. Structural lumber is sold either by the board foot or by the lineal foot.
8. Cedar lining and manufactured board (plywood, hardboard, and wallboard, for example) are sold by the square foot. The price of this type of board is scaled according to grain pattern.
9. Some building materials, such as clapboard, shingles, and flooring, are sold by the **square.** A square is a unit covering 100 square feet of surface.

Standards and Results

- All measurements and figures should be accurate.

Specifying and Ordering Lumber

Topic 4.

In ordering lumber, the kind and grade of lumber must be specified. If the pieces in the object are to be built with stock that is relatively long (3′ to 4′), FAS (First and Second) grade lumber may be the most economical, as it provides for large, clear cuttings. If the object is to be built with short stock (2′ or smaller) it may be more economical to buy #1 Common and cut between the defects.

The next decision to be made is whether to use kiln-dried or air-dried lumber. A good general rule to follow is this: If the article is to be used inside a heated building, kiln-dried lumber should be used, as there will be less shrinkage. If the object is to be used outside, air-dried lumber is preferable. Kiln-dried stock is usually dried to 6-8% M.C. Air-dried usually has 12-14% M.C.

In some woods, it may be advantageous to purchase quartersawed stock. In this type of lumber, the medullary rays will be visible on the face, and the shrinkage and swelling will be half the width of slash-sawed lumber. However, the pieces are generally narrower. Plain-sawed stock may be desirable because of its well-defined grain pattern. However, plain-sawed wood is not as strong as that which is quartersawed. Plain-sawed wood also has a greater tendency to warp.

Lumber is cut in multiples of 1/4″ thickness. For example, 4/4 = 1″ and 6/4 = 1-1/2″. If the finished thickness is to be 13/16, you should purchase 4/4 lumber. If the finished thickness is 1-1/8″, you may need to buy 6/4 lumber so that each piece can be finished to 1-1/8″ thickness.

When ordering lumber, you must also consider the surface preparation of the wood. Lumber can be purchased in rough form, S2S (surfaced two sides), or S4S (surfaced four sides). Rough stock is that which has not undergone any surface preparation after being sawed into lumber. Surfaced stock, on the other hand, has been planed or surfaced on a specified number of sides so that those sides will be straight and relatively smooth. Although rough lumber is the least expensive type, surfaced stock is recommended if a jointer-planer is not available. If you specify certain lengths and widths when ordering lumber, you will pay more per board foot than if you order random lengths and widths. Some lumber outlets allow the buyer to select individual pieces of stock.

Topic 5.

Manufactured Board

The complete utilization of wood has led to an expansion in the production of manufactured board. This development has come about in an attempt to meet competition from other manufactured materials and in an effort to make use of the residue produced in the manufacture of lumber and lumber products.

Lumber is divided into three classifications: **hardwood, softwood,** and **manufactured board.** Manufactured board, as the name implies, is made of wood that does not appear in its natural state. There are three common kinds of manufactured board: **plywood, hardboard,** and **particleboard.**

Plywood is made up of an odd number of veneer sheets glued together face-to-face. The grain on adjacent pieces intersects at right angles.

Hardboard (pressed wood) is made from wood chips. These wood chips are exploded into fibers under high-pressure steam, then pressed into sheets. The lignin (natural cement) in the fibers holds the material together without additional adhesives. The result is a reconstituted product. This type of paneling is called **untempered** hardboard. **Tempered** hardboard is impregnated with a special adhesive, then baked to become harder and more moisture resistant. Some of these sheets are embossed with patterns resembling tile or are grained to resemble simulated leather.

Particleboard (called flakeboard, chipboard, splinterboard, and crumbleboard in different geographic areas) is manufactured from many types of organic material. Some of the materials used are chips, curls, fibers, flakes, shavings, slivers, strands, wood wool (excelsior), and wafers of wood. The types of raw materials commonly used in the manufacture of particleboard are green logs, veneer cores, cull lumber, slabs and edgings, veneer clippings, pulp chips, shavings from planers, sawdust, and plywood sander dust. Vegetable fibers such as bagasse, esparto, and lemon grass are also used. These materials are bonded with either urea-formaldehyde-resin glue or phenolic-resin glues. (The type of glue used depends upon whether the board is for interior or exterior use.) The fibers are pressed either into sheets or into other molded shapes. These shapes are used to form a number of familiar products. Chair seats, cores for irregular shapes, parts for upholstered furniture, molded tabletops, and siding for homes are but a few of the common products constructed of particleboard.

All three types of manufactured board have the following qualities: (a) more dimensional stability than wood in its natural state, (b) greater design potential, (c) good rigidity, and (d) good impact strength. Because of these qualities, particleboard may be covered with veneer or plastic laminate on only one side without producing problems of warpage.

Plywood

Topic 6.

Classification

Manufactured board

Composition or Description

Plywood is made up of an odd number of veneer sheets, glued together face-to-face. The grain of adjacent pieces intersects at right angles. See Fig. 1-30.

There are two basic types of plywood — **softwood** and **hardwood.** Softwood plywood is made with softwood veneers cut from conifers (needle-bearing trees). This type of plywood is very common and is used extensively for construction and structural purposes.

Hardwood plywood is made with hardwood face veneers cut from deciduous (broad-leaved) trees. This type of plywood is used for decorative purposes such as in furniture and paneling applications.

Properties

Tests at the Forest Products Laboratories have shown that plywood shrinks less than half of 1% in drying from the point of saturation to 6% moisture content. This shrinkage is substantially less than that which occurs in solid woods of the same species under similar conditions. Weight-for-weight, plywood is stronger than steel. Screws and nails can be driven close to the edges without danger of splitting, but it is difficult to glue plywood edge-to-edge unless a spline is used. Exterior and marine plywoods are made for exterior use. Plywood is

Hardwood Plywood Manufacturers' Association.

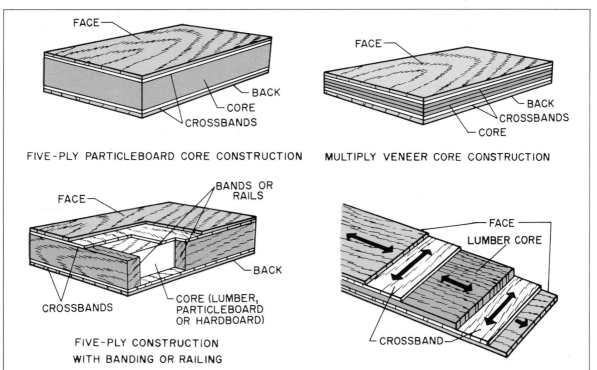

FIVE-PLY PARTICLEBOARD CORE CONSTRUCTION

MULTIPLY VENEER CORE CONSTRUCTION

FIVE-PLY CONSTRUCTION WITH BANDING OR RAILING

Fig. 1-30. Typical plywood constructions.

light in weight and resists twisting and buckling. It may be bent to slight curves, but fixed shapes are best achieved through the process of gluing up in the desired form.

Uses

Plywood is used for home and office furnishings, for toys, sports equipment, kitchen cabinets, drawer bottoms, door panels, wall and roof sheathing, forms, floors, boats, aircraft, boxes, caskets, and radio and television cabinets.

Market Analysis

Shapes

Plywood is available in various panel sizes.

Sizes

```
1/8" thick, 3-ply — 36" × 72", 84", 96"
                    48" × 96"
3/16" thick, 3-ply — 24" × 72"
                     30" × 72"
                     36" × 72", 84", 96"
                     48" × 96"
1/4" thick, 3-ply — 24" × 48", 60", 72",
                       84", 96"
                    30" × 60", 72", 84",
                       96"
                    36" × 60", 72", 84",
                       96"
                    48" × 60", 72", 84",
                       96", 108", 120",
                       144"
5/16" thick, 3-ply — 30" × 84"
                     48" × 96", 108", 120"
3/8" thick, 3-ply — 24" × 48", 60", 72",
                       84", 96"
                    30" × 60", 72", 84",
                       96"
                    36" × 60", 72", 84",
                       95", 120"
                    48" × 60", 72", 84",
                       96", 120", 144",
                       168", 192"
```

Plywood is also available in five-ply panels in 1/2", 5/8", 3/4", and 1" thicknesses, ranging in size from 24" × 60" to 60" × 108". Seven-ply panels of 1-1/8" and 1-3/16" thicknesses, are available in 36" × 84" and 48" × 96" sheets.

Grades — Softwood Plywood

(Softwood plywood is the most common type for structural use.)

Within each type of plywood, there is a variety of grades. These grades are determined by the grade of veneer (N, A, B, C, or D) used for the face and back of the panel. Grades of plywood are designated by the type of glue used and by the veneer grade. Plywood is manufactured from any of 30 different species of varying strength. These species are grouped into any of five categories, according to their degree of stiffness. These categories are designated as Group I, II, and so on. The strongest woods are in Group I.

Structural I and II

This category consists of unsanded, construction-grade plywood, made only with exterior glue. This type of plywood withstands great shearing force, has good nail-holding ability, and bears a high degree of compression and tension.

Standard with Exterior Glue

Interior type C-D sheathing is available with waterproof adhesives of the same type as those used in exterior-type grades. These panels will retain their structural strength under most conditions. However, when this grade of plywood is subjected to wet or highly humid conditions, the presence of D-grade veneers in the inner plies and backs may result in weakness along the glue line.

Class I and Class II

This classification applies only to plyform-grade plywood, used for concrete form applications. The name of this grade indicates the species mix permitted in this grade. Class I is limited to Group I for the faces, and Group I or II for the core. Class II is limited to Group I or II for the faces and the inner plies from any group.

Identification Index Number

Two numbers, separated by a dash, appear in the grade mark on Structural I and II and on

Exterior C-C. The number on the left indicates spacing (in inches) for rafters. This information is required when the panel is used for roof sheathing. The number on the right shows the spacing (also in inches) for floor joists. This information is necessary when the panel is to be used for subflooring.

Grades — Hardwood Plywood

(Hardwood plywood is the most common type for cabinetmaking and architectural use.)

Hardwood plywood is commonly constructed with veneer cores, lumber cores, and particleboard cores. In addition to these basic materials, hardwood plywood is constructed with a hardwood face veneer and softwood inner plies.

Hardwood plywood is graded according to veneer, core, and adhesive. The veneer grades are as follows:

Premium Grade A

In this grade, each face of the panel must be smooth and tight. The veneer must be the outside face of the slice. (The outside face is that side of the sheet which was farthest from the knife as the sheet was being cut.) This face should contain no cutting checks. The veneer should be a smooth, full-length cut. When the face consists of more than one piece, it must be edge matched. The face veneer may contain small burls, occasional pin knots, color streaks or spots, inconspicuous small patches, and the usual characteristics inherent to the particular species. **Large knots, wormholes, rough-cut veneer, splits, shakes, and decay are NOT permitted.**

Good Grade A

The face veneer in this grade must be made of tight-cut veneers. When the face consists of more than one piece, the edges must be tight and approximately parallel to the length of the panel. The pieces need not be matched for color or grain, but **sharp contrasts between adjacent pieces of veneer, with respect to grain, figure, and natural character markings are NOT permitted.**

> INTERESTING FACT: In 1830, the piano industry became the first industry to use plywood.

(Natural character markings include large knots, wormholes, rough-cut veneer, splits, shakes, and decay.) Face veneer in this grade may contain small burls, pin knots, color streaks, inconspicuous patches, and the usual characteristics inherent to the particular species.

Sound Grade 2

The face veneer in this grade must be free of open defects. This grade provides for a sound, smooth surface. Matching for grain and color is not required. The natural characteristics and other characteristics that are permitted are as follows: sapwood, discolorations and stains, mineral streaks, wormholes that have been filled or patched, green spots, and sound, tight knots 3/4″ or less in diameter. **Large knotholes, open splits or joints, cross breaks, and joint laps are NOT permitted.**

Utility Grade

This grade allows the following defects: sound, tight burls; sapwood discoloration and stain; mineral streaks; and sound, tight knots up to 3/4″ in diameter. It also permits knotholes up to 1″ in diameter, wormholes, open splits or joints 3/16″ wide (for half the length of the panel), shakes, brashness, a small area of rough-cut veneer, cross breaks 1″ in length, bark pockets, green spots, and lapped joints. **Some decay is allowed in the back and in the inner plies.**

Backing Grade

All the defects allowed in the preceding grades are permitted in backing-grade plywood. However, the maximum size for knotholes is 3″. The sizes permitted for open splits and joints are as follows: 1″ wide for one-fourth the length of the panel, 1/2″ wide for one-half the length of the panel, and 1/4″ for the full length of the panel. Shakes, brashness, and decay are allowed in small areas of the face, and in large areas on the back and in the inner plies.

Specialty Grade or Custom Grade

The actual description of this grade is up to the judgment of the manufacturer, or can be
(Text continued on page 28.)

Table 1-1
Guide to Appearance Grades of Plywood[1][8]

American Plywood Association

Type	Grade Designation[2]	Description and Most Common Uses	Typical Grade-trademarks	Face	Back	Inner Plies	1/4	5/16	3/8	1/2	5/8	3/4
Interior Type	N-N, N-A, N-B INT-APA	Cabinet quality. For natural finish furniture, cabinet doors, built-ins, etc. Special order items.	N N G1 INT APA PS174 / N A G2 INT APA PS174	N	N,A, or B	C						3/4
	N-D-INT-APA	For natural finish paneling. Special order item.	N D G3 INT APA PS174	N	D	D	1/4					
	A-A INT-APA	For applications with both sides on view. Built-ins, cabinets, furniture and partitions. Smooth face; suitable for painting.	AA G4 INT APA PS174	A	A	D	1/4		3/8	1/2	5/8	3/4
	A-B INT-APA	Use where appearance of one side is less important but two solid surfaces are necessary.	AB G4 INT APA PS174	A	B	D	1/4		3/8	1/2	5/8	3/4
	A-D INT-APA	Use where appearance of only one side is important. Paneling, built-ins, shelving, partitions, and flow racks.	A-D GROUP 1 INTERIOR PS174 000	A	D	D	1/4		3/8	1/2	5/8	3/4
	B-B INT-APA	Utility panel with two solid sides. Permits circular plugs.	BB G3 INT APA PS174	B	B	D	1/4		3/8	1/2	5/8	3/4
	B-D INT-APA	Utility panel with one solid side. Good for backing, sides of built-ins. Industry: shelving, slip sheets, separator boards and bins.	B-D GROUP 3 INTERIOR PS174 000	B	D	D	1/4		3/8	1/2	5/8	3/4
	DECORATIVE PANELS—APA	Rough-sawn, brushed, grooved, or striated faces. For paneling, interior accent walls, built-ins, counter facing, displays, and exhibits.	DECORATIVE B D G1 INT APA PS174	C or btr.	D	D		5/16	3/8	1/2	5/8	
	PLYRON INT-APA	Hardboard face on both sides. For counter tops, shelving, cabinet doors, flooring. Faces tempered, untempered, smooth, or screened.	PLYRON INT APA			C & D				1/2	5/8	3/4
Exterior Type[7]	A-A EXT-APA	Use where appearance of both sides is important. Fences, built-ins, signs, boats, cabinets, commercial refrigerators, shipping containers, tote boxes, tanks, and ducts. (4)	AA G3 EXT APA PS174	A	A	C	1/4		3/8	1/2	5/8	3/4
	A-B EXT-APA	Use where the appearance of one side is less important. (4)	AB G1 EXT APA PS174	A	B	C	1/4		3/8	1/2	5/8	3/4
	A-C EXT-APA	Use where the appearance of only one side is important. Soffits, fences, structural uses, boxcar and truck lining, farm buildings. Tanks, trays, commercial refrigerators. (4)	A-C GROUP 1 EXTERIOR PS174 000	A	C	C	1/4		3/8	1/2	5/8	3/4
	B-B EXT-APA	Utility panel with solid faces. (4)	BB G1 EXT APA PS174	B	B	C	1/4		3/8	1/2	5/8	3/4
	B-C EXT-APA	Utility panel for farm service and work buildings, boxcar and truck lining, containers, tanks, agricultural equipment. Also as base for exterior coatings for walls, roofs. (4)	B-C GROUP 2 EXTERIOR PS174 000	B	C	C	1/4		3/8	1/2	5/8	3/4
	HDO EXT-APA	High Density Overlay plywood. Has a hard, semi-opaque resin-fiber overlay both faces. Abrasion resistant. For concrete forms, cabinets, counter tops, signs and tanks. (4)	HDO 60/60 BB PLYFORM I EXT APA PS174	A or B	A or B	C or C plgd		5/16	3/8	1/2	5/8	3/4
	MDO EXT-APA	Medium Density Overlay with smooth, opaque, resin-fiber overlay one or both panel faces. Highly recommended for siding and other outdoor applications, built-ins, signs, and displays. Ideal base for paint. (4)	MDO BB G4 EXT APA PS174	B	B or C	C		5/16	3/8	1/2	5/8	3/4
	303 SIDING EXT-APA	Proprietary plywood products for exterior siding, fencing, etc. Special surface treatment such as V-groove, channel groove, striated, brushed, rough-sawn. (6)	303 SIDING 16 oc GROUP 1 EXTERIOR PS174 000	(5)	C	C			3/8	1/2	5/8	
	T 1-11 EXT-APA	Special 303 panel having grooves 1/4" deep, 3/8" wide, spaced 4" or 8" o.c. Other spacing optional. Edges shiplapped. Available unsanded, textured, and MDO. (6)	303 SIDING 16 oc T 1-11 GROUP 1 EXTERIOR PS174 000	C or btr.	C	C					5/8	
	PLYRON EXT-APA	Hardboard faces both sides, tempered, smooth or screened.	PLYRON EXT APA			C				1/2	5/8	3/4
	MARINE EXT-APA	Ideal for boat hulls. Made only with Douglas fir or western larch. Special solid jointed core construction. Subject to special limitations on core gaps and number of face repairs. Also available with HDO or MDO faces.	MARINE AA EXT APA PS174	A or B	A or B	B	1/4		3/8	1/2	5/8	3/4

(1) Sanded both sides except where decorative or other surfaces specified.
(2) Available in Group 1, 2, 3, 4, or 5 unless otherwise noted.
(3) Standard 4x8 panel sizes, other sizes available.
(4) Also available in Structural I (all plies limited to Group 1 species) and Structural II (all plies limited to Group 1, 2, or 3 species).
(5) C or better for 5 plies; C Plugged or better for 3-ply panels.
(6) Stud spacing is shown on grade stamp.
(7) For finishing recommendations, see form B407.
(8) For strength properties of appearance grades, refer to "Plywood Design Specification," form Y510.

Table 1-2
Guide to Engineered Grades of Plywood
Specific Grades and Thicknesses May Be In Locally Limited Supply. See Your Dealer for Availability Before Specifying.

American Plywood Association

	Grade Designation	Description and Most Common Uses	Typical Grade-trademarks	Veneer Grade Face	Back	Inner Plies	Most Common Thicknesses (inch) (1)				
Interior Type	C-D INT-APA	For wall and roof sheathing, subfloor, industrial uses such as pallets. Commonly available with exterior glue. Specify exterior glue for better durability in somewhat longer construction delays, and for treated wood foundations. (2) (9)	C-D 32/16 INTERIOR APA PS 1-74 000 / C-D 32/16 INTERIOR APA PS 1-74 000 EXTERIOR GLUE	C	D	D	5/16	3/8	1/2	5/8	3/4
	STRUCTURAL I C-D INT-APA and STRUCTURAL II C-D INT-APA	Unsanded structural grades where plywood strength properties are of maximum importance: structural diaphragms, box beams, gusset plates, stressed-skin panels, containers, pallet bins. Made only with exterior glue.	STRUCTURAL I C-D 24/0 INTERIOR APA PS 1-74 000 EXTERIOR GLUE	C(6)	D(6)	D(6)	5/16	3/8	1/2	5/8	3/4
	UNDERLAYMENT INT-APA	For underlayment or combination subfloor-underlayment under resilient floor coverings, carpeting. Specify exterior glue where moisture may be present, such as bathrooms, utility rooms, or if construction may be delayed, as in site-built floors. Touch-sanded. Also available in tongue and groove. (2) (3) (8)	UNDERLAYMENT GROUP 1 INTERIOR APA PS 1-74 000	C Plugged	D	C(7) & D	1/4		3/8	1/2	5/8	3/4
	C-D PLUGGED INT-APA	For built-ins, wall and ceiling tile backing, cable reels, walkways, separator boards. Not a substitute for UNDERLAYMENT as it lacks UNDERLAYMENT's indentation resistance. Touch-sanded. (2) (3) (8)	C-D PLUGGED GROUP 2 INTERIOR APA PS 1-74 000	C Plugged	D	D	5/16	3/8	1/2	5/8	3/4
	2·4·1 INT-APA	Combination subfloor-underlayment. Use 2·4·1 with exterior glue in areas subject to moisture, or if construction may be delayed as in site-built floors. Unsanded or touch-sanded as specified. (2) (5) (10)	2·4·1 GROUP 1 INTERIOR APA PS 1-74 000	C Plugged	D	C & D	1-1/8"				
Exterior Type	C-C EXT-APA	Unsanded grade with waterproof bond for subflooring and roof decking, siding on service and farm buildings, crating, pallets, pallet bins, cable reels. (9)	C-C 42/20 EXTERIOR APA PS 1-74 000	C	C	C	5/16	3/8	1/2	5/8	3/4
	STRUCTURAL I C-C EXT-APA and STRUCTURAL II C-C EXT-APA	For engineered applications in construction and industry where full Exterior type panels are required. Unsanded. See (8) for species group requirements.	STRUCTURAL I C-C 32/16 EXTERIOR APA PS 1-74 000	C	C	C	5/16	3/8	1/2	5/8	3/4
	UNDERLAYMENT C-C Plugged EXT-APA / C-C PLUGGED EXT-APA	For underlayment or combination subfloor-underlayment under resilient floor coverings where severe moisture conditions may be present, as in balcony decks. Use for tile backing where severe moisture conditions exist. For refrigerated or controlled atmosphere rooms, pallets, fruit pallet bins, reusable cargo containers, tanks and boxcar and truck floors and linings. Touch-sanded. Also available in tongue and groove. (3) (8)	UNDERLAYMENT C-C PLUGGED GROUP 2 EXTERIOR APA PS 1-74 000 / C-C PLUGGED GROUP 3 EXTERIOR APA PS 1-74 000	C Plugged	C	C(7)	1/4		3/8	1/2	5/8	3/4
	B-B PLYFORM CLASS I & CLASS II EXT-APA	Concrete form grades with high re-use factor. Sanded both sides. Mill-oiled unless otherwise specified. Special restrictions on species. Also available in HDO. (4)	B-B PLYFORM CLASS I EXTERIOR APA PS 1-74 000	B	B	C				5/8	3/4

(1) Panels are standard 4x8-foot size. Other sizes available.
(2) Also made with exterior glue.
(3) Available in Group 1, 2, 3, 4, or 5.
(4) Also available in STRUCTURAL I.
(5) Made only in woods of certain species to conform to APA specifications.
(6) Special improved grade for structural panels.
(7) Special construction to resist indentation from concentrated loads.
(8) Also available in STRUCTURAL I (all plies limited to Group 1 species) and STRUCTURAL II (all plies limited to Group 1, 2, or 3 species).
(9) Made in many different species combinations. Specify by Identification Index.
(10) Can be special ordered in Exterior type for porches and patio decks, roof overhangs, and exterior balconies.

Typical Back-stamp

Typical Edge-mark

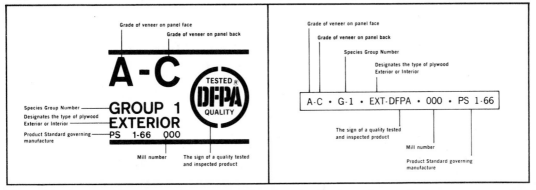

American Plywood Association

Table 1-3
Classification of Species
Used in Plywood

Group 1	Group 2	Group 3	Group 4	Group 5
Apitong	Cedar, Port	Alder, Red	Aspen	Basswood
Beech,	Orford	Birch, Paper	Bigtooth	Fir, Balsam
American	Cypress	Cedar, Alaska	Quaking	Poplar,
Birch	Douglas	Fir,	Cativo	Balsam
Sweet	Fir 2[a]	Subalpine	Cedar	
Yellow	Fir	Hemloc,	Incense	
Douglas	California	Eastern	Western	
Fir 1[a]	Red	Maple,	Red	
Kapur	Grand	Bigleaf	Cottonwood	
Keruing	Noble	Pine	Eastern	
Larch,	Pacific	Jack	Black	
Western	Silver	Lodgepole	(Western	
Maple, Sugar	White	Ponderosa	Poplar)	
Pine	Hemlock,	Spruce	Pine	
Caribbean	Western	Redwood	Eastern	
Ocote	Lauan	Spruce	White	
Pine, South	Almon	Black	Sugar	
Loblolly	Bagtikan	Engelmann		
Longleaf	Mayapis	White		
Shortleaf	Red Lauan			
Slash	Tangile			
Tanoak	White Lauan			
	Maple, Black			
	Mengkulang			
	Meranti, Red[b]			
	Mersawa			
	Pine			
	Pond			
	Red			
	Virginia			
	Western			
	White			
	Spruce			
	Red			
	Sitka			
	Sweetgum			
	Tamarack			
	Yellow			
	poplar			

(a) Douglas Fir from trees grown in the states of Washington, Oregon, California, Idaho, Montana, Wyoming, and the Canadian provinces of Alberta and British Columbia shall be classed as Douglas Fir No. 1. Douglas Fir from trees grown in the states of Nevada, Utah, Colorado, Arizona and New Mexico shall be classed as Douglas Fir No. 2.

(b) Red Meranti shall be limited to species having a specific gravity of 0.41 or more based on green volume and ovendry weight.

Table 1-4
Summary of Veneer Grades
Used in Plywood

N	Smooth-surface, natural-finish veneer. Select, all heartwood or all sapwood. Free of open defects. Allows not more than 6 repairs, wood only, per 4 × 8 panel, made parallel to grain and well matched for grain and color.
A	Smooth, paintable. Not more than 18 neatly made repairs, boat, sled, or router type, and parallel to grain, permitted. May be used for natural finish in less demanding applications.
B	Solid surface. Shims, circular repair plugs and tight knots to 1″ permitted. Wood or synthetic patching material may be used. Some minor splits permitted.
C (Plugged)	Improved C veneer with splits limited to ⅛″ width and knotholes and borer holes limited to ¼″ × ½″. Admits some broken grain. Synthetic repairs permitted.
C	Tight knots to 1½″. Knotholes to 1″ and some to 1½″ if total width of knots and knotholes is within specified limits. Synthetic or wood repairs. Discoloration and sanding defects that do not impair strength permitted. Limited splits allowed.
D	Knots and knotholes to 2½″ width and ½″ larger within specified limits. Limited splits are permitted.

agreed upon by the buyer and seller. This grade may include veneer that does not conform to any of the other grades. It may permit either more or fewer characteristics and defects. It may also permit different characteristics. Species such as wormy chestnut, bird's-eye maple, and English brown oak, which have unusual decorative features, are considered Specialty Grade.

Weyerhaeuser Company

Fig. 1-31. Veneer plies being cut from peeler logs.

Fig. 1-32. Applying glue to veneer sheets.

Fig. 1-33. Particleboard chips in raw and finished form.

The thickness of veneers most commonly used in hardwood plywood is as follows: 1/50″, 1/36″, 1/32″, 1/28″, 1/26″, 1/24″, 1/20″, 1/16″, 1/12″, 1/10″, 1/8″, 1/7″, 1/6″, 3/16″, and 1/4″.

Unless otherwise specified, the species of lumber cores is optional. However, all wood used in a single core must be of the same species. The maximum width for core strips is as follows: 2-1/2″ for high-density woods, 3″ for medium-density woods, and 4″ for low-density woods. For all grades, end-grain-glued finger joints are allowed as full-length strips.

There are three grades of lumber core: clear grade with full-length strips, sound grade with full-length strips, and regular grade.

1. **Clear grade.** This grade is free of knots and from other defects that resist shaping or molding. Neither wood patches nor plugs are permitted, but wood filler is allowed.

2. **Sound grade.** With a few exceptions, wood strips must be free of defects. The defects permitted are as follows: small, open knots, discoloration, and small, open defects that have been securely patched or plugged with wood or filler.

3. **Regular grade.** In this grade, wood strips must be of sound grade. However, random lengths with tightly butted end joints are permitted. In all grades, lumber-core edges must be of clear stock. Also, all edges must be free of defects so as to permit shaping or molding to a depth of 1-1/2″.

Particleboard and Hardboard Cores

Particleboard cores must be of the type, grade, and class specified, and must be in accordance with the most recent commercial standard. Hardboard cores must be of the type specified and must be in accordance with the most recent commercial standard. The following are the four types of core:

1. **Type I** has a fully waterproof bond, making it able to withstand extreme moisture conditions.

2. **Type II** is water resistant and is suitable for most interior applications.

3. **Type III** will withstand only occasional moisture. This type should be used in plywood that will not be subjected to moisture or high humidity.
4. **Technical Type** core is fully waterproof. It is suitable for use where conditions of extreme moisture exist.

Sales Units

Plywood is sold by the square foot.

Maintenance

Plywood should be stored in a dry place, in either a vertical or a horizontal position. Panels of plywood should be stacked one directly on top of another. They should not be stuck. If stored vertically, plywood should be supported in such a manner as to minimize buckling.

> INTERESTING FACT: A single panel of plywood for structural use is constructed of 29 plies. The record number of plies used in a plywood panel is 93.

Topic 7.

Hardboard (Pressed Wood)

Classification

Manufactured board

Composition or Description

Hardboard (usually referred to by its trade name, **Masonite**) is made from wood chips exploded into fibers under high-pressure steam. The fibers are refined, felted (joined), and then pressed into heated, hydraulic-bed presses to form sheets. No fillers or artificial adhesives are used. Hardboard is held together by the wood's own lignin. Tempered hardboard is made by saturating the formed sheet with a special tempering compound and then baking. This increases the board's strength and its resistance to abrasion. It also reduces the rate of moisture absorption. Tempered hardboard is darker in color and has more sheen than untempered hardboard. Hardboard varies in color from light brown to dark brown. It is very hard and smooth, and is free from resin and oil.

Properties

Hardboard is equally strong in all directions, but is very brittle. It is moisture resistant, moldproof, and fungus proof. It resists dents, scuffing, abrasion, splitting, splintering, shrinking, and swelling. Hardboard can be sawed, shaped, routed, and drilled with hand- or power-operated woodworking or metalworking tools. It can be punched, die-cast, and laminated. Although hardboard can be bent into simple curves, compound curves cannot be made. Hardboard can be painted, enameled, stained, or varnished. It can be glued or bolted, and it is well able to hold nails and screws. Resin glue, casein glue, and hide glue are satisfactory adhesives for this material. Hardboard cannot be toenailed or used for base nailing.

Uses

Hardboard is used for food containers, signs, chair seats, toys, trays, house trailers, sink cabinets, card tables, baby carriages, and playpens. It is also used for templates, jigs, control-switch panels, and the interiors of buses, trucks, railroad cars, and airplanes.

Market Analysis

Shapes

Hardboard is produced in sheets.

INTERESTING FACT: *The first hardboard was developed accidentally. William Mason was attempting to produce a strong paper or insulating board, using fibers heated in a steam-heated press. One day a faulty valve permitted the steam to continue heating, and the fibers were pressed into a smooth, strong board, which today we call hardboard or Masonite.*

Grades

1. **Untempered** hardboard is the standard type of hardboard. It is smooth on one side only and has a screen impression on the reverse side.
2. **Tempered** hardboard can either be smooth on one side, with a screen impression on the back, or it can be smooth on both sides. Tempered hardboard is suitable for exterior use.

Types

1. **Tile-marked.** This is a type of tempered hardboard that has lines scored on the surface, forming 4″ × 4″ squares.
2. **Embossed.** This is a type of tempered hardboard that has been embossed with a pattern such as simulated leather.
3. **Die stock.** This is the most dense of all types of hardboard. Working with die stock requires the use of high-speed tools.

4. **Benelex®.** This is a structural, electrical-insulating panel.
5. **Perforated hardboard (pegboard).** This is patterned hardboard, perforated with small holes.

Sizes

1. Tempered and untempered are available in 1/10″, 1/8″, 3/16″, 1/4″ and 5/16″ thickness in 1′ × 4′, 1-1/2′ × 4′, 2′ × 4′, 3′ × 4′, 4′ × 4′, 4′ × 6′, 4′ × 8′, and 4′ × 12′.
2. Smooth, two-sides-tempered hardboard and tile-marked hardboard are made only in 1/8″ thickness. Smooth-two-sides hardboard is made in sheets 1′ × 4′, 1-1/2′ × 4′, 2′ × 4′, 3′ × 4′, 4′ × 4′, 4′ × 6′, 4′ × 8′, and 4′ × 12′. Tile-marked hardboard is made only in sheets 4′ × 8′ and 4′ × 12′.
3. Embossed, tempered hardboard is made in 1/8″ sheets 1′ × 4′, 1-1/2′ × 4′, 2′ × 4′, 3′ × 4′, 4′ × 4′, 4′ × 6′, 4′ × 8′, 4′ × 10′ and 4′ × 12′.
4. Die stock and Benelex® are made in thicknesses from 1/4″ to 2″, in sheets 3′ × 4′, 4′ × 6′ and 4′ × 12′.

Sales Units

Hardboard is sold by the square foot.

Particleboard

Topic 8.

Classification

Manufactured board

Composition or Description

Particleboard (also known as **flakeboard, chipboard, splinterboard,** and **crumbleboard**) is made from a number of wood products. Some of these materials are wood chips, curls, fibers, flakes, shavings, slivers, strands, wood wool (excelsior) and wood wafers. It also contains vegetable fibers such as bagasse (sugar cane), esparto, and lemongrass. The wood fibers are residue from fir, pine, aspen, hemlock, poplar, gumwood, redwood, cedar, maple, and oak. **Low-density woods are preferred for particleboard.** In some particleboard products, as much as 5% hardwood bark may be included without harmfully affecting the properties of the product. The particles are arranged to control dimensional stability. The controlled distribution of particles assures that the board will have the correct physical and surface properties. The particles are formed into sheets and other shapes, under high pressure and at a temperature of 165° C (325° F). They are then bonded with resin glue. The pressure is controlled to assure that the product will have an even density. A small amount of petroleum wax (1%) is placed in particleboard. There are three reasons for doing this: (1) to make removal from the press easier, (2) to help ensure dimensional stability, and (3) to make the product more water resistant.

Properties

In a given cross-sectional area, particleboard has equal strength in all directions. It is not brittle, and it resists warping. Particleboard is easily worked both with hand tools and machine tools. It shapes and finishes well, but should not be run through a surfacer, as it chips out. It may, however, be run through a bed sander with good results. Particleboard has good rigidity, dimensional stability, and water resistance, as well as good impact strength and superior acoustical properties. In high-density particleboard, unbalanced construction (covering or coating one surface without covering the opposite surface) is not harmful as it is in solid or veneered construction.

Uses

Particleboard is used as a core for veneer, plastic laminates, and solid-core doors. It is also used for making tables, desks, bench tops, and counter tops. Particleboard is used as well in the manufacture of floors, store fixtures, panels, furniture, cabinets, and underlayments. Particleboard that has been molded into various shapes can be observed in many common products. Some examples of molded particleboard are as follows: drawers, boxes, phonograph cabinets, foundation parts for upholstered furniture, chair seats, cores for irregular curves to be veneered, and siding on structures.

Market Analysis

Shapes

Particleboard is available both in sheets and molded shapes.

Sizes

Thickness	Lengths and Widths				
	2½' × 4'	4' × 8'	4' × 10'	4' × 12'	4' × 18'
¼"		•			
⅜"		•	•	•	•
½"		•			
9/16"		•			
⅝"		•			
11/16"		•			
¾"	•	•	•		
13/16"		•			
1"		•	•		
1⅛"		•	•		
1¼"		•	•		
2"		•	•		

Standards

Particleboard is identified according to (a) type, (b) grade, and (c) class. There are two types of particleboard, classified by the type of binder used:
1. **Type I** board is **urea bonded** and composes 90 to 95% of the particleboard produced. It is intended for interior use.
2. **Type II** is made with a **phenolic-resin binder** and is suitable for both exterior use and interior use. It can be subjected to high temperatures.

Each type is made in three grades. Grades are determined by density. (The higher the density, the harder and heavier the panel will be).
1. **Grade A** (high density). This grade has a density range of 50 or more pounds per cubic foot.
2. **Grade B** (medium density). Grade B particleboard has a density range of 37 to 50 pounds per cubic foot.
3. **Grade C** (low density). The density range of this grade is below 37 pounds per cubic foot.

There are two **classes** for each grade of particleboard. Classes of particleboard are determined by properties such as **modulus of rupture, modulus of elasticity, internal bond, expansion,** and **screw-holding power** (on both the face and the edge). **Class I** has a lower range than **Class II.** However, both classes have a higher modulus of rupture and modulus of elasticity in the higher-density grades than in either the medium- or low-density grades.

Maintenance

Particleboard should be stored flat and in a dry place.

The Garrett Wade Company

SECTION TWO.

Layout and Getting Out Stock

Topic 9.

Tools

Over the centuries, jigs and devices have been improvised for the purpose of making work easier and more efficient. These devices are commonly known as **tools.** Tools are of many types. Some are quite simple in their design, while others are rather complex. Complex tools are generally classified as **machines.**

Tools and machines provide increased mechanical advantage, accuracy, efficiency, speed, and, in many cases, safety in the work operation. Through the proper selection and use of tools, the worker is able to perform tasks more effectively. Many of these tasks would be impossible to do if the worker had to rely only on the use of the hands or on crude, primitive implements.

In the search for greater efficiency, new tools are always being invented, and modifications are continually being made on existing tools. The introduction of new materials and the application of contemporary design methods have together improved both the quality and the efficiency of tools.

Tools are classified according to their particular function and in terms of the simple machines of science. Thus, in woodworking, there are cutting tools (knives, saws, planes, and chisels), which are **wedges;** driving tools (hammers, spiral screwdrivers, and bit braces), which are examples of the **lever, inclined plane,** and **wheel and axle** respectively; and boring tools, which are applications of the **wedge, inclined plane,** and **screw.** See Figs. 2-1 through 2-5. Obviously, some tools are a combination of several of the simple machines. Complicated power tools contain applications of each of the six simple machines of science: the wedge, the lever, the inclined plane, the screw, the wheel and axle, and the pulley.

Both the name and the functional classification of woodworking tools indicate their use and purpose. Thus, a screwdriver is a **driving tool,** a saw is a **cutting tool,** and a square is a **testing and layout tool.** A knowledge of the particular class of simple machine to which a tool belongs should provide some insight into the basic principle by which that tool and its principal parts are operated. This understanding will enable the worker to use the tool to its best mechanical advantage and efficiency.

Students of woodworking classify tools functionally as any of the following: measuring, layout, and testing tools; cutting, drilling, and boring tools; driving, striking, holding, and clamping tools; and sharpening tools. All but the measuring, layout, and testing tools are examples of the wedge, lever, inclined plane, screw, wheel and axle, and pulley.

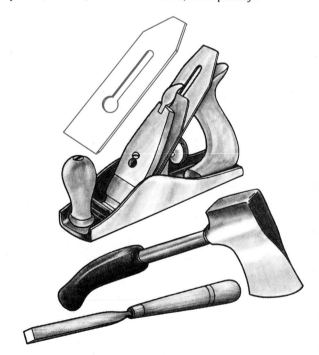

Fig. 2-1. Examples of wedges used on simple woodworking tools. The wedge is the actual cutting portion of the tool.

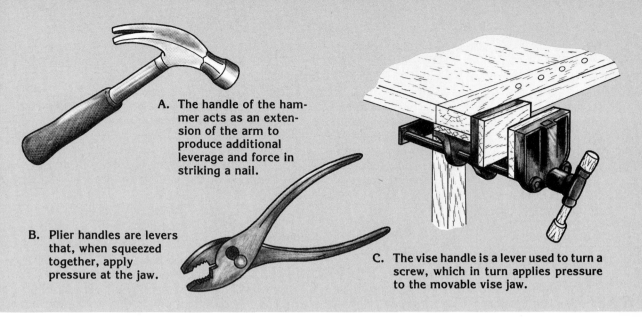

A. The handle of the hammer acts as an extension of the arm to produce additional leverage and force in striking a nail.

B. Plier handles are levers that, when squeezed together, apply pressure at the jaw.

C. The vise handle is a lever used to turn a screw, which in turn applies pressure to the movable vise jaw.

Fig. 2-2.   Applications of the lever.

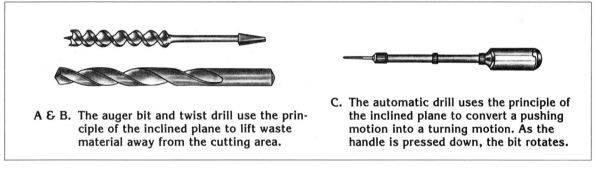

A & B. The auger bit and twist drill use the principle of the inclined plane to lift waste material away from the cutting area.

C. The automatic drill uses the principle of the inclined plane to convert a pushing motion into a turning motion. As the handle is pressed down, the bit rotates.

Fig. 2-3.   The application of the inclined plane is easily recognized in many drilling and boring tools.

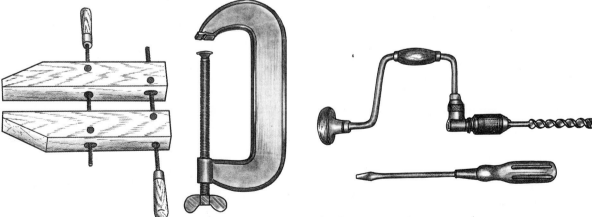

Fig. 2-4.   Tools utilizing the principle of the screw include the hand screw and C-clamp. By turning the screw, force is applied to the clamp jaws.

Fig. 2-5.   The bit brace and screwdriver are examples of tools that use the principle of the wheel and axle. The handles of these tools act like a large-diameter wheel driving an axle.

Wedge

All edge and toothed tools such as knives, planes, chisels, gouges, files, saws, hatchets, and the cutting edges of drills and bits are examples of the wedge. Those with teeth contain a series of cutting wedges. The wedges of woodworking cutting tools separate the wood fibers by processes of shearing, slicing, shredding, scraping, and splitting.

Lever

Leverage is applied in the operation of a number of hand tools requiring strength or pressure. Sometimes the **fulcrum** (or pivot point) is a part of the worker's arm. Sometimes it is a specially designed feature of the tool. Pinch bars, nippers, pliers, vise handles, and hammers are all examples of first class levers on which the forces pivot about a fixed fulcrum. Tools such as scrapers, chisels, and planes are levers and wedges used in various combinations to increase mechanical advantage. The wedge is the cutting part, and the handle helps the user to obtain leverage.

When the hammer is used to drive nails, it becomes a lever arm of force. The handle length multiplied by the weight of the hammerhead times the effort equals the force applied to the nail in the direction of the path of the hammerhead.

Using a 16-ounce hammer with a 10″ handle to drive a nail, you strike the nail with 100 pounds force when you apply 10 pounds of force at the handle end.

Example:
Weight of hammerhead × effort applied at handle × length of handle = force
$$1 \times 10 \times 10 = 100 \text{ lbs.}$$

When the hammer (a first class lever) is used to withdraw nails, the fulcrum is located between the effort and the force. Effort times distance to fulcrum equals force distance to fulcrum.

Example:
Hammer handle 10″
Claw   1-1/2″
Effort   25 lbs.
$$25 \times 10 = 1\text{-}1/2 \times \text{force F}$$
$$250 = 1\text{-}1/2\text{F}$$
$$F = 166 \text{ lbs.}$$

Inclined Plane

Auger bits, drill bits, twist drills, and spiral screwdrivers are examples of the inclined plane. Mechanical advantage and efficiency are obtained by distributing the resistance or weight in such a way as to effect an indirect, gradual pull or lift as on an incline or spiral.

Screw

A number of tools have a threaded section or screw by which heavy pressure can be exerted with a minimum of effort. The application of the screw is found in such clamping and holding tools as handscrews, vises, clamps, and chucks. The screw is a form of inclined plane and is used to ease the operation of adjustment mechanisms (adjusting wheel of plane) or to lessen resistance (screw portion of boring tools).

A bench vise is a good example of this simple machine. In terms of the simple machine, the handle represents the wheel and the bolt shaft the axle. The thread of the bolt is the inclined plane.

Combining the formula for the wheel and axle and the formula for the inclined plane, we have the following: weight of closing jaws (W) × pitch distance traveled in one revolution (P) = effort to turn handle (E) × the distance effort travels in making one turn (circumference of circle vise handle describes — 2πr).

$$W \times P = E \times 2\pi r$$
Pitch of screw = 1/4″
Effort to turn = 10 lbs.
$$W \times .25 = 10 \times 2 (3.14) \times 8$$
$$W = 2009 \text{ lbs.}$$

In the preceding problem, no allowance was made for friction. The bearing on the screw sets up tremendous friction, which reduces the push of the closing jaws and leaves about 10% working efficiency. This would give a closing push of 2009 × .10 or 200 pounds push.

Wheel and Axle

In some tools, great leverage is obtained by the act of twisting, winding, or cranking in such a manner that force is distributed in a circular motion around a fixed point or pivot. Screwdrivers, hand drills, bit braces, and ratchets are examples of the application of the principle of the wheel and axle.

Radius of wheel × effort =
radius of axle × wt.

This principle of driving force is used in the turning of the bit brace.

A five-pound push on the crank arm produces a force of 50 pounds on the auger cutters.

Radius of crank × effort = radius of
auger (axle) × force
5 × 5 = .5 × force
$$\frac{25}{.5} = \text{force}$$
50 lbs. = force

Pulley

Belt-driven machines use single or cone pulleys to transmit power. The cone pulley also serves to vary the rates of speed. See Fig. 2-6.

The pulley attached to the driving force (usually a motor) is called the **driver,** and transmits power by means of a belt to another pulley, called the **driven.** If both pulleys are of the same diameter, the driven will rotate at the same speed as the driver. If the driven is smaller than the driver, it will be rotated at a **higher** speed than the power source (motor). If the driven is larger than the driver it will rotate at a **lower** speed than the driving force (motor).

As the driver pulley rotates one revolution, it causes the belt to advance a distance

equal to the circumference of the driver. This may be computed using the formula for the circumference of a circle. Circumference (C) equals pi (π) times the diameter (D) or:

$$C = \pi D$$

Thus, a 2″ diameter driver has a circumference of 3.1416 × 2″ or 6.2832″, and will advance the belt 6.2832″. Since the belt is responsible for turning the driven pulley, a 6.2832″ advance of the belt will drive the driven pulley 6.2832″ of circumference. Thus, a 2″ driven pulley will rotate one revolution. (C = πD or C = 3.1416 × 2) for each revolution of the driver pulley.

To compute speed of pulleys:
Driver   Driven
πD = πDx

Example: A 2″ driver driving a 1″ driven would be:
π2″ = π1″x
3.1416 × 2″ = 3.1416 × 1x
6.2832″ = 3.1416x
$$\frac{6.2832″}{3.1416″} = x$$
2 = x or two revolutions of the driven for each revolution of the driver

Example: A 2″ driver driving a 4″ driven would be:
πD = πDx
π2″ = π × 4x
3.1416 × 2″ = 3.1416 × 4x
6.2832″ = 12.5664x
$$\frac{6.2832″}{12.5664} = x$$
1/2 = x or a half revolution of the driven for each revolution of the driver

Combinations of Simple Machines

Many woodworking hand tools are combinations of several of the simple machines of science. One principal part may function as a screw and another as an inclined plane or wheel and axle. The jack plane, for example, contains applications of the wedge, the lever, the inclined plane, and the screw. Power tools and woodworking machines represent the application of a variety of combinations of the simple machines.

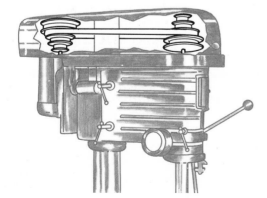

Fig. 2-6. Machine speeds may be altered (as on this drill press) by changing the belt location on the cone pulleys.

Topic 10.

Introduction to Measurement and Layout

Linear measure (measure in inches and feet) is the basic system used in woodworking. Although measurement in this area is less precise than in some other fields, accuracy is still imperative. The worker must ensure that parts fit, that joints are tight, and that individual members are square and sit flat. These are a sample of the demanding requirements that must be met.

In furniture making, the tolerance may be 1/32″. In patternmaking, it may be 1/64″ or less. However, in carpentry and in other rough work, the tolerance may be 1/16″ or greater. An accomplished woodworker is accurate at all times and is capable of performing within the necessary tolerance.

Metric Measure

Every major country in the world has switched to a system of measurement called the International System of Units (abbreviated SI). This is a modernized version of the metric system established by international agreement. Use of metric weights and measures was legalized in the United States in 1866, yet we have been slower than other countries in making the conversion. This system provides a logical and interconnected framework for all measurements in science, industry, and commerce. Most manufacturing industries have found it necessary to adopt the metric system in order to remain competitive on the international market. Thus, almost all other industries are well ahead of the woodworking industries in making this conversion.

Major manufacturers of woodworking measuring tools produce instruments such as rules, tapes, marking gauges, and squares that are calibrated in the metric system, but they have not yet begun to describe other tools listed in their catalogs (such as planes, chisels, saws, hammers, drills, and bits) in the metric system. Manufacturers of plywood, hardboard, particleboard, and other manufactured board indicate they have worked out new standard

sizes of length, width, and thickness, but will not make the conversion until the construction industry adopts new standards. Paint manufacturers still mark containers with U.S. Customary measurement, such as half pint, pint, quart, and gallon, but some manufacturers now indicate the metric equivalent of these measures. For example:

    1 pint   - 473 ml (milliliters)
    1 quart - 946.33 ml
    1 gallon - 3.78 l (liters)

Eventually, the U.S. measures will be dropped and products sold in metric units only. This will involve a slight change in sales units. For example, a quantity of liquid will not be sold by the quart (.95 l) but by the liter (1.06 qts.) That which is now sold by the gallon (3.78 l) will be sold in 5-liter (1.32 gal.) quantities.

Weight will also be measured in metric units. The units that will be used in packaging are grams (1 g = .035 oz.) and kilograms (1 kg = 2.45 lbs.), replacing the current sales units of (dry) ounces (28.35 g) and pounds (.45 kg).

The student of woodworking is advised to learn the metric system because it is the measuring system of the future. The system is very simple to learn and use since measurements of length, weight, and volume are all interrelated. The simplicity of the system is demonstrated in the following examples: In order to convert from inches to feet, you must divide by 12, but to convert from millimeters to centimeters you simply move the decimal point one place to the left. To convert from feet to yards, you must divide by three, but to convert from centimeters to meters you simply move the decimal point two places to the left. Thus:

    1000.   millimeters (mm) which is the same as
     100.0   centimeters (cm) which is the same as
      10.00   decimeters (dm) which is the same as
       1.000   meter (m)

The interrelatedness of the system is shown in the following example: A cube that is 10 cm × 10 cm × 10 cm is 1,000 cubic centimeters. A cube of this size will hold exactly one liter of water, and one liter of water weighs exactly one kilogram.

The student is advised to learn the metric system of measurement and to **think metric!** The student is also advised to purchase measurement tools that are calibrated in both U.S. and metric graduations.

Making Parts Straight, Square, and Parallel

Woodworkers are concerned with such matters as whether parts are straight, square, and parallel. Many wood products contain parts that are either square or rectangular. Boards, planks, cants, and turning squares are all basic geometric forms having surfaces that are relatively straight and either perpendicular or parallel.

The principle of **parallelism** is basic in laying out and cutting stock (or even in processes such as turning or boring holes). Stock is milled to parallel thickness and cut to parallel widths. It is typical procedure in processing stock to select or prepare a surface that is reasonably flat, to prepare an edge that is straight and at right angles (90° to the surface), and to prepare an end that is straight and 90° to both the edge and the surface. Once those working planes are established,

measurements and layouts can be made from them and opposite surfaces, edges, and ends can be cut parallel and square. The principle of parallelism also applies in shaping irregular and circular cutouts.

In making measurements and layouts, the woodworker starts with a straight surface as a reference for all measurements. Layout tools, such as gauges and squares, are designed with the principles of both the perpendicular and parallel planes. The adjacent parts (blade) of these tools form a right angle (to the handle), and all marks or lines made with them are readily made perpendicular to the handle or parallel to the blade. All squares and marking gauges exemplify in their operation standard geometric theorems such as these:

- Two lines are parallel if they lie in the same plane and do not intersect, even if extended.
- Two lines parallel to a third line are parallel to each other.
- Two lines perpendicular to a third line are parallel.
- If a line is perpendicular to one of two parallel lines, it is perpendicular to the other.

It may thus be said that gauges and squares are instruments of mathematics. Certainly their correct applications in measuring, marking, layout, and testing are based on the acceptance of mathematical principles or theorems.

Rules	**Topic 11.**

Classification

Linear measuring instruments

Application

Principle of Operation

Rules are used for duplicating measurements and testing against standard units of measure. Woodworking rules are usually graduated in 1/4″, 1/8″, and 1/16″. Accurate measurements are best made by holding the rule on edge so that the graduations are next to the work. Because the ends of rules often get worn, it is advisable to make measurements from one of the inch marks to ensure accuracy.

Kinds and Uses

1. **Bench rules** and **folding rules,** Figs. 2-7 and 2-8, are instruments used in layout to measure relatively short distances. They are made of boxwood, maple, brass, or steel, and are available in 1′, 2′, and 3′ lengths.
2. **Steel rules** and **tapes** are usually made of flexible steel, in lengths from 6′ to 100′,

Stanley Tools

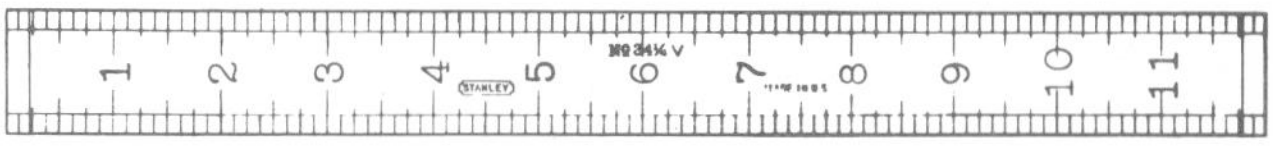

Fig. 2-7. Bench rule.

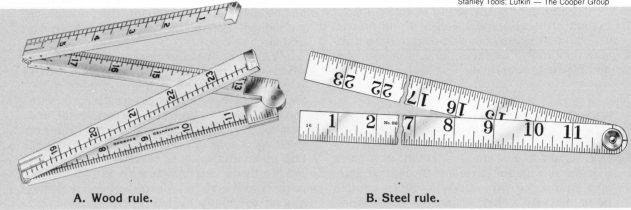

A. Wood rule.   B. Steel rule.

Fig. 2-8.   Two-foot folding rules:

Fig. 2-9.   Flexible steel rule.

Fig. 2-11. Slide caliper rule.

Fig. 2-12. Board rule.

Fig. 2-10. Extension rule.

Fig. 2-13. Log rule.

and are used for measuring longer distances. See Fig. 2-9.

3. **Extension rules** are made of boxwood or maple, in lengths of 4′ and 8′. They are used for inside measurements, such as door and window openings, or for measuring distances greater than the capacity of a bench rule. See Fig. 2-10.

4. **Hook rules** and **caliper rules,** Fig. 2-11, are made of boxwood and are used to measure diameters of cylindrical pieces.

5. **Shrink rules** are made of steel or boxwood and are used by patternmakers. The divisions of a shrink rule are made slightly greater than those of standard rules, to allow for shrinkage of metals in casting. Thus, a 1/4″ shrink rule would be 12-1/4″ long. They are available in 1′ and 2′ lengths with shrinkage allowances of 1/10″, 1/8″, 3/16″, and 1/4″ to the foot.

6. The **board rule** is used to measure footage of lumber. It is made of hickory and is 3′ in length, Fig. 2-12.

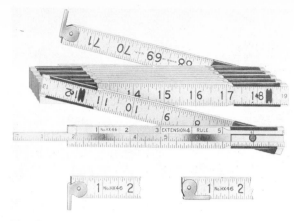

Fig. 2-14. Folding extension rule or zigzag rule.

7. **Log rules** are used to determine the lumber footage in a log. They are made of hickory and are available in 3', 4', 5', and 6' lengths, Fig. 2-13.
8. The **folding extension rule** or **zigzag rule,** Fig. 2-14, is available in 4', 6', and 8' lengths, with locking joints that permit each member to fold either way. Each member is graduated in **inches** and **sixteenths** on both edges of both sides. Because of the number of joints, its accuracy is limited. It is the most common rule used by carpenters for rough layout.

Principal Parts and Function of Each

1. **Hinges** on folding rules permit a more compact unit.
2. **Tips** on the ends, made of harder material, prevent wearing, which could make the rule inaccurate.

3. **Hooks** on hook rules and caliper rules make the measurement of diameters easier.
4. **Cases** on steel tapes provide housing for the tape. The tape winds into a compact unit inside the case.

Maintenance

Cleaning

Rules should be kept clean from dirt or rust so that divisions and figures can be easily read. It is sometimes necessary to use steel wool and oil to clean metal rules. Mild soap and warm water can be used to clean rules made of wood.

Storing

Steel rules should be stored in a dry place to prevent rusting. They should be coated with a film of oil before being left unused for a long period of time.

Lubricating

Joints on folding rules should be lubricated with light machine oil.

Market Analysis

Attachments

Some two-foot folding rules have a **protractor** and a **level** attachment.

Gauges

Topic 12.

Classification

Marking and layout tools

Application

Principle of Operation

A wedge-shaped spur marks or scores a line to a set distance from the head.

Kinds and Uses

1. **Marking gauges** are used to make lines parallel to an edge. They are usually 8" long, Figs. 2-15A and 2-15B.
2. The **butt gauge** is used for laying out hinges. It has two bars, each 2-1/2" long. One bar has a spur on each end. The other bar has a spur on only one end. With a screw, an oval spur is attached to the end of the

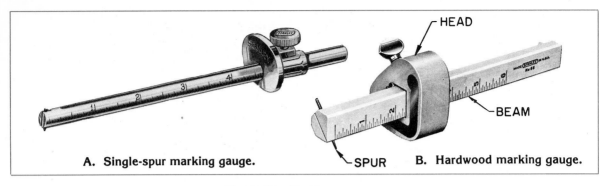

Stanley Tools

A. **Single-spur marking gauge.**

B. **Hardwood marking gauge.**

HEAD

BEAM

SPUR

Fig. 2-15. **Marking gauges.**

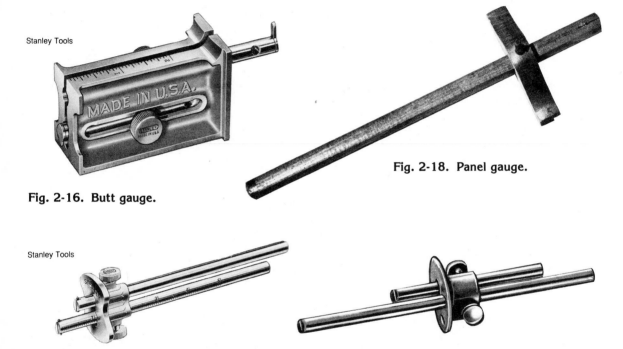

Stanley Tools

Fig. 2-16. **Butt gauge.**

Fig. 2-18. **Panel gauge.**

Stanley Tools

Fig. 2-17. **Double-spur marking and mortise gauge.**

Fig. 2-19. **Roller marking gauge or pattern-maker's gauge.**

bar. This makes internal marking possible. The body holds the bars, and the knurled nut locks the bar. See Fig. 2-16.

3. **Mortise gauges** are used for laying out mortises and tenons. These are similar to marking gauges except that they have two spurs. Both sides of the mortise can be marked with a single stroke. One type of mortise gauge has a bar within a bar. Another type has a double or split bar with a spur on each, Fig. 2-17.

4. **Parallel gauges** or **panel gauges** have a longer bar and a larger head. They are used to lay out lines at a greater distance from the working edge than the marking gauge would allow. See Fig. 2-18.

5. The **roller marking gauge** or **patternmaker's gauge** is similar to a marking gauge. It has a spur at one end of the beam and a roller cutter at the other end, Fig. 2-19. This roller cutter scores lines on concave and convex surfaces.

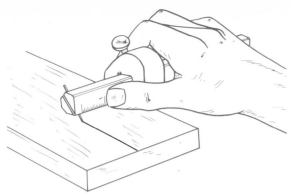

Fig. 2-20. Using the marking gauge.
　　The beam of the marking gauge is laid flat on the wood, the spur to the rear. With the spur in contact with the wood, the gauge is then pushed, scoring a line. This method permits observation of the line as it is being scored.

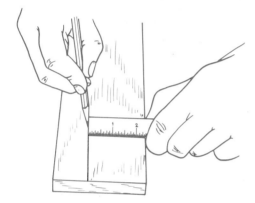

Fig. 2-21. Marking a line with a rule and pencil.
　　Slide the rule along the length of the stock, keeping the pencil against the end of the rule. (This method is not recommended for accurate gauging.)

Principal Parts and Function of Each

1. The **head** or **block** of marking gauges, parallel gauges, and mortise gauges is made of either beech, maple, boxwood, or rosewood. The better gauges have brass insets to prevent wear at the bearing surface.
　　The block or head slides along the beam or bar, and may be set at any point by means of a thumbscrew. The block serves as a guide.
2. The **beam** or **bar** of the marking gauge is usually 8″ long and is graduated in inches by sixteenths. It is made of hard wood or steel.
3. The **spur** is a steel pin fastened near the end of the beam. This pin scores a line on the board.

Fig. 2-22. Utility knife with retractable blade — used for normal cutting, delicate work, and scoring.

Fig. 2-23. Finger gauging.
　　This is a fast, inaccurate method of gauging. It is used in cases where scoring a line with the marking gauge would mar the face of the work. Care must be taken to avoid contracting splinters.

Maintenance

Adjusting

　　The spur may need to be adjusted. It should protrude 1/16″ to 1/8″ below the beam.

Shaping of Spur

　　Spurs may need to be shaped with a mill file. Either a chisel point or a knife point is acceptable.

　　Note: Defective parts may be replaced.

Market Analysis

Capacity

　　The capacity of a gauge is determined by the length of the bar.

Topic 13.

Squares

Classification

Measuring, layout, and testing tools

Application

Principle of Operation

The right angle of the **square** is used in testing the squareness (right angles) of adjacent sides of a piece or adjacent parts of an object.

The square is also used as a guide for a pencil or knife when guide lines are being drawn. The combination square may be used with a pencil to gauge lines parallel to a surface.

Kinds and Uses

Squares are used in testing 45°, 90°, and 180° angles, for laying out straight lines and angles, and for measuring.
1. The **try square,** Fig. 2-24, usually has a 6″ or 10″ blade. Smaller try squares, with 3″ or 4″ blades, are also available.
2. The **miter square,** Fig. 2-25.
3. The **combination square** has a 6″, 8″, 10″, or 12″ blade, Fig. 2-26.
4. The **combination set** (see "Attachments"), Fig. 2-27.
5. The **steel square** usually has a 12″ or 24″ body and an 8″ or 16″ tongue, Fig. 2-28.

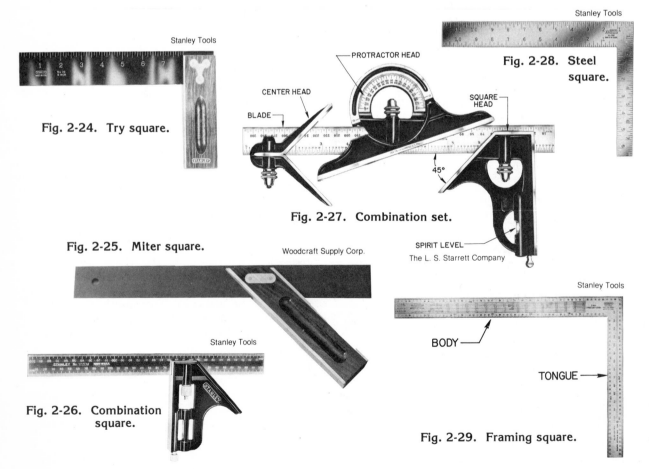

Stanley Tools

Fig. 2-24. Try square.

Fig. 2-25. Miter square.

Woodcraft Supply Corp.

Stanley Tools

Fig. 2-26. Combination square.

PROTRACTOR HEAD

CENTER HEAD

BLADE

SQUARE HEAD

45°

Fig. 2-27. Combination set.

SPIRIT LEVEL

The L. S. Starrett Company

Stanley Tools

Fig. 2-28. Steel square.

Stanley Tools

BODY

TONGUE

Fig. 2-29. Framing square.

6. The **framing square** usually has a 24″ body and a 16″ tongue. It has tables to assist in calculation. See Fig. 2-29.
7. The **center square,** Fig. 2-30, is used to find the center of a cylinder. It can also be used as a protractor to find a given angle.

Fig. 2-30. Center square.

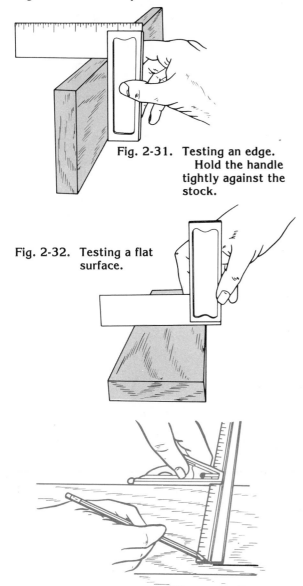

Fig. 2-31. Testing an edge. Hold the handle tightly against the stock.

Fig. 2-32. Testing a flat surface.

Fig. 2-33. Scribing a line, using a combination square.

Fig. 2-34. Scribing a line, using a try square and a sloyd knife.

Principal Parts and Function of Each

1. The **handle** or **butt** is the shortest part of a try square. It is made either of rosewood or of cast iron. The shorter member on a steel framing square is called the **tongue.** On the combination square it is called the **square head.** This head is made of cast iron, and the working surfaces are machined.
2. The **blade** or **beam** of the try square is the flat steel part, which is graduated into sixteenths or eighths of an inch. It is longer than the handle. The blade of a combination square is graduated into eighths, sixteenths, thirty-seconds and sixty-fourths of an inch, and serves as a base for any of its sliding heads. (See "Attachments.")
3. Framing squares are made of either polished, blued, or stainless steel, royal copper, or aluminum. The edges are ground true. There are four tables that often appear on framing squares. These are as follows: (1) **Rafter** or **framing tables,** which are used to determine the length and angle of the common, valley, hip, and jack rafters. (2) The **Essex board-measure table,** which lists board measure for standard lengths and widths. (3) The **octagon scale,** for laying out eight-sided figures. (4) The **brace table,** which shows the length for common braces. See Fig. 2-29.
4. **Take-down** framing squares have a tongue that can be removed from the body. This makes it easier to store the square in a tool box.

Maintenance

When storing tools for an indefinite period of time, first apply a light coating of oil to all metal parts to prevent rust. Care should always be taken not to drop or give rough treatment to the square, as this may cause it to get out of alignment, thereby limiting its use. As a result of gradual wear on the slide, the combination square may not remain accurate. Therefore, it should be checked periodically for accuracy.

Market Analysis

Capacity

The capacity of a square is determined by the length of the blade.

Fig. 2-35. Early forms of testing and layout tools.
Note the ingenuity displayed in the construction of the dividers — a single, bent piece of wood is regulated in radius by a turnbuckle.

Attachments

A combination set includes three types of heads: The **square head** has a level glass in the head and is used for testing levelness and for laying out 90° and 45° angles. The **center head** is used for finding the center of a cylinder. The **protractor head** is used to determine or to lay out any angle from 0° to 360°. See Fig. 2-27.

Stops for framing squares (called **gauges** or **clips**) are used in laying out stair stringers. See Fig. 2-37.

Fig. 2-36. All-purpose layout tool.
This tool may be used as a level, a plumb, a square, a marking gauge, a protractor, a depth gauge, a beam compass, a stud marker, a screw gauge, a dowel gauge, or a nail gauge.

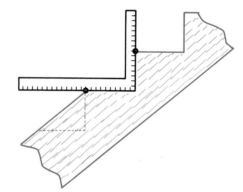

Fig. 2-37. Framing square with stops.

Topic 14.

Laying Out and Testing Angles

Classification

Measuring, marking, and checking

Procedure

Angles of 45° and 90°

1. Angles of 90° are laid out and tested with a try square. Angles of 45° and 90° are laid

out and tested with the aid of the framing square, steel square, miter square, or combination square.

2. A short bevel of 45° may be laid out or tested with the aid of the miter square (Fig. 2-38) or the combination square (Fig. 2-26).

3. A larger bevel of 45° may be laid out by using the framing square or by measuring an equal distance on the sides of a 90° angle and connecting with a diagonal as illustrated in Fig. 2-39.

Using the T-Bevel

The **T-bevel** is the most common tool for laying out angles other than 90°. These are angles such as bevels, chamfers, miters, and various kinds of polygons. The protractor head of the combination set may also be used for laying out these angles.

1. Set the T-bevel to the required angle. The blade is moved by loosening the clamping screw, and is set to the desired angle with the aid of a protractor or a framing square.

(See Table of Angles, which follows.) The T-bevel is used in the same manner as the try square, but not as a substitute for it. See Figs. 2-40 and 2-41.

2. For convenience in laying out the above angles, attach a wood fence to the framing square. See Fig. 2-42. Set the fence at an angle from the table reading.

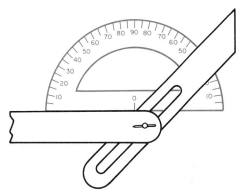

Fig. 2-40. Setting a T-bevel with a protractor.

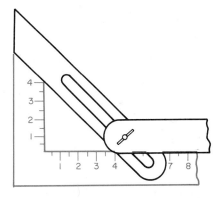

Fig. 2-41. Setting a T-bevel, using the table of angles and a steel or framing square.

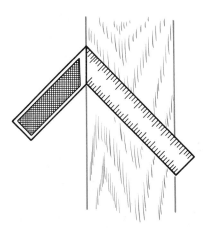

Fig. 2-38. Using the miter square at a 45° angle.

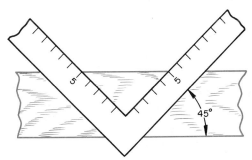

Fig. 2-39. Using the steel or framing square to lay out a 45° angle.

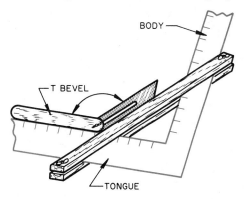

Fig. 2-42. Setting a T-bevel with a framing square and fence.

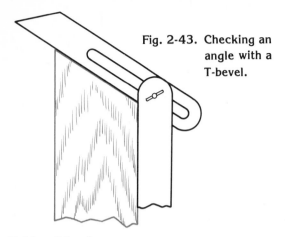

Fig. 2-43. Checking an angle with a T-bevel.

Table of Angles

The table below indicates the angle that is formed when a line is drawn between given pairs of measurements on the framing square. The T-bevel may be set according to this angle.

The table could be used to lay out the included angles of a given polygon. Half these angles would be used in laying out the miter for the cut.

Angle Divider

The angle divider, Fig. 2-44, may also be used for testing and laying out angles. This tool has two blades that form the bevels for the miter cut for polygons having four, five, six, eight, nine, or ten sides.

Standards and Results

- The tool must be set at the proper angle.
- In testing the angle, care must be taken that the set or adjustment is not changed.

Table 2-1
Table of Angles

Polygon No. of Sides	Angle (Degree)	Tongue (Inches)	Body (Inches)
3	30	12	$20^7/_8$
5	54	12	$8^{25}/_{32}$
6	60	12	$6^{15}/_{16}$
7	$64^2/_7$	12	$5^{25}/_{32}$
8	$67^1/_2$	12	$4^{31}/_{32}$
9	70	12	$4^3/_8$
10	72	12	$3^7/_8$

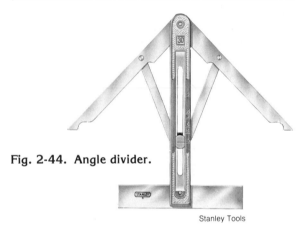

Fig. 2-44. Angle divider.

Stanley Tools

Topic 15.

Laying Out Irregular Shapes, Curves, and Geometric Forms

A. Transferring or Laying Out Irregular Designs, Using Proportional Squares

Classification

Enlarging and reducing designs

Procedure

Most project ideas pictured in books and magazines are scaled drawings that must be enlarged to full size if a pattern is necessary. If the design is symmetrical (the same on either side of the center line), only half the design must be drawn. See Fig. 2-45.

1. Determine how much larger or smaller the pattern is to be in relation to the original drawing or picture. Keep in mind that the

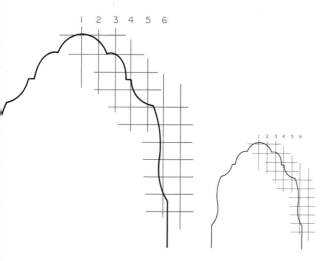

Fig. 2-45. Use of proportional squares on an irregular design.

B. Other Methods of Layout

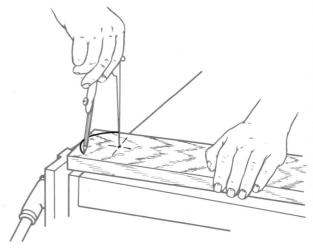

Fig. 2-46. Using a wing divider to scribe a circle.

grid squares in the larger figure should not normally exceed 1".

2. When this scale has been determined, secure a piece of wrapping paper or cardboard large enough to make the full-size pattern.
3. Lay out the vertical and horizontal lines for each of the figures in accordance with the predetermined scale. It will help if the corresponding lines both on the original and on the enlargement are marked with matching numbers.
4. On the full-size grid, carefully duplicate all the intersecting lines of the scaled pattern. Indicate the direction of the curved lines at the points of intersection.
5. Sketch the curves as indicated by the directional lines on the grid. In order to produce a sharp line drawing, use an irregular (French) curve to go over the contours.
6. Transfer this pattern onto the material by tracing with carbon paper or by carefully cutting out the profile and tracing around it. If the pattern is to be used frequently, one made of sheet metal should be used, as it will retain its original shape for a longer period of time.

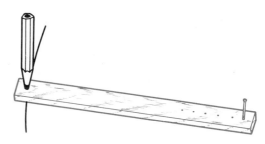

Fig. 2-47. Method of laying out a circle, using trammel points.

Standards and Results

- Lines should be sharp and clear-cut.
- The finished pattern should be in proper proportion to the original drawing.

Fig. 2-48. Laying out a long curve, using a flexible stick and two brads.

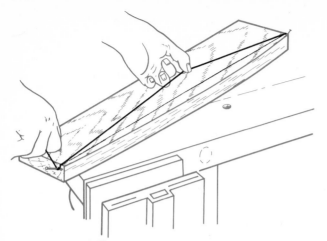

Fig. 2-49. To produce a straight line on a long board, snap a taut chalk line square with the surface.

Fig. 2-50. Dividing stock into equal parts.

Place a rule diagonally across the stock so that the diagonal distance spanned by the rule is a distance easily divisible by the number of equal parts desired. (Example: to divide a piece of 4-7/8″ stock into seven equal parts, place a rule diagonally across the stock so that the distance from one edge to the other is 7″ on the rule.) Mark off each of the divisions on the rule with a sharp pencil. (In the example given, make the pencil mark at each 1″ mark on the rule.) Draw lines parallel to the edge through each of the points marked.

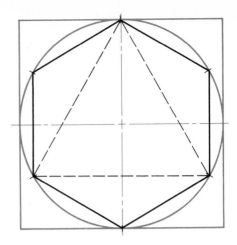

Fig. 2-52. Laying out a hexagon or an equilateral triangle within a circle.

Using the radius of the circle, step off six equal parts around the perimeter of the circle. Use straight lines to connect each point to adjacent points. To form a triangle, connect alternate points as shown by the broken line.

If many pieces must be laid out, construct a simple jig out of sheet metal.

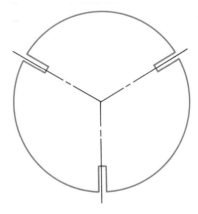

Fig. 2-53. Laying out 120° angles for pedestal legs.

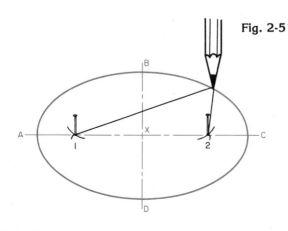

Fig. 2-51. Laying out an ellipse — pin-and-string method.

Lay out the major axis AC and the minor axis BD. Set a compass equal to the distance AX and, using B as the center point, scribe an arc to locate points 1 and 2. Insert pins at points 1, 2, and B. Tie a string to form a loop around the three pins, allowing no slack in the string. Remove the pin at point B and replace it with a sharp pencil. Keeping tension on the string, draw a steady line to form the ellipse.

Getting Out Stock

Topic 16.

Classification

Selecting, measuring, laying out, and cutting

Procedure

1. Determine the required kind of stock, the correct dimensions, and other necessary data from the drawing or the stock bill.
2. Look in a short-piece storage container for the material. Very often, satisfactory material is available there.
3. If you cannot find suitable material in the short-piece container, go to the material storage center. As well as checking the type and grade of the stock, check its dimensions. Examine the stock for warp, defects, or blemishes and determine if these will interfere with the use of that particular material for the job. Select stock that will result in the least amount of waste. Take into consideration qualities such as color, texture, figure, and grain, and be sure each piece is best suited for the purpose it is to serve.
4. Lay out stock, keeping in mind such essential considerations as waste, defects, strength, and beauty.

Stock that has a **waney** (beveled) **edge** may be usable if the wane is removed. Using a straightedge or a chalk line, mark a line on the surface of the board as close to the wane as possible.

See Fig. 2-49. With either a ripsaw or a band saw, cut on the waste side (wane) of the board. Plane the edge to the line, or joint on a jointer.

Stock that has a **crook** may be straightened in the same manner. See Fig. 2-54.

Stock that has either a **bow** or a **wind,** Figs. 2-55 and 2-56, should first be faced. This may be done either by hand planing or with a jointer. If a hand plane is used, it is best to plane the convex surface. If a jointer is used, it is best to face the concave surface. This will give a better bearing surface in both cases.

On stock that has a **cup,** Fig. 2-57, it may be necessary to rip the piece down the center, square the joint, and then glue to achieve the desired width. If narrower

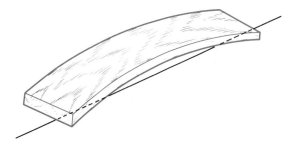

Fig. 2-55. Stock with bow.

Fig. 2-56. Stock with wind.

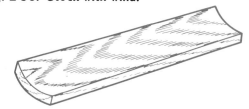

Fig. 2-57. Cupped stock.

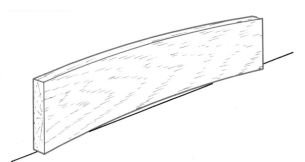

Fig. 2-54. Stock with crook.

pieces are required, rip to rough widths before facing and surfacing. Whether stock has bow, crook, or wind, maximum dimensions in thickness and width are obtained by cutting in **short lengths.** Be careful, however, not to cut the stock too short for later machine cutting and shaping.

In the case of stock that has **end checks** (lengthwise cracks), it may be necessary to cut off the defective end. If narrower pieces are required, the checks may be ripped out.

Knots may be eliminated either by laying out the pieces between the knots, or by ripping out the knots and then gluing to get the desired widths. The same procedure may be followed in eliminating grub holes, wormholes or shakes (splits across the growth rings).

5. Record on your stock bill all the material you have taken. Be sure all necessary dimensions and specifications are noted.

6. Secure the instructor's approval before you cut any stock.

7. Support stock properly and avoid overcutting, tearing, bending, or in any other way damaging the stock or equipment.

8. Use the proper tools and be certain the cut is correct.

9. Store unused material in the proper place and in a safe, neat, and appropriate way.

10. Return tools to their proper places.

The age-old craft of canoe-building is a good illustration of wood selection from available sources. The Ojibwa Indians of northern Michigan used various parts of the trees native to them to construct an ingenious lightweight and watertight vessel. The following excerpt describes the elements used to make such a canoe.

The Song of Hiawatha
by Henry Wadsworth Longfellow

"Give me of your bark, O Birch-Tree!
Of your yellow bark, O Birch-Tree!
Growing by the rushing river,
Tall and stately in the valley!
I a light canoe will build me,
Build a swift Cheemaun for sailing,
That shall float upon the river,
Like a yellow leaf in Autumn,
Like a yellow water-lily!

With his knife the tree he girdled;
Just beneath its lowest branches,
Just above the roots, he cut it,
Till the sap came oozing outward;
Down the trunk from top to bottom,
Sheer he cleft the bark asunder,
With a wooden wedge he raised it,
Stripped it from the trunk unbroken.

"Give me of your boughs, O Cedar!
Of your strong and pliant branches,
My canoe to make more steady,
Make more strong and firm beneath me!"

Down he hewed the boughs of cedar,
Shaped them straightway to a framework,
Like two bows he formed and shaped them,
Like two bended bows together,

"Give me of your roots, O Tamarack!
Of your fibrous roots, O Larch-Tree!
My canoe to bind together,
So to bind the ends together
That the water may not enter,
That the river may not wet me!"

Thus the Birch canoe was builded
In the valley, by the river,
In the bosom of the forest;
And the forest's life was in it,
All its mystery and its magic,
All the lightness of the birch-tree
All the toughness of the cedar,
All the larch's supple sinews;
And it floated on the river,
Like a yellow leaf in Autumn,
Like a yellow water-lily.

Selected Wood Species

Larger wood species photographs were provided by the Fine Hardwoods/American Walnut Association; smaller wood species photographs were provided by the Frank Paxton Company.

Modern desk made of birch and goncalo alves.

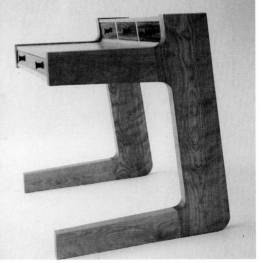

Alder

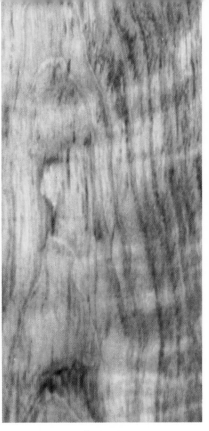

Amazaque

Ash, White (Brown Heart)

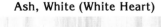

Ash, White (White Heart)

Alder. Origin: Pacific coast. Lightweight, fine texture, good impact resistance. Good machining and finishing qualities. Often stained to blend with walnut, mahogany, or cherry veneer. Used mainly for furniture frames.

Amazaque. Origin: West Africa. Contrasty grain, often figured. Veneer used for furniture and plywood; lumber used for furniture and flooring.

Ash. Origin: Eastern, central U.S. Straight, open grain, moderate workability. Hard, shock-resistant. Used for tool handles, cabinets, furniture, doors, sports equipment.

Banak. Origin: Central and South America. Medium weight; soft, close grain. Easily worked. Used for furniture, cabinets, veneer, and plywood.

Basswood. Origin: Eastern U.S. Lightweight, close grain; soft, fine texture. Easily worked with hand tools; resists warpage. Very stable. Used for patterns, templates, drawing boards, and core stock in veneered panel.

Beech. Origin: Eastern U.S. Moderately hard; even textured. Straight, close grain. White sapwood; reddish brown to white heartwood. Excellent tensile strength and nail- and screw-holding power. Moderately workable. Used for flooring, furniture, crates, dowels, musical instruments, veneers.

Birch. Origin: Eastern U.S., Canada. Close-grained, uniform texture, often curly or wavy figure. Sapwood white; heartwood reddish brown. Strong, hard. Machines and finishes well. Many uses, including furniture, cabinets, dowels, instruments, flooring.

Banak   **Basswood**

Mitchell Azoff, Waukesha, WI
Mindscape Gallery and Studio, Evanston, IL

Cherry rocking bug.

Beech, American   **Birch**   **Birch (Rotary Sliced)**

 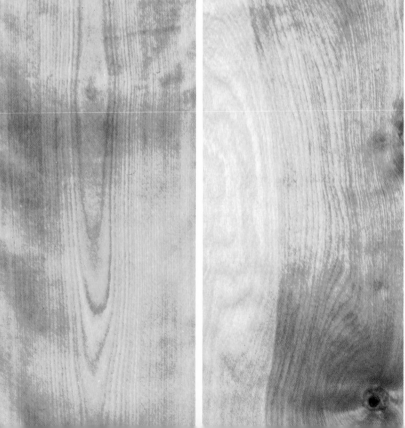

**Bubinga
(Quarter Sliced — Figured)**

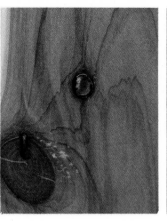

Cedar, Aromatic Red

Cedar, Western

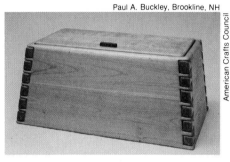

Stuff Box, made of cherry and rosewood.

Cherry

Cherry (Gummy)

Bubinga. Origin: West Africa. Fine-textured, hard. Sometimes has a purplish cast. Dark, uniform stripe pattern. Easily worked. Used for cabinetwork and decorative plywood.

Cedar, Aromatic Red. Origin: Southern, eastern U.S. Actually not a cedar, but a member of the juniper family. Medium-density softwood. Non-porous, close grained, knotty. Sapwood white; heartwood red. Highly fragrant. Easily worked. Used for chests, closet linings, novelty items.

Cedar, Western. Origin: Northern Pacific coast. Lightweight, fragrant. Straight, close grain. Very durable under a variety of weather conditions. Stains well; machines, seasons easily. Used for shingles, exterior construction, interior construction and trim.

Cherry. Origin: Eastern U.S. Moderately heavy, hard, and strong. Must be carefully worked to avoid knots. Close-grained, very stable. Machines and sands well. Not easily worked with hand tools. Used for furniture, interior trim, gunstocks, paneling.

Chestnut (Wormy)

Cypress

Chest, made of cherry, padauk, rosewood, and birch.

Ebony, Macassar

Cocobolo

Cottonwood

Chestnut. Origin: Eastern U.S. Coarse texture, wormy. Very stable and durable. Works and machines easily. Once plentiful but most destroyed by blight. Used for paneling, chests to give rustic effect. Also used for plywood core stock.

Cocobolo. Origin: Central America. A rainbow-streaked rosewood, oily and very hard. Red when cut but darkens quickly. Difficult to work due to interwoven grain. Decorative uses such as small boxes, knife handles. Only heartwood used.

Cottonwood. Origin: Eastern U.S. Lightweight; small pores. Excellent nailing properties, hard to split. Machines easily but dulls cutting edges. Does not finish well. Best worked when very dry. Used for boxes, crates; crossbanding, cores for plywood.

Cypress. Origin: SE U.S. coast. Medium to coarse grain. Lightweight. Heartwood strong and very durable, termite and decay resistant. Easily worked. Superior paint-holding qualities. Used for exterior applications, paneling.

Ebony, Macassar. Origin: Macassar. Extremely hard, dense. Black and brown streaks, very patterned. Difficult to work. Larger work likely to check. Used for wall paneling, inlay, marquetry, ornamental work.

Coffee table, made of bird's-eye maple.

Elm, Gray

Elm, Red

**Gaboon
(Quarter Sliced — Figured)**

Gum, Red (Figured)

Gum, Tupelo

Elm, Gray. Origin: Eastern U.S., SE Canada. Also called "white elm" or "American elm." Strong, shock resistant. Excellent bending properties. Machines well but somewhat difficult to season. Finishes well. Used for veneer, paneling, handles.

Elm, Red. Origin: Eastern U.S., SE Canada. Heartwood reddish to dark brown; sapwood light grayish brown. Hard, strong, durable, and shock resistant. Excellent bending properties; machines and finishes well. Used for cabinetwork and paneling. Often marketed as "northern gray elm."

Gaboon. Origin: West Africa. Lightweight but relatively strong. Low density. Straight-grained; quartersliced wood has interesting figure. Not easily worked; carbide-tipped edge recommended. Used primarily for furniture.

Gum, Red. Origin: SE U.S. Also called "sweet gum." Close-grained, uniform texture. Medium hardness, density, strength. Excellent turning and finishing properties. Can be stained to match more valuable woods such as maple or walnut. Used in cabinetwork, furniture, plywood, veneer, doors.

Gum Tupelo. Origin: SE U.S. Often referred to as "tupelo." Fine, uniform texture. Interlocked grain; low stability. Has good machining and finishing properties. Requires careful seasoning to prevent warpage. Used for furniture structures, crates, cabinetry, and novelties.

David Holmes, Racine, WI
Mindscape Gallery and Studio
Evanston, IL

"Ritual Racer," pine/canvas construction.

Hackberry. Origin: Eastern U.S. A member of the elm family. Medium density and strength. Machines, turns, finishes well; excellent gluing properties. High resistance to shrinking and warpage. Excellent bending properties. Used for furniture frames, tables and chairs, crates.

Hickory. Origin: Eastern U.S. Member of walnut family, very close resemblance to pecan. Very heavy, hard, and shock resistant. Elastic but strong. Heartwood reddish brown; sapwood white. Very durable if kept dry. Machines, turns, bends well. Used for handles of striking tools, ladder rungs, skis.

Koa. Origin: Hawaii. Fine texture, similar to walnut but not as hard. Easily worked; finishes extremely well. Requires moderate care to avoid lifting grain. Used for musical instruments, art objects, furniture, and paneling.

Hackberry

Hickory (Narrow Heart)   **Hickory (Character Marked)**   **Koa**

Lacewood. Origin: Australia. Silvery hue; small, flaky grain due to large rays. Coarse texture. Usually quartered to produce attractive pattern. Used for decorative work on small areas of furniture and paneling.

Limba. Origin: Congo. Often sold under tradename, Korina®. Fine-textured blond wood. Few pores but large enough to give interesting grain. Easily worked with hand or machine tools. Used for furniture and paneling.

Locust, Honey. Origin: East central U.S. Fairly coarse, heavy. Bends well and has high compression strength and shock resistance. Somewhat difficult to work and will check if not carefully seasoned. Used for furniture frames, containers, and structures.

Louro Preto. Origin: Florida through Brazil. Also called "canalete" or "canaletta." Very hard; medium texture. Looks like Brazilian rosewood when red toner applied. Used for fine face veneers, tool and knife handles.

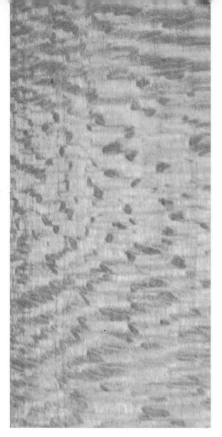

Lacewood (Quarter Sliced)

Prairie Woodworks
Bloomington, IL

Dining table and benches.

Limba (Quarter Sliced)   **Locust, Honey**   **Louro Preto**

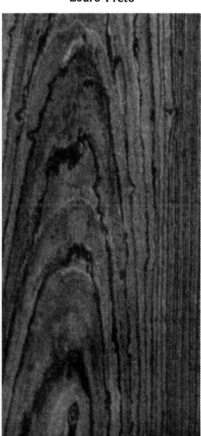

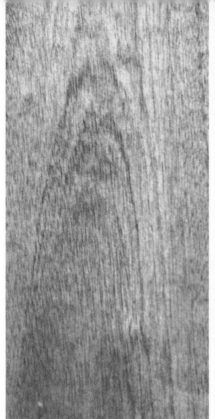

Mahogany, African

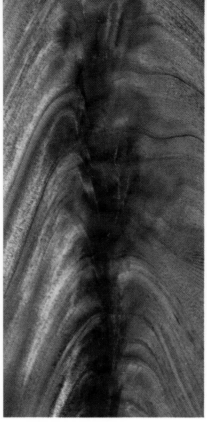

Mahogany, African (Crotch)

Mahogany, African (Swirl)

Mahogany, African. Origin: West Africa. Medium weight and hardness. Open-grain pore structure. Very stable. Available in a variety of attractive grain patterns and figures. Excellent workability and finishing qualities. Good turning and carving properties. Considered the ideal cabinet wood. Used for fine furniture and cabinetry and in boat building.

Mahogany, African
(Quartered — Ribbon Striped)

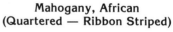

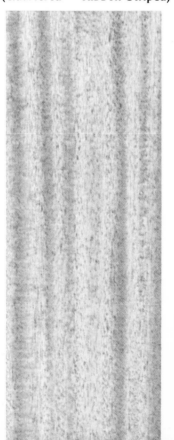

Mahogany, African
(Quartered — Mottled)

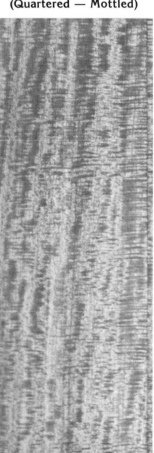

Swing.

Mitchell Azoff, Waukesha, WI
Mindscape Gallery and Studio, Evanston, IL

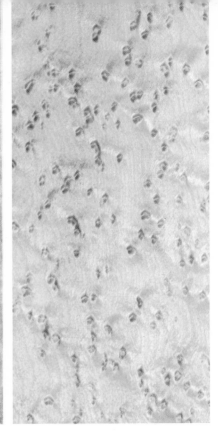

Mahogany, Red Philippine
(Quarter Sliced)

Mahogany, White Philippine
(Quarter Sliced)

Maple (Bird's-eye — Half Round)

Maple (Half Round — Plain)   **Maple (Figured)**

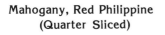

Mahogany, Philippine. Origin: Philippine Islands. Not a true mahogany; also called "lauan." Strong and elastic. Has a ribbon-stripe interlocking grain structure; coarse in texture. Works well and resists decay and warpage. Used for furniture, doors, cabinetmaking, paneling, and boats.

Maple, Hard. Origin: Eastern U.S. and Canada. Heavy, strong, and hard. Very fine grain, often figured as in curly or bird's-eye maple. Has high shock resistance and wears very well. Moderate workability; tends to split when nails or screws are applied. Turns well and takes a high polish. Used for furniture, flooring, cutting boards, workbenches, bowling pins.

Cabinetmaking bench, made of hard maple.

Glenn Gordon, Chicago, IL

Mappa. Origin: Central Europe. Whitish with burly characteristics. Quite sound. Used for face veneer for furniture.

Myrtle. Origin: U.S. Pacific coast. Hard, strong, highly figured. Machines, turns, finishes easily; can be polished to a high luster. Hard to kiln-dry. Timber used for furniture; burls used for veneer. Also for novelty items.

Oak, Red. Origin: Eastern U.S. Heavy, hard, open-grained wood. Has a reddish hue, distinguishing it from white oak. Very strong, and has great wear resistance. Has moderate workability and excellent bending and turning characteristics. Finishes well, but pores must be paste filled. Used for flooring, paneling, house trim, and furniture.

Oak, White. Origin: Eastern U.S. and California. Same characteristics as red oak, except wood is lighter in color, and has greater resistance to decay and water. Pores of white oak are filled with a substance called **tyloses,** which imparts water resistance to the wood. Used in all areas of woodworking. Examples of uses are barrels, shipbuilding, flooring, furniture, and house trim.

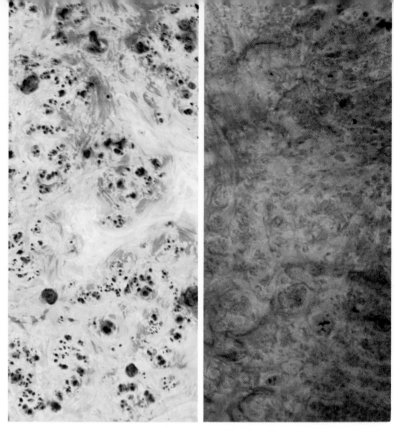

Mappa (Burl — Half Round)   Myrtle (Burl — Half Round)

Oak, Red   Oak, White   Oak, White (Rift Cut)

Padauk, Burma (Quarter Sliced)

Prairie Woodworks, Bloomington, IL

Oak pie safe.

Pecan   **Pecan (Pecky)**

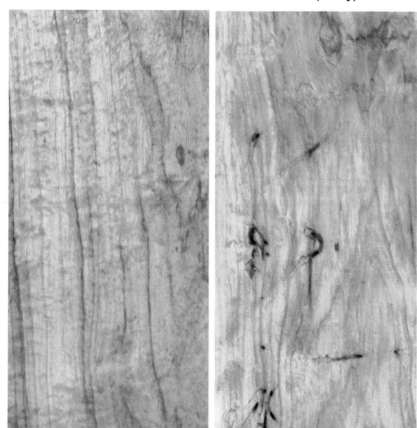

Padauk. Origin: Burma. Also called "vermillion." Hard, firm texture. Very stable and durable. Seasons well but difficult to work because of interlocked grain. Used for art objects and novelty items.

Pecan. Origin: Eastern and Southern U.S. Heavy close-grained wood; hard and strong. Bends, finishes, and machines well, but has poor gluing and nailing characteristics. Used for furniture, flooring, wall paneling, and novelties.

Dining table made of cherry and padauk.

Mark Levin, Chicago, IL

63

Pine, Southern Yellow. Origin: SE U.S. Includes many species of southern-grown pines. Heavy and coarse in texture. Close-grained. Strong and hard. Moderate workability. Used for furniture, structures, paneling, telephone poles, and crates.

Pine, White. Origin: Western U.S. A soft, dimensionally stable wood. Fine, uniform texture. Heartwood tan or brown; sapwood white. Easily worked and can be carved to intricate detail. Used for light construction, patternmaking, interior trim work, and Colonial furniture.

Primavera. Origin: Mexico, Northern South America. Also inaccurately called "white mahogany." Very stable. Medium density; moderately lightweight. Has excellent finishing properties and is used for fine cabinetwork.

Redwood. Origin: N. California to Oregon. Lightweight, close-grained, soft, and moderately strong. Highly resistant to decay and fire. Contains no pitch. Easily worked and stable. Used for exterior trim, shingles, siding, fences, structural timbers, and lawn furniture.

Rosewood, Brazilian. Origin: Brazil. Very stable, hard, and durable. Fairly workable, finishes very smoothly and has a high natural polish. Used for furniture, musical instruments, paneling, art objects. Only heartwood used.

Pine, Southern Yellow   **Pine, White (Knotty)**

Primavera

Mark Lindquist, Henniker, NH

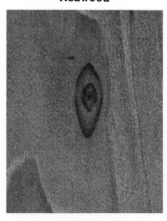

Container turned from cherry burl.

Rosewood, Brazilian

Redwood

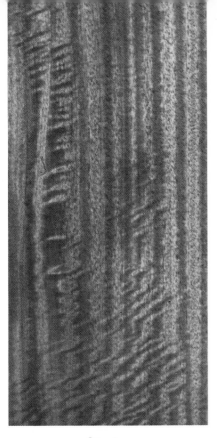

Sapele
(Quarter Sliced — Figured)

Canopy bed.

Sassafras

Satinwood, East Indian
(Quartered — Figured)

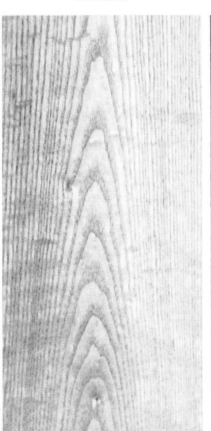

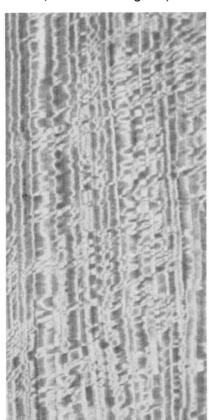

Sapele. Origin: West Africa. Resembles African mahogany though harder, heavier, and not as dimensionally stable. Medium durability and stability. Works quite well with hand and machine tools. Used for furniture and cabinetwork.

Sassafras. Origin: Central to eastern U.S., southern Ontario. Soft and brittle, light, nonporous. Stable and durable. Quite workable but care must be taken in planing not to lift grain. Used for paneling, boats, novelty furniture.

Satinwood, East Indian. Origin: East Indies, Ceylon. Also called "Ceylon satinwood." Hard, dense; interlocking grain. Oily and fine-textured. Fairly workable but inclined to check. Used primarily for furniture.

65

Spruce, Sitka

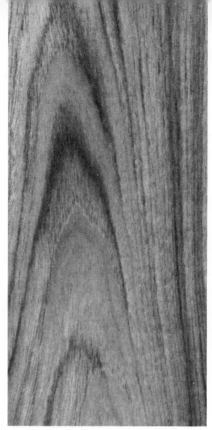

Teak (Half Round)

Tigerwood (Quarter Sliced)

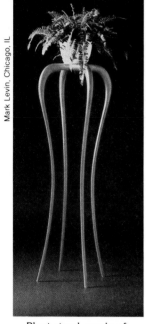

Plant stand, made of cherry and walnut.

Spruce, Sitka. Origin: Alaska to N. California. Lightweight, soft, close-grained. Has highest strength-to-weight ratio of any wood in the world. Does not machine well. Used for general carpentry, ladders, scaffolding, and sail masts.

Teak. Origin: Burma, India, Thailand, Java. Hard, strong, and extremely durable. Dimensionally stable. Has an oily appearance. Fairly workable but dulls tools quickly. Relatively rare and expensive. Used for fine furniture, paneling, ship and boat building.

Tigerwood. Origin: West Africa. Member of the mahogany family. Sometimes called "African walnut." Has a ribbon-stripe pattern; irregular, scattered pores. Good stability when properly seasoned. Easily worked, good finishing qualities. Used for cabinetwork and paneling.

Walnut lamp tables.

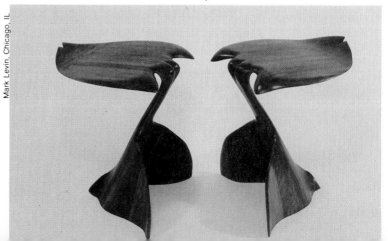

Walnut (Narrow Heart)   Walnut (Wide Heart)   Walnut (Character Marked)

Walnut. Origin: Eastern U.S. Also called "American walnut" or "black walnut." Medium heavy, strong, very stable. Has fine texture and open grain. Heartwood chocolate brown, often with purple cast. Sapwood white. Easily worked and has excellent finishing and carving qualities. Most valuable U.S. furniture wood. Yields a wide variety of grain and figure patterns. Primary uses include fine furniture and cabinets, gunstocks, musical instruments, paneling, and veneers.

Walnut
(Quarter Sliced — Pin Knotty)   Walnut (Butt)   Walnut (Figured)

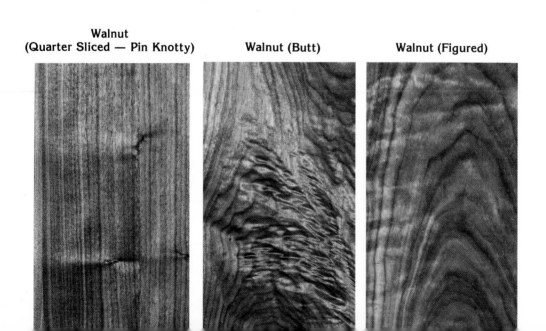

Ejner Pagh, Rockford, IL
Mindscape Gallery and Studio, Evanston, IL

Birch swivel mirror.

Yellow Poplar

Zebrawood (Quarter Sliced)

Yellow Poplar. Origin: SE U.S. Not actually a poplar but a member of the magnolia family. Straight, soft, even-textured. Close-grained. Lightweight but moderately strong. Works and finishes well. Used for furniture construction, siding, interior molding, doors, and novelties.

Zebrawood. Origin: Central, West Africa. Also called "zebrano." Heavy, hard, and coarse. Highly decorative grain pattern. Can be polished to a high luster. Used as quartered veneer for decorative effect as wall paneling, inlay.

Mark Levin
Chicago, IL

Doug Ayers, Little River, CA
Mindscape Gallery and Studio, Evanston, IL

Sling chair, white oak/leather construction.

Bowl, turned from laminated walnut and maple.

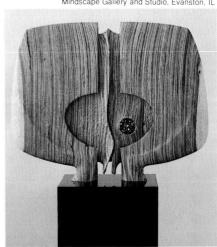

Standing form, made of zebrawood.

John Fossum, Allston, MA
American Crafts Council

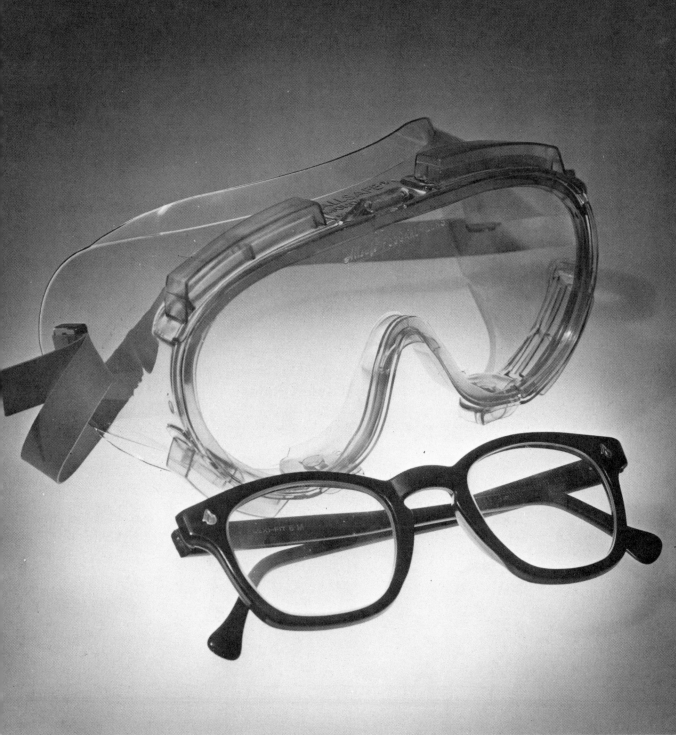

SECTION THREE.

Safety

Topic 17.

Safety

The most important factor in safety is the attitude of the worker. Modern tools and machines are designed to be as safe as possible but it is the careless use of these machines that causes accidents. By developing safe work habits and an awareness of good safety practices, accidents may be avoided. The worker must recognize the dangers involved in each particular operation. An appreciation of good work skills will develop an understanding of the need for proper maintenance of tools. A broken or dull tool should never be used. Both the difficulty of controlling a broken tool and the extra force needed to operate a dull tool restrict the safe control of a particular operation.

You will find that there are more safe ways to do a job than unsafe ways. **Don't take chances. Become familiar** with an operation and **always** follow the correct procedure.

Personal Safety Rules

Fig. 3-1.   **A student dressed properly for working safely around machinery.**

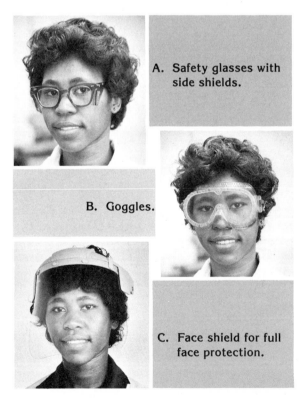

A. Safety glasses with side shields.

B. Goggles.

C. Face shield for full face protection.

Fig. 3-2.   **Your eyes cannot be replaced. Choose the right equipment to protect them.**

Fig. 3-3. Long, loose hair must be tied back so that it will not get caught in the machinery.

Fig. 3-4. Always notify the instructor when an injury occurs and get first-aid treatment as soon as possible.

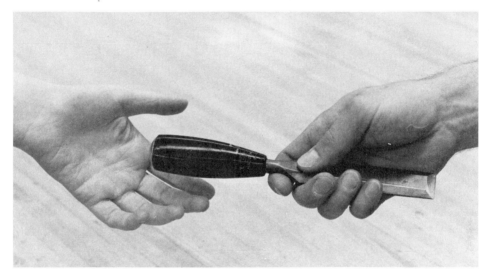

Fig. 3-5. When handing someone a sharp tool, offer it handle first.

Fig. 3-6. In order to avoid injuring someone or damaging the equipment, ask for help in handling long pieces of stock.

Fig. 3-7. So that you will not strain the muscles in your back, learn to lift heavy objects using the strength in your legs.

1. Clothing: (a) Avoid loose clothing. (b) Wear clothing that has short sleeves. (c) Remove items such as ties, rings, watches, and any other article that might get caught in the tool or machine.
2. Eye safety: It is a good practice to wear safety glasses when you are doing any cutting operation. Many state laws require that safety glasses be worn by all students in the vicinity of any cutting operation.
3. Long hair should be tied back and should be well out of the way of the rotating cutterheads and the spindles.
4. Any injury should be reported to the instructor immediately.
5. Never put fasteners or hardware of any kind in your mouth.
6. Avoid throwing tools (or anything else) to another person.
7. Keep the work area free of waste material such as shavings and pieces of wood.
8. When you are carrying long stock, have someone help you so that you will be able to maintain proper control.
9. Handle rough stock carefully so as to avoid painful splinters.
10. Use good judgment in attempting to lift any heavy object. When you lift such an item, exert strength from the legs, not from the back.

Hand-Tool Safety Rules

Fig. 3-8.   For safety, make sure the workpiece is firmly secured in a holding device. Remember to direct sharp cutting tools away from your body.

Fig. 3-9.   Store clamped stock in assigned areas and make sure that clamps do not protrude.

1. Keep your fingers away from the edges of sharp cutting tools. It is a good practice, when using a sharp cutting tool, to direct the tool away from your body. The work should be secured in a holding device. This will free both hands to control the tool.
2. The cutting edge of sharp tools should be protected when these tools are being carried or are in storage.
3. Do not use dull or broken tools.
4. Be sure that tool handles are in good condition and are securely fastened to the body of the tool.
5. Store clamped stock so that the protruding clamps do not present any danger.
6. Tools that have ragged or mushroomed edges should not be used as they are. They must first be ground to produce a smooth edge. Rough edges are dangerous as particles of metal may come loose and fly out.
7. Observe all special safety considerations for each tool or operation.

Machine Safety Rules

Rockwell International

Fig. 3-10. Before starting a machine, make certain all safety shields are in place.

Fig. 3-11. Brush chips away from a machine only after it has come to a complete stop.

Fig. 3-12. Processing long stock requires two people. Give your helper instructions before beginning the operation.

1. Do not use any machine before you have (a) been instructed as to its use, and (b) received specific permission to operate the machine.
2. Make sure all guards and eye shields are in place.
3. Examine all stock for physical defects and unwanted matter.
4. Clean the machine and/or remove chips **only** when the machine is not running. Use a brush, bellows, or a vacuum to do this.
5. Check all adjustments to make sure the machine is in proper operating condition.
6. Do not converse with others while you are (or while they are) operating the machine.
7. Normally, there should be only one person at a machine at any given time. However, when you are processing large or long pieces, secure the assistance of a helper. Before you begin, explain to your helper what you would like him or her to do.
8. Make sure that spectators do not stand in direct line with the revolving cutters or with the stock.
9. Make adjustments while the machine is not in operation. There is one exception to this rule: On machines equipped with variable-speed control, adjustment of the speed should only be made while the machine is running.
10. Repairs should only be made while the machine is not in operation and when the electrical circuit to the machine is disconnected.
11. If oil is spilled on the machine or on the floor, be sure to remove it completely.
12. Do not walk away from the machine until it has stopped.
13. While the machine is running, be attentive to any sound that may indicate that the machine is not operating properly.
14. Be alert for any odor that may signal that the machine or the stock might be overheating.
15. Do not touch moving stock or any cutting tool that is in motion.
16. Observe all special safety considerations for the particular machine you are using.
17. Report any defective electrical outlets and/or cords.

Fire Safety Rules

Fig. 3-13. Oily rags could easily catch fire. To prevent this, always be sure to place them in an approved metal container.

Fig. 3-14. Sweep up chips and sawdust from the floors and remove this waste material from the shop.

Wood shavings and finishing materials are highly combustible. With this in mind, be especially certain that you adhere to the following safety and cleanliness considerations:

1. Flammable liquids should be stored in covered metal containers. These containers should always be stored in a safe place, where they will not be tipped or come near heat.
2. Rags that have been used in oil or paint should either be destroyed or should be stored in covered metal containers.
3. Sawdust and shavings should be swept up regularly and removed from the shop.

Topic 18.

Occupational Safety and Health Administration (OSHA)

In 1970, Congress passed the Occupational Safety and Health Act "to assure so far as possible every working man and woman in this Nation safe and healthful working conditions and to preserve our human resources."

The purpose of the Act was as follows: (a) To encourage employers and employees to reduce hazards in the place of work and to implement improved safety and health programs. (b) To establish separate but interdependent responsibilities and rights for employers and employees, for the achievement of better safety and health conditions. (c) To establish reporting and record-keeping procedures to monitor job-related injuries and illnesses. (d) To develop mandatory job-safety and health standards and to effectively enforce these standards. (e) To require each state to establish and administer its own occupational safety and health program that is at least as strict as the federal program.

In order to enforce its standards and regulations, OSHA is authorized to conduct workplace inspections. Every establishment covered by the Act is subject to inspection by OSHA officers. These officers are trained in

OSHA standards and in recognition of hazardous conditions.

The OSHA Act encourages each state to develop and operate its own job safety and health programs. Once a state plan is approved, OSHA will fund 50% of the plan's operating costs.

Schools are considered political subdivisions of the state and are required to comply with OSHA standards. This means that both professional and nonprofessional staff members must be provided with safety training.

Students do not come under the law since they are not employees. However, since students are developing specific skills, attitudes, and knowledge relating to the world of work, they should develop the proper attitude toward safety. Students should be provided with a safety program in their respective occupational learning clusters. The learning activities should be concerned with general safety principles and should be included as an integral part of specific programs in woodworking.

General Requirements for Woodworking Machinery

General Machine Standards

1. All woodworking machinery, including circular saws, radial-arm saws, band saws, jointers, drill presses, mortisers, shapers, surfacers, lathes, sanders, and other miscellaneous woodworking machinery shall have proper guards (consistent with OSHA requirements) to protect the operator from hazards inherent to the machine's operation. The guard shall be such that it does not itself present an accident hazard.
2. Each machine shall be free of noticeable vibration when the largest-size tool is mounted and is run idle at full speed.
3. Arbors and mandrels shall be free from play.
4. All belts, pulleys, gears, shafts, and other moving parts shall be guarded in accordance with specific machine requirements.
5. Machines designed for a fixed location shall be securely anchored to prevent "walking" or other random movement.

6. No saw, cutterhead, or tool collar shall be placed or mounted on a machine arbor unless the tool has been accurately machined to a size and shape to fit the arbor.
7. Combs (featherboards) or suitable jigs shall be available at the workplace for use in cases where a standard guard cannot be used. Examples of procedures in which a standard guard cannot be used are: dadoeing, grooving, jointing, molding, and rabbeting.
8. It is recommended that each power-driven woodworking machine be provided with a disconnecting switch that can be locked in an "off" position.

Machine Controls

1. A mechanical or electrical-power control shall be provided on each machine to make it possible for the operator to cut off the power from each machine without leaving his or her position at the point of operation.
2. On machines driven by belts and shafting, a locking-type belt shifter or equivalent positive device shall be used.
3. To allow for conditions in which the operator might be injured if the motors were to restart after a power failure, provision shall be made to prevent machines from automatically restarting upon restoration of power.
4. Power controls and operating controls should be located within easy reach of the operator's regular work location, making it unnecessary for him or her to reach over the cutter to make adjustments.
5. On each machine operated by electric motors, positive means shall be provided for rendering such controls or devices inoperative while repairs or adjustments are being made to the machine.
6. Each operating treadle shall be protected against unexpected or accidental tripping.

Inspection and Maintenance of Woodworking Machinery

1. Dull, badly set, improperly filed, or improperly tensioned saws shall be immediately removed from use, so they will not cause the material to stick, jam, or kick back as it

is being fed into the saw at normal speed. Gum that has adhered to the sides of a saw shall be removed immediately.

2. All knives and cutterheads of woodworking machines shall be kept sharp, properly adjusted, and firmly secured. Where two or more knives are used in one head, these knives shall be properly balanced.

3. Bearings shall be kept free from lost motion and shall be kept well lubricated.

4. Arbors of all circular saws shall be free from play.

5. Sharpening or tensioning of saw blades or cutters shall be done only by persons who are skilled in this kind of work.

6. Cleanliness must always be maintained around woodworking machinery. This is particularly important with regard to the effective functioning of guards and as it concerns the prevention of fire hazards in switch enclosures, bearings, and motors.

7. All cracked saws shall be removed from use.

8. Push sticks or push blocks shall be provided at the workplace in the several sizes and types suitable for the work to be done.

Portable Power Tools

1. The following portable power tools shall be equipped with a constant-pressure switch or control: hand-held power drills, fastener drivers, disk sanders with disks greater than 2" in diameter, and belt sanders. This also applies to reciprocating saws, saber saws, scroll saws, circular saws, and jigsaws having blade shanks greater than a nominal 1/4", and other, similarly operated power tools. These tools may have a lock-on control, provided that turnoff can be accomplished with a single motion of the same finger or fingers used to start the tool.

2. All other hand-held power tools, such as (but not limited to) the following, may be equipped with either a positive on-off control or other controls: platen sanders, disk sanders with disks 2" or less in diameter, routers, planers, laminate trimmers, nibblers, and shears. This applies as well to saber saws, scroll saws, and jigsaws that have blade shanks equal to or less than a nominal 1/4" in width.

3. The operating control on hand-held power tools shall be so located as to minimize the possibility of its being started accidentally.

4. Portable electric hand-operated woodworking tools that operate at more than 90 volts shall be grounded with a separate ground wire and a polarized plug and receptacle. Double-insulated, plastic-housed tools require only a two-prong plug.

5. All cracked saw blades shall be removed from use.

Specific and more detailed regulations applying to individual machines or tools may be found under the topic describing that particular tool. Machines that do not have additional OSHA regulations are considered to be adequately covered by the general regulations.

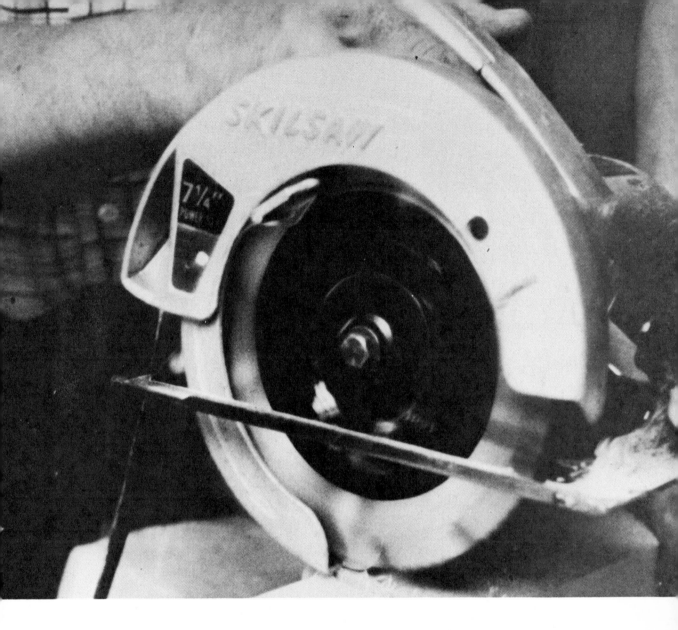

SECTION FOUR.

Cutting Stock With Saws

Topic 19.

Handsaws

Handsaws are divided into two main classes: crosscut saws and ripsaws. Broadly speaking, however, the term **handsaw** includes all hand-operated, special-purpose saws.

Classification

Reciprocating, toothed cutting tool

Application

Principle of Operation

1. The **crosscut saw** cuts both as a knife and as a chisel. The extreme points on either side of the saw score parallel lines. This action is like two knives cutting parallel lines across the face of the wood, Fig. 4-2.

   As the sawing action continues, the cutting edge on the inside of the teeth comes into contact with the wood, shearing it out of the kerf, Fig. 4-3.

   When a full bite is taken, the points of each tooth continue to score the outside of the kerf, and the sharpened, beveled sides of the teeth shear and crumble the wood left between the cutters.

   With each stroke of the saw, the sawdust is carried out of the kerf in the throat or gullet formed between the teeth of the saw.

The teeth of a saw are set alternately to the right and left so that the cut, or **kerf,** is wider than the thickness of the saw blade. This offsetting of the teeth is known as **set.** See Fig. 4-2.

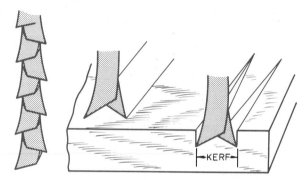

Fig. 4-2.   Top view of a crosscut saw, showing set and cutting action of teeth.

Fig. 4-3.   Side view of the cutting action of a crosscut saw.

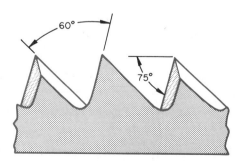

Fig. 4-1.   Crosscut-saw teeth — side view.

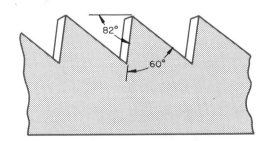

Fig. 4-4.   Ripsaw teeth — side view.

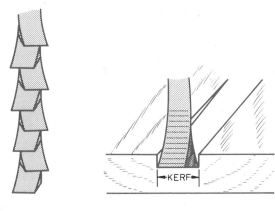

Stanley Tools

Fig. 4-7.   Crosscut saw.

Stanley Tools

Fig. 4-8.   Backsaw.

Disston, Inc.

Fig. 4-9.   Dovetail saw.

Fig. 4-5.   Top view of a ripsaw, showing set and cutting action of teeth.

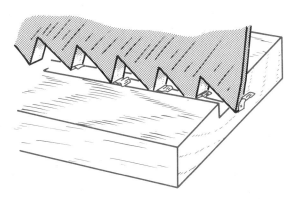

Woodcraft Supply Corp.

Fig. 4-10.   Veneer saw.

Fig. 4-6.   Side view of the cutting action of a ripsaw.

2. The teeth of a **ripsaw** are chisel-shaped, Fig. 4-5. These teeth have a straight front and sever the fibers at only one place. They do not score either side of the cut. The front edges of the tooth cut the fibers of the wood, Fig. 4-6. As sawing continues, the fibers on the bottom and sides of the cut give way and the chips are carried out in the teeth gullets, Fig. 4-6.

Kinds and Uses

Saws with Crosscut Teeth

1. The **crosscut saw** is considered an all-purpose saw, but it is specially designed to cut across the grain of the wood or at an angle to the grain. It is used to cut boards to length. A crosscut saw with large teeth is used for rough work. A crosscut saw with fine teeth is used for finish work.

2. A **panel saw** is a short, fine-toothed, crosscut saw, used for doing fine work.
3. The **backsaw,** Fig. 4-8, has fine, crosscut teeth, a thin blade, and a steel reinforcing bar on the back. This saw is used for fine cutting or wherever a straight, even cut is required.
4. A **dovetail saw** is similar to a backsaw except that it has a thinner blade and a straight handle, Fig. 4-9. It is used for cutting dovetails and for doing other fine work.
5. The **miter-box saw** is similar to the backsaw except it is wider and larger. It is used in a miter box.
6. A **veneer saw** has crosscut teeth on both edges of the saw and has a very slight set, Fig. 4-10. It is used for cutting veneer.
7. The **flooring saw** eliminates the need for boring or chiseling in the process of sawing into flat surfaces. The blade comes to a point and the bottom edge is curved. Crosscut teeth are filed on both edges.

8. A **half backsaw** combines the action of the handsaw and the backsaw. It gives the advantages of a stiffened cutting edge and makes it possible to cut all the way through the work.

Saws with Rip Teeth

1. The **ripsaw** is used for cutting **along** the grain of wood. In the hands of a skilled worker, a fine ripsaw may be used for cutting **across** the grain of wet or green lumber.
2. The **compass saw,** Fig. 4-11, has rip teeth and a narrow blade, making it possible for this saw to cut to a curve.
3. The **keyhole saw** is a fine compass saw.
4. A **turning saw** has a narrow blade with rip teeth. The blade is held under tension in a frame. This saw is used for cutting curves.
5. A **coping saw** has a narrow blade with rip teeth. The blade is held under tension in a steel frame, Fig. 4-12. The coping saw is used for cutting along a curve.

Saw with Crosscut and Rip Teeth

The **cabinet saw** is similar in size and shape to a backsaw, but it has no back. One edge of the blade has crosscut teeth and the other has rip teeth.

Stanley Tools

Fig. 4-11. Compass saw.

Millers Falls Co.

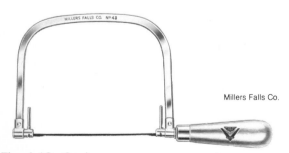

Fig. 4-12. Coping saw.

Principal Parts and Function of Each

1. The **handle** is shaped to fit the worker's grip. By gripping the handle, the worker can apply pressure on the cutting stroke. Handles are made either of beech, applewood, or plastic.
2. The **blade,** made of high-grade tool steel, is the part in which the teeth are located.
3. The **toe** is the end of the blade opposite the handle.
4. The **heel** is the portion of the blade nearest the handle.
5. The **back** is the edge of the blade opposite the teeth. Saws are made with either a straight or a skew (slanted) back.

Some blades are **taper-ground.** That is, the blade is made thinner at the back than at the teeth. This allows for a narrower kerf and less set in the teeth.

Maintenance

To give good service, a saw must have a smooth blade. Rust pits roughen a saw blade, causing wood fibers to bind against it. To prevent rust, wipe the saw blade with oil or wax.

Storing

Saws should be stored in a dry place. Make sure the saw is stored in such a way that there is no possibility of the cutting edge coming into contact with other objects.

Adjusting

Saws are sharpened either by hand filing or by machine filing. Sharpening a saw correctly requires precision and skill. See Topic 196, "Sharpening Saw Blades."

As well as being sharpened, the teeth of saws must also be set. This is done with a special tool that bends the teeth alternately to the right and left. Setting is done so that the saw kerf will be wider than the thickness of the blade.

The probable use of the saw should be kept in mind as it is being filed and set. Soft, wet woods require a saw with greater set than do hard, dry woods.

Market Analysis

Sizes

Handsaw blades are described by a "point" system. That is, the blade is classified according to the number of full teeth in one inch — plus one.

Usually the number of points is stamped on the heel of the saw. A large number of points indicates a fine saw. A low number of points indicates a coarse saw. A six-point saw would be fairly coarse and would give a rough, rapid cut. A ten-point saw would produce a fine cut but would cut more slowly. Backsaws and miter-box saws have 12 to 16 points to the inch.

The length of blades varies from 20″ to 26″ for crosscut and ripsaws, 8″ to 16″ for backsaws, and 22″ to 30″ for miter-box saws.

Sawing a Board with a Handsaw

Topic 20.

Classification

Cutting by scoring and shearing with specially shaped teeth

Procedure

1. Lay out a guide line to follow as you are handsawing. Use a rule, a straightedge, or a marking gauge, together with a pencil or a knife. A chalk line may be used for long pieces.

2. When sawing, hold short pieces either in a vise or on a bench hook. Longer pieces are usually placed on a sawhorse. Use your knee to help hold the work.

3. Grasp the saw with your right hand, extending the thumb and index finger along the two sides of the handle. This helps to guide the saw in a straight line.

4. Stand so that your forearm, shoulder, and eye follow the line of the saw blade.

5. When using a sawhorse, place your knee on the piece that is to be cut. Start the cut on the waste side, as close to the line as possible. The line should be barely visible after the cut is made. Grasp the edge of the board with your left hand. Keep this hand close to the saw so that some part of the thumb will bear against the saw and act as a guide. See Fig. 4-13. Raise your thumb to prevent it from being cut by the saw teeth. Start the saw by drawing it back

two or three times. This will engage the teeth. After the starting stroke has been made, take a few short strokes in order to deepen the groove. Remove your left hand from the edge of the board. Take full-length strokes, applying downward pressure with the arm and body. Applying wrist pressure results in a jerky motion and makes it more difficult to follow the line.

Fig. 4-13. Correct position for starting the saw cut. Notice the use of the thumb to control the position of the blade.

Fig. 4-14. Twist the saw to get back to the line.

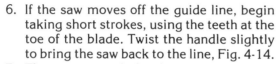

Fig. 4-16. The angle of the saw blade for ripping should be about 60°.

6. If the saw moves off the guide line, begin taking short strokes, using the teeth at the toe of the blade. Twist the handle slightly to bring the saw back to the line, Fig. 4-14.
7. The correct angle for the saw in crosscutting is about 45° to the face of the work. In ripping, an angle of about 60° is considered more efficient. See Figs. 4-15 and 4-16.
8. The saw must be guided to cut along the line and to cut at right angles to the surface.
9. If the saw binds while being used for ripping, force some type of wedge into the kerf to free the saw blade. See Fig. 4-17.
10. As you near the end of the cut, hold the piece with your left hand and take short, easy strokes until the piece is cut free, Fig. 4-18. Make sure the piece you are cutting off is properly supported so that the wood will not break off as you reach the end of the cut.

Fig. 4-17. A wedge spreads the kerf, preventing sticking.

Fig. 4-15. The angle of the saw blade for crosscutting should be about 45°.

Fig. 4-18. Finishing a cut.

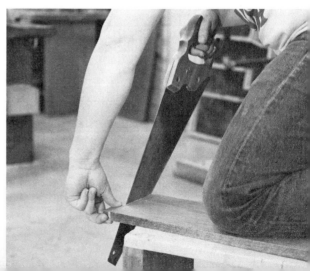

Fig. 4-19. A hand screw may be used to hold stock to the sawhorse. This provides increased control and mobility in sawing.

Fig. 4-21. Using a keyhole saw.

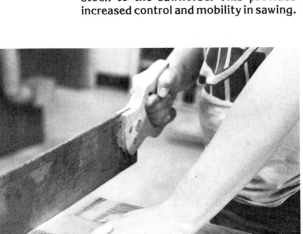

Fig. 4-20. Using a bench hook and backsaw.

Standards and Results

- Saw cuts should be made on the waste side of the line.
- Unless otherwise specified, the cut should be square with the face of the board.
- The stock should not be chipped or split at the end of the cut.

Safety Considerations

- Wear safety glasses when sawing.
- Be careful not to cut your thumb as you start the cut.
- Take care not to catch your clothing in the teeth of the saw.
- Be careful not to cut into the bench.

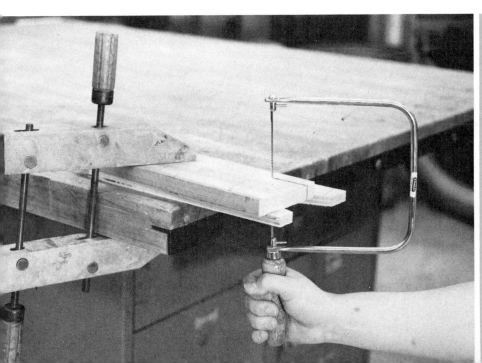

Fig. 4-22. Using a coping saw.

Topic 21.

Miter Box

Classification

Jig for cutting angles

Application

Principle of Operation

The **miter box** is a jig that guides a fine-toothed crosscut saw in making accurate angle cuts. The saw slides between guides, which may be set to certain predetermined angles without the use of any other layout tool. These guides keep the saw in a vertical position. See Fig. 4-23.

Kinds and Uses

The miter box is used for squaring ends (cutting a 90° angle) and for cutting miter joints and polygons. A miter guide may be purchased for use with a handsaw. Wooden miter boxes may either be constructed by hand or may be purchased ready-made. They are usually only used as a temporary measure, as their accuracy is short-lived.

Principal Parts and Function of Each

1. A specially made carbon-steel **miter-box saw** is used in the miter box. This differs from the conventional backsaw only in length and width. It has a heavy, rigid back, which stiffens the blade and rides in the miter-box sleeves. Miter-box saws are made from 22″ to 30″ long. They are available in widths of 4″, 5″, 5-1/2″, 6″, and 6-1/2″.
2. The **frame** holds the board to be cut.
3. **Saw guides** reduce friction and wear. They control the angle and the depth of cut.
4. **Saw-guide catches** lock the saw in a raised position so that both hands may be used to adjust the work.
5. The cast-iron or steel **quadrant** is graduated in degrees and is numbered for sawing 3-, 4-, 5-, 6-, 8-, 12-, and 24-sided figures.
6. The **board-length stop** can be used on either end of the frame as a gauge to cut duplicate lengths.
7. Some miter boxes are made with a **depth stop,** which controls the depth of cut.
8. **Stock guides** hold the stock firmly against the frame back.

Maintenance

1. The bearings in the guides should be oiled periodically.
2. Before leaving the miter box unused for an extended period of time, coat all metal parts with a film of oil or wax so that they will not rust.
3. The saw should be kept sharp.

Market Analysis

Capacity

The capacity is determined by two factors: (1) the width and thickness of the maximum-

Stanley Tools

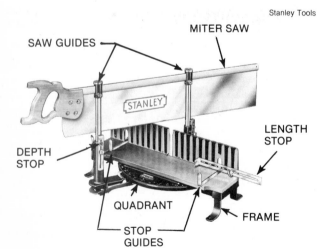

SAW GUIDES • MITER SAW • DEPTH STOP • LENGTH STOP • QUADRANT • STOP GUIDES • FRAME • STANLEY

Fig. 4-23. Miter box.

size board that can be cut, and (2) the angle to which the saw may be moved.

1. **Width** — usually 8″ to 10″ at a 90° angle, 5″ to 7″ at a 45° angle, 3″ to 4″ at a 30° angle.
2. **Thickness** — up to 3″ or up to 4″.
3. **Angle** — Miter boxes are constructed to cut an angle either to the right or to the left. The most common type of miter box cuts from 0° through 45°, at 15° intervals. Some miter boxes cut from 0° through 60°, at 15° intervals. Another type of miter box will make cuts between 0° and 45°, but may be set at any angle within this range.

Attachments

1. **Length gauge.** The length gauge is used to ease the cutting of duplicate lengths.
2. **Stock guides.** These hold the pieces tightly against the back of the frame.
3. **Segment arm.** This attachment pulls out from the back of the frame to permit angles of less than 45° to be cut.

Motorized Miter Box

Topic 22.

Classification

Rotary cutting tool for cutting angles

Application

Principle of Operation

The rotary cutting saw blade cuts at a predetermined angle of between 45° and 90°, to either the right or left. It is held in position above the wood and is pivoted downward to make the cut.

Kinds and Uses

The **motorized miter box,** Fig. 4-24, is used to cut angles on stock as thick as 2-1/2″. It will cut wood, manufactured board, plastics, and lightweight aluminum, all of widths up to 4″.

Principal Parts and Function of Each

1. The motorized **head,** similar to a portable electric saw, drives a 9″-diameter crosscut or combination-tooth blade.
2. The wooden **table,** 4″ × 17″, holds the material that is to be cut.

3. The **base,** made of cast iron, supports the table and the fence.
4. The **fence,** made of cast iron, holds the wood at the proper cutting position.

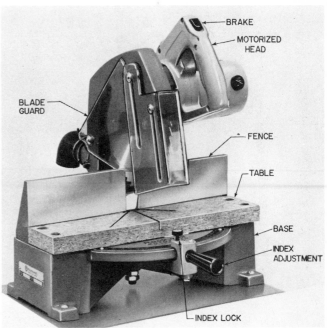

Rockwell International

Fig. 4-24. Motorized miter box.

5. The spring-loaded **index** adjusts to position for angle cuts.
6. The **index lock** secures the mitering arm in position for the cut.
7. The retractable **blade guard,** made of clear plastic, covers the blade.
8. The push-button **brake** permits the operator to stop the rotation of the blade.

Maintenance

1. Saw blades should be kept sharp.
2. Clean any sawdust from the miter pivot so that the guide will move easily.

3. Wax bright surfaces. Keep surfaces free of rust and dirt.

Market Analysis

Capacity

Crosscuts 90°—2-1/2″ × 4″
Miter 45°—2-1/2″ × 3-5/8″
Miter 45°, right or left on edge—5/8″ × 3-5/8″

Attachments

The only attachment for the motorized miter box is a **mounting stand.**

Topic 23.

Jigsaw or Scroll Saw

Fig. 4-25. Jigsaw.

Rockwell International

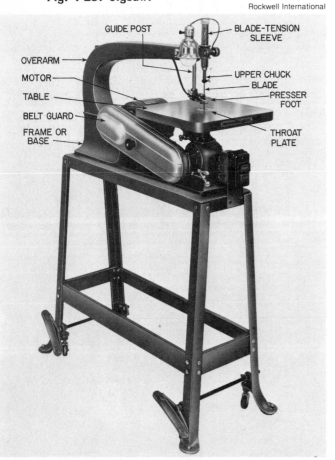

GUIDE POST
BLADE-TENSION SLEEVE
OVERARM
MOTOR
TABLE
BELT GUARD
FRAME OR BASE
UPPER CHUCK
BLADE
PRESSER FOOT
THROAT PLATE

Classification

Power-driven, reciprocating, toothed cutting tool

Application

Principle of Operation

Rip teeth are formed on one edge of a steel blade. This blade reciprocates at approximate speeds of either 600, 950, 1325, or 1750 strokes per minute. As the blade moves downward, the teeth cut as a series of cutting wedges.

Kinds and Uses

The **jigsaw** is used to cut curves and irregular shapes. One of the primary advantages of the jigsaw is that the blade can be easily removed and inserted into a workpiece to do internal sawing. The jigsaw is also suitable for doing very fine, detailed cutting.

1. The **plunger**-type jigsaw is the most common in school shops. It works on the principle of the wheel and axle. The belt-driven pulley is connected to a cam-and-pitman mechanism. As the cam rotates, the pitman

pushes and pulls the lower chuck up and down. The upper end of the blade may be held in a chuck, which is attached to the plunger-and-spring tension control. See Fig. 4-25.

2. The **vibrating**-type jigsaw is operated by a circuit breaker. In the power stroke, an electromagnet pulls down the lower chuck, which holds one end of the blade. When the chuck reaches the lower limit of its stroke, the circuit is broken and a spring in the tension sleeve returns the blade to its upper limit. The cycle is then repeated. See Fig. 4-26.

3. The **rocker-arm**-type jigsaw works on the principle of the wheel and axle. The belt-driven pulley is connected to a cam, which drives a rocker arm to produce an up-and-down motion.

Jigsaws are made in sizes from 12″ to 24″, measured from the blade to the overarm. The most common sizes are 18″ and 24″. The maximum thickness of cut ranges from 3/4″ to 4″, depending on the make.

Principal Parts and Function of Each

1. The cast-iron **frame** or **base** consists of two sections, bolted together. The upper part of these two sections is the deep-throated yoke called the **overarm,** to which the guidepost is fastened. The **base,** also fastened to the overarm, houses the pitman and cam. The frame may be mounted either on a bench or on a stand.

2. The **table,** made of machined cast iron, supports the work as it is being cut. The table tilts 45° to the left or to the right of the horizontal.

3. The **tension sleeve,** made of pressed steel, contains a spring, which regulates the tension on the blade.

4. The **throat plate,** a movable insert in the table, is located above the lower chuck. It supports the work close to the blade. The throat plate is made of aluminum or wood. If the blade should run out of line, the throat plate will keep it from being damaged.

5. The upper and lower **chucks,** made of machined steel, hold the blade at the ends. Saber blades, files, and spindle sanders are all held in the lower chuck. The upper chuck holds the tension sleeve.

6. The hardened-steel **blade guides** prevent the blade from twisting during cutting.

7. The **guidepost,** made of machined steel, adjusts to the thickness of the stock.

8. The **blades,** made of heat-treated steel, are available in widths of between .022″ and 3/8″. They are made from .007″ to .035″ thick, and have between seven and 32 teeth per inch.

9. The **hold-down foot** or **presser foot** is fastened to the bottom of the guidepost. It rests on the stock, preventing it from moving up and down with the motion of the saw.

10. The **cam-and-pitman** mechanism converts rotary motion into reciprocating motion.

11. The **plunger** acts as a blower, keeping sawdust away from the saw.

12. The electric **motor** provides the power.

13. The **cone pulleys** (variable-speed mechanism) regulate the speed.

14. The **belt guard,** a protective device, covers the belt and the pulleys.

Maintenance

1. The oil level of the driving mechanism should be maintained.
2. Unless it is equipped with sealed bearings, the motor should be oiled periodically.
3. When the jigsaw is not in use, release the tension on the blade.
4. Whenever the jigsaw is to be left unused for a long period of time, all machined parts should be coated with a thin coat of oil in order to prevent rusting.

Fig. 4-26. Vibrating-type jigsaw.

Dremel Manufacturing Co.

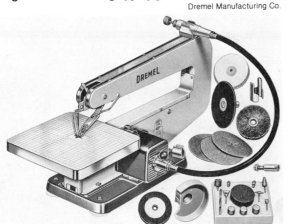

Market Analysis

Capacity

The capacity of a jigsaw is determined by two factors: (1) the distance between the over-arm and the blade (called throat capacity), and (2) the maximum thickness of stock allowed by the guidepost.

Attachments

The only attachment for the jigsaw is a **lamp,** providing better light on the work.

Topic 24.

Using the Jigsaw

Classification

Cutting by shredding and shearing with a rapidly reciprocating toothed blade

Procedure

General Operation

1. Select the blade appropriate to the particular kind of work.

   There are two types of blades. One is the **jewelers' blade,** which is held in the upper and lower chucks, and is used for fine work. The other type is the **saber blade,** which is held only in the lower chuck. This type of blade is used for heavier work.

   Jigsaw blades have rip teeth. These blades vary in length, in thickness, and in the number of teeth they have per inch. The finer the cut to be made, the more teeth per inch and the finer the thickness of the blade. Blades vary from seven teeth to the inch (for soft woods) to 32 teeth to the inch (for cutting metals and other hard materials). See Table 4-1. A blade with about 15 teeth per inch is considered an all-purpose blade.

2. Insert the blade into the upper and lower chucks, the teeth pointing toward the table.
3. Adjust the tension on the upper chuck to keep the blade taut.
4. Adjust the blade guide.
5. Determine the proper speed. The number of cutting strokes per minute can be regulated by changing the belt on the cone pulleys. Speeds range between 600 and 1750 rpm. At low speeds, it is easy to follow the guide line, but a rough cut is produced. Much finer work can be done at high speeds.
6. Adjust the hold-down presser foot so that the spring tension holds the work on the table.
7. Before starting the machine, turn the drive shaft by hand, one revolution, in order to check all adjustments.
8. Start the machine and evenly feed the work forward. Apply downward pressure so as to prevent the work from jumping with the

Fig. 4-27. Treadle-operated jigsaw.

Fig. 4-28. Cutting outside curves on the jigsaw. Note the position of hands away from the path of the blade.

Table 4-1
Jigsaw-Blade and Speed Selection

89

Material to Be Cut	Speed	Up to 1/16	1/16-1/8	1/16-1/4	1/16-1/2	1/8-1/4	1/8-1/2	1/8-2	1/4-2
		Thickness to Be Cut (in Inches)							
		Number of Teeth per Inch on Blade							
Hardwood	1000-1750	20	16	16		15	15	15	10
Softwood	1750	20	18			15	15	10	skip tooth 7
Hardboard, Plywood, etc.	1300-1750	20	18	18		15	15	10	10
Veneer	1300-1750	20							
Inlays	650- 900	20	18						
Paper	1300-1750	32	20			15	15	15	15
Bakelite® Plastics	650- 900	20	18	16		15	skip tooth 14	14	
Laminated Plastics, Micarta®, Fibertex®	650- 900					15	15	15	skip tooth 7-10
Mica	900-1300	30	20	20	20	20	20		
Hard Leather	900-1300	30	20	12		12			
Hard Rubber	650- 900	20	16	15	15	14	14		skip tooth 7
Felt	650- 900	32	20			15	15	15	15
Brake Lining	650- 900		20	20	20	20	20		
Asbestos	900-1300	32	20	20	20	15	20		
Ivory	650- 900	20	18	16	15	skip tooth 14	14		7
Bone	650- 900								
Pearl	900-1300	30	20	12		15	15	15	15
Aluminum, Brass	650- 900	20-32	20	20	20	15	15		
Copper	650- 900	32	20	20	20	15	15		
Pewter, Lead	650- 900	32	20	20	20	15	15		
Sheet Iron, Mild Steel	650	32	20	20		15			

motion of the saw blade. Always examine the stock before cutting, to make certain it is free of nails, grit, or any other foreign material. When making a turn, maintain a forward cutting motion. See Fig. 4-28.

Cutting Inside Work

1. Small holes are drilled in the waste stock at points of abrupt change of direction in the curves, Fig. 4-29.
2. Insert the saw blade through one of the drilled holes and secure it in place in the chucks.
3. Follow Steps 3-8 as for regular outside cutting.
4. Raise the presser foot and remove the blade from the upper chuck, freeing the work.

Cutting With a Saber Blade, Filing, or Sanding

1. A saber blade may be used in the jigsaw, Fig. 4-30. Because of the stiffness of the blade, it need only be attached in the lower chuck. The upper chuck and guides may be removed for extra work space.
2. To do machine sanding and filing, replace the saber blade with a jewelers' file or a sanding strip.

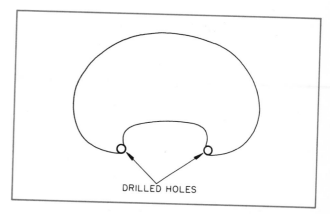

DRILLED HOLES

Fig. 4-29. Location of drilled holes for cutting inside curves.

Fig. 4-30. Saber blade in lower chuck.

Rockwell International

- Saw cuts should be on the waste side of the line. The line should be barely visible on the stock after cutting.
- Saw cuts should follow the curve of the line and should not be jagged.
- The saw blade selected should be suited to making a smooth cut for the particular type of work being performed.

Safety Considerations

- Wear safety glasses when using the jigsaw.
- Make all adjustments before starting the machine.
- Use the presser foot to apply pressure on the work.
- Keep your fingers out of the saw line.
- Do not force the work into the saw. This might cause the blade to bend and break.

Standards and Results

- Saw cuts should be smooth and at the desired angle to the surface.

Topic 25.

Portable Electric Saber Saw (Bayonet Saw)

Classification

Power-driven, reciprocating cutting tool

Application

Principle of Operation

The **portable electric saber saw** is driven by a high-speed electric motor. It has a mechanism for changing from rotary to reciprocating motion. This motion is transferred to a saber-shaped blade, resulting in a stabbing-like cutting action.

Kinds and Uses

1. Saber saws are designed to cut scrolls and patterns in wood and in other workable materials. They are rated according to amperes under load. Heavy-duty saber saws have the highest number of amperes under load. The saws have a tilting base so that cuts can be made at an angle. These saws can also cut flush to a vertical or a horizontal surface. Some saber saws have a knob on the top of the driving mechanism. This knob allows the operator to manually control the cutting direction of the blade without rotating the saw. This gives the saw greater maneuverability for cutting sharp corners and for doing scrolling operations.

2. Saber saws are available in both single-speed and variable-speed models.

The saber saw was originally designed to cut wood. It has become a very versatile tool, as it has variable-speed adjustments and blades designed for use on metal, plastic laminates, and composition materials. Some blades can be used to start a hole in the center of the stock, making it unnecessary to drill a pilot hole.

Principal Parts and Function of Each

1. The **housing,** made of aluminum or of plastic, is designed to be held with ease. It guides the cutting action.

Millers Falls Co.; Stanley Tools

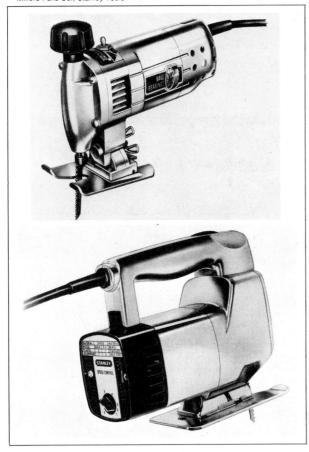

Fig. 4-31. Two styles of portable electric saber saws.

2. The **motor** is the driving power unit.
3. The **cam-and-pitman** unit changes rotary motion into reciprocating motion.

4. The **chuck,** made of hardened steel, holds the blade. Some chucks can be adjusted to four positions.
5. The **handle** is usually part of the housing. It is the means by which the tool is carried and by which it is guided during cutting operations. An extra side handle or knob is available on some machines.
6. The **trigger** or **toggle switch,** the starting control, is constructed into the handle for easy access.

Maintenance

1. The chuck should be kept free of sawdust.
2. The conductor cords should be handled carefully to prevent wear or cable breaks.

Market Analysis

Capacity

The length of blade the machine will accommodate determines the maximum depth of cut.

All-purpose saws accommodate blades 2-1/4″ to 12″ long, with a length of stroke 5/8″ to 1″, and speeds of 800 to 2400 strokes per minute.

Saber saws accommodate blades 2-1/4″ to 2-3/4″ long, with a length of stroke 7/16″ to 5/8″, and speeds of 3000 to 4500 strokes per minute.

Attachments

Guides are available for ripping, crosscutting and miter-cutting operations.

Table 4-2
Selection of Saber-Saw Blades

No.	Length	Teeth Per 1″	Thickness	Shank Width	Use
S-7	3½″	7	.050	.250	Fast-ripping woods, plywood to 2½″
S-10	3½″	10	.050	.250	Medium cuts woods, plywood to 2½″
S-F	3″	10	.040	.250	Finish cuts woods, plywood to 2½″
SHD	6″	7	.050	.250	Fast-ripping woods, up to 4″
S-14	3½″	14	.050	.250	Heavy metals over $^3/_8$″ thick
S-24	3″	24	.040	.250	Metals $^1/_8$″ to $^5/_8$″ thick
S-32	3″	32	.040	.250	Metals $^1/_{16}$″ to $^3/_8$″ thick

Patterson Brothers, a Subsidiary of Frank Paxton Lumber Company, Kansas City, Missouri

Safety Considerations

- Wear safety glasses.
- The saber saw should never be raised from a cut while still in operation. This could cause the saw to kick away from the operator's hand, resulting in possible injury or blade breakage.

Topic 26.

Circular Saw — Table Type

Classification

Power-driven rotary cutting tool with toothed, circular blade

Application

Principle of Operation

A circular-saw blade revolves at an arbor speed of approximately 3450 rpm. (The rim speed of a saw should be approximately 9000 FPM.) The saw cuts on the principle of a continuous set of cutting wedges.

Kinds and Uses

The **circular saw** is used to cut stock to length and width and to cut rabbets, grooves, dadoes, and tenons. (See "Using the Circular Saw.") There are two basic types: the **variety saw** (also called **tilting-arbor saw**), and the **universal saw.** The tilting-arbor saw is a single-blade, general-purpose saw that is widely used in industry and school shops, Fig. 4-32. The universal saw (or **double-arbor saw**), Fig. 4-33, is equipped with two blades, which may be used alternately by raising one or the other into position. This type of saw enables the operator to make two different types of cuts without having to change blades.

Fig. 4-32. Tilting-arbor table saw.

Oliver Machinery Co.

Fig. 4-33. Double-arbor bench saw.

Oliver Machinery Co.

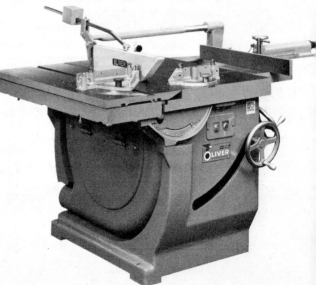

1. Tenons may be cut on the circular saw without the use of a dado head. This is done by using a tenoning attachment.
2. Several pieces may be cut to the same length by using one of the following attachments: (a) a **length gauge** (or **stop rod**) attached to the miter gauge, (b) a **clearance block** attached to the rip fence, (c) a **stop block** attached to the miter gauge.

Circular saws are made to accommodate saw blades of 6", 7", 8", 10", 12", and 14" diameters. Larger sizes are not usually found in school shops. The saw-table size increases with the diameter of the saw blade.

Principal Parts and Function of Each

1. The **base** supports the table.
2. The **table,** made of cast iron or pressed steel, supports the miter gauge, the rip fence, the attachments, and the stock that is to be cut.
3. The **miter gauge,** made of cast iron or aluminum, serves as a guide for crosscutting stock. The miter gauge may be equipped with a **length gauge** for cutting duplicate lengths.
4. The **rip fence,** made of cast iron or of pressed steel, serves as a guide for ripping stock.
5. The **tilting wheel,** made of cast iron, is used to tilt the saw blade.
6. The **handwheel,** as it is turned, regulates the height of the saw.
7. The **saw blade** cuts the stock. The saw blade is made of high-grade steel. Some saw blades have carbide-tipped teeth. Saws with this feature are much more expensive, but they stay sharp longer.
8. The **arbor** is a round shaft made of high-grade steel. The saw blade is fastened to the arbor.
9. The **guards,** made of plastic, cast iron, or aluminum, cover the saw blade, protecting the operator from possible injury.
10. The **splitter,** made of sheet steel, keeps the stock from binding against the saw while the cut is being made.
11. The **motor** provides the power (1 HP or greater).

OSHA Regulations

Hand-Fed Circular Table Saws

1. Each circular hand-fed saw shall be guarded by a hood. This hood shall completely enclose that portion of the saw which is above the table and that portion of the saw which is above the material being cut. The hood and the mounting shall be arranged in such a way that the hood will automatically adjust itself to the thickness of the material being cut and will remain in contact with this material. This hood shall not offer any notable resistance to the insertion of material into the saw and shall not block the passage of the material being sawed.
2. All portions of the saw blade beneath or behind the table shall be covered by an exhaust hood or a guard, which shall be so arranged as to prevent accidental contact with the blade.
3. Each hand-fed circular saw shall be furnished with a spreader to prevent material from being thrown back toward the operator and to keep the material from squeezing the saw. The spreader shall be attached so that it will remain in true alignment with the saw even when the saw or the table is tilted. This spreader should be placed so that there is not more than a 1/2" space between the spreader and the back of the saw when the largest saw is mounted in the machine.
4. Each hand-fed circular ripsaw shall be provided with anti-kickback fingers or dogs, which are located where they will oppose the thrust of the saw as well as its tendency to pick up the material and/or to throw it back toward the operator.

Maintenance

1. Circular-saw blades should be kept sharp and set. Sharpening should be done only by an experienced person. This process includes jointing, sharpening, setting, and gumming. See Topic 196, "Sharpening Saw Blades."

Mechanical parts of some circular saws require periodic greasing. Others have sealed bearings.

CAUTION: If you use a pin to hold an arbor or a saw blade in locked position as you are changing blades, be certain to remove the pin before starting the saw.

2. Check the alignment of the miter gauge and/or fence.
3. Before a saw is left unused for an extended period of time, all machined parts should be coated with a film of oil or paraffin wax.
4. Sawdust should be blown from the motor and the machine with a blower or with bellows.

Market Analysis

Attachments

These are the attachments (accessories) available for the circular table saw: **dado** **heads, tenoning attachment, molding head, length gauge, stop block, sanding disk,** and a **throat plate** for dado heads and molding heads.

Capacity

Size of Saw Blade	Maximum Cut
7"	2" above the table
8"	2¼" above the table
10"	2¾" above the table
12"	3¼" above the table

The capacity for the width of ripping is determined by the extent of travel of the rip fence.

Topic 27.

Selecting and Changing Circular-Saw Blades

Classification

Rotary edge-cutting tool

Circular saws are classified according to the type and number of teeth, the gauge thickness of the blade, the arbor-hole size, and the grade of steel from which they are made.

To prevent binding and to minimize friction between the saw blade and the edges of the stock being cut, the kerf or groove that the saw cuts must be wider than the thickness of the blade. This clearance is obtained by the use of spring-set teeth, swage teeth, carbide-tip teeth, and a hollow-ground blade. See Fig. 4-34.

1. **Spring-set** teeth are made by bending the tip of each tooth alternately to the right and left. **The set is no more than twice the thickness of the blade.** More set is used for coarse wood than for finished wood. The more teeth on a blade, the finer the cut.

Spring-set teeth are the most common type, and are found on crosscut saws (sometimes called **cutoff** saws), ripsaws, and combination saws.

2. **Swage teeth** (chippers) are obtained by upsetting (or swaging) the tips of all the teeth in order to increase their width. This type of set is used on large-diameter production ripsaws, and as a backup seat for cemented carbide-tip blades. Safe-edge saws and easy-cut saws also have swage teeth.

3. **Carbide-tip teeth** have carbide tips, cemented to a seat formed by swaging the ends of a saw blade.

4. The **hollow-ground blade** (planer blade) has a taper, making the blade thicker at the rim than near the center. These saws are used in smooth surfacing and have teeth that are sharpened on alternate top- and face-bevel as in spring-set teeth.

Application

In selecting a saw blade, one must consider the following: The greater the number of teeth in contact with the wood, the greater the degree of power required to drive the saw or to keep the saw running at the correct speed.

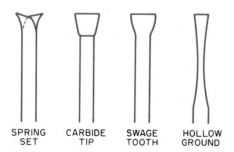

| SPRING SET | CARBIDE TIP | SWAGE TOOTH | HOLLOW GROUND |

Fig. 4-34. **Cross sections of saw blades.**

Table 4-3
Selection of Circular-Saw Blades

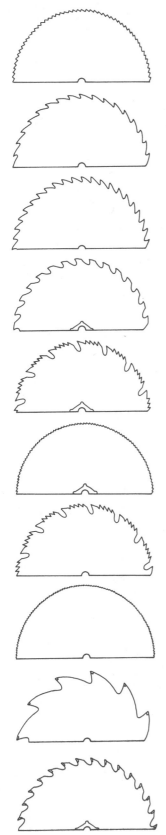

Cutoff Blade
Flat-ground. Fine teeth are set for fast, smooth cutting across the grains of hard or soft wood, sheeting, flooring and wood molding. Easily resharpened.

Rip Blade
Flat-ground. Designed for cutting hard and soft woods with the grain. Teeth set for clearance. Easily resharpened.

All-Purpose Combination
Flat-ground. A blade for all general-purpose work. Smooth cutting in any direction, through all types of wood. Easily resharpened.

Chisel-Tooth Combination
Flat-ground. For fast, rugged, general-purpose cutting. Rips, crosscuts, miters hard and soft wood, wallboard, and heavy construction-gauge plywood. Easily resharpened.

Planer Combination
Flat-ground. Economical blade for smooth crosscutting, ripping, and mitering. Fast-cutting teeth are set for clearance. Resharpenable.

Plywood Blade
Flat-ground. Smooth, economical cutting of paneling, plywood, and laminates. Also used where occasional nails are found, such as old flooring. Easily resharpened.

Planer Combination — Hollow-Ground
Premium blade offers fast, smooth crosscutting, ripping, and mitering. Fast-cutting teeth, hollow-ground for clearance. Excellent blade for all furniture- and cabinetwork where exceptionally smooth cutting is required. Resharpenable.

Plywood Blade — Hollow-Ground
A premium blade, hollow-ground for clearance, designed for virtually splinter-free cutting of plywood, paneling, and laminated woods. Easily resharpened.

Carbide-Tipped Blade (12-Tooth)
Long-lasting premium blade — fast, rugged, general-purpose cutting of wood, wallboard, and heavy construction-gauge plywood. Longer-lasting than conventional blades.

Carbide Tipped Blade (Multi-Tooth)
A premium blade for faster fine cutting, mitering, and finishing. Stays sharper and lasts longer than conventional blades.

Disston, Inc.

Theoretically, a saw blade that extends above the surface of the board will tend to hold the board down on the table and will give less feed resistance. However, the more the blade surface is exposed, the greater the danger to the operator. Thus, the required safety rule for a blade that is not covered by a guard is a projection of 1/8" to 1/4" above the board.

Kinds and Uses

There are three basic classifications of circular-saw blades: crosscut blades, rip blades, and combination blades.

Crosscut Blades

Crosscut (or Cutoff) Blade. This type of blade is designed like that of the hand crosscut saw, for cutting across the grain, Table 4-3. Because of the greater number of teeth in contact with the wood, it will heat up quickly if used for ripping. Overheating the teeth or rim of the saw blade will cause the blade to warp and to run with a wobble. An inaccurate cut will result.

Plywood Blade. The plywood blade is used to cut plywood and other laminates. Because this blade has very small teeth, it produces a fine, smooth cut and reduces splintering along the kerf. The plywood blade is easy to sharpen.

Rip Blades

Rip blades are designed to cut along the length of the grain (with the grain) as is done in cutting boards to width. The chisel-shaped teeth remove a series of chips to make the cut, Table 4-3.

Combination Blades

Combination Rip and Crosscut Blade. This blade is a combination of a crosscut tooth and a rip tooth. The tooth angle, the top bevel, and the front bevel allow this saw to cut (a) across the grain, (b) at a miter to the grain, and (c) with the grain (rip). It is a fast-cutting saw, and produces a rough cut.

Hollow-Ground Combination Blade. This saw is sometimes called a **planer blade.** It is used in finish work done on crosscutting, mitering, and ripping. The name (planer) comes from the smooth surface it produces. The disadvantage of this saw is the small clearance allowed by the hollow-ground design. The saw blade must be allowed to project above the surface of the stock. This is done to ensure that the minimum blade contact in the cut is obtained, preventing overheating. See Table 4-3.

Carbide-Tipped Blades. Carbide-tipped blades are made for both crosscutting and ripping (and in a combination type). The initial cost is greater for a carbide-tipped blade than for a standard steel blade, but it stays sharp up to ten times longer and, therefore, costs less. The most common styles found in smaller sizes are the swage-tooth rip blade and the swage-tooth safe-edge blade. Large sizes (for production purposes) are found in all tooth shapes. The carbide tip may either be resharpened by special machines, or the tips may be replaced. Carbide-tip saws are used on hardboard, laminates, and other materials that would quickly dull a regular saw.

Easy-Cut Blade or Safe-Edge Blade. This is a **controlled-cut** saw blade. The back of the swaged tooth acts as a stop guide to control the amount of feed. It also reduces the tendency of the stock to kick back. Because the blade has fewer teeth, it requires less power and thus is quiet to operate.

Molding Head and Cutters

There are many styles of molding heads designed for use on the circular saw. Each has

Rockwell International

Fig. 4-35. Molding head for the circular saw.

Disston, Inc.

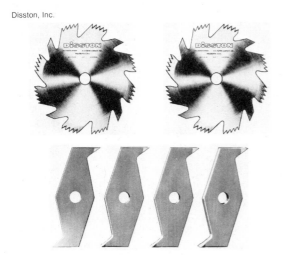

Fig. 4-36. Dado-blade set.

Rockwell International

Fig. 4-37. Adjustable dado head.

a set of matched knives with profile-cutting edges used to form various molded shapes. The replaceable blades are held in place in the molding head by a self-aligning safety lock. The blades are changed easily and quickly.

The rip fence of the saw table must have either a cutout or an attached wood face above the cutterhead in order to clear the cutters when they project to the highest point above the table. The saw-table throat plate must be replaced by a plate that has a slot wide enough to accommodate the width of the cutter knives, Fig. 4-35.

Dado-Blade Set

The dado-blade set consists of two hollow-ground 1/8" combination saws and a series of inside chippers. There are usually four chippers in a set: one 1/4" thick, two 1/8" thick, and one 1/16" thick. See Fig. 4-36. The dado-blade set is used to cut grooves (dadoes and rabbets), in any grain direction, of between 1/8" and 13/16" in width.

On table saws and radial-arm saws, a single combination saw blade will cut a groove 1/8" wide. A series of chippers can be used in combination so that grooves wider than 1/4" may be cut. These grooves must have 1/16" increments. Sets may be larger on heavy equipment. However, it is best to make multiple cuts on dadoes larger than 1".

To position the outside saws, arrange them so that the raker tooth is opposite the cutting teeth of the other blade. Chipper teeth should be in line with the gullets of the saw's raker tooth. They should form an even pattern around the perimeter of the saw blade.

Adjustable Dado Head

An adjustable dado head makes it possible to regulate or to change the width of cut by turning the center section of the blade unit. This changes the angle of the blades, altering the cutting area, Fig. 4-37. Work should be fed very slowly into this type of dado head.

Changing Saw Blades

1. Disconnect the power supply to the saw.
2. Remove the throat plate by raising the leading edge from the table.
3. To prevent it from rotating, lock the blade by inserting a scrap piece of stock between the front edge of the throat opening

Fig. 4-38. Changing the saw blade, using wood scrap to hold blade while turning the arbor nut.

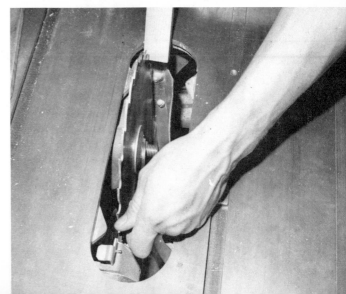

and the teeth of the blade. (Some saws have a pin that may be inserted in the saw to hold the arbor or blade in a locked position.) See Fig. 4-38.

4. Remove the arbor nut by turning it in the direction of the saw's rotation. Use the proper size wrench to fit the nut. Be careful not to drop the nut, the flange, or the saw blade.

5. Store the blade in such a way that the teeth will neither be damaged nor present a safety hazard.

6. Place the new saw blade on the arbor, pointing the teeth in the direction of the rotation, toward the front of the table.

7. Replace the flange and the nut and tighten the nut with the wrench. Lock the blade to prevent it from rotating. This is done by inserting a scrap piece of stock between the rear of the throat opening and the saw teeth. (If a pin was used to remove the blade, it will still be in position and the blade or arbor will already be locked in position.)

8. After the blade is fastened in position, be sure to remove the locking pin (if one was used).

9. Replace the throat plate.

10. Reconnect the power supply to the saw.

Simonds Saw & Steel

Fig. 4-39. Cut-in-half saw.
Saws of this type are used in gang-saw setups so that individual saws can be removed without disturbing any of the other saws on the arbor.

Table 4-4
Blades for the Circular Saw

Diameter in Inches	Crosscut Saws		Ripsaws		Combination Ripsaw and Crosscut Saws		Easy-Cut Saws Carbide-Tip	
	Gauge	No. of Teeth	Gauge	No. of Teeth	Gauge	No. of Teeth	Gauge	No. of Teeth
6	18	100	18	36	18	44	14	8
7	18	110	18	36	18	44	14	8
8	18	100	18	36	18	44	14	8
9	16	100	16	36	16	44	14	8
10	16	100	16	36	16	44	13	8
12	14	100	14	36	14	44	13	12
14	14	100	14	36	14	44	12	12
16	14	100	14	36	13	44	12	12
18	13	100	13	36	12	44		
20	13	80	13	36				
22	12	70	12	36				
24	11	70	11	36				
26	10	70						
28	10	70						
30	10	70	10	36				

Using the Circular Saw

Topic 28.

Classification

Cutting by scoring, shearing, shredding, and chipping with a toothed, circular blade

Procedure

Examine the stock to determine whether it contains nails, grit, or other foreign matter. If it does, do not cut the stock on the circular saw because these elements will dull the saw blade and may cause injury.

Stock that is to be cut on the circular saw should have a straight edge and a flat surface. (See Topic 16, "Getting Out Stock.") The flat surface should be down (against the table). The straight edge should be held against the miter gauge for crosscutting, and against the ripping fence for ripping. If it is necessary to cut cupped stock, the concave face should be facedown.

Crosscutting or Squaring an End

1. Use either a crosscut blade or a combination blade. Adjust the height of the saw blade so that it is about 1/8" above the stock to be cut.
2. Set the miter gauge at right angles to the saw blade. Usually, a graduated scale will indicate this 90° position. It may be checked with a framing square.
3. Use the saw guard and splitter. The rip fence must be moved clear of the work to prevent binding and kickback.
4. One edge of the work to be cut must be straight. Keeping the straight edge against the face of the miter gauge, move the stock to cutting position. Hold the stock firmly against the face of the miter gauge. Start the machine and allow it to reach full speed. Make a test cut by nicking the stock. Make any necessary minor adjustments to the stock. Then, using both hands to hold the stock firmly against the miter gauge, feed the stock steadily through the saw, Fig. 4-40.

5. Turn off the saw. Allow the blade to come to a complete stop before clearing the saw area of trimmings. Return the guide to the starting position.

Cutting to Length With a Clearance Block Fastened to the Rip Fence

1. When many pieces of the same length are to be cut, a clearance block may be used for measuring. The location for placement of the block is determined by the length and width of the work to be cut.
2. For short pieces, use a clamp to fasten a clearance block to the rip fence, near the front edge of the table. The length of the piece to be cut is measured from this block to a saw tooth set toward the fence. See Fig. 4-41.
3. Secure the rip fence to the table at the correct cutting position.
4. Holding the work against the miter gauge, slide it along the table until the square end strikes the block. Hold the stock firmly in place and feed it into the saw, cutting the work to length. Repeat this process for all remaining pieces.

Fig. 4-40. Crosscutting on the circular saw. (Guard removed to show operation.)

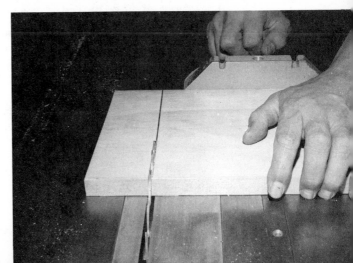

Fig. 4-41. Crosscutting using a clearance block and a rip fence. (Guard removed to show operation.)

Cutting to Length With a Stop Block Fastened to the Miter Gauge

1. Fasten a straight, flat piece of stock (called a **wood fence** piece) to the face of the miter gauge. The stock should just clear the saw on one end, and extend a convenient length (slightly longer than the pieces to be cut) on the other end.

2. The length of the stock to be cut is measured from a tooth set to the left of the saw. Mark this length on the face of the wood fence piece. At this point, attach a stop block with a square edge by using nails, screws, or a lightweight clamp, whichever is suitable.

3. The rip fence must either be moved or must be removed from the table so as to allow a 2″ minimum clearance between the fence and the stock to be cut.

4. Square one end of the work. Then, holding the squared end against the stop block, cut the piece to length. Repeat until all pieces have been cut. Both edges must be square.

5. Some miter gauges are equipped with a length gauge or a stop rod for measuring lengths. However, when a wood fence piece is used to extend the working face of the guide, it is not convenient to use the rod.

Cutting a Miter or Angle Between 30° and 90°

1. The miter gauge may be set to cut angles of between 30° and 90°. The work is held against the miter gauge (which is set at the required angle) and the cut is made in the same manner as is done in crosscutting. See Fig. 4-42.

2. A stop block, fastened to the miter gauge, may be used in cutting pieces to length in the manner described above.

3. It is very important that the work be held securely against the miter gauge in order to ensure a straight cut.

4. To obtain a smooth cut, make sure the angle points to the front of the table so that the cut will be made **with the grain.** The long edge of the work will be against the gauge.

5. When cutting miters on wide stock, tilt the saw or table to the desired angle and proceed as for square crosscutting.

6. When cutting compound angles, first set the miter gauge to the desired angle on the face of the stock. Then, set the blade or table to the desired angle of the thickness of the stock, Table 2-1. Feed the stock into the saw as described above.

Fig. 4-42. Cutting a miter at 45° using the miter gauge. (Guard removed to show operation.)

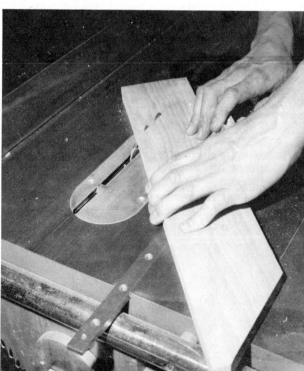

Ripping or Cutting to Width

1. A ripsaw or combination saw is adjusted to 1/8″ above the thickness of the stock. Some workers prefer to have the saw blade at its full height for ripping, but this practice is not recommended here for safety reasons.
2. Use the saw guard and splitter.
3. One edge of the stock must be straight. This edge is held against the rip fence. A board with a wind or an uneven edge should not be cut.
4. Set the rip fence the required distance to the right of the saw. This distance may be gauged by the scale on the saw table and then checked with a rule. Make this check by measuring between the rip fence and a tooth set to the right, Fig. 4-44.
5. Stand to one side of the saw (usually to the left). Start the saw running. With the straight edge of the board held against the fence, push the board. Use a firm, even motion to make the cut.
6. If the cut is made close to the rip fence, use a push stick to move the board, Figs. 4-45 and 4-46. Do not reach over the blade to remove the pieces. The section of board between the fence and the saw should always be pushed clear of the saw.
7. Long boards should be supported by a stand the same height as the saw table.
8. A device used to keep the board firmly against the fence is called a **feather strip** Figs. 4-47, 4-48. (This is a piece of hard wood that has a series of saw kerfs.) The springing action of the fingers pushes the board against the fence, still allowing it to be moved in the direction of the cut.

Fig. 4-43. Cutting a miter at 45° using a sliding table.

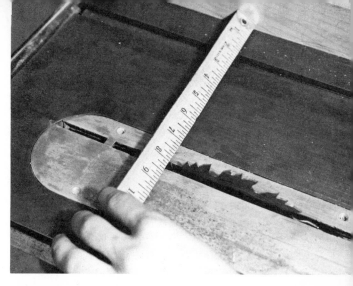

Fig. 4-44. Using a rule to adjust the fence square with the saw blade. (Saw must be Off.)

Fig. 4-45. Using a push stick for ripping narrow stock. The saw guard may interfere with this operation. (Guard removed to show operation.)

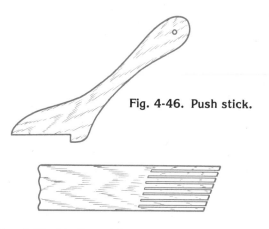

Fig. 4-46. Push stick.

Fig. 4-47. Feather strip.

Fig. 4-48. Using a feather strip in ripping. (Guard removed to show operation.)

Fig. 4-49. Resawing on the circular saw — note feather strip.

Resawing on the Circular Saw

1. Set the saw blade 1/8″ to 1/4″ higher than half the width of the stock. The saw should not be set to make any single cut more than 2″ deep.
2. Adjust the feather strip to hold the stock firmly against the rip fence.
3. Start the saw and make a cut along one edge, Fig. 4-49.
4. Turn the stock end-for-end and make the second cut. Make sure the face side is against the fence at all times.
5. Boards more than 4″ wide should be cut in four steps. This will make it necessary to cut through, on each edge, slightly more than one-quarter of the width of the piece (Steps 1 and 2). After this has been done,

Fig. 4-50. Adjustable tapering jig.

Fig. 4-51. Using an adjustable tapering jig. (Guard removed to show operation.)

Fig. 4-52. Fixed tapering jig for cutting leg tapers.

Fig. 4-53. Using a fixed tapering jig. (Guard removed to show operation.)

raise the saw blade to just over half the width of the piece and cut again on each edge (Steps 3 and 4).

6. If the stock is more than twice as wide as the maximum width the saw will cut, the remaining portion may be cut with a band saw or with a hand ripsaw.

Cutting a Taper

A jig may be made as a handy attachment for cutting tapers on the circular saw, Figs. 4-50 and 4-52.

1. Hold the straightedge of the jig against the rip fence. The piece to be cut is held against the notch of the jig.
2. Push the jig and the board (as a unit) past the saw, making the cut at the desired angle or taper. See Figs. 4-51 and 4-53.

Cutting a Bevel or Chamfer

1. Most saws may be tilted so that an angle of between 45° and 90° may be cut.
2. On the tilting-arbor saw, the fence may be on either side of the blade while the work is being cut.
3. If the desired angle is less than 45°, the saw should be adjusted to the supplement of the angle. For example, if the desired angle is 30°, set the saw for 60°. The trial cut should be checked for the desired angle.

Cutting Grooves, Rabbets, or Dadoes

1. Although grooves or rabbets may be cut by making a series of closely spaced cuts, a dado-head attachment will do the job much more quickly. A dado head consists of two saws similar to combination saws (having both crosscut and rip teeth) and a series of chippers, which act as waste cleaners between the saws. These saws may be set to cut grooves from 1/8" to 13/16" on most popular saws. See Fig. 4-36. The throat plate must be replaced either with one supplied with the machine or one made from hard wood.
2. Cut the grooves in the same way as is done in crosscutting or in ripping. The guards and splitter cannot be used.
3. A rabbet may also be made by making cuts — at right angles — on the adjacent edge and face of the stock. See Fig. 11-36.

Cutting Stop Grooves and Dadoes

1. Cuts that do not extend to the end of the board may be started by lowering the work over the saw, Figs. 4-54 and 4-55.
2. To limit the travel or cutting length, attach two stop blocks to a board that has been fastened to the rip fence.
3. Hold the board in contact with the fence. One end should be facedown on the table and against the stop block nearest the operator. Slowly lower the board over the saw until it rests flat on the table. Push the board the length of the cut until it strikes the opposite stop block. Raise the end farthest from the operator until it clears the saw. Be careful to maintain contact with the rip fence until the board is clear of the blade.
4. To minimize the possibility of kickback, maintain a firm grasp on the stock. Keep your hands out of the direct line of the blade.

Fig. 4-54. Cutting stop dadoes. (Guard removed to show operation.)

Fig. 4-55. Completed stop dado.

Standards and Results

- All stock should be cut to dimension. No test marks should show on the finished piece.
- Cuts should be square or of the correct angle.
- Grooves and rabbets should be even in depth and width and should be parallel with the edge of the board.
- All stop cuts should run up to the length marks.
- No saw burns should show.

Safety Considerations

- Wear safety glasses when using the circular saw.
- Use all guards, except when the blade is covered by the work.
- Keep the blades sharp and set so that they will produce clean cuts.
- The concave side of a cupped board should rest facedown on the table.
- Do not force the saw to stall. A sharp blade running at full speed will do a better job.
- To keep from being struck if the stock should kick back, stand to one side of the work when using the saw.

- No one should stand in direct line with the saw blade.
- The blade should not project more than 1/8" above the work.
- Let waste pieces fall off the table, or else stop the saw so that you can remove them. Never reach over the blade while the saw is in operation.
- Always use a guide to make a cut. Never saw freehand.
- Use a stand to aid in handling long boards.
- When using a fence and a miter gauge to cut stock to length, always use a clearance block.
- Always make adjustments while the machine is stopped.
- Plan your work before starting the machine.
- Never talk to the operator while the machine is running.
- Narrow boards (2" or less in width) should not be pushed through with the fingers. Instead, always use a push stick.
- Never allow stock that has already been cut to remain between the blade and the fence.
- The operator should have firm footing.
- Make sure the saw blade is lowered beneath the table when the cutting operation is completed.

Topic 29.

Circular-Saw Operator

The **circular-saw operator** is a semiskilled worker, most commonly employed by trade and industry. This person is able to use one or many of the different types of circular saws used in various fields.

Table saws used in the schools are of the same type used in trade and industry. Circular saws are available in a variety of types and sizes. In most industries, the crosscut saw and the ripsaw are separate, single-purpose machines. However, double-arbor saws are some-

times used for both crosscutting and ripping. Among the specialized variations of the table saw are cutoff saws, trimmers, straight-line ripsaws, matching saws, edgers, and sawmills.

Swing saws, radial saws and portable saws are used extensively in lumber yards, in mills, and in construction work.

There are also a great many types of saw blades. Each type is specially designed to serve a specific function.

Radial-Arm Saw

Classification

Power-driven rotary cutting tool with toothed, circular blade

Application

The **radial-arm saw** is a refinement of the overhead swing saw. The saw arbor and the motor unit are mounted in a pivoting yoke, which rides in a track on a radial arm. The radial arm is adjustable for height and for radius angle. Combining the adjustments of the yoke and the radius arm makes it possible to swing the saw unit so that any given angle may be set either for plain or for compound-angle cutting.

Principle of Operation

Circular cutters revolve at an arbor speed of between 3450 and 3600 rpm. The saw cuts on the principle of a continuous set of cutting wedges.

Kinds and Uses

The radial-arm saw is used to cut stock to length and width and to cut grooves, dadoes, and tenons. When combined with the attachments necessary to do other specific jobs, the machine becomes a power shop. See Fig. 4-56.

Radial-arm saws are made in sizes that accommodate blades 8″, 9″, 10″, 12″, 14″, 16″, 18″, and 20″ in diameter. These are the common blade sizes found in shops where cabinetwork is done. Models up to 44″ in diameter are used in industry.

Principal Parts and Function of Each

1. The **base,** made of pressed metal, supports the table and the column.
2. The hollow, steel **column** supports the cantilever arm.
3. The **column lock** fastens the column at the desired height.
4. The **arm** supports the yoke and the motor. It also provides the track for the movement of the saw.
5. The **arm lock** fastens the arm in position.
6. The cast-steel **yoke** holds the motor. It rides in the arm track.
7. The **yoke lock** fastens the yoke in position on the arm.
8. Two **swivel locks** secure the yoke in position between the vertical and the horizontal, making it possible to cut miters and bevels.
9. The **motor** drives the saw and its attachments.
10. The **saw guards,** made of cast iron, cover the saw, protecting the worker. They also direct the sawdust away from the cut.
11. The **anti-kickback fingers** keep the work from being thrown back during the ripping operation.

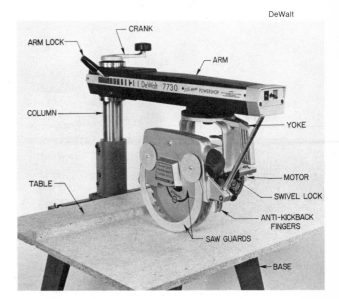

DeWalt

Fig. 4-56. Radial-arm saw.

12. The **crank** raises and lowers the cantilever arm to the correct operating position.
13. The **table,** made of wood, supports the stock. It has an insert or guide strip for doing crosscutting and ripping.

OSHA Regulations

Radial Saws

1. The upper hood shall completely enclose the upper portion of the blade and the saw arbor. It will protect the operator from such things as flying splinters and broken saw teeth, and will deflect sawdust away from the operator. The sides of the lower, exposed portion of the blade shall be guarded to the full diameter of the blade by a device that will automatically adjust itself to the thickness of the stock. This device will remain in contact with stock being cut, to give maximum protection possible for the operation being performed.
2. Each radial saw used for ripping shall be provided with anti-kickback fingers or dogs. These will be located on both sides of the saw so that they may oppose both the thrust of the saw and its tendency either to pick up the material or to throw it back toward the operator.
3. An adjustable stop shall be provided in order to prevent the blade from traveling forward, beyond the position necessary to complete the cut in repetitive operations.
4. Installation shall be done in such a manner that the front end of the unit will be slightly higher than the rear. This is necessary to cause the cutterhead to return gently to the starting position when released by the operator.
5. Ripping and plowing shall be done in a direction opposite that of the turning motion of the saw. The direction of the saw's rotation shall be conspicuously marked on the hood. In addition, a permanent label, measuring not less than 1-1/2" × 3/4", shall be affixed to the rear of the guard, at approximately the level of the arbor. This label shall read as follows: "Danger: Do Not Rip or Plow From This End." Such a label should be colored standard danger red.

Maintenance

1. All cutters should be kept sharp, in true shape, and in balance.
2. Worn tabletops and table guides should be replaced so that a true edge will be maintained.
3. Most machines have sealed bearings and ball-bearing guides for the traverse.
4. All machined parts should be coated with a thin film of oil to provide protection from rust.

Market Analysis

Capacity

The capacity for the width of ripping is determined by the arm length and the table width.

Attachments

The following are the attachments (accessories) available for the radial-arm saw: **dado heads, molding heads, shaper cutters, rotary planes, router, drill chuck, saber saw, wood lathe, belt sander, disk sander,** and **grinder.**

Table 4-5
Radial-Arm-Saw Cuts

Blade Size	Depth of Cut	Length of Crosscut
8"	2"	11¾"
9"	2½"	12"-15"
10"	3"	12"-16"
12"	3"-3½"	14⅜"
14"	4½"	20"-24"
16"	4"-5"	19"-31"
18"	6"	depends on length of arm
20"	7"	depends on length of arm

Using the Radial-Arm Saw

Topic 31.

Classification

Cutting by scoring, shearing, shredding and chipping with toothed, circular blade

Procedure

Crosscutting (90°)

1. The radial arm must be at right angles to the back guide strip on the saw table. The miter scale will register "0" (zero). Make a trial cut and then test this cut with a steel square.
2. To make a through cut, the saw blade must be set to cut slightly below the surface of the wooden saw table, Fig. 4-57.
3. Mark the position at which the stock is to be cut. Then, place the piece against the insert or guide strip.
4. Adjust the saw guard so that it will be near the location of the cut you are going to make. Make certain the saw guard does not obstruct vision.
5. Raise the kickback device so that it clears the face of the work.
6. Set the saw to the rear, against the stop, making sure that it is not in contact with any wood.

7. Start the machine and allow it to reach maximum speed.
8. Hold the stock firmly against the guide strip with one hand and grasp the handle of the motor yoke with the other hand. Draw the blade forward, making the cut.
9. After cut has been made, return the saw to the starting position and turn off the motor.
10. To cut several duplicate pieces, clamp a stop to the guide strip at the desired position and proceed as above, holding the squared end of each piece against the stop. Never put one piece of stock on top of another as it will kick over the fence, Fig. 4-58.
11. Because of the direction of rotation of the saw blade, the saw pulls itself into the work and in some cases must be held back. This is especially true when the saw is dull, or when hard wood or planks are being cut.

Cutting Miters

1. Release the arm lock and the motor latch. Raise the saw blade above the table and swing the arm to the desired angle, Fig. 4-59.

Fig. 4-57. Crosscutting.

Fig. 4-58. Crosscutting using a stop block to cut duplicate pieces.

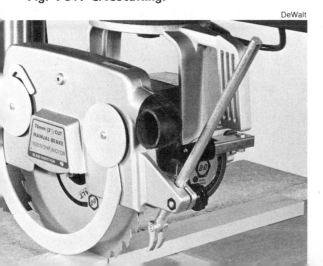

DeWalt

DeWalt

Fig. 4-59. Miter cut. DeWalt

Fig. 4-60. Righthand ripping. DeWalt

2. With the saw in the back position, lower the column until the saw will cut completely through the stock.
3. Adjust the saw guard so that it clears the work and does not obstruct the operator's view.
4. Check the setup by cutting a scrap piece of stock.
5. If the cut is satisfactory, follow the procedure outlined for crosscutting.

Cutting Bevels

1. Raise the column sufficiently for the blade to clear the saw table when the motor is tilted.
2. Release the bevel latch and the bevel clamp lever and tilt the motor to the desired angle. Lock in this position.
3. Start the saw and lower the column until the saw blade comes in contact with the table. Stop the motor.

4. Adjust the saw guard so that it clears the work and does not obstruct the operator's view.
5. Check the setup by cutting a scrap piece of stock.
6. If the cut is satisfactory, proceed as in crosscutting.

Ripping

1. The radial arm must be at right angles to the guide strip, and the miter scale on the column must register "0" (zero). Lock in this position.
2. Raise the column until the saw blade clears the table. Draw the saw to the front of the radial arm. Lock in this position.
3. Rotate the motor yoke 90° so that the saw blade is parallel with the guide strip. Lock in position.
4. Move the motor assembly to the desired width of cut and lock in position.
5. Adjust the safety guard on the infeed end until it clears the surface of the stock being cut, Fig. 4-60.
6. Lower the blade until it comes into contact with the table.
7. Lower the anti-kickback fingers until they rest lightly on the surface of the stock. Lock in this position. See Fig. 4-60.
8. Start the motor. Slide the stock on the table, keeping the straight edge in contact with the guide strip. Slowly feed the stock against the rotation of the saw. As the cut nears the end of the board, use a push stick. Do not extend your arm beyond the blade.

Bevel Ripping

1. Set the machine for normal ripping.
2. Raise the column, release the bevel clamp, and rotate the motor on the yoke to the desired angle; relock the clamp.
3. Move the motor assembly to the desired width and lock in position.
4. Lower the column until the saw blade touches the table.
5. Adjust the guard so that it clears the work. Lock the guard in position.
6. Place the stock in position for ripping and start the motor. Slide the stock along the table, keeping it in contact with the guide strip.

7. Feed the stock slowly into the blade. As the cut nears the end of the board, use a push stick and do not extend your arm beyond the blade.

Cutting Dadoes

The procedure described below is also used for cutting rabbets.

1. Remove the saw blade and replace it with a dado head of the desired width.
2. With the elevating crank, lower the dado head to the desired depth.
3. Lower the saw guard to about one inch above the cut. This will not obstruct the operator's view, Fig. 4-62.
4. Place a scrap piece of stock against the guide strip and start the motor. Make a test cut.
5. Make any necessary adjustments.
6. Place the stock against the guide strip. Make sure it is in the correct position for the dado to be cut.
7. Start the motor, grasp the yoke, and slowly feed the dado head into the work. After the cut has been made, return to the original position and turn off the motor. Wider dadoes may be made by repositioning the work and taking additional cuts.
8. Angular dadoes may be made by releasing the arm lock and yoke swivel latch, turning the motor to the desired angle, and relocking in position.

Cutting Grooves

1. Remove the saw blade. Replace it with dado heads of the desired width.

Fig. 4-61. Cutting a compound angle.

DeWalt

Fig. 4-62. Cutting a dado. DeWalt

Fig. 4-63. Cutting grooves. DeWalt

2. Release the yoke clamp and swing the motor parallel to the guide strip. Relock.
3. Move the motor assembly on the arm to the desired location. Lock in position.
4. Lower the column to make the desired depth of cut. Lock in position.
5. Adjust the guard so that it clears the work, then lock in position, Fig. 4-63.
6. Make a test cut on a scrap piece of wood.
7. Place the stock against the guide strip and slowly feed it into the dado head. Keep your hands clear of the dado heads. As the cut nears the end of the board, use a push stick.

Shaping

A **molding head,** which has assorted shapes and sizes of cutters, is available as an attachment for some types of radial-arm saws.

1. Insert the desired cutters in the cutterhead and lock in position.

2. Remove the saw blade and replace it with the cutterhead and special shaping guard. Lock in position.
3. Release the bevel clamp and the bevel latch. Rotate the motor 90° to a position vertical to the table. Lock in this position. See Fig. 4-64.
4. Adjust the column height to the desired position. Lock in this position.
5. Release the rip lock and make adjustments for the correct depth of cut. Lock in position.
6. Start the motor. Make a trial cut on scrap stock by moving the piece along the guide strip. Stop the motor. Make any necessary adjustments.
7. Slowly feed the stock into the cutters. Keep your hands at least four inches away from the cutters.

Routing

Routing attachments are available for some radial-arm saws.
1. Remove the saw guard. When doing edge routing, use the special shaper guard.
2. Release the bevel clamp and bevel latch. Rotate the motor 90° to a position perpendicular to the table.
3. Select the desired router bit and secure it to the motor arbor with a chuck adapter.
4. Start the motor. Place the stock on the saw table under the cutter, and lower the bit to the desired depth by turning the elevating crank. Lock the motor in this position.

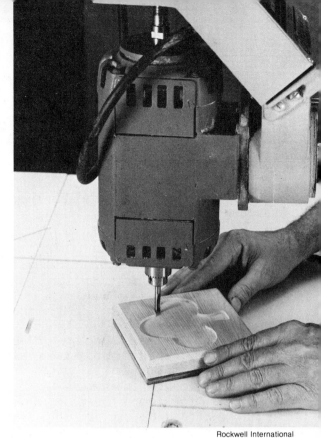

Rockwell International

Fig. 4-65. Routing with the radial-arm saw.

5. Slowly move the work against the revolving bit until all the desired stock has been removed. See Fig. 4-65.
6. If the stock is not free when the routing is completed, shut off the motor, raise the bit, and remove the work from the table.

Standards and Results

- Saw cuts should be made on the waste side of the line.
- Saw cuts should be of the desired angle.
- Dadoes and rabbets should be of the desired size and in the proper location.
- Molding cuts should be smooth.
- Dadoes, grooves, and rabbets should be of an even depth.

Safety Considerations

- Wear safety glasses when using the radial-arm saw.
- Keep your hands out of the line of the rotation of the cutters.
- Guards should be in proper position and should be locked in place.

Fig. 4-64. Using the shaping attachment on the radial-arm saw.

DeWalt

- All adjustments should be made before the machine is started.
- All adjustment mechanisms should be locked before the machine is started.
- Use a push stick when ripping or when cutting grooves or rabbets. When ripping, feed the work against the cutting edge. Do not push the board past the saw without using a push stick.
- When moving stock, do not reach over the

path of the saw unless it is completely stopped.
- The saw should not cut more than 1/16" into the table.
- Allow the saw to obtain maximum speed before making any cuts.
- When crosscutting, be sure to return the saw to the starting position after you have completed a cut.

Portable Electric Saw

Topic 32.

Classification

Power-driven rotary cutting tool with toothed, circular blade

Application

Principle of Operation

A circular blade (usually a combination blade) revolves at an arbor speed of between 3200 and 4600 rpm. The speed varies according to the type of machine. The saw cuts on the principle of a continuous set of cutting wedges.

Fig. 4-66. Portable electric saw.

Rockwell International

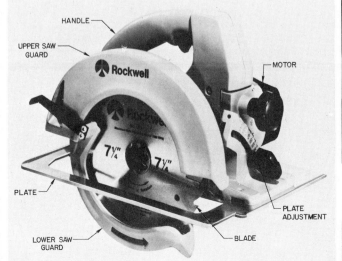

Kinds and Uses

The **portable electric saw** is a handy piece of equipment for construction work. It is used to cut stock to length and width and to make angular cuts such as those on roof rafters and on stairjacks.

Saws are classified according to blade size. They are available in a variety of sizes. See Figs. 4-66 and 4-67.

Principal Parts and Function of Each

1. The **soleplate, shoe,** or **base,** supports the saw and can be adjusted, with the motor

Fig. 4-67. Cutting off stock with the portable electric saw.

Rockwell International

Simonds Saw & Steel

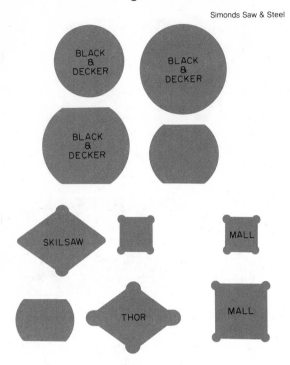

Fig. 4-68. Shapes of arbor holes of portable electric saws.

housing, to control the depth of cut and the angle of the blade.

2. The **base, housing, guards,** and **handles** are usually made of aluminum or of plastic. They are designed and balanced to permit easy handling of the tool in the cutting position.
3. The **motor** provides the power.
4. The **handle** provides the method of controlling the operation of saw.
5. The **front knob** (on some saws) provides for two-hand control.
6. The **trigger switch** is built into the handle for quick control of the cutting action.
7. The **upper saw guard** covers that portion of the blade which is above the soleplate.
8. The **lower saw guard** is retractable so that the saw is covered when not in use. Either removing this guard or tying it back is a very dangerous practice.
9. The **saw blade,** made of high-grade steel, cuts the stock. Saw blades must be selected so that the arbor hole will match the arbor seat, Fig. 4-68. Inserts are available to convert to various shapes.

OSHA Regulations

Portable Circular Saws

All portable, power-driven circular saws that have a blade diameter greater than 2″ shall be equipped with guards above and below the base plate or shoe. Except for the minimum arc required to permit the base to be tilted for bevel cuts, the upper guard shall cover the saw to the depth of the teeth. Except for the minimum arc required to allow proper retraction and contact with the work, the lower guard shall cover the saw to the depth of the teeth. When the tool is withdrawn from the work, the lower guard shall automatically and instantly return to the covering position.

Maintenance

1. Circular-saw blades should be kept sharp and set.
2. The gear reduction unit should be checked periodically to see if it needs lubrication.
3. Most saw housings are made of a rust-resistant material. However, steel parts (such as saw blades) should either be coated with oil film or wax or should be stored in proper containers to prevent them from rusting when they are not in use.

Market Analysis

Capacity

A 6″ saw will cut to a depth of 1-7/8″.
A 7″ saw will cut to a depth of 2-1/2″.
An 8″ saw will cut to a depth of 2-3/4″.
A 9″ saw will cut to a depth of 3-1/4″.
Any width cut or length cut may be made freehand by following a line or by guiding the side of the saw base against a straightedge.

Attachments

1. **Special-purpose blades** may be used for cutting many materials other than wood.
2. A **rip fence** may be attached and adjusted for cutting widths of up to 12″ on some materials.
3. An **adjustable saw track** can either be constructed or, for some machines, can be purchased ready-made. This attachment makes it possible to cut true and square and

to cut bevels and bevel miters. With this device, the portable saw can be used in much the same way as the radial-arm saw.

Safety Considerations

- Wear safety glasses when using the portable electric saw.
- When using the portable electric saw, adjust the saw guard so that the blade projects no more than 1/8″ to 1/4″ below the thickness of the board to be cut.
- Use the portable electric saw **only** when the saw guard is in place.
- It is dangerous to cut short pieces on the saw.
- If the guard catches while you are making diagonal cuts, stop the saw before attempting to free the guard.
- Be sure to keep the electric cord out of the path of the saw.

Band Saw   Topic 33.

Classification

Power-driven, endless, toothed-band cutting tool

Application

Principle of Operation

An endless, flexible-steel belt with rip teeth filed on one edge moves at a speed of between 3,000 and 5,000 feet per minute (600 to 1,200 wheel rpm). This saw cuts on the principle of a continuous set of cutting wedges.

Kinds and Uses

The **band saw,** Fig. 4-69, is used to cut curves and for resawing. When a circular saw is not available, the band saw may be used for crosscutting and ripping. It is available in the following wheel sizes: 12″, 14″, 16″, 18″, 24″, 30″, 36″, and 40″. The larger machines are not usually found in school shops. The table size increases with the size of the wheels. Fourteen-inch machines have a table 14″ × 14″ in size. Blade widths of 1/8″, 3/16″, 1/4″, 3/8″, 1/2″, 5/8″ and 3/4″ are available.

The band saw usually has a 1/2-HP, 1725-rpm, 60-cycle motor, which is either single-phase or three-phase.

Rockwell International

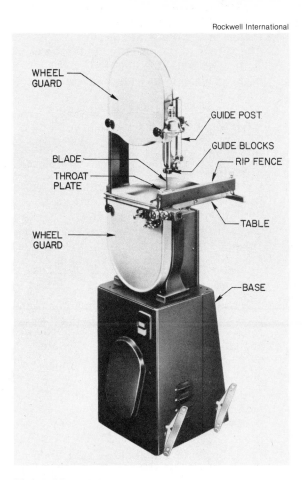

Fig. 4-69. 14″ band saw.

Principal Parts and Function of Each

1. The **wheels** are made of cast iron, aluminum, or pressed steel. Although there are some three-wheeled band saws, most band saws have two wheels. The outer rims of the wheels are covered with a band of rubber (a **tire**). The saw runs on these rubber tires, which serve to protect the teeth, to act as a cushion for the blade and to prevent the blade from slipping.

2. The machined-cast-iron **table** supports the work as it is being cut. The larger band saws have two tables. The table on the right is larger and can be tilted 45° to the right and about 10° to the left. The left table is stationary. Smaller band saws have only one table. This table usually tilts 45° to the right and 10° to the left.

    The table through which the saw blade runs has a slot for insertion of the blade. This table is kept in alignment by means of a **table-aligning pin.**

3. The **throat plate,** usually made of aluminum, prevents damage to the blade if breakage occurs or if the saw runs off the track.

4. The **guide blocks,** made of hardened steel, are positioned above and below the table. They prevent the blade from being twisted during the cutting operation.

5. The **thrust wheels,** made of pressed steel or cast iron, prevent the blade from being pushed off the wheels. They also serve as an indicator for saw's tracking.

6. The **tension mechanism** is made of spring steel and is used to put the proper tension on blade. Some saws have a tension indicator, which gives proper tension for each size blade.

7. The **tracking mechanism** is an adjustment that pivots the upper wheel so that the saw blade will track in the middle of the wheels.

8. The **blades** are made of high-carbon chromium steel. They have rip teeth.

9. The **wheel guards** cover the wheels, protecting the operator. These guards are made either of pressed steel or of sheet metal.

10. The adjustable **guidepost** is made of steel and may be moved up or down to accommodate different thicknesses of work.

11. The cast-iron **frame** or **yoke** serves as a mounting for the two wheels.

12. The **base** or **stand,** made of cast iron, pressed steel, or wood, supports the machine.

13. The **motor** provides the power.

14. The **blade guard** covers the portion of the blade between the guide blocks and the upper wheel.

OSHA Regulations

Band Saws

1. All portions of the saw blade shall be enclosed or guarded, except for the working portion of the blade between the bottom of the guide rolls and the table.

2. Each band saw shall be provided with a tension-control device to indicate the proper tension for the standard saw blades used on the machine.

3. Effective brakes should be provided to stop the wheel in the case of blade breakage.

4. To avoid vibration, brazed joints in band-saw blades shall be of the same thickness as the saw blade.

5. Twists or kinks in band-saw blades should be promptly and carefully removed with a hammer.

6. The use of wooden band-saw wheels (other than those of commercial manufacture) is prohibited.

Maintenance

1. Band-saw blades should be kept sharp. Sharpening should be done by someone experienced in performing this task.

2. The saw should be maintained at the proper tension. It should also be kept tracking in the center of the wheels.

3. The upper and lower guide blocks should be properly adjusted so that two-thirds of the width of the saw blade runs between the blocks, Fig. 4-70.

4. The blade should be 1/64″ away from the upper and lower thrust wheels when the saw is not cutting.

5. Broken saw blades should be repaired by an experienced person.

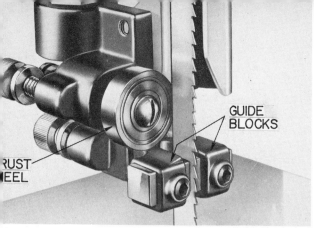

Fig. 4-70. Detail of upper guide blocks and thrust wheel.

6. Some band saws require periodic greasing; others have sealed bearings.
7. Whenever a band saw is to be left idle for a long period, machined parts should first be coated with a thin film of oil and the tension on the blade should be released.
8. Sawdust should be blown from the motor and the machine.
9. So that proper clearance can be maintained, the throat plate should be replaced when it becomes worn.

Market Analysis

Capacity

The size of a band saw is determined by the diameter of its wheels.

A 12" band saw usually has an adjustable guidepost opening of 4-1/2". A 14" band saw has an opening of 6-1/4". However, stock more than 3" thick is rarely cut on this size of machine. (For resawing, the guidepost opening may be raised to its maximum width, although the actual amount of stock cut will be approximately 3".)

Attachments

1. **Miter gauge.** The miter gauge is used for square, miter, and compound-angle crosscutting.
2. **Fence.** The fence is used for straight ripping.
3. **Sand belts.** These are used in place of the saw blade for sanding the edges of curved stock.
4. **Template guide pins** and **pivot pins.** These are used for cutting circles.

| **Band-Saw Blades** | **Topic 34.** |

Classification

Continuous-band-shaped cutting tool

Band-saw blades have one of two types of teeth:
1. The standard **rip tooth,** Fig. 4-71.
2. The **raker tooth,** used on saber-tooth and skip-tooth blades, Fig. 4-72. Blades designed for cutting wood are generally set for both crosscutting and ripping.

Application

Band-saw blades can be purchased either in welded lengths (for a specific machine) or in coils 100' or 250' in length.

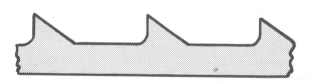

Fig. 4-71. Standard tooth shape for rip band saws.

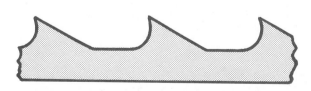

Fig. 4-72. Raker tooth for rip band saws.

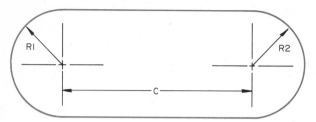

Fig. 4-73. Determining the length of a band-saw blade.

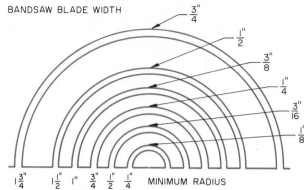

Fig. 4-74. Chart shows the minimum cutting radius for each common width of band-saw blade.

To determine the blade length, follow this procedure:

1. Measure the radius of the band wheels. See **R1** and **R2** in Fig. 4-73.
2. Adjust the upper wheel to the halfway take-up position. Measure the center distance between the two wheels. See **C** in Fig. 4-73.
3. Use this formula to determine the band length:

   (R1 × 3.1416) + (R2 × 3.1416) + (2 × C) = band length

The width of the band-saw blade selected is determined by the curve the band saw is to cut. See Fig. 4-74. For resawing, the blade should be as wide as possible.

Kinds and Uses

Regular Rip-Tooth Blade

This is an all-hard blade, designed to be long-lasting. It may be resharpened for longer use. The rake angle of the rip-tooth blade is between 8° and 10°. This blade has round gullets and is designed for all types of cutting and alternate set.

Skip-Tooth Blade

The skip-tooth (raker-shaped) blade generally has a hardened cutting edge. This blade is designed to be thrown away when the cutting edge becomes dull. The large gullet gives extra capacity for the chips, permitting a fast cut.

Table 4-6
Regular Rip-Tooth Blade Size

Width	Gauge	Teeth/In.
1/8″	25	6
3/16″	21	3-4
	22	4-5-6
	25	5-6
1/4″	21	2-3-4-5
	22	4-5-6
	25	5-6
5/16″	21	3
3/8″	20	2
	21	2-3-4-5
	22	4-5
	25	5-6
1/2″	20	2-3
	21	2-3-4-5
	22	3-4-5
	25	5-6
3/4″	19	2
	25	4-5
1″	19-22	2-3-4-5

Table 4-7
Skip-Tooth Blade Size

Width	Gauge	Teeth/In.
3/16″	23	4
1/4″	23	4-6
3/8″	23	3-4
1/2″	23	3-4
3/4″	21	3
1″	20	2-3

Table 4-8
Saber-Tooth or Hook-Tooth Blade Size

Width	Gauge	Teeth/In.
1/4″	23	4-6
3/8″	23	3-4-6
1/2″	23	2-3-4-6
3/4″	21	2-3-6
1″	20	2-3-6

Saber-Tooth or Hook-Tooth Blade

This blade is similar in design to the skip-tooth blade, but the face of the tooth has a 10° hook or rake angle. The tooth edge is flame-hardened and is designed as a throw-away blade. The angle of the tooth, with its chip-breaker design, permits fast feed and prevents soft, gummy materials from sticking in the gullets.

Using the Band Saw

Topic 35.

Classification

Cutting by shearing and shredding with an endless, toothed blade

Procedure

Cutting Curves

1. Determine the width of the saw blade suitable for cutting the curve, Table 4-9. Outside curves less than 1″ in diameter should either be made using relief cuts or should be cut on a jigsaw. Inside curves of less than 1″ should either be drilled or bored.

Table 4-9
Saw-Blade Width for Cutting Curves

Width of Saw Blade	Minimum Diameter of Circle
1/8″	1″
3/16″	1 1/2″
1/4″	2″
3/8″	2 1/2″
1/2″	3″
5/8″	3 1/2″

Note: The saw must be sharp and properly set in order to make cuts of the diameter given.

Fig. 4-75. Proper position and stance at band saw.

2. Make sure all outlines are clearly marked. When several pieces are to be cut, they may be fastened together with brads. Do this in the waste stock. Check the stock for grit and nails.

3. Adjust the saw guide to give about 1/4″ clearance above the thickness of the stock.

4. Stand slightly to the left of the center of the table, Fig. 4-75. Start the machine and apply even, forward pressure with the right hand. Guide the stock with the left hand, Flg. 4-76.

5. To cut a sharper curve than the width of the blade will permit, make relief cuts in the

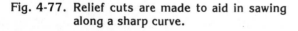

Fig. 4-76. Cutting to a line.
Left hand pushes stock while right hand serves as a pivot.

Fig. 4-77. Relief cuts are made to aid in sawing along a sharp curve.

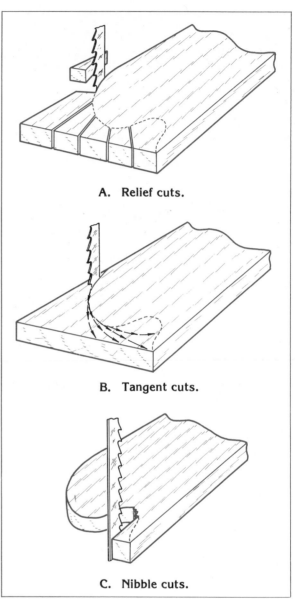

A. Relief cuts.

B. Tangent cuts.

C. Nibble cuts.

Fig. 4-78. Methods of cutting sharp curves with the band saw.

waste stock, Figs. 4-77 and 4-78. Relief cuts should not touch the line.

It is not a recommended practice to back the blade out of the cut while the machine is running. The work should be planned in such a way that you can saw out on each cut. Backtracking tends to run the blade away from the guide.

Fig. 4-79. Using a pivot guide for resawing.

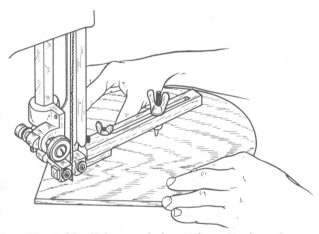

Fig. 4-80. Using a circle-cutting attachment on the band saw.

Resawing or Ripping to Thickness

Thin stock may be resawed from thicker boards or planks. It is sometimes advisable to start the cuts on the circular saw.

1. Both one side and one adjacent edge of the work to be resawed must be straight and square.
2. For resawing, select the widest saw blade available. This will help prevent the saw from following its natural tendency to run to the softest part of the wood grain.
3. Secure a rip fence or a wooden guide to the table. The distance from the fence to the blade should equal the thickness of the resawed piece. See Fig. 4-82.
4. For clearance and safety, set the upper guide 1/4" above the work.
5. A line along the edge to be cut will aid in guiding the work.
6. Hold the stock against the fence and guide it steadily past the saw.

Ripping or Crosscutting

Ripping or crosscutting may be done on the band saw when a circular saw is not available. It is important to use a sharp saw and proper guides. A dull saw will have a tendency to follow the grain.

| A | B |

Fig. 4-81. Diagonal cutting on the band saw using (A) a fence and tilting table and (B) a V-block.

Standards and Results

- All saw cuts should be made on the waste side of the line.
- When cutting two or more pieces that have been fastened together, make certain that no nail holes will be visible in the finished piece.
- Band saws cut rapidly but should not be forced, as this will cause the cut edges to be burned.

Safety Considerations

- Wear safety glasses.
- Use the machine only when all guards are in place.
- Adjust the upper guide for clearance. Too high a setting will leave the saw unguarded.
- Keep your hands away from the moving blade and out of line with the saw's rotation.

- Small chips that lodge in the guide blocks may jam the blade. Stop the saw and remove them.
- Avoid backtracking. Whenever possible, cut the saw clear. If backtracking is unavoidable, turn off the saw before pulling the stock clear.
- Check the blade-guide adjustments.
- All observers should stand clear of the working area.
- Cylindrical stock should not be cut on the band saw.
- Stop the saw and investigate any unusual noise.
- No one should stand to the right of the saw. If the saw were to break, it would be most likely to fly to the right.
- If the blade breaks, turn off the saw. Wait until the machine has come to a complete stop before attempting to dislodge the blade.

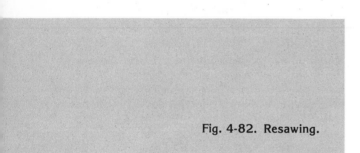

Fig. 4-82. Resawing.

B. Completing the cut on the band saw.

A. Cuts made from each edge on the circular saw, in preparation for finish cutting on the band saw.

C. Two pieces cut — the result of resawing. Note the symmetry of the matching pieces.

Replacing a Band-Saw Blade

Topic 36.

Procedure

1. Remove the upper and lower wheel guards, the throat plate, and the table-aligning pin.
2. Release the tension on the blade by lowering the upper wheel.
3. Remove the saw blade by slipping it off the wheels and out of the table slot.
4. Coil the blade that has been removed, Fig. 4-83.
   a. With the blade almost touching your body, grasp it at arm's length in front of you. The back of the blade should be resting in the palm of each hand and the teeth of the blade should be pointing up.
   b. Twist the wrists up and in, then bring them together. This will automatically form three loops in the blade.
   c. Place the loose loop flat on bench top and release your hands. The blade is now coiled.

5. Select the proper blade for the job to be done. (See "Cutting Curves" under Topic 35, "Using the Band Saw.")
6. If necessary, clean the tires by turning the wheel against a piece of 100-grit sandpaper.
7. Grasp the blade so that the teeth are facedown and pointing toward you. If the teeth point up, the blade is inside-out and must be reversed.
8. Insert the blade in the slot in the table and position it on the upper and lower wheels.
9. Make sure the blade is between the upper and lower guide blocks.
10. Apply tension by raising the upper wheel. Most modern band saws are equipped with a gauge for checking tension of various widths of blades. If the band saw is not equipped with this gauge, the tension may be checked by gently plucking the blade. If the blade feels slack, the upper wheel should be raised until the blade is taut.

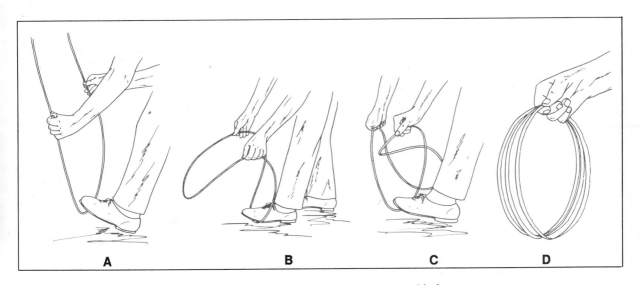

A   B   C   D

Fig. 4-83. Steps in coiling a band-saw blade.

11. When changing blades, back off the upper and lower thrust wheels and guide blocks.
12. Rotate the upper wheel by hand. Note whether the blade is tracking properly.
13. If the blade is running toward the back or the front of the wheel, adjust the tracking mechanism until the blade tracks in the center of the wheel.
14. Adjust the guide blocks so that they are behind the set of the teeth and close to the blade. They should not, however, be close enough to the blade to cause friction. One-half to two-thirds of the blade width should run between these guide blocks.
15. Position the thrust wheels behind the blade, in such a way that they are free when the saw is not cutting but make contact when the saw is cutting.
16. Replace the upper and lower guards, the throat plate and the table-aligning pin.

Topic 37.

Band-Saw Operator

Classification

The band saw has numerous industrial applications. It is used in the general woodworking shop, the small cabinet shop, the sample maker's shop, and the pattern shop. Practically all woodworkers require some skill in operating the band saw.

In larger factories and cabinet shops, the **band-saw operator** is a machine attendant who cuts shapes to a template. The use of templates[1] and jigs[2] reduces the need for the attendant to have very specialized skills. However, some band-saw operators are skilled in resawing.

In lumber manufacture, the band-saw operator (or **sawyer**) is in charge of cutting the logs into lumber forms such as cants, timbers, planks, and boards.

[1]**Template** — a profile shape used to make duplicate parts or to match test profiles. Templates are usually made of cardboard, metal, or, when they are to be used to trace or test a profile, of thin wood. When a template is to be used to guide the direction of movement of the work or of the cutting tool, thicker material should be used.

[2]**Jig** — a device used to aid in setting up (positioning or securing) work to do a particular operation accurately and more efficiently.

Heywood-Wakefield Co.

Fig. 4-84. Worker trimming a chair back on a large industrial band saw.

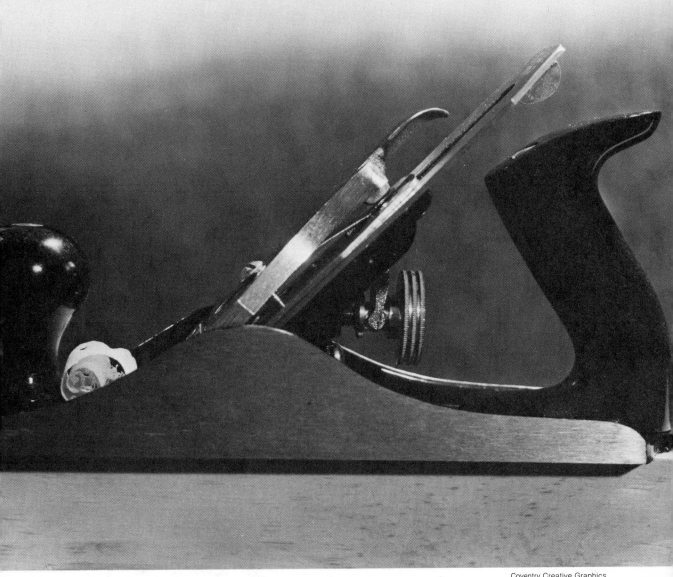

Coventry Creative Graphics

SECTION FIVE.

Hand Cutting to Basic Form

Topic 38.

Hand Planes

Classification

Edge-cutting tools

Application

Principle of Operation

All **hand planes** work on the principle of the cutting wedge.

Kinds and Uses

1. **Smooth planes** are used for smoothing and finishing work, Fig. 5-1. They are either 7″, 8″, 9″, or 10″ long and have cutters that are 1-5/8″, 1-3/4″, 2″, and 2-3/8″ wide, respectively. The cutter is set at an angle of 45°, and the bevel faces down.
2. **Jack planes** can be used to true edges, but are most commonly used as all-purpose planes, Fig. 5-2. They are either 14″ or 15″ long, and have cutters 2-3/8″ wide. The **junior jack plane** is a smaller version of the jack plane. It was designed for use by junior high school industrial-arts students, with

the intention of providing them with a jack plane that is easier to manipulate than the standard jack plane. The junior jack plane is 11-1/2″ long and has a cutter 1-3/4″ wide.
3. **Fore planes** are used for planing large surfaces and edges, Fig. 5-3. They are 18″ long and have a 2-3/8″ cutter.
4. **Jointer planes** are used to plane large surfaces and to joint edges on long pieces. Like all members of the plane family except the block plane, the cutter is set at an angle of 45°, with the bevel facing down. These planes are either 22″ or 24″ long and have a 2-3/8″ or 2-5/8″ cutter, Fig. 5-4.

Stanley Tools

Fig. 5-2.   Jack plane.

Stanley Tools

Fig. 5-3.   Fore plane.

Stanley Tools

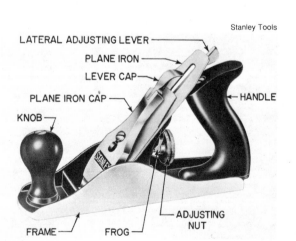

LATERAL ADJUSTING LEVER

PLANE IRON

LEVER CAP

PLANE IRON CAP

KNOB

HANDLE

FRAME   FROG

ADJUSTING NUT

Fig. 5-1.   Smooth plane.

Stanley Tools

Fig. 5-4.   Jointer plane.

Stanley Tools

Fig. 5-5.   Block plane.

5. **Block planes** are used for planing end grain, Fig. 5-5. The block plane differs from the preceding planes in that the cutter is set at an angle of 20° with the bevel facing up. Another difference is that it does not have a cap iron. The lever cap is shaped to fit the hand, and serves as a handle. This plane is either 6″ or 7″ in length. The cutters of the block plane are 1-3/8″ or 1-5/8″ wide, respectively.

Principal Parts and Function of Each

1. The **frame** is the body of the plane and is the part that determines its size. It is usually made of a casting of gray iron or aluminum, or sometimes of pressed steel. The bottom of the frame is called the **sole** and may be either smooth or corrugated.
2. The **frog,** made of cast iron, determines the angle at which the plane iron is held. It also positions the plane iron at the rear of the mouth.
3. The **lateral adjusting lever,** made of pressed steel, is used to regulate an even shaving thickness.

4. The **adjusting nut,** made of plastic or brass, is used to increase or decrease the depth of cut or the shaving thickness.
5. The **plane iron,** or cutter, is made of the finest tool steel, which has been tempered, hardened, and sharpened to a bevel. This part of the plane does the cutting.
6. The **plane-iron cap,** made of steel, is shaped to give stiffness to the cutting edge and to prevent chattering. It breaks the back of the shaving, causing it to curl. The plane-iron cap prevents the tool from splintering or digging into the surface. It is attached to the plane iron with a **cap screw.**
7. The cast-iron **lever cap** holds the plane iron securely in place and prevents chatter.
8. The **knobs** and **handles** are made either of plastic, cast aluminum, or rosewood. They are the means by which pressure is applied and direction controlled.

Maintenance

1. Planes should be cleaned of all shavings before being returned to the tool cabinet. This is best done with a brush.
2. Keep screws tight in the handle, the knob, and the frog.
3. Replacement parts are available from most manufacturers.
4. Planes should be stored in a dry place. The blade should not protrude below the base surface. When planes are to be left unused for a long period of time, all metal parts should first be coated with a film of oil.
5. For information on sharpening, see Section 19, "Sharpening" — Topic 191, "Grinding Edge Tools," and Topic 193, Whetting or Honing a Cutting Tool."

Market Analysis

Capacity

The only capacity for planes is the width of cut and depth of cut. The width of cut is determined by the width of the blade. This width ranges from 1-5/8″ to 2-5/8″. The operator may vary the thickness of cut, according to the type of job to be done and the kind and condition of the stock.

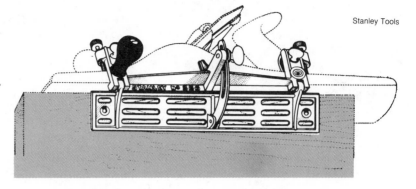

Stanley Tools

Fig. 5-6.   Jointer gauge.

Attachments

The **jointer gauge** may be used on any plane except the block plane, but it is most practical to use it on a fore plane or a jointer plane. It is used as a jig in planing any bevel from 30° to 90° and as an aid in jointing an edge, Fig. 5-6.

Topic 39.

Special-Purpose Planes

Classification

Edge-cutting tools

Application

Principle of Operation

All types of planes cut on the principle of the cutting wedge.

Kinds and Uses

1. The **router plane** has two knobs, a depth gauge, and an adjustment for cutter depth, Fig. 5-7. This plane is equipped with three cutters — 1/4″ and 1/2″ square cutters and a "V" cutter. The router plane is used for surfacing the bottom of grooves, of dadoes, and of recesses parallel with the surface of the stock.
2. The **rabbet plane,** Fig. 5-8, has no knob, and the handle is part of the plane. The plane iron is the full width of the base. The rabbet plane is fitted with a spur and a detachable depth gauge. It is 8″ long and has either a 1″, 1-1/4″, or 1-1/2″ plane iron. This plane is used to plane rabbets.
3. The **cabinetmaker's rabbet plane** is made in two pieces in order to permit increase or decrease in the throat opening, Fig. 5-9. It has an adjusting screw and cap. This plane is available in 5-1/2″ and 6″ lengths and has 3/4″ or 1″ cutters. It is used for fine work.

Stanley Tools

Fig. 5-7.   Router plane.

Stanley Tools

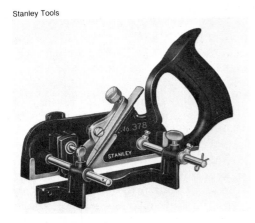

Fig. 5-8.   Rabbet plane.

Stanley Tools

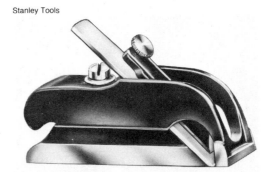

Fig. 5-10. Bullnose rabbet plane.

Stanley Tools

Fig. 5-9.   Cabinetmaker's rabbet plane.

Stanley Tools

Fig. 5-11. Bench rabbet plane.

Stanley Tools

Fig. 5-12. Duplex rabbet plane.

4. The **bullnose rabbet plane** is much like a cabinetmaker's rabbet plane but is shorter and its plane-iron seat is close to the front end of the plane. See Fig. 5-10. It is 4″ long and has a 1″ plane iron. It is used for working into corners or other restricted places.

5. The **bench rabbet plane** is like a smooth plane except that the frame has a portion cut out and the plane iron is full width, Fig. 5-11. It is available in 9″ and 13″ lengths and has a 2-1/8″ plane iron. It is used to cut rabbets.

6. The **duplex rabbet plane** Fig. 5-12, is similar to a rabbet plane, but instead of one seat for the plane iron, it has two — one for regular work and one for bullnose work. It is equipped with an adjustable fence for making parallel cuts. It is 8-1/4″ long and has a 1-1/2″ plane iron.

7. The **skew-cutter rabbet plane** is similar to

a rabbet plane, but the plane is wider and the plane iron is set on an angle. The angle makes it possible to take a shearing cut. The plane is 8-1/2″ long and has a 1-7/8″ plane iron. It is used to cut rabbets on cross-grain stock. The spur scores the stock ahead of the blade in order to prevent chipping.

Stanley Tools

Fig. 5-13. Side rabbet plane.

Stanley Tools

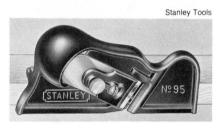

Fig. 5-14. Edge-trimming block plane.

8. The **side rabbet plane** has a 5-1/2" body and two 1/2" cutters, which are held by clamps and thumbscrews, Fig. 5-13. It is used to increase the width of dadoes, rabbets, and grooves.

9. The **edge-trimming block plane,** Fig. 5-14, is similar to a side rabbet plane. It has a body, cap iron, and screw. A 1-1/16" plane iron is held at an angle on the side of the 6" plane. It is used in trimming and squaring the edge of end rabbets.

10. The **double-end block plane** serves a dual purpose. One end is used to do common end-grain planing, while the other is used for corner work. It is 8" long and has a 1-5/8" cutter.

11. The **dado plane** is comparable to the skew-cutter rabbet plane. The plane iron is 8" in length and is set on an angle. It has 1/2" to 3/4" cutters, and is used to cut dadoes. On either side of the frame, there is a spur that scores a path for the blade. The spurs score the sides of the cut and the skew cutter removes the waste material. This plane is also equipped with a depth gauge.

12. The **plow plane** is much like a dado plane, but the plane iron is set square instead of at an angle. See Fig. 5-15. It has spurs and a depth gauge, as well as an adjustable fence. This plane is 9-1/2" long and its

cutters are 1/8", 5/32", 3/16", 7/32", 1/4", 5/16", and 3/8" wide. It is used to cut grooves. The depth gauge and the fence are used for doing work requiring accuracy.

13. The **combination plane** is used for cutting various shapes of moldings, Fig. 5-16. It is 9-1/4" long.

14. The **tongue-and-groove** (or **matching**) **plane** has a handle on each end, making it possible to push the plane either way. See Fig. 5-17. The frog is designed in such a way that the cutter can be set for either direction. The plane is 9" long and is equipped with two 1/4" plane irons — one to cut the tongue and one to cut the groove.

15. The **model maker's plane,** Fig. 5-18, has either a flat or a curved bottom. It has a curved handle, similar to that of a cabinet scraper. It has no knob. This plane is

Stanley Tools

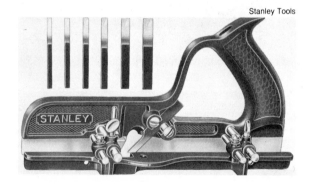

Fig. 5-15. Plow plane.

Stanley Tools

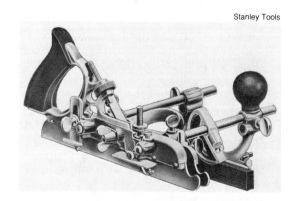

Fig. 5-16. Combination plane.

3-1/2″ to 5″ long and has 1-1/4″ to 1-5/8″ cutters. It is designed for one-handed use in the construction of scale models such as boats and airplanes.

16. The **scraper plane** has two handles, which project from the sides of the frame, Fig. 5-19. The pivoting frog enables the plane to be set at any angle between 15° and 90°. Changing the angle of the blade changes the depth of cut. The scraper plane has a 2-7/8″ blade, sharpened on the cutting edge to produce a burr. This plane is used for final preparation of the surface prior to sanding. It is especially suitable for scraping around knots and for scraping cross-grained woods such as curly maple or bird's-eye maple. Because the bearing surface of this plane is larger than that of the cabinet scraper, a flatter surface will be produced.

17. The **circular plane** is similar to the smooth plane except that the bottom is made of flexible steel and, at each end, is fastened to the frame on a pivot, Fig. 5-20. The bottom curvature of the plane is changed from concave to convex by means of a threaded shaft. It is 10″ long and has a 1-3/4″ cutter. The circular plane is used for either concave or convex surfaces, and may be adjusted for various types of curves by means of an internally threaded wheel.

Stanley Tools

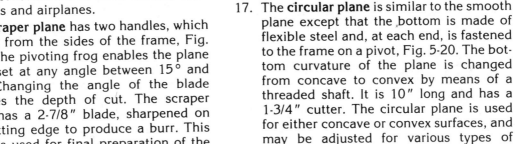

Stanley Tools

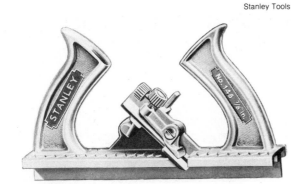

Fig. 5-17. Tongue-and-groove plane.

Fig. 5-19. Scraper plane.

Stanley Tools

Fig. 5-18. Model maker's planes.

Woodcraft Supply Corp.

Fig. 5-20. Circular plane.

Fig. 5-21. Core-box plane.

Stanley Tools

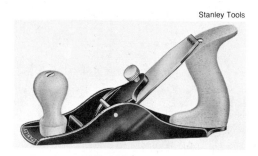

Fig. 5-22. Scrub plane.

Fig. 5-23. Worker using a 1737 side-handle wooden scrub plane.
   For extra-heavy work, a second worker pulled forward on a rope that was attached to the dowel pin at the front of the plane.

Old Sturbridge Village, Inc.

curves by means of an internally threaded wheel.

18. The **core-box plane** is 10″ long, has a 7/8″ cutter, and is used to rough out concave surfaces such as cores. See Fig. 5-21. The frame is shaped like a square trough.

19. The **fiberboard plane** is much like a smooth plane except that the plane iron is parallel to the sides of the plane. It also has an adjustable fence. It is 10″ long and has shaped plane irons for trimming and grooving.

20. The **scrub plane,** Fig. 5-22, is similar to a smooth plane, but is narrower and has no plane-iron cap, adjusting nut, or lateral adjusting lever. It has a 1-1/4″ plane iron with a rounded, beveled end. The plane is 9-1/2″ long. It is used for roughing down thick stock to dimension.

Principal Parts and Function of Each

For a description of common parts, see Topic 38, "Hand Planes."

Fig. 5-24. Old-time 6′ jointer plane.
   This jointer plane was commonly operated by two workers. When used by one worker, however, the plane was secured in an inverted position and the stock was moved over the blade.

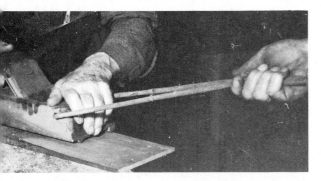

Fig. 5-25. Two-person molding plane.

1. **Plane irons** on all planes are made from high-grade tool steel that has been tempered and hardened. The plane iron does the cutting.
2. The **fence** on special-purpose planes is made of machined cast iron. It serves as a guide during planing.
3. The **spurs** are made of steel that has been tempered and hardened. They score the wood ahead of the cutter to prevent tearing and chipping.
4. Steel **depth gauges** limit the depth of cut.

5. Circular planes have a flexible steel bottom that can be adjusted to conform to the contour of the surface being cut.

Maintenance

See "Maintenance," Topic 38, "Hand Planes."

Market Analysis

Capacity

The only capacity for planes is determined by the length and width of the plane and by the depth of cut. Some planes are equipped with an adjustable fence that limits the width of cut. The plane iron may be adjusted to vary the shaving thickness according to the kind of job to be done and the condition of the stock.

Attachments

Specially shaped **plane irons,** designed for making moldings, are available for combination planes.

Squaring a Board — Hand Process

Topic 40.

Squaring is the process of cutting stock to dimension, making certain that adjacent surfaces form right angles.

Classification

Laying out, cutting, and testing surfaces

Procedure

Planing a Face True and Smooth

1. Select the better of the two faces and examine the board for twist by placing a

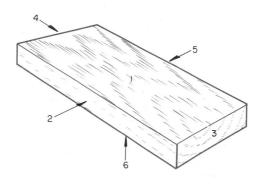

Fig. 5-26. Numbered surfaces of board.
1 & 6 — Faces
2 & 5 — Edges
3 & 4 — Ends

straightedge across the corners or by sighting across the corners. Mark any high corners, and check by turning the board over on the bench and rocking it on the high corners.

2. Determine the direction of the grain on the edge and on the face of the board. Draw an arrow in the direction of the grain, as shown in Fig. 5-27.

3. Clamp the board end-to-end between the vise dog and a bench stop, Fig. 5-28. If the bench is not drilled for bench stops, the board may be held between the vise dog and a piece of waste stock clamped to the bench top, Fig. 5-29. Never clamp a board edge-to-edge, as pressure applied in this manner would compress the board and cause it to cup. A board planed flat in this position would very likely develop a curve that would be evident when the pressure was released.

Fig. 5-29. One method of holding a board.

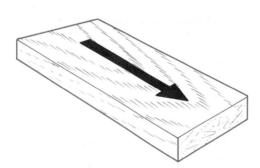

Fig. 5-27. Direction of grain.

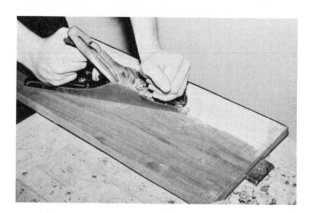

Fig. 5-30. Planing the working face.

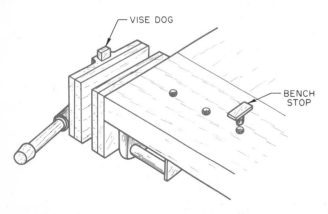

Fig. 5-28. The vise dog may be used in conjunction with a bench stop to hold stock on the work table.

4. Set the plane to cut a fine shaving. If, in testing the board, you find high corners, first remove sufficient material from these corners to flatten the board. Then, plane enough to produce a clean surface. Always be sure to plane **in the direction of the grain. Remember:** when starting to plane, apply pressure on the knob end of the plane. When the entire plane is on the board, bear down equally on both the knob and the handle. Then, as the plane begins to pass off the board, relieve the pressure on the knob. See Fig. 5-30.

5. Test this surface frequently with a straightedge or try square. Always looking toward

Fig. 5-31. Testing the face for flatness.

Fig. 5-32. Planing an edge.

the light, hold the straightedge lengthwise, crosswise, and then diagonally. Repeat this procedure at several points on the board. Wherever light shows under the straightedge, Fig. 5-31, the surface is low. Further planing must be done where the straightedge touches the wood. Be careful, as one thin shaving is often sufficient.

6. Mark this surface or face so you will recognize it later. It is called the **working face.**

Planing an Edge True With the Face

1. Select the better of the two edges and test it to see if it is square with the working face. Mark any high points, as material will be removed first from these areas.

2. Fasten the board securely in the vise with the marked edge parallel to the bench top.

3. Grasping the handle, place the left thumb on the front of the plane, just behind the knob. Slide your fingers against the face of the board in order to keep the plane and board parallel. This will also aid in holding the plane steady. See Fig. 5-32.

4. Take full-length strokes, holding the plane level so that any high spots will be removed first. Remember to press down on the knob at the beginning of each stroke and on the handle at the end of each stroke. You should finish with a full-width shaving.

5. Holding the board in your left hand, sight carefully down the edge to see that you are keeping the edge straight. To test whether

Fig. 5-33. Testing an edge for squareness with face.

the edge is square with the working face, hold the head of the try square snugly against the working face, keeping the blade against the edge of the board, as shown in Fig. 5-33. Where light shows under the blade, the edge is low. Further planing must be done where the blade touches the wood. This should be done carefully, as one thin shaving may be all you need to remove. Work for a full-width shaving that is the full length of the board, and you will have little difficulty getting a true edge.

6. Mark this edge so that you will recognize it later. It is called the **working edge.** The working face and working edge may be marked **1** and **2** respectively. See Fig. 5-26.

Cutting or Planing an End True With the Face and Edge

1. If the end grain is not going to be seen from the outside of the project, squaring may be done by cutting the end in a miter box. A cut should be made about 1/4″ from the end of the board to prevent the saw from tearing the edge.

2. If the end grain is to show, it is best to prepare it by planing, as this will give a much smoother surface than sawing. End-grain planing may be done in several ways. The preferred method is to begin from one edge, planing half the distance across the end, then to plane the remaining half from the opposite edge. This is done to prevent chipping of corners. Figures 5-34 and 5-35 show this method. Chipping may also be

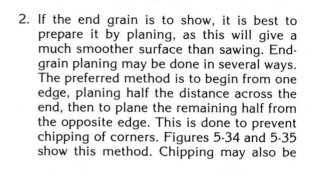

Fig. 5-34. Planing end grain — note angle of plane.

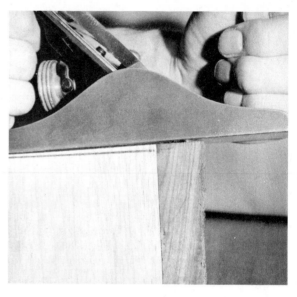

Fig. 5-36. Scrap used to prevent chipping on back edge during end planing.

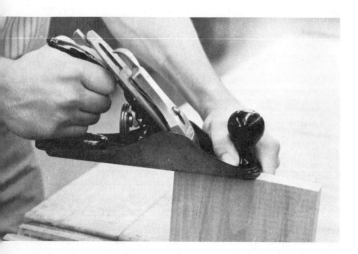

Fig. 5-35. Planing from the opposite edge to the center.

Fig. 5-37. Testing an end for squareness with face.

Fig. 5-38. Testing an end for squareness with edge.

prevented by clamping a scrap piece of wood to one edge of the stock, Fig. 5-36. This makes it possible to plane the entire length of the end in one direction.

3. Hold the plane as in edge planing but at an angle with the side of the board, as shown in Fig. 5-34. This will result in a shearing cut across the wood fibers.

4. Test the end with the try square, both from the face and from the edge, Figs. 5-37 and 5-38, carefully planing any high places that you find.

5. Mark this end so that you will recognize it later. It is called the **working end.**

Cutting to Length

1. Measure the desired length from the working end and mark across the stock with a sharp pencil or knife. If the end grain is not to be seen from the outside, the end may be cut square by using a miter box. Cut just outside the line.

2. Stock that is to be planed must be cut at least 1/16″ longer than the required finished length of the board. Secure the stock either in a vise or on a bench hook, then cut off the waste stock with a fine crosscut saw.

3. To plane the end smooth and square, work to the line in the same manner as you planed the working end, using a try square to test it carefully from both the working face and the working edge.

Planing to Width

1. Set a marking gauge to the desired width. Check the width on the gauge with a rule, measuring from the spur to the head. Mark the desired width on both faces of the stock, being careful to keep the head of the marking gauge against the working edge while gauging, as shown in Fig. 5-39. Be sure to push the gauge away from you so that you can see the line being scribed. If the board is more than 3″ or 4″ wide, a panel gauge should be used.

    A combination square may also be used. The blade is allowed to project from the head the required width of the board. Keeping the head of the square firm against the working edge, hold a pencil against the end of the blade while you push the square along the length of the board.

    For a very wide board, use a ruler to measure the width at two points, one near each end. Then draw a knife along a straightedge aligned with these two points.

2. Fasten the stock in the vise and plane to the middle of the gauge line or knife line.

3. Test from the working face with the try square as in Fig. 5-33. If you have been careful in planing to the middle of the gauge line, this edge should test true.

Fig. 5-39. Using the marking gauge.

Planing to Thickness

1. With the marking gauge, measure the desired thickness on both edges of the stock, being careful to keep the head of the gauge against the working face while marking. Connect the ends of these gauged lines with a pencil and straightedge. The line that is produced will be the guide line to which you should plane.
2. Clamp the stock on the bench against the stop and then plane to the middle of the gauge line.
3. Test this surface with a straightedge. If you have been careful in planing to the gauge line, this surface should be reasonably flat and square.

Standards and Results

- Each planed surface should be flat, smooth, square with the adjacent surfaces, and of correct dimension.
- There should be no chipped edges.

Safety Considerations

- Wear safety glasses when using a plane or a saw.
- Stock should be adequately secured.
- All adjustments to the plane or the saw should be made with caution.

Topic 41.

Spokeshave

Classification

Edge-cutting tool

Application

Principle of Operation

The **spokeshave** works on the principle of a controlled cutting wedge, in much the same way as the plane.

Stanley Tools

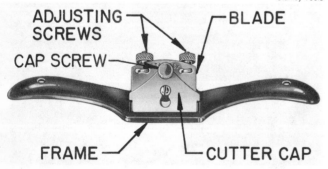

Fig. 5-40. Spokeshave.

Kinds and Uses

1. Spokeshaves are made with any of three face shapes: flat, convex, or hollow.
2. In cutting or shaping a curved surface, the spokeshave is usually pushed. The flat-face type, Fig. 5-40, is used to cut flat edges, while the convex face is used to cut concave edges. The hollow-face spokeshave is used for rounding edges, Fig. 5-41.

Principal Parts and Function of Each

1. The **frame,** made of cast iron or wood, consists of a short face and two handles. The face may be either round or flat. It is made short so that it will follow contours with ease.
2. The **blade,** made of fine carbon steel, is shaped to a beveled cutting edge, like the blade of a plane iron.
3. The **cutter cap** is made of cast iron. It holds the blade in position.
4. The steel **cap screw** locks the cutter cap and the blade in the frame.

5. The steel **adjusting screws** regulate the cutting depth and serve as a lateral adjustment of the cutter blade. Only the more expensive types have this adjustment.

Maintenance

Sharpening

Like the plane iron, the cutting edge of the spokeshave is first sharpened to a 25° to 30° angle, then is whet on an oilstone to achieve an angle of between 30° and 35°. See Section 19, "Sharpening" — Topic 191, "Grinding Edge Tools" and Topic 193, "Whetting or Honing a Cutting Tool."

Market Analysis

Capacity

Spokeshaves are usually made with cutters 1-3/4" and 2-1/16" in width, and with frames of 9" and 10", respectively.

Woodcraft Supply Corp.

Fig. 5-41. Hollow-face spokeshave.

Drawknife   Topic 42.

Classification

Edge-cutting tool

Application

Principle of Operation

The **drawknife,** Fig. 5-42, works in much the same way as a chisel, using the principle of the wedge.

Kinds and Uses

The drawknife is used for quick removal of large amounts of stock and for doing rough shaping on molded work. It is often used to remove corners from billets prior to spindle turning on the lathe. The tool is held in both hands, with the bevel edge down and at a slight angle to the work. It is then firmly drawn toward the worker. This removes a thin chip from the wood. The wood should always be worked **in the direction of the grain.**

Principal Parts and Function of Each

1. The long, chisel-shaped, hollow-ground cutting blade does the cutting. It is made of high-grade tool steel.
2. Wooden **handles** are attached to each end of the knife, forming a U-shaped tool.

Attachments

The only attachments for the drawknife are **chamfering attachments.**

Fig. 5-42. Drawknife.

Maintenance

Storing

Drawknives can be suspended horizontally over two hooks on the tool panel. The cutting edge should be protected with a wood or leather sheath.

Sharpening

The cutting edge is hollow ground on the grinding wheel to achieve an angle of 25° to 30°, then is whet on the oilstone to an angle of between 30° and 35°. See Section 19, "Sharpening" — Topic 191, "Grinding Edge Tools" and Topic 193, "Whetting or Honing a Cutting Tool."

Market Analysis

Capacity

Drawknives are available with blade lengths of between 6" and 13-1/4". Blade widths range from 1" to 2". Most drawknives have a 1"- or a 1-3/8"-wide blade.

Topic 43.

Scrapers — Hand, Cabinet, Hook

Classification

Edge-cutting tools

Application

Principle of Operation

Scrapers work on the principle of the sharp wedge. In this case, the wedge is a fine burr that cuts a very light shaving. A dull scraper produces dust rather than a shaving.

Kinds and Uses

Scrapers are used to remove paint and varnish and to smooth wood surfaces. They are usually used in the final preparation of the surface prior to sanding. All scraping must be done before sanding, as abrasive grit left in the pores or on the surface of the wood will dull the edge of a scraper.

1. The **hand scraper,** Fig. 5-43, has an alloy-steel blade. The edges are sharpened to a right angle, then are turned with a bur-

Disston, Inc.

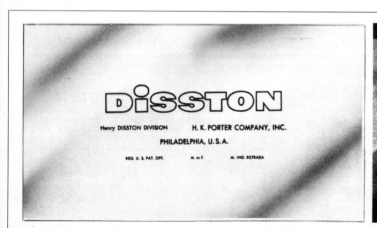 

Fig. 5-43. Hand scraper.

Stanley Tools

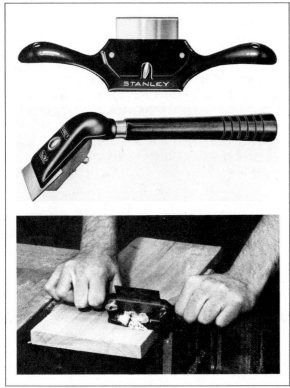

Fig. 5-44. Cabinet scrapers.

Red Devil Tools

nisher (rolled to a burr) to form a cutting edge.

2. The **cabinet scraper,** Fig. 5-44, has an alloy-steel blade similar to that of a hand scraper. The blade is sharpened to a bevel of 45°, then is turned with a burnisher.

3. The hook-shaped blade of the **hook scraper** is designed for rough, heavy work such as scraping floors and surfaces that are painted or varnished. See Fig. 5-45. The handle, made of hard wood, holds the blade firmly in position.

Fig. 5-45. Hook scrapers.

Principal Parts and Function of Each

1. Scraper **blades** are made of the finest carbon steel.

2. Cabinet scrapers have a cast-iron **frame** holding the blade at an angle of about 75°.

3. Hook scrapers are held in a metal or hard wood **frame.**

Maintenance

Storing

1. Blades of cabinet scrapers should be retracted in storage.

2. Cabinet scrapers should be stored in such a way that the cutting edges will neither be

susceptible to damage nor present a safety hazard.

Sharpening

1. Sharpening of hand scrapers and cabinet scrapers is done by filing, whetting, and burnishing the blade.
2. Hook scrapers are sharpened by draw filing the cutting edge to an angle of 35°.

   See Section 19, "Sharpening" — Topic 194, "Sharpening Hand Scrapers and Cabinet Scrapers."

Market Analysis

Capacity

1. Hand scrapers are 2-1/2" or 3" in width and are 5" or 6" in length. They are available in various shapes for scraping irregular surfaces.
2. Cabinet scrapers have a blade width of 2-3/4".
3. Hook scrapers are available with blades 1-1/2", 2", 2-1/2", or 3" wide, and with handles 5", 7-1/2", 8-3/4", or 12" long.

Topic 44.

Chisels, Gouges, and Carving Tools

Classification

Edge-cutting tools

Application

Principle of Operation

Edge-cutting tools work on the principle of the cutting wedge, using a shearing and forcing action.

Kinds and Uses

Chisels and **gouges** are used in chipping, paring, trimming, mortising, and carving. They are divided into two groups, according to the method used to attach the handle. **Socket** chisels have a hollow, cone-shaped end. The handle is shaped to fit into this socket, thereby joining the handle to the tool. **Tang**-type chisels have a thin, tapered end (the tang), which is forced into an opening in the handle, joining the handle and tool together.

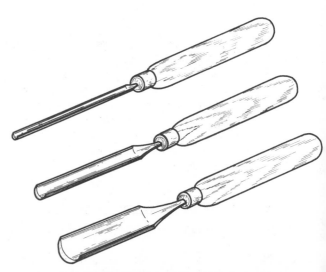

Fig. 5-47. Gouges are available with many different degrees of sweep to suit a wide variety of applications.

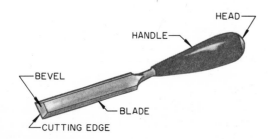

Fig. 5-46. Chisel nomenclature.

Buck Brothers

Fig. 5-48. Firmer chisel.

Buck Brothers

Fig. 5-49. Paring chisel.

Greenlee Tool Co.

Fig. 5-50. Framing chisel.

Greenlee Tool Co.

Fig. 5-51. Socket framing chisel.

Buck Brothers

Fig. 5-52. Short-tang butt chisel.

Buck Brothers

Fig. 5-53. Socket butt chisel.

Woodcraft Supply Corp.

Fig. 5-54. Mortise chisels.

Buck Brothers

Fig. 5-55. Inside-bevel gouge.

Buck Brothers

Fig. 5-56. Outside-bevel gouge.

A gouge is a chisel with a concave blade. This curve of the blade is called **sweep.** Gouges are manufactured with various degrees of sweep to suit different working applications. See Fig. 5-47.

1. The **firmer chisel** has a thick blade and is used for general work, Fig. 5-48.
2. The **paring chisel** has a thin, beveled blade and is used for fine work, Fig. 5-49. The handle usually has a tang set.
3. The **framing chisel** has a heavy blade suited for use in framing construction and shipbuilding. A ferrule, replacing the leather cap on the handle, helps prevent the handle from splitting under heavy blows. See Figs. 5-50 and 5-51.
4. The **butt chisel** has a short blade. This gives the tool the control necessary for doing fine work and for doing work that is in awkward positions. See Figs. 5-52 and 5-53. This chisel is used for cutting gains in setting hinges.
5. The **mortise chisel,** Fig. 5-54, is used in cutting the mortise portion of mortise-and-tenon joints. Its thick blade makes it suitable for use as a lever in making deep cuts.
6. The **inside-bevel gouge,** Fig. 5-55, has a bevel ground on the inside of the blade and is used for hollowing out concave surfaces.

7. The bevel of the **outside-bevel gouge** is ground on the outside of the blade. It is used for cutting grooves, Fig. 5-56.
8. The **offset chisel** and **offset gouge** both have an offset handle, an aid in doing close work. See Figs. 5-57 and 5-58.
9. **Carving tools** is the name given to chisels and gouges that have a variety of cutting-edge shapes and that are used for making angular or curved cuts. Some carving tools are the **straight chisel,** the **skew chisel,** the **offset shank chisel,** the **part-**

Buck Brothers

Fig. 5-57. Offset chisel.

Buck Brothers

Fig. 5-58. Offset gouge.

Buck Brothers

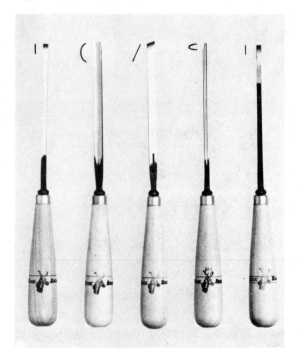

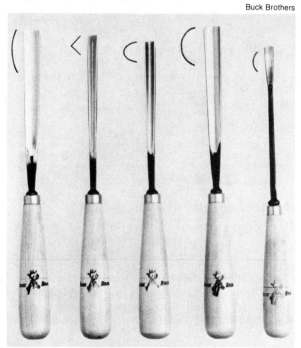

Fig. 5-59. Carving tools.

Greenlee Tool Co.

Fig. 5-60. Socket slick.

Greenlee Tool Co.

Fig. 5-61. Glazier's chisel.

ing tool, the straight gouge, and the veining tool. See Fig. 5-59.

10. The socket slick, Fig. 5-60, is a special-purpose chisel, used in heavy construction work. Its long handle provides better control for fitting heavy timbers.

11. The glazier's chisel, Fig. 5-61, is used in setting glass. It is used for removing old putty, for setting glazier's points, and for reputtying.

Principal Parts and Function of Each

1. The carbon-tool-steel **blade** is the body of tool. Some blades have chamfered sides.
2. The **bevel** on the blade forms the cutting wedge.
3. The **handles** serve to hold the blade and enable the worker to control the cutting action. They are made either of plastic or of hardwood such as maple or hickory.

4. The leather or steel **head** and/or the steel **ferrule cap** help reduce the possibility of the handle splitting as it is struck with a mallet.

Maintenance

Storing

1. Chisels should be individually stored in a rack or case to ensure safety and to prevent the keen edge from becoming dull. When the chisel is to be left unused for a long period of time, the steel should be coated with a film of wax or oil to prevent rusting.
2. To remove rust, pitch, and other foreign substances from blades, wipe with light oil or kerosene.

Sharpening

1. The blade or cutting edge should be reshaped when it becomes nicked or broken or when the bevel becomes too short. The chisel is first ground to an angle of between 25° and 30°, and then is whet to a razor edge on a fine oilstone. Gouges and carving tools are dressed with a slipstone. See Section 19, "Sharpening"—Topic 191, "Grinding Edge Tools" and Topic 193, "Whetting or Honing a Cutting Tool."
2. Damaged handles, both on tang chisels and on socket chisels, may be replaced.

Market Analysis

Capacity

1. Chisels are commonly made with blades 3″ to 6″ long, and in widths ranging from 1/8″ to 2″. (Lengths given do not include the handle.)
2. Gouges range from 1/8″ to 2″ in width.
3. Carving tools are sold either individually or in sets.

Using Chisels, Gouges, and Carving Tools

Topic 45.

Classification

Cutting and shaping stock by wedging and paring

Procedure

The chisel is an essential tool in shaping and joining. It must be kept sharp and must always be used with caution. To obtain a smooth cut, always work **in the direction of the grain.** The work must be held securely, either in a vise or clamped to a sturdy surface. This will free both hands to be used for controlling the cutting action of the tool.

Paring Horizontal Surfaces with a Chisel

Making a fine cut or trimming to a finish line is called **paring.**

1. The chisel is generally held with the bevel facing up and with the back of the chisel parallel to the surface that is to be cut.

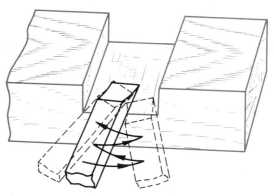

Fig. 5-62. Technique of paring the bottom of a cross-lap joint.

2. Grasp the handle of the chisel in the right hand, the left hand resting against the stock. Hold the chisel so that its direction may be guided and the depth of cut may be controlled.

3. Using one hand as a pivot, force the chisel from side to side in a shearing motion, Fig. 5-62.

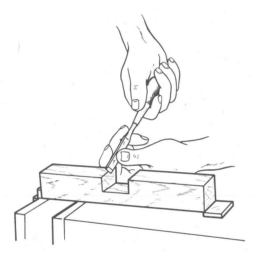

Fig. 5-63. Paring the shoulders of a cross-lap joint.

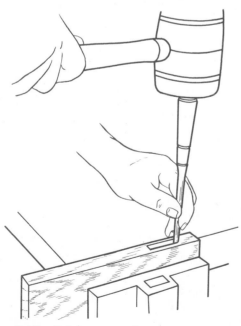

Fig. 5-64. Cutting a mortise.

Cutting End Grain or Shoulders With a Chisel

1. Secure the stock to the bench, protecting the bench top with a bench hook or a scrap piece of stock.

2. Hold the chisel in a vertical position, with the bevel facing outward from the finish line.

3. Assume a position that enables you to sight the direction of cut.

4. Using the left hand to guide the chisel, apply pressure with the right hand, Fig. 5-63. The palm of the right hand is usually held over the end of the chisel handle.

5. Use only part of the chisel's width to cut; use the remainder as a guide for maintaining a straight line or edge.

6. For deep cuts, use a mallet to strike the handle, Fig. 5-64.

Removing Surplus Stock When Cutting a Mortise or Gain (See Topic 85)

1. Select a socket-type chisel of proper width for the cut.

2. Hold the blade of the chisel in the left hand. The bevel should face the waste side so that the cut may be controlled.

3. Use a mallet to strike the chisel. Make a series of close cuts into the waste material, Fig. 5-64.

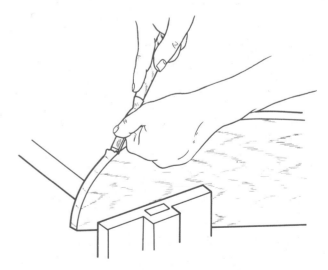

Fig. 5-65. Rounding an edge with a chisel.

4. Remove these chips with a shearing cut, as is done in horizontal trimming.
5. Continue this process until the surplus stock has been removed.

Trimming to a Curved Surface

1. Convex surfaces are trimmed in the same manner as horizontal trimming, with the bevel side of the chisel up, Fig. 5-65.

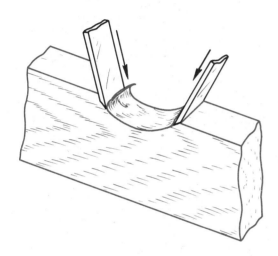

Fig. 5-66. **Making a concave cut with a chisel.**

2. Concave surfaces are trimmed with the bevel of the chisel down. It is important in both these operations that the cutting be done **with the grain.** See Fig. 5-66.

Using a Gouge

In making a curved surface, the gouge is used in the same manner as a chisel. A gouge with an inside bevel is used to shape the edge of curved stock. A gouge with an outside bevel (most common) is used for making grooves and for fluting.

1. Select a gouge of the proper width and shape.
2. Hold the gouge in one hand so that it may be guided as pressure is applied with the other hand, Fig. 5-67.
3. Use a mallet, Fig. 5-68, to strike the gouge when making heavy cuts or roughing out.
4. Always finish with a light cut **in the direction of the grain.**

Using Carving Tools

1. Use extreme care when doing fine, intricate work with carving tools.
2. Hold the tool in much the same way as you would hold the chisel or the gouge. Control is especially important in carving.

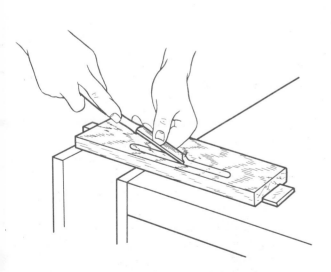

Fig. 5-67. **Using a gouge.**

Fig. 5-68. **Types of mallets.**

3. Use very light, even cuts to remove material. Never try to remove all the material in one cut.
4. Work from the profile of the pattern to the deepest recess.

Standards and Results

- All trimming should be done to a guide line.
- All cuts should be smooth and true.

Safety Considerations

- Wear safety glasses.
- Secure the stock firmly.
- Always keep both hands behind the cutting edge of the tool.
- Always direct the tool away from your body.
- Keep tools sharp.
- Protect the bench top from cuts.
- Always store the tool in such a way that the sharp edges are covered or concealed.

Old Sturbridge Village, Inc.

Fig. 5-69. Wooden mauls.
These wooden mauls are examples of early mallets made of burls and cross-grained tree sections.

Woodcraft Supply Corp.

Vincent G. Mack

Fig. 5-71. The carved wooden eagle and shield were made by gluing up 2″ stock, cutting to shape on the band saw, then carving with a gouge and chisel.

Fig. 5-70. Carving tools may be used to carve a variety of decorative designs, enhancing the appearance of furniture and other wooden articles.

Vincent G. Mack

Fig. 5-72. The weapon at the right is a modern version of the ancient crossbow. Sculpturing was done by means of the band saw, gouges, rasps, and files.

SECTION SIX.

Machine Cutting to Basic Form

Topic 46.

Jointer

Classification

Power-driven rotary cutting-edge tool

Application

Principle of Operation

A round cutterhead with two, three, or four knives (usually three) revolves at a speed of approximately 4000 rpm. The knives cut on the principle of a continuous set of cutting wedges, each cutting a small arc, Fig. 6-2.

Kinds and Uses

The **jointer** is used for planing faces and edges straight and smooth and for planing tapers, chamfers, and bevels. It is also used for

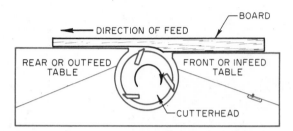

Fig. 6-2.   Cross section of a jointer.

cutting rabbets and for making specialty cuts. Jointers are made in 4″, 6″, 8″, 10″, 12″, 14″ and 16″ blade and table widths. The wider jointers usually have longer tables. Some brands are available with extra-long tables.

Principal Parts and Function of Each

1. The adjustable **front table** or **infeed table,** made of machined cast iron, supports stock as it is fed into the knives. The height of the table regulates the depth of cut. Some jointers have an extension of the front table, called a **rabbeting arm,** which is used to support the stock while rabbets are being cut.
2. The **rear table** or **outfeed table** is also made of machined cast iron. Though adjustable, it is usually fixed at the height of the knives. It is used to support the stock after it has been cut.
3. The **front-table adjustment wheel,** made of cast iron, is used to raise and lower the front table to adjust the depth of cut.
4. The **rear-table adjustment wheel,** made of cast iron, is used to raise and lower the rear table.
5. The **fence,** made of machined cast iron, is used as a guide to support the stock at the correct angle.
6. The **guard,** made of either cast iron or aluminum, covers the knives, protecting the operator.

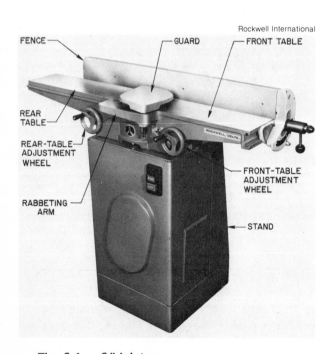

Rockwell International

Fig. 6-1.   6″ jointer.

7. The steel **cutterhead** is the unit into which the knives are inserted and are locked in position.
8. The high-speed steel **knives** do the cutting.
9. The **motor** supplies the power.
10. On those other than direct-drive machines, a rubber fiber-composition **belt** transmits the power.
11. The **stand** supports the machine. It may be made of cast iron, pressed steel, or wood.

OSHA Regulations

Jointers

1. Each hand-fed jointer with a horizontal head shall be equipped with a cylindrical cutterhead.
2. The clearance between the edge of the rear table and the cutterhead shall be not more than 1/8".
3. Each hand-fed jointer with a horizontal head shall have an automatic guard that will cover the entire section of the head on the working side of the fence or gauge. This guard shall effectively keep the operator's hands from coming into contact with the revolving knives. The guard shall automatically adjust itself to cover the unused portion of the head, and shall remain in contact with the material at all times.
4. Each hand-fed jointer with a horizontal cutterhead shall have a guard that will cover the section of the head in back of the gauge or fence.
5. Push sticks or push blocks shall be provided at the workplace in the several sizes and types suitable for the work to be done.

Maintenance

Adjusting

As a result of continuous use, the jointer may vibrate out of adjustment. When the knives are at their highest point, the rear (outfeed) table should be the same height as the cutting edge of the knives. (This is true except in the case of specialty cuts.) See Topic 47, "Setting Knives and Aligning Rear Jointer Table."

Oiling

1. Some jointers are equipped with sealed bearings, while others require periodic greasing.
2. Whenever a jointer is to be left idle for a long period of time, all machined parts should first be coated with a thin film of oil.

Sharpening

Honing

Knives may be honed with an oilstone while they are still in the cutterhead. Select an oilstone that has a fine, flat face. Place it on the infeed table at a right angle to the cutterhead. To keep the table from becoming scratched, place paper between the table and the stone. Hold the cutterhead in such a way that the blade is slightly off top-center (the highest point). Place the stone so that the uncovered section extends beyond the cutting edge. To remove burrs and to produce a sharp edge, move the stone along the length of the blade. Count the number of strokes you use so that you can treat each blade in the same manner. When the new bevel exceeds 1/32", the knives should be reground. Both sharpening and regrinding should be done only by an experienced person.

Jointing

When the knives are too dull to be honed quickly, and there is not sufficient time to have them reground, they may be jointed. This is done by lowering the outfeed table slightly below the knives (1/64") when the knives are at the highest point. The infeed table is raised to the level of the outfeed table. With the knives off center, check the level positions with a straightedge. To prevent the tables from becoming scratched, wrap a piece of paper around each end of a medium oilstone. Place the stone at a right angle across the knives. One end should rest on the infeed table and the other end on the outfeed table. Start the machine and slowly move the stone across the blades, from one end of the blades to the other. Stop the machine and examine the blades for sharpness. This operation should be done only in an emergency and only by an experienced person.

Market Analysis

Capacity

The capacity of the jointer is determined by the length of the knives (width of the table), the length of the table, and the depth of cut.

Attachments

Some jointers have a **grinder attachment,** which permits the knives to be sharpened without being removed from the cutterhead.

Topic 47.

Setting Knives and Aligning Rear Jointer Table

Classification

Adjustment of tables for true cut

Procedure

Setting Jointer Knives

1. Remove the guard and the fence to expose the cutterhead.
2. Remove the dull knives from the cutterhead by loosening the blade clamp (gib) bolts with a wrench.
3. Wrap a cloth around a screwdriver blade. Then, clean the cavity (in the cutterhead) that houses the blade and the blade clamp. If you find pitch or gum in the cavity, use a solvent to loosen it.
4. Position one sharp blade and the blade clamp in the cutterhead cavity. The bevel of the blade should face the rear table.
5. Hold the blade in position by tightening the blade clamp bolts finger-tight.
6. Adjust the blade so that, at its highest point, it is as high as the rear table. (This should not exceed 3/16" above the cutterhead.) The blade may be adjusted by placing a strong horseshoe magnet or a block of previously jointed hard wood on the rear table. See Fig. 6-3. Raise the blade until it comes in contact with the magnet or the wood. Check to make sure the full length of the blade is even with the rear table.

   Jointer blades may also be adjusted to the proper height with a special gauge made for that operation. See Fig. 6-4.

7. Using a wrench, tighten the blade clamp bolts.
8. Repeat Steps 3 through 7 for each of the remaining knives.
9. With the knife at its highest point, recheck to see that each blade is the same height as the rear table.
10. Recheck to see that each knife clamp bolt is **tight.**
11. Replace the guard and the fence.
12. Make a trial run. A smooth, even cut should be produced.

Aligning Rear Jointer Table

The outfeed (or rear) table of the jointer must be adjusted so that it is level with the cutting edge when the knives are at their highest

Fig. 6-3.   Using a hardwood block to adjust the height of jointer knives.

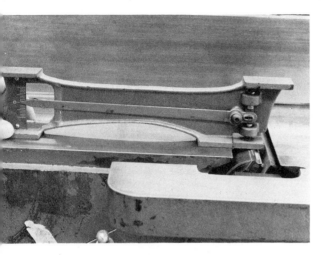

Fig. 6-4.   Setting the height of a jointer knives, using a special gauge.

point. If this is not done accurately, the resulting cut will not be true.

1. Turn the cutterhead so that one of the blades is at its highest point.
2. Unlock the outfeed table and lower it until it reaches a point below the height of the cutter blade.
3. Place a hard wood straightedge on the table so that one end rests on the table and the other end rests on the edge of the cutter blade.

4. Raise the table slowly until the straightedge rests evenly on the table and on the edge of the cutter. Move the straightedge back and forth across the cutter. This movement should cause the cutterhead to make a slight rotating motion. This motion should not raise the straightedge or cause the cutterhead to move excessively.
5. Lock the outfeed table in position and recheck the alignment on both sides of the table as well as in the center. Do this for each of the blades.
6. Replace all guards.
7. Set the infeed table for a light cut.
8. Start the jointer and make a cut several inches into the face of the flat board.
9. The stock should slide onto the rear outfeed table without hitting the table. No light should show between the table and the surface of the board that has just been cut.

Safety Considerations

- Always disconnect the power supply before making adjustments or removing guards.
- Check to see that the blades are even with the rear table and securely fastened in the cutterhead.
- Tighten all adjustments before use.
- Replace all guards.
- Make only light cuts on the face of stock.

Smoothing a Surface on the Jointer

Topic 48.

Classification

Removing stock by shearing with rotating edge cutters

Procedure

Planing an Edge

CAUTION: This machine should not be used to surface any board less than 12" long or 1/4" thick. Be sure the stock is free of nails, grit, paint, and other foreign materials.

1. Adjust the fence so that it is at the desired angle to the table, Fig. 6-5.
2. Set the front infeed table for a light cut. It is better to make several light cuts than one heavy cut, as this reduces the possibility of kickback and chipping.
3. Be certain all guards are in position.

Fig. 6-5.   Testing a fence for squareness.

4. Standing to one side, start the machine. Hold the trued face of the board against the fence, the grain pointing down and to the rear. Push the edge of the board over the cutter in a slow, even motion, Fig. 6-6. The speed at which the work is fed over the cutterhead will determine the spacing between the cuts. (Cuts are seen on the surface as machine marks.) Be sure that enough downward pressure is applied to keep the board flush against the table.
5. If the stock has high spots or an uneven edge, it will need to be passed over the cutters several times in order to remove the high spots and to true the edge.

Planing a Surface

The length of the jointer knives will determine the width of the board that may be planed. Jointers are commonly made with knives from 4″ to 16″ in length. The width and hardness of the board will determine the depth of cut. The maximum cut should not normally exceed 1/16″.
1. Lay the board on the infeed table with the grain pointing toward the infeed table and away from the knives.
2. Using downward pressure, push the board forward and across the cutters, Fig. 6-7. Always use a push shoe, Fig. 6-8.
3. When you have passed the stock partway across the cutter, transfer one hand to the stock on the outfeed table. Continue the cut, applying downward and forward pressure. In the case of cupped stock, the concave face should face downward.
4. Stock that has high places or an uneven surface will need to be passed over the cutter several times to true the surface.

Fig. 6-6.   Jointing an edge correctly — with the grain. (Guard removed to show operation.)

Fig. 6-7.   Jointing a face — note use of push shoe. (Guard removed to show operation.)

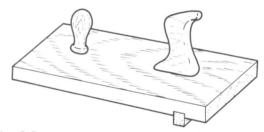

Fig. 6-8.   Push shoe.

5. Warped or twisted pieces should be held in one position and run across the cutter. Make sure to keep the stock from rocking as you do this. This is especially important on the first few cuts and until a flat surface has been made.
6. Take care to distribute even hold-down pressure across the width of the board.

"Squaring" Stock on the Jointer

Stock cannot actually be squared on the jointer, however it is common practice to true up the four sides of stock that is to be used for legs or that is square in a cross-sectional view.
1. Check the position of the fence to assure that it is square with the table.

Fig. 6-9. Cutting a rabbet. Guard cannot be used.

2. Plane the better face first. To produce a good, smooth cut, point the grain downward and to the rear of the table.
3. Holding this true face against the fence, joint the adjacent edge.
4. Joint to width. If you are going to be removing a great deal of stock, cut it first on the circular saw, leaving 1/16" for full-finish cut on the jointer.
5. With one of the previously jointed edges against the fence, joint the remaining surface.

Cutting a Rabbet

1. The depth of the rabbet that may be cut on any particular make of jointer is limited to the travel and the bearing surface of the rabbeting arm. Most smaller machines will cut a rabbet the width of the knives and 1/2" deep.
2. Set the fence to the width of the rabbet. This width is measured from the outside edge of the cutters.
3. The cutter guard must be removed on most machines in order to allow the board to pass by the end of the cutterhead. See Fig. 6-9.

Fig. 6-10. Cutting a bevel.

4. For shallow rabbets, lower the infeed table so that the full depth of cut may be made in one operation. If the rabbet is both wide and deep, it is advisable to make several cuts.

Cutting a Bevel or Chamfer

1. Most fences may be tilted to angles of between 30° and 90°. The angle may be measured with the protractor on the locking mechanism or by measuring with the protractor head of a square or a T-bevel.
2. After the desired angle has been obtained, proceed as in regular jointing, Fig. 6-10.
3. Stop chamfering may be done by lowering both the infeed and outfeed tables to the depth of the chamfer. Clamp stop blocks to the fence to limit the length of cut. With one end of the stock against the infeed block, slowly lower the work over the revolving cutters to the required depth. Then, gradually push the stock forward until the outfeed stop block is reached. Then, lift the work from the cutters. It is better to take several light cuts when making a heavy chamfer. To do this, adjust both tables to produce a series of lighter cuts instead of a single heavy cut.

Cutting Tapers

1. The taper should be laid out on one side of the workpiece. If the taper requires a heavy cut, it should be divided into equal segments so that a series of thinner cuts can be made.
2. Lower the front (infeed) table a distance equal to the size of the laid-out taper. If the taper is to be cut in steps, lower the table to the depth of the first cut.
3. With the jointer turned off, position the workpiece in such a way that the cutter will contact the stock about 3/8" in from the starting line of the taper. At the end of the stock, clamp a stop block to the fence or front table so that the length of the taper will be uniform on successive cuts. (**Note:** If the taper is longer than the front table, a stop block cannot be used.)
4. Start the machine. Butt the end of the workpiece to the stop block and slowly lower the front end of the stock onto the cutters until it rests on the rear (outfeed) table, Fig. 6-11. Using a push shoe and/or push sticks, run the entire taper across the

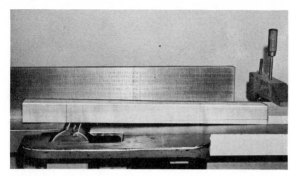

Fig. 6-11. Leg in position for cutting a taper. Note the stop block, used to ensure uniform taper length. (Guard removed to show setup.)

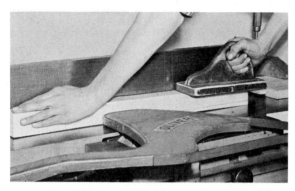

Fig. 6-12. When cutting tapers, the stock should be fed slowly across the cutterhead with a push shoe and/or push sticks.

cutters, Fig. 6-12. Repeat if more than one cut is to be made.

5. The starting edge of the taper may be surfaced by hand planing, by sanding, or, as for an ordinary edge, by jointing.

6. The surface of a taper that has previously been cut on the circular saw may be smoothed in the same manner as would be done in jointing an edge.

Standards and Results

- Light, even cuts will produce a smoother surface than will a heavy cut.
- All surfaces should be smooth and the mill marks should be very small.
- Always plane **in the direction of the grain.**

Safety Considerations

- Wear safety glasses when operating the jointer.
- Before the machine is started, make all necessary adjustments for the correct depth of cut.
- Boards less than 12″ should not be planed.
- Be sure the stock is free of nails, grit, paint, loose knots, or any other foreign material.
- Setups for specialty cuts such as bevels, chamfers, stop chamfers, and tapers should be checked by the instructor before cuts are made.
- Always have a guard over the knives when the jointer is running.
- Stand to one side while operating the machine.
- Always keep your hands above the surface of the board.
- Never run your hands directly over the cutterhead when planing the face of stock.
- Always use a push shoe when planing a surface.
- Use a push stick when jointing narrow stock.

Topic 49.

Uniplane®

Classification

Power-driven rotary edge-cutting tool

Application

Principle of Operation

The **Uniplane**®, Fig. 6-13, is a round, disk-shaped cutterhead with eight quick-change,
high-speed cutting bits. It revolves around a stationary faceplate at a speed of 4000 rpm. The eight cutting bits act as a continuous series of cutting wedges, making 32,000 cuts per minute.

The eight cutting bits are divided into two sets — one for scoring and the other for shearing. The blades are set alternately (scoring, shearing, scoring, shearing, etc.) in the cut-

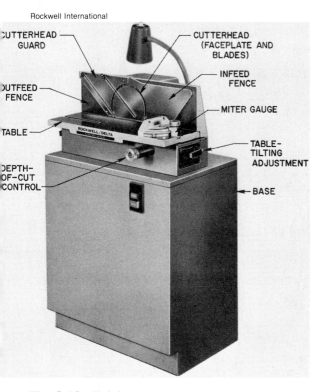

Rockwell International

CUTTERHEAD GUARD

CUTTERHEAD (FACEPLATE AND BLADES)

OUTFEED FENCE

INFEED FENCE

TABLE

MITER GAUGE

DEPTH-OF-CUT CONTROL

TABLE-TILTING ADJUSTMENT

BASE

Fig. 6-13. Uniplane.

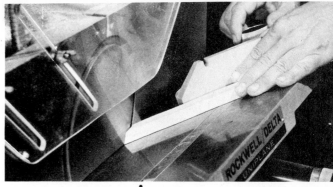

A

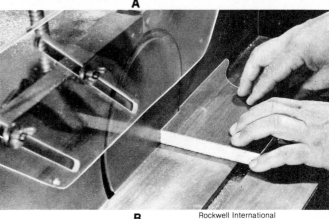

B

Rockwell International

Fig. 6-14. The Uniplane may be used to plane end grain (A) or small stock that could not be surfaced on the jointer (B).

terhead. The first cutting bit entering the wood surface scores the depth of cut. The second follows, shearing out of the chip. This allows the cut to be made, either with or across the grain, without splintering.

Kinds and Uses

The Uniplane is used for planing faces, edges, and ends straight and smooth. See Fig. 6-14. It is also used to cut bevels, chamfers, and tapers.

Principal Parts and Function of Each

1. The **table,** made of cast iron, tilts to an angle of 45°. This design enables it to cut chamfers and bevels. A slot is provided for the miter-gauge guide.
2. The **table trunnions** support the table when it is tilted.
3. The **infeed fence,** made of cast iron, is adjustable for depth of cut.
4. The **cutters** are made either of high-speed steel or of solid carbide. They are available in sets of eight — four cutters for shearing and four for scoring.

5. The cast-iron **faceplate** supports the wood that is being cut.
6. The **outfeed fence,** made of cast iron, supports the wood being fed through the machine.
7. The cast-iron **cutterhead** is dynamically balanced. It contains eight cutting tools.
8. The **base,** made of cast iron, supports the trunnion guides for the table pivot.
9. The **stand** houses the motor and the belt drive.
10. The **belt guard** covers the driving pulleys and the belt.
11. The **depth-of-cut control** is graduated into 64ths of an inch. It is used to adjust the depth of cut.
12. The transparent, plastic **guard** covers the cutterhead.

Maintenance

Adjusting Cutter Bits

Cutter bits are set with a guide to project either .003″ or .005″ from the surface of the stationary faceplate.

Sharpening Cutter Bits

Sharpen the cutter bits by shaping them on a grinder and then honing them to a keen edge on an oilstone. The original shape must be maintained.

Preventing Rust

Finished surfaces should be protected from rust with either paste wax or oil.

Market Analysis

Capacity

The Uniplane will surface to a maximum width of 6″ and a maximum depth of 1/8″.

Topic 50.

Single-Surface Planer

Classification

Power-driven, rotating edge-cutting tool

Application

Principle of Operation

Three full-width knives are set equal distances apart along the circumference of the cutterhead. The cutterhead revolves at speeds from 3600 to 7200 rpm. The knives cut on the principle of a continuous set of cutting wedges. On some surfacers, the rate of feed may be varied. Generally speaking, the slower rate of feed results in more cuts per inch, producing less pronounced machine marks, Fig. 6-16.

Kinds and Uses

Planers (surfacers), Fig. 6-15, are used to plane the surface of stock to parallel and uniform thickness. The most common planer is the single-surface planer.

1. The **single-surface planer,** Fig. 6-15, has one cutterhead, located above the stock.

Powermatic Houdaille, Inc.

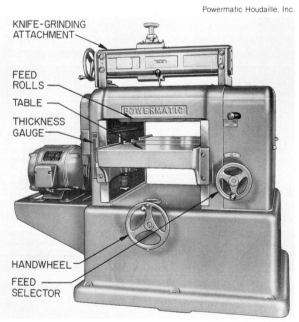

KNIFE-GRINDING ATTACHMENT
FEED ROLLS
TABLE
THICKNESS GAUGE
HANDWHEEL
FEED SELECTOR

Fig. 6-15. Surfacer.

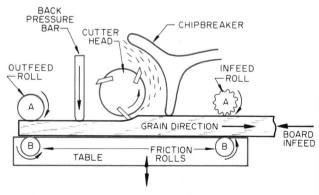

BACK PRESSURE BAR — CUTTER HEAD — CHIPBREAKER
OUTFEED ROLL
INFEED ROLL
A
GRAIN DIRECTION
BOARD INFEED
B   TABLE — FRICTION ROLLS   B

Fig. 6-16. Cross section of a single surfacer. Table raises and lowers for depth of cut.

This planer surfaces one face of the stock at a time.

2. The **double-surface planer** has two cutterheads, one above the stock and one below it. These cutterheads surface both the top and bottom of the stock at the same time.

Principal Parts and Function of Each

1. The cast-iron or machined-steel **table** is a flatbed that supports the stock as it passes under the knives. The amount of stock removed is determined by the difference between the thickness of the stock and the size of the opening between the knives and the table. The cut is made parallel to the bed.
2. The **feed rolls,** made of machined steel, feed the stock into the machine. The upper infeed roll is usually sectional and is corrugated to provide better traction on narrow stock or on pieces of uneven thickness.
3. The **chip breaker,** made of steel or cast iron, breaks the shavings and directs them away from the infeeding stock. It prevents splintering and helps to hold the stock flat against the table.
4. The **cutterhead,** made of alloy steel, holds the knives. (There are usually three knives.)
5. The **knives** are made of high-speed, oil-hardened steel. They do the cutting.
6. The **back pressure bar** is made of either cast iron or steel. It holds the stock firmly against the bed after the cut has been taken and the stock has been reduced in thickness. The back pressure bar keeps the stock from chattering.
7. The **outfeed rolls** or **delivery rolls,** made of machined steel, carry the stock out of the machine.
8. The cast-iron **handwheel** raises and lowers the table. This regulates the size of the cut, producing the desired stock thickness.
9. The **motor** size varies according to the size of the machine. The larger surfacers have two motors — one for the cutterhead and one for the feed and delivery rolls.
10. The **feed selector** increases or decreases the rate of feed (15 to 45 feet per minute). Adjustments should be made to the variable-speed selector only while the machine is running.

11. The **thickness gauge** indicates the approximate thickness that will result from any given setting.

OSHA Regulations

Planing Machines

1. The cutterhead on each planing machine shall be covered by a metal guard.
2. Feed rolls shall be guarded by a hood or a guard suitable to prevent the operator's hands from coming into contact with the in-running rolls at any point. So that it will remain in adjustment for any thickness of stock, the guard shall be fastened to the frame that carries the rolls.

Maintenance

1. Follow the manufacturer's recommendations for adjusting the rolls, the chip breaker, and the back pressure bar.
2. Sharpening should be done only by an experienced person.
3. Surfacers should be greased periodically. See manufacturer's specifications to find out which SAE number of grease to use.
4. The feed rolls, the chip breaker, and the back pressure bar should be kept free of pitch.

Market Analysis

Capacity

Small single-surface planers will plane stock up to 4″ thick and 12″ wide. Larger ones will plane stock up to 8″ thick and 50″ wide.

Small double-surface planers will plane stock as thick as 7″ and as wide as 30″. Larger machines will handle stock of up to 14″ in thickness and 40″ in width.

Attachments

1. **Grinding attachments.** These attachments are used to grind the knives. The knives do not need to be removed from the cutterhead in order to be ground.
2. **Honing attachments.** These are used to hone the knives. Honing can be done while the knives are still in the cutterhead.

Topic 51.

Using the Single-Surface Planer

Classification

Reducing stock to uniform thickness by passing it through an adjustable opening and under a revolving cutterhead

Procedure

For accurate work on single-surface planers, one side of the stock must first be faced on the jointer, then run through the surfacer, face-side down, until parallel thickness is established.

Stock less than 12" in length or 1/4" in thickness should not be run through the surface planer. The stock should be clean and free of all foreign material such as grit, paint, and other finishes.

1. Set the table to the desired opening. In planing soft woods or narrow boards, you may take a heavier cut than may be taken on hard woods or on wide stock. The maximum amount recommended for removal in a single cut is 1/16". Check the thickness along the board and set the table in accordance with the thickest section. On most surfacers, one complete, clockwise revolution of the handwheel will raise the bed 1/16".

2. Check the grain of the stock. Try to determine direction and feed the stock so that the cut will be made in the direction of the grain. See Fig. 6-16.

3. Feed the stock in at right angles to the cutterhead.

4. Run the stock through as many times as necessary to achieve the desired thickness. Once parallel thickness has been established, successive cuts should be taken off alternate faces. In doing this, stock must be turned end-for-end so that planing will always be in the direction of the grain.

5. Boards should not be allowed to drop on the floor. Long boards should be supported at each end.

Fig. 6-17. Surfacing a board.

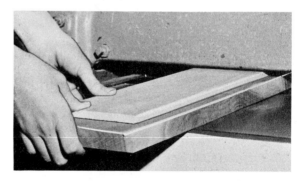

Fig. 6-18. Using a backing board to plane thin stock.

6. In planing square stock, two adjacent faces are first planed straight and square (jointed). The two remaining faces are then planed parallel to these squared faces.

7. Stock that is to be used in carpentry work or that is impractical to surface on the jointer should be placed on the surfacer table with the concave surface facedown. Only a light cut should be taken.

Fig. 6-19. Butt the ends of short pieces together. Turning these pieces at an angle will provide a smoother feed.

8. Stock that has a thickness of less than 3/8" should be placed on top of a backing board before it is run through the planer. The backing board should be a smooth, flat piece of stock, at least 3/4" thick. The thickness of the backing board should be added to the stock thickness before the table height is adjusted. See Fig. 6-18.
9. When a number of short pieces of stock are planed at one time, they should be butted end-to-end and fed into the planer in this fashion, Fig. 6-19. This keeps the stock moving through the planer and reduces the possibility of taper on the trailing edge of each piece.

Standards and Results

- Stock should be smooth and free from chips, excess cutter marks, and wind.
- Long pieces should be free of chip impressions.

Safety Considerations

- Wear safety glasses when operating the planer.
- Loose knots should be removed before the board is run through the surfacer.
- Stock that is shorter than the distance between the feed and the delivery rolls (this is usually 12") should not be surfaced. Stock less than 1/4" thick is apt to break if not supported by a backing board.
- Cross-grained stock should never be fed through the surfacer.
- Locate the stopping mechanism before starting the machine. If the stock gets stuck, turn off the machine and, when the machine has completely stopped, lower the table and remove the board.
- Stand to one side of the stock when you are feeding or receiving.
- Keep your hands away from the feed rolls.
- When surfacing wet stock, lubricate the table with kerosene or wax.

Portable Electric Plane

Topic 52.

Classification

Power-driven rotary cutting-edge tool

Application

Principle of Operation

A small-diameter, spiral-edged cutter revolves at speeds of between 20,000 and 25,000 rpm. Cutting is done on the principle of continuous-motion shearing.

Kinds and Uses

The **electric plane** is used to plane edges and surfaces smooth and true. This operation is similar to that done with the hand plane, but requires less effort and time. Electric planes are made in two sizes — the **block plane** (for short surfaces) and the regular **power plane** (for longer surfaces), Fig. 6-20.

Principal Parts and Function of Each

1. The **body,** made either of cast aluminum or of plastic, houses the motor and the cutter.
2. The **handle** includes a trigger switch. Handles vary in style according to make.
3. The **cutter blade,** made of high-speed steel, usually has a fluted, spiral cutting edge.

Rockwell International

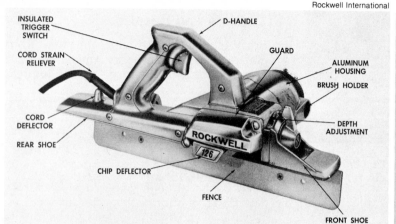

INSULATED TRIGGER SWITCH

D-HANDLE

CORD STRAIN RELIEVER

GUARD

ALUMINUM HOUSING

BRUSH HOLDER

CORD DEFLECTOR

DEPTH ADJUSTMENT

REAR SHOE

ROCKWELL

126

CHIP DEFLECTOR

FENCE

FRONT SHOE

Fig. 6-20. Portable electric plane.

The length of the edge varies, so cuts from 1-13/16″ to 6-1/8″ can be made.

4. The **chip deflector** is designed to deflect chips to the side of the operation.

5. The **rear shoe** is made of aluminum. It supports the electric plane as the plane is moving over the path of the cut.

6. The **front shoe** adjusts for depth of cut.

7. The **depth-adjustment mechanism** controls the position of the front shoe. It is calibrated in such a way that cuts of between 1/64″ and 1/8″ can be made.

8. The **bevel adjustment** positions the guide fence for both outside-bevel and inside-bevel cuts. The guide fence may be removed for planing wide surfaces.

Maintenance

1. Blades can be honed or sharpened with a special jig available from the manufacturer.

2. Blades should be kept clean of pitch and chips.

Topic 53.

Smoothing a Surface with the Portable Electric Plane

Classification

Removing stock by shearing with a rotary cutter

Procedure

1. The work must be held securely and in a convenient position on a bench or work area so that both hands will be free to hold the plane.

2. Set the front shoe for the correct depth of cut. (Make light cuts until you are familiar with controlling the plane.) Always plane in **the direction of the grain.**

3. Make sure that the electric cord is long enough and is properly grounded to the power supply.

4. Hold the plane over the work, placing one hand on the handle trigger and the other on the front-shoe knob.

5. With the planer in operation, hold the front shoe down on the work as you would a hand plane and proceed to make the cut. When the plane is over the work, transfer equal pressure to both hands. Finish the cut with pressure on rear shoe.

Rockwell International

Fig. 6-21. Planing a bevel with a portable electric block plane, using the adjustable guide fence.

Rockwell International

Fig. 6-22. Planing a surface with a large portable plane.

6. A bevel cut is made by adjusting the fence to the proper angle and using the above procedure. See Fig. 6-21.
7. To plane surfaces that are wider than the width of the cutter, remove the fence and guide the plane over the work. Both hands must be used in order to properly hold and control the position of the plane.

Standards and Results

- The cut should be relatively smooth and free from chips.
- The depth of cut should be uniform across the workpiece.

Safety Considerations

- Wear safety glasses while operating the electric plane.
- Always use the proper plug to ground the tool.
- Before inserting the plug into the power supply, **always** make sure the planer switch is in the "off" position.
- Lift the plane from the bench before turning on the power.
- Keep your fingers and your clothing away from the revolving cutters **at all times.**
- Before you put the plane down after making a cut, make sure the motor of the plane has come to a **complete** stop.

Squaring a Board — Machine Process

Topic 54.

Classification

Cutting to dimension with adjacent sides at right angles, removing warp (includes wind or twist, cup, crook, and bow)

Procedure

Lumber for cabinetwork is usually purchased rough, then planed to specific thickness. Full-length boards with warp must be handled in smaller sections if these distortions are to be removed. Simply passing a board

through the thickness planer will not remove its distortion or flaw. See Figs. 6-23, 6-24, and 6-25.

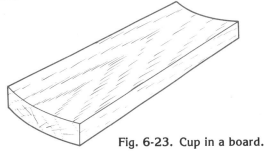

Fig. 6-23. Cup in a board.

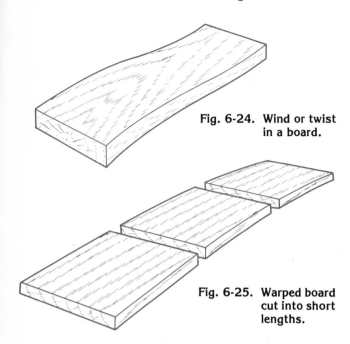

Fig. 6-24. Wind or twist in a board.

Fig. 6-25. Warped board cut into short lengths.

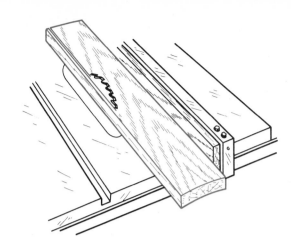

Fig. 6-26. Ripping a cupped board to width. (Guard removed to show operation.)

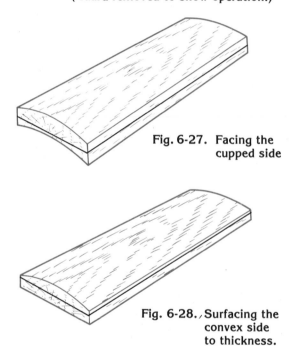

Fig. 6-27. Facing the cupped side

Fig. 6-28. Surfacing the convex side to thickness.

Getting Out Stock

1. Determine the rough length (desired finish size plus 1/2″) of the required pieces of stock. Be sure that the sections that are to be surfaced are longer than 12″, as this is the minimum for safe work on the jointer or surfacer.
2. Crosscut to rough length. Use the radial-arm saw, the portable circular saw, the table saw, or the hand crosscut saw.
3. Rip to rough width. Allow about 1/4″ more than the finished dimension. Note that if there is cup in the board, the dish is placed facedown on the table saw, Fig. 6-26. This operation will cut out some of the warp. If a board has excessive cup, it is advisable to rip the board into several equal sections, face the cup side on the jointer, then glue up to the necessary width. A band saw may also be used to rip to rough width. Use the saw to follow a pencil line.

Jointing One Face

Use a jointer if it is wide enough. If not, joint by hand plane. Plane one side flat and straight. The cup side is the one that should be straightened, Fig. 6-27.

Note: When performing this operation on warped stock, remember that the thickness planer alone will simply plane to the original

warp. The pressure rolls flatten the board while the cutters do the work. As the board passes the rolls and the pressure is relieved, the board springs back to its original shape. When using a jointer on which the pressure is controlled by hand, one side can be cut perfectly flat.

Jointing One Edge

Hold the face that has just been planed against the jointer fence and joint an edge square and straight.

Surfacing to Thickness

With the finished face against the table, the board is passed through the thickness planer until the desired thickness is obtained, Fig. 6-28. If a thickness planer is not available, use a marking gauge to scribe the desired thickness around the perimeter of the board. Then, surface the board on the jointer, cutting as close to the scribed line as possible. Finish by hand planing.

Ripping to Finished Width

Set the rip fence of the circular saw to the proper dimension, allowing 1/16″ for finished jointing. With the jointed edge against the rip fence, pass the board through the saw.

Jointing to Finished Width

With one face against the fence, joint the second edge to the finished width.

Cutting to Finished Length

1. Square one end of the board on the circular saw. Keep the jointed edge against the miter gauge.

2. Lay out and square a line at the finished length. If several pieces are to be cut to the same length, a length gauge or stop blocks should be used with the miter gauge to ensure that pieces will be of identical size and shape.

3. Cut the board to finished length. Use the same jointed edge next to the miter gauge as was used in squaring the first end.

Standards and Results

- All distortion should be removed from the board. It should test square on all surfaces.
- All surfaces should be smooth and of correct dimension.
- The rotary cutters should not leave chipped edges nor an excessive number of planer marks.

Safety Considerations

- Wear safety glasses.
- Get the instructor's approval before proceeding with any operation.
- Observe all safety practices pertaining to the particular machine you are using.

Portable Hand Router

Topic 55.

Classification

Power-driven rotary shaping tool

Application

Principle of Operation

The bits of the **router** revolve at a spindle speed of 5,000 to 27,000 rpm. They shape on the principle of a continuous set of cutting wedges. See Fig. 6-29.

Kinds and Uses

Routers are classified by size, determined by the horsepower of the motor and the diame-

Stanley Tools

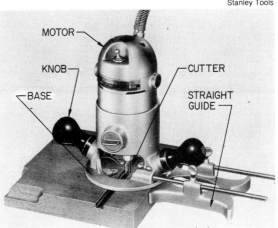

Fig. 6-29. Hand router.

ter of the cutter shaft. The router is used to cut moldings, to cut gains for inlay, to cut decorative edges, and to cut dovetails, dadoes, and rabbets. It is also used for doing fluting and beading.

Principal Parts and Function of Each

1. The **motor** provides the power.
2. The **base** is made of machined cast aluminum and is adjusted to determine the depth of cut.
3. **Straight** and **circular guide,** made of cast aluminum, acts as a fence for routing out or shaping parallel to either a straight or a curved edge.

Stanley Tools

Fig. 6-30. Air-cooled production router.

4. The **bits,** made of tempered, high-carbon tool steel, shape the stock, Fig. 6-31.
5. The rosewood or plastic **knobs** serve to hold and to guide the router.

Maintenance

1. Router bits should be kept sharp. Sharpening should be done by an experienced person. See Section 19, "Sharpening" — Topic 191, "Grinding Edge Tools" and Topic 193, "Whetting or Honing a Cutting Tool."
2. Some routers require periodic oiling, while others have sealed bearings.

Market Analysis

Capacity

The capacity of a router is determined by the depth and diameter of the bit that may be used.

Attachments

1. **Dovetail template.** This attachment is used to cut dovetails on case or box work.
2. **Grinding wheels** and **attachment for sharpening bits.**
3. **Carving attachment** or **pantograph attachment.** This is used to follow a pattern in routing the irregular shapes of duplicate parts.
4. **Rotary files.**
5. **Circle-cutting device,** Fig. 6-33.

Stanley Tools

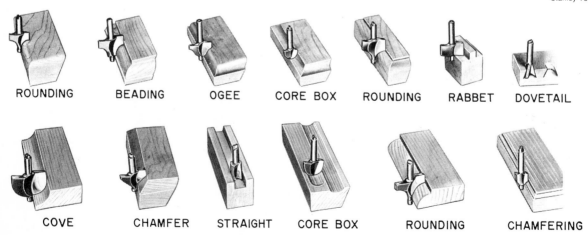

ROUNDING   BEADING   OGEE   CORE BOX   ROUNDING   RABBET   DOVETAIL

COVE   CHAMFER   STRAIGHT   CORE BOX   ROUNDING   CHAMFERING

Fig. 6-31. Shapes and uses of router bits.

6. **Fluting and beading attachment.**
7. **Router table.** This is used to position the router so that it may be used as a shaper.

Fig. 6-33. Circle-cutting device.

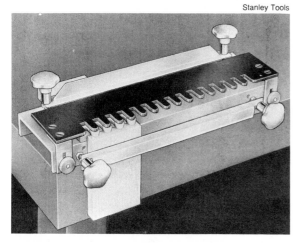

Fig. 6-32. Setup for doing dovetailing with the router.

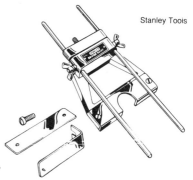

Fig. 6-34. Straight gauge used for routing.

<table>
<tr><td>

Using the Portable Hand Router

</td><td>

Topic 56.

</td></tr>
</table>

Classification

Shaping, molding, and recessing with a rotary cutter

Procedure

The hand router may be used for cutting gains for inlay lines and insets, for cutting rabbets and dadoes, for cutting gains for hinges, for cutting molded edges, and for cutting dovetails. It is also used for doing beading and fluting (see Topic 107, "Reeding and Fluting") and for cutting gains for inlay lines and insets (see Topic 128, "Applying Inlay and Insets").

Fig. 6-35. Router setup for cutting a rabbet.

Cutting a Rabbet or a Dado

1. Select a straight router bit of the proper size (Fig. 6-31), and secure it in the chuck. See Fig. 6-35.
2. Adjust the base to produce the desired depth of cut.
3. Adjust the straight guide to give the desired width of cut, Figs. 6-35, 6-36.
4. The stock to be rabbeted should be securely fastened to a bench.
5. Start the motor. Slowly move the router over the stock, making sure that the base is held flat against the stock and that the gauge is tight against the edge.
6. Rabbets that are wider than the diameter of the bit may be made by moving the gauge and taking two cuts. (Dadoes and grooves are cut as above with bits the same size as the width of the groove or dado.)

Cutting Gains for Hinges

A special bit is available for cutting gains for hinges. This is used with a special metal template designed for this type of work. It is adjustable for two or three hinges and for any standard-size door.

1. Follow the manufacturer's specifications in setting up this template, Fig. 6-38.
2. Set the base of the router to yield the desired depth of cut.
3. In following the template, keep the base tight against the template surface.

Stanley Tools

Fig. 6-37. Straightedge forms a guide — edge block prevents splitting.

Stanley Tools

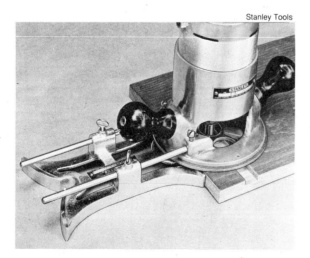

Fig. 6-36. Using the straight gauge to cut a dado.

Stanley Tools

Fig. 6-38. Cutting gains for hinges.

4. Remove the material that is within the hinge area.
5. When square-cornered hinges are used, it will be necessary to cut out the corners with a chisel.

Molding

1. Select the desired bit. Some bits have a pilot, which serves to limit the depth of cut, Fig. 6-39.
2. Lock the bit in the router and adjust the base to the desired height.

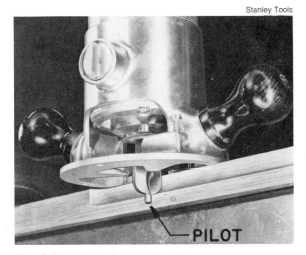

Fig. 6-39. Pilot-tip molding bit.

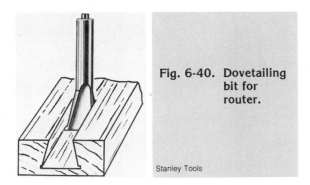

Fig. 6-40. Dovetailing bit for router.

Stanley Tools

3. If the bit has no pilot, the straight or circular gauge must be attached and adjusted to give proper depth of cut.
4. Start the machine and move it slowly along the edge of the stock. Make sure that the base is held flat against the surface of the stock that is being molded. Also assure that either the pilot or the straight and circular gauge is in contact with the edge at all times. See Fig. 6-39.
5. When the bit has a pilot, care must be taken to prevent too much pressure against the edge, as this will cause burning. Burning may also occur if the cutter is dull or if the router is moved too slowly.

Dovetailing

Cutting dovetails with a router requires a dovetail jig, guide template, and dovetail bit.
1. Attach the guide tip to the base of the router.

2. Insert the dovetail bit in the chuck.
3. Adjust the base so that the bit extends the correct depth. (See manufacturer's specifications as furnished with attachment.) A 9/16″ dovetail should extend from the base exactly 9/32″.
4. Mount the dovetailing attachment on a bench. This may be done either with screws or with clamps. The base should project slightly beyond the front edge.

The following instructions refer to parts of a drawer, since this is the most common dovetailing application. It is good

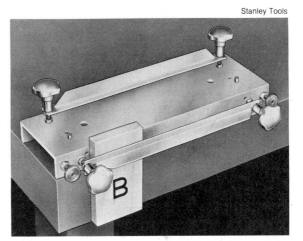

Fig. 6-41. First piece mounted in the dovetail attachment. *B* **is one side of the drawer.**

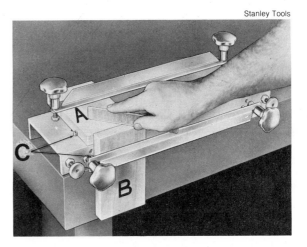

Fig. 6-42. Mounting the second piece in the dovetail attachment. *A* **is the drawer front;** *C* **points to the locating pins.**

practice to secure scrap stock of the same dimensions as the drawer parts and to make the setup using this scrap stock for testing.

5. Clamp the board that is to be one side of the drawer, **B** in Fig. 6-41, with the inside surface facing the operator. Make sure it is in contact with the locating pin so that it protrudes above the surface of the base a distance equal to the thickness of the drawer front.

6. Place the drawer front, **A** in Fig. 6-42, with the inside surface faceup and in contact with the locating pin and with the full width of drawer side. Clamp the drawer front to the top surface of the base, Fig. 6-42.

7. Fasten the template to the base, making certain that it is flat on the inside of the drawer front, Fig. 6-43.

8. To cut the dovetail, hold the base of the router flat against the template and follow the recesses with the guide template. See Fig. 6-44.

9. After the cut has been made, fit the two pieces together. If the fit is too loose, lower the bit slightly. If it is too tight, raise the bit slightly in relationship to the base. When the fit is satisfactory, the drawer pieces may be cut. See Fig. 6-45.

The foregoing instructions apply to the making of any blind dovetail with the aid of a dovetailing attachment.

Fig. 6-44. Cutting the dovetail.

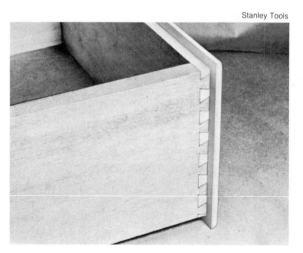

Fig. 6-45. Assembled dovetail joint.

Standards and Results

- Rabbets should be parallel to an edge or an end and should be of equal depth.
- Stock at the end of dadoes, grooves, and rabbets should not be chipped.
- Hinges should fit snugly into the gains.
- The surface of the leaf hinge should be flush with the surrounding area.

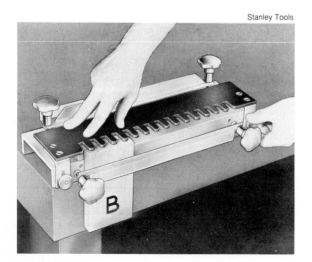

Fig. 6-43. Placing the template in position.

- No burn marks should show on the routed stock.
- Dovetail joints should fit snugly and the bottom edges should be even after assembly.

Safety Considerations

- Wear safety glasses while operating the router.
- Always use the proper plug to ground the tool.

- Before inserting the plug into the power supply, **always** make sure the router switch is in the "off" position.
- Lift the router from the bench before turning on the power.
- Keep your fingers and your clothing away from the revolving cutters **at all times.**
- Before you put the router down after making a cut, make sure the motor of the router has come to a **complete** stop.

Shaper

Topic 57.

Classification

Power-driven rotary cutting tool

Application

Principle of Operation

Standard sets of cutters, revolving at a spindle speed of 5,000 to 12,000 rpm, cut shapes on the principle of a continuous set of cutting wedges.

Kinds and Uses

The **shaper** is used to cut moldings, to make grooves and rabbets, and to smooth curved edges.

Shapers are sized according to the diameter of the spindle and the size of the table. Most shapers used in school shops are equipped with a 5/16″ to 3/4″ spindle and have a table size of 20″ × 28″. See Fig. 6-46.

Principal Parts and Function of Each

1. The **base,** or **frame,** is made of either pressed steel, cast iron, or wood. It supports the motor and the table.
2. The **table,** made of machined cast iron, supports the fence and the stock that is to be shaped.

3. The adjustable **fence** is used as a guide in shaping. It is made of cast iron and has a maple facing.
4. The **spindle,** made of machined, high-grade steel, is a round drive shaft. The cutters are attached to the spindle.
5. The **cutters,** made of alloy steel, shape the stock.

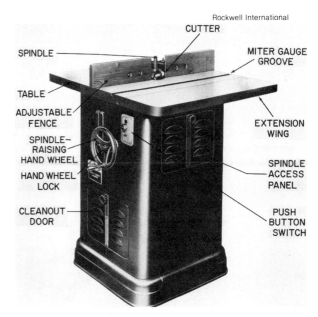

Fig. 6-46. Floor-model shaper.

C. O. Porter Machinery Co.

Fig. 6-47. Automatic multiple-spindle shaper.

6. The **spindle-raising handwheel** is made of machined cast iron. It is used to raise and lower the spindle or the table.
7. The **guard** is made of either pressed steel, hard rubber, or plastic. It protects the operator from injury. See Fig. 6-48.
8. The electric **motor** provides the power. The shaper motor should be reversible.
9. The **miter gauge** is made either of cast iron or cast aluminum. It is used as a guide in shaping end grain.
10. The **taper pin and collar** is made of machined steel. It is used as a guide for circular and irregular shapes whenever a fence cannot be used. See Figs. 6-49, 6-50, and 6-51.

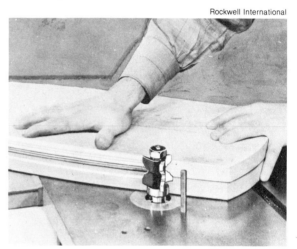

Rockwell International

Fig. 6-50. Shaping top and bottom edges, using a template, collar, and pin.

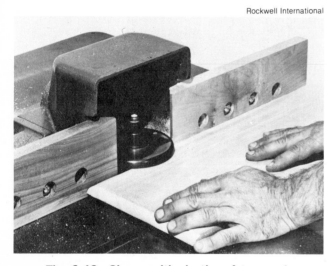

Rockwell International

Fig. 6-48. Shaper with plastic safety guard.

Fig. 6-49. Circular shaping using a collar and pin.

Fig. 6-51. Smoothing a curved surface, using collar above cutter, collar below cutter, two templates, and pin.

Rockwell International

Rockwell International

OSHA Regulations

Shapers

1. The cutterhead of the wood shaper, or of any other machine that is not automatically fed, shall be enclosed with a cage or an adjustable guard designed to keep the operator's hand away from the cutting edge.
2. The diameter of circular shaper guards shall be not less than the maximum diameter of the cutter. In no case shall it be acceptable to attach a warning device, made of leather or of any other material, to the spindle.

Maintenance

1. Shaper cutters should be kept sharp. Sharpening should be done only by an experienced person.
2. Some shapers require periodic greasing, while others have sealed bearings.
3. Whenever a shaper is to be left unused for a long period of time, all machined parts should first be coated with a film of oil to prevent rusting.

Market Analysis

Capacity

The capacity of a shaper is determined by the size of the largest cutter (the cutter of max-

Rockwell International

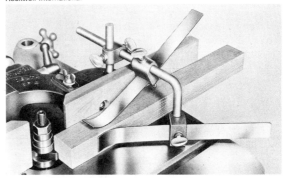

Fig. 6-52. Molding an edge, using spring hold-downs. (Guard removed to show operation.)

imum diameter and height) that the machine will accommodate.

Attachments

1. **Sliding shaper jig** (miter gauge). This jig is used as a guide in cutting moldings on end grain.
2. **Spring hold-downs.** The spring hold-downs, made of spring steel, are used to hold straight stock firmly against the fence and table while shaping is being done. See Fig. 6-52.
3. **Safety-ring guard.** The safety-ring guard protects the operator from the knives. It also serves to press the work against the table when neither a fence nor a miter gauge can be used.

Cutting Moldings, Molding an Edge, Making Special Cuts for Joining Edges with a Shaper

Topic 58.

Classification

Shaping a profile with an edge cutter

Procedure

There are four methods used in shaper operations:

- Straight stock is run against a fence.
- Curved stock is shaped by using collars and a pin.
- Stock is fastened to a template. (This procedure is used when a number of duplicate parts are required.)
- A miter gauge is used.

Rockwell International

Fig. 6-53. Profiles of shaper cutters.

Shaping Straight Stock Using a Fence

1. Select the proper cutter, Fig. 6-53. A collar may be placed either above or below the cutter or both above and below the cutter. Lock the assembly in place on the spindle.
2. Adjust the cutter or the table to the desired height. Lock after adjustment is made.
3. Adjust the fence to produce a cut of the desired depth. Lock in position. See Fig. 6-52.
4. Single-spindle shapers are equipped with reversible motors. A check should be made to see that the motor is turning in a direction opposite that of the feed.
5. Make a trial run on scrap stock before cutting the finished piece.

Shaping Curved Stock Using a Collar and Pin

1. Select the desired cutter and the proper size collar. Lock these in place on the spindle. (The diameter of the collar determines the depth of cut the cutter will make.) Collars may be placed either above or below the cutter or both above and below the cutter.
2. Adjust the spindle or the table until the cutter is at the desired height. Position the guard.
3. If the cutter has been set up to turn in a clockwise direction, the pin should be inserted in the hole on the lefthand side of the spindle. If it has been set up to turn in a counterclockwise direction, the pin should be inserted in the hole on the righthand side. The pin should always be on the infeed side of the table. See Figs. 6-49, 6-50, 6-51.
4. A check should be made to see that the motor is turning in a direction opposite to that of the feed.
5. Make a test cut on a piece of scrap stock. Take a scrap piece of wood the same thickness as the piece to be cut. Place it against the pin. Feed the stock into the cutter by gradually pivoting it on the starting pin until it comes in contact with the collar.
6. Check the cut on the scrap stock. If it is satisfactory, make the cut on the piece that is to be used.
7. Feed the stock for the entire length of cut, making certain that the stock is in contact with the collar at all times. The feed should be continuous. A stop will cause a surface burn. **Keep your hands well away from the cutters.**

Shaping Stock Using a Template

This method is very similar to the process of using a collar and pin. The difference is that the template is run against the collar rather than against the stock itself. See Figs. 6-50, 6-51, and 6-54.

1. Prepare a template that is either slightly smaller or slightly larger than the piece to be shaped but of the same outline as this piece. The size of the template is determined by the size of the collar, the size of the cutter, and the size of the required depth of cut.

2. Fasten the stock to the template in such a way that the overhang is equal on all sides. Pieces may be held in position with pins or clamps.
3. Follow the same procedure as that described for shaping with a pin and collar.

Shaping End Grain Using a Miter Gauge and a Hold-Down Attachment

1. Select the proper cutter and lock in place on the spindle.

Rockwell International

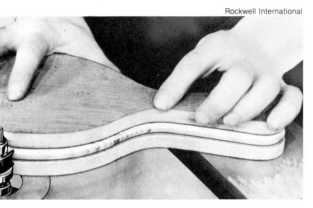

Fig. 6-54. Shaping using a template and collar.

Fig. 6-55. Double-spindle shaper.
   Round, oval, irregular, bent, and ogee shapes, as well as numerous other shapes, can be made on the shaper. Thousands of identical parts can be accurately duplicated on this machine. The knives of the shaper shown in this illustration operate at a remarkable speed of 7200 rpm. The use of a frequency changer doubles the usual speed of the driving motors. The faster the knives turn, the better the edge of the cut.

Heywood-Wakefield Co.

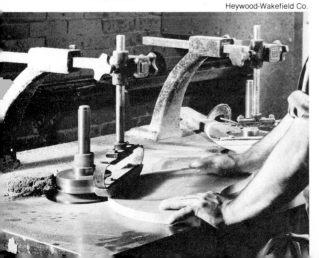

Old Sturbridge Village, Inc.

Fig. 6-56. Early form of hand seat saddler used in shaping seats of Windsor chairs.

2. Adjust the fence to produce the desired depth of cut.
3. Adjust the cutter height or table height to the desired position.
4. Make a trial run on scrap stock before final shaping of finished stock.
5. Place stock against miter gauge and secure with the hold-down attachment.
6. Feed the stock into the cutter in a direction opposite that of the cutter rotation. In order to avoid splitting the stock, feed slowly at the end of the cut.

Fig. 6-57. Seat saddler and scooper.
   The stack of seat blanks feeds automatically into the cutter knives. At the time this picture was taken, the machine was set up for a simple scooping operation. A different arrangement of the knives would produce a saddling effect in addition to the scooping.

Heywood-Wakefield Co.

Mattison Machine Works

Fig. 6-58. High-speed molder.
This production molding machine is used to make all sizes of quarter- and half-round moldings, small-bead moldings, and venetian-blind slats. This molder has several sets of knives, which make it possible to mold the entire surface in a single run through the machine.

Standards and Results

- Cuts should be free of chips and burn marks.
- Cuts should be of the desired shape and depth.
- Cuts should be uniform.

Safety Considerations

The shaper is generally considered to be one of the most dangerous machines in the school shop.
- Wear safety glasses when using the shaper.
- Keep your hands away from the cutter **at all times.**
- Make certain that the shaper is secured so that it will not move during operation.
- Make certain that the floor area is clear of debris and that the surface is not slippery.
- Make certain the spindle nut is tight.
- Check all attachments and safety devices.
- Do not make cuts on stock less than 10″ in length.
- Always feed the stock into the cutter opposite the direction of the cutter rotation.

SECTION SEVEN.

Filing

Topic 59.

Wood Files and Rasps

Classification

Serrated cutting tools

Application

Principle of Operation

In making a cut, the teeth of a **file** or **rasp** employ the principle of the cutting wedge. The teeth are cut diagonally across the face of the file, permitting a shearing cut. See Fig. 7-1.

Kinds and Uses

1. The rasp and file should be used only where space and shapes do not allow the use of sharp-edged tools. The various shapes of files are used to file corresponding curves and cuts in wood.
2. The file is used to achieve a smoother cutting, Fig. 7-2.
3. The rasp is used for roughing off surfaces, Fig. 7-3.
4. Files and rasps are described by length and shape as well as by **cut**. See Fig. 7-4. The cut of a file or rasp is the shape of the teeth.

Simonds Saw & Steel

Fig. 7-2.   Wood file.

Simonds Saw & Steel

Fig. 7-3.   Half-round rasp.

Nicholson — The Cooper Group

Fig. 7-4.   Files, left to right: single-cut file, double-cut file, rasp.

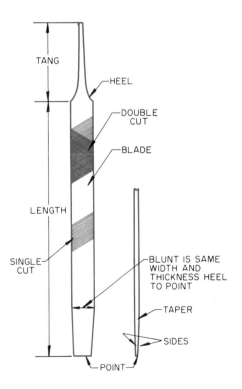

Fig. 7-1.   Nomenclature of files.

HALF ROUND   CABINET   ROUND   FLAT   PILLAR   SQUARE

CROSSING   PIPPIN   KNIFE   SLITTING   CANT   3 SQUARE

Fig. 7-5.   Cross section of file shapes.

Fig. 7-6.   Half-round file.

Nicholson — The Cooper Group

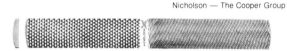

Fig. 7-7.   Shoemaker's rasp.

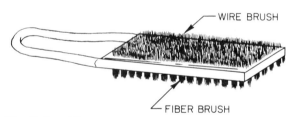

WIRE BRUSH

FIBER BRUSH

Fig. 7-8.   File card.

5. Files are made in the following shapes: half-round, cabinet, round, flat, pillar, square, crossing, pippin, knife, slitting, cant, and three-square. See Fig. 7-5. The length of a file is measured from the shoulder of the tang to the tip of the blade. Files range in size from 4″ to 18″.

6. Files are made in the following degrees of coarseness: coarse, bastard, second-cut, and smooth.

7. Files are also made with two shapes of teeth — single-cut and double-cut, Fig. 7-4. The single-cut file has parallel lines of teeth running diagonally across the file face. The double-cut file has a double series of teeth, crossing each other at an oblique angle. Single-cut files have a series of chisel edges, while double-cut files have staggered cutting points. Some files have no teeth on the edge. These are called **safety-edge** files.

8. Wood rasps are made in two shapes: flat and half-round, Fig. 7-6. They are made in four degrees of coarseness: rough, bastard, second-cut, and smooth. They are from 6″ to 16″ in length.

Principal Parts and Function of Each

Files and rasps are made of high-grade carbon steel. File handles (which do not come with files) are made of maple or birch.

1. The **blade** is the part on which the teeth are formed.

2. The **tang** is the tapered end onto which the handle is attached.

Maintenance

Cleaning

After use, files and rasps should be cleaned with a wire brush called a **file card,** Fig. 7-8. This cleaning process is illustrated in Fig. 7-9. When files and rasps are used on woods that contain a great amount of pitch, it is wise first to cover the teeth with chalk dust to prevent particles from clogging the spaces between the teeth.

Nicholson — The Cooper Group

Fig. 7-9.   Cleaning the file with a file card.

Storing

Files and rasps should be stored so that they do not come in contact with other files, hard surfaces, or moisture. For safety, make certain that the tangs are concealed or that there is a handle covering each one.

Market Analysis

Attachments

A **handle** should be attached to the file, making it possible to achieve better control of the cut. There are two types of handles for the file — those that are driven onto the file, and those that are twisted onto the file. The second type has screw threads, which cut threads on the tang as the handle is attached.

> *INTERESTING FACT: There are more than 3,000 types of files. They are classified according to length, shape, and spacing of teeth.*

Topic 60.

Shaping with a File or Rasp

Classification

Removing stock by shearing and shredding with a series of wedges

Procedure

Note: The rasp is used for quick removal of stock when roughing to a line. Finishing cuts usually follow this operation.

Fig. 7-10. Filing a convex curve.

Fig. 7-11. Filing end grain.

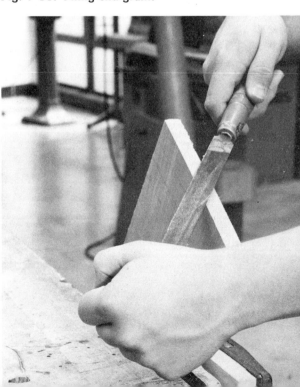

1. The size and shape of the file to be used is determined by the surface of the work (half-round, flat, square, and so on).
2. Secure the work so that it is parallel to the height of your elbow.
3. Grasp the handle of the file in the right hand, extending the index finger along the top of the file. See Figs. 7-10, 7-11, and 7-12. As illustrated, hold the point of the file with the thumb and first two fingers of the left hand, keeping the thumb on top. (Hand positions are reversed for left-handers.)
4. The file cuts on the forward stroke, so release pressure on the back stroke.
5. Filing end grain or curved surfaces is done with a forward, sweeping motion. Work diagonally across the grain to avoid cutting grooves, flat spots, or hollow places. See Figs. 7-10, 7-11.

   In filing a concave surface, the file must be held at right angles to the work, Fig. 7-12. In filing a flat or convex surface, the file may be pointed parallel to the surface.
6. When the file serrations become clogged, clean them out with a file card. If the file is to be used on resinous wood, fill in the serrations with chalk dust. A solvent may be used to clean the file.

Fig. 7-12. Filing a concave surface.

Standards and Results

- The file cut should be clean and smooth.
- The filed surface should conform to the specified shape and dimension.
- There should be no file marks showing.

Safety Considerations

- Wear safety glasses when using a file or a rasp.
- To avoid being injured by the tang, use a file that has a handle.
- Clamp the work securely for filing.
- Allow sufficient clearance for a full stroke. This clearance is necessary to prevent injury to the hand, to the work surfaces, to the benches, or to the holding devices.

Surform®

Topic 61.

Classification

Multi-edge cutting tool

Note: The name **Surform**® is derived from its use as a **sur**face **form**ing tool.

Application

Principle of Operation

Each Surform uses a thin steel blade that has been specially corregated to form rows of cutting edges. Each cutting edge works on the principle of the wedge.

Kinds and Uses

The various types of Surform tools use a patented blade, designed to remove material quickly. Although there are no adjustments for controlling the depth of cut, by experimenting, one may become skilled at controlling the size of the shaving. This is done by positioning the tool at an angle to the work, Fig. 7-15. Surform tools do not generally produce as smooth a surface as a file or plane. They may be used on wood, plaster, plastic, aluminum, and painted surfaces.

1. The **file type** is available in either a flat or a half-round shape. The leading end of the body has a ribbed section that permits two-handed use. It is used in the same manner as a file or rasp for quick removal of stock. See Fig. 7-13.

2. The **plane type,** Fig. 7-14, is shaped and is used in much the same way as the hand plane. The dimensions of the plane type and the blades that it uses are the same as those of the file type. It is used to remove stock from flat or convex edges and surfaces.

3. The **two-way type** (file-plane) Surform has an adjustable handle (two positions) to ac-

Stanley Tools

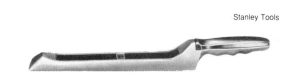

Fig. 7-13. File-type Surform.

Stanley Tools

Fig. 7-14. Plane-type Surform.

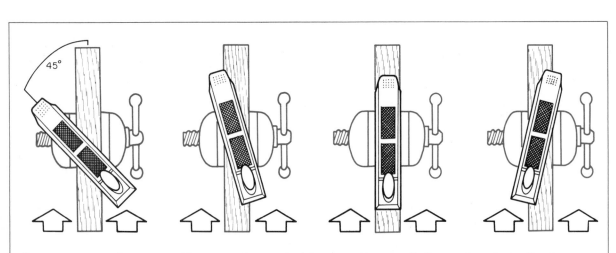

To remove a maximum amount of material, hold the tool at 45° to the direction of the stroke.

To remove less material and obtain a smoother surface, reduce the angle.

To smooth the work surface, direct the tool parallel to the surface or at a slight reversed angle to it.

Fig. 7-15.

commodate its use as either a file or a plane, Fig. 7-16. It has a knob on the leading end and uses the same blades as the file type.

4. The **pocket plane** is shaped to fit the palm of the hand, Fig. 7-17. It is used in the same manner as a block plane.

5. The **Mini File**™ has a thin blade secured to a molded plastic body, Fig. 7-18. It is used to file grooves, joints, and notches, and to square corners.

6. The **round-file type,** Fig. 7-19, has a 5/8"-diameter blade that is threaded to a handle. It is used to enlarge holes and to shape tight curves.

7. The **Shaver**™ Surform has a handle-shaped body and is designed to cut on the pull stroke, Fig. 7-20. Its design permits it to be used on curves, in corners and in tight places.

8. The **drum** Surform tool is designed to be used in an electric drill or drill press, Fig. 7-21. It is commonly used for shaping contoured stock.

Principal Parts and Function of Each

1. The **body** of the different types of Surform tools is die-cast of either zinc alloy or hard plastic. They are designed to hold and support the blade.

2. The **handles** provide comfortable control of the tool. The file, plane, Mini File and Shaver have die-cast handles that are made as part of the tool. Other handles or knobs attached to the body are made of wood or plastic.

Stanley Tools

Fig. 7-16. Two-way-type Surform.

Stanley Tools

Fig. 7-19. Round-file-type Surform.

Stanley Tools

Fig. 7-17. Pocket-plane Surform.

Stanley Tools

Fig. 7-20. Shaver Surform.

Stanley Tools

Fig. 7-18. Mini-File Surform.

Stanley Tools

Fig. 7-21. Drum Surform.

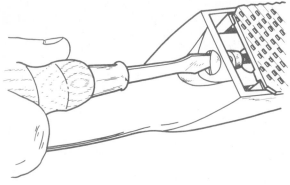

Stanley Tools

Fig. 7-22. Attaching a new Surform blade.

3. The **blades** are made of tool steel that has been hardened and tempered. Blades for the file-type and plane-type Surform are made in both flat and half-round shapes. They are available with either regular or fine-cut surfaces. The razor-sharp teeth are raised from a series of diagonal ridges. Holes at the base of each tooth permit the shavings to escape, producing a nonclogging cutting edge.

4. The **locking device** consists of fixed and adjustable hooks. Fitting the blade into position over these hooks secures the blade to the body. The position of the blade is secured as the adjustable hook is tightened, Fig. 7-22. Round-file-type blades are screwed into the handle. Shaver-type blades snap over the base of the body.

Maintenance

1. A light tap on the back of the body will remove shavings. This should be done frequently.
2. Keep the locking screws tight.
3. Replace dull blades.
4. Store in such a way that the cutting edge is protected.

SECTION EIGHT.

Sanding

Topic 62.

Coated Abrasives

Coated abrasives are used exclusively in the sanding process. In this process, abrasive material is rubbed against an object to remove stock from the object's surface. Many sharp grains of abrasive material, acting as tiny cutting wedges, produce the cutting action.

Classification

Natural or manufactured abrading materials adhered to flexible backing

Composition or Description

Abrasive Used

1. **Flint quartz** is a natural mineral, generally of a yellowish color.
2. **Garnet** is a natural mineral, reddish brown in color.
3. **Emery** is a natural mineral that is very dark or black in color.
4. **Silicon carbide** is composed of silicon (sand) and carbon, fused in an electric furnace. Silicon carbide ranges in color from steel gray to black.
5. **Aluminum oxide** is composed of bauxite, iron filings, and carbon, fused in an electric furnace. Aluminum oxide is light brown in color.

Backing Used

There are five general classes of backing used for abrasives: **paper, cloth, fiber, plastics,** and a **combination of paper and cloth.** Paper is the most common backing material used with abrasives. To aid its versatility, backing paper is produced in four general weights, classified as **A, C, D,** and **E. A** is the lightest and **E** is the heaviest and most durable. Abrasives with paper backing are used on almost all hand sanding jobs and on many short-term machine sanding jobs. Abrasives that have other backings, such as cloth, are used in many heavy-duty machine applications because of their strength, their pliability, and the ease with which they conform to curved surfaces.

Grit cloth uses a plastic screen for backing material. The screen is coated with an adhesive and is covered with either silicon carbide or aluminum oxide.

Adhesive Used

Coated abrasives have two adhesive layers, which bond the abrasive to the backing. The first is called the **bond coat** and the second the **size coat.** The bond coat is used to bond (adhere) the abrasive to the backing. The size coat is used as a filler-sealer to provide heat resistance and/or moisture resistance, depending on the type of bond coat used. There are five types of adhesives in use: animal glue, glue and filler, resin over glue, resin over resin and waterproof glue.

1. **Animal glue** is an animal-hide glue, used both for bond coat and size coat.
2. **Glue and filler** is an animal-hide glue to which a fine filler has been added to produce a bond that is both durable and strong.
3. **Resin over glue** is a combination of hide glue (for the bond coat) and a synthetic resin (for the size coat). The result is a highly heat-resistant bond.
4. **Resin over resin** is a synthetic-resin glue, used for both the bond and size coat. This bond is resistant to both heat and moisture.
5. **Waterproof glue** is a synthetic-resin glue, used for both bonding and sizing. It is used on a waterproof backing so that water or other liquid lubricants may be used in the sanding process.

Properties

1. Flint quartz lacks the hardness and durability of other abrasives and the cutting action is short-lived.

2. Garnet is a fairly hard, tough mineral that makes an ideal abrasive for woodworking.
3. Emery has a very hard and durable cutting edge. It is usually bonded to a cloth backing and is relatively expensive. Emery is generally used for hand sanding and polishing.
4. Silicon carbide is extremely hard and sharp. It is second to the diamond in hardness, but it is brittle. This brittleness limits its usefulness in machine sanding.
5. Although aluminum oxide is not quite as hard as silicon carbide and its crystals are not as sharp as those of silicon carbide, it is tough. This enables it to stand up under the most severe working conditions, making it an ideal material for sanding belts.

Uses

Coated abrasives are used in both hand and machine sanding for removing excess stock and for cleaning and polishing. Both resinous woods and stock that has been coated with paint or varnish are apt to clog the paper before it has become worn. For this reason, and since there would be greater waste with the more expensive types of coated abrasive, flint quartz (the cheapest form of coated abrasive) is recommended for use on such surfaces.

Market Analysis

Shapes

Coated abrasives are available in a variety of shapes. The most common of these shapes are **sheets, belts, tapes, disks, rolls,** and **cylinders.** In addition to these, there are coated abrasives that have been manufactured into rotary sanding attachments for use on the electric drill. See Figs. 8-1 and 8-2.

Sizes

Coated abrasives are available in the following sizes:
Sheets — 9″ × 11″ and 4-1/2″ × 5-1/2″
Belts — from 1″ to 12″ in width
Tapes — 1″ and 1-1/2″ widths
Disks — from 3″ to 18″ in diameter
Belts for Bandsaws — 1″ in width × 93-1/2″ in length

Larger-size and special-purpose abrasive materials are available for industrial machinery.

Types

1. On **open-coat** abrasives, roughly 50% to 70% of the surface is covered with abrasive material. This provides greater flexibility and keeps the paper from becoming clogged (with pitch, paint, or other such materials) before the cutting edges of the grit have worn down.

Merit Abrasive Products, Inc.

Fig. 8-1.   Grind-O-Flex® sanding wheel.

Merit Abrasive Products, Inc.

Fig. 8-2.   Sand-O-Flex® contour sanding wheel.

2. On **closed-coat** abrasives, the abrasive grains cover the surface of the backing. This type gives longer service in cases where the material does not clog.

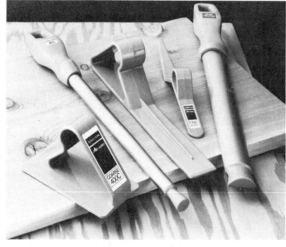

Fig. 8-3.   The Disston® abrader is a unique sanding tool that may be used, instead of sandpaper or files, for many hand shaping operations. The tool's surface is made up of hundreds of tiny, sharp-edged pillars, etched from stainless-steel sheet. A chrome-plated finish gives the abrader a durable edge.

Abraders are available with either fine or coarse surfaces. So that they can be used for a number of different applications, they are available in a variety of shapes, as shown.

Grades

1. **Cabinet paper** is used for sanding out machine marks and preparing the surface for finish. The grit number ranges from 20 (very coarse) to 150 (fine).
2. **Finishing paper** is used for sanding that is done just prior to the application of finish. It is also used for sanding between coats. The grit number ranges from 80 (medium) to 600 (very fine).
3. **Self-cleaning cloth** is used in belt sanders for removing glue from surfaces. This type of abrasive cloth has soap between the grains to prevent the grit from clogging.
4. **Self-cleaning paper** is a nonclogging paper that is coated with stearate and silicon carbide. Stearate is a salt of stearic acid, which comes from the solids of animal fats (beef and lamb). It is also found in milk and in some vegetable fats. Stearate itself is white. However, when it is applied to silicon-carbide paper, it gives the paper a grayish color.

Sales Units

1. Sheets of coated abrasive may be purchased in any quantity. The most economical way to buy coated abrasives is in packages of 50 or 100. Handy assorted packages come with 12 quarter-sheets to the package.
2. Belt-, disk-, and cylinder-shaped coated abrasives may be purchased in a variety of sizes to fit standard machines.
3. Tape abrasives are available in 100' rolls.

It is generally true that the coarser an abrasive is, the more expensive it will be.

Maintenance

1. Extreme dryness makes the bonding adhesive brittle, while dampness softens the adhesive. Either condition will affect the grain-holding properties of the adhesive, shortening its life.
2. For best results in tearing coated-abrasive paper, fold it both ways and tear it over a square edge. Or, use a special jig made for tearing and cutting coated abrasives.
3. Coated-abrasive paper that has become clogged with wood dust may be cleaned with a stiff brush. Another cleaning method is to slap the coated abrasive, grit side up, against a piece of stock.

**Table 8-1
Abrasive-Grit Sizes**

General Uses		Screen Grit*	Number	
Hand or Light Machine Sanding	Polish sanding or sanding between coats of finish.	600 400	10/0	Extra-Fine
	Final sanding prior to finishing.	360 320 280 240 220	8/0 7/0 6/0	
	Final sanding prior to painting. Intermediate finish sanding.	180 150 120	5/0 4/0 3/0	Fine
	Sanding mill marks or machine marks smooth. Sanding rough spots and minor defects.	100 80 60	2/0 0 $^{1}/_{2}$	Medium
Machine Sanding	Rough shaping and leveling. Belt sanding.	50 40 36	1 $1^{1}/_{2}$ 2	Coarse
	Rapid removal of stock. Rough shaping. Removal of old finish. Floor finishing.	30 24 20 16 14 12	$2^{1}/_{2}$ 3 $3^{1}/_{2}$ 4	Extra-Coarse

* Grit numbers apply to silicon carbide, aluminum oxide and garnet abrasives.

Sanders — Spindle, Belt, Disk

Topic 63.

Classification

Power-driven abrading tool (rotary or reciprocating)

Application

Principle of Operation

1. A **spindle sander** has a rubber-coated spindle to which the coated-abrasive sleeve is fitted. The spindle rotates and, at the same time, oscillates (moves up and down), Fig. 8-4.
2. The **belt sander,** Figs. 8-5 and 8-6, has a cloth-coated abrasive belt that revolves on one driver and one idler pulley. As it is doing this, it passes over a flat table on which stock has been placed for sanding.
3. The **disk sander** has a coated-abrasive disk that is attached to a metal disk. This metal disk revolves in a clockwise direction, Fig. 8-7.

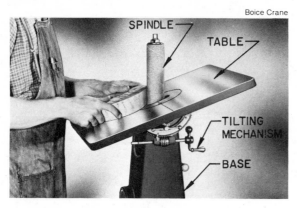

Boice Crane

Fig. 8-4.   Spindle sander.

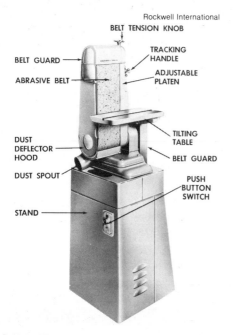

Rockwell International

Fig. 8-5.   Floor-model belt sander.

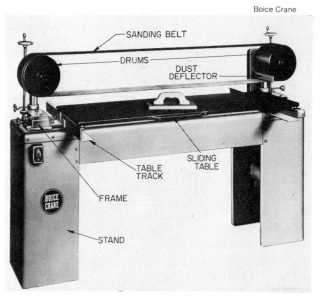

Boice Crane

Fig. 8-6.   Horizontal belt-stroke sander. (Drum guards have been removed.)

Principal Parts and Function of Each

Spindle Sander (Fig. 8-4)

1. The **base** (made of either cast iron, pressed steel, or wood) supports the motor, table, spindle, and oscillating mechanism.
2. The **motor** provides the power.
3. The **table,** made of machined cast iron, supports the work.
4. The **spindle,** made of machined steel, transmits the motion.
5. The **oscillating mechanism,** made of hardened steel, moves the spindle up and down as it rotates.
6. The **rubber spindle** is covered with a coated-abrasive sleeve.

Belt Sander (Fig. 8-5)

1. The **stand** is made either of cast iron, pressed steel, or wood. It supports the motor and the sanding unit.
2. The adjustable **table** supports the work during sanding operations. It tilts 45° away from the belt and 30° toward the belt.
3. The **motor** provides the power.
4. The **drums** are made of pressed steel or aluminum. The **lower drum** is connected to the motor and provides turning force for the belt. The **upper drum** adjusts to track and keeps tension on the belt.

Kinds and Uses

1. Belt sanders are used to sand flat surfaces. Belt widths range from 1″ to 12″, and belt lengths from 4′ to 26′.
2. Disk sanders are used to sand straight and convex curves on the edge of stock. The diameters of disks range from 3″ to 18″.
3. Spindle sanders are used to sand concave curves on the edge of stock. Sleeve diameters range from 3/4″ to 3-1/2″, and lengths range from 6″ to 9″.

Rockwell International

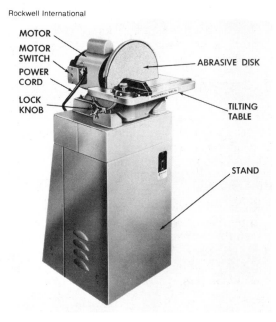

Fig. 8-7. Disk sander.

Fig. 8-8. Combination belt-and-disk finishing machine.

5. The **belt-tension knob** and **tracking handle** are used to adjust the tension and position of the belt on the sanding drums.
6. The adjustable **platen** supports the belt so that it will not sag when pressure is applied.
7. **Belt guards** and **pulley guards,** made of pressed steel, protect the operator.
8. The **dust deflector** and **spout** collect and reroute sanding dust.

Belt-Stroke Sander (Fig. 8-6)

1. The **stand** is made either of cast iron, pressed steel, or wood. It supports the motor, bed, and table.
2. The **frame,** made of cast iron, supports the drums.
3. The **drums** are made of turned aluminum. One drum is connected to the motor and provides turning force for the belt. The other drum is adjustable to track and keep tension on the belt. Both drums can be raised or lowered to sand stock of various thicknesses.
4. The **motor** provides the power.
5. The **sliding table** supports the work and allows lateral movement during sanding operations.
6. The **belt guards** and **pulley guards** protect the operator.

Disk Sander (Fig. 8-7)

1. The **stand** is made either of pressed steel, cast iron, or wood. It supports the motor, table, and disk.
2. The **table,** made of machined cast iron, supports the work and tilts 45° away from and 20° toward the disk.
3. The **motor** provides the power.
4. The **disk,** made either of machined cast iron or of aluminum, serves as a faceplate to which the abrasive is fastened.

OSHA Regulations

Sanding Machines

1. Each drum sanding machine shall have an exhaust hood or other guard. This guard shall be arranged in such a way as to enclose the revolving drum, excluding that portion of the drum above the table (if a table is used).
2. Each disk sanding machine shall have an exhaust hood or other guard. This guard shall be arranged in such a way as to enclose the revolving disk, excluding that portion of the disk above the table (if a table is used).

3. Belt sanding machines shall be provided with guards at each nip point where the sanding belt runs onto a pulley. These guards shall effectively prevent the operator's hands or fingers from coming into contact with the nip points. The unused run of the sanding belt shall be guarded against accidental contact.

Maintenance

1. All moving parts should be kept oiled unless they are equipped with sealed bearings.
2. Whenever a sander is to be left unused for a long period of time, all machined parts should first be coated with a thin film of oil to prevent rusting.

3. When abrasive belts, disks, or cylinders become worn, torn, or clogged, they should be replaced.

Market Analysis

Capacity

The capacity is usually determined by the size and/or diameter of the belt, disk, or cylinder the machine is capable of using.

Attachments

1. Dust collector. This attachment serves to minimize dust. Dust is a hazard to your health, to the machinery, and to the work.
2. Miter gauge. The miter gauge is used as a guide in doing accurate work on belt and disk sanders.

Topic 64.

Portable Sanders — Belt, Disk, Finishing

Classification

Power-driven abrading tool (in-line or rotary)

Application

Principle of Operation

There are three basic types of portable sanding machines, each designed to meet a specific need.

1. On the **belt sander,** Fig. 8-9, a coated-abrasive belt is run over a pad area by an idler and driving drum.
2. On the **disk sander,** Fig. 8-10, a coated-abrasive disk rotates on a motor spindle.

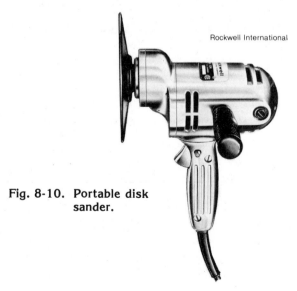

Rockwell International

Fig. 8-10. Portable disk sander.

Black & Decker

Fig. 8-9.   Portable belt sander.

Black & Decker

Fig. 8-11. Portable finishing sander.

3. On **finishing sanders,** a coated-abrasive strip, fitted over a pressure pad, is powered either in an orbital or an in-line oscillating motion. See Fig. 8-11.

Kinds and Uses

The belt sander is used to do flush or regular sanding. Belts are available in various grit numbers and in a variety of widths and lengths to fit a specific make of machine. Sizes of belts range in width from 3″ to 4″, and in length from 21″ to 27″.

The disk sander is used in rough sanding for fast removal of stock. It is used where a scratch-free surface is not essential. A pad may be fitted over the disk, making it possible for the disk to be used in polishing operations.

Finishing sanders are classified according to the type of sanding motion they use. There are two basic types of finishing sanders:
1. **Orbital-motion sander,** used in finish sanding, has a fast, ovular pattern. It removes stock quickly and is used primarily on flat surfaces.
2. The **in-line sander's** cutting action is back and forth in a straight line. This is ideal for the final sanding of wood surfaces. It leaves no sanding marks on the surface as does the orbital sander.

Principal Parts and Function of Each

Belt Sander

1. The **housing** is an aluminum or plastic die-casting, designed for efficient and minimum-effort handling.

2. A **universal motor** provides the power.
3. The **driving mechanism** connects the motor to the driving drum by means of a direct gear, a rubber timing belt, a spur gear, or a chain-worm gear drive.
4. The **driving drum,** made of aluminum, is covered by a rubber tire. The belt rides on this tire.
5. The **tracking mechanism** controls the alignment of the tracking drum so that the belt will ride within the proper path.
6. The **tension device,** a spring unit, automatically maintains the correct belt tension by positioning the idler drum.
7. The **striker bar,** made of hardened steel, prevents the belt from riding against the housing.
8. The **sanding shoe** is positioned in line with the rim of the pulleys and is covered by a pad and spring-steel wear strip. It maintains even pressure on the belt during the sanding operation.
9. The **vacuum system** (on dustless models) collects the sanding dust. It helps prevent the belt from clogging, resulting in longer belt life and smoother sanding.
10. The **handles,** made of plastic, are designed to provide positive control in any position.
11. The **trigger switch** is built into the handle. It provides on-off control.

Rockwell International

Fig. 8-12. Speed Bloc® finishing sander.

Disk Sander

1. The **housing,** an aluminum or magnesium die-casting, is designed for efficient handling.
2. A **universal motor** provides the power.
3. The **driving unit** varies according to the type of machine. Most small disk sanders have the disk mounted directly on the motor shaft. In some others, a reduction unit provides high torque. On some disk sanders, the disk is at right angles to the motor shaft. This requires a straight gear reduction. On others, the disk is mounted on a shaft that is parallel to the shaft of the motor. This type is smaller in height, but it requires an angle driving unit containing bevel gears.
4. The **backing disk** is made of steel. The abrasive disk rotates on the surface pad of the backing disk.
5. The **disk-retaining nut** fastens to the center of the disk and is used to hold the abrasive disk in place.
6. There are two types of **handles.** One type is built into the housing and the other, made of plastic, is attached to the housing. An auxiliary handle fits on the side for easy control.
7. The **trigger switch,** built into the handle, provides on-off control.

Finishing Sander

1. The **housing,** an aluminum or plastic die-casting, is designed for easy handling during the sanding operation.
2. A **universal motor** provides the power.
3. The **driving mechanism** provides either in-line or orbital motion for the sanding operation.
4. The **sanding pad,** a felt or rubber backup pad, causes pressure to be evenly distributed on the abrasive paper.
5. **Pad clamps,** made of spring steel, secure the abrasive paper in place.
6. The **handles** are constructed into the housing to provide easy control during the sanding operation. On some makes, there is an extra knob, made of plastic, which attaches to the front or side of the housing to provide further control.

7. The **trigger switch** is built into the handle. It provides on-off control of the machine.

OSHA Regulations

Portable Belt Sanding Machines

Belt sanding machines shall be provided with guards at each nip point where the sanding belt runs onto a pulley. These guards shall effectively prevent the operator's hands or fingers from coming into contact with the nip points. The unused run of the sanding belt shall be guarded so as to prevent accidental contact.

Maintenance

1. All worn or torn sanding papers should be replaced.
2. Although most bearings are self-lubricating, the level of the oil reservoir on the belt sander must be maintained.
3. The pressure pad must be kept in working condition so that it will continue to sand efficiently.
4. To avoid cable breaks, exercise care in handling the conductor cord.

Market Analysis

Capacity

The sanding area of portable sanders is determined by the amount and shape of the sanding surface of the machine.
1. Belt sanders are made to handle belts 3″ or 4″ in width and 21″, 24″, or 27″ in length.
2. Disks sanders are made for disks measuring 3″, 6″, 7″, and 9″ in diameter.
3. Finishing sanders are made to use sanding sheets 3″ × 8″, 3-5/8″ × 9″, and 4-1/2″ × 11″.

Safety Consideration

• All machines should either be double-insulated or grounded with a third wire.

Using Sanders — Spindle, Belt, Disk

Topic 65.

Classification

Removing stock by abrasion

Procedure

Sanders should not be used to remove large amounts of material unless facilities exist for complete dust control.

Using Spindle Sander to Sand Inside or Concave Curves

1. Place the work on the table.

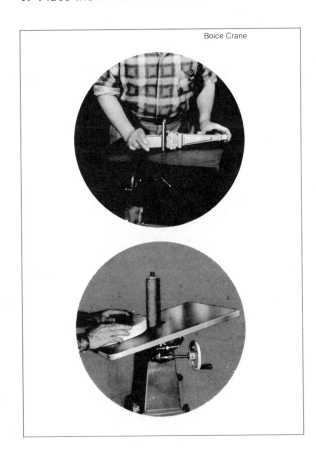

Boice Crane

Fig. 8-13. Using the spindle sander.

2. Holding the work securely, move it into contact with the revolving spindle. Guide the work to sand the contour of the edge, Fig. 8-13. The oscillating motion tends to prevent grooves being formed in the edge being sanded. This motion also causes the wear on the abrasive to be distributed over the surface. Stopping the movement of the stock at any given point causes the edge to hollow out at the point of contact.

3. Sand until all the waste stock is removed. Because of the speed at which machine sanders revolve, coarser abrasives may be used and still produce a smoother surface than would result from hand sanding with an abrasive of the same coarseness.

4. If a drill press or lathe is used as a spindle sander, adjust the belt to the proper speed. The spindle sander attachment for the shaper is not recommended because of the high speed of the spindle's movement. This rapid motion often causes burning of the stock.

Using Disk Sander to Sand Convex and Small Surfaces

1. Place the work on the table.
2. Move the work into contact with the sanding disk.
3. Slowly move the work along until all waste stock has been removed. Keep in mind that sanders are intended mainly to smooth surfaces and edges and not to remove large quantities of stock. See Fig. 8-14.
4. Resinous woods should be sanded close to the center of the disk, where the peripheral speed is not so great. This will minimize clogging and heating.
5. To convert a lathe into a disk sander, cement a coated-abrasive disk to the faceplate and build the table up to the height of the center of the disk.

Rockwell International

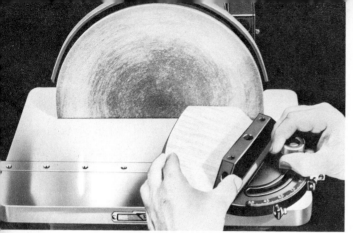

Fig. 8-14. Using a disk sander to sand small surfaces.

6. There are also disk attachments and spinner attachments available for electric hand drills. Care must be taken in using the spinner attachment, as this is harder to control and is likely to leave circular scratches on the surface.

Using Belt Sander to Sand Flat Surfaces

1. To sand a flat surface, place the belt sander in a horizontal position. The table should be in a vertical position. See Fig. 8-15.
2. Start the machine and hold the stock flat against the moving belt. Care must be taken to keep an even pressure on the entire surface. Examine the work often to see that there is not an excessive amount of material being removed from any one section.

Using Belt Sander to Sand Straight, Beveled, or Convex Edges

1. To sand straight or convex edges, place the belt sander in a vertical position. The table should be in a horizontal position. See Fig. 8-5. For sanding a bevel or an angle, the table and/or sanding unit may be repositioned at the desired angle, Fig. 8-16.
2. Holding the work firmly against the table, gradually bring the stock into contact with the belt.
3. Slowly move the work along until all waste stock has been removed.

Using Belt Sander to Sand Concave Surfaces

1. Place the belt sander in a horizontal position and remove the top guard.

Rockwell International

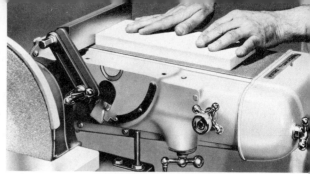

Fig. 8-15. Using a belt sander to sand a flat surface.

Rockwell International

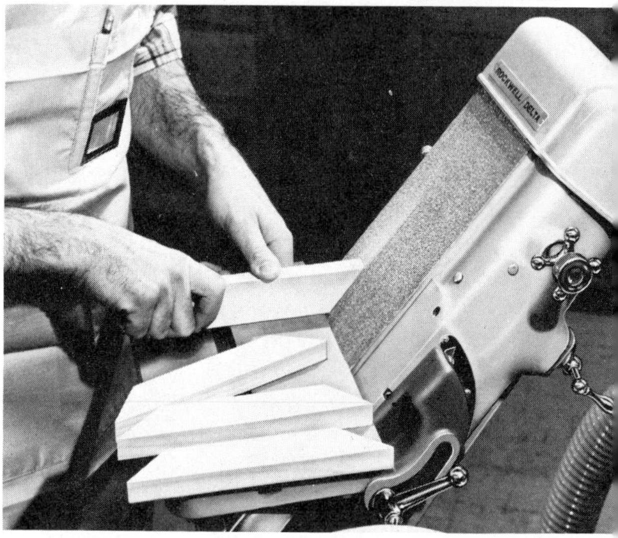

Fig. 8-16. Belt sanders may be set up for angle sanding by adjusting the angle of the table or sanding unit.

2. The concave surface should be brought gently into contact with the curved top section of the belt sander, Fig. 8-17.
3. Care should be taken to support the stock firmly with both hands during the sanding operation.
4. The top guard should be replaced immediately after the sanding is completed.

Using Belt-Stroke Sander to Sand Flat Surfaces

1. Secure the stock to the sliding table and adjust the drums so that the belt is just above the surface to be sanded.
2. Using a stroker, press the belt down on the workpiece, Fig. 8-18. Constantly move the stroker or the sliding table to avoid sanding too much material in one area.
3. Continue sanding until the entire surface is sanded to a uniform level and texture.

Fig. 8-17. Contour sanding with the belt sander.

Fig. 8-18. The stroker is used to apply pressure to the back side of the sanding belt.

Fig. 8-19. Sanding tabletops with an automatic belt sander.

Fig. 8-20. Sanding a flat surface with a portable belt sander.

Fig. 8-21. Large belt-stroke sander.
This sander is used to sand ornate table pedestals. The wooden stroker has been cut to conform to the curvature of the pedestal.

Using Portable Belt Sander to Sand Flat Surfaces

1. Secure the stock to the bench top.
2. Select the proper-grade abrasive belt for the sanding job. See Table 8-1.
3. Start the machine, slowly moving it back and forth over the surface. See Fig. 8-20. Always keep the belt running **in the direction of the grain.** It is better to start at the end and work in the direction opposite to that of the rotation of the sanding belt. This will pick up the sanding dust and will allow you, as the work progresses, to inspect the surface you have just sanded without having to stop the machine.
4. Do not hold the machine in one place or tilt the machine while it is in contact with the surface. This will produce deep sanding marks in the surface.
5. As you operate the machine, be careful not to cut the electrical cord or the dust bag.

Fig. 8-22. Drum sanding.

Heywood-Wakefield Co.

Planers and other high-speed machines beat the fibers down, producing a glazed surface. These fibers must then be roughed or softened somewhat so that a stain will taken evenly. Sanding, using any type of sander, will accomplish this.

Drum sanders are usually used on irregularly-shaped parts. The common procedure is to use two grades of sandpaper (coarse and fine) on a single horizontal drum. This makes is possible to do both rough and finished sanding in one operation.

Fig. 8-23. Multiple-drum sander.

The multiple-drum sander is used for production-sanding of flat surfaces. Because each sanding drum may have a different-grit abrasive, it is possible for stock to be both rough- and fine-sanded in a single pass through the machine.

Norton Company

Norton Company

Fig. 8-24. Pneumatic drum sander.

The pneumatic drum sander is used for production-sanding of curved shapes.

Standards and Results

- Surfaces and edges should be sanded smooth.
- Finished work should be of the predetermined size and shape. The work should also be free of burn marks caused by the application of too much pressure or by a clogged, worn abrasive.
- Surfaces should be free of cross-grain scratches.

Safety Considerations

- Wear safety glasses when sanding.
- Use portable machines only in dry areas and only when the machines have been grounded. Make certain your hands are dry.
- Before inserting the plug of a portable sander into the power supply, make sure the switch is in the "off" position.
- Keep your hands away from all moving parts.
- Belt sanders should be properly tracked so that the belt will stay on the rolls.
- When using the disk sander, sand on the downward rotation.
- Make sure the material that you are going to sand is well secured.
- Do not use belts that are torn.
- Exercise care in sanding splintered stock.
- Before setting a portable belt sander on the bench, be sure the switch is in the "off" position and the belt has stopped running.

SECTION NINE.

Drilling, Boring, and Mortising

Topic 66.

Selecting the Proper Tool to Cut a Hole

The type of tool and cutter best suited to cut a particular hole is determined by two factors: the desired shape and diameter of the hole and the method that will be used to drive the cutter.

There are two basic types of boring tools. In one type, the bit has side spurs that cut the wood fibers on the perimeter of the hole. The cutting lips clean out the center of the hole. This type of boring tool is best used on face or side grain. In the other type, the cutting lips shear off the ends of the wood fibers as the hole is cut. For this reason, the twist bit is best suited for boring into end grain. This type of bit will cut a rough hole in face or side grain.

Driving tools for hand operations include the push drill, the hand drill, and the bit brace. Cutters designed for machine use are driven by the portable electric drill (Topic 72) and the drill press (Topics 74 and 75).

Table 9-1
Selecting Cutting Tools for Holes

	Hole Size	Cutting Tool*
HAND OPERATION	$1/_{32}''$-$1/_8''$	Brad or finish nail
	$1/_{16}''$-$11/_{64}''$	Straight-shank drill points
	$1/_{16}''$-$1/_4''$	Twist drills or twist bits
	$3/_{16}''$-2$''$	Auger bit, Forstner bits, or dowel bits
	$5/_8''$-3$''$	Expansive bits
MACHINE OPERATION	$1/_{16}''$-$1/_2''$	Twist drill, machine or multi spurs
	$3/_8''$-1$''$	Power bore or Forstner bits
	$3/_8''$-1$1/_2''$	Spade bit
	1$3/_4''$-2$1/_8''$	Lock-bit sets
	Pilot Hole by Screw Size	
	$1/_8''$-$1/_4''$	Screw Mate®
	1$''$-5$1/_2''$	Fly cutter
	$3/_4''$-7$''$	Hole saw

* Many of these cutting tools are illustrated in Section 9.

| **Bit Brace** | **Topic 67.** |

Classification

Rotary driving tool

Application

Principle of Operation

The **bit brace** operates on the principle of the wheel and axle. The pressure on the swing of the bow is in direct proportion to the amount of force applied to the cutters of the auger bit. (Refer to Topic 9, "Tools", and the discussion of the wheel and axle.)

The design of the bit brace makes it possible to apply downward pressure on the boring tool at the same time as a constant revolving motion is directing the cutting action.

Kinds and Uses

The bit brace or bit stock is used for holding and driving all kinds of boring tools that have squared, tapered tangs, screwdriver bits, dowel pointers, and countersinks.

Braces are made in three types: (1) the **plain brace,** (2) the **ratchet brace,** and (3) the **corner brace.** See Figs. 9-1, 9-2, and 9-3.

Fig. 9-2.   Open ratchet bit brace.

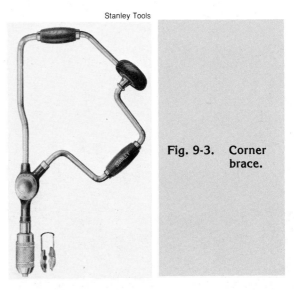

Stanley Tools

Fig. 9-3.   Corner brace.

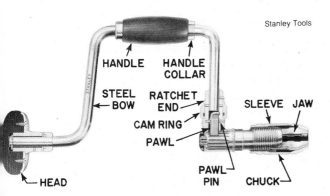

Stanley Tools

HANDLE   HANDLE COLLAR
STEEL BOW   RATCHET END
CAM RING
PAWL
SLEEVE   JAW
PAWL PIN   CHUCK
HEAD

Fig. 9-1.   Plain bit brace.

Millers Falls Co.

Fig. 9-4.   Ratchet auger handle.

Principal Parts and Function of Each

1. The **head,** made of cocobolo, aluminum, or plastic, is fastened to the bow and turns freely on ball bearings. It controls the direction and pressure.
2. The steel **bow** forms the outer rim of the wheel and axle. It carries the power from the operator's hand to the chuck. This bow shape permits a controlled or continuous operation. The larger the bow, the greater the mechanical advantage. (See page 37.)
3. The **handle,** made of cocobolo, aluminum, or plastic, is fastened to the bow but turns

Stanley Tools

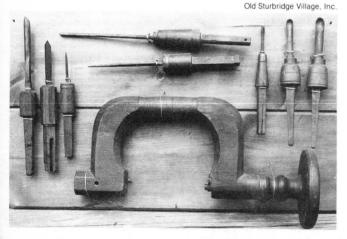

UNIVERSAL INTERLOCKING SPRING ALLIGATOR PIN ALLIGATOR

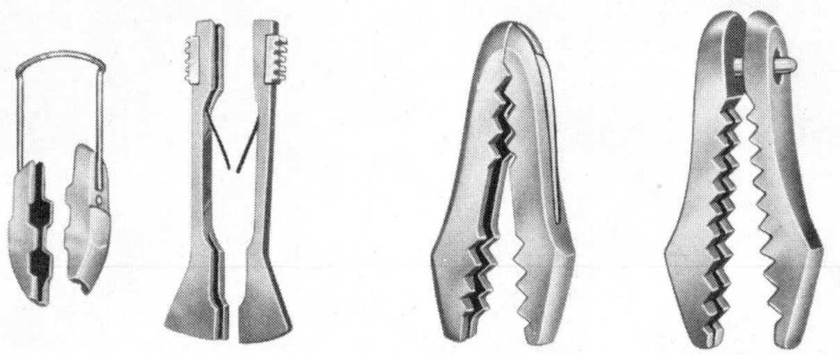

Fig. 9-5.   Types of jaws on bit braces.

Old Sturbridge Village, Inc.

Fig. 9-6.   Early bit brace, wooden.
One step in the development of the modern bit brace was this bit stock and chuck, made entirely of wood. The bit is secured in its own chuck, which in turn is held in the bit brace by a wooden thumbscrew. Note that the head turns, but the handle does not.

freely on it. Force applied to the handle causes the brace to turn.

4. The hardened-steel **jaws** of the **chuck** are held in position by the use of a screw and wedge. Tightening the **sleeve** of the chuck forces the jaws to close.
   There are three types of jaws, Fig. 9-5: (1) **Universal** jaws are used for round-shank and tapered-tang bits and drills. (2) **Interlocking** jaws fit square-taper tang bits and drills. (3) **Alligator** jaws may be used with regular-sized tapered-tang and medium-sized round-shank drills.
5. The **ratchet** engages the handle for the proper drilling rotation. There are three types of ratchets: (1) The **concealed type** of ratchet has a **sleeve,** which seals the ratchet mechanism and the lubricant. This sleeve also prevents other foreign materials from entering the ratchet. (2) The **open ratchet** is not as strong as the concealed or box ratchets, nor is it as easily worked. (3) The **box ratchet** is the strongest of the three types.
   Turning the cam ring to the right (clockwise) engages a pawl with the **ratchet wheel.** This causes the bit to turn with the brace in a clockwise direction, but permits the bow to be turned in the opposite direction while the bit is stationary in the wood. Thus, a hole may be bored in a place where the full swing of the bow is not possible.

Maintenance

Cleaning

Rust on the bow or the chuck should be removed with an abrasive (steel wool or emery cloth). The tool should be oiled with machine oil.

Replacing Parts

Jaws wear out from continued use. They may be replaced by unscrewing the shell of the chuck. New heads and bows are available, but proper care will make replacement of these unnecessary.

Storing

Bit braces should either be stored in boxes designed for this purpose or should be hung up securely.

Oiling

The bearings (between the head and the bow and between the ratchet and the chuck) should be oiled regularly. Before the brace is put away for a long period of time, all metal parts should be covered with oil.

Market Analysis

Capacity

1. The **sweep** (or swing) is the diameter of the swing of the handle. It ranges from 6″ to 16″. The average sweep is between 8″ and 10″.
2. The capacity of chucks ranges from 0 to 1/2″.

Wood Bits

Topic 68.

Classification

Boring tool (rotating edge tool)

Application

Principle of Operation

All **bits** work on the principle of the wedge and the inclined plane.

Kinds and Uses

Bits are used for boring round holes in wood.
1. **Auger bits** are made with three twist types (single, double, and solid-center) and three types of screws (coarse, medium, and fine). The coarser the screw and the coarser the twist, the faster the cutting action and the rougher the cut. An auger bit with a fine screw is recommended for boring holes in hard, close-grained woods as a finer screw will minimize splitting of the workpiece.

Solid-center auger bits are stronger than single- and double-twist auger bits. See Figs. 9-7, 9-8, and 9-9.
2. A **Forstner bit** is used to bore flat-bottomed holes. It is suitable for this because it has no screw projecting below the cutting edges, Fig. 9-10.
3. **Plug-cutter bit** is used to cut wooden plugs used to cover screws, dowels, or defects. See Fig. 9-11.

Stanely Tools

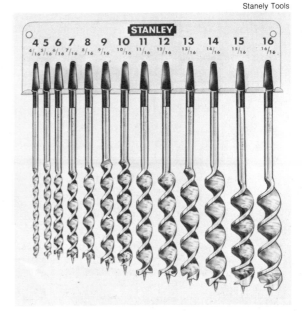

Fig. 9-8.   Double-twist auger bits.

Stanley Tools

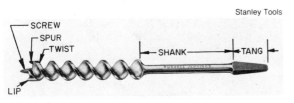

Fig. 9-7.   Auger bit.

Stanley Tools

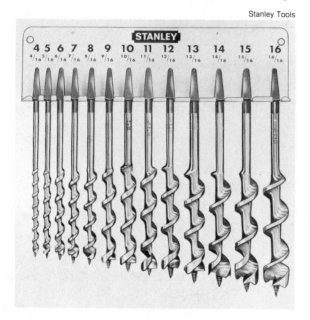

Fig. 9-9.   Solid-center auger bits.

Connecticut Valley Manufacturing Co.

Fig. 9-10.   Forstner bit.

Greenlee Tool Co.

Fig. 9-11.   Plug-cutter bit.

Stanley Tools

Fig. 9-12.   Rose machine countersink.

Stanley Tools

Fig. 9-13.   Rose countersink with square tang.

4. **Countersinks** are used to provide clearance for screwheads, Figs. 9-12 and 9-13.
5. An **expansive bit** may be adjusted to cut large holes. The cutter is adjusted by turning a screw, Fig. 9-14.
6. The **dowel bit** is used to bore holes for dowels, Fig. 9-15.
7. The **spade bit** is used for rapid machine cutting of general-purpose holes, Fig. 9-17.
8. The **Screw Mate®** is used to produce a pilot hole, a clearance hole, and a countersink or counterbore hole all in one operation, Figs. 9-18 and 9-19.

Stanley Tools

Fig. 9-14.   Expansive bit.

Stanley Tools

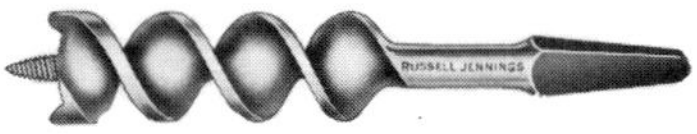

Fig. 9-15.   Dowel bit.

Stanley Tools

Fig. 9-16.   Dowel pointer.

The Irwin Auger Bit Company

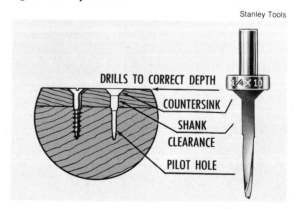

Fig. 9-17.   Spade bit.

Stanley Tools

DRILLS TO CORRECT DEPTH

COUNTERSINK

SHANK
CLEARANCE

PILOT HOLE

Fig. 9-18.   Screw Mate countersink.

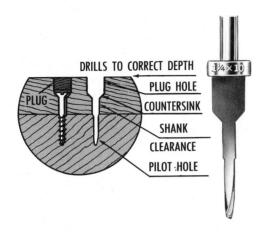

DRILLS TO CORRECT DEPTH
PLUG HOLE
PLUG
COUNTERSINK
SHANK
CLEARANCE
PILOT HOLE

Fig. 9-19. Screw Mate counterbore.

Principal Parts and Function of Each

Auger Bit

1. The **screw** is the first part to touch the wood. It draws the bit into the wood, using the principle of the inclined plane. See Figs. 9-7, 9-8 and 9-9.
2. The **spurs** or **nibs** score the edge of the hole, using the principle of the wedge.
3. The **lips** cut the material from within the scored circle, also using the principle of the wedge.
4. The **twist** carries the wood chips to the surface. It works on the principle of the inclined plane.
5. The **shank** is the part that connects the twist and the tang.
6. The **tang** is the square, tapered part, which locks within the chuck, causing the bit to revolve as the bow is turned. The number engraved on the tang of the bit indicates the bit's size (in sixteenths of an inch).

Forstner Bit

1. The sharpened, circular **steel ring** scribes the circumference of the hole, using the principle of the wedge. See Fig. 9-10.
2. The two **lips** cut the wood within the circle, using the principle of the wedge. These lips then carry the shavings up the inclined plane and out of the hole. Forstner bits 3/8" and smaller have only one cutting lip.
3. The **shank** connects the cutter and tang or, on machine Forstner bits, is the surface that is held in the chuck.

4. The **tang** is the square, tapered end that is locked in the chuck. The number stamped on the tang indicates the size of the bit (in sixteenths of an inch).

Plug-Cutter Bit

1. The **cutter disk** scores and cuts a ring, using the principle of the wedge. The remaining disk or cylinder is used as a plug to fill holes, Fig. 9-11.
2. The connecting parts of the plug-cutter bit are similar to those of the auger bit.

Countersink Bit

On the countersink bit, a cone-shaped **cutter** widens a hole, using the principle of the wedge. See Figs. 9-12 and 9-13. Three kinds of countersink bits are available: single, double, and rose-type.

Expansive Bit

The expansive bit (sometimes called an **expansion bit**) has two adjustable **cutters,** which may be set at different positions to cut holes 5/8" to 3" in diameter. This bit works on the same principle as the auger bit, Fig. 9-14. Some expansive bits have a **screw adjustment,** which regulates the diameter of the hole to be cut.

Dowel Bit

The dowel bit is similar to the auger bit, but is shorter in length and has a finer twist, Fig. 9-15.

Spade Bit

The spade bit consists of a flat **blade** and a center **spur.** The width of the blade determines the size of the bit. See Fig. 9-17.

Screw Mate®

This is a combination drill and countersink. It makes the pilot, clearance, and countersunk hole for the length and wire size of a

Greenlee Tool Co.

Fig. 9-20. Machine bit.

given screw, Fig. 9-18. The head of the screw is sunk below the surface in a hole made by the **counterbore.** The counterbore also makes a clearance hole, a pilot hole, and a countersunk hole for the length and size of a given screw, Fig. 9-19.

Machine Bit

The **machine bit** is similar to the auger bit, but has a brad point instead of a screw point, Fig. 9-20. The screw point is not necessary on the machine bit, due to the speed and the amount of pressure applied by the machine.

Multi-Spur Bit

The **multi-spur bit** is used for machine cutting large holes. It consists of (a) **saw teeth,** cut into the rim, (b) a single **cutter,** and (c) a **spur center.** See Fig. 9-21.

Maintenance

So that the cutting edges will not be damaged, bits should either be mounted in-

Greenlee Tool Co.

Fig. 9-21. Multi-spur machine bit.

Stanley Tools

Fig. 9-22. Bit gauge.

Fig. 9-23. Bit gauge.

Stanley Tools

Stanley Tools

Fig. 9-24. Bit extension.

The Irwin Auger Bit Company

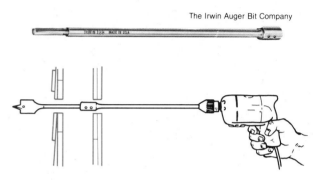

Fig. 9-25. Electric-drill bit extension. (Note: Do not use in drill press.)

dividually on a board or should be stored in a canvas roll or a container.

Bits get dull from use and may be sharpened. This is done by filing the inside of the spurs and the top side of the lips. See Section 19, "Sharpening," Topic 195.

When bits are to be left unused for a long period of time, they should be oiled to prevent rusting.

Market Analysis

Capacity

The capacity of a wood bit is usually determined by the size of hole it will cut. However, other factors, such as the bit length, the shank type, the twist angle, the number of spurs on the bit, and the type of the end screw, must be taken into account in determining the capacity of a wood bit.

Attachments

1. **Bit gauge.** This attachment is used to control the hole depth. See Figs. 9-22 and 9-23.
2. **Bit extensions.** These permit the user to bore through walls or floors. See Figs. 9-24 and 9-25.

Boring a Hole with Bit and Brace

Topic 69.

Classification

Driving a boring tool to score and remove stock

Procedure

1. A hole should be cut in such a way that the sides are square with the surface or at the prescribed angle to the surface.
2. Locate the center of the hole by making intersecting lines on the surface of the stock. It is a good practice to make an awl mark to indicate the center point.

Through Boring

1. Select the proper size auger bit for the hole and secure it in the jaws of the bit brace. (See Topic 68, "Wood Bits" and Topic 67, "Bit Brace" for uses and names of parts of the auger bit and bit brace.)
2. Secure the stock. The surface must be at right angles to the natural boring position

Fig. 9-27. Using the T-bevel to check an angle. A straightedge is used to bridge the recess in the stock.

in order that the hole may be cut perpendicular to the surface. The same principle applies when boring at an angle to the surface. A control must be established to maintain accuracy at any given angle.

3. Place the point of the screw at the intersection point of the lines. Hold the head of the bit brace so that the auger bit is at the desired angle with the surface of the work. With your left hand, rotate the swing of the brace in a clockwise direction. Apply pressure to the head as you swing the handle.
4. When the bit has started to cut, check to see that the hole is being cut at the desired angle. This may be done by sighting from two directions (not opposite) or by holding a try square or a T-bevel (depending on the angle) against the surface close to the bit. See Figs. 9-26 and 9-27.
5. Continue to bore the hole until the point of the screw comes through the opposite side.

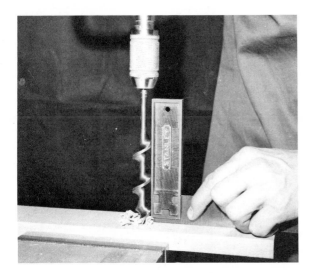

Fig. 9-26. Using a try square to check squareness.

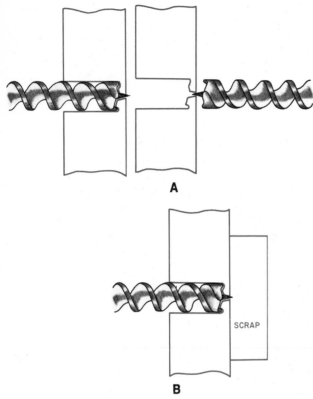

Fig. 9-28. Through boring — two ways to prevent splitting out.

Remove the bit by reversing two turns of the swing, then turning in a clockwise direction. Pull up on the head as you turn. Do not reverse the motion as you are withdrawing the bit, as this will cause the cuttings to remain in the hole.

6. Turn the board and complete the hole from the opposite side. This method will help prevent the wood from breaking or splitting at the edges of the hole. See Fig. 9-28A.

7. Another method of preventing the wood from breaking on the back surface is to clamp the work over a piece of scrap material and bore into the scrap piece. Care must be taken not to drill too deeply into the second piece. See Fig. 9-28B.

8. In boring through a long piece, it is advisable to bore halfway from one side and halfway from the other side.

9. If the hole to be bored is longer than twice the length of the bit, a bit extension may be added for increased depth, Figs. 9-24 and 9-25.

Stop Boring

Stop boring is the process of boring a hole to a predetermined depth. The surest method of stop boring is to use some type of depth gauge attached to the bit, Figs. 9-22, 9-23, and 9-29. There are two types of gauges that can be used. One type is an adjustable bit gauge, which clamps to the auger bit. The other type is made in the shop. This type of depth gauge is made by boring a hole into a piece of wood. This hole is fit over the bit. The wood used to make this gauge is cut to length so the bit will extend through the hole far enough to bore to the required depth. (The depth of the hole is determined by the amount the bit extends below the gauge to the cutting lips.)

When boring a series of holes of approximately the same depth, count the number of turns needed to make one hole. Make each hole in the series using this same number of turns.

Using Jigs

Jigs are used to aid in locating and boring straight holes, Figs. 9-30, 9-31, 9-32, 9-33.

Counterboring

Counterboring is done to recess screwheads. In effect, it is the process of making a

Fig. 9-29. Bit stops.

Stanley Tools

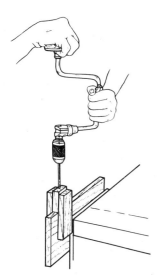

Fig. 9-30. Homemade
doweling
jig.

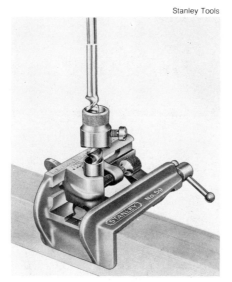

Fig. 9-31. Doweling jig
with inter-
changeable
drill sleeves.

Fig. 9-32.   Self-
centering
doweling
jig.

smaller hole within a larger hole, Fig. 9-34. In counterboring, the larger hole must always be cut first. Care should be taken that the size of the bit selected matches the size of the plug. A plug that fits the larger hole covers the screwhead.

Countersinking

A **countersink** cuts a tapered hole. The taper matches the bevel on the underside of screwhead. See Fig. 9-18. The hole should be cut in such a way that the diameter of the countersunk hole at the surface equals the outside diameter of the screwhead.

Standards and Results

- All holes should have clean-cut edges and sides.
- The sides should be of the proper angle to the surface.
- Holes should be properly located.
- Care should be taken not to mar benches or holding devices.

Safety Considerations

- Wear safety glasses.
- Be certain the stock is properly secured.
- Avoid applying excess pressure.

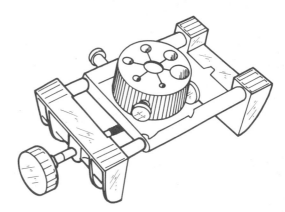

Fig. 9-33. Turret-type doweling jig.

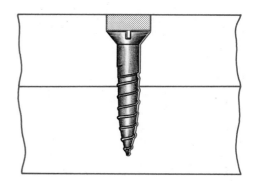

Fig. 9-34. Plugged, counterbored hole.

Topic 70.

Hand Drill and Breast Drill

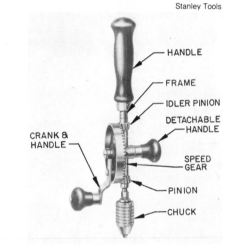

Fig. 9-35. Nomenclature of open-gear hand drill.

Classification

Rotary driving tool

Application

Principle of Operation

The hand drill works on the principle of the wheel and axle and the inclined plane. Each tooth of the gear is one of a series of inclined planes that combine their mechanical advantage to increase the speed and turning power. This speed ratio is in direct proportion to the number of teeth on the pinion gear as compared to the number of teeth on the speed gear. The more teeth on the pinion gear, in relation to the speed gear, the greater the turning speed of the drill. Decreasing the number of teeth on the pinion gear will result in greater torque (turning force) but slower speeds. On the 1/4" hand drill, the speed ratio is generally 4 or 5 to 1. On the 3/8" and 1/2" breast drills, there are two pinion gears. One is used for the slow speeds required for large drills, while the other obtains the higher speeds necessary for smaller drills. See Figs. 9-35 and 9-36.

Kinds and Uses

The **hand drill** and **breast drill** are used in driving a twist drill to drill small holes. The size of each of these drills depends on the diameter of the chuck opening. This opening is usually either 1/4", 3/8", or 1/2".

Principal Parts and Function of Each

1. The **handles** are usually made of wood or plastic. They make it possible to control the force and direction of the drilling operation.
2. On the breast drill, a metal **breastplate** is used to apply pressure.
3. The **frame** is cast or drop-forged to a shape designed for holding attachments.

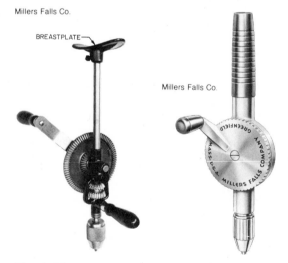

Fig. 9-36. Breast drill.   **Fig. 9-37. Enclosed hand drill.**

4. The **speed gear** provides mechanical advantage to increase speed and the turning power. There are several styles of wheels for the speed gear. Some have open spokes, while others have a disk wheel. See Figs. 9-36 and 9-37.

5. The **crank** and **handle,** attached to speed gear, form the outer diameter of the wheel and axle and provide leverage.
6. The **pinion gear** is attached to the opposite end of the spindle chuck. It meshes with the speed gear.
7. The **idler pinion gear,** Fig. 9-35, has the

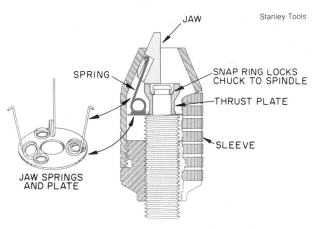

Fig. 9-38. Nomenclature of chuck.

same size and number of teeth as the pinion gear. It is located on the upper section of the frame and meshes with the speed gear opposite the pinion gear. Its function is to balance the thrust of force applied to the handwheel speed gear, and is usually found only on better-quality hand drills.
8. The hard, carbon-steel **chuck** holds the drill. It has three jaws and is tightened with a clockwise turn of the sleeve. (The sleeve uses the inclined plane of the jaws as a wedge.) This locks the jaws around the drill, Fig. 9-38. The three jaws will always center a properly gripped drill. Some breast drills have two-jaw chucks.
9. Some breast drills have a **level** built into the frame.

Maintenance

The hand drill requires periodic oiling and checking. The screws that fasten the crank arm and breastplate should be kept tight.

Market Analysis

Capacity

There are three sizes of hand drills: those that have chucks of 0-1/4″ (for light work), those with chucks 0-3/8″ (for medium work), and those that have 0-1/2″ chucks (for heavy work).

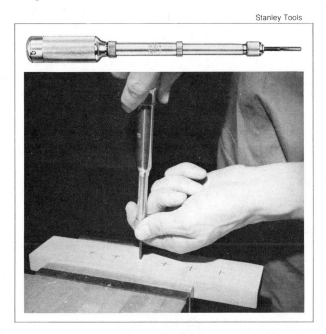

Fig. 9-39. Push drills or automatic drills are used to drill small pilot holes for screws. The handle is pumped up and down to operate the drill. This action gives a turning force to the drill bit. Push-drill bits are available in sizes from 1/16″ to 11/64″.

Fig. 9-40. Wooden spiral hand drill.
This is the forerunner of the modern spiral push drill. Note the carved, spiral thread. The driving barrel, shown at the bottom of the spindle, was run up and down, causing the drill to turn.

Old Sturbridge Village, Inc.

Topic 71.

Twist Drill

Classification

A spiral-fluted tool with a tip ground to two cutting wedges, used in making round holes in wood and other materials

Application

Principle of Operation

As the drill is turned and pressure is applied, the cutting lips of the drill remove the material, using the principle of the wedge. The material is removed from the hole by the flutes. This is done on the principle of the inclined plane.

Kinds and Uses

Drills are used for making round holes in wood, metal, plastics, and other materials. They are made of carbon steel (for general use) and of high-speed steel or with carbide tips (for drilling hard materials).

Three different classification systems are used to designate drill size:

1. **Numerical** — 1-80 (1 = .2280″ in diameter, 80 = .0135″ in diameter).
2. **Alphabetical** — letters from A to Z (A = .234″ in diameter, Z = .413″ in diameter).
3. **Fractional** — incremented by 64ths of an inch.

There are three types of shanks. These types are: **straight, tapered,** and **tang.**

Principal Parts and Function of Each

1. The **cutting lips** cut the material.
2. The **flute** carries the material out of the hole and allows lubrication of the cutting edge. No lubrication is necessary for drilling wood.
3. The **shank** is shaped to permit the chuck to grip the drill securely.

Maintenance

Storing

Drills should be kept in graduated stands. This is done to prevent damage to the cutting edges and so that easy selection can be made. Drills should be kept oiled to prevent rusting.

Sharpening

The process of sharpening a drill is really a shaping process performed on a grinding wheel. For general use, the cutting lips should form an angle of 118°. The clearance angle should be from 12° to 15°. Sharpening should

Union Twist Drill Co.

Fig. 9-41. Straight-shank drill.

Huot Manufacturing Company

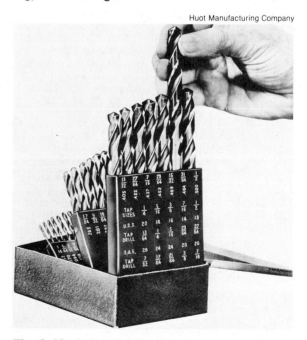

Fig. 9-42. Indexed drill set.

not be attempted by beginners. See Section 19, "Sharpening," Topic 195.

Market Analysis

Capacity

Twist drills are made in various lengths and in diameters of between 1/32" and 2".

They can be purchased either individually or in indexed sets. High-speed drills are more expensive, but they last longer than carbon-steel drills. The drill's size and material of construction are stamped on the shank.

Attachments

The only attachment for the twist drill is a **depth gauge,** used for drilling to predetermined depth.

Portable Electric Drill   **Topic 72.**

Classification

Motorized rotary driving tool

Application

Principle of Operation

The **portable electric drill** is operated by a small, high-speed electric motor that has a gear-reduction driving unit. See Fig. 9.43.

Kinds and Uses

Electric drills are made in many sizes to accommodate a wide range of rotary cutting tools. Although these drills are used primarily in drilling operations, they may be equipped with attachments enabling them to be used for sanding, polishing, and grinding.

Principal Parts and Functions of Each

1. The **housing,** made of aluminum or plastic, is designed for holding, guiding, and applying pressure to the twist drill.
2. The **motor** is a rotary power unit.
3. The **reduction gears** reduce the speed of the motor to high-torque driving force. See Table 9-2.
4. The **chuck** is a three-jaw, nonslip gripping unit made of hard-carbon steel. It works on

Fig. 9-43. Portable electric drill and chuck key.

Table 9-2
Electric-Drill Sizes and Speeds

Drill Size	Speeds (rpm)
1/4"	to 2000 - 2450 - 5000
5/16"	to 1000
3/8"	to 750 - 1000
1/2"	to 450 - 750
5/8"	to 300
3/4"	to 250
1"	to 200 (This drill has a #3 taper sleeve for drills up to 1" in diameter.)

the principle of the inclined plane, wedging the jaws on the drill shank.

5. The **handle,** made of aluminum or plastic, is designed to give maximum holding power for each drill according to its size. A pistol grip is part of the housing design and a side handle, made of plastic or of a solid rod, is used to guide the drill and to over-come torque. A D-shaped handle is used on large drills.

6. The **trigger switch** is the starting control. It is constructed into the handle for on-off control.

7. Some drills have a **variable-speed unit** incorporated into the trigger-switch unit. The variable-speed unit permits speeds of between 0 and 2250 rpm.

Maintenance

Jaws should be cleaned and oiled for trouble-free operation. Conductor cords should be handled with care so as not to cause wear or breaks in the cable.

Portable electric drills should be both used and stored in a dry place.

Market Analysis

Capacity

The maximum opening of the chuck indicates the size of the electric drill. Electric drills of the following sizes operate in the speed ranges shown in Table 9-2.

Attachments

1. **Chuck.** A chuck is used to increase the capacity of a drill from 1/4" to 1/2".
2. **Friction clutch.** A friction clutch may be added for the purpose of driving screws.
3. **Flexible unit.** A flexible unit is used for drilling in close quarters and at angles.
4. **Drill stand.** The portable drill may be mounted on a drill stand, enabling it to be used as a drill press. See Fig. 9-44.
5. **Drill fixture.** A drill fixture can be attached to the portable drill, making it possible to drill holes at 90° or at predetermined angles.
6. **Offset right-angle attachment.** This attachment is used for drilling holes in close quarters. See Fig. 9-45.
7. Other attachments are available that equip the drill to be used as a grinder, a buffer, a polisher, a jigsaw, a circular saw, a plane, a lathe, or a sander.

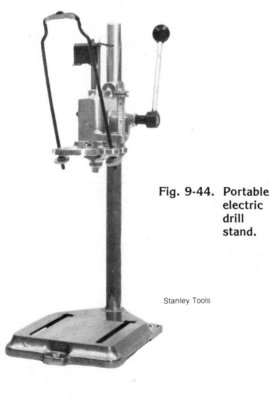

Fig. 9-44. Portable electric drill stand.

Stanley Tools

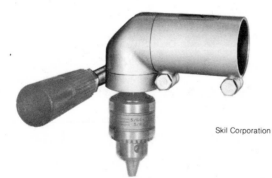

Skil Corporation

Fig. 9-45. Right-angle attachment may be used to drill in hard-to-reach places.

Drilling a Hole

Topic 73.

Classification

Driving an edged cutting tool in a circular motion

Procedure

Holes less than 1/4" are usually drilled with a twist drill. This twist drill is driven with a hand drill, a breast drill, a portable electric drill, or a drill press.

1. Using intersecting lines, locate the center of the hole. Score the exact center with a center punch or an awl, depending upon the hardness of the material.
2. Select the drill bit and secure it in the chuck.
3. Place the drill on the center point. Position the drill in such a way that the hole will be drilled at the desired angle to the work surface.
4. Operate the drill in a clockwise direction, applying light pressure to the handle. Operating the drill in this direction will guide the drill downward as the hole is being cut.
5. Check to see that the drill is square with the work, continuing to drill until the desired depth has been reached. If the hole is to go completely through the board, relieve pressure as you near the bottom so that the drill will not break through the bottom surface.

6. To remove the drill, continue operating the drill as you pull up on the handle. As you do this, make sure you do not reverse the direction of the drill's rotation, as this will sometimes cause the jaws of the chuck to open.
7. If a drill tends to wander from the starting point, tip the drill slightly until the center is reached. Then, set the drill at a right angle to the surface and continue drilling the hole.

Fig. 9-47. Drilling a hole with a portable electric drill.

Stanley Tools

Fig. 9-48. Hand-held drill guide, used to keep drill straight while hole is being drilled.

Fig. 9-46. Drilling a hole with a hand drill.

Standards and Results

- Holes should have clean-cut surfaces and sides.
- The hole should be started on the exact center point and at the desired angle to the surface.

- Care should be taken not to drill into the bench top.

Safety Considerations
- Wear safety glasses.
- Observe all safety practices pertaining to the particular tool or machine you are using.

Topic 74.

Drill Press — Floor and Bench Models

Classification

Power-driven rotary driving tool

Application

Principle of Operation

The **drill press** provides the rotary power for driving drills, bits, and plug cutters. It also provides power for many auxiliary attachments, such as mortise chisels, grinding wheels, and shaper cutters. The vertical power is applied through the feed wheel or lever (wheel and axle) to a pinion gear, which engages a rack on the quill (an inclined plane). The speed of the drill press may vary from 300 to 7000 rpm. Speed is controlled by shifting the drive belt on a set of cone pulleys. These cone pulleys operate on the principle of the wheel and axle. See Fig. 9-50. Some drills have a variable-speed unit, which regulates the speed, Fig. 9-51.

Kinds and Uses

The drill press is used for rotating cutting bits and drills and for controlling the depth and angle of holes. When used in combination with various attachments, it can substitute as a sander, a planer, a shaper, a router, or a mortiser.

School shops usually have single-spindle drill presses, with table sizes ranging from 10″ × 10″ to 11″ × 16″. Industrial drills often have multiple spindles, Fig. 9-54.

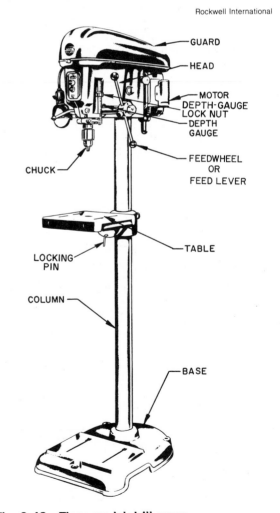

Rockwell International

GUARD
HEAD
MOTOR
DEPTH-GAUGE LOCK NUT
DEPTH GAUGE
FEEDWHEEL OR FEED LEVER
CHUCK
TABLE
LOCKING PIN
COLUMN
BASE

Fig. 9-49. Floor-model drill press.

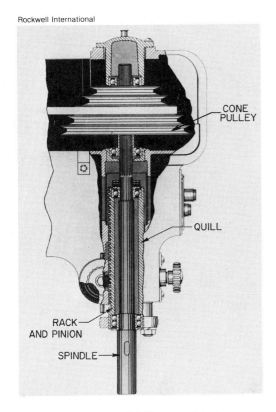

Rockwell International

Fig. 9-50. Cutaway of drill-press head.

4. The machined-steel **chuck** (three-jaw) grips bits and drills securely, and attaches the cutter to the driving spindle. The chuck is tightened with a chuck wrench or a key.
5. The **feed lever** or **feed wheel,** made of steel or cast iron, raises or lowers the spindle during drilling. See Fig. 9-49.
6. The **quill,** made of machined cast steel, permits vertical motion without interfering with the rotary drive. See Fig. 9-50.
7. The **depth gauge** indicates (or limits) the travel of the spindle.
8. The cast-iron **head** houses the pulleys, the bearings, the spindle, and the quill.
9. The **motor** provides the power.
10. The **V-belt,** made of fiber composition and rubber, transmits the power.
11. The cast-iron or pressed-steel **guards** protect the operator from the belt.
12. A steel **feed-wheel spring** returns the spindle to its original position.
13. The **spindle lock** holds the spindle at any desired position.
14. The cast-aluminum **cone pulley** transmits the power and regulates the speed. See Fig. 9-50.

Rockwell International

Fig. 9-51. Variable-speed unit on drill press.

Principal Parts and Function of Each

1. A cast-iron **base** supports the machine.
2. The **column,** made of machined steel, holds the table, head, and motor.
3. The cast-iron **table** holds the work. The table is adjustable for height. Some tables may be tilted to angles other than 90°.

OSHA Regulations

Boring Machines

1. Only safety-bit chucks that have no projecting screws shall be used.
2. If the machine is equipped with an operating treadle, the treadle shall be covered by an inverted-U-shaped metal guard. This guard shall be fastened to the floor and shall be of adequate size to prevent accidental tripping.

Maintenance

Some drill presses require periodic greasing, while others have sealed bearings. Whenever a drill press is to be left idle for a period of time, all machined parts should first be coated with a film of oil.

Market Analysis

Capacity

The capacity of the drill press is determined by the distance from the center of the chuck to the column. For instance, a 17" drill press will drill a hole in the center of a workpiece 17" in diameter.

Drill presses generally range in sizes from 11" to 20". The vertical distance is determined by the length of the column and by the travel of the spindle. See Fig. 9-50.

Attachments

1. **Mortising attachment.** This attachment is used for cutting mortises, Fig. 9-52.
2. **Rotary planer.** The rotary planer is used for surfacing stock, Fig. 9-53.
3. **Footfeed.** The footfeed enables the operator to use both hands for production.
4. **Shaper attachment.** The shaper attachment is used for cutting moldings. See Fig. 9-64.
5. **Router attachment.** This attachment is used for performing routing operations. See Fig. 9-65.

Barron Tool Co., Inc.

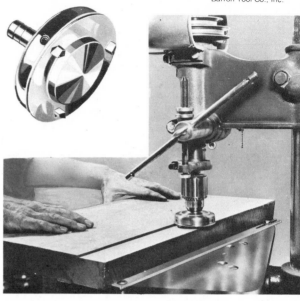

Fig. 9-53. Using a planer attachment on the drill press.

6. **Sanding drums** and **sanding disks.** These attachments are used for sanding irregular curves. See Fig. 9-66.
7. **Slow-speed attachment.** This attachment is used on large drill presses for drilling large-diameter holes.

Rockwell International

Fig. 9-52. Mortising attachment for the drill press.

Heywood-Wakefield Co.

Fig. 9-54. Multiple-spindle drill.
Note the fixture rigged to guide the chair seat into position. Hold the chair seat firmly while holes are bored (five at a time) for spindles.

Using the Drill Press

Topic 75.

Classification

Drilling, boring, mortising, routing, shaping, sanding

Procedure

Inserting the Drill

1. Select a round-shank drill of the correct size for the hole to be cut.
2. Open the chuck. The opening must be slightly larger than the diameter of the drill shank. (Turn the sleeve counterclockwise.)
3. Insert the drill in the chuck, making sure that the shank is centered between the three jaws. Tighten the chuck with the key.
4. Remove the key from the chuck before making any further adjustments.
5. Some large drill presses have tapered sleeves, which will receive only a tapered-shank drill or a tapered chuck. These are held in place by friction and pressure and are removed by insertion of a tapered drift into a slot in the spindle above the shank.

Adjusting the Table

1. Raise or lower the table to the proper height by loosening the table clamp at the column. Care should be taken that the table does not drop. Some tables are adjusted with a hand-wheel.
2. The distance the table should extend below the point of the drill is as follows: This distance should be equal to the combined length of the drill and chuck plus the thickness of the stock to be drilled. This distance should also include the thickness of the stock being used as a table pad.
3. The center or clearance hole on the table should line up with the center of the drill bit.
4. Some drill-press tables may be tilted at an angle on either side of the horizontal. Pins are used to lock the table at predetermined angles.

Adjusting the Spindle Travel Depth Gauge

1. Holes that are to be bored to a specific depth, as in stop boring, can be measured and regulated by the spindle-travel depth gauge.
2. To determine the proper adjustment, mark the desired depth on the stock to be drilled and position the stock next to the drill. Lower the spindle until the drill reaches the depth mark, then adjust the lock nuts.
3. Drill presses that have a calibrated depth gauge may be easily adjusted. This is done by lowering the spindle until the tip of the drill touches the surface of the stock to be drilled. Using this as a reference point, the lock nuts are adjusted for the proper depth using the calibrated scale.

Selecting Proper Speed for Drill Size

1. Adjust the belt to the spindle speed that is correct for the size drill to be used and for the material that is to be bored. A 1725-rpm motor will give spindle speeds of 600, 1250, 2440, and 5000 rpm. In general, large-

Fig. 9-55. **Using a V-block to hold the cylinder for drilling. Note that entire setup is clamped to table.**

diameter drills are used at low speeds; very fine drills are run at high speeds. The hardness of the stock to be drilled is also a factor to be considered in the selection of the correct speed. Generally speaking, the harder the material, the slower the speed.

Securing Stock to the Table

1. When drilling small holes in a long piece of stock, you may use your hand to hold the stock firmly against the table.
2. Short stock must be held in a drill-press vise that has been fastened to the table. An alternative procedure is to clamp the work in position on the table.

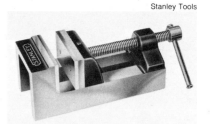

Fig. 9-58. Drill-press vise.

Fig. 9-59. The tilting table of the drill press may be adjusted to drill holes at angles other than 90° to the surface of the stock.

Fig. 9-56. Drilling a hole in an irregularly shaped piece. Note use of clamps.

Fig. 9-57. Boring a dowel hole in the end of an apron — table is rotated. Note use of clamp and fence.

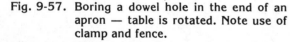

3. Round stock may be held in the drill-press vise or in a V-block, Fig. 9-55.
4. It may be necessary to use a jig to secure irregular stock in the proper position, Figs. 9-56 and 9-57.

Drilling a Hole

1. Make an indentation at the exact center. Start the drill into this indentation.
2. Apply a constant feed so that the shavings will be carried out of the hole and the drill will operate efficiently. Too slow a feed will cause friction and overheat the drill, and too fast a feed may cause excessive pressure, which could break the drill or tear the stock.
3. When doing through boring, release pressure on the feed as you approach the opposite surface.
4. When you are making deep holes, you may find it necessary to withdraw the drill from

Millers Falls Co.

Fig. 9-60. Hole saw.

Stanley Tools

Fig. 9-61. Circle cutter.

the hole several times in order to clean the cuttings from the flutes.

5. When drilling a series of parallel holes, use a fence as a guide.

6. Large holes may be cut with a hole saw or a circle cutter. See Figs. 9-60 and 9-61.

Using the Mortising Attachment

1. Most attachments require a special spindle to accommodate the bit and chisel. The chisel is fastened to an extension of the quill. See Fig. 9-62.

2. Select the proper size bit and chisel and insert them in their respective holders. Make sure that the bit projects 1/8″ below the chisel.

3. Mount the fence and the hold-down fingers on the table so that the work is in line with the sides of the chisel.

4. Adjust the table to the desired height.

5. Adjust the spindle-travel depth gauge to the correct mortise depth.

6. Select the speed that is correct for the size of bit being used. (Normally, a slower speed is used than that used for regular boring.) The larger the hole, the slower the speed.

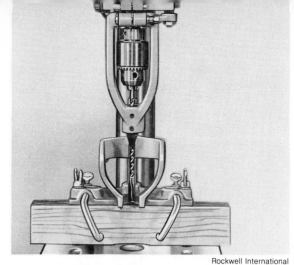

Rockwell International

Fig. 9-62. Mortising attachment ready for use.

HOLD DOWN FINGERS

FENCE

Fig. 9-63. Cutting a mortise in the end of a pedestal, using the mortising attachment.

7. Start the cuts at the end of the mortise and continue making parallel cuts until all waste material has been removed. If the mortise is deep, the first cut may be made to only about half the required depth. Next to the first cut, make a full cut. Then, bore the first cut to full depth.

Using the Shaper Attachment

1. Insert the special spindle or adapter used to hold the shaper cutters. A regular chuck should not be used for this operation.

2. Select the shaper cutter that is correct for the shape to be cut and select the collar of the correct diameter to control the depth of cut. Fasten these in place on the spindle adapter. Lock the spindle in position.

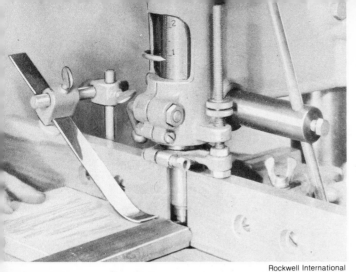

Fig. 9-64. Using a shaper attachment on the drill press.

Fig. 9-66. Using a sanding attachment on the drill press. The chuck has been secured with a cap screw.

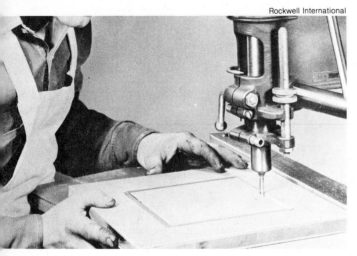

Fig. 9-65. Using a router attachment on the drill press.

3. If a collar is not to be used, fasten the shaper fence in the desired position on the table. This is done to produce the depth of cut that is correct in relation to the vertical axis of the cutter.
4. Raise the table to the desired height and lock it in this position.
5. Adjust the spring-tension guides to hold the work against both the fence and the table.
6. Adjust the speed to 5000 rpm.
7. Using a scrap piece of stock, make a trial cut. Feed the work slowly into the cutter from the left side of the table. See Fig. 9-64.
8. If a deep cut is required, it is sometimes necessary to make several light cuts to prevent splintering. When you are cutting on all four sides of a board, shape the end grain before the edges.

Using the Router Attachment

1. Select the router bit and insert it in the special spindle adapter.
2. Lock the table at the desired height.
3. Locate the special fence in position or clamp scrap stock, straightedges, or guides on the table.
4. Set the drill press at the highest possible speed (5000 rpm).
5. If a full-length cut is to be made, lock the spindle at the desired cutter depth. Make several light cuts to remove the material in the groove.
6. Feed the work from the left side of the table. If a stop cut is to be made, use stop blocks or make marks in the face of the work to indicate the limit of the length of travel. See Fig. 9-65.

Using a Sanding Drum

1. Secure the sanding drum in the special chuck.
2. Secure a wood table plate on the drill-press table. If the drum has a thrust bearing on the bottom end, this should fit into a hole in the wood plate.
3. Adjust the table to the proper height and lock it in this position.
4. Lock the spindle at the desired position.
5. Adjust the speed to about 1200 rpm.
6. Hold the work flat on the table and, using light pressure, begin sanding. Be sure to maintain even pressure and steady movement throughout the sanding operation. See Fig. 9-66.

Standards and Results

- Holes and cuts should have clean-cut surfaces and sides and should be of proper size.
- Holes and cuts should be in correct position and should be of the desired angle.
- Drill bits should not become overheated.

Safety Considerations

- Wear safety glasses when using the drill press.
- Insert only round-shank drills in a three-jaw chuck and round, tapered-shank drills in a tapered-shank spindle.
- Change belt speeds only while the machine is stopped.
- Use the correct speed for each operation.
- Protect the table with a table board.
- Hold the table securely while you are making table adjustments.
- When using the drill press as a mortiser, shaper, router, or sander, use a fence or fixtures to guide the work in the correct position.

Vertical Hollow-Chisel Mortiser

Topic 76.

Classification

Power-driven, rotary cutting tool within a hollow square chisel

Application

Principle of Operation

The cutting action is a combination of that of the screwless auger bit and the chisel. Machine principles used are those of the wedge, the inclined plane, and the lever.

Kinds and Uses

The **hollow-chisel mortiser** is used to cut the mortise portion of mortise-and-tenon joints. It is used principally for the production mortising done in furniture factories and in sash-and-door plants. Numerous mortiser styles and sizes are available to meet the varied production requirements. See Figs. 9-67 and 9-68.

Principal Parts and Function of Each

1. An electric **motor** provides the power.
2. The **table** and **fence** are made of machined cast iron. They are used in conjunction to support and align the stock.
3. The **frame,** made of steel, holds the motor and table.

4. The **handwheels,** made of machined cast iron, are used to make height and tilt adjustments to the table.

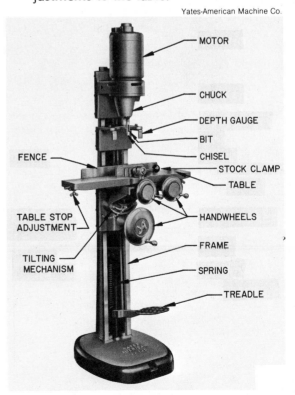

Yates-American Machine Co.

Fig. 9-67. Hollow-chisel mortiser.

5. A high-carbon-steel **bit** bores a hole and carries the shavings through the hollow chisel.
6. The **chuck,** made of machined steel, holds the bit.

Powermatic Houdaille, Inc.

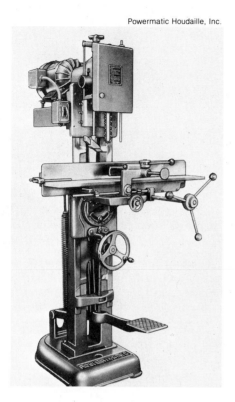

Fig. 9-68. The chain mortiser is a variation of the hollow-chisel mortiser. It uses a chain-type saw to cut the mortise.

Greenlee Tool Co.

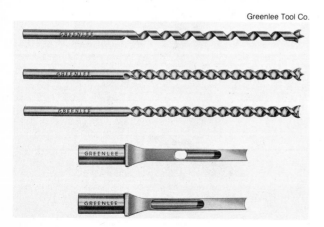

Fig. 9-69. Hollow chisels and bits.

7. Adjustable **table stops,** made of machined steel, regulate the travel of the table to the right and left.
8. The **treadle,** made either of steel or of cast iron, lowers the chisel and the auger.
9. The **spring,** made of spring steel, returns the treadle to the "up" position.
10. The **tilting mechanism,** made of machined cast iron, is used to tilt the table 45° to the right or left.
11. The **depth gauge,** made of steel, regulates the depth of cut.
12. The **chisel,** made of high-carbon steel, trims the corners of the hole, producing a square opening, Fig. 9-69.
13. The **chisel holder** is made of machined cast iron.
14. The **blower** is made of steel and has a cast-iron casing. This part removes waste material from the cut.

OSHA Regulations

Mortising Machines

1. Only safety-bit chucks that have no projecting set screws shall be used.
2. The top of the cutting chain and driving mechanism shall be enclosed.
3. Each operating treadle shall be covered by an inverted-U-shaped metal guard. This guard shall be fastened to the floor and shall be of adequate size to prevent accidental tripping.

Maintenance

1. Unless bearings are the sealed type, they must be lubricated.
2. When a mortiser is to be left unused for a long period of time, all machined parts should first be covered with a thin coat of oil.
3. Mortising bits and chisels should be kept sharp. Sharpening should be done only by an experienced person.

Market Analysis

Capacity

The capacity of a mortiser is determined by the following: (a) The distance from the end of the chisel (at its highest point) to the surface of the table (in its lowest position). (b) The distance between the chisel's center line and the fence. (c) The range of chisel sizes that can be accommodated. (d) The vertical travel of the chisel.

Matched bits and chisels are available in the following sizes: 1/4", 5/16", 3/8", 7/16", 1/2", 9/16", 5/8", 11/16", 3/4", 13/16", 7/8", and 1".

Attachments

A **bit guide** and a **spindle extension** can be used to convert the machine into a drill press.

Using the Hollow-Chisel Mortiser

Topic 77.

Classification

Driving a rotary cutting tool within a hollow square chisel to produce a square hole

Procedure

1. Select the proper size bit and chisel for the job. (The mortise width should be one-third to one-half the thickness of the thinner piece.)
2. Insert the bit in the chuck and the chisel in the holder. The bit should protrude below the chisel about 1/8" so that the bit will bore a round hole before the chisel cuts a square hole. This prevents overheating and exertion of excessive pressure on the chisel.
3. Adjust the table height to produce a mortise about 1/8" deeper than the length of tenon.
4. Secure the workpiece with the table clamp, Fig. 9-70.
5. Adjust the table either away from or toward the frame so that the mortise will be cut in the proper position.
6. Adjust the stops so that each mortise will be the correct length.

Fig. 9-70. Adjust the table height so that the mortise will be cut 1/8" below the length of the tenon.

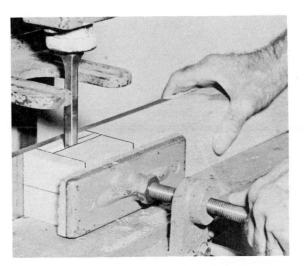

Fig. 9-71. When cutting each side of the mortise, cut only to about half the finished depth.

Fig. 9-72. Cutting a mortise.
The numbered areas show the sequence and depth of the cuts required in starting a mortise. After these cuts are made, the center portion is hollowed out.

7. Start the cuts at one end of the mortise, Fig. 9-71. The first cut should be made only about 3/8″ to 1/2″ deep, so that the workpiece will not be raised as the chisel is withdrawn from the stock. See **1,** Fig. 9-72. Make the second cut adjacent to the first cut. This cut should be deeper. See **2,** Fig. 9-72. Return to the first position and make a full-depth cut. See **3,** Fig. 9-72.

8. Move the table so that the opposite end of the mortise will be cut in the same manner. This will ensure a straight cut at each end of the mortise. See Fig. 9-72.

9. Continue by mortising out the stock between the two end cuts.

Standards and Results

- The mortise should be in the proper location and should be cut to the proper length and depth.

Safety Considerations

- Wear safety glasses when using the mortiser.
- Clamp the stock securely to the table.
- Keep your fingers out from underneath the chisel and bit.

The Garrett Wade Company

SECTION TEN.

Shaping Circular Forms on the Lathe

Topic 78.

Wood Turning

Oliver Machinery Company

Fig. 10-1. Turning area in a school shop.

Either plastic guards, mounted on the lathe, or full-face shields should be used in addition to safety glasses when operating a lathe.

Wood turning is the process of shaping stock into cylinders, disks, and other round and out-of-round forms. This turning is achieved in a lathe (or turning machine). The lathe is a power-driven spindle to which stock may be attached and thereby be given rotary motion.

When a sharpened tool enters the path of the stock's rotation, it is brought into contact with the high points of the wood, producing the arc of a circle on those points. Further lengthening of these arcs occurs as the tool advances. This process continues until the circumference of a circle is formed.

The repetition of this procedure to some predetermined distance along the axis of the rotating stock will increase the length of the cylinder to that dimension. The profile of the turning is determined by (a) the distance from the axis to the cutter, (b) the shape of the tool, and (c) the angle, motion, and sweep of the tool as it is advanced into the work.

Most turnings are **concentric.** That is, the turned piece has one common axis. It is possible, however, to turn eccentric pieces on the lathe. An **eccentric** turning is one on which the

John Lindbeck

Fig. 10-2. Objects turned from wood.

stock is turned along two or more axes. This may be done on special machines (in industry) or on a small lathe. On a small lathe, this operation is done by changing the turning axis at each end of the piece.

Lathes can also be set up to turn duplicate parts. Industrial lathes are capable of producing an unlimited number of identical parts used in the mass production of many different products. School lathes can be set up to turn duplicate parts by adding a duplicating attachment. Duplicate parts can be made without the benefit of duplicating attachments, but this requires constant testing and measuring and is therefore quite time-consuming.

Speed is an important factor in turning. One of the factors governing the selection of the speed is the balance of the stock. Once the stock is in balance, the speed of the lathe should be regulated in accordance with the diameter, length, and hardness of the stock that is to be turned. Because peripheral (rim) speed is a factor in cutting, small-diameter pieces may be turned at higher spindle speeds than are recommended for pieces of large diameter. The beginning cuts made in soft wood may be made at higher speeds than would ordinarily be used with hard wood, because soft wood gives less resistance to the cutting action.

Hillerich & Bradsby Co.

Fig. 10-3. **Industrial turnings — baseball bat on semi-automatic lathe.**

Olin-Mathieson Chemical Corp.

Fig. 10-4. **Industrial turnings — gunstocks.**
This automatic stock-carving machine, known as a "Salstrom," performs a carving operation on eight gunstocks at one time.

Wood Lathe

Topic 79.

Classification

Powered rotary driving tool

Application

Principle of Operation

A **lathe** is a machine on which a faceplate or a spur center is attached to a motor-driven spindle that revolves at adjustable speeds. The work is mounted on the faceplate or between centers. Shaping takes place as the work turns against chisels or special cutters. These chisels or cutters cut on the principle of the cutting wedge. The speed of the belt-driven lathe is maintained by step pulleys or by a variable-speed mechanism. When the driving pulley is smaller than the driven pulley, the speed is reduced. When the driven pulley is smaller than the driving pulley, the speed is increased. Speeds may be regulated between 300 and 3600 rpm. See Fig. 10-5.

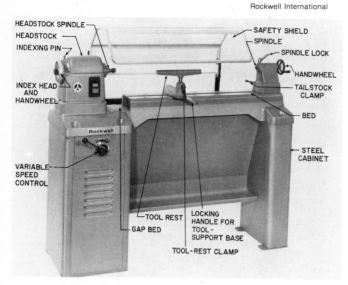

Rockwell International

HEADSTOCK SPINDLE
HEADSTOCK
INDEXING PIN

SAFETY SHIELD
SPINDLE
SPINDLE LOCK
HANDWHEEL

INDEX HEAD
AND
HANDWHEEL

TAILSTOCK
CLAMP

BED

Rockwell

STEEL
CABINET

VARIABLE-
SPEED
CONTROL

TOOL REST
GAP BED

LOCKING
HANDLE FOR
TOOL-
SUPPORT BASE

TOOL-REST CLAMP

Fig. 10-5.   Variable-speed gap-bed wood lathe.

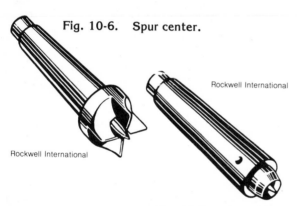

Fig. 10-6.   Spur center.

Rockwell International

Rockwell International

Fig. 10-7.   Cup center.

Rockwell International

Fig. 10-8.   Ball-bearing dead centers.

Kinds and Uses

The lathe is used to rotate stock for shaping, sanding, or polishing operations. It is also used as a holding jig for fluting, reeding, and drilling holes.

Some lathes are made with a gap bed, which provides a greater swing (distance from the center to the bed), permitting larger faceplate turnings. Fig. 10-5.

Principal Parts and Function of Each

1. The **headstock,** which contains the driving mechanism, is made of cast iron and has two sealed bearings. If the lathe is a direct drive, the motor is part of the headstock. If it is belt-driven, the pulleys are located in the headstock. The driving-mechanism spindle is hollow and extends beyond the headstock at both ends. The inboard end has a righthand thread for attaching a faceplate for regular turning. The outboard end has a lefthand thread for attaching a faceplate for outside turning of diameters larger than the swing of the lathe will accommodate.

2. The **live center** or **spur center** is made of unhardened tool steel. It has a tapered shank so that it will fit the spindle. The spur center supports the left end of the stock as turning is being done between centers, Fig. 10-6. It is called the live center because it turns with the headstock spindle and drives the work.

3. The cast-iron **tailstock** holds the dead center.

4. The hardened-tool-steel **dead center** serves as a pivot, as it does not move. It supports the workpiece on the right side when turning is being done between centers. There are two types of dead centers: cup-center and cone-center. Ball-bearing centers are also available. These allow the cup or cone to rotate with the workpiece, thus reducing friction. Dead centers have a tapered shank to fit the spindle. See Figs. 10-7 and 10-8.

5. The **tool rest,** made of machined cast iron, provides support for the lathe tool.

6. The cast-iron **bed** supports the headstock, tailstock, and tool-rest holder.

7. The cast-iron **tailstock handwheel** increases or decreases the distance of the protrusion of the dead center from the tailstock.

Rockwell International

Fig. 10-9.   Index head.

8. The **tailstock clamp** secures the tailstock to the bed.
9. The **alignment screw** on the tailstock adjusts the center turning.
10. The **tool-rest holder** secures the tool post to the bed.
11. The **tool-rest clamp** secures the tool rest at the desired height.
12. The adjustable **index head** locks the spindle for reeding or fluting operations. See Fig. 10-9.
13. The **safety shield** mounts on the lathe and helps protect the operator from flying debris.
14. The **motor** provides the power.
15. The **belt** transmits the power.

OSHA Regulations

Lathes

1. Cutting areas on wood-turning lathes shall be covered as completely as possible with a hood or shield. This hood or shield should be hinged to the machine so that it can be moved back for making adjustments.
2. Lathes that are used for turning long pieces of stock held only between the two centers shall be equipped with long, curved guards. These guards shall extend over the top of the lathe so that they will be able to prevent loose workpieces from being thrown out of the machine.

Maintenance

1. The spurs and points of live centers should be kept sharp.
2. The working edge of the tool rest should be kept smooth. Recondition this edge by draw filing.
3. The original shape of the cup center should be maintained. A cone center should be ground only by an experienced person.
4. Bearings should be kept lubricated.
5. Before a lathe is left unused for long periods, all machined surfaces should first be coated with a protective film of oil or wax.
6. The tailstock may vibrate out of line. If it does, it will need adjusting.
7. Belts may need adjusting or replacing.
8. Wood dust should be blown from the motor periodically.

Market Analysis

Capacity

The capacity of a lathe is determined by two factors: (1) the maximum length of stock that can be turned between the centers and (2) the distance from the live center to the bed of the lathe. This distance is called **swing.**

These are the usual lathe capacities:

9" swing — 30" between centers.
11" swing — 36" between centers.
12" swing — 36" between centers.
14" swing — 36" between centers.

Larger lathes are not usually found in school shops, but there are lathes that measure as much as 6' between centers.

Rockwell International

Fig. 10-10. Sanding disk.

Attachments

1. **Sanding disk.** This attachment fastens onto the faceplate and is used for sanding convex curves on the edges of stock, Fig. 10-10.
2. **Sanding drum or cylinder.** This is mounted between the centers and is used for sanding concave curves on the edges of stock, Fig. 10-11.
3. **Faceplate.** The faceplate holds the stock during faceplate turning. The stock is secured with screws driven through the slots or holes in the faceplate. Faceplates are available with righthand threads (for inboard turning) or lefthand threads (for outboard turning). See Fig. 10-12.

4. **Screw center.** This attachment is used to turn knobs or to do small faceplate turnings, Fig. 10-13.
5. **Drill chuck.** The drill chuck has a tapered shank so that it will fit either the headstock spindle or the tailstock spindle. The drill chuck serves to hold a drill being used to drill holes in turnings.
6. **Four-jaw chuck.** This chuck is used, in place of the live center, for holding square or irregularly shaped pieces. See Fig. 10-15.
7. **Screw** or **arbor.** This is used to attach a grinding wheel or buffing wheel, Fig. 10-16.
8. **Steady rest.** The steady rest provides support on long between-center turnings, Fig. 10-17.
9. **Right-angle tool rest.** This attachment makes it possible to turn both the edge and the face on the faceplate without changing the setup of the tool-rest holder, Fig. 10-18.

Fig. 10-11. Sanding drum attachment.

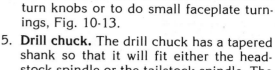

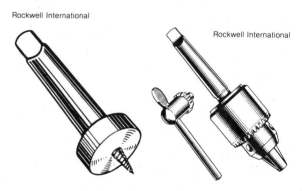

Fig. 10-13. Screw-point face-plate.

Fig. 10-14. Jacobs chuck.

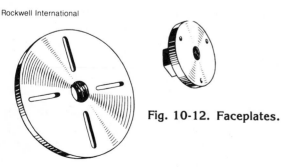

Fig. 10-12. Faceplates.

Fig. 10-15. Four-jaw chuck for holding square or irregularly shaped pieces.

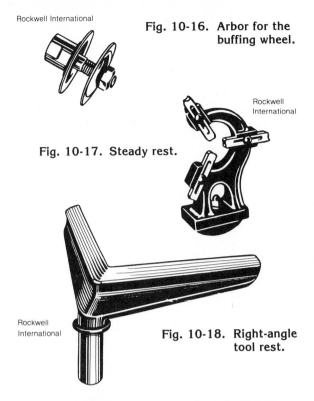

Fig. 10-16. Arbor for the buffing wheel.

Fig. 10-17. Steady rest.

Fig. 10-18. Right-angle tool rest.

Fig. 10-19. A large faceplate turning can be mounted to the outboard position of the lathe. A floor-supported tool rest is used to support the cutting tool.

Fig. 10-20. Double-post tool rest.

Fig. 10-21. Turning duplicator.

Fig. 10-22. Model of a bow lathe.

The most primitive lathe, the bow lathe, was in fact not a lathe at all. It was an arrangement by which one or two loops of a bow string were wrapped around a piece of round stock held between two pivot points.

Moving the bow back and forth across the stock and at a right angle to it caused the stock to rotate. This rotation moved alternately clockwise and counterclockwise. The cutting was done as the bow was drawn toward the operator. The worker had to operate the bow with one hand and hold the cutting tool with the other.

10. **Floor stand.** The floor stand holds the tool rest for outside faceplate turning. See Fig. 10-19.

11. **Double-post tool rest.** This is used for long-spindle turning, Fig. 10-20.

12. **Duplicating attachment.** This attachment supports a sample turning or a template so that identical turnings can be made, Fig. 10-21. A cutting tool, much like one used for metal turning, is held in a sliding

tool rest. This tool rest moves along the length of the stock while moving in and out along the contour of the template. As the contour is followed, material is removed from the workpiece, reproducing the original pattern.

Old Sturbridge Village, Inc.

Fig. 10-23. Seventeenth-century Cape Cod foot-powered lathe.

Springfield Armory NHS

Fig. 10-24. The Blanchard stocking lathe, made by Thomas Blanchard in 1822, truly automated the manufacture of irregularly shaped wooded parts. The Blanchard lathe was used extensively in the making of gunstocks, which, until then, had had to be hand carved.

Topic 80.

Turning Chisels

Classification

Edge-cutting tools

Application

Principle of Operation

The outside, beveled wedge on **turning chisels** is a cutting wedge. The rotating motion of the lathe provides the driving force. The long handle of the tool provides the lever arm necessary to control the cutting edge. The speed of the turning sets up centrifugal force in the stock, and the turning chisel (cutting wedge), adjusted at the proper angle, serves to release the stock as it is revolved (forced) against it.

Kinds and Uses

The shape or type of turning chisel selected for work with the lathe is determined by the contour or design that is to be turned, as well as by the cutting method used.

There are two cutting methods that are related to the shape of turning chisels. These two methods are called **scraping** and **shearing**.

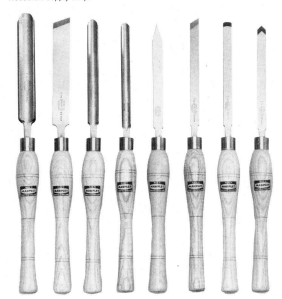

Fig. 10-25. Turning chisels.

Scraping is done with a tool sharpened to an angle of between 40° and 45°. In scraping, the bevel of the chisel faces down and the chisel is moved into the stock at right angles to the center line. (For procedure, see Topic 81, Step 12 under "Procedure.") A rough surface is produced as the scraping action tears the wood fibers. The squarenose chisel, roundnose chisel, diamond-point chisel, and parting tool are all designed specifically as scraping tools. However, scraping cuts can also be made with the turning gouge and the skew chisel.

Shearing is a cutting process done using turning gouges and skew chisels. Shearing differs from scraping in that the wood fibers are cut (rather than scraped) from the stock. This produces fine wood shavings. This cutting technique is more difficult to master than the scraping method but it results in a much smoother, finished surface. For shearing, the cutting edges of turning gouges and skew chisels are sharpened to an angle of 30° and then are brought into contact with the stock as described in Step 13 of "Procedure," Topic 81. Turning gouges and skew chisels will remain sharp much longer when used for shearing than when used for scraping.

1. The **turning gouge** is a turning chisel used in roughing out cylinders and in turning concave surfaces on spindles, Fig. 10-26. Its blade is concave-convex in cross section and has a rounded, beveled cutting edge. The cutting edge is rounded to prevent the tool from digging into the work being turned. The bevel, approximately 30°, aids in making scraping or shearing cuts. Turning gouges are commonly made in sizes of 3/8", 1/2", 3/4", and 1".

2. The **skew chisel** is a flat turning chisel used in smoothing cylinders, rounding edges, and in making V-cuts and shoulder cuts, Fig. 10-27. It can be used with either a shearing or a scraping action. The end of the skew forms a 60° to 70° profile, beveled on both sides to form a cutting angle of approximately 40°. (There are also righthand and lefthand skew chisels, beveled on one face only, which are scraping chisels used in pattern turning.) The common skewchisel sizes are 1/4", 1/2", and 1".

3. The **roundnose chisel** is a flat scraping chisel used in roughing and shaping concave surfaces, Fig. 10-28. The end is rounded and has a single bevel of about 30°. Roundnose chisels are available in 1/8", 1/4", 1/2" and 1" sizes.

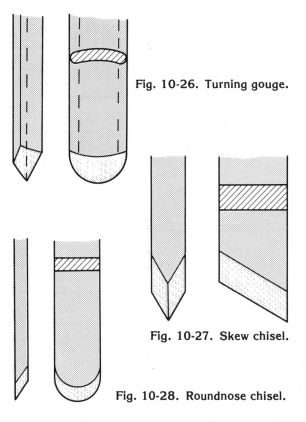

Fig. 10-26. Turning gouge.

Fig. 10-27. Skew chisel.

Fig. 10-28. Roundnose chisel.

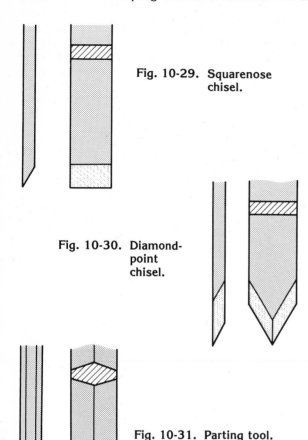

Fig. 10-29. Squarenose chisel.

Fig. 10-30. Diamond-point chisel.

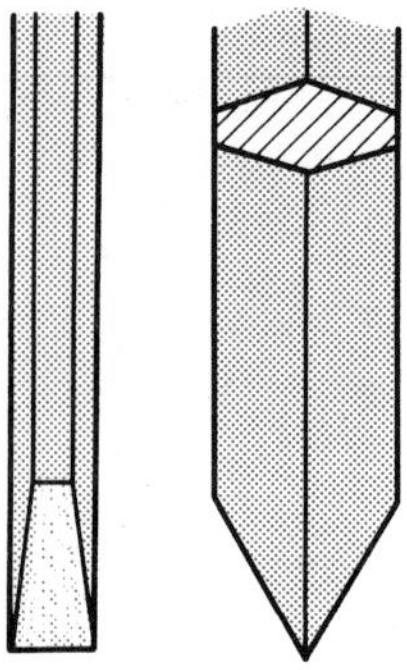

Fig. 10-31. Parting tool.

at an angle, from each edge to the center. This forms a flat, pointed cutting edge, which reduces binding and friction or heating during the cutting process. The common sizes of parting tools are 1/8″ and 3/16″.

Principal Parts and Function of Each

1. The **blade,** made of carbon tool steel, is the body of the tool.
2. The **bevel** on the blade forms the cutting wedge.
3. The **tang** (tapered end) fits into the handle.
4. The hardwood **handle,** 4″ to 9″ long is the means by which the tool is held and the cutting action is controlled and directed.
5. The brass **ferrule** reinforces the handle to protect against splitting.

Maintenance

Sharpening

The blade or cutting wedge should be reshaped when it becomes nicked or broken or when the bevel becomes too short. The bevel should be between two and two-and-a-half times the thickness of the blade. Turning chisels are dressed with a slipstone. See Section 19, "Sharpening" — Topic 191, "Grinding Edge Tools," and Topic 193, "Whetting or Honing a Cutting Tool."

Repairing

Damaged handles should be replaced.

Storing

Turning chisels should be stored individually in a rack or case in order to prevent the keen edge from becoming dull and to ensure safety. When the tool is to be left unused for a long period of time, the steel should be coated with a film of oil or wax to prevent rusting.

4. The **squarenose chisel** is a flat scraping chisel used to make flat, straight cuts, Fig. 10-29. It resembles a standard wood chisel in shape but has a thicker and longer blade. The end is square and has a single bevel of about 30°. Squarenose chisels are most commonly made in sizes of 1/2″ and 3/4″.
5. The **diamond-point chisel** is a flat scraping chisel used to make V-cuts or beads, Fig. 10-30. The pointed cutting edges are formed by grinding the sides to the desired angle at a bevel of 30°. The most common size for the diamond-point chisel is 1/2″.
6. The **parting tool** is a scraping chisel used to make deep, narrow cuts and depth cuts for sizing in shaping profiles, Fig. 10-31. The thickness of the blade is greater at the center than at the edges. The blade is ground,

Market Analysis

Attachments

A **woodturner's gauge** is available for use with the parting tool.

Spindle or Between-Center Turning

Topic 81.

Classification

Shaping stock that is revolving against a cutter

Procedure

1. After the stock has been selected, cut it to size. Include a waste allowance of 1" in length and 1/4" in diameter. Square the ends and find the center of each end by marking intersecting diagonal lines. Methods of locating centers are shown in Figs. 10-32 through 10-38.
2. The corners on pieces of stock 2" square or larger should be removed before the piece is placed in the lathe. The preferred methods of doing this are to use a plane, a spokeshave, a drawknife, or a jointer.
3. Select one end for the live center. Using a backsaw, cut this end on the lines to a depth of 1/8". On the other end, center punch at the point where the lines intersect. When using hard woods, a hole 1/8" in diameter and depth may be drilled at each center.
4. Slide the tailstock out of the way.
5. Remove the live center from the headstock. Hold the live center in your right hand. With your left hand, insert the drive-out rod through the headstock spindle and drive out the center. Next, use a wooden

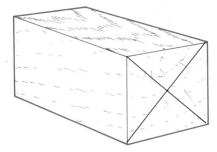

Fig. 10-32. Locating the center with diagonal lines.

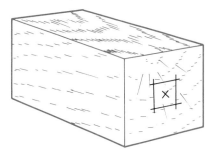

Fig. 10-34. Locating the center of a regular block, using lines drawn with dividers.

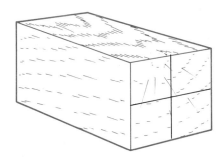

Fig. 10-33. Locating the center with lines drawn using a square or a marking gauge.

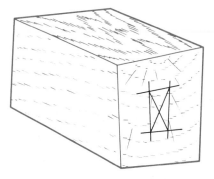

Fig. 10-35. Locating the center of irregular block, using lines drawn with dividers.

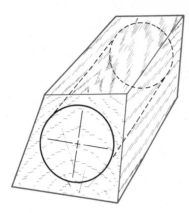

Fig. 10-36. Circle drawn on an uneven block, using compasses.

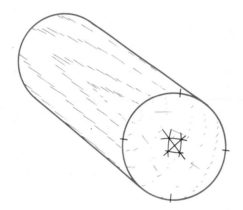

Fig. 10-37. Scribed arcs made to locate the center on a cylindrical piece.

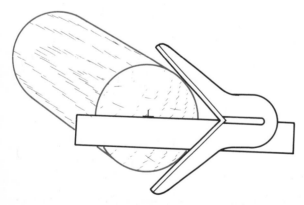

Fig. 10-38. Locating the center of a cylinder with a center head.

mallet to drive the live center into the wood so that the spurs enter the kerf made by the saw.

6. With the spur quite firmly imbedded in the stock, replace the live center in the spindle of the headstock.

7. Adjust the tailstock spindle so that it advances 1″ beyond the tailstock housing. Slide the tailstock until the point of the dead center enters the hole. Lock the tailstock in position. Turn the tailstock spindle-feed handle until the dead center is seated in the wood. Release the pressure slightly and apply a little wax, oil, or soap to the impression that has been made on the end of the wood by the dead center.

Turn the feed handle until the dead center is fairly tight in the original position. Then, back off until the stock turns freely. Lock the spindle in place.

8. Adjust the tool rest so that it is 1/8″ above the center of the stock. Lock in position. Rotate the stock by hand and adjust the tool rest so that it clears every corner of the stock by at least 1/8″ and is reasonably parallel to the stock. Lock the tool-rest holder in position. The tool rest should be maintained at a distance of no more than 3/8″ away from the work as stock decreases in diameter.

9. Assume a natural position. The feet should be spread slightly, one foot a little behind the other, and the weight should be evenly distributed.

10. Select a large gouge. Using your right hand, grasp the handle well out toward the end. Hold the blade in your left hand and guide it along the tool rest. Work out from the center. It is advisable to get the feel of this position before you start the lathe.

11. Start the lathe on the slow speed (600 rpm). If the lathe is a variable-speed model, the speed should be set while the machine is running and before the work-piece is mounted.

The diameter, length, and hardness of the stock will influence the speed of rotation. Large-diameter pieces should be turned and sanded at slow speeds. Stock 2″ to 3″ in diameter may be turned at higher speeds after the stock has been turned round. Soft woods are more apt to tear at slow speeds than are hard woods.

12. If a scraping cut is to be made, hold the gouge in a horizontal position, using the tip end of the tool to do the cutting, Fig. 10-40. This will produce a rough cut. To

avoid long splinters, make a series of cuts with the narrow gouge. Do this by placing the gouge at approximately 45° on the tool rest, with the tip over the work. Raise the handle to make a 1/4" cut. Repeat this about every two inches.

13. If a shearing cut is to be made, lower your right hand about 10°. Turn the gouge to make a slight angle toward the direction of the cut. Move the tool along the tool rest, taking a fine cut, Fig. 10-41. If the chisel is not held properly, the tool may catch, taking a "bite" or chunk out of the workpiece.

14. When the stock has been turned down and is in balance, the speed may be increased to 1200 rpm.

15. Finish turning with a wide skew chisel. A higher speed makes a smoother cut and is therefore used for finish turning.

Select a wide skew chisel. With your right hand, grasp the handle close to the end of the chisel, placing your left hand on the blade. The slope of the bevel should point in the direction of the cut you are going to make. The blade should be resting on the stock. With the bevel protruding beyond the stock, draw back on the tool until the center of the bevel is in contact with the stock. Adjust the tool by turning the blade to approximately 120° to the axis of the stock. Raise the tool handle until the cutting edge begins to cut. (A sharp tool will cut a shaving.) Raising the handle

Fig. 10-39. Spindle turning using the clear plastic guard.

Form-All Corporation

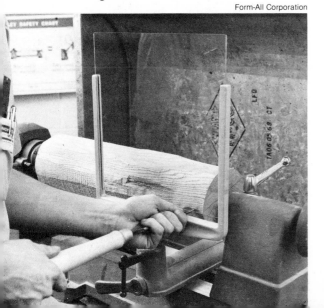

Fig. 10-40. Rough turning with a gouge, using a scraping cut.
Note the horizontal position of the tool, the placement of the fingers, and the manner in which the gouge cuts the wood being turned.

Fig. 10-41. Making a shearing cut with the gouge.
Note the angle of the cutting tool, the position of the fingers, and the shearing action of the gouge.

Fig. 10-42. Scraping with the skew chisel.
Observe how wood chips and dust are scraped off the stock, resulting in a rather rough turning. Scraping is a forced, tearing action, which rapidly wears away the cutting edge, thus necessitating frequent whetting of the chisel.

increases the depth of cut. (Beginners should not try to make a heavy cut.) Slide the tool along the tool rest, maintaining the proper angle. Reverse the tool and repeat the process until all stock has been turned to proper dimension. See Fig. 10-43.

Note: On long, thin spindle turning, a steady rest may be used to reduce vibration or chatter. See Fig. 10-17.

Making V-Cuts

1. Using a sharp pencil and a rule, lay out the center line and the width of the "V."
2. Place the edge of the skew on the tool rest. The heel should be down and the cutting edge should be on the center line of the "V," Fig. 10-44. Score the center line.
3. Slide the skew along the tool rest, about 1/8" from the center line, turning the skew chisel at a slight angle toward the center line. Cut into the center line. Do the same on the opposite side of the center line. Repeat the steps of this operation until the desired "V" is obtained.
4. If the scraping method is used, use a diamond-point chisel of the proper size, holding it in a horizontal position and at a right angle to the stock. Advance the chisel until the desired width and depth are obtained.

Fig. 10-43. Shearing with the skew chisel.
Shearing is accomplished by holding the face of the chisel's bevel edge flat against the stock. The cut is made from the center of the bevel. A sharp tool will pare off shavings, resulting in a smooth surface requiring very little sanding.

Fig. 10-44. Cutting a "V" with the heel of a skew chisel.
The size of the "V" is determined by the angle at which the skew is held.

Cutting Beads

1. With a sharp pencil and a rule, a template, or dividers, lay out the width of the bead. On a wide bead it is advisable to have a center line.
2. Set the calipers to the respective diameters of the crest and of the base of the bead.
3. To shape a bead, place the edge of the skew on the tool rest with the heel facing down and the cutting edge on a width line. Score the width line on each side of the bead.
4. From the width lines of the bead, move the skew chisel 1/8" along the tool rest, toward the center of the bead. As the heel is cutting, roll the skew chisel to the width line. Repeat this process on both sides until the desired bead is formed. See Figs. 10-45 and 10-46.

Fig. 10-45. Cutting beads with the skew chisel.
The bead is being shaped from the high point to the scored width lines.

Fig. 10-46. Scraping a large bead with the skew chisel.
   After depth cuts have been made on each side of the bead, the skew is held flat on the rest and is fed in from the high point to the width lines.

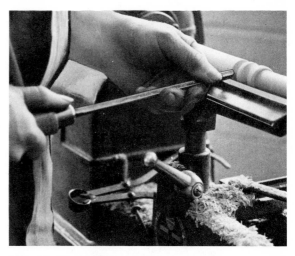

Fig. 10-48. Making shearing cut, using the small gouge.
   The turner who has mastered this method can produce accurate cuts with a minimum of tearing.

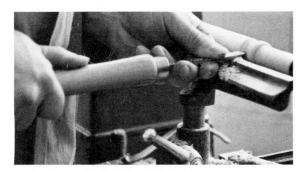

Fig. 10-47. Making a scraping cut with the round-nose chisel.
   Holding the chisel flat on the tool rest, pivot the handle to form the arc.

Fig. 10-49. Making a depth cut with the parting tool.
   Set the calipers to the desired diameter (make a small allowance for sanding). Test frequently as you cut to size with the parting tool.

Making Concave or Cove Cuts

1. With a sharp pencil and a rule or template, mark the center and width lines of the cove.
2. Set the caliper to 1/16″ greater than the desired diameter.
3. With the parting tool, cut to this dimension at the center line.
4. If the scraping method is used, take a roundnose chisel of the appropriate size and place it, in a horizontal position, bevel down on the tool rest. Sweeping the tool from side to side, cut to the desired shape and dimension, Fig. 10-47.
5. If the shearing method is used, place the gouge on its side on the tool rest. It should extend about 1/8″ from either side of the cut that has already been made by the parting tool. With a rolling motion, cut to the center. Continue this process until you have

obtained the desired shape and dimension. See Fig. 10-48.
6. If the concave cut is long and gradual (as the handle of a baseball bat), lay out cuts at every inch with a pencil and rule or a template.
   With a parting tool, cut to the desired depth at each mark, Fig. 10-49. Calipers should be set for each dimension. A woodturner's gauge may be attached to the parting tool after rough cutting. Rough off the

Fig. 10-50. Roughing out a long taper by shearing with the large gouge.
     Work from the larger diameter to the smaller.

Fig. 10-51. Sanding in the lathe.
     Sanding may be done by holding the paper either above or below the turning. Holding the paper below the turning (as shown) makes it easier to observe the progress of the sanding. Note: The tool rest is removed.

surplus stock with a turning gouge. Use a skew chisel to make either a scraping cut or shearing cut to the finished dimension.

Cutting a Long Taper

1. Lay out the length of the taper with a pencil and rule, dividers, or trammel points.
2. Set the calipers 1/16″ greater than the largest diameter and 1/16″ greater than the smallest diameter of the taper.
3. If a full-size drawing is not available, lay out the taper on paper to determine the correct dimensions of the taper at several points. At these intervals, cut the proper depth with a parting tool. Make certain that these cuts are made on the side of the line with the smaller diameter.

4. Rough off surplus stock with a turning gouge. See Fig. 10-50.
5. Set the tool rest parallel to the taper.
6. Using a skew chisel, make either a scraping cut or a shearing cut to the correct finished dimensions.
7. Check the taper with a straightedge.

Sanding

1. Remove the tool rest. See Fig. 10-51.
2. After a final scraping cut, use 50-, 60-, and 100-grit garnet paper. After a final shearing cut, very little sanding should be required, and then only with 100-grit abrasive.
3. For cylindrical sanding, hold a long piece of sandpaper between both hands and at right angles to the stock. Place your right hand over the work. Bear down evenly, moving the paper back and forth and lengthwise with the grain of the stock.
4. To sand beads, V-grooves, and coves, form the paper to fit a small section of the contour of the turning. Sand from beneath the piece so that you can observe the sanding operation as it progresses, Fig. 10-51.

Standards and Results

- Stock must be turned to the prescribed shape and dimension. Beads should be round, contours should be sharp, sides of "V's" should be straight, and shoulders should be flat.
- Surfaces must be smooth and free of sanding marks, defects, and stains.

Safety Considerations

- Wear eye-protective devices when operating the lathe.
- When selecting stock for turning, avoid stock that has loose knots, checks, and cross grain. Also avoid stock that is splintery or improperly glued.
- Be careful not to drop the live center when you are removing it from the headstock.
- Check to see that the stock is properly centered.
- Check the tailstock to see that it is locked in position. Secure the work firmly between the centers.
- Rotate the stock by hand in order to determine the clearance of the tool rest.

- Avoid wearing loose or dangling clothing.
- Maintain the tool rest at the proper height and distance from the work.
- Rough turning should be done only at a slow speed.
- Avoid making heavy cuts.
- Keep your hands off rough stock that is revolving.
- The turning chisel should always be held firmly and at the proper angle.

- Periodically check the heating, lubrication, and adjustment of the dead center.
- Tools should not be left on the bed of the lathe while the lathe is in operation.
- Tools should be kept sharp at all times.
- The tool rest should be removed before sanding is done.

Faceplate Turning on a Lathe

Topic 82.

Classification

Shaping stock that is revolving against a cutter

Procedure

In faceplate turning, the stock is mounted on a flat, metal plate that is attached to the headstock spindle of the lathe. As the plate revolves, the stock is shaped by scraping cuts. The tools used are: (a) the roundnose chisel (for concave cuts), (b) the skew chisel (for convex cuts), (c) the squarenose chisel (for straight cuts), (d) the diamond-point chisel (for V-cuts), and (e) the parting tool (for depth cuts).

1. On the band saw, cut a disk slightly larger in diameter and length than the required finished dimensions. Square stock should be made as nearly round as possible.
2. Select a faceplate that is smaller than the disk being turned.
3. If screw holes are undesirable in the bottom of the finished turning, or if there is a possibility of the turning tools striking the screws, a block of wood should be glued to the base of the work. In gluing, place a piece of heavy paper between the glued surfaces in order to make separation easier and to prevent damage to the finished turning.
4. Attach the stock to the faceplate. Select screws of adequate length and diameter to hold the work and still ensure that there is

no possibility of the turning tools striking the screws. The heads of the screws must be flush with the back surface of the faceplate. Make sure that the centers coincide. Small objects may be turned on a screw center. (A screw center is a faceplate that has one screw in the center.)

5. Remove the live center from the lathe and screw the faceplate to the spindle. For easier removal, it is advisable to place a piece of heavy paper between the shoulder of the spindle and the faceplate.
6. Adjust the tool rest so that it is slightly below the center and is clear of the turning.
7. Turn the stock one revolution to see that it clears the tool rest at every point.
8. Adjust the lathe to the proper speed. It is customary to use the slow speed (600 rpm), however, pieces 3″ or less in diameter may be turned at a speed of 1200 rpm.
9. In turning to diameter, you should assume a natural position, facing to the bed of the lathe at an angle of approximately 45°. Your weight should be evenly distributed on both feet. Grasp the turning chisel with the right hand near the end of the handle. With your left hand, hold the blade and guide it along the tool rest. Get the feel of this position before starting the lathe.
10. True up the edge with a skew chisel. This is done by holding the tool, in a horizontal position, flat against the tool rest. Start at either axis and move the tool across the

Fig. 10-52. Inboard faceplate turning.
Shaping the inside of a bowl by scraping with the roundnose chisel is a typical application of inboard turning.

thickness of the stock. Continue this procedure, taking small cuts and keeping the full width of the blade in contact with the work, until the edge is true.

11. To produce convex cuts on an edge, rest the flat side of the skew chisel in a horizontal position on the tool rest and pivot to form the desired arc.

12. To produce a concave cut on an edge, rest the flat side of the roundnose chisel in a horizontal position. Pivot to form the desired arc.

13. To produce convex cuts on the face, position the skew chisel as in Step 11 and pivot out from the center.

14. To produce concave cuts on the face, position the roundnose chisel as in Step 12. Start the cut at the center and work out. Keep the tool perpendicular to the arc of the cut so that the cutting will be done with the end of the tool. See Figs. 10-52 and 10-53.

15. To produce straight cuts, use a squarenose chisel. Keep the full width of the blade in contact with the work.

16. To produce V-cuts, use the diamond-point chisel.

17. As stock is removed from the turning, the tool rest should be advanced and adjusted to an angle that will keep it within safe working distance.

18. After the turning has been completed, it must be sanded. Use 50-grit garnet cabinet paper to start removal of turning-chisel marks. Make the finish sanding with 100- to 120-grit garnet paper, depending on the hardness of the wood. Too fine an abrasive may glaze the surface of the wood, preventing proper penetration of finishing materials. See Fig. 10-54. Be sure to

Fig. 10-53. Outboard faceplate turning.
For diameters too large for inboard turning, the outboard faceplate may be used. Observe that the tool is worked from the center to the right, opposite to the direction of inboard turning.

Fig. 10-54. Sanding a concave surface on a faceplate.
Sanding is done below the center and on the downward slope of the stock's rotation. A sanding pad is recommended.

remove the tool rest before beginning the sanding operation.

19. When the turning has been completed, remove the work from the lathe. Then, remove the faceplate from the turning. If a backing block was glued on, remove it by splitting on the glue line with a mallet and chisel. Do not damage the turning.

Standards and Results

- Turnings should be smooth and free of defects.
- Turnings should be of the specified dimensions and shape.
- The backing block should be split off cleanly on the glue joint.

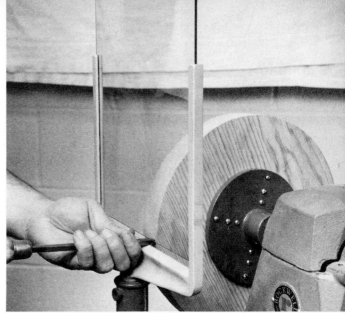

Fig. 10-55. Outboard faceplate turning using clear plastic guard.

Safety Considerations

- Wear eye-protection devices when operating the lathe.
- Rotate the stock by hand to determine the clearance of the tool rest.
- Avoid wearing loose or dangling clothing.
- The lathe must be operated at the proper speed. The larger the diameter of the stock, the lower the speed and the greater the need for accurate balancing.
- Rough turning should be done at a slow speed.
- Avoid making heavy cuts.
- Tools should be kept sharp and properly shaped.
- Care must be taken not to get the chisel caught in the work, as this would damage the work and the tool and could cause injury to the operator.
- The turning chisel should always be held firmly and at the proper angle.
- Maintain the tool rest at the proper height and distance from the work.
- The tool rest should be removed before sanding is done.
- Tools should not be left on the bed of the lathe while the lathe is in operation.
- A safe minimum thickness for bowl sides and bottoms is 3/16″.

Fig. 10-56. Portable special-purpose machine for faceplate turning up to 16″ in diameter.

- Screws should be of the correct size to fit into the countersunk holes in the faceplate. These screws should be inserted in such a way that they are straight, tight, and flush.
- To prevent accidents, remove the live center before doing outboard turning.

Topic 83.

Industrial Turning

Whether it is done by hand or by machine, turning is performed using the same principle. In hand turning, the cut is made from the larger diameter to the smaller; the tool shears the stock in the direction of the grain. Automatic shaping lathes follow exactly the same procedure. Rotating cutterheads, containing a great number of knives, shear the stock along the entire length of the turning sequence. See Fig. 10-57.

In forming a head or other ornamental shape, the knives always start at the highest point and shear downward, toward the right

Heywood-Wakefield Co.

Fig. 10-57. Back-knife lathe.
The back-knife lathe is used to turn spindles, legs, rounds, and to make slight contour cuts. In this lathe, the stock revolves at a high rate of speed in a counterclockwise direction. The single knife is the length of the pattern and is ground to the profile of the finished piece. This knife is fed mechanically into the revolving stock, cutting the entire turning to shape.

and toward the left. Thus, the cut is made as much with the grain as across it, and a smooth surface is produced. See Fig. 10-58.

The knives are staggered along short sections of the cutterhead. These knives are inserted into knife holders designed to hold them at the proper angle in back of the center line. This position gives the knives a forward shearing cut. Very rarely are more than one or two knives involved in cutting at the same time. Thus, the strain on the stock is reduced.

Some lathes have uniform, double-end drive, which provides a synchronized turning motion on both ends of the stock. This feature also makes it possible to turn exceptionally delicate pieces with little danger of their breaking, chattering, or twisting. As a result, the work that is produced requires very little or no sanding. All pieces are turned true and are uniform in size and shape.

A hollow chuck attachment supports long and slender turnings, permitting the stock to be revolved either with or opposite to the rotation of the knives without danger of loosening. The knives revolve at a high speed (2700 rpm) and are advanced into the work, which turns slowly (2-30 rpm).

An automatic stock-centering device saves time in centering blanks. The head center holds the turning, allowing the cut to be completed over the end of the work. This eliminates the need for an extra inch of stock. As the carriage is pushed forward, the centering device automatically recedes out of the way of the knives.

The swing of the automatic lathe is 14" to 18". These lathes can accommodate a cut up to 62" long in a single operation. Horizontal steady rests, extension plates, and other special attachments can be used, making it possible for longer, thinner stock to be turned.

Shaping the knives is a special task. A profile of the desired turning is made into a pattern board. This pattern board is clamped into a special marking machine and setup box

Fig. 10-58. The Mattison lathe.
Large shaper-like knives revolve at a high rate of speed
and are advanced into the slowly revolving stock by a
series of cams that turn the entire piece in one operation.

in which the knife blanks are marked. A perfect fit, corresponding to the pattern board, can then be ground on the knife blanks.

The automatic shaping lathe will handle practically any type of plain or decorative turning. It will produce round, square, octagonal, hexagonal, or most any other polygonal shape. The following are among the more common uses for the automatic shaping lathe: shaping of table legs, pedestals, piano pillars, lamp standards, standards and posts for bureaus, chiffoniers, table and toilet stands, bedposts and rails, chair legs, casket corners, coffin handles, tenpins, Indian clubs, dumbbells, ball bats, lawn-mower handles, and rollers. Many odd-shaped turnings, such as gunstocks and golf-club heads, are also produced on this machine.

The automatic lathe can produce between 100 and 600 pieces per day, depending on the size, kind, and style of work being turned. Round turnings are produced an average of three to ten times faster on the automatic lathe than they are on a hand-operated lathe. Production of square and many-sided patterns takes only a fraction of the time that would be required to produce these patterns by hand sawing.

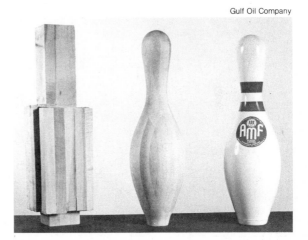

Fig. 10-59. Steps in producing a bowling pin. Stock is glued to the basic shape, turned on a lathe, and then painted.

The knives are fed in behind the stock by means of a lever that is controlled by the operator. The skill of the operator is very important. This person must be able to feel the cutting action as the knives come in contact with the wood. If the operator forces the cut, a poor turning will result.

Topic 84.

The Woodturner

Only a very small number of hand wood-turners are employed in industry today. Most woodworking plants do only mechanized wood turning, using automatic lathes. As a result, job opportunities in hand turning are extremely limited. However, there are still some highly skilled woodturners employed in the furniture industry. Their training period is between three and four years in length. Wood-turning skills are also needed in patternmaking shops, custom shops, specialty shops, and small general-woodworking shops.

In addition to the common woodworking lathe (the type found in schools and home workshops), industry uses semi-automatic and automatic shaping lathes. See Figs. 10-3, 10-4, 10-57, and 10-58.

Glenn Gordon, Chicago, IL

SECTION ELEVEN.

Joinery

Topic 85.

Joinery

The term **joinery,** in its older, restricted sense, meant the art of constructing doors, windows, stairs, panels, and other closely fitted items of interior woodwork. As commonly used, the word **join** means to connect, unite, or combine. In woodworking, **join** means to connect pieces of wood in order to extend dimension (length, width, or thickness), for the purpose of changing direction, or to couple pieces for the purpose of allowing for motion.

Definition of Wood Joint

A woodworking **joint** is the place or part in which two separate pieces of wood are joined, either rigidly or with allowance for motion. There are 10 or 12 basic joints, and more than 24 variations of these basic joints. Strength and appearance are the basic qualities required of a joint.

Types of Wood Joints

Woodworking joints are divided into two basic types: **lay-up** joints and **assembly** joints. Lay-up joints are those used for building up the dimensions of stock. Assembly joints are those used in assembling members that have been cut to specified shape and dimension. Each type of assembly joint has a specific function, although some types are used interchangeably depending upon strength considerations and character of design.

Reinforcement of Wood Joints

Practically all joints are held in place by some type of fastener. Nails, screws, pins, wedges, splines, dowels, corrugated fasteners, mending plates, and other such forms of hardware all serve to reinforce joints. Glue is the common adhesive used in wood joints consisting of separate members that have been fitted.

The strength of the joint is determined largely by the accuracy of the fit, the quality of the glue, and the quality of gluing and clamping.

The strength of any given joint depends upon the following factors:

1. The ability of a specific kind of wood to stay in shape and in place. That is, the degree to which the wood will resist twisting, cupping, bowing, swelling, and shrinking.
2. The degree to which the wood has been dried and the extent to which natural factors, such as swelling and shrinking, have been considered in making a joint. Some examples of products made with these considerations in mind are boats, barrels, and tubs. The expansion dowel and Valiton compressed tenon are joints that work specifically on the principles of expansion and contraction. See Fig. 11-80.
3. The degree to which the fibers of a particular type of wood can withstand compression by such things as nails, corrugated fasteners, dowels, and splines.
4. The degree of effectiveness of using adhesives with a particular kind of wood.
5. The degree of precision observed in cutting and shaping the joint surfaces. Dull or vibrating cutting tools can leave a poor, uneven gluing surface.
6. The dimensions of the separate members of the joint.
7. Standard of work quality.

These are some of the terms used in joinery:

Arris — a sharp edge formed by the meeting of two surfaces.
Bevel — a full-edge cut, at an angle other than 90°, connecting two surfaces in the same plane.
Chamfer — a sloping angle, cutting two intersecting surfaces but not an entire edge.

Cheek — the broad face or surface of a tenon.
Corner — point where three arrises meet.
Dado — a recess running across the grain of a piece of lumber.
Edge — the narrow faces running with the grain.
Gain — a recess cut in one member to enable it to receive another piece (locks, hinges, timber, tenons, and tongues, for example).

Groove — a recess in a piece of lumber, running with the grain.
Resawing — decreasing the thickness of stock by sawing into thinner pieces of the same length and width.
Shoulder — the end of the stock adjacent to the end of the tenon, where increase in dimension takes place.

Common Wood Joints

Topic 86.

Butt Joint

A **butt joint** is produced by butting (bringing together) the end, edge, or surface of one member to the end, edge or surface of another member. The two parts of the joint are then secured and reinforced with glue, nails, screws, plates, corner blocks, splines, dowels, or other fasteners. The butt joint is a common joint, and is used alone in conditions where great strength is not a primary consideration, Figs. 11-1 and 11-2. **Reinforced butt joints** lock in one or more directions and provide additional gluing surfaces. These are such joints as the tongue-and-groove joint, Fig. 11-3, the rabbet joint, Fig. 11-4, the scarf joint, Fig. 11-12, the half lap joint, Fig. 11-13, the cross lap joint, Fig. 11-14, the finger joint, Fig. 11-15, the dovetail joint, Fig. 11-16, and the mortise-and-tenon joint, Fig. 11-18. See also Figs. 11-112, 11-113, and 11-114.

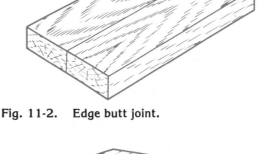

Fig. 11-2.   Edge butt joint.

Fig. 11-3.   Tongue-and-groove joint.

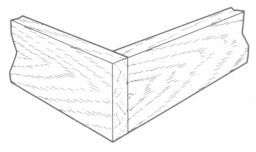

Fig. 11-1.   End butt joint.

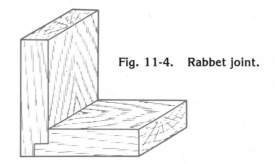

Fig. 11-4.   Rabbet joint.

Rabbet Joint

A **rabbet joint** is a corner joint, made by cutting a recess on the end or on the edge of one or both members to be joined, Fig. 11-4. This is an easily made joint, widely used in the construction of boxes and simple furniture.

Dado Joint

A dado is a groove cut perpendicular to the wood grain. This recess provides a seat for a connecting member. The joining of these two members forms a **dado joint,** Fig. 11-5. The dado joint is similar to the rabbet joint. It must, however, have a shoulder on each side of the groove and therefore cannot be cut along the end of the stock. This type of joint is strong and easy to make. Dado joints are used extensively for shelving and in cabinet construction.

Dado-Rabbet Joints

A good general rule to follow in laying out **dado-rabbet joints** is that the rabbet should be equal to about half the thickness of the piece. If the cut is to be made by machine, select the dado head nearest in dimension to half the thickness of stock. Since most dadoes are cut with dado heads on the circular saw, this cut should be made first, and the rabbet should be fitted to the dado. Because of the shoulder on the dado-rabbet joint, this type of joint is stronger than a regular dado. Dado-rabbet joints are used in fastening case fronts and backs to ends (as in cedar chests), top-drawer frames to cases, drawer sides, and drawer backs. See **A,** Fig. 11-6. A modified type of dado-rabbet joint is used in drawer construction for fastening drawer fronts to ends, **B,** Fig. 11-6. In this case, the dado in the drawer side is usually 1/8″ wide and 1/8″ deep.

Stop dado-rabbets do not run through to the front edge. For this reason, they look like butt joints.

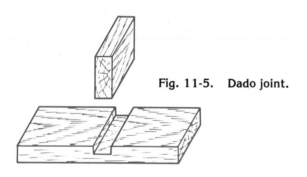

Fig. 11-5.   Dado joint.

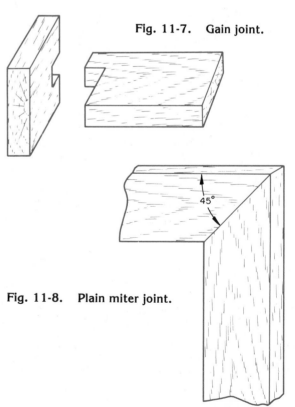

Fig. 11-7.   Gain joint.

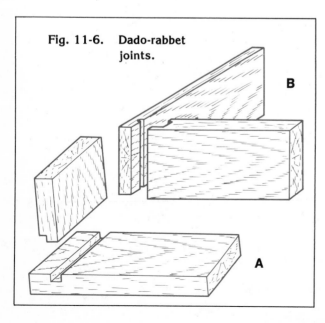

Fig. 11-6.   Dado-rabbet joints.

45°

Fig. 11-8.   Plain miter joint.

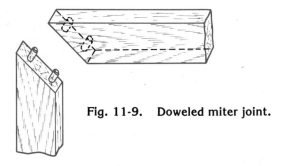

Fig. 11-9.   Doweled miter joint.

Miter Joint

A **miter joint** is a butted joint. Two members of equal width are cut at the same angle (less than 90°), and are usually fastened together with glue and reinforced with nails, corrugated fasteners, dowels, or a spline. See Figs. 11-8, 11-9, 11-10, and 11-11.

Scarf Joint

A **scarf joint** is used for extending length. Two members of equal width and thickness are joined at an acute angle (about 15°), in order to obtain maximum bearing surface at the joint, Fig. 11-12.

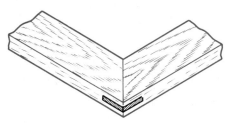

Fig. 11-10.   Splined side miter joint.

Half Lap Joints

In a **half lap joint,** two members of approximately equal thickness and usually of the same width are joined in a modified butt joint. Half the thickness of each member is cut away so that, when the two parts are lapped together, a thickness equal to that of one member is formed. The **end lap joint** is used to extend length or to change direction, Fig. 11-13. The **cross lap joint** is an interlocking joint, Fig. 11-14. Wooden Christmas-tree stands, coatracks and clothes-tree bases are often made using cross lap joints.

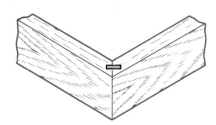

Fig. 11-11.   Splined edge miter joint.

Finger, Box, or Multiple Slip Joint

This joint is made by cutting notches so that the resulting fingers and sockets will alternate and the two sections will interlock when joined together, Fig. 11-15. **Finger joints** are strong and are used extensively in fine box construction.

Fig. 11-12.   Scarf joint.

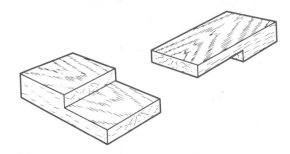

Fig. 11-13.   End lap joint.

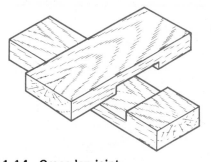

Fig. 11-14.   Cross lap joint.

Dovetail Joints

Dovetail joints are modified finger joints, consisting of reversed-wedge-shaped fingers that fit into matched sockets. The shape of the fingers resembles the spread of a dove's tail. See Figs. 11-16 and 11-17. Dovetail joints are very strong, interlocking joints, used in furniture construction.

Mortise-and-Tenon Joints

Mortise-and-tenon joints consist of a finger or tenon, cut on one member and fitted into a socket or mortise of corresponding dimension in the other member, Fig. 11-18. There are many modifications of the mortise-and-tenon joint. As a result, this is a versatile joint, very popular in furniture construction. See Figs. 11-19 through 11-25.

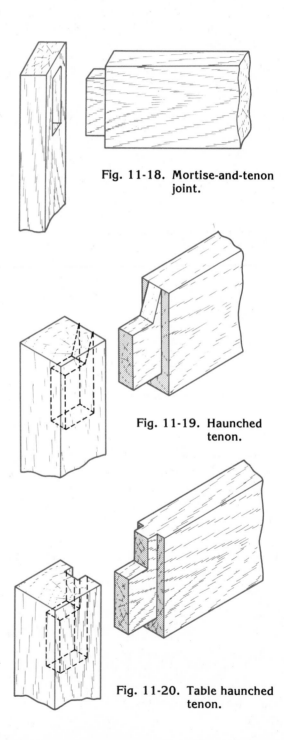

Fig. 11-18. Mortise-and-tenon joint.

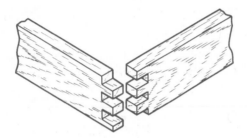

Fig. 11-15. Box or finger joint.

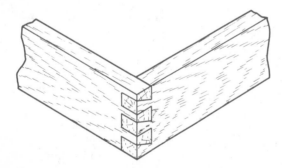

Fig. 11-16. Through dovetail joint.

Fig. 11-19. Haunched tenon.

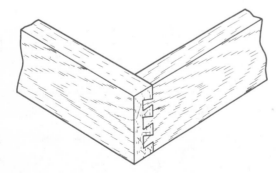

Fig. 11-17. Half-blind or stop dovetail joint.

Fig. 11-20. Table haunched tenon.

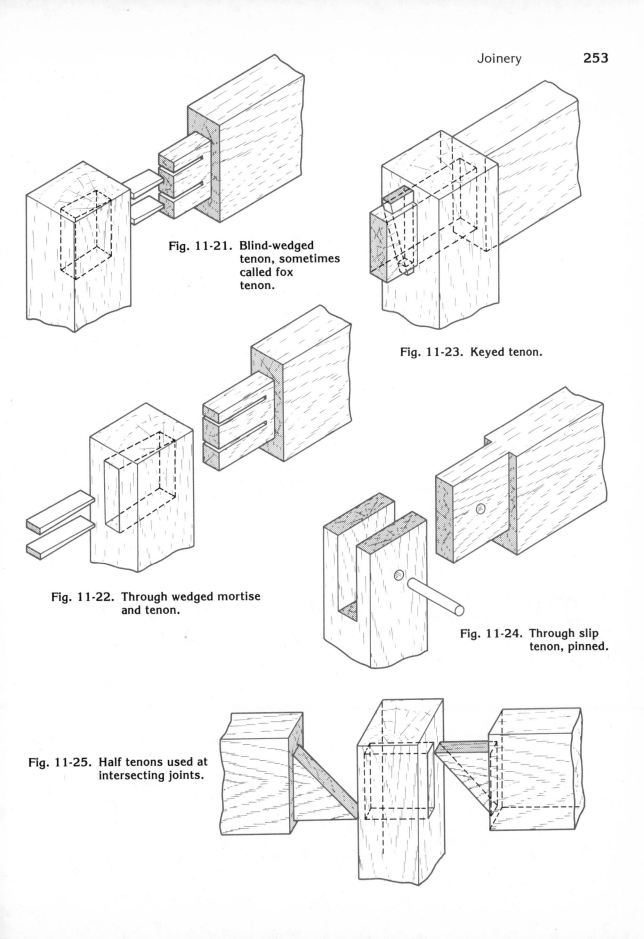

Fig. 11-21. Blind-wedged tenon, sometimes called fox tenon.

Fig. 11-23. Keyed tenon.

Fig. 11-22. Through wedged mortise and tenon.

Fig. 11-24. Through slip tenon, pinned.

Fig. 11-25. Half tenons used at intersecting joints.

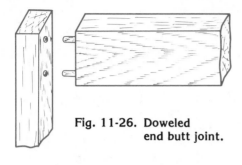

Fig. 11-26. Doweled end butt joint.

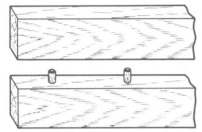

Fig. 11-27. Doweled edge butt joint.

Dowels

Dowels are used to give added strength to a butted joint by providing resistance to cross strain and increasing the gluing surface. Properly fitted dowel pins serve to provide· better alignment in assembly. See Figs. 11-26 and 11-27.

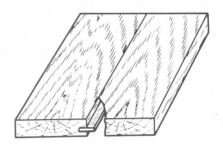

Fig. 11-28. Splined edge butt joint.

Splines

A **spline** is a narrow strip of thin stock. It is inserted in a groove or keyway in a butted joint, with the grain at right angles to the adjoining surfaces, Fig. 11-28. Thus, the spline adds strength to the joint by giving greater resistance against twist or torsion. When the spline is used in panel construction or in applications where strength is not a major consideration, the grain usually runs with the length of the spline. In making a spline, cut the thickness by resawing across the end of a board. The length (with the grain) will be equal to the combined depths of the grooves cut in the joint.

Topic 87.

Making an Edge-to-Edge Spring Joint

Classification

Joining by fitting and gluing

Production methods in industry rarely involve use of a hand plane on edge-to-edge joints. Stock to be glued is jointed on a jointer. Many furniture manufacturers simply use a hollow-ground circular-saw blade to square up and smooth edges before gluing. With proper care, joints made in this manner do not have a visible glue line, and the bond between the two pieces is stronger than the wood itself.

Procedure

In a well-made edge-to-edge joint, the glue line is hardly distinguishable. If the joint tends to open, it is most likely to do so at the extreme ends. This occurs as a result of shrinkage of members. In order to minimize this tendency, each member of the joint must be planed in a very slight concave arc, Fig. 11-29. This is done by using the plane to take a very fine shaving, applying greatest pressure in the center. When the members are brought togeth-

Fig. 11-29. A slight "spring" is desirable in an edge-to-edge joint.

er, there is a slight opening at the center. This will disappear, however, as pressure is applied through clamping. This clamping sets up compression in the ends, which lessens as shrinkage occurs. The spring joint will not open at the ends under normal use.

In gluing up slash- or plain-sawed stock, it is recommended that adjacent pieces be alternated so that the annual rings will be opposite on adjoining pieces. This reduces cupping. Cupping may also be reduced by using narrow widths of slash-sawed stock.

Plain-sawed lumber shrinks more on the sap side than on the heart side. If panels consist of wide boards, or if several boards are glued together with the sap side facing one surface, the panel will warp toward the sap side if the moisture is lowered. If boards making up a panel are 4" or less in width, and the annual ring direction is reversed on adjoining boards, the cupping will be less noticeable.

1. Match the pieces, giving attention to color, figure, and grain. Mark the members in their respective positions.
2. Joint (straight and square) all edges to be joined.
3. Set the hand jointer plane to take a fine shaving, then plane the two edges slightly concave.

    Note: This slight concave may be produced on the jointer by lowering the rear table **very slightly** below the cutters (at their highest point) and then making a **light** cut. This should be done only by an experienced worker.
4. Place the pieces edge-to-edge in a vertical position. Sight through from the face side to see if any trace of light shows in the center.
5. Test the joint by swinging each end alternately from side to side. This is done to

determine whether the board pivots on the ends.
6. If greater strength is desired, use dowels to reinforce an edge-to-edge joint. (See Topic 92, "Reinforcing Joints with Dowels.")
7. Uniformity of pressure is important in gluing two or more pieces together. Frequently, clamps are spaced about 2" from the ends and 12" to 15" apart, divided alternately on each side of the panel, Fig. 11-30. In gluing up several pieces to make up a panel, narrow boards should be in the center rather than at the edges. This will help prevent future warpage and will provide for better distribution of pressure during clamping. Too much clamping pressure may result in glue starvation, the result of glue being squeezed from the joint. This produces a weakened panel.

Note: It is advisable, on any assembly containing highly figured grain patterns or alternate arrangements of slash-sawed stock, to smooth the surface with a cabinet scraper or a scraper plane. Use of a plane may cause the grain to tear.

Fig. 11-30. Position of clamps in gluing spring joint. Note use of straightedges and hand screws to ensure flatness of surface.

Standards and Results

- There should be no rocking in the joint.
- The pieces should be in the same plane.
- The opening in the joint should show only a ray of light before the joint is glued.
- After gluing, the joint should be tight and should not be noticeable.

Topic 88.

Making a Lap Joint — Hand Process

Classification

Joining by fitting and reinforcing with fasteners or adhesives

Procedure

An end lap joint is used to extend length or change direction of two pieces of stock. See Fig. 11-31. Half the thickness of each member is cut away so that the surfaces are flush. This joint is used in the construction of houses, sills, and plates, as well as in the manufacture of stretchers, bases, stands, and frames.

1. Square the ends of the stock. The two pieces of stock on which the joint is to be made must be of equal thickness. Lay these pieces side by side, one member faceup and the other facedown, Fig. 11-32.

2. From the squared end of each, measure and mark with a sharp knife the width, **W**, Fig. 11-32.

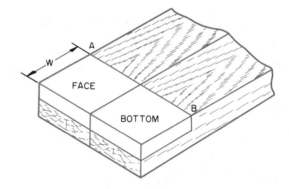

Fig. 11-32. Laying out an end lap joint.

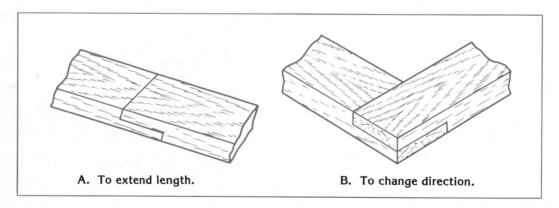

A. To extend length.   B. To change direction.

Fig. 11-31. End lap joints.

3. Using a try square, mark a knife line, **AB**, across the surface of the two boards. To check accuracy, lay one piece over the other at right angles.
4. From points **A** and **B**, square lines down the edge, half the thickness of the board. Do this on both edges of each piece.
5. Set a marking gauge to an amount one-half the thickness of the stock. Measure from the face. Mark along the edges and ends of each piece to be cut.
6. Secure stock in vise with the end grain faceup. Using a backsaw, cut on the waste side of the line to make the cheek cut.
7. Lay the piece on a bench. With the backsaw, cut on the waste side of the cross lines to the depth of the cut just made. If the cuts have been accurate, the two pieces should fit together to make an extended surface or a right angle. If the pieces are not even, pare the cut surface with a chisel.
8. In making a cross lap joint, the same layout procedure is used, but the measurements are made away from the edge of each piece. The depth cut is made in several places and the waste material is removed with a chisel. See Fig. 11-14.
9. Make lap joints secure by reinforcing them with glue, nails, or screws.

Standards and Results

- The two members of this joint should fit together snugly. There should be no space between surfaces or edges, or between lapping surfaces at the center point.
- The joint should not be forced together.
- A loose-fitting joint, or one that is too tight, is an indication of poor work.

Safety Considerations

- Wear safety glasses when using woodworking equipment.
- Observe all safety practices pertaining to the particular tool or machine you are using.

Making a Dado Joint — Hand Process

Topic 89.

Classification

Joinery by fitting and gluing

Procedure

A dado is a recess, cut across the grain, into which another board is to fit. It is commonly found in case construction.

1. Locate the position of the joint by measuring the desired distance from the nearest end.
2. With a try square and sharp knife, mark a line across the width of the board.
3. From the line just made, measure and mark the thickness of the board that is to fit into the dado.
4. With the try square and knife, mark this line to define the width of the dado. Continue these lines to the depth of the joint on the sides of the board.
5. A marking gauge, set to the depth of the joint, is used to mark the depth of cut on both edges, Fig. 11-33.
6. The dado cut is made in much the same manner as a cross lap cut. A stop is clamped to the cutting line to enable the backsaw to be guided squarely and on the waste side of the line. Several cuts are made into the waste material.

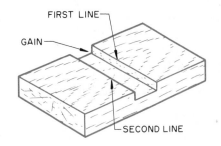

Fig. 11-33. Dado joint.

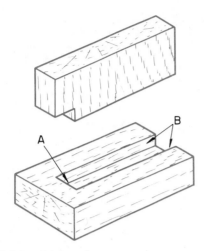

Fig. 11-34. Making a stopped or blind dado joint.
1. **Cut with a chisel at point A.**
2. **Cut with a backsaw at point B.**
3. **Remove waste with a chisel.**
4. **Trim bottom of gain with a router plane.**

7. To remove waste material, use a chisel with a blade somewhat narrower than the width of the dado.
8. Set a router plane to the depth of the dado and trim the bottom surface.
9. Try the second piece for fit. If the fit is too tight, it can be made perfect by removing a few shavings from the underside of the shelf. Too loose a fit will have to be repaired. This can be done by gluing a thin strip of wood to one side of the dado, on the underside of the joint.
10. A **stopped dado** is one on which the joint does not appear on the front edge, Fig.

11-34. It has a neater appearance than an ordinary dado joint. The same layout procedure is followed, but the dado stops 3/8″ to 1/2″ from the edge.
11. Use a chisel to remove the waste material from the stopped edge of the dado. Cut the remainder with the backsaw.
12. The board that is to fit the stopped dado is notched on the front edge. This notch must be equal to the width of the stop on the front edge of the dado and must be the same depth as the dado.
13. The joint may be reinforced with glue, nails, or screws. See Topic 114, "Gluing a Joint," Topic 117, "Driving Nails," and Topic 121, "Driving Wood Screws."

Note: For information on making a dado by machine process, see Topic 28, "Using the Circular Saw" and Topic 56, "Using a Portable Hand Router."

Standards and Results

- A dado joint must fit snugly.
- The depth of the recess must be even.
- The notched edge should fit snugly to the surface of the second piece.

Safety Considerations

- Wear safety glasses when using woodworking equipment.
- Always direct the chisel away from your body as you work.
- Keep both hands on the chisel.
- Observe all safety practices pertaining to the particular tool or machine you are using.

Topic 90.

Making a Rabbet Joint — Hand Process

Classification

Laying out and cutting a recess

Procedure

A rabbet is the recess that is cut along the end or edge of a board. It is commonly used in

the construction of panels and drawers. The recess is usually one-half to two-thirds the thickness of the stock. See Figs. 11-35 and 11-36.
1. Square the end or edge on which the joint is to be made.
2. Lay the board (on which the rabbet is to be cut) facedown.

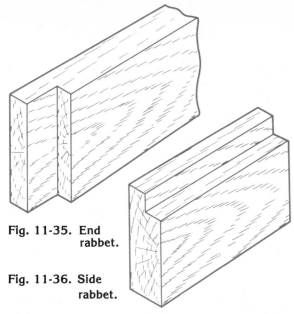

Fig. 11-35. End rabbet.

Fig. 11-36. Side rabbet.

3. From the squared end or edge, measure the thickness of the board that is to fit the rabbet. Mark this thickness on the upper surface of the board.
4. Using a try square and a sharp knife, square a line across the length of the rabbet for the cut.
5. Square a line down each edge to the depth of the rabbet.
6. Set a marking gauge to this depth and mark the sides and the end.

Cutting an End Rabbet

1. With the board held securely on a bench hook, use a backsaw to make several cuts to the depth of the rabbet. Make sure the saw kerf is on the waste side of the line. It is good practice to clamp a piece of stock to the line to ensure a square cut.

2. Remove the waste with a chisel.
3. Smooth the bottom with a chisel, rabbet plane, or plow. Make a square edge, being careful not to pare beyond the line.

Cutting a Side Rabbet

The side rabbet is usually cut on a machine. However, in a hand operation, the side rabbet may be cut with a rabbet plane.
1. Set the rabbet plane to cut an even shaving.
2. Gauge a depth line with the marking gauge. This process is described under the preceding heading, "Cutting an End Rabbet."
3. A stop may be clamped along the surface to act as a guide in planing parallel to the edge.
4. Plane until the desired depth is reached.

Note: For information on making a rabbet by machine process, see Topic 28, "Using the Circular Saw," Topic 48, "Smoothing a Surface on the Jointer," and Topic 56, "Using a Portable Hand Router."

Standards and Results

- The rabbet should form a 90° angle and should be parallel to the surface of the face.
- The rabbet should be of the correct width and depth.

Safety Considerations

- Wear safety glasses when using woodworking equipment.
- Observe all safety practices pertaining to the particular tool or machine you are using.

Dowels — Wood and Metal

Topic 91.

Classification

Aligning and reinforcing pins

Composition or Description

Wood dowels are cylindrical pieces of birch, beech, maple, or oak. They sometimes have grooves or flutes, cut or pressed into the surface, Fig. 11-37.

Metal dowels, sometimes called **dowel pins,** are made of brass or steel. They are constructed in two pieces and are screwed into the wood. Patternmakers use metal dowels on split patterns.

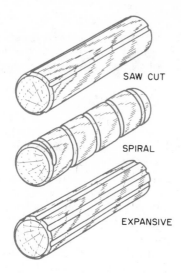

Fig. 11-37. Types of dowels.

Properties

Wood dowels add strength to an edge-to-edge joint and reduce twisting. Dowels with spiral cuts in the surface permit better glue distribution, resulting in a stronger joint. Dowels with flutes pressed into the surface are called **expansion dowels.** They are made of lumber that has been compressed but not thoroughly dried. When used with hot or cold animal glue they expand and make a stronger joint.

Uses

Wood dowels are used in applications similar to those of the mortise-and-tenon joint, as well as in edge-to-edge and miter joints, in segments, in reinforcements, in pinning, and in temporary joints (as in table leaves). In addition to their applications in joinery, wood dowels are used in the construction of spindles, crates, racks, and other articles requiring wood pieces of this shape and size.

Metal dowels are used to prevent sideslip and are not intended for use on a glued joint.

Market Analysis

Shapes

Wood dowels can be either smooth, spiral, fluted, or grooved.

Metal dowels are smooth. The male piece has a square shoulder on the end, and the female piece has flutes. This design permits each part to be fastened into the wood.

Sizes

Wood dowels are available in the following diameters: 1/8", 3/16", 1/4", 5/16", 3/8", 7/16", 1/2", 9/16", 5/8", 3/4", 7/8", and 1". They are also available in various other diameters, up to 3". The lengths available are 12", 18", 2', 3', and 4'. Metal dowels are available in the following sizes: 11/64", 3/16", 7/32", 5/16", 13/32", 9/16", and 13/16".

Sales Units

Dowels may be bought in any quantity, but the most economical way to purchase them is in bundles of 100. (Metal dowels are always packed in lots of 100.) Dowels may be made using a dowel cutter.

Maintenance

Store dowels in a dry place, in either a horizontal or a vertical position.

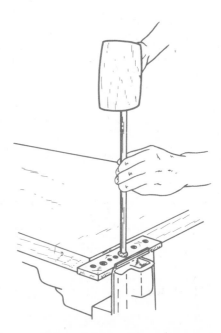

Fig. 11-38. **Reducing the diameter of a dowel and scoring it along its length by driving it through a dowel plate.**

Reinforcing Joints with Dowels

Topic 92.

Classification

Joinery by fitting and reinforcing

Procedure

A dowel is used to strengthen a butt joint. It also serves as a substitute for mortise-and-tenon joints in joining aprons and legs in the construction of tables and chairs.

Making an Edge Dowel Joint

1. The two surfaces to be fitted together are squared to proper dimension. The pieces should fit closely together.

Fig. 11-39. Butt dowel joint.

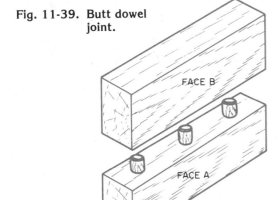

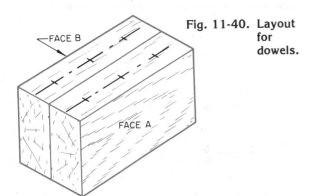

Fig. 11-40. Layout for dowels.

2. Set a marking gauge to draw a center line along the edge to be joined, as in Fig. 11-40. Make sure all measurements are taken from the same face of each piece.

3. Measure and mark the position of each dowel. Place the two pieces together in such a way that the jointed edges are as in Fig. 11-40. With a try square and a sharp pencil or knife, mark the position of the dowels on each member. Do this by drawing a line across the jointed edge of each piece. On edge jointing, dowels should be about 2″ from the end and should be 12″ to 14″ apart.

   Another method of determining dowel-hole location is this: Mark and drill the dowel holes in one piece, insert dowel centers, and assemble the joint. A light tap or squeeze on the adjacent pieces will cause the dowel centers to make an impression on the undrilled member. These impressions indicate the correct drilling points for proper dowel location, Fig. 11-41.

4. Select the size of dowel to be used. It should be approximately one-third to one-half the thickness of the board.

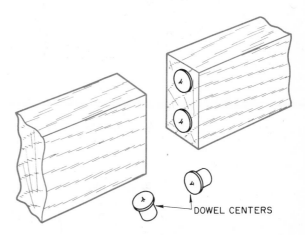

Fig. 11-41. Using dowel centers to determine dowel-hole location.

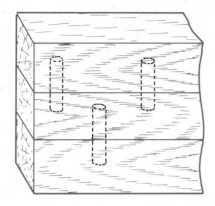

Fig. 11-42. Alignment of dowels — butt joint.

and 11-46. Protect the surface from marks that may be left by the jig. Bore the holes with an auger bit or dowel bit the size of the dowel. After the hole has been started, check with a try square to see that the holes are being cut accurately. In each piece, countersink the holes slightly to make insertion of the dowel easier and to allow space for excess glue.

7. Dowels should not exceed 3″ in length. A stop gauge, used with an auger bit, will ensure even depth of holes, Figs. 11-47, 11-48, 11-49.

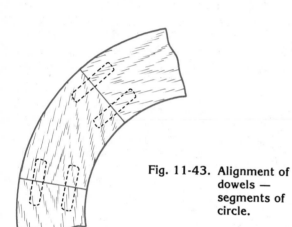

Fig. 11-43. Alignment of dowels — segments of circle.

Stanley Tools

Fig. 11-45. Doweling jig.

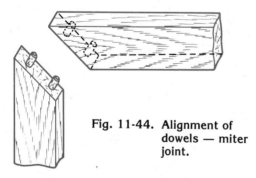

Fig. 11-44. Alignment of dowels — miter joint.

Fig. 11-46. Self-centering doweling jig.

5. With a brad awl, make a small hole at the point where the lines intersect. In order for the dowels to line up, this step must be done very accurately.

6. Set the dowel jig so that it will guide the bit to the proper position. See Figs. 11-45

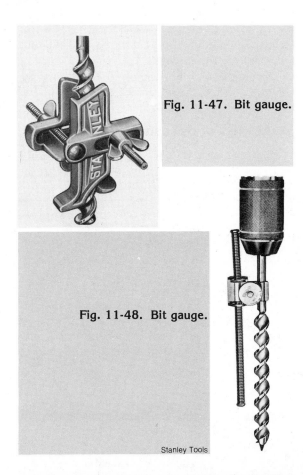

Fig. 11-47. Bit gauge.

Fig. 11-48. Bit gauge.

Stanley Tools

Fig. 11-49. Bit stops.

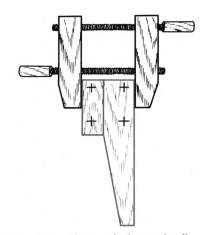

Fig. 11-50. Dowel layout in leg and rail.

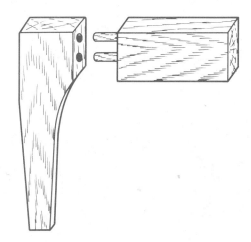

Fig. 11-51. Assembly of leg and rail.

8. Cut each dowel slightly shorter than the total depth of both holes. A dowel that is too short might cause a depression in the wood surface if the wood ever shrinks. If spiral dowels are not used, a groove should be cut along the length of the dowel. This will make it possible for glue and air to escape from the hole while the dowel is being inserted. See Fig. 11-37.

9. Except on expansion dowels, which are smaller on the ends, the tip of the dowel should be chamfered to allow for easy insertion into the hole.

10. Make a dry run to test the fit.

11. With a small, chisel-like stick, put glue inside the holes of one member of the joint.

12. Dip the end of the dowel in glue and drive it in firmly with a mallet, using light blows.

13. Spread a thin, even layer of glue in the matching holes and on the surface of each member of the joint.

14. Fit the joint together and tighten it with clamps.
15. With a square and straightedge, check to see that members of the joint are in line.
16. Wipe off all surplus glue with a damp paper towel and put the work aside to dry.

Using Dowels to Reinforce a Butt Joint on a Leg and Rail

1. Be sure the two pieces that are to fit together form a tight joint.
2. Locate the position of the rail on the leg.
3. Clamp the rail to the leg. See Fig. 11-50.
4. Locate dowel holes in the end of rail, as done in Step 2 of "Making an Edge Dowel Joint." Dowels should be no closer to the edges than two-and-a-half times their diameter.
5. Determine the distance you want the rail to set back from the face of the leg. Add this distance to the previous setting of the marking gauge. Mark the legs.

6. Square the lines across from the end of the rail to the leg. Lines will intersect at the center of the dowel holes.
7. Proceed as outlined under the heading "Making an Edge Dowel Joint." See Fig. 11-51.

Standards and Results

- All joints should fit snugly. A correctly glued joint will not show a hairline.
- All excess glue should be removed.
- All pieces should be in the same plane.
- Dowel holes should be correctly positioned and square with working surfaces.
- Stock should not show clamp marks.

Safety Considerations

- Wear safety glasses when using woodworking equipment.
- Observe all safety practices pertaining to the particular tool or machine you are using.

Topic 93.

Making a Miter Joint

Classification

Joinery by reinforced, matched, angular butting

Procedure

A miter joint is used where all end grain is to be covered. This type of joint is used to obtain a continuous profile of moldings. It is usually thought of as a 45° joint, but the term "miter joint" includes all joints made up of beveled edges or ends. The miter joint is a weak joint if not strengthened by a spline, dowel, miter nails, or corrugated fasteners. Miter joints are used on picture frames, door casings, moldings, and in segment construction.

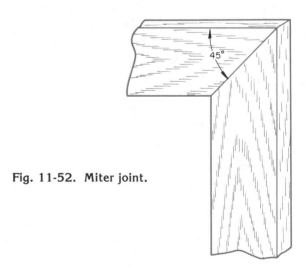

Fig. 11-52. Miter joint.

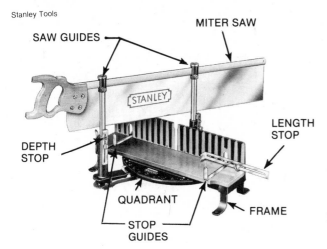

Stanley Tools

SAW GUIDES

MITER SAW

STANLEY

LENGTH
STOP

DEPTH
STOP

QUADRANT

FRAME

STOP
GUIDES

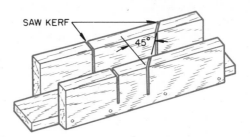

SAW KERF

45°

Fig. 11-54. Homemade miter box.

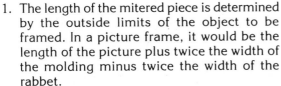

Fig. 11-53. Miter box.

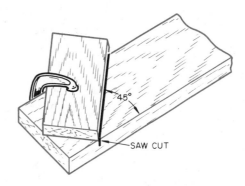

45°

SAW CUT

Fig. 11-55. Using a board as a guide to cut a miter.

1. The length of the mitered piece is determined by the outside limits of the object to be framed. In a picture frame, it would be the length of the picture plus twice the width of the molding minus twice the width of the rabbet.

2. A miter is cut most accurately in a miter box, Figs. 11-53 and 11-54. The miter box can usually be set to cut at any angle between 30° and 90° with stops at increments of 5°. Locks are provided on some miter boxes to lock the saw guide at any angle within the limit of the box. A wooden miter box can be constructed, as shown in Fig. 11-54. The work should be held securely in the miter box while the cut is being made.

   When a board is to be cut at a 45° angle, and no miter box or jig is available, the board is laid out by squaring a pencil line across its width. Measure the width of the board along one edge and, using this measurement, square another line parallel to the first line. Diagonals from the corners of this square will form the 45° angle for the miter. This joint may be cut accurately by clamping a board close to the diagonal line to act as a saw guide, Fig. 11-55.

   Note: For information on cutting a miter by machine process, see Topic 28, "Using the Circular Saw" and Topic 31, "Using the Radial-Arm Saw." Also see Topic 21, "Miter Box," and Topic 22, "Motorized Miter Box."

3. The joint should fit snugly. If there is any opening, the joint may either be resawed or planed. To resaw, clamp the joint in posi-

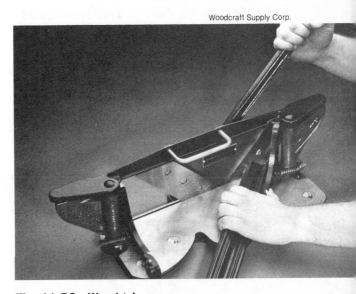

Woodcraft Supply Corp.

Fig. 11-56. Wood trimmer.
     The wood trimmer is used for cutting cross grain square with the face and at angles from 45° to 90°.

tion on a board and run a backsaw or a fine-toothed crosscut saw between the joint. This will trim high spots from each piece. This operation may also be done while the stock is in a miter vise. Never try to trim a miter joint by sanding or filing.

If a miter joint is to be fitted by planing, the plane should be set for a very fine cut and used to smooth the high spots.

Another method of trueing the ends of mitered pieces is to use a wood trimmer, Fig. 11-56. Wood trimmers use a shearing action to remove small amounts of wood. The wood trimmer should not be used to make initial dimension cuts.

4. In gluing a miter joint, most of the exposed surface to be glued is end grain. To prevent this porous surface from absorbing all the glue, a sealer coat of glue is applied and then allowed to set on the open pores. After this sealer coat has hardened sufficiently, a good coating of glue is applied. Some sort of jig, miter clamp, or clamping board should be used to hold the joint in position, Figs. 11-57, 11-58, and 11-59.

5. The glued joint must be reinforced in some way. Nails, screws, special miter hardware (corrugated fasteners or chevrons), dowels, or splines may be used, depending on the purpose of the joint. Nails, screws, or dowels may be inserted in the open ends of the joint. This is done while the joint is held in the clamping jig and before the glue is set. See Figs. 11-60, 11-61, and 11-62.

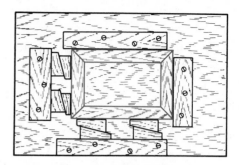

Fig. 11-58. Homemade miter frame.

Fig. 11-59. Method of clamping a mitered joint.

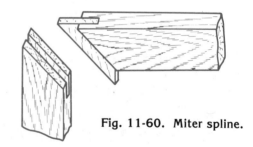

Fig. 11-60. Miter spline.

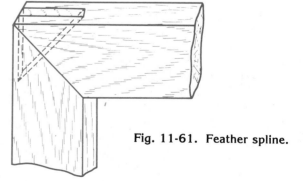

Fig. 11-61. Feather spline.

Stanley Tools

Fig. 11-57. Miter vise.

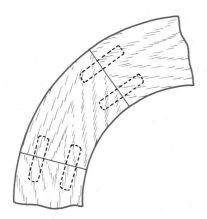

Fig. 11-62. Doweled miter joint.

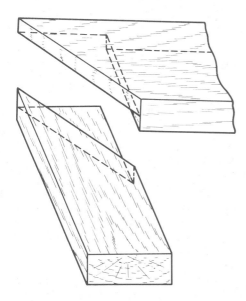

Fig. 11-63. Lap miter joint.

Stanley Tools

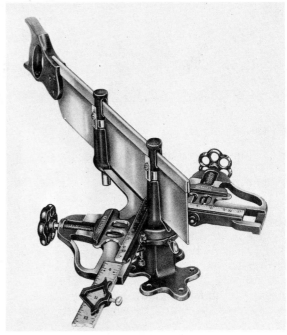

Fig. 11-64. Miter machine.

7. The dowels of a doweled miter joint are always at right angles to the miter cut. A lap miter joint is sometimes used with fasteners such as nails, screws, and corrugated fasteners. These are inserted from the back surface to increase strength.

Standards and Results

- In a good miter joint, no space should appear between the adjoining wood surfaces.
- The inside and outside corners should be flush, and the face surface should be in the same plane.
- In figured grain, the markings should be matched as closely as possible.
- In splines, the grain should be at right angles to the frame parts.

Safety Considerations

- Wear safety glasses when using woodworking equipment.
- Observe all safety practices pertaining to the particular tool or machine you are using.

6. If a spline is to be used to reinforce the miter joint, a kerf may be cut in each member. This kerf should equal the width of each joint face before assembly. A spline is then fitted and glued in the joint, Fig. 11-60.

   In an alternate method, which uses a **slip feather spline,** Fig. 11-61, the frame is first assembled and glued. When the joint is dry, a kerf is cut in each outer corner and a spline is fitted and glued into the kerf.

   In both methods, the grain of the spline should be at a right angle to the face of the joint. This will provide strength.

Topic 94.

Making a Mortise-and-Tenon Joint — Hand Process

Classification

Joinery by fitting and gluing

Procedure

The mortise-and-tenon joint is used in door construction to join rails and stiles, and in table construction to join legs and aprons, Fig. 11-65. It is one of the oldest joints and is very strong when constructed so that the tenon and the stock remaining on each side of the mortise are of equal strength. A standard practice is to make the tenon between one-third and one-half the thickness of the thinner piece of the joint, with the width no more than six times the thickness of the tenon, Fig. 11-66. Wider tenons weaken the mortise. Multiple-tenon construction is recommended because it provides greater strength. It is advisable to leave a space between the mortises. Make this space equal to the thickness of the thinner piece.

There are many variations of the tenon joint, such as the through tenon, the haunched tenon, the miter tenon, and the blind tenon. The following steps outline the procedure for making a blind tenon.

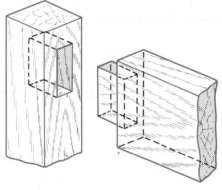

Fig. 11-65. Mortise-and-tenon joint.

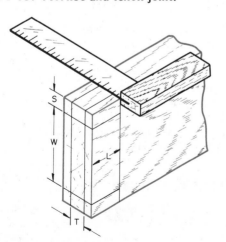

Fig. 11-66. Layout of tenon.

Laying Out the Tenon

1. Select the face side of each piece on which mortise and tenon will be laid out. Work from this side.
2. Determine the length of the tenon. In a blind tenon joint, the tenon should be no longer than two-thirds the width of the thicker piece. Square a line around the length of the tenon, using a sharp knife and a try square, **L** in Fig. 11-66.
3. Set the marking gauge to the desired thickness of the cheek. (This is determined by subtracting the thickness of the tenon from the thickness of the rail and dividing by two.) From the face side, mark the sides and ends of the tenon. Reset the marking gauge by adding the thickness of the tenon to the original setting. Holding the head against the same face, mark the opposite side. (This may be done in one operation if a mortise gauge is used.) See **T** in Fig. 11-66.
4. The shoulder, **S,** is determined by the position of the tenon. Generally, the shoulder of a tenon is equal to its thickness. However, some workers prefer to make all shoulders 1/2" wide. If more than one tenon of a particular size is to be made, the rails should be laid side by side and clamped together so that the length and shoulders can be marked at the same time, Fig. 11-67.

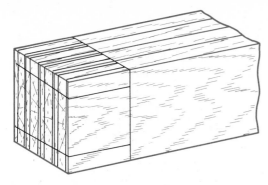

Fig. 11-67. Layout of tenons on four pieces.

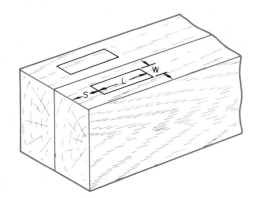

Fig. 11-68. Layout of mortise.

Laying Out the Mortise

If more than one mortise is to be made, the pieces should be clamped together and marked at the same time to ensure alignment. In determining the size of the mortise, the length **(L)** is determined by the width of the tenon, the shoulder **(S)** is equal to the shoulder of the tenon, and the width **(W)** is equal to the thickness of the tenon. See Fig. 11-68. Do all laying out from the face side of the stock.

1. Using a sharp knife and a try square, mark the length of the mortise.
2. Set the marking gauge to the width of the tenon shoulder and gauge the width (W). Each shoulder must be gauged from the same face. (Again, this may be done in one operation if the mortise gauge is used.)

Cutting the Mortise

The mortise is cut first because it is easier to fit the tenon to the mortise than to do the reverse.

1. A doweling jig is a convenient tool for removing waste stock. Select a bit that is

1/16" smaller than the width of the mortise, and set the doweling jig so that the bit is centered in the waste. Attach a bit gauge to the bit so that all holes will be bored 1/8" deeper than the length of the tenon. Bore the hole at the end nearest the end grain, then bore the hole at the opposite end. Continue to bore holes close together until all waste has been removed, Fig. 11-69.

2. With a reasonably wide, sharp chisel, carefully pare the sides of the mortise. A straight, evenly cut mortise is necessary for a good joint. Do not make the mortise wider than the width lines.
3. The ends of the mortise are cut to the straight shoulder with a chisel narrower than the width of the mortise.
4. Another method of cutting a mortise by hand is to use a mortise chisel 1/16" narrower than the width of the mortise. Start the cut from the center and work to each end, as shown in Fig. 11-70.

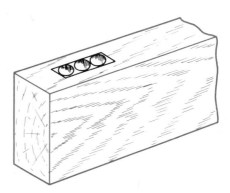

Fig. 11-69. Holes bored for mortise.

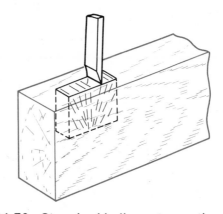

Fig. 11-70. Steps in chiseling out a mortise.

Cutting the Tenon

1. Cut the cheeks of the tenon with a backsaw, Fig. 11-71. Fasten the rail in the vise at a convenient angle, as illustrated. Be sure to start the saw cut on the waste side of the gauged line and stay within the limits.
2. Cut the width of the tenon.
3. Cut the shoulders on the face and on the back side. These shoulders are determined by the length of the tenon. It is best to use a miter box with a stop to ensure equal length and to ensure a square shoulder on each member.
4. Cut shoulders on the top and bottom, using the same stop as above for length.
5. Chamfer the ends of the tenon, as in Fig. 11-72, to allow for easier insertion and for a small glue pocket.

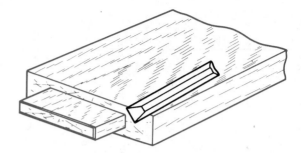

Fig. 11-73. Paring the shoulders of a tenon with a chisel.

Fitting the Joint Together

1. The members should make a snug fit. A joint that is too tight will cause the mortise to bulge or the wood surrounding the mortise to split. A joint that is too loose will not hold.
2. The shoulders of the tenon must be perfectly square around the rail so that a snug fit is made with the adjoining surface. An uneven tenon shoulder may be pared with a sharp chisel, Fig. 11-73.

Standards and Results

- The joint should be tight and at the correct angle.
- Opposite shoulders should be parallel.
- The tenon should not be forced into the mortise, as this will cause splitting.

Safety Considerations

- Wear safety glasses when using woodworking equipment.
- Observe all safety practices pertaining to the particular tool or machine you are using.

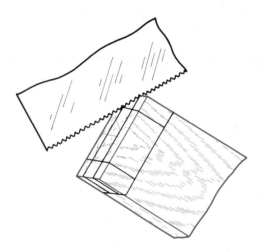

Fig. 11-71. Cutting cheeks of tenon.

INTERESTING FACT: The mortise and tenon, as used in millwork and furniture making, dates back to days before written history. This construction is evident in objects excavated from tombs of ancient Egyptian rulers.

Although the mortise and tenon is still the standard method of construction in Europe, dowel construction is more commonly used in this country, principally because the development of production equipment for the latter method has proceeded more rapidly than has high-production mortising equipment.

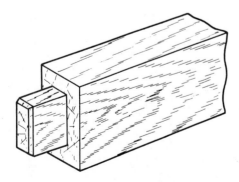

Fig. 11-72. Completed tenon.

Making a Mortise-and-Tenon Joint — Machine Process

Topic 95.

Classification

Joinery by fitting and gluing

Procedure

Follow the layout procedure as in hand joining. See Figs. 11-74 and 11-75.

Cutting the Mortise

1. Select the proper size hollow chisel for the width of the mortise. Insert it either in a mortiser, Fig. 9-67, or in an attachment on the drill press, Fig. 11-76. Adjust the table and guide so that the shoulders for the cut will be at right angles to the table guide. To prevent overheating, the bit should be about 1/8" below the cutting edge of the chisel.
2. Locate the work on the table so that when the chisel is lowered, the cut will be made between the gauged lines. Adjust the fence so that the gauge lines will be parallel to the cutting edges of the chisel. The face side of the work usually faces the fence. All pieces must be set in the same position.
3. Secure the lock-down lever so that the work will not be raised when the chisel is withdrawn.
4. Set the depth gauge or the stop to cut to the desired depth.
5. When making more than one mortise, clamp stops to the table to limit the length of the mortise in each member.
6. To keep from binding the chisel on withdrawal, start the cut at one end of the mortise and make a partial depth cut at the first position. Make repeated adjacent cuts until all waste has been removed. On the last cut, there should be enough stock for the chisel to take a full bite, thereby ensuring a straight cut.

Cutting the Tenon on a Circular Saw

1. The surfaces on all tenon stock must be square with each other and must be of the same thickness and length. Any variation in these dimensions will cause a variation in the size of the tenon.

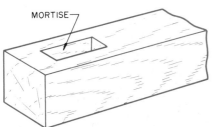

Fig. 11-74. Mortise.

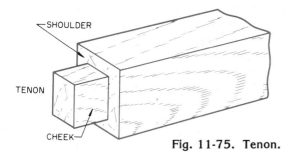

Fig. 11-75. Tenon.

Fig. 11-76. Mortising attachment.

Rockwell International

2. If more than one tenon is to be cut, and all pieces of stock are of proper dimension, it is necessary to lay out only the first piece to the exact dimensions.

3. To cut the cheeks, set the rip fence in such a way that the distance from the fence to a saw tooth bent away from the fence is equal to the length of the tenon. Lock in position.

4. Set the crosscut or combination saw to a height, above the table, equal to the waste stock to be removed. It is good practice to make a test nick near the end of the tenon to ensure the correct height. A saw blade that is too high will make too thin a tenon. When the correct height has been obtained, the stock should be moved to its cutting position against the miter gauge and a nick should be made to check the proper length of the tenon. When the setting is correct, lock the blade-raising mechanism in position.

5. Make the shoulder cheek cuts first. Then, by repeated cuts (close together), remove the waste on one side.

6. Turn the stock over and repeat these steps on the opposite side.

7. After opposite cheeks have been cut to the same dimension on all pieces, reset the saw height to cut the shoulders on the edges of the stock. Do not move the rip fence.

8. Repeat the waste-removal operation by starting at the shoulder cut and working toward the outside end.

9. The cheeks of the tenon may be smoothed by carefully paring with a sharp chisel. Do not remove too much material, or the tenon will be too thin.

10. If a dado head, Fig. 4-36, is available, it can be used to speed the process of waste removal, as fewer cuts are needed with the dado head.

Cutting Identical Tenons

1. Cut all shoulders as in the above process.

2. Two rip or combination blades of the same size are mounted in such a way that the space left between the blades during cutting is equal to the thickness of the tenon.

   Note: The spacer must take up allowance for the saw set. See Fig. 11-77.

3. Set the stock to be cut upright in a tenoning jig, so that it will be held securely while the work is being passed over the saw blade. See Fig. 11-78.

   Regardless of how the tenon is cut, a 1/8″ chamfer should be cut on the end of the tenon.

Fig. 11-78. Tenoning jig.

Rockwell International

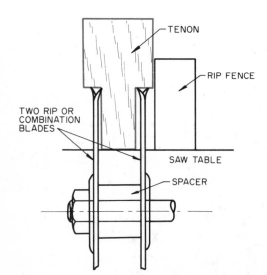

Fig. 11-77. Setup for cutting a tenon on the circular saw, using two saw blades.

Oliver Machinery Co.

Fig. 11-79. Mortising machine.

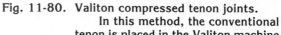

Heywood-Wakefield Company

Fig. 11-80. Valiton compressed tenon joints.

In this method, the conventional tenon is placed in the Valiton machine and, in one operation, is compressed toward the center from three different directions. When the tenon compressed in this manner is inserted into a glue-lined hole, the moisture of the glue causes the tenon to expand back to its original size. The swelling of the tenon makes a tight joint. This process requires a glue that has a high moisture content.

Standards and Results

- Cuts should not run into the shoulder of the tenon.
- Edges of both the mortise and the tenon should be smooth.
- The tenon should fit the mortise snugly.
- To allow for glue, the mortise should be 1/8″ deeper than the tenon.
- The end of the tenon should have an 1/8″ chamfer on all edges.
- The shoulder of the tenon should fit flush against the mortised members.

Safety Considerations

- Wear safety glasses when using woodworking equipment.
- Observe all safety precautions regarding the use of the circular saw, the drill press, and the mortiser.
- Stock should be clamped securely on the mortiser.
- Keep your fingers out from under the mortising chisel.

Making a Through Dovetail Joint — Hand Process

Topic 96.

Classification

Joinery by lock fitting

Procedure

1. Study Fig. 11-82, noting particularly the names of the parts of the dovetail joint.

2. The **pins** may be the same size as or smaller than the tails, and are usually designed this way for better appearance. However, more strength is gained by having the tails wider than the pins. This type of layout is recommended for softwood construction.

3. A good rule to follow in laying out the tails is to make the base width of the tail three-

Fig. 11-81. A through dovetail chest.

Mark Levin

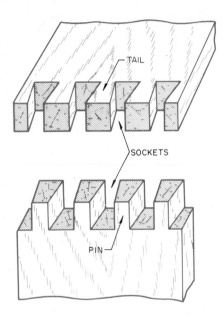

Fig. 11-82. Nomenclature of dovetail joint.

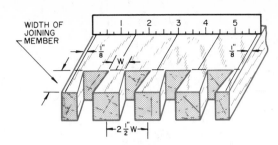

Fig. 11-83. Layout of tails.

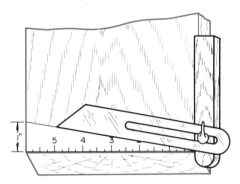

Fig. 11-84. Adjusting the T-bevel for a one-to-six ratio.

procedure for setting the T-bevel is explained in detail in Step 7 of "Laying Out the Tails," which follows.

Laying Out the Tails

1. Square the ends of the two members to be joined.
2. Square a line around the ends of each piece at a distance equal to the thickness of the opposite member. Use a sharp knife or a sharp, hard pencil.
3. Determine the number of tails. Applying the formula recommended above on a board 6" wide and 3/4" thick (W = 3/4t), you would have 3/4 × 3/4", which is 9/16". Use 2-1/2 as the midpoint between two and three, in order to determine the center-to-center spacing (CC = 2-1/2W), and apply the dimensions — 2-1/2 × 9/16" = 1-13/32", or, in round numbers, 1-1/2".

   To determine the number of tails, divide the width of the side, in this case, 6", by 1-1/2". The result will be four tails. Since there is to be a half tail on each edge, there will be three full tails and two half tails.
4. Since each outside tail will be 1/8" wider than one-half the center tails, lay out a 1/8" line along the outside edges.

quarters the thickness of the thinner piece (W = 3/4t). The center-to-center distance of the tails is between two and three times that width (CC = 2-3 W). The outside tails are 1/8" wider than one-half the width of the center tail. No tail should be less than 1/4" wide. See Fig. 11-83.

It is important to note that the width of the tails and pins must be such that one-half of the tail (plus 1/8") will be left on each edge of the tail side. To achieve this result, it may be necessary to make some alteration either of the tail or pin sizes, or of the center-to-center dimensions.

The tails are laid out with a T-bevel that has been set to an angle having a ratio of one to six (79°), as shown in Fig. 11-84. The

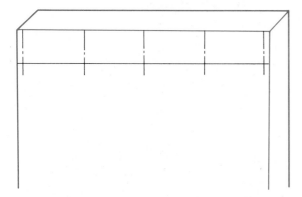

A. Marks indicating center-to-center spacing and depth of tails.

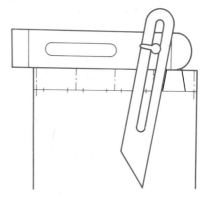

C. Laying out the slope of the tails with a T-bevel.

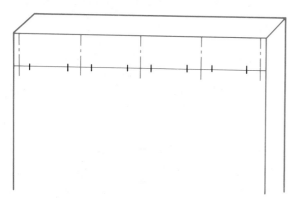

B. Marks indicating base width of tails.

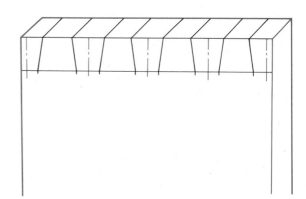

D. Steps in laying out the tails for a through dovetail joint.

Fig. 11-85. Steps in laying out the tails for a through dovetail joint.

5. Divide the remaining space into four equal parts and mark on the line laid out in Step 2. These marks indicate the center of the tails. See Fig. 11-85A.

6. Measure and mark one-half the width of each tail (in this case, half the width is 9/32") on each side of the points located in Step 5. Do this also on the inside of the 1/8" marks on both edges. See Fig. 11-85B.

7. Set a T-bevel to a ratio of one to six. This may be done by squaring a line across the width of a board. At the 6" mark, square a line at a right angle and measure in 1" on this line. Draw a line from this 1" mark to the beginning of the 6" line. With the head of the T-bevel against the edge of the board, adjust the blade so that it coincides with the line. See Fig. 11-84.

8. Placing the head of the T-bevel against the square end of the tails, mark the slope of each tail, Fig. 11-85C.

9. Complete the layout of the tails on one surface. Square lines across the end with a try square. Complete the layout on the other surface. See Fig. 11-85D.

Cutting the Tails

1. Select a small auger bit to bore into the waste at the base of the socket. This makes it easier to remove the stock at the base.

   CAUTION: Take care not to split the stock.

2. With a backsaw or a dovetail saw, cut on the waste side of the layout of the tails. See Fig. 11-86.

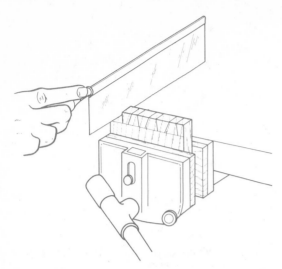

Fig. 11-86. Cutting the dovetails, using a dovetail saw.

3. The sockets formed by cleaning the waste between the tails may now be removed with a coping saw or by chiseling halfway on one side then turning the face stock over and removing the remaining half. Care must be taken to keep the sides of tails square, with no undercutting.

   Note: For information on cutting dovetails by machine process, see Topic 56, "Using a Portable Hand Router."

Laying Out the Sockets on Adjoining Side

1. The cut dovetailed piece is used as a template to mark the sockets and pins on the second member.
2. Stand the two boards on edge and at right angles to each other in the position they will take in the finished joint.
3. Use a sharp knife or a sharp, hard pencil to mark the shape of the sockets by tracing around each cut tail. See Fig. 11-87.

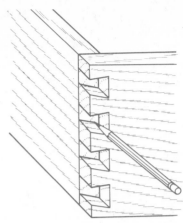

Fig. 11-87. Tracing the sockets on the adjoining side.

4. Along the width of the board, square the depth of the tails with a sharp knife and a try square.
5. Using the T-bevel and square, duplicate the markings on the reverse side.
6. Cut the sockets as on the first piece, making sure to cut on the waste side of the line.
7. Fit the pieces together, taking care not to force any part out of position.

Standards and Results

- The joint should fit tightly and at the correct angle.
- The tails should not be forced into the sockets, as this will cause splits.
- The width of the joining pieces should fit flush.

Safety Considerations

- Wear safety glasses when using woodworking equipment.
- Observe all safety practices pertaining to the particular tool or machine you are using.

Topic 97.

Making a Half-Blind or Stop Dovetail — Hand Process

Classification

Joining by lock fitting

Procedure

1. Study Fig. 11-88, noting particularly the names of the parts of the blind- or stop-dovetail joints used in drawer construction.

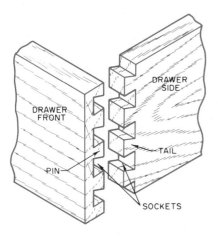

Fig. 11-88. Half-blind or stop dovetail joint.

2. The tails are usually twice the size of the pins. They are designed this way to give more strength.

3. A good rule to follow in laying out the tails is to make the width of the tails (at the widest point) between two and three times the thickness of the drawer side. The pins at the narrowest part should be half the width of the tail at the widest part.

The width of the tails and pins must be such that, when laid out on the drawer pieces, half a pin will be left on each outer edge of the drawer front. See Fig. 11-88.

The length of the tails is usually two-thirds to three-quarters the thickness of the drawer front. The angle of the tails is laid out with a T-bevel that has been set at an angle having a ratio of one to six (79°). See Fig. 11-89.

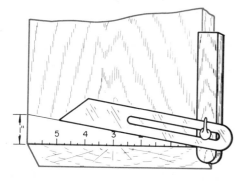

Fig. 11-89. Adjusting the T-bevel for a one-to-six ratio.

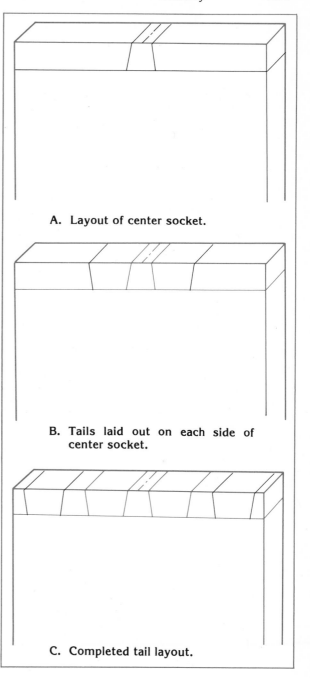

A. Layout of center socket.

B. Tails laid out on each side of center socket.

C. Completed tail layout.

Fig. 11-90. Steps in laying out the tails of a half-blind dovetail joint.

Laying Out the Tails on the Drawer Sides

1. Square the ends of the members to be joined.
2. On each end of the piece that is to become the drawer front, measure in from the inside surface (the surface opposite the face of the

drawer front) a distance equal to two-thirds to three-quarters the thickness of the stock. Square this line the width of the piece on each end of the stock.

3. Measure an equal distance from one end on each of the two pieces that will be used to make the drawer sides. Using a sharp, hard pencil, square these lines across the width of the pieces. These lines indicate the length of the tails.

4. Determine the width of tails by applying the formula recommended in Step 3. In a drawer 6″ deep with a 13/16″-thick drawer front and a 1/2″-thick drawer side, two to three times the thickness of the drawer side would be between 1″ and 1-1/2″. The width of the tail at the widest point should be 1″. This provides the proper placement of tails so that one half of a socket will be left on each edge of the drawer side. See Fig. 11-88.

5. To lay out the tails and sockets on the drawer side, first measure on the end from one edge to find the center of the piece. Then, on each side of this center line, measure 1/4″, or one-quarter the width of a tail at its widest point. Square these lines across the end and, using a T-bevel set at a ratio of one to six (79°), continue the lines down each side of the stock to the line indicating the base of the tails, Fig. 11-90A. These lines indicate the center socket.

6. On the end of the stock, measure 1″, or twice the thickness of the drawer side, on each side of the socket laid out in Step 5. Mark these lines on the face of the stock, using the T-bevel as in Step 5. These lines indicate two full tails. See Fig. 11-90B.

7. Using the T-bevel as in Step 5, lay out a socket the same size and shape on each side of the tails that were laid out in Step 6.

8. Using the same dimensions, lay out another tail on each side of the sockets that were laid out in Step 7.

9. If the layout has been accurate, there should be four tails, three full sockets, and a half socket on each edge, Fig. 11-90C.

Cutting the Tails and Pins

1. On the socket side of the line, use a backsaw or a dovetail saw to cut down the sides of each tail to the base line, Fig. 11-91. This step may also be done on a band saw.

2. Select a small auger bit and bore into the waste at the depth of the tail. This makes it easier to remove the stock.

   CAUTION: Take care not to split the stock.

3. Cut the remainder of the waste between the tails and on the edges. This is done either with a coping saw or scroll saw or by chiseling halfway on one side, then turning the stock over and chiseling from the other side.

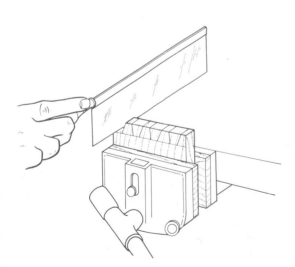

Fig. 11-91. Cutting the dovetails, using a dovetail saw.

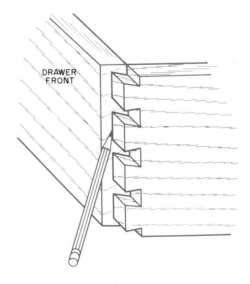

DRAWER FRONT

Fig. 11-92. Marking the sockets on a drawer front, using the drawer side as a template.

4. With a chisel, pare the sides of the tails to the lines. Care must be taken to keep the sides of the tails square (no undercutting).

Laying Out and Cutting Sockets on the Drawer Front

1. Use the dovetailed drawer side as a template to mark the sockets on the ends of the drawer front, Fig. 11-92.
2. Position the two pieces at right angles to each other in the position they will take in the finished joint.
3. Mark the shape of the pin by tracing around the tails with a sharp, hard pencil.
4. Square the lines on the inside of the drawer front, as far as the base line.
5. Using a sharp chisel, backsaw, or dovetail saw, remove the waste to form the socket. Make sure to cut on the waste side of the line.
6. Fit the pieces together, being careful not to force any part out of position.

   Note: For information on cutting dovetails by machine process, see Topic 56, "Using a Portable Hand Router."

Standards and Results

- The joint should fit tightly and at the correct angle.
- The tails should not be forced into the sockets, as this may cause splits.
- The edges and face of the drawer side should be flush with the end and edges of the drawer front.

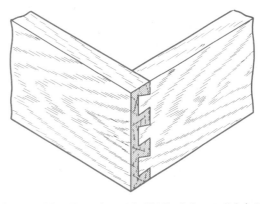

Fig. 11-93. Completed half-blind dovetail joint.

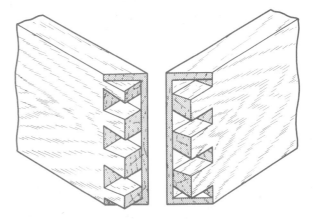

Fig. 11-94. Blind miter dovetail.

Safety Considerations

- Wear safety glasses when using woodworking equipment.
- Observe all safety practices pertaining to the particular tool or machine you are using.

Laying Out and Cutting Dovetails on a Pedestal Leg

Topic 98.

Classification

Joinery by lock fitting

Procedure

The general rules for determining the size of dovetails are as follows: (a) Make the length of the tail one-quarter the diameter of the pedestal. (b) Make the width of the tail (at the widest point) three-quarters the thickness of the leg. (c) Make the taper of the pin on a ratio of six to one.

Example:
a. L = 1/4d   1/4 × 3 = 3/4
b. W = 3/4 × 1-1/4 = 15/16
c. Taper = 6 to 1 ratio

Note: The tail is cut first. The socket is then laid out and cut to fit.

Laying Out and Cutting the Tail on the Leg

1. Lay out the center lines on the ends of the legs, Fig. 11-95. Using a square, a knife, a marking gauge, and a T-bevel, lay out the tails. See Topic 96, "Making a Through Dovetail Joint — Hand Process."
2. With a backsaw, cut the shoulder and the cheek. Make sure that the cuts are made on the waste side of each line. Trim to the line with a sharp chisel, Fig. 11-96.
3. A cut such as that in Step 2 may also be made on the circular saw. This is done by

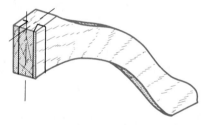

Fig. 11-95. Layout of tail on leg.

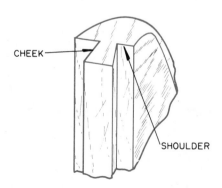

CHEEK

SHOULDER

Fig. 11-96. Shoulder and cheek.

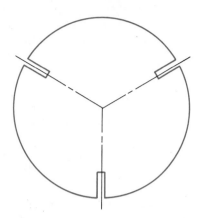

Fig. 11-97. Layout of 120° angles for template.

first making the cheek cuts and then the shoulder cuts. To do this, tilt the saw to the proper angle and adjust the fence to the desired distance. With the joint end of the leg down, make the cheek cut.

Adjust the saw blade to the vertical position and the proper height. Set the rip fence to the required distance. Place the leg on its side and make the shoulder cut. Repeat for the other shoulder.

Laying Out the Center Lines of the Socket Cuts

1. Divide the end of the cylinder into three equal parts. See Fig. 11-97. This may be done by setting a compass or dividers to the radius of the cylinder and stepping off the six equal divisions on the outer circumference.
2. Using a square and a pencil, mark the center lines at alternate points along the face of the spindle (a distance equal to the length of the shoulder of the leg).

Laying Out and Cutting the Flats

1. On the end of the cylinder, measure one-half the thickness of a leg on each side of the center lines. This will locate the proper position and width of each leg around the cylinder.
2. Square these lines down the face of the cylinder a distance equal to the length of the shoulder of the leg, Fig. 11-98.

3. Set the combination square a distance equal to the length of the shoulder of the leg. With a knife, mark the length of the shoulder for the flat by connecting the lines. Using a sharp knife, make an undercut on the line just made.
4. With a backsaw, cut at right angles along the undercut just made, until the saw kerf reaches the width lines.
5. With a chisel and mallet, remove all waste stock within the area just laid out. Finish with a shearing cut.

Laying Out and Cutting the Sockets

1. On the end of the pedestal, lay out the socket the same size as the leg tail. This may be done with a knife and a T-bevel, Fig. 11-99. Square these lines down the face of the flats the length of the shoulder. Remove the waste for the socket by boring or by using a mortiser. Trim to the exact size with a chisel.
2. Make a partial fit by testing and paring with a chisel where necessary.

To test for proper fit, coat the sides and end of the tail with chalk and assemble the joint. Surfaces of the socket most heavily marked by chalk indicate spots that need trimming. A well-fitted joint will have a light, even coating of chalk on all contacting surfaces.

Standards and Results

• The tail should fit snugly in the socket.

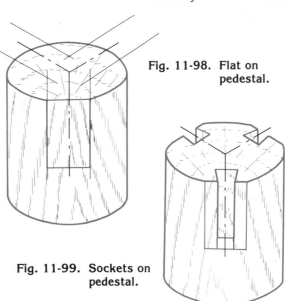

Fig. 11-98. Flat on pedestal.

Fig. 11-99. Sockets on pedestal.

• The shoulder of the leg and the flat cut on the spindle should make a tight joint.
• Legs should be properly spaced on the spindle — at right angles and perpendicular to the axis of the pedestal.
• All feet should rest evenly on a flat surface.

Safety Considerations

• Wear safety glasses when using woodworking equipment.
• Observe all safety practices pertaining to the particular tool or machine you are using.

Making a Coped Joint

Topic 99.

Classification

Joinery by profile butting

Procedure

A **coped joint** is usually used as a substitute for a miter joint in joining inside corners of moldings and molded baseboards. It is used for this purpose because it will not open up as the pieces are fastened in place. See Fig. 11-100. The end of one member is cut to fit the contour of the shaped surface of the other member.

Mitering Method

1. After the first member has been squared at one end and has been cut to length, fasten it

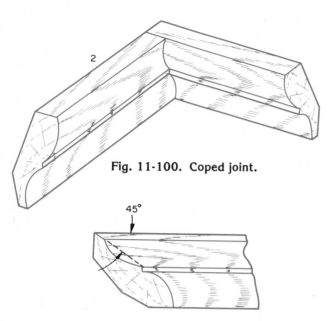

Fig. 11-100. Coped joint.

Arco Tools, Inc.

45°

Fig. 11-101. Miter cut made, ready for cope cut.

COPY BASIN &
PLUMBING CONTOURS

MEASURE MOLDINGS

CHECK DIMENSIONS

Fig. 11-103. Molding comb or contour gauge.

in place. The two inside faces should fit snugly and should be straight and square.

2. Place the second member in the miter box in the position it will take when fitted. The back of the molding should be against the miter fence. A 45°-angle cut should be made so that the contour of the work will show a profile on the face of the molding. See Fig. 11-101.

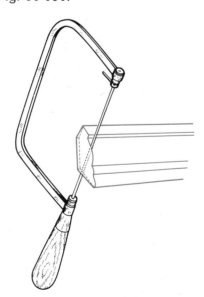

Fig. 11-102. Undercutting the coped edge to make a tight fit on the face.

3. With a coping saw, cut along the profile of the face. Hold the coping saw parallel to the top edge of the molding and undercut at a slight angle. This is done so that a tight fit will be made with the first piece. See Fig. 11-102.

4. Place the second member in position. It should fit the contour snugly. If any obstructions exist, they may be undercut with a knife or file. Be sure that the top edge and the back are held in such a way that the members form a 45° angle with the corner.

5. Fasten the second member in place. Nails should be driven into two adjacent surfaces. (Nailing will not open up a joint that has been properly fitted.) The finished joint should look like a mitered joint.

Template Method

1. A molding comb, Fig. 11-103, or a piece of thin sheet material is fitted to the molding to form a template.

2. The profile made in this manner is used to transfer the contour to the piece to be joined.

Standards and Results

• There should be no openings in the fitted members.

- The pieces should form a perfect corner with no gaps.
- No hammer marks or splits should show on the face of the work.
- Nails should be set below the surface.

Making Finger Joints to Support Table Leaves

Topic 100.

Classification

Joinery by fitting and pinning

Procedure

Finger joints are used on a swing leg or rail, to support drop leaves of a table. To use this type of joint, it is necessary to have an apron that is fixed and solid. The apron with the finger joint (or joints, if more than one support is used) should be on the outside and should be adjacent to the fixed apron. See Fig. 11-104.

Laying Out the Arcs on the Ends of the Pieces

1. On both pieces of stock to be used to make the joint, locate the center of the thickness on the top and bottom edges and near the end of each piece.

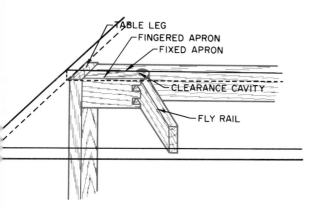

Fig. 11-104. **Construction of fly rail, using a finger joint.**

Labels: TABLE LEG, FINGERED APRON, FIXED APRON, CLEARANCE CAVITY, FLY RAIL

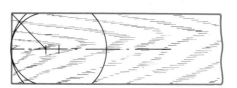

Fig. 11-105. **Determining the arc of the ends.**

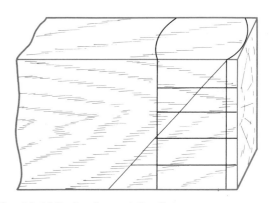

Fig. 11-106. **Laying out the fingers.**

2. Set a pair of dividers to an opening equal to one-half the thickness of the fixed apron.
3. Place one leg of the dividers on the center line. This leg should be positioned in such a way that the distance between it and the end of the pieces is equal to the radius of the circle. See Fig. 11-105.
4. Using the same center, increase the radius to a distance from the center to a corner.
5. Relocate the center so that the new radius scribes an arc tangent to the end of the piece.
6. On the edge of the stock, draw as much of a complete circle as the thickness permits.

Do this on the opposite edge and on both pieces.

7. Where the arcs meet the faces, square lines down both faces to the opposite edge. See Fig. 11-106.

Laying Out the Width of the Fingers

For maximum strength, fingers are usually laid out as close to 1″ in width as possible. There should be an odd number of fingers so that the apron has a finger at each edge.

1. Divide the width of the apron into an odd number of equal sections. This may be done either with a pair of dividers or with a rule. Figure 11-106 shows a diagonal line that has been drawn in such a way that it can be conveniently divided into five equal parts. (The diagonal-rule method is illustrated in detail in Fig. 2-50, Topic 15.)
2. On these divisions, square lines in from the end to the line previously drawn on the faces, as shown in Fig. 11-106.
3. Lay out the matching fingers on the fly rail.

Cutting the Fingered Apron

1. Shape the arc on the end of the pieces, using a smooth plane, a file and sandpaper, or, if available, a suitable shaper cutter.
2. Using either a backsaw and chisel or a band saw, remove the stock from within alternate

divisions. Be careful to stay on the waste side of the line.

3. To cut the inside arcs in the center cavities, clamp the stock upright in the vise. Place a hand screw across the stock at a position even with the inside end of the fingers. (The hand screw prevents the stock from splitting.) See Fig. 11-107.
4. Select a chisel slightly narrower than the width of the finger. Hold the bevel side down and work from each face toward the center. Cut the concave arc in the center cavities. See Fig. 11-108.

Cutting the Fly Rail

1. Cut the cavities to match the fingers previously cut. See Fig. 11-109.
2. Use an inside-bevel gouge to cut the inside arcs on the top and bottom edges.
3. Repeat Steps 3 and 4 (under the preceding heading) for cutting the inside arc on the center cavity.
4. The two pieces should fit together as shown in Fig. 11-110.
5. If the fingers need trimming, do this with a chisel.
6. After the pieces have been properly fitted, and while they are in the correct position, use the center point of the arc to bore a 1/4″-diameter hole from the top edge to a point halfway through the bottom finger. Care must be taken to bore the hole at right angles to the edge of the apron. Otherwise, the fly rail will not swing plumb.
7. Apply a coat of wax to a 1/4″ hardwood dowel or steel pin. Insert the dowel or pin into the hole just drilled.

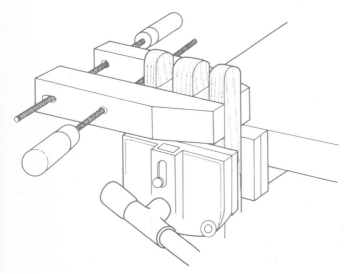

Fig. 11-107. A hand screw should be used to reinforce the bottom edge of the fingers. This reduces the chances of splintering during the process of chiseling between the fingers.

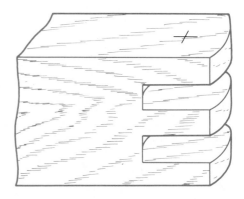

Fig. 11-108. Cutting the fingered apron.

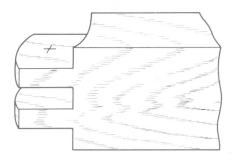

Fig. 11-109. Cutting the fly rail.

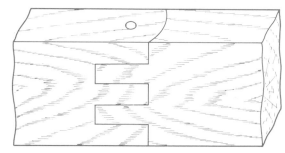

Fig. 11-110. The assembled joint on the fly rail.

Laying Out and Cutting a Clearance Cavity

In order for the fingers to clear the fixed apron, a cavity must be cut in it.

1. Clamp the movable apron to the fixed apron in the exact position these parts will occupy when in use.
2. The cavity may be laid out by setting the dividers at the same arc as that of the ends of the fingers. Placing one point at the center of the dowel pin, scribe the arc on the top edge of the inner apron. Using the center on the lower edge, scribe an arc of the same size on the underside of the inner apron. See Fig. 11-111.
3. Remove the clamps and separate the pieces.

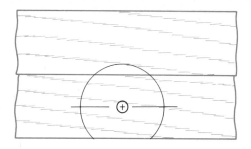

Fig. 11-111. Laying out the clearance cavity of the fixed apron.

4. Square lines down the face, connecting the ends of the two arcs.
5. Cut and smooth the cavity, using a chisel, file, and sandpaper.
6. With the two aprons clamped in the correct position, check to see if the fly rail swings smoothly. If it does, fasten it permanently with glue and reinforce it with screws driven from the inside of the aprons.

Standards and Results

- If layout and cutting have been done accurately, the fly rail should swing out to an angle 90° from the inner apron and should be in a plumb position.
- Joints between the fingers should be reasonably tight.
- The top and bottom edges of the fly rails and aprons should be flush.

Safety Considerations

- Wear safety glasses when using woodworking equipment.
- Observe all safety practices pertaining to the particular tool or machine you are using.

Joints Commonly Used in Table Construction

Topic 101.

1. **Edge-to-edge spring joint** (Topic 87) or **dowel butt joint** (Topic 92), used in joining tops.
2. **Mortise-and-tenon joint** (Topics 94 and 95) or **dowel joint** (Topic 92), used to assemble legs, rails, and aprons.
3. **Dovetail joint** (Topics 96 and 97), **rabbet joint** (Topic 90), and **dado-rabbet joint,** Fig. 11-6, used in drawer construction.
4. **Reinforcing joints,** Figs. 11-112 through 11-114.

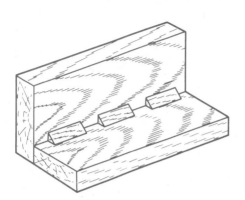

Fig. 11-112. Edge butt joint reinforced with glued corner blocks.

Fig. 11-113. End butt joint reinforced with corner brace fastened with screws.

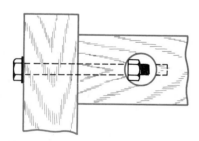

Fig. 11-114. End butt joint reinforced with through bolt.

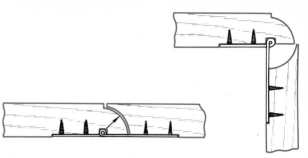

Fig. 11-115. Rule joint on a drop leaf.

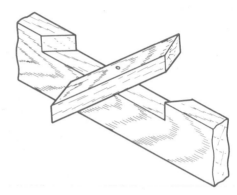

Fig. 11-116. Pivot support for drop leaf.

Fig. 11-117. Pullout support for drop leaf.

5. **Rule joint,** used between the center board and the drop leaf on a table. This provides a movable joint with an attractive molded edge on the center board when the leaf is down, and closes to a flat, horizontal surface when the leaf is raised. This joint must be used in conjunction with a pair of table-leaf hinges. See Fig. 11-115.

6. **Finger joint** (Topic 100), **pivot support,** Fig. 11-116, or **pullout support,** Fig. 11-117, used for supporting the drop leaves of a table.

7. **Dado joint** (Topic 89), used for fastening drawer frames to sides or aprons.

8. Figure 11-119 shows tabletop fastening methods that allow for expansion.

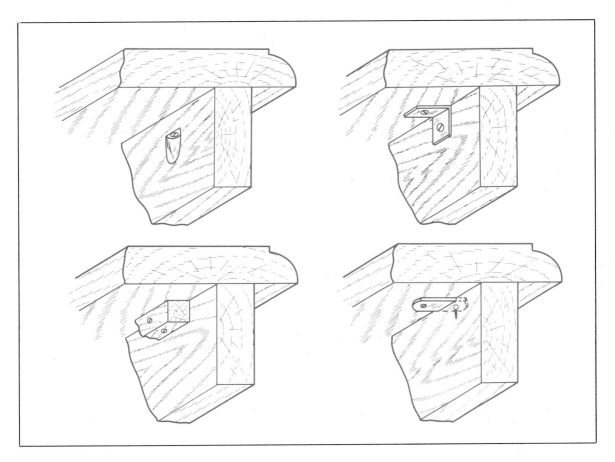

Fig. 11-118. Methods of fastening tabletops to frames.

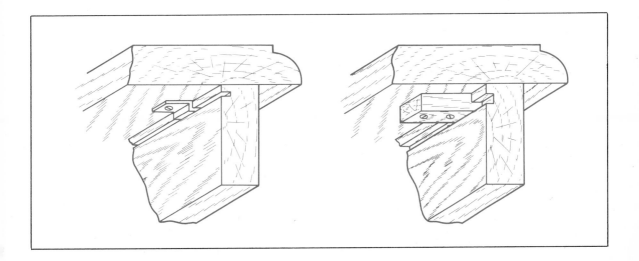

Fig. 11-119. Tabletop fasteners that allow for expansion.

Topic 102.

Drawer Guides, Shelf Supports, and Sliding Doors

Drawer Guides

Drawer guides are used to support and to guide a drawer squarely into its opening. There are several types of drawer guides. Some are made of wood and may be constructed in the wood shop, and others, made of metal and other materials, are purchased in a hardware store.

1. **Corner drawer guides** are L-shaped wood guides that support the drawer along its bottom edges, Fig. 11-120. Corner guides may be made with strips of wood that have been rabbeted on one edge. The rabbet forms a lip, which, when attached to the cabinet, forms the sliding surface for the drawer.

2. **Side drawer guides** support the drawer on each side by means of guide strips and matching grooves, Fig. 11-121. The guide strips are usually 1/2″ to 3/4″ thick and 1″ wide (depending on the size of the drawer) and are the length of the drawer side. These guide strips are attached to each side of the drawer frame. Grooves are then cut in the drawer sides to accommodate the guide strips. (These grooves should be cut before the drawer is constructed.)

Another method of constructing side drawer guides is to cut the grooves in the drawer frame and add the strips to the sides of the drawer, Fig. 11-122.

3. **Center drawer guides** use a guide strip and groove much like those of side drawer guides. However, the groove is cut on an additional piece of stock and is mounted on the underside of the drawer, Fig. 11-123. The grooved strip of this guide system should be 1/2″ thick, 1-1/2″ wide, and the same length as the drawer. Cut a groove 1/2″ deep and 3/4″ wide in the center of this strip, and attach this portion to the underside of the drawer.

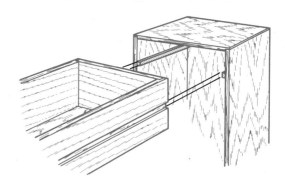

Fig. 11-121. Side drawer guides (grooved-drawer method).

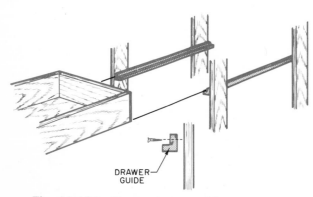

DRAWER GUIDE

Fig. 11-120. Corner drawer guides.

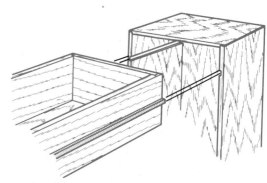

Fig. 11-122. Side drawer guides (grooved-frame method).

The guide strip, or ungrooved portion of this guide system, is made with 3/4"-wide by 1/2"-thick stock, with a 1/4" rabbet cut on each end. This piece is attached to the center of the drawer-frame cross members in such a way that it protrudes 1/4" above the surface of the frame. It should be centered to enable the grooved strip to slide properly along its length.

4. **Manufactured drawer guides** generally consist of metal tracks supported by metal or plastic rollers, Fig. 11-124. These are attached to the drawer and frame to assure smooth and accurate drawer movement. Follow the manufacturer's specifications for installation.

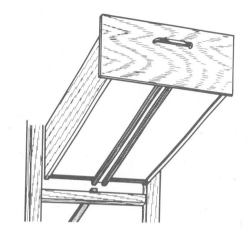

Fig. 11-123. Center drawer guide.

Shelf Supports

Shelf supports hold shelves and permit them to be raised or lowered to accommodate different needs. Many shelves are permanently joined to the upright members and cannot be adjusted. The decision to make shelves adjustable or permanent must be made prior to construction, as this may change the overall design.

1. **Dowel supports** can be made by cutting short lengths of dowel rod and inserting these into holes drilled in the sides of the case. The dowel pins protrude from the sides to support the shelves. See Fig. 11-125.

   Dowel supports are generally made with 1/4" dowel rod, cut 5/8" to 3/4" long. These supports fit into blind holes, which are drilled 3/8" to 1/2" deep and are usually spaced 1-1/2" in from each edge of the side. Extra holes, to allow for shelf adjustment, are usually spaced 1-1/2" apart along the length of the sides.

2. Two types of manufactured shelf supports are available. One type consists of metal strips, punched to accept special support clips, Fig. 11-126. These strips are attached, in pairs, to each side of the case. Grooves are usually cut in the case sides so that the strips will mount flush with the inside surface.

   The second type of manufactured support is a metal or plastic variation of the dowel support. These metal or plastic pins are used in the same way as dowel supports, but are less conspicuous. See Fig. 11-125.

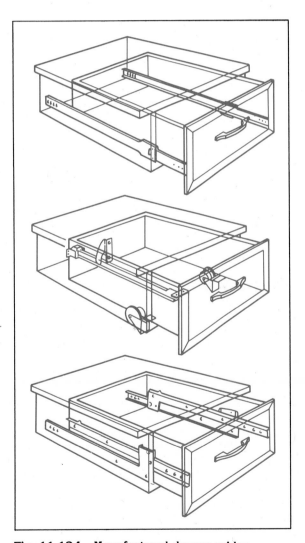

Fig. 11-124. Manufactured drawer guides.

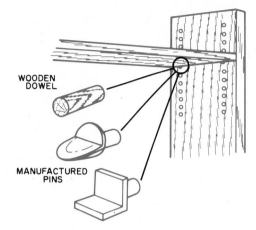

Fig. 11-125. Shelf-support pins.

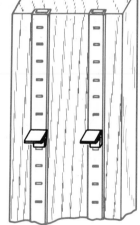

Fig. 11-126. Manufactured clip-type shelf supports.

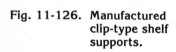

Sliding Doors

In many cabinet designs, a **sliding door** is used instead of a conventional hinged door. Although this is usually done to conserve space, it can also improve the cabinet's style and utility. For these reasons, sliding doors are also used in home construction, particularly in the design of closets and in areas where space is at a premium.

Sliding doors can be made of many materials, such as wood, glass, plastic, and hardboard. They are fitted into tracks at the top and bottom of the door opening.

The tracks can either be cut directly into the cabinet frame or can be made separately and then attached. Manufactured guides are also available for a wide range of applications. See Fig. 11-127.

In cutting grooves for wood guides, it is important that the top guide be cut twice as deep as the bottom guide. This allows the door to be lifted into the top guide and then to be lowered into position in the bottom guide. The grooves must also be wide enough to allow easy movement of the doors. For thick doors, a rabbet cut should be made in each end. This will reduce the width of the grooves needed and will reduce the space between the doors.

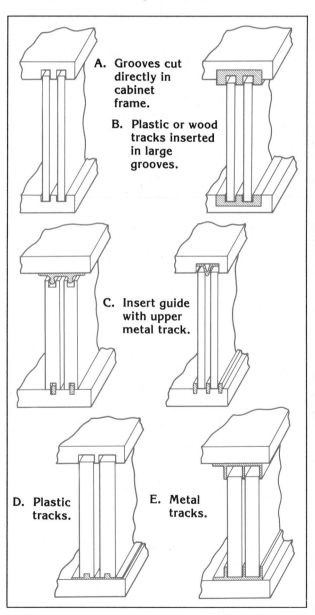

A. Grooves cut directly in cabinet frame.

B. Plastic or wood tracks inserted in large grooves.

C. Insert guide with upper metal track.

D. Plastic tracks.

E. Metal tracks.

Fig. 11-127. Common tracks used for sliding doors.

Woodcraft Supply Corporation

SECTION TWELVE.

Cabinetmaking and Decorative Shapes

291

Topic 103.

Cabinetmaking

Cabinetmaking is a general term in the wood fabrication industry for the making of furniture. Today all furniture makers working in wood are loosely classified as cabinetmakers. Most of these workers are machine operators. In former times there was a distinction made between the categories of cabinetmaker, joiner, and chairmaker.

In the 18th and 19th centuries, the cabinetmaking shops were small and the owners were the principal workers. They were usually artisans who designed and made furniture on order. Under their direction, helpers or apprentices learned the craft. An expert cabinetmaker was skilled in all phases of cabinetmaking, including joinery, carving, and finishing. Quality construction, beauty, and durability were characteristics of the furniture of reputable cabinetmaking firms. Individual pieces of furniture were expected to last not only a lifetime but were handed down from one generation to the next. Sometimes family possessions of this type were shipped from abroad. The top cabinetmakers of this earlier period were truly artists, expressing their ideas and skills in the medium of wood. They selected their materials carefully and enhanced natural beauty with attractive elements of functional design. Woodworkers of various specialties also made furniture that filled the needs of the average household. Though plain in style and made only from the wood available in the region, this furniture was attractive and durable.

There are many furniture factories today, all over the United States. Like all modern industries, furniture making is highly mechanized and is organized for mass production. Only a small number of expert cabinetmakers are employed in these factories. These are the sample makers, who translate the plans of the designer into the initial sample or new model. Upon completion, this model is thoroughly analyzed to determine whether production will be possible and the product can be marketed. Once the design has been approved and the decision has been made to go into production, jigs and fixtures are made to simplify production. In the mass-production process, each part can be made in great number, with a minimum variation in size, shape, and detail.

The various operations by which lumber is shaped into furniture are performed by machine operators, skilled in the specific techniques of their job. As a rule, these workers are not concerned with the overall factory setup. They are not likely to be highly skilled in the operations performed by the workers on other machines or in other departments of the factory. The employees are, for the most part, specialists in one kind of work. This type of work might include such things as tending a particular machine, assembling parts, setting

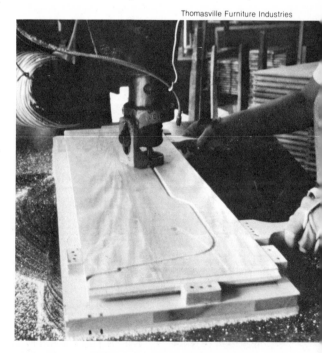

Thomasville Furniture Industries

Fig. 12-1.   Machine cutting basic furniture components in production manufacturing.

Thomasville Furniture Industries

Fig. 12-2.   Assembly operations in a production furniture shop.

uct. In fact, many times quality is reduced in the attempt to maintain a lower cost. Pricing must be competitive if furniture is to be affordable to the average consumer. Durability is not a major consideration today. Style, function, and cost are the concerns of consumers, and most of today's furniture is not expected to last more than a decade. With care, most furniture will hold up beyond that time, but it is not generally built to withstand generations of use.

There are many amateur cabinetmakers who make their own furniture. There are also skilled cabinetmakers — present-day counterparts of the 18th- and 19th-century artisans — who operate their own small businesses in much the same fashion as cabinetmakers of the earlier period. Custom-made furniture can be obtained if the customer is willing to wait for it to be made and is willing to pay a higher price. Although the cost is high, a well-crafted product will be a prized possession having timeless quality.

up machines, making jigs and fixtures, maintaining equipment, finishing, upholstering, or performing duties essential to some division of the production line. Improved machinery, power tools, and new materials have resulted in the mechanization of most operations. There is a minimal amount of hand work done. Many parts that were once produced by highly skilled workers such as wood-carvers are now either mass-produced by machines or are molded from plastic and incorporated in the finished product.

The production line is based on a sequence of operations. This sequence begins with the cutting of boards to required dimension. Operations that follow are shaping, assembling, joining, and finishing. The factory is organized by departments or divisions, and efficiency is sought in the handling of materials and the flow of work.

Cost is a prime consideration, and every aspect of design, production, sales distribution, and management is influenced by the need for a competitive overall product cost. Improved production methods, automation, and cost-saving features have not always resulted in a better design or an improved prod-

Woodcraft Supply Corp.

Fig. 12-3.   Skilled artisans still exist today, designing and making individual pieces of furniture.

Topic 104.

Design

In the field of wood processing, **design** involves not only the planning and construction of a project, but also a consideration for the natural design of the wood. All wood possesses a unique design. This design will be apparent whether or not it has been considered in the overall planning of the product. In shape and size, as well as in grain, figure, texture (or even blemish), wood presents to the woodworker many natural qualities of design. To enhance these natural characteristics, woodworkers and designers have created numerous methods of working and finishing wood to give it character, beauty, and distinctiveness.

Consider how wood products come into being. Wood is usually fabricated into form in response to some need or with some end use in mind. Style, ornamentation, and motif are also considered.

While most woods are appropriate for numerous applications, the selection of the most suitable wood for a given use is based on both scientific findings and traditional practice. Often, a particular wood is best known by some specific use. For example, ash is known for use in the construction of baseball bats; mahogany, maple, and cherry for furniture; knotty pine for paneling; oak for floors; and hickory for handles. The experienced woodworker is quite well informed about the properties of the different woods and the suitability of these types of wood for particular applications. Both the woodworking student and the amateur woodworker should investigate available data about woods and should consider the specific properties of wood types in planning and designing objects to be made of wood.

A.W. Marlow

Fig. 12-5.   Queen Ann highboy.

Mark Levin

Fig. 12-4.   Contemporary table design.

Fig. 12-6.   Governor Winthrop desk.

Fig. 12-8.   Candlestand.

Fig. 12-9.   Piecrust
tilt-top table.

Fig. 12-7.   Drop-leaf
table.

In addition to considering the functional aspects of construction, the worker should keep in mind the overall appearance of the finished product. Wood products can and should be attractive as well as being practical and technically sound.

There are many wood products that are considered objects of beauty because of their shape, style, grain pattern, finish, and other qualities. Still, as an art medium, wood has not been fully utilized. Although much has been done in this regard, there is still much that could be done with wood. Because wood has such a variety of characteristics, it has great potential for use as an art medium.

Throughout the years, imaginative workers have discovered that wood can be fashioned readily into a variety of shapes. These shapes may have many degrees of inside and outside curves, either sharp or rounded edges and corners, bevels and tapers, and an almost infinite variety of turnings. Countless designs of panels, beading, carvings, fretwork, inlay, marquetry, and molding are also employed to impart a unique character to wood products.

In recent times, formfitting molded shapes and laminations have contributed further variety to woodworking designs. Improved types of appliques such as decals, transfers, wood tapes, and manufactured panels have added great variety to wood decoration. The development of new finishes has increased the attractiveness and utility of wood products, particularly furniture and household woodware.

Every product made of wood is the result of some need, interest, idea, or inspiration. Sometimes little thought is given to the factor of design. Usually, however, design considerations accompany every stage of the development of a project.

In preliminary sketching, functional qualities usually receive greatest attention. Certain fundamental considerations must be included. Some of these considerations are as follows:

a. Technical knowledge about properties of particular wood species.
b. Performance characteristics of glues, nails, screws, hardware, and other fasteners.
c. Methods of joinery and construction.
d. Shape and dimension of wood.
e. Kinds of finishes.
f. Intended function of the product.

Some technical considerations have as much to do with the product's appearance as they have to do with its function. For example, in determining the particular kind of wood to be used, texture, grain, color, and figure are considered. At the same time, fabricating properties and suitable physical characteristics are considered. Construction is determined mainly on the basis of functional considerations, but often is greatly influenced by characteristics of the wood's appearance. In the refinement of a design, the method of construction is sometimes altered, and strength becomes less important than beauty, or is at least sacrificed to some degree.

Thus, it can be seen that both technical decisions and decisions regarding the work's appearance are made at every stage of the development of a product. The application of sound technical thinking often results in a very attractive product. The attempt to make a product that is visually pleasing results in an emphasis on good design. On the other hand, an object that is well constructed has a particular beauty of its own.

Woodware

Many useful objects are made of wood. They are classified as **woodware.** A few examples of woodware are wooden plates, bowls, lamps, serving trays, sewing boxes, jewelry boxes, knife boxes, stepladders, and clothespins. The design requirements of many of the more inexpensive woodware products are quite simple. They concern mainly such things as size, shape, function, finish, and cost. Woods are selected on the basis of suitable properties, availability, and cost. The price an object of woodware will bring on the market is a very important consideration. Sometimes, therefore, it is necessary to compromise somewhat in strength and beauty in order to meet a particular price level. In cases where natural wood beauty is not important, opaque finishes are employed to completely obscure blemishes and defects. Utility, style, and color are probably the consumer's main concerns in selecting a wood product. Both the student of woodworking and the amateur woodworker should keep in mind all these considerations when designing a woodware project.

Fig. 12-10. Windsor chair.

Drexel Heritage Furnishing, Inc.

Fig. 12-11. Dining table and chairs

Mark Levin

Fig. 12-12. Contemporary chair design.

Furniture Design

There has been considerable experimentation done in the area of wood-furniture design. Efforts have been made to introduce new and different shapes and styles. Many pieces have been simplified and streamlined by rounding corners and by bending and molding parts. New finishes and fabrics appropriate to the newer shapes have given a new look to many pieces of furniture. There has been a definite increase in the use of metal in combination with wood. Sheet iron, stainless steel, brass, copper, aluminum, and expanded metal have been used for legs, feet, frames, shelves, and drawer guides. Plastic and glass have also been used in combination with wood.

Most furniture manufactured today is mass-produced. It is made to serve the style and characteristics of contemporary living. Modern furniture is usually light in weight, compact, and readily cleaned and maintained. Either traditional or modern finishes may be used, according to preference. However, the advantages of modern finishes are becoming widely recognized. The covering of upholstered goods must possess beauty of design, color, and texture, as well as being practical. Latex foam and other new fillers are sought after for their resilience, their good wearing qualities, and their attractive appearance and comfort. Ap-

pearance, sometimes called "customer appeal," is a primary consideration in furniture design.

In planning their furniture projects, students and amateur furniture makers would do well to study the characteristics of good furniture of all periods. They should try to identify the qualities that give a piece character and attractiveness. In so doing, the woodworker will likely discover that the best in both contemporary and traditional furniture is not only suited to its intended use, but has a quality of harmony and unity that is found both in individual parts and in the work as a whole. The style of the best furniture represents a fashion rather than a fad.

A chair presents an excellent challenge in furniture design. The relation of the chair to the human body is intimate. The chair must both fit the body and provide comfort and rest. A chair must be relatively easy to handle, portable, and strong enough to resist complex stresses. It must also be attractive. All chairs must be functional, which is to say that the user must be able to sit relaxed, in comfort and safety.

The Windsor chair, Fig. 12-10, is an interesting study in wood structure. The back spindles act as an openwork, cantilevered truss with the bow member serving as a tie rod. The combination of the sweep of the bow and the arc of the spindles as they come forward on the sides creates flanges like those of a channel beam. Finer and longer back spindles, somewhat bowed instead of straight, provide greater support and comfort.

A Windsor chair has exceptional stability. The cant of the legs assures this feature. Their angle stiffens the entire base against sidesway. The stretchers are always arranged in the form of an "H," with the front part open between the legs. This design provides both horizontal and vertical bracing against the outward diagonal strain of the splayed legs. This reduces the likelihood of the joints pulling apart. The saddle seat provides formfitting comfort.

Many articles of furniture, like the Windsor chair, are designed with an open, visible structure. This type of design, although suitable for many chairs, tables, stools, and benches, is not suitable for cabinetry. Cabinets, dressers, desks, and other articles of enclosed furniture are not made primarily for support, as are tables and chairs, but rather are designed to provide decorative storage space. This difference in purpose is accommodated by major differences in design and construction.

Cabinet Construction and Design

Cabinet design is based on three basic methods of cabinet construction. Each method requires different design considerations with regard to materials, use, and the overall strength and stability of the finished product.

Box construction is the most basic cabinet design. It consists of four sides, a base, and sometimes a top or cover, Figs. 12-13, 12-14. This type of cabinet is constructed of solid material. As a result, grain direction becomes a consideration. The width of the boards and the direction of the grain should be used in the same position on each side so that shrinkage will be equalized among all members and no opposing forces will be built into the construction. Simple butt joints may be used to join the corners. Where strength and appearance must be considered, more complex joints such as finger joints or dovetail joints may be used. The bottom or cover is usually fitted into a side rabbet to conceal the edges and to give added strength. Blanket chests and drawers are examples of box construction in cabinetwork.

Case construction is sometimes thought of as resembling a box on its side, Fig. 12-15. This type of construction is used in the manufacture of bookcases, television cabinets, desks,

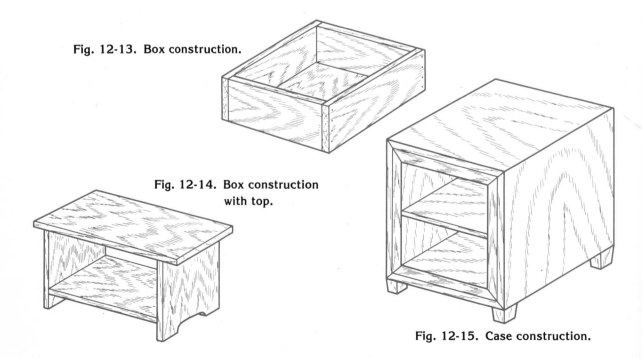

Fig. 12-13. Box construction.

Fig. 12-14. Box construction with top.

Fig. 12-15. Case construction.

and storage cabinets. When solid wood is used to provide the inner and outside surfaces, the shrinkage must be equalized, as in box construction. Case construction in larger units, such as kitchen cabinets, is often done using panels of manufactured board such as plywood. The use of plywood minimizes shrinking and gives great stability. For surface appearance, however, the grain pattern of the exterior surface is used in the same direction throughout. When plywood is used on the sides, top, and bottom of a structure, the front lip must be covered with solid wood strips to hide the end grain.

Carcase construction is similar to case construction, but is used for larger units having many partitions. It is a more detailed construction. Carcase construction generally employs a front frame to support and divide doors and drawers in articles such as breakfronts, highboys, secretaries, and hutches.

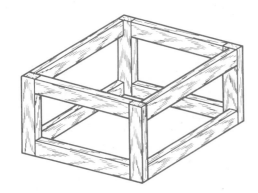

Fig. 12-16. Frame construction.

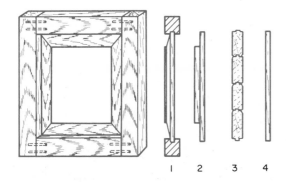

Fig. 12-17. Raised-panel construction.
   1 & 2 — Raised panel.
   3 — Tongue and groove.
   4 — Plywood.

Frame construction is designed with an internal framework that is later covered with wood panels or manufactured board, Fig. 12-16. Kitchen cabinets are often built using this type of construction because they can be made both strong and very lightweight.

Raised-panel construction is another type of frame construction that involves the insertion of decorative panels between the framing members, Fig. 12-17. The lightweight panels are fitted into grooves or rabbets on the inside edges of the frame. No glue is required in attaching the panels. This permits expansion and contraction of the panels without distortion of the framework. Raised-panel doors are an example of this type of frame construction.

Decorative Design

Aspects of the design of Greek and Roman architecture have been used so extensively over the years that they are now recognized and referred to as "classic shapes." These classic shapes are used, in combination, to make moldings, turnings, aprons, and other decorative and structural forms. See Fig. 12-18.

Moldings enhance the character of cabinetwork, whether on furniture or on interior woodwork. In paneling a door, attaching a base, or fitting a bonnet to a grandfather clock, the blending of curves and lines gives highlights that either attract attention to that portion of the piece or visually blend all of the parts together.

In the early days of cabinetmaking, the profile of the various moldings was cut by specially designed cutters used in molding planes. Today, most moldings are cut on a shaper or with a router, using specially shaped cutters or sets of cutters. These shapes are obtained with a single pass over a cutter, or by making a series of passes over different cutters.

Design in Turning

Although the general principles of design apply to turning, unique effects can also be obtained. The general profile of a turned design is a combination of basic molds and/or angular lines complementing each other in a unified design. Many spindle turnings are adaptations of the classic shapes found in columns and pedestals. Turnings are normally composed of

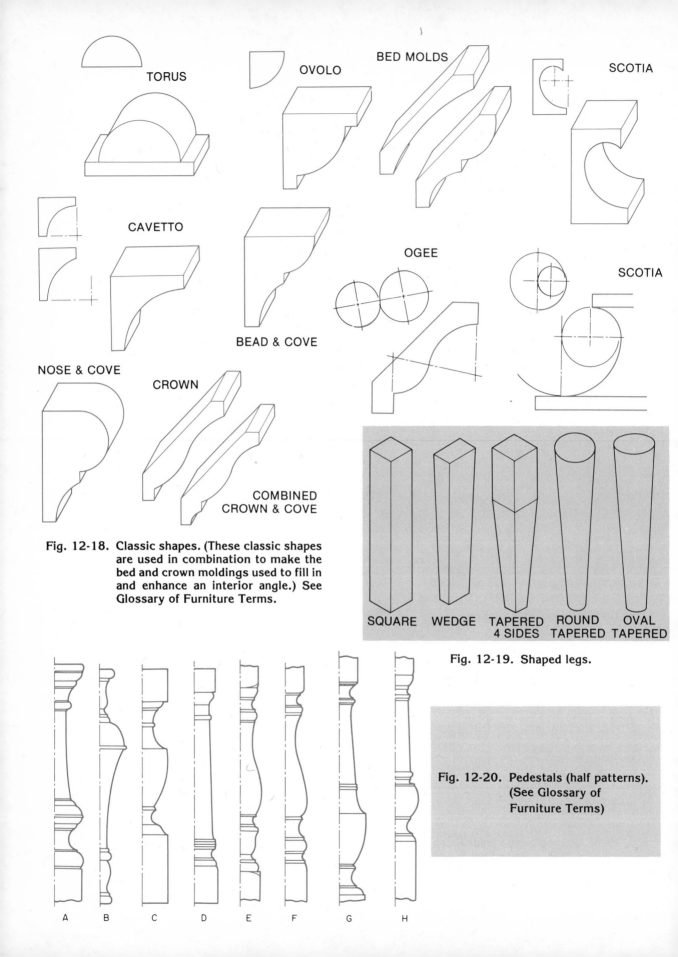

TORUS

OVOLO

BED MOLDS

SCOTIA

CAVETTO

BEAD & COVE

OGEE

SCOTIA

NOSE & COVE

CROWN

COMBINED
CROWN & COVE

Fig. 12-18. Classic shapes. (These classic shapes
are used in combination to make the
bed and crown moldings used to fill in
and enhance an interior angle.) See
Glossary of Furniture Terms.

SQUARE   WEDGE   TAPERED   ROUND   OVAL
                   4 SIDES   TAPERED TAPERED

Fig. 12-19. Shaped legs.

Fig. 12-20. Pedestals (half patterns).
(See Glossary of
Furniture Terms)

A   B   C   D   E   F   G   H

two or three divisions, one of which is dominant. Each division should be distinct yet related, and should contribute to the overall pattern. The flow of curves should be graceful and in harmony with the mass. Long curves should terminate with an abrupt change of direction. Reverse curves should be broken by a square shoulder or a bead. Subdivisions usually consist of well-formed beads, flutes, and "V's."

In developing a design for a turning, a profile of half the object is drawn and a mirror is placed on edge along the axis. The mirror will reflect the image of a completed object. Tilting or moving (shifting the axis of) the mirror creates the effect of increasing or decreasing the diameter and permits the designer to select the most pleasing proportion. Experienced woodturners sometimes design turnings with the intention of bringing out and focusing on the natural beauty of a particular grain pattern.

Turned pedestals, legs, stretchers, finials, and drops are all combinations of the classic shapes. See Figs. 12-20, 12-21, 12-22, 12-23, and 12-24. In examining the profile of these turnings, it is easy to identify the individual shapes of the ogee, cove, scotia, torus, and ovolo as they are joined together to form the complete unit.

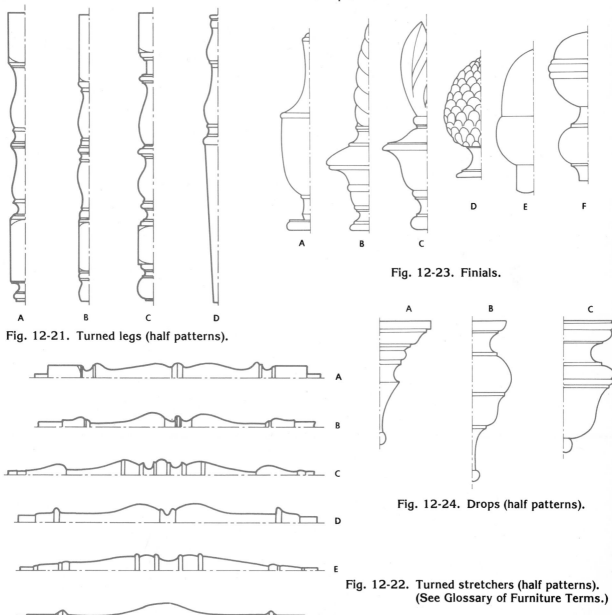

Fig. 12-23. Finials.

Fig. 12-21. Turned legs (half patterns).

Fig. 12-24. Drops (half patterns).

Fig. 12-22. Turned stretchers (half patterns).
(See Glossary of Furniture Terms.)

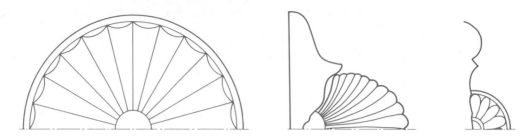

Fig. 12-25. Shells and sunbursts.

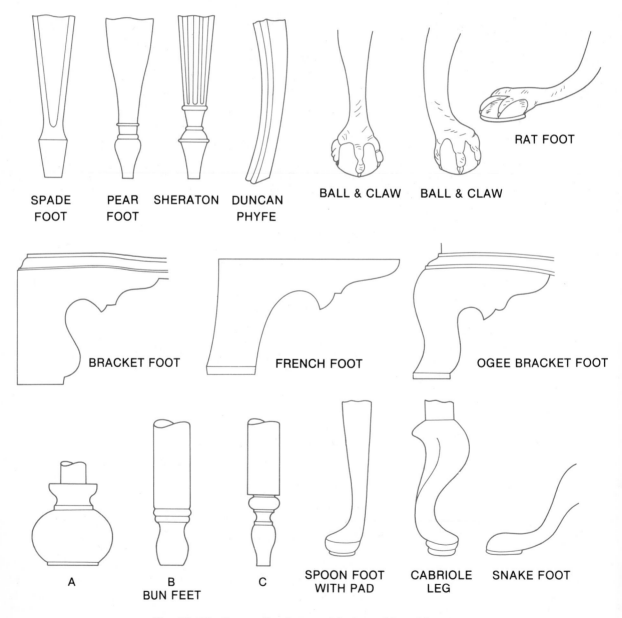

SPADE FOOT

PEAR FOOT

SHERATON

DUNCAN PHYFE

BALL & CLAW

BALL & CLAW

RAT FOOT

BRACKET FOOT

FRENCH FOOT

OGEE BRACKET FOOT

A

B
BUN FEET

C

SPOON FOOT WITH PAD

CABRIOLE LEG

SNAKE FOOT

Fig. 12-26. Decorative legs and feet used in cabinetry.

Table 12-1
Dimension Reference Chart

This table has been compiled to give a suggested range of sizes for many common household and sports articles. Each has been proportioned in relation to the average human body to provide comfort, convenience, and maximum utility. The dimensions also take into account the compatibility of one item in relation to another. A desk chair, for instance, must be compatible with the desk with which it is to be used. Sports equipment is dimensioned to provide maximum performance and to comply with any set regulations.

Although the sizes listed below are considered standard, they are intended only to serve as guides in designing a project. Innovative projects, or projects which are designed to adapt to a specific situation, may not fall within the size ranges provided in this table.

Home Furnishings

Name	Width	Length	Height
Beds			
Cribs	31″-37″	53″-55″	22″ to mattress
Twin	39″	75″	''
3/4	48″	75″	''
Double	54″	75″	''
Queen	60″	80″	''
King	76″	80″	''
Benches			
work			30″-34″
Bookcases	7³/₄″-12″	15″-36″	9″-14″ between shelves 18″-84″ high
Buffets	17″-25″	4′-6′6″	42″
Chairs (wooden)	seat width 13″-32″ arm height 23″-25″	depth 13″-19″ back height 30″-48″	15″-18″ seat
Chests, cedar	17″-21″	35″-47″	15″-21″
Chests of drawers	18″-22″	34″-42″	28″-48″
China cabinets	18″-22″	36″-48″	5′ and up
Clocks, grandfather:			6′3″-7′6¹/₂″
base	16″-18″	8″-9¹/₄″	
waist	12″-14¹/₂″	7″-7¹/₂″	
bonnet	16″-18″	8″-9¹/₄″	
grandmother:			4′4″-5′2″
base	12″-13″	6¹/₂″-7″	
waist	10″	6″	
bonnet	12″-13″	6¹/₂″7″	
Desks	15″-31″	30″-60″	28″-34″ to the writing surface

At least 22″ between legs or sides, to provide room for chair.

Name	Width	Length	Height
Dry Sinks	19″-20″	38″-46″	37″-40″
Tables,			
Bedside	14″-24″	12″-24″	20″-28″
Card	2′6″-3′ sq.		28¹/₄″
Cocktail — Same as coffee table			

Name	Width	Length	Height
Coffee	15″-36″	22″-60″	15″-19″
Console			
rd., sq.	14″-22″	30″-48″	29″-32″
Dining	30″-48″	40″-8′10″	29″-30″
Dressing	15″-22″	36″-50″	29″
End	10″-14″	18″-36″	20″-29″
Harvest	41″-44″	48″-96″	29″-30″
Lamp	16″-28″	16″-30″	22″-29″
Living room	14″-36″	36″-72″	28″
Nest of	12″-20″	14″-24″	18′-29″
Night	16″-20″	16″-20″	24″
Tea, oval, rd., sq.	20″-36″	24″-30″	24″-29″
Telephone	12″-24″	14″-24″	22″-30″
Tilt-top	16″-30″	20″-36″	26″-30″
TV (table)	20″-24″	24″-30″	17″-24″
Typing	14″-16″	18″-44″	27″
Sewing boxes	8″-11″	10″-14″	2¹/₂″-5″
Sewing cabinets	12″-18″	20″-30″	26″-28″
Footstools	8″-17″	11″-24″	4″-15″
Hall trees			4′-6′
Hutches	19″-20″	46″-75″	69″-77″
Ironing boards	12″-19″	36″-56″	30″-36″
Ironing sleeves	2¹/₂″-4³/₄″	17″-24″	4″
Kitchen stools	8¹/₂″-12″		35″
Luggage racks	17″	22″	22″
Magazine racks	7³/₄″-12″	10″-17″	14″-18″
Shelves for wall	3″-6″	18″-26″	22″-26″
Shoeshine kits	7″-10″	10″-16″	8″-14″
Smoking stands			25″-26″

Name	Width	Length	Height
Stepladders	12″ between steps, width varies with height		
Step stools	12″-14″, 8″ between steps, 9″-24″		
Serving trays	8″-16″	14″-24″	

Sports Equipment

Name	Width	Length	Height
Arrows			
Men		25″-31″	
Women		24″-27″	
Bows			
Men		5′8″-6′	
Women		5′2″-5′10″	
Basketball backboards	4′	6′	9′ from floor
Hoop must be mounted 12″ up from bottom of backboard			
Bats baseball	2³/₄″ max. 42″ max. diam.		
The general rule for weight of baseball bats is about 1 oz. to each inch of length.			
Little League	2¹/₄″ max. 32″ max.		
Softball	2¹/₈″ max. 34″ max. diam.		
Bobsleds, 2-person		7′-11″	10¹/₂″
4-person		9′	''
Packracks	10″ at the top, 16″ at the bottom, 23″ long		
Paddles canoe		4′-5¹/₂′	
ping-pong	5¹/₄″ across the blade, 5¹/₄″ handle, 6¹/₂″ length of blade, total length is 11³/₄″.		
Tables, ping-pong	5′	9′	30″
Skis, water	The size of the water ski is determined by the weight of the rider and the power towing the skier.		

Glossary of Furniture Terms

This list defines popular forms of feet, legs, spindles, moldings, and ornamentation, as well as structural elements. It also provides suggestions for designing and identifying designs.

Applique — applied ornaments, such as carvings and turnings, which are fastened to a surface and closely resemble moldings.

Apron — a horizontal member that joins legs and supports the tabletop or chair seat.

Arrow foot — an arrow-shaped turning at the base of the leg of some styles of Windsor chairs.

Ball and claw — a carved foot common to Chippendale designs. This design is representative of a bird's claw grasping an egg, Fig. 12-26.

Ball foot — a spherical foot, usually quite large in diameter. It is normally used on chests. (In England this is called a **bun foot**.) See Fig. 12-26.

Bracket foot — a foot formed of two pieces equal in size and shape. These pieces are joined at a 90° mitered angle reinforced with dowels or splines, Fig. 12-26. Also see Topic 106, "Making a Flat Bracket, Ogee Bracket, or French Foot."

Cabriole leg — a furniture leg shaped like the calf of a human leg, Fig. 12-26. Also see Topic 105, "Making a Cabriole Leg."

Cavetto — a quarter-round concave molding, also called a "cove," Fig. 12-18.

Chest-on-chest — a chest of drawers divided into two sections by a prominent horizontal molding. The upper chest is slightly smaller in width and depth.

Comb back — a double-splatted Windsor chair back, the upper section of which resembles a high comb, Fig. 12-10.

Cornice — a protruding portion of a roof or a cabinet top, composed of moldings.

Cove — a concave molding, Fig. 12-18.

Crow's nest — a cage-shaped arrangement found on tilt-top tables (between pedestal and top), which permits the tabletop to be rotated as well as tilted.

Dish top — a tabletop with a raised rim, having the effect of a large, shallow dish.

Drake foot — a three-toed carved foot.

Drop — a turned ornament, fastened to the bottom edge of the apron of a lowboy or highboy, Fig. 12-24.

Escutcheon — a brass, bone, or ivory keyhole plate, Fig. 12-27.

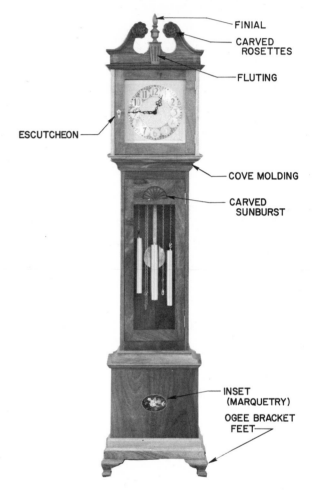

Fig. 12-27. Grandfather clock, illustrating many decorative components.

Finial — a turned, carved, cast, or pressed ornament, used in the break of pediments and at the top of chair posts, highboys, mirrors, and four-poster beds. A finial may be one of a number of different shapes such as a torch, a pineapple, or an acorn of bulbous fruit. See Figs. 12-23 and 12-27.

Fluting — a series of concave grooves or channels, extending along the length of a flat or turned surface, Fig. 12-27. See Topic 107, "Reeding and Fluting."

French foot — a slender, flared-out cabinet foot, similar to the ogee bracket foot, but with a more pronounced flair, Fig. 12-26.

Fretwork — the ornamental cutout of interlaced woodwork.

Hood — the semicircular top found on William and Mary cabinet furniture.

Intarsia — pattern of woods of natural but different coloring, inlaid on wood or other materials.

Marquetry — flat, pictorial pattern of natural, different-colored veneer woods, glued on a core, Fig. 12-27.

Muntin — the molding or division between panes of glass in a door or window.

Ogee — a shape that is formed like the letter "S," Fig. 12-18. The ogee shape is used in moldings, legs, pedestals and turnings, to separate or connect designs.

Ogee bracket foot — a decorative cabinet foot using the ogee shape. See Figs. 12-26 and 12-27. Also see Topic 106, "Making a Flat Bracket, Ogee Bracket, or French Foot."

Ovolo — a quarter-round convex molding, Fig. 12-18.

Pad foot — a pad or base underneath a shaped foot.

Pear foot — a foot turned to resemble the shape of a pear, Fig. 12-26.

Pedestal — the main supporting column of kidney and tilt-top tables, Fig. 12-20.

Piecrust — the raised, scalloped rim of a tabletop, bearing a resemblance to the thumbprint design of a piecrust, Fig. 12-9.

Piegeonholes — open compartments in the cabinet of a desk or secretary.

Pilaster — a flat-back column fastened to a wall or cabinet.

Quarter column — a fourth of a column, usually placed into a niche at the corner of a lowboy or at the base of a highboy, chest of drawers, or grandfather clock.

Plinth — the lower square base of a column or pedestal.

Rat foot — a slender ball-and-claw foot on a splayed leg, Fig. 12-26.

Reeding — a carved ornament, composed of a series of convex molds and resembling parallel rows of reeds. See Topic 107, "Reeding and Fluting."

Rosette — a carved decoration resembling a rose. See Fig. 12-27.

Rule joint — a joint on table leaves in which a cove molding on one leaf slides over a thumbnail molding on the other leaf.

Saddle seat — a recessed, formed seat.

Scotia — a deep molding, used in the base of a pillar or column, Fig. 12-18.

Serpentine — a series of alternate concave and convex curves, suggesting the effect of a serpent in motion.

Shell and Sunburst — both carved decorations. The shell design resembles a seashell; the sunburst design resembles the sun and its rays. These designs are used primarily on door and drawer panels on Queen Anne, lowboy, highboy and pigeonhole desk units, Fig. 12-25. Also see Topic 108, "Laying Out and Carving a Sunburst or Shell."

Shield back — a chair back, the outline of which resembles a heart-shaped shield. This design is characteristic of Hepplewhite furniture.

Snake foot — a foot shaped like a modified snake head, Fig. 12-26.

Stretcher — the cross braces on table and chair legs, Fig. 12-22.

Torus — a large bead shape, used primarily in moldings and turnings to separate or combine other shapes, Fig. 12-18.

Trumpet turning — a turned leg, resembling a trumpet, used on William and Mary style furniture.

Turnip foot — similar to a ball foot, but with a base lip.

Making a Cabriole Leg

Topic 105.

Classification

Joining and shaping using edged cutting tools

A **cabriole leg** is shaped in a double curve and resembles the hind leg of an animal such as a dog. The upper part of the leg swells out, and the lower part swings in toward the foot, which turns out. Cabriole legs, commonly called Queen Anne legs, are used on such pieces as lowboys, highboys, chairs, tables, and chests. They are characteristic of early Chippendale furniture. The profile is the same when viewed from either of the two adjacent sides. See Figs. 12-5 and 12-7.

Procedure

1. If a flat pattern of a cabriole leg is not available, one must be designed. Cabriole legs may be from 5″ to 30″ long, and may be made from stock 1″ to 5″ thick. This stock is usually glued up to form the knee and foot. In designing a cabriole leg, two principles should be observed to ensure that the center of gravity will be such that the leg, after being shaped, will stand by itself on a flat surface. These principles are as follows: (1) the inside surface of the leg must be in the same plane at both the top and bottom, and (2) the outside surface must protrude slightly (1/8″ to 1/4″) at the top. See Fig. 12-28.

2. Begin with a square piece of stock that is the length, width, and thickness of the top of the finished leg. Two adjacent sides should be jointed smooth and flat. Place the flat pattern on the basic part of leg, flush with one edge. Mark the areas where extra stock is needed to form the shape of the knee and foot, Fig. 12-29. The portion of the basic leg that is too small for the pattern at the knee and foot is built up by gluing blocks to the basic leg at those points, as described in Steps 3 and 4.

3. Using one side of the basic leg as a guide, measure and cut two blocks. These blocks, when glued to the leg, will be flush on

each side and will be long and thick enough to provide needed material at the knee and foot. Glue these pieces to the basic leg, using the marks made in Step 2 as guides for placement, Fig. 12-30.

4. On the adjacent side of the leg, two more blocks must be cut and glued in place, Fig. 12-31. The blocks on this side will be the same length and thickness as the first two blocks. They must, however, be wide enough to cover both the basic leg and the pieces that have just been glued to the leg. All edges must be flush.

   Note: The position of the blocks on a right-side leg should be reversed as compared to a left-side leg. See Fig. 12-32. This is done so that glue joints will not be visible from the front of the finished piece.

5. Place the flat pattern flush on the bottom and on the edge opposite that to which the blocks are glued. Trace around the pattern. Turn the pattern over and trace on the adjacent side, opposite the face to which the blocks are glued. See Fig. 12-33.

6. Use the band saw to cut on the waste side of the line. Cut from one end about half the length of the leg. Then, back the band saw out of the saw cut and begin cutting from the opposite end. Stop the cut about 1/8″ from the previous cut. This 1/8″ piece of uncut stock will keep the pieces together, maintaining the lines needed to

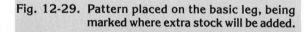

Fig. 12-28. Flat pattern of a cabriole leg.

Fig. 12-29. Pattern placed on the basic leg, being marked where extra stock will be added.

Fig. 12-30. Blocks are glued to the base piece of the leg to add material for the knee and foot.

Fig. 12-31. Second set of blocks for the knee and foot, glued to adjacent surface.

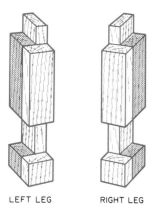

LEFT LEG   RIGHT LEG

Fig. 12-32. Proper position of blocks for front cabriole legs.

Fig. 12-33. Pattern being traced on a cabriole leg.

Fig. 12-34. The band saw is used to cut the basic shape of the leg. Note: The band-saw cuts should not connect to remove waste material.

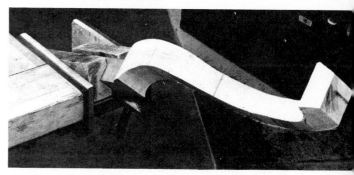

Fig. 12-35. Band-sawed cabriole leg, ready for final shaping. Notice the use of V-blocks to hold the leg in the vise.

cut the adjacent side and to preserve the square shape of the leg. Be sure to stop the band saw before backing the blade out of the saw cut. See Fig. 12-34.

7. Repeat Step 6 on adjacent side of leg.

8. After all cuts have been made on adjacent sides, cut through the previous 1/8″ left on each saw cut. The rough form of the leg will now be visible.

9. Place the square end of the leg in a vise. File all curved surfaces until saw marks are removed and all curves have a good flow (no bumps).

10. It is much easier to shape a cabriole leg if V-blocks are used. These are made of soft wood and are used to clamp the leg in the vise. See Fig. 12-35. Make up two blocks

about 4″ wide and 8″ long. The "V" should be slightly less than the size of the basic leg.

11. Place the square end of leg in the V-blocks and clamp in a vise. With a spokeshave or rasp, chamfer the front edge of the leg. The chamfer should flare out from the square part of the leg, to a 3/4″ to 7/8″ width at the high part of the knee. The chamfer should gradually decrease in width (to about 3/8″ at the ankle) and should taper off to the end of the foot. This will vary with the size of the leg. See Fig. 12-36.

12. Remove the leg from the corner blocks and clamp it squarely in the vise. With a spokeshave or a rasp, chamfer the outside curves to a 45° angle. Chamfers should flare from the squared section and foot to a width of about 1/8″ at the center of the leg. See Fig. 12-37.

13. Draw a center line the length of the chamfered surface made in Step 11. Using this line as a reference, gently round the cham-

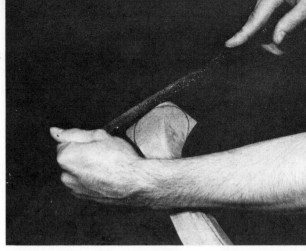

Fig. 12-38. Shaping the perimeter of the foot with a rasp.

Fig. 12-39. Final sanding of the cabriole leg to finished form.

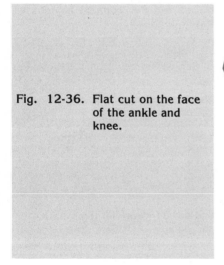

Fig. 12-36. Flat cut on the face of the ankle and knee.

Fig. 12-37. Chamfering the outside curves of the cabriole leg.

fers away from the center line along the complete length of the leg.

14. With a rasp, shape the perimeter of the foot. The foot should form three fourths of a circle, Fig. 12-38.

15. To remove file marks, sand all parts and sides of the leg and foot, using 50-grit coated abrasive. Then, use 100-grit abrasive to sand to finished form, Fig. 12-39.

16. For added decoration, many cabriole legs have a wing attached to each side of the knee. The wings are cut to the desired shape and then attached with dowels and glue, Fig. 12-40. This is usually done after the basic leg has been completed.

17. Cabriole legs are attached as part of the basic case construction. The square portion of each leg serves as the corner section of the article. Front, back, and end panels are attached to this square part of the leg. Common joints used are tongue-and-groove joints, dowel joints, and multiple mortise-and-tenon joints.

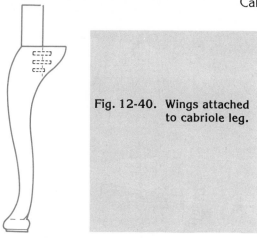

Fig. 12-40. Wings attached to cabriole leg.

- Blocks glued to the basic leg should be flush with each edge.
- Blocks glued to that part of the basic leg which is to become the foot should be flush with the bottom.
- Blocks glued on to permit design of the knee should be placed in the correct position by matching the pattern profile marks.
- All file and machine marks should be removed by sanding with coated abrasive.
- An unsupported leg should remain standing upright when placed on a flat surface.

Standards and Results

- All joints should be well glued and should have a tight fit.

Safety Considerations

- Wear safety glasses.
- Observe all safety practices pertaining to the particular tool or machine you are using.

Making a Flat Bracket, Ogee Bracket, or French Foot

Topic 106.

Classification

Joining and shaping

The **bracket foot** and **French foot** are widely used in the construction of period furniture such as bureaus, chests, and grandfather clocks. (See Topic 104, "Design.")

Procedure

Making Front Feet

Note: Because making a flat bracket foot is the first step in the process of making an ogee bracket foot or French foot, this information must be followed for making any of the front feet.

The stock selected for the flat bracket foot must be 13/16″ thick, and that selected for the ogee bracket foot must be 1-5/8″ thick. For the French foot, the thickness of the stock will be equal to 13/16″ plus the thickness of the flare at the base of the foot. The procedure for shaping the flare is similar to that for shaping the ogee bracket foot.

A.W. Marlow

Fig. 12-41. Secretary with ogee bracket feet.

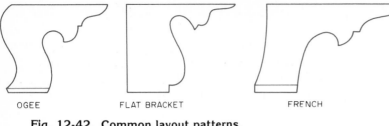

OGEE   FLAT BRACKET   FRENCH

Fig. 12-42. Common layout patterns.

Fig. 12-43. Layout using a template on a wood block.

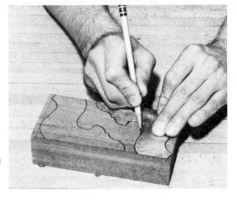

Fig. 12-44. Cut each end of the traced block in the miter box.

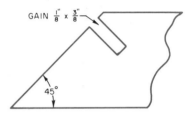

GAIN $\frac{1}{8}$" x $\frac{3}{8}$"

45°

Fig. 12-45. Gain layout.

1. If a flat pattern is not available for any of the above feet, one must be designed. Some common shapes are shown in Fig. 12-42. These feet are usually 3" to 6" high. Their length is proportionate to their height.

2. Get out enough stock for the two feet. The width of the stock should be finished to the desired height of the foot. If you are making an ogee bracket foot, the thickness should be 1-5/8" to 1-7/8" thick, depending on the size of the foot. The length of the stock should be long enough to permit all parts of both front feet to be made. To conserve stock, trace the pattern on the stock, as shown in Fig. 12-43.

3. Using the table saw or miter-box saw, cut a 45° angle to the top surface on each end of the workpiece, Fig. 12-44. The miters should start at the front edge of each traced foot and extend back toward the center of the stock.

4. Use a band saw or jigsaw to cut the section of the feet opposite the mitered ends.

5. File and sand all band-sawed ends. (Use an abrasive of between 50 and 100 grit.)

6. With a sharp, smooth plane set for a fine cut, plane the mitered ends to make a tight fit. Before gluing, make a spline to increase the strength of the joint. (This process is explained in Steps 7 through 9.)

7. Lay out the gain for the spline. For strength, this should be as close as possible to the heel of the miter. The cut is usually 1/8" wide and 3/8" deep on each piece of the foot. See Fig. 12-45.

8. Using the table saw, cut the gain for the spline. Set the fence at the proper position and lock. Raise the saw blade 3/8" above the table. With the miter flat on the saw table and the point of the miter against the fence, feed the stock through the saw. See Fig. 12-46. Cut gains on all pieces needed for the front feet.

9. Make the hardwood spline on the table saw, keeping in mind that the grain of the spline should run at right angles to the miter joint. This minimizes splitting of the spline, providing greater strength, Fig. 2-47. Splines should fit snugly in the gains and should be as wide as the height of the foot. The pieces are now ready to be glued together.

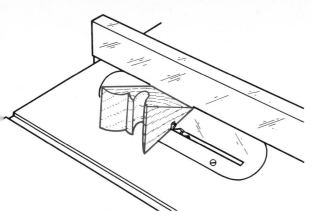

Fig. 12-46. Setup for cutting gains on the circular saw.

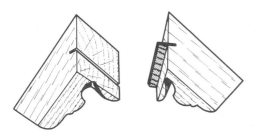

Fig. 12-47. Spline joint ready for gluing. Notice the direction of grain on the spline.

Fig. 12-48. Two sides of the foot glued and clamped using corner blocks and the hand screw.

Fig. 12-49. Cutting the outside contour of the foot on the band saw. Note use of support block.

Fig. 12-50. Finished front ogee bracket foot.

10. To aid in the process of gluing up the pieces, construct corner blocks of soft wood. Position and glue the corner blocks onto those pieces that are to be the feet. This is done so that clamping pressure can be applied through the middle of the joint. See Fig. 12-48.
11. Apply a thin layer of glue to each miter and to both surfaces of the spline. Clamp and set aside to dry for a minimum of one hour, Fig. 12-48.
12. Remove the hand screw. Using a chisel, remove the corner blocks and plane smooth.

Note: For making a flat bracket foot, the above procedure is complete except for final smoothing and sanding. In making an ogee bracket foot or a French foot, additional shaping is required.

13. For an ogee bracket foot or a French foot, it is necessary to shape the outside surfaces of the foot. This is done by supporting the foot on a block and cutting the contours on the band saw. See Fig. 12-49. If the pattern lines made in Step 2 are not clear, it may be necessary to retrace the foot lines so that you will have clear reference line in sawing.
14. Both sides may be sawed by repositioning the foot on the supporting block. Saw on the waste side of the lines.
15. Using a plane, file, and sandpaper, hand shape until the foot has a smooth, graceful contour, Fig. 12-50.

Making Back Feet

1. Get out enough stock for two side pieces of the back feet. The finished dimensions should be the same as for the front feet.

2. Place the flat pattern on the piece of stock in such a way that it is flush on the top, the bottom, and the square end. Trace around the pattern as for front feet. Do not trace along the front edge of each foot. See Fig. 12-51. These will be the side pieces of the rear feet.

3. Using a band saw, cut along the traced lines, staying on the waste side of the line.

4. File and sand to the line. (Use an abrasive of between 50 and 100 grit.)

5. Get out enough stock for the rear pieces of the back feet. This stock is usually 13/16" thick and is the same width as the front feet. The stock must be long enough to make two rear pieces for the back feet. These pieces do not have to be ornate, since they cannot be viewed from either the front or side of the furniture. To save time, use a simple pattern for layout, as shown in Fig. 12-52. Place the pattern flush on the squared stock. Trace the pattern on the top, the bottom, and the end.

6. Use a band saw to cut the pieces out, staying on the waste side of the line.

7. File and sand rough curves to the line.

8. The two pieces that make up the two rear feet are held together with glue and dowels, Fig. 12-53. The back pieces are connected to the side pieces so they will not be visible from the side, Fig. 12-54.

9. Using a marking gauge, lay out the dowel holes. See Topic 92. The dowels are usually 3/8" in diameter and are located 3/4" to 1" down from the top edge and up from the bottom edge. The depth of the dowel is usually 1" in the back piece and 1/2" in the side piece. Dowel holes may be made

either by boring with a bit and brace or by using a spur bit in a drill press.

10. Check the joint for squareness and a tight fit. Apply glue to the dowels and the joint surfaces and then clamp.

11. After removing the hand screw, lay out the contour of the back feet. This is done by using the front-foot pattern and marking the end grain of the side piece, Fig. 12-55.

12. Block up the foot with scrap wood, as done in Step 13 for band sawing the front feet, under the heading, "Making Front Feet."

13. Use a band saw to cut the contour of the foot, sawing on the waste side of the line.

14. Remove saw marks by filing and sanding to the line. (Use an abrasive paper of 50 to 100 grit.) See Fig. 12-56.

15. All types of bracket feet are attached to the base of the case with dowel joints. The dowels should be located on the thicker part of the foot. Usually each foot is fastened with two dowels.

Fig. 12-52. Metal back-foot pattern being used to lay out the rear pieces of the back feet.

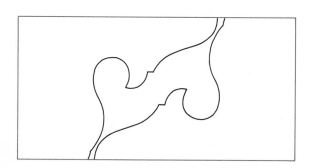

Fig. 12-51. Pattern layout for side pieces of back feet.

Fig. 12-53. Rear-foot assembly showing dowel joints.

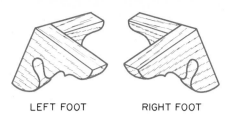

LEFT FOOT   RIGHT FOOT

Fig. 12-54. Back pieces must be assembled in such a way that no joints will be visible from the side.

Fig. 12-56. Finished rear ogee bracket foot.

Fig. 12-55. Laying out for a contour cut on the side piece of the rear foot.

Standards and Results

- All joints should be well glued and should have a tight fit.
- The two pieces making up the foot should be flush on the top and bottom edges.
- The grain in the spline should run at right angles to the miter.
- The spline should fit snugly in the gains.
- All machine and file marks should be removed by sanding with coated abrasives.

Safety Considerations

- Wear safety glasses.
- Observe all safety practices pertaining to the particular tool or machine you are using.

Reeding and Fluting

Topic 107.

Classification

Surface decoration

Reeding, sometimes called **beading,** consists of two or more reeds or beads, cut close together in parallel lines. These reeds or beads are either flush with the surface or are raised above the surface they decorate. The cross section of a reed is convex in shape. See Fig. 12-57.

Fluting, the reverse of reeding, is concave in cross section. See Fig. 12-58.

Fig. 12-58. Fluting, end view of stock.

In furniture making, fluting and reeding operations are done on pilasters, legs, bedposts, friezes, and aprons.

Procedure

Flat Stock

Reeding or fluting may be done on a flat surface by using an electric router with a reeding or fluting bit and a straight guide.

Fig. 12-57. Reading, end view of stock.

1. Select the proper size bit and insert it to the proper depth in the router chuck. Cut an arc between 1/8″ and 1/4″ deep. (This is the usual depth.)
2. Determine the length of cut. Either clamp stop blocks on the workpiece (to assure correct length) or use a pencil to clearly mark where cuts are to be made.
3. Adjust the straight guide to regulate the distance of the cut from the edge of the piece.
4. Make a test cut on a scrap piece of wood. This is done by holding the straight guide against the edge of the piece being cut and, with the router in a horizontal position, lowering the router until its base rests flat against the stock.
5. Move the router slowly, making sure the straight guide is in contact with the edge of the piece.
6. If the test cut is of the proper dimension, make cuts on the piece to be used. If stop blocks are used, move the router until its frame touches the block at each end of the cut. If a pencil line has been used, stop the movement of the router when the bit touches the line.
7. After each flute is cut, the straight guide is readjusted to the desired amount for the next flute.
8. If reeds are to be cut, the profile of the router bit must be such that it cuts half of one bead and half of the adjacent bead.

Round Stock

Reeding and fluting may be done on round stock by mounting the workpiece between centers on a lathe equipped with an indexing head. The indexing head holds the stock in a fixed position and makes it possible to accurately and evenly space adjacent reeds or flutes. A router is mounted in a special attachment used to support the router in the proper position for cutting. A collar is then placed above the cutter. This collar determines the depth of cut and guides the cutter along the contour of the stock. The cutter selected determines the shape and size of the flutes or beads.

If a lathe with an indexing head is not available, a fluting jig may be made. This jig is made of wood and has a live center on one end

and a dead center on the opposite end. The jig must be made with a pin lock on the end on which the live center is located and with an indexing plate to hold the workpiece in a stationary position. Fig. 12-59. This jig may be used with a router or with a shaper that has a movable base.

Router Method

The procedure for reeding and fluting using the lathe is the same as that for using the fluting jig.
1. Divide the circumference by the number of flutes or reeds desired (usually six to eight). Mark both ends of the cuts. Indicate the position of the cut on the indexing head and lock in place.
2. Place a fluting or reeding bit in the chuck of the router and tighten securely.
3. Place the router in the router attachment. This attachment is used to do reeding and fluting on a turned leg. Adjust the router to the proper height in the base. The center of the bit should be in line with the center of the turning.
4. Adjust the bit for the proper depth of cut.
5. Place the router attachment on the bed of the lathe or on the base of the fluting jig. Make one cut to the proper length.
6. Release the indexing pin and turn the workpiece the proper distance. (This distance is determined by the number of cuts needed in the design.)
7. Lock the spindle in a fixed position and make a second cut.

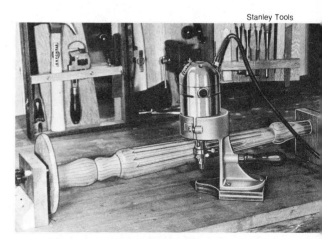

Fig. 12-59. Fluting-and-beading setup for round stock.

Rockwell International

Fig. 12-60. Using the fluting jig for cutting flutes on a table leg.

8. Continue until all beads or flutes are cut. The ends of the beads or flutes may need to be touched up. This is done either with carving tools, rifler files, or sandpaper.

Shaper Method

For reeding and fluting round stock on the shaper, a pattern board must be made and attached to the base of the fluting jig. The pattern is cut to the same contour as the workpiece. This serves as a cutting guide, keeping the workpiece a fixed distance from the shaper spindle as the flutes or reeds are being cut, Fig. 12-60.

1. Lay out the length and number of flutes or reeds. Set and lock the indexing head of the jig. Blocks may be clamped to the shaper table to act as stops at each end of the flute.
2. Mount the proper cutter on the shaper spindle in conjunction with depth collars, Fig. 12-61. The pattern board will slide against the collar, following the contour of the workpiece. Adjust the height of the cutter to the exact midpoint of the workpiece.

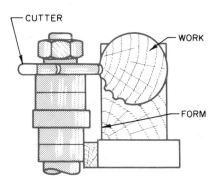

Fig. 12-61. Setup of shaper spindle for cutting flutes on round stock.

3. Move the stock into the cutter in the direction opposite that of the cutter rotation.
4. After each complete cut, rotate the workpiece and relock the indexing head for the next cut.
5. Touch up cut flutes or beads with a chisel and sandpaper.

Standards and Results

- Beads and flutes should be equally spaced.
- Beads and flutes should be the same length and depth.
- Beads and flutes should be smooth and should have no burn marks.

Safety Considerations

- Wear safety glasses.
- Observe all safety practices pertaining to the particular tool or machine you are using.

Laying Out and Carving a Sunburst or Shell

Topic 108.

Classification

Surface decoration

Procedure

One characteristic that Queen Anne, Georgian, and Chippendale furniture have in common is that their design is often enhanced with a carving of a **shell** or **sunburst**. Traditionally, these carvings are located on the center drawer front of a lowboy or highboy, on the top rail of the pendulum door of a grandfather or grandmother clock, or on the door in the center of cubby holes in a Governor Win-throp desk. In some cases, a shell is carved on the knee of a cabriole leg.

Laying Out a Sunburst

1. Determine the size of the carving and its location on the piece of furniture.
2. Lay out the base line. This is usually 3/4″ to 1-1/4″ from the bottom edge of the drawer fronts or the top rails.
3. Locate the center point of the base line. Using a compass, draw a half circle. The top of the circle should be no closer than 1″ to the top of a door.
4. With a compass set to the desired dimension of the ray at the widest point, mark the divisions of the rays on the circumference line of the semicircle. To determine the compass setting, first find the circumference of the circle (c = π d). Then, divide this figure by two to find the circumference of the half circle. Divide the result by the desired number of rays. Set the compass to this measurement.
5. With a sharp pencil and a straightedge, draw lines from the center point of the base

line to the points laid out around the circumference.

In some cases, a half button about 1″ in diameter is drawn at the center point of the base line. The rays start at the circumference of the button.

6. Reset the compass to 1/4″ less than the radius of the semicircle. Using the center point of the base line, draw another semicircle within the one drawn in Step 3. See Fig. 12-63. This distance may vary depending on the size of the sunburst.
7. Reset the compass again, in such a way that the arcs can be drawn tangent to the smaller semicircle and to the widest part of the rays. Lay out an arc at the end of each ray. See Fig. 12-64.

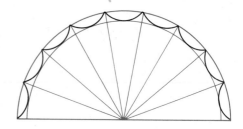

Fig. 12-64. Layout of arcs at end of rays.

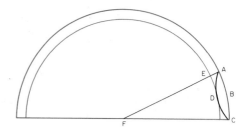

Fig. 12-65. Guide cuts on one ray.

Fig. 12-66. Carving the contour of a ray.

Fig. 12-62. Typical assortment of carving tools.

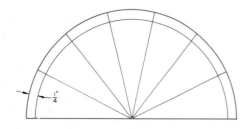

Fig. 12-63. Layout of second semicircle.

Carving a Sunburst

1. With a thin-bladed knife, cut straight down on the line, beginning at point **F,** Fig. 12-65. At point **E,** gradually increase the depth of cut to 3/16″. Decrease the depth of cut to point **A** (repeat for all rays). With the same knife, cut the outside arc at the end of the ray beginning at point **A,** cutting to a depth of 3/16″ at point **B,** and decreasing the depth of cut to point **C.** (Repeat for the ends of all rays.)

2. With a 3/8″ short-sweep gouge, cut the arcs at the ends of the rays. These cuts should be about 3/16″ deep in the center. The cut should have a curved bottom with no depth at the ends.

3. To cut the rays, make a V-cut on each side of the knife line made in Step 1.

4. Using either a 3/8″ skew chisel or a bent squarenose chisel, carve the rays. The rays should have very little depth (less than 1/16″) at the narrow end, and a depth of about 3/16″ at the wide end. See Fig. 12-66. Rays should have a convex curve between one side and the other.

5. To avoid chipping, carve in the direction of the grain. The center vertical ray may be cut in either direction, as it will run at right angles to the grain of the wood. Tight cuts should be made to the proper profile of the ray to avoid undercutting.

6. Rays may be touched up for roundness with a rifler (wood-carver's file). To preserve the knife cuts, do not sand the carving.

Fig. 12-68. Typical shell designs.

Fig. 12-69. Secretary with carved shells.

A.W. Marlow

Fig. 12-67. Example of a carved sunburst on a buffet.

Fine Woodworking Magazine   Donald F. Eaton   R.E. Bushnell
(photographer)   (craftsman)

Laying Out and Carving a Shell

A shell is a decorative type of carving, which, as the name implies, resembles the outer surface of a seashell (scallop). Shell carvings are often found on the knees of cabriole legs and on chair fronts. They are also used as decorative additions on many types of furniture.

Because there is a wide variation of shell designs, there is no set procedure for laying out a shell. Generally speaking, the rays of a shell radiate from a bell-shaped base and usually curve to the right or left, away from the center. The rays are also made in different lengths and widths, which further limits set layout techniques.

A typical layout may consist of a freehand sketch on the surface of the wood or may be transferred to the wood from a drawing or from a previously carved shell, using a French curve or template. Some examples of common shells are found in Fig. 12-68. Also see Fig. 12-25.

Carving a shell is much like carving a sunburst. Shells, however, are often carved to protrude above the surface of the wood. See Fig. 12-69. This process requires removal of stock around the shell. It also requires convex rather than recessed shaping of the ends of the rays. A shell carved below the surface of the wood is carved in the same manner as a sunburst.

Standards and Results

- All layout cuts should be made on the lines.
- All rays should be the same shape and size and should have the proper profile.
- Carving should be clean and distinct.

Safety Considerations

- Wear safety glasses.
- Clamp the stock to the bench so that both hands will be free to manipulate the tool during carving.
- When making cuts, carve away from your body.
- Observe safety precautions pertaining to the use of hand tools.

Topic 109.

Occupations in the Furniture Industry

Most of the furniture manufactured in the United States is done by mass production. The majority of workers doing this type of work are semiskilled. Only a short training period is required of these workers, whose jobs are usually limited to a single operation or to the tending of a machine.

The making of furniture is divided into three basic processes — wood processing, assembly, and finishing. In each operation, work is sped through specialized machines. Both cutting and shaping of parts are done on special saws and shapers. Jigs and fixtures make assembly machines highly efficient for mass production. Finishing is also sped up by the use of machines, although certain operations, such as shading, wiping, and rubbing, are still performed by hand.

Workers in the largest occupational group in furniture making operate either manual or automatic machines such as cutoff saws, hand shapers, belt sanders, and boring machines. A worker just beginning in such a job is usually assigned as a helper. When this person has acquired adequate skill and has met certain other requirements, he or she is advanced to other jobs. These requirements include such things as demonstrating the ability to follow direc-

tions, getting along with fellow workers, taking responsibility, and showing initiative.

Many of the occupations in furniture making or in the woodworking industry have counterparts in the jobs and operations performed in the school shop. Some of the operations done in the school shop are almost exactly the same as those performed in industry; others are similar only in principle. The following are examples of jobs that have a counterpart in the school shop:

Band-saw, scroll-saw, and jigsaw operators
Boring-machine operator
Assembler
Furniture repairer
Table-saw operator
Cutoff-saw operator
Dado operator
Gluer
Jointer operator
Layout person
Setup person
Sander operator
Shaper operator (single-spindle shaper only)
Single-surfacer operator
Woodturner

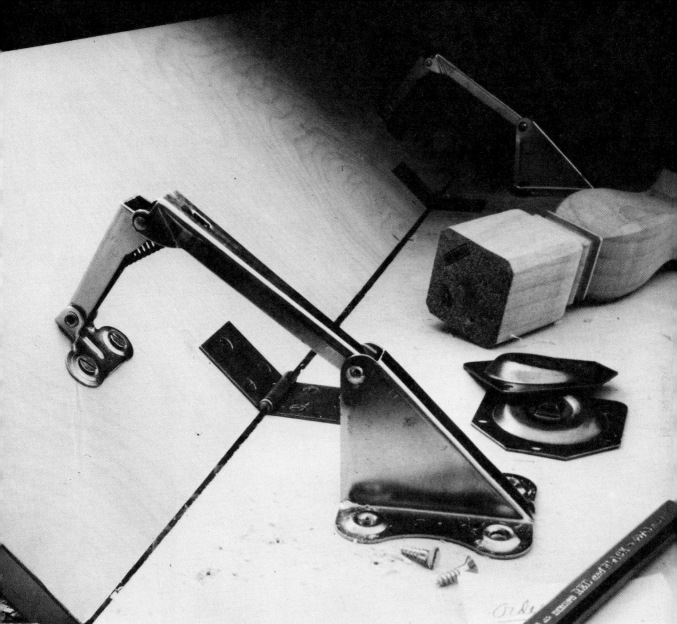

The Woodworker's Store

SECTION THIRTEEN.

Fastening

Topic 110.

Adhesives (Glue)

Classification

Adhesives

Composition or Description

Glues may be grouped into two basic categories, according to the materials from which they are made. The two basic kinds of glue are **synthetic-resin glue** and **natural glue.**

Synthetic-resin glues

Synthetic-resin glues are made of **urea** (a compound of carbon dioxide, ammonia, and formaldehyde), **phenol resin** (a coal-tar derivative), and **melamine formaldehyde.**

There are two types of synthetic-resin glue, classified according to the method in which they set or cure. These types are called **thermoset** and **thermoplastic.** Thermoset glues set by catalytic action and, once set, they cannot be reworked. These include resorcinol-, phenol-, melamine-, and urea-formaldehyde glues, as well as epoxy-resin glues.

Thermoplastic glues cure by evaporation of the solvent. They may be reworked by adding heat or by adding the solvent. These glues include polyvinyl acetate, aliphatic resin, and hot-melt adhesives.

Natural glues

The following are the basic types of natural glue:
1. **Animal glue** is made from hides, hoofs, bones, sinews, and hide fleshings.
2. **Casein glue** is made from curds of milk (called **casein**), hydrated lime, and sodium hydroxide.
3. **Fish glue** is made from the scales, heads, backbones, fins, and tissues of fish.
4. **Vegetable glue** is made from starch and soybean protein.
5. **Blood-albumin glue** is made from beef blood to which an alkali has been added.

Properties

Synthetic (thermosetting)-resin glues

1. **Resorcinol-formaldehyde glues** are liquid and are resistant to moisture, chemicals, and microorganisms.
2. **Phenol-formaldehyde glues** are available in two types — **hot-press** and **intermediate.** These glues hold under prolonged or alternating exposure to moisture, heating, and cooling. They are highly resistant to heat.
3. **Melamine-formaldehyde glues** are of two types — **hot-press** and **intermediate.** The intermediate type may be used at room temperature if the assembly is left un-

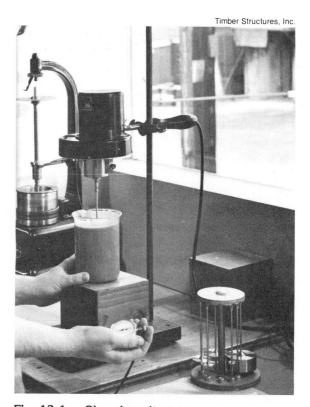

Timber Structures, Inc.

Fig. 13-1.   Glue-viscosity test.

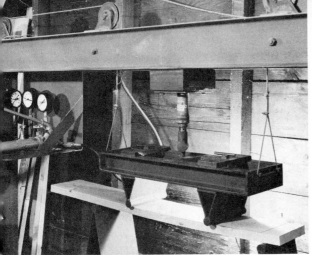

Fig. 13-2.　Scarf-joint test.

Timber Structures, Inc.

clamped for half an hour after the glue is applied. (This permits proper penetration and curing.) The assembly must then be closed and clamped for one hour. Hot-press melamine glue requires greater heat for setting, but is more durable than the intermediate type.

4. **Urea-formaldehyde glues** are of two types — **hot-press** and **cold-press.** They are not recommended for use on wood with a temperature of below 21° C (70° F). They resist cold water but cannot withstand high temperatures and humidity.

5. **Epoxy-resin glues** can be used to bond metal, wood, glass, ceramics, plastics, and hard rubber. They have excellent strength and good resistance to weather, moisture, weak acids, corrosive salts, and petroleum products.

Synthetic (thermoplastic)-resin glues

1. **Polyvinyl-acetate resin emulsion** (white glue) sets in approximately one hour, makes a colorless glue joint, and is durable. White glues remain elastic, which limits their use in joints having high stress. These glues are not water resistant and cannot withstand high temperatures.

2. **Aliphatic resin glues** have good heat resistance, cold flow, and creep resistance. They may be used at temperatures as low as 10° C (50° F), and they can withstand temperatures up to 120° C (248° F) without loss of strength.

3. **Hot-melt adhesives** are solid prior to heating. The application of heat changes the material to a liquid. After removal of heat, the adhesives set by cooling. Hot-melt glues are waterproof, flexible, and require no surface preparation or clamping. This type of glue is good for filling gaps in loosely fitted parts, but it is not shock resistant. Its strength is much lower than that of most other glues, but is ample for some gluing jobs. Wood materials to be glued should be 21° C (70° F). Hot-melt adhesives set in 60 seconds (joint must be assembled in 20 seconds). For best results, the stock should be preheated in one of the following ways: (a) in a caul box, (b) with a flat iron, or (c) with a heat lamp. This will keep the glue from chilling before the joint is tight. Some hot-melt adhesives cannot withstand temperatures over 55° C (131° F). Lacquer finishes will soften the glue and cause the joint to open.

Natural glues

1. All **animal glues** other than liquid hide glue must be soaked in water overnight and then heated. Repeated heatings cause loss of strength. Hot glue sets quickly. Liquid hide glue is ready to use at room temperature, but it sets slowly. Hide glue has great strength and does not stain. It has poor resistance to moisture.

2. **Casein glue** has fair resistance to moisture, but some types will stain wood.

3. **Fish glue** is ready to use at room temperature. It is slow to set and is good for joining wood. Fish glue has poor resistance to moisture and crystallizes with age.

4. **Vegetable glue** is ready to use at room temperature and it sets rapidly. It is excellent for interior plywood and veneers but has poor resistance to moisture.

5. **Blood-albumin** flakes are dissolved in water. This glue sets rapidly, and is waterproof and stainless. The wood must be preheated for use with this type of glue.

Dielectric gluing

The principle behind dielectric heating is based on the fact that disturbed molecules cause friction and create heat. This disturbance is caused by a very high-frequency cycle charge, which moves the molecules of glue at such a high speed that the friction generates heat and the glue bond is completed in a matter of seconds.

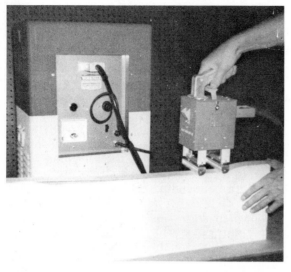

Fig. 13-3.   Dielectric gluing of edge banding.

Fig. 13-4.   Dielectric gluing of miter joint.

Resorcinol, phenol-formaldehyde, and urea-formaldehyde resins are relatively unaffected by weather conditions and can easily be cured with dielectric heating.

Uses

Many synthetic-resin glues have widespread use in woodworking. Each type of synthetic-resin glue develops approximately the same initial strength when used under proper conditions. All synthetic-resin glues are capable of producing joints that are at least as strong as the wood itself. Because they are so durable, these glues have been used in the pro-

U.S.M. Corporation

Fig. 13-5.   Glue gun for hot-melt adhesives.

duction of products intended for use under severe conditions. These glues can withstand more severe conditions than can nonresin glues. Plywood for buildings, signs, railroad cars, laminated ship keels and frames, wooden aircraft, and prefabricated house panels are among the many products that have demonstrated improved performance through the use of synthetic-resin glues.

Although glue is primarily an adhesive, it is widely used as a sizing. The best glue for a given use is determined by the materials to be sized or joined and the conditions of use. Under ideal conditions, a properly fitted joint should withstand a tension of approximately 1000 psi (pounds per square inch).

In the woodworking industry, the three most common uses of hot-melt adhesives are (1) edge banding of veneer, (2) plastic lamination of furniture tops made of plywood cores or particleboard cores, and (3) the application of corner blocks, drawer stops, and decorative objects. Hot-melt adhesives are not recommended for joining structural members such as furniture joints. Hot-melt adhesives are also used on ceramics, leather, cloth, metal, glass, and most types of plastic. The glue is usually melted and then applied with an electric glue gun. See Fig. 13-5.

Market Analysis

Selection of a glue for a particular use must be made with consideration for strength, resistance, and durability. In addition, glues should be selected according to specific conditions that will affect the glue's performance. These conditions include such things as joint tightness, moisture content of the wood, clamping time and procedure, glue application, and curing time. See Table 13-1.

Shapes

1. Synthetic-resin glue is available in powder, liquid, or paste form; in the form of a powder requiring the addition of a catalyst; and in paper-film form. Hot-melt adhesive is available in sticks, tapes or ribbons, films or thin sheets, granules, pellets, cylinders, cubes, blocks, and cords.
2. Animal glue is available in liquid, flake, pearl, bead, sheet, stick, powder, cake, ground, or shredded form.
3. Casein glue is available in powder form.
4. Fish glue is available in liquid form.
5. Vegetable glue is sold in either powder or liquid form.
6. Blood-albumin glue is sold in flakes.

Grades

All types other than animal glue are ungraded. Packer's glue is considered the best grade of animal glue, followed by render's glue and extracted bone glue.

Sales Units

1. Synthetic-resin glue in powdered form is available in 4-ounce, 8-ounce, 1-pound, 5-pound, 10-pound, and 25-pound cans. Liquid-form synthetic-resin glue is available in 1/4-pint, pint, quart, gallon, and 5-gallon cans, and in 55-gallon drums. In paper-film form, this glue is available in sheets. Epoxy-resin glue is available in small (1-ounce) containers.
2. Powdered or flaked animal glue is available in 1-pound, 10-pound, and 25-pound packages, and in 100-pound barrels. Liquid animal glue is available in tubes and in 1/4-pint, 1/2-pint, pint, quart, and gallon cans.
3. Casein glue is available in 4-ounce, 8-ounce, 1-pound, 5-pound, 10-pound, 25-pound, 50-pound, 100-pound, and 300-pound containers.
4. Fish glue is sold in tubes and in 1/4-pint, 1/2-pint, pint, quart, and gallon cans.
5. Vegetable glue is not commonly used in school shops.
6. Blood-albumin glue requires extensive equipment and is not commonly used in school shops.

The United States is presently undergoing a transition from U.S. Customary measure to metric (or SI) measurement. This change will affect not only linear measure (feet and inches) but weight and volume as well. This will affect packaging of adhesives in that those sold by dry weight — synthetic-resin glue, for example — will be sold in grams (g) and kilograms (kg). Adhesives sold in liquid measure — for example, fish glue — will be sold in milliliters (ml) and liters (l). For more information, see Topic 10.

Storage

The storage life of resin glues varies from a few weeks for some to a few years for others. The higher the temperature, the shorter the storage life. Generally, the faster-curing glues will have a shorter storage life than the slower-curing resins. Some liquid resins require storage under refrigerated conditions to prolong their usable life. The storage life of powdered resins that have not been mixed with a catalyst is longer than that of those that have been mixed with a catalyst. When the storage life has been exceeded, properties are altered.

All liquid glues other than hot animal glue should be kept tightly covered. When thermoplastic synthetic resin, animal glues, and fish glues become too thick for use, add warm water to bring them to the thickness of light cream.

Table 13-1   Glues and Their Properties

Type of Adhesive	Durability	Color	Form and Mixing Procedure	Setting Time	Temperature	Stain	Cost	Shelflife	Use*
Resorcinal	Waterproof	Reddish	Liquid, mix with powdered catalyst.	2-1/2 Hours	21°C (70°F)	No	High	1 year unmixed, 3 hours mixed	AEF GH
Phenol	Waterproof	Red	Liquid, no mixing required.	2 to 5 minutes	149°C (300°F)	No	Medium	3 months	ADG
Phenol Resorcinal	Waterproof	Red	Liquid, mix with powdered catalyst.	2 to 6 Hours	21°-32°C (70°-90°F)	No	High	1 year unmixed, 3 hours mixed	ADG
Melamine	Waterproof	Clear	Powder, mix with water.	16 to 18 Hours at 24°C (75°F)	Hot Press 116°-127°C (240°-260°F)	No	High	1 year unmixed, 10-15 hours mixed	ADG
Epoxy	Waterproof	Clear	Liquid, mix with catalyst.	6 to 8 Hours	21°C (70°F)	No	High	Unlimited unmixed, 1-2 hours mixed	CH
Blood Albumin	Waterproof	Dark brown	Powder, mix with water.	2 to 5 minutes	110°-138°C (230°-280°F)	Yes	Low	Unlimited unmixed, 4-12 hours mixed	ADE GH
Casein	Water resistant	Cream	Powder, mix with water.	4 to 6 Hours	1°-32°C (34°-90°F)	Some	Low	1 year unmixed, 4-6 hours mixed	AEFH
Urea (Powder)	Water resistant	Cream	Powder, mix with water.	4 to 6 hours	21°C (70°F)	No	Low	1 year unmixed, 4-6 hours mixed	AEFH
Urea (Liquid)	Water resistant	Cream	Liquid, mix with powdered catalyst.	2 to 6 hours	21°C (70°F)	No	Low	1 year unmixed, 2-12 hours mixed depending upon catalyst used	AEFH
Melamine Urea	Water resistant	Clear	Powder or liquid, mix powder type with water.	4 Hours at 24°C (75°F)	Hot Press 121°-149°C (250°-300°F)	No	Medium	1 year unmixed, 3-10 hours mixed	ABDE
Aliphatic Resin	Slightly water resistant	Yellowish	Liquid, no mixing required.	20 to 40 minutes	5°-32°C (40°-90°F)	No	Medium	1 year	ABEF
Vegetable (starch)	Non water resistant		Powder or liquid. Mix powder with water, use liquid as purchased.	4 to 6 Hours	21°C (70°C)	Yes	Low	1 year	AED
Vegetable (soybean)	Non water resistant		Powder, mix with water.	2 to 3 Hours	21°C (70°F)	Yes	Low	1 year unmixed, 3 hours mixed	E
Hot Animal Glue	Non water resistant	Amber	Sheets, flakes, or chips. Soak in water for 8 hours. Heat in double boiler to 60°-71°C (140°-160°F)	2 minutes	21°C (70°F)	No	Medium	Unlimited before heating	AE
Liquid Animal Glue	Non water resistant	Amber	Liquid, no mixing required.	4 Hours	21°C (70°F)	No	Medium	6 months	ABEF
Polyvinyl Acetate	Non water resistant	White	Liquid, no mixing required.	20 Minutes to 1 Hour	21°C (70°F)	No	Medium	1 year	ABE
Contact Cement	Water resistant		Liquid, no mixing required.	Bonds on contact	21°C (70°F)	—	High		BF
Fish Glue	Non water resistant	Amber	Liquid, no mixing required	6 Hours	21°C (70°F)	Some	Low	1 year	AB

*Use: A. Wood to Wood
B. Cloth or Paper to Wood
C. Wood to Metal
D. Plywood
E. Veneers
F. Plastic Laminates to Wood
G. Marine
H. Exterior

Hand Screw

Topic 111.

Classification

Adjustable holding tool

Application

Principle of Operation

The **hand screw** works on the principle of the screw and lever, Fig. 13-6. It is designed to hold stock under pressure. The two jaws are adjusted for size opening by simultaneously revolving the two spindles. Compression is applied by tightening the middle spindle. Tightening the end spindle causes the jaws to pivot on the middle spindle. This results in leverage, which produces additional compression at the open end of the jaws. (See discussion of the screw, Topic 9, "Tools.") In order to secure with uniform pressure, the jaws must be parallel.

Kinds and Uses

Hand screws serve as an adjustable pressure device and are used extensively in gluing and other joining operations. Hand screws are also used for securing stock and fixtures in position for work.

There are two types of hand screws available — fully adjustable and nonadjustable. The adjustable hand screw is designed to permit adjustment of the jaws to different angles. This design has many advantages and is generally preferred. The nonadjustable hand screw is designed in such a way that the jaws remain parallel to each other. This feature limits its usefulness in some applications, but it can save time in many standard clamping operations.

Principal Parts and Function of Each

1. The **jaws** are made to serve as gripping levers. Stock is held between the openings of the jaws. Jaws are made of oiled maple or are cast of a magnesium alloy steel.
2. **Adjustment spindles** are made of cold-drawn steel. One half of the spindle has righthand threads. The other half has lefthand threads. Revolving the spindle advances or retracts the jaws simultaneously. Wooden spindles are made of ash or hickory and have righthand threads throughout their length.
3. **Pivot nuts,** made from cold-drawn steel, are fitted into the jaws to hold the threaded spindle.
4. The maple **handle** is fastened to the spindle to provide a better grip.

Maintenance

Hand screws should be stored on racks. The jaws must not be under pressure. Keep the jaws clean and free from glue (coat them with wax). Periodically, a drop of oil should be applied to the spindle.

Market Analysis

Capacity

Hand screws are available with jaw lengths from 4″ to 24″ and jaw openings of up to 17″.

Adjustable Clamp Co.

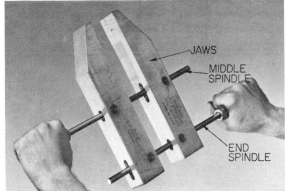

JAWS

MIDDLE SPINDLE

END SPINDLE

Fig. 13-6.   Hand screw.

Topic 112.

Bar Clamps

Adjustable Clamp Co.

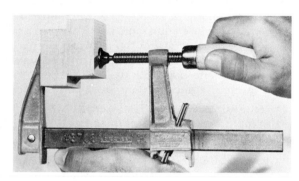

Fig. 13-7.   Types of steel bar clamps.

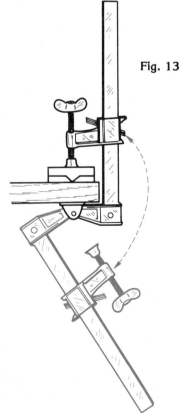

Fig. 13-8.   Hinged bar clamp.

Classification

Adjustable, rigid holding tools

Application

Principle of Operation

Clamps operate on the principle of the screw. Pressure is applied and maintained by means of tightening a screw.

Kinds and Uses

Bar clamps are used in clamping wide, glued-up sections such as tabletops, and in holding parts in assembly.

1. **Steel bar clamps** are made in various styles to suit many clamping needs. See Figs. 13-7 and 13-8. Steel bar clamps are made in deep throat sizes, with jaw openings from 4″ to 60″. Standard bar clamps have capacities ranging from 2′ to 8′.

Adjustable Clamp Co.

Fig. 13-9.   I-bar clamp with clutch-operated rear jaw.

Adjustable Clamp Co.

Fig. 13-10.   I-bar clamps used to assemble frame.

Adjustable Clamp Co.

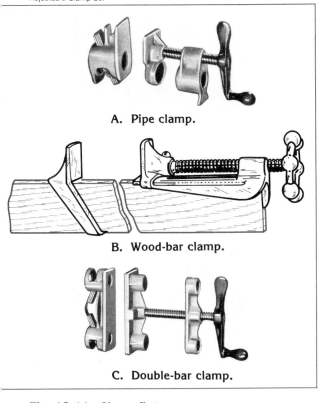

A. Pipe clamp.

B. Wood-bar clamp.

C. Double-bar clamp.

Fig. 13-11. Clamp fixtures

Adjustable Clamp Co.

Fig. 13-12. Pipe clamps used to glue window frame.

2. **I-bar clamps** use an I-shaped bar for greater strength and rigidity. See Figs. 13-9 and 13-10. Sizes range from 2' to 8' in length.

3. **Clamp fixtures** may be purchased separately to fit strips of wood or pipe. This type of clamp is less expensive than manufactured bar clamps and less restrictive in size. The clamp capacity may easily be altered by using different lengths of pipe or wood. See Figs. 13-11A, 13-11B, and 13-12.

Wetzler Clamp Co., Inc.

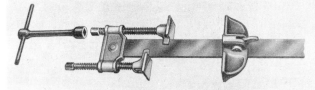

Fig. 13-13. Piling clamp.

Wetzler Clamp Co., Inc.

Fig. 13-14. Piling clamps in stack.

Clamp fixtures are also available for constructing **double-bar clamps,** Fig. 13-11C. This type of clamp assures even pressure on both sides of the work, which reduces the chance of buckling in thin or wide stock.

4. **Piling clamps** allow stock to be clamped on each side of the bar. This type is a production clamp, used where many pieces of stock of the same size are glued and are piled one on top of another. See Figs. 13-13 and 13-14. Piling clamps range in size from 2' to 6' maximum opening.

Principal Parts and Function of Each

1. The **bar** is made either of wood, rectangular steel, pipe, or an I-shaped bar. It holds and guides the clamping mechanism and serves both to regulate the length of opening and to provide stiffness.

2. Movable, forged-steel **dogs** grip the bar and adjust for length of opening.

3. The **clutch** or **pressure plates,** made of tempered steel, grip the bar or pipe. (Some bars have notches into which the steel dogs catch at fixed intervals.)

4. The **jaws** transmit pressure from the screw to the stock being clamped.

Wetzler Clamp Co., Inc.

5. A **screw,** made of cold-drawn steel, transmits pressure to the dogs or jaws.

6. A **handle, crank, wing,** or **wheel** aids in turning the screw.

Maintenance

Bar clamps should be oiled before storage to prevent damage and rusting. The screw should be oiled periodically.

Market Analysis

Capacity

The size of bar clamps is determined by the length of the bar or pipe and by the depth of the jaws. Pipe or wooden bars may be of any convenient length.

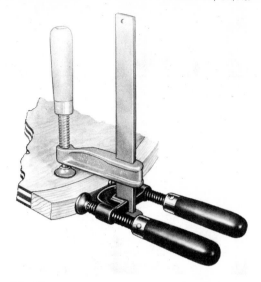

Fig. 13-15. Cross clamp — used with quick-action clamp to clamp edge material.

Topic 113.

C-, Band, Miter, and Spring Clamps

Classification

Adjustable holding tools

Application

Principle of Operation

Pressure is applied by means of a screw or spring. See discussion of the screw, Topic 9, "Tools."

Kinds and Uses

1. **C-clamps** are used in clamping small work. See Figs. 13-16 through 13-20.

2. **Miter clamps** provide a right angle for squaring and clamping flat, mitered corners. There are three basic types: **miter vise, miter frame,** and **miter clamp.** See Figs. 13-21 through 13-23.

3. **Band clamps,** made of canvas or flexible steel, are used in clamping round and irregularly shaped objects such as furniture, tanks, and columns. See Figs. 13-24 and 13-25.

4. **Spring clamps** are quick-release clamps used for holding small pieces, Figs. 13-26 and 13-27.

Fig. 13-16. C-clamp.

Fig. 13-17. C-clamp, regular-throat.

Adjustable Clamp Co.

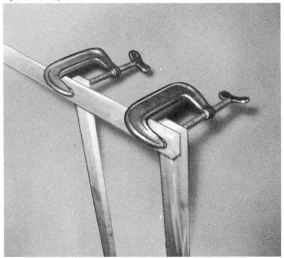

Fig. 13-18. C-clamps used in assembly.

Cincinnati Tool Co.

Fig. 13-22. Miter frame, four-corner.

Fig. 13-19. C-clamp, deep-throat.

Adjustable Clamp Co.

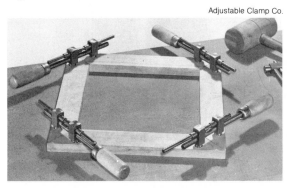

Fig. 13-23. Miter clamps requiring a blind hole to be drilled in each piece of the stock to be joined. The pins of the clamp fit in the holes and, by means of a screw handle, the joint is pulled tightly together.

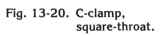

Fig. 13-20. C-clamp, square-throat.

Fig. 13-24. Band clamp.

Adjustable Clamp Co.

Stanley Tools.

Fig. 13-21. Miter vise.

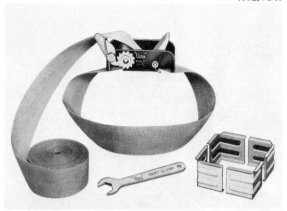

Fig. 13-27. Spring clamps.

Fig. 13-25. Band clamp and steel corners used for clamping square corners.

Fig. 13-26. Use of spring clamps.

Fig. 13-28. Universal clamp used for miter joints with both square and irregualr angles.

Principal Parts and Function of Each

C-Clamps

1. The **frame,** made of iron or forged steel, forms the opening between the fixed jaw and the adjustable jaw.
2. A **screw,** made of cold-rolled steel, transmits pressure to the steel swivel or plate.
3. A steel **swivel** serves as an adjustable jaw.

Band Clamps

1. The **frame,** made of pressed steel, secures the flexible-steel or canvas **band**.
2. The **screw,** or **ratchet mechanism** tightens the flexible band.

Miter Clamps

1. The steel **jaws** serve as pressure plates.
2. The **screws** transmit pressure to the jaws.

3. The **corner miter clamps** have four aluminum-alloy corner blocks and four screws and nuts.

Spring Clamps

1. The steel **jaws** grip the surface of the workpiece.
2. A steel **spring** transmits pressure to the jaws.

Maintenance

Clamps should be stored on racks when not in use. The screw should be oiled periodically.

Adjustable Clamp Co.

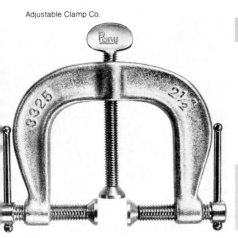

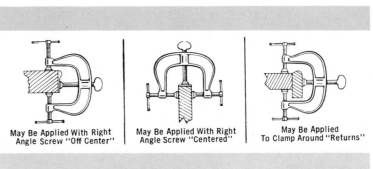

May Be Applied With Right Angle Screw "Off Center" | May Be Applied With Right Angle Screw "Centered" | May Be Applied To Clamp Around "Returns"

Fig. 13-29. Three-way edging clamp.

Market Analysis

Capacity

1. C-clamps are made with 5/8" to 6-1/4" throat openings and depths of 3/4" to 12".
2. In band clamps, the band length determines the size of the object that can be clamped.

Bands are from 10' to 30' long.
3. Spring clamps are made with overall jaw lengths of 4" to 12", with maximum jaw openings from 1" to 4-1/4".
4. Miter clamps are limited to the opening of the jaws.
5. The miter vise will open to a width of 3-1/2".

Gluing a Joint

Topic 114.

Classification

Fastening by adhesion

Procedure

1. Test all surfaces to be glued together for accuracy of fit. Glue cannot compensate for a poor fit. The closer the members fit together, the better the glue will hold. A properly glued joint is generally stronger than the wood itself.
2. After members of the joint have been properly fitted, they should be assembled in a dry run. Check to see that adjacent pieces are marked with corresponding numbers or letters so that exact reassembly will be quick and easy.

3. Adjust the clamps to tighten the joints. Protective blocks should be used under clamp jaws to prevent marring of the wood surface. Check to see that the work is locked square and flat. See Fig. 13-30. Clamps

Fig. 13-30. Position of clamps in gluing spring joint.

Fig. 13-31. Clamping stock, using bar clamps. Stock is clamped on both sides to provide even pressure. Light showing under the bars indicates warp in the boards.

Fig. 13-32. Gluing a frame, using bar clamps.

Fig. 13-33. Taylor clamps.
Previously fitted stock is joined into large blanks for tabletops, case tops, and other long furniture surfaces. The stock is held in large Taylor clamps until dry. It takes these revolving clamp gluers about 30 minutes to complete the cycle.

Fig. 13-34. Industrial assembly — frame being clamped in pneumatic press.

Fig. 13-35. Industrial assembly — clamping a dresser in a hand-operated press.

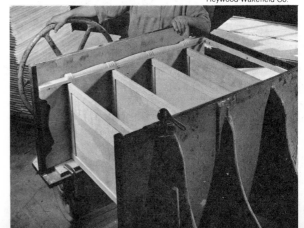

should be located close to the ends and should be spaced not more than 12″ apart on alternate sides. See Fig. 13-31.

4. Disassemble the joint and apply a thin layer of glue to each member. Some glues set in a short time. If the glue you are using is fast-setting, work quickly. Use paper inserts or some other means of ensuring that hand screws, straightedges, or protective blocks are not unintentionally glued to the work.

5. Quickly apply pressure with clamps, bringing the joint together. Do not force out the glue by applying excessive pressure. **Check to see that your work is flat and square.**

6. Wipe all excess glue from the surface with a damp paper towel. If this glue is left to harden, it will have to be removed with a glue scraper or a chisel. This causes additional work and may cause trouble in finishing.

7. Set the work aside, allowing time for the glue to dry. Some glues harden in one hour, while others take four to eight hours to harden. Follow the manufacturer's directions.

8. The room temperature should be 21° C (70° F) for the most desirable gluing conditions.

Standards and Results

• A properly glued joint should fit so closely that no glue line shows between the pieces.

• There should be no warp clamped into the assembly. See Fig. 13-31.
• Work should be square.
• There should be no excess glue left on the surface.

Safety Considerations

• Wear safety glasses when handling glues.
• Excess pressure should not be applied to any clamp fixture, as this may cause deformation or breakage of the workpiece.
• Use a helper when handling awkward or heavy projects.

Claw Hammer

Topic 115.

Classification

Driving and withdrawing tool

Application

Principle of Operation

Both in driving and withdrawing nails, the **hammer** works on the principle of the lever.

Kinds and Uses

The hammer is used to drive and withdraw nails. It is also used as a lever in driving apart pieces that have been nailed, Figs. 13-36 and 13-37. Claw hammers are available with head weights of 5, 7, 10, 13, 16, and 20 ounces. They are available with either straight or curved claws.

Principal Parts and Function of Each

1. The **handle** is the means by which the hammer is held. Handles can be made of hickory, ash, fiberglass, or steel. Fiberglass and steel handles are covered with a neoprene, leather, or vinyl grip to absorb shock.

2. The **head** of the hammer is made of high-grade steel that has been drop-forged to

Stanley Tools

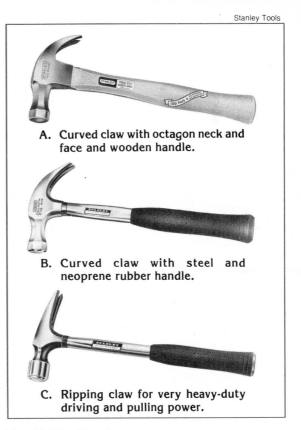

A. Curved claw with octagon neck and face and wooden handle.

B. Curved claw with steel and neoprene rubber handle.

C. Ripping claw for very heavy-duty driving and pulling power.

Fig. 13-36. Claw hammers.

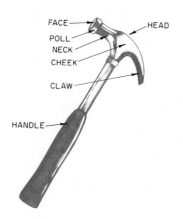

Fig. 13-37. Nomenclature of claw hammer.

shape, then semihardened and tempered. The head of the hammer does the driving or withdrawing. The heavier the head, the greater the force exerted in driving nails. The hammerhead is composed of several parts, Fig. 13-37.

Maintenance

Cleaning

The face of a hammerhead may become gummy from use. This gum may be cleaned off with steel wool or fine sandpaper. Handles may also get dirty and sticky and may be cleaned with sandpaper.

Repairing

Wooden handles may dry out and shrink, resulting in a loose head. This may be overcome by driving the wedges further into the handle. Immersion in water provides only a temporary solution. The problem may be resolved more permanently by soaking the handle in a commercial wood stabilizer such as polyethylene glycol 1000. (See discussion of wood stabilization, Topic 1.)

Replacing Parts

Wooden handles may break and need replacement.

Market Analysis

Attachments

An attachment that can be used with the hammer is the **hammer nail clip.** This fits onto the head of a hammer, holding the nail until the first blow is struck. This attachment is used in overhead nailing, freeing one hand to hold the stock.

Topic 116.

Nails

Classification

Fasteners

Composition or Description

Steel is the most common material used to make **nails.** Nails made of copper, brass, bronze, aluminum, and stainless steel are also available. They are used for applications in which corrosion is a problem. Steel nails are often galvanized or coated to improve their corrosion resistance.

Nails are most commonly produced by feeding coiled wire into production machines. These machines straighten, head (make a head on), and cut the formed nail to length. The burrs are then removed. When necessary, the nails are then galvanized, plated, or resin coated so that they will be resistant to corrosion.

Properties

Nails are designed in such a way that, when driven into wood, they force, bend, break, or

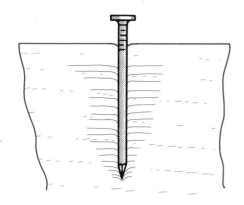

Fig. 13-38. Action of wood fibers to hold nail.

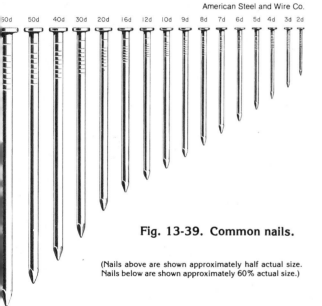

American Steel and Wire Co.

60d 50d 40d 30d 20d 16d 12d 10d 9d 8d 7d 6d 5d 4d 3d 2d

Fig. 13-39. Common nails.

(Nails above are shown approximately half actual size. Nails below are shown approximately 60% actual size.)

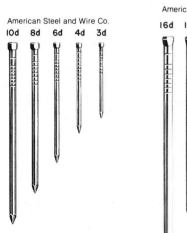

American Steel and Wire Co.
10d 8d 6d 4d 3d

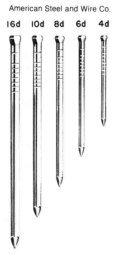

American Steel and Wire Co.
16d 10d 8d 6d 4d

Fig. 13-40. Finishing nails.

Fig. 13-41. Casing nails.

split the fibers. The bent fibers tend to return to their normal position, thus pressing against the nail and wedging and gripping it tightly, as shown in Fig. 13-38. See "Factors Affecting the Holding Power of Nails," under Topic 117.

Uses

Nails are usually used to fasten two or more pieces of wood or other material. The nails fasten by driving into or through the separate pieces.

Market Analysis

Shapes

Head Form and Wire Diameter of Nails

1. **Common nails.** These are large, flat-headed wire nails, of a standard gauge wire for any given length, Fig. 13-39. They are usually plain, but they may have spiral grooves or ring grooves. Common nails are used primarily in construction, where strength is of major importance.
2. **Spikes.** Spikes are large common nails, 16d to 60d in size, Fig. 13-39.
3. **Box nails.** These are similar to common nails, but are smaller in diameter and have a thinner head. Box nails are used in place of common nails in light construction because they are less likely to split thin or narrow stock. Box nails are commonly used in making wooden boxes and crates.
4. **Wire nails.** Wire nails are similar to common nails, but the gauges of wire differ from those of common nails. These nails are classified by length in inches and by gauge of wire.
5. **Finishing nails.** These are wire nails that have small heads. The small head makes it possible to set the nail below the surface of the wood on finish work, Fig. 13-40. Finishing nails are classified by the standard penny system.
6. **Brads.** Brads are small finishing nails that are classified, like wire nails, by length in inches and by gauge of wire.

INTERESTING FACT: Nails and staples are known to have been produced in Egypt as early as 2700 B.C.

7. **Casing nails.** These nails are similar to finishing nails, but have larger heads, Fig. 13-41. The larger head provides greater holding power. Casing nails are used where both strength and appearance must be considered. House trim, door frames, and windows are usually fastened with this type of nail. Casing nails are classified by the standard penny system.

Nail Points
(See Fig. 13-42)
1. **Regular diamond point.** Nails with this type of point are of medium sharpness and are for general use.
2. **Long-diamond point.** This type of point is found on nails used for speed driving.
3. **Blunt point.** Nails with a blunt point are used for dense wood and masonry.

4. **Chisel point.** This point is a large spike and is used for hard wood.
5. **Round point** or **pointless.** A nail with this kind of point is used on fabric and carpeting to prevent tearing.
6. **Needle point.** Nails with a needle point are used to prevent tearing. They are also used for speed nailing.
7. **Duckbill point.** This type of point is usually found on smaller nails that are to be clinched.
8. **Side point.** Nails with this type of point are used for clinching in hard wood. The side point minimizes splitting.

Special Nails
1. **Stronghold® nails.** This type of nail has threads, providing extra holding power. See Fig. 13-43.

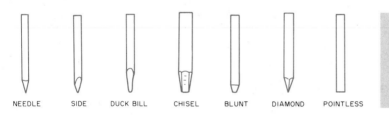

NEEDLE   SIDE   DUCK BILL   CHISEL   BLUNT   DIAMOND   POINTLESS

Fig. 13-42. Types of points.

Independent Nail Corp.

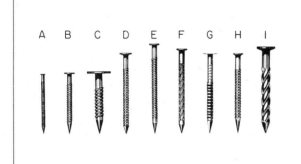

A   B   C   D   E   F   G   H   I

Fig. 13-43. Special-purpose Stronghold nails.
A. Wood-shingle face nail.
B. Nail for applying siding to plywood.
C. Nail for applying roofing to plywood.
D. Annular-ring nail for general use.
E. Spiral nail for general use.
F. Hard-tempered nail for concrete.
G. Drywall nail.
H. Underlay floor nail.
I. Roofing nail with neoprene washer.

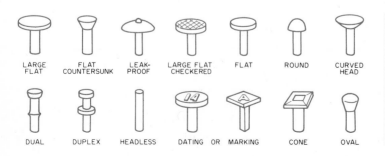

LARGE FLAT   FLAT COUNTERSUNK   LEAK-PROOF   LARGE FLAT CHECKERED   FLAT   ROUND   CURVED HEAD

DUAL   DUPLEX   HEADLESS   DATING OR   MARKING   CONE   OVAL

Fig. 13-44. Types of heads.

2. **Duplex nails.** These nails have two heads. They are used in temporary construction (for example, scaffolding and making cement forms). The lower head allows the nail to be driven tight and the upper head allows for easy removal. See Fig. 13-44.
3. **Round, curved, cone,** and **oval-head nails.** These nails are used for decorative purposes. See Fig. 13-44.
4. **Dating nails** or **marking nails.** These nails have numbers or letters on the head. They are used on telephone poles and railroad ties to number and date the time of installation. They are also used to match wooden storm windows and screens to the proper window opening. See Fig. 13-44.
5. **Roofing nails.** Large, flat nails are commonly referred to as roofing nails. They are usually galvanized or coated and are used in applying shingles and roll roofing. See Fig. 13-44.
6. **Escutcheon pins.** Escutcheon pins are very small nails, used for intricate decorative work.
7. **Scotch truss nails.** These are made in most sizes and can be substituted for most common nails. These nails have a ribbed shank, which provides extra holding power, Fig. 13-45.
8. **Staples.** Staples, Fig. 13-46, are used to secure wire or thin metal to wood.

Sizes

1. The size of most ordinary nails is indicated by a combination of numbers and the term **penny** (abbreviated **d**). A 2d nail is 1" in length. Each increase in the penny value represents a 1/4" increase in the length of the nail. Thus, a 6d nail would be 2" in length. This general rule applies to nails up to 16d. Above 16d, the size of nails increases disproportionately with each penny size.
2. Sizes of all wire brads and of wire nails that deviate from the penny system are usually indicated by length in inches and by gauge of wire. For example, a wire nail that is 1" long and made of #15 wire is actually classified as a 2d common nail, but a wire nail that is 1" long and made of #17 wire is classified as a 1", #17 wire nail.

Sales Units

1. Most nails may be purchased by the pound, but they are sometimes sold in 5-pound packages. Nails may also be purchased in 100-pound units, sold in a cardboard carton.
2. Small wire nails, brads, and escutcheon pins are usually sold in 1/4-pound, 1/2-pound, and 1-pound packages.

Maintenance

Nails should be stored in a dry place to prevent rusting.

Armco Steel Corporation

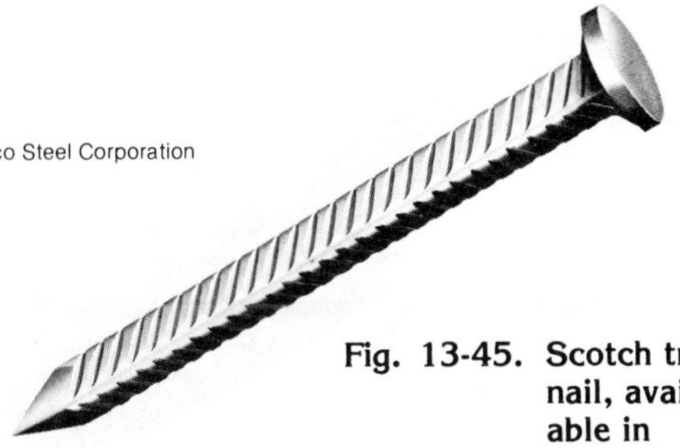

Fig. 13-45. Scotch truss nail, available in many sizes and designs.

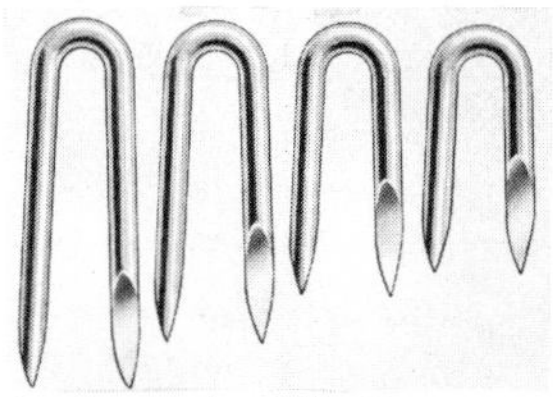

Fig. 13-46. Staples.

American Steel and Wire Co.

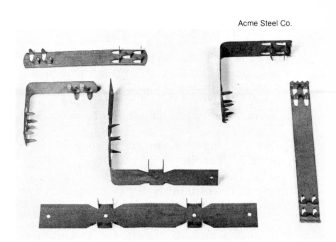

Acme Steel Co.

Fig. 13-47. Fasteners for crate corners.

Stanley Tools

Fig. 13-48. Corrugated fasteners.

Everard Tap and Die Corp.

CHEVRONS WOOD FASTENER   JOINT WITH CHEVRONS FLUSH   JOINT WITH CHEVRONS COUNTERSUNK (Slots filled with putty)

THE CHEVRONS COUNTERSINK

Fig. 13-49. Chevrons.

INTERESTING FACT: In America, nails were hand-forged until 1790, when Jacob Perkins of Newburyport, Massachusetts invented a nailmaking machine. This took the place of the hand manufacture of cut nails. This nailmaking machine could make 200,000 nails per day, and was a major step in pioneering an industry that today has the capacity to produce annually more than 1.2 million tons of nails and staples.

The Pilgrims did not use nails in the construction of their buildings. Instead, they used wooden pegs called trunnels.

Topic 117.

Driving Nails

Classification

Fastening

Procedure

Nails are used to fasten materials such as wood, metal, asbestos, slate, plasterboard, and composition board to wood. The wood usually serves as a base into which the nails are driven.
1. Select the proper nail. (Refer to Topic 116, "Nails.")
2. Select a hammer in accordance with the size of the nail.

Locating Position of Nail

1. If conditions permit, it is best to locate nails at least 3/4" from the edge or end of the board. If this is not possible, a hole slightly smaller than the diameter of the nail should be drilled through the first piece to prevent splitting.
2. If strength is the only consideration, the nails should be staggered so that adjacent nails in the same grain are not in line with each other.

Fig. 13-50. Driving a nail — note how hammer is held.

3. If appearance is a major consideration, the nails should be in perfect alignment and should be equally spaced.
4. Avoid nailing into knots or other defects.

Driving Nails

1. Take a position that allows you to sight the nail and to drive it at the proper angle.
2. Hold the nail with the forefinger and thumb of one hand. With the other hand, grasp the handle of the hammer so as to gain maximum leverage, Fig. 13-50.
3. The nail should be struck squarely on the head, using forearm action. Use light taps to start the nail and increase the force of the blows as the nail penetrates deeper. Lessen the force as the head approaches the surface. Light hammer blows cause the nail to hold better because the wood fibers (into which the nail is being driven) are bent rather than torn.
4. Splitting may be prevented and nails driven more easily if holes slightly smaller than the diameter of the nails are drilled in the piece being fastened.
5. If the nail bends while being driven, remove and discard it.
6. If a nail tends to follow the grain, either withdraw and relocate it or drill out the hole.
7. Heads of most nails are usually driven flush with the surface of the material being held.
8. Finish and casing nails are usually set below the surface with a **nail set,** Fig. 13-51.

Fig. 13-51. Setting finish nail with a nail set.

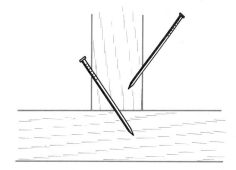

Fig. 13-52. Toenailing.

Toenailing is the method used to fasten two pieces of stock together when the contact of the butted surface is small and the pieces are running at an angle that would not permit the straight driving of nails. See Fig. 13-52. Nails driven at an angle greater than 30° from the perpendicular do not permit enough depth of penetration into the second piece. Nails driven at an angle less than 30° may cause splitting of the first piece. Contrary to popular opinion, toenailing does not provide as much holding power as straight nailing. Toenailing is usually used in house construction, to fasten the lower ends of studs to the sole, to fasten fire stops to studs, or to fasten corner braces to studs.

Factors Affecting the Holding Power of Nails

The following statements apply only if there is no splitting in the wood:
1. As the length of the nail is increased, the holding power is increased.
2. As the diameter of the nail is increased, the holding power is increased.
3. The sharper the point, the greater the holding power.
4. The density of the material into which the nail is driven affects the holding power. For example, a nail driven into oak has a greater holding power than an identical nail driven into pine.
5. The surface of the nail affects the holding power. For example, smooth nails do not have as great a holding power as sandblasted, galvanized, or spirally or annually grooved nails.
6. The driving force affects the holding power. In general, a moderately slow blow is preferred.

7. Maximum holding power is obtained when the nail is driven at right angles to the fibers.
8. Nails driven into dry wood have greater holding power than those driven into wet wood.

Standards and Results

- There should be no splitting of the material being fastened.
- The heads of nails should not protrude above the surface of the work.
- Nail points should neither protrude from any surface nor force out stock.
- There should be no hammer marks on the face of the material.
- There should be no bent nails driven into the surface.

Safety Considerations

- Wear safety glasses when nailing.
- Points of nails should not protrude through a board unless they are clinched.
- Avoid careless blows. Flying nails are very dangerous.

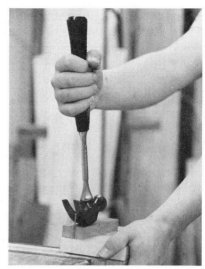

Fig. 13-53. Withdrawing a nail, using a block of wood to protect the surface of the stock and to provide greater leverage.

- When the nail is started, move your fingers out of the way so they will not get hit.
- Never hold nails in your mouth.
- Whenever possible, avoid driving against a springy surface.

Topic 118.

Automatic Nailers and Staplers

Classification

Driving tool

Application

Principle of Operation

A plunger unit drives nails, staples, or corrugated fasteners into the materials being fastened. These units may be powered manually, electrically, or pneumatically.

Large, manual units are activated by striking the plunger with a hammer, Fig. 13-54. Some manual units are operated simply by striking the head of the gun on the surface being fastened or by squeezing a trigger.

Electric and pneumatic units are powered (respectively) by electricity and by compressed air. These guns are trigger-activated.

Kinds and Uses

There are over 800 different models, designed to perform a wide variety of fastening jobs. All operate by one of three basic methods. These methods are as follows:
1. Individual nails, corrugated fasteners, or staples are fed into place and are driven either manually or with each squeeze of the trigger.

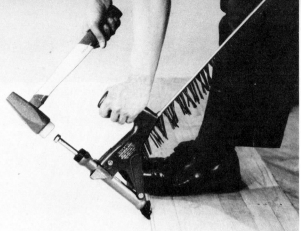

Independent Nail and Packing Co.

Fig. 13-54. Production technique of floor nailing. This machine feeds nails at the proper angle, drives and sets nails, and drives flooring strip snugly into place. All this is done in one operation. Tongue-and-groove floors may be laid accurately, quickly, and without dented or mashed edges.

2. Wire is cut to length from a roll of wire and is driven into the material with each squeeze of the trigger.
3. Nails are fed, from a feeder unit, point-first through a hose and are driven into the material with each squeeze of the trigger.

Some common types of fastening guns are as follows:
1. The **pneumatic stapler** drives a heavy-gauge wire staple. See Fig. 13-55.
2. The **pneumatic tacker** is commonly used in upholstering furniture, fastening paneling and trim, and attaching protective felt lin-

ing to crates. It is also used in the furniture industry to fasten glue blocks; drawer backs, bottoms, and sides; composition board, boxes, and pallets.
3. The **disk stapler** drives staples through prepunched holes in metal disks. These staples are used for stapling roofing paper or felt paper. The metal disks prevent the staples from pulling through the paper, Fig. 13-56.
4. The **pin tacker** is used for attaching overlays and decorative trim to furniture, paneling, and other finish work, Fig. 13-57. Pin tackers are often used in gluing operations to hold pieces in position until the glue has set.

Bostitch Div. of Textron Inc.

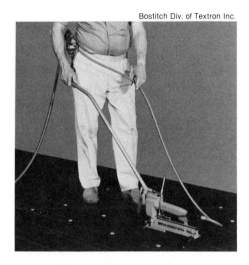

Fig. 13-56. Disk stapler.

Bostitch Div. of Textron Inc.

Fig. 13-55. Pneumatic stapler used to assemble furniture.

Bostitch Div. of Textron Inc.

Fig. 13-57. Pin tacker.

Fig. 13-58. Pneumatic nail gun, used to assemble crate sections.

The length of pin is determined by adjusting a screw on the side of the unit. When the trigger is squeezed, a pin is cut from a coil of wire to the predetermined length. The pin is then driven into the materials being fastened. Holes made by the pins are so small that they are covered in the finishing process and do not need filling.

5. The **automatic nailing machine** is used for many applications in the construction industry. Examples of these applications are fastening butt joints in sash and door units and fastening framing members, wood panels, and siding. These nailing machines come in a wide variety of sizes and can be used for either flat nailing or toenailing.

There are several types of automatic nailers. One type can be adjusted to fire automatically at fixed intervals when the trigger is held down. Another type, called a **gang nailer,** is multiheaded and can discharge several nails at one time.

Principal Parts and Function of Each

1. The steel **frame** contains the fastener and the plunger mechanisms.
2. The **plunger** drives the nail, stapler, or corrugated fastener.
3. The **magazine** holds the fasteners until the **feeder unit** supplies them to the plunger.
4. The **trigger** (on pneumatic, electric, and small manual units) activates the plunger.
5. The **cutter** on wire-roll units cuts the wire to the proper length and shapes the ends.
6. The **screw adjustment** on wire-roll units determines the length of a pin being cut from the roll.

On automatic nailing machines, the screw adjustment sets the time interval between each discharge.
7. Some staplers and nailing machines have a **safety head.** This prevents the gun from firing (when the trigger is depressed) unless the head is pressed firmly against the surface being fastened.

Maintenance

Moving parts should be oiled periodically.

Market Analysis

Capacity

1. Some nail guns will handle nail sizes ranging from 2d to 20d.
2. Some staple guns drive staples 1/8″ to 1-1/4″ wide and 1/8″ to 2-1/2″ long.
3. Pin tackers drive pins 1/4″ to 1″ in length.

Sales Units

1. Nails are sold attached, in coils of 100 to 400.
2. Staples are sold in boxes of 1000 and 5000.
3. Wire is sold by the pound.

Topic 119.

Screwdrivers

Classification

Driving and withdrawing tools

Application

Principle of Operation

The **screwdriver** works on the principle of the wheel and axle. The handle is equivalent to the wheel, and the blade and tip are equivalent to the axle. Hence, the larger the diameter of the handle, the greater the mechanical advantage. The manner in which the hand, wrist, and arm are used may also increase the mechanical advantage. See Fig. 13-59.

Kinds and Uses

1. The **common screwdriver** is used to drive and withdraw screws. It is available in blade lengths from 1-1/4" to 18" and in blade diameters from 1/16" to 1/2".
2. The **screw-holding screwdriver** is similar to the common screwdriver, but is equipped with tempered-steel jaws. These jaws are used to hold the screw to the screwdriver blade for easy starting in hard-to-reach places.
3. The **offset screwdriver** is used for driving or loosening screws in areas where there is little space. The body of the offset screwdriver has one or two tips at each end, Fig. 13-60.
4. The **ratchet screwdriver** is similar to a common screwdriver, but has a ratchet, located at the handle end of the blade. This permits the handle to be turned a full turn of the wrist and then returned to the original position without the need for removal of the screwdriver tip from the screw.
5. The **offset ratchet screwdriver** is similar to the regular offset screwdriver, but the ratchet action permits back-and-forth motion with no need for removal of the screwdriver tip from the screw, Fig. 13-61.

Fig. 13-59. Nomenclature of screwdriver.

Fig. 13-60. Offset screwdriver.

Fig. 13-61. Offset ratchet screwdriver.

Fig. 13-62. Stubby screwdrivers.

Fig. 13-63. Spiral ratchet screwdriver.

Fig. 13-64. Screwdriver bit.

6. The **stubby screwdriver** is identical to a common screwdriver, but its blade and handle are much shorter. This permits use in close quarters, Fig. 13-62.
7. The **spiral ratchet screwdriver** is used to speed up the operation of driving or withdrawing screws. It works on the principle of the inclined plane, Fig. 13-63. As the handle is pushed down, the double-spiral grooves in the shaft turn the blade. The turning action of the blade either drives or loosens the screw, depending on the position of the ratchet. Some types have a spring on the handle for quick return. Spiral screwdrivers are equipped with a chuck, which makes it possible to change bits.
8. **Screwdriver bits** are available with tip widths of 3/16" to 3/4", graduated by 16ths. They are used in bit braces to provide greater force in driving or withdrawing screws and also to speed up the operation, Fig. 13-64.

Fig. 13-65. Replaceable-bit stubby ratchet screwdriver.

Fig. 13-66. Electric screwdriver.

9. The **replaceable-bit screwdriver** is recommended for driving case-hardened screws, which might cause wear on the tip of ordinary screwdrivers. Bits are made in a number of sizes, all of which fit a common handle. Fig. 13-65.

10. The **electric screwdriver** is used in production work. It is equipped with a clutch, which slips when the screws are properly seated, Fig. 13-66.

11. The **pneumatic screwdriver** is similar to the electric screwdriver, but is driven by air pressure.

12. The electric drill may be used as a **power screwdriver** if it is equipped with a clutch and/or speed-reduction device. Variable-speed drills may be used to drive screws without conversion. However, the driving power is limited.

All of the above screwdrivers come with either regular, Phillips, or cross tips, Figs. 13-64 and 13-67.

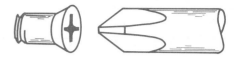

Fig. 13-67. Phillips-head screw and Phillips-head screwdriver tip.

Phillips screwdriver tips are available in five sizes — #0, #1, #2, #3, and #4. Screws with a wire size of between 2 and 4 use a #1 bit. Screws with a wire size of between 5 and 9 use a #2 bit. Screws having a wire size of between 10 and 16 use a #3 bit, and those with a wire size over 18 use a #4 bit.

Principal Parts and Function of Each

1. The wooden or plastic **handle** is shaped to provide a firm grip during twisting.
2. The **ferrule,** made of pressed steel or brass tubing, strengthens wooden handles against splitting under great pressure.
3. The **tip** is the part of the blade that fits the slot of the screw. The **blade** is made of carbon steel and has a hardened tip.

Maintenance

1. Keep screwdriver handles clean and smooth.
2. Screwdriver tips should be ground so that the sides are straight and parallel.
3. The metal blade and tip should be covered with a thin coat of oil when they are to be left unused for long periods of time.
4. Spiral and ratchet screwdrivers should be lubricated periodically.

Market Analysis

Capacity

Screwdrivers should fit the slot of the screw snugly, and the tip should not protrude beyond the diameter of the screwhead.

Wood Screws

Topic 120.

Classification

Spiral fasteners

Composition or Description

Wood screws are almost always made of either steel or brass. Special-purpose screws are also available in copper, bronze, aluminum, and stainless steel.

Properties

Screws made of steel are strong and brittle. They are often plated with zinc or cadmium to prevent rusting. Screws made of brass, copper, or aluminum are not as strong as steel screws, but have better resistance to corrosion.

Uses

Screws fasten as they are turned into or through a piece of material. They are used when strength greater than that of a nailed joint is desired. Screws tap their own internal threads while being driven into wood. This makes it possible to take the pieces apart without injury to either member. **Drive screws,** Fig. 13-68, can be driven in at least partway with a hammer. These screws, therefore, combine the driving ease of a nail with some of the holding power of a screw. Most screws must be seated with a screwdriver. Full-bodied threaded screws can be used for fastening wood or composition board, providing greater holding power.

Market Analysis

Shapes

There are many specialty shapes of screws. The common shapes, however, are usually referred to by the head shape. **Flat head, round head,** and **oval head** are the three basic head types. See Fig. 13-69. Some screws are made of hardened steel and are self-tapping, Fig. 13-68.

Sizes

Screws range in length from 1/4" to 6" and in wire gauge from 0 to 18. See Table 13-2. A 1/4" screw is made in wire gauges of between 0 and 4, while a 1-1/4" screw is made in gauges of between 4 and 16. The larger the gauge number, the larger the diameter of the wire.

Sales Units

Screws may be bought in any quantity, but the most economical way to purchase them is by the box of 100. Handy assortments may be purchased in smaller quantities.

Cost

For any given size, flat-head screws are cheapest. Round-head and oval-head screws usually cost about 10% more than flat-head screws.

FLAT HEAD   ROUND HEAD   OVAL HEAD

Fig. 13-69. Screwheads.
There are many special shapes of screwheads, but the most common are flat, round, and oval.

Fig. 13-68. Drive and self-tapping screws.

Table 13-2
Screw Availability Chart

● Steel Screws, readily available in the sizes listed   □ Brass Screws, readily available in the sizes listed
■ Steel Screws, manufactured, but not readily available   ☆ Brass Screws, manufactured, but not readily available

WIRE SIZE	0	1	2	3	4	5	6	7	8	9	10	12	14	16	18
APPROX. DIAM.	1/16″	5/64″	5/64″	3/32″	7/64″	1/8″	9/64″	5/32″	5/32″	11/64″	3/16″	7/32″	15/64″	17/64″	19/64″
1/4″	■ ☆	■ ☆	● □		●										
3/8″	■ ☆	■ ☆	● □	● □	● □	●	● □								
1/2″	■ ☆	■ ☆	● □	● □	● □	● □	● □	●	● □						
5/8″			● ☆	● ☆	● □	● □	● □	●	● □						
3/4″					● □	● □	● □	● □	● □	● □	● □	●			
7/8″					●	●	● □	● □	● □	● □	● □	●			
1″					● □	● □	● □	● □	● □	● □	● □	● □	●		
1 1/4″					●	●	● □	● □	● □	● □	● □	● □	● □	●	
1 1/2″							● □	●	● □	●	● □	●	●	●	
1 3/4″							● ☆		● □	●	● □	● □	● □	●	
2″									● □	●	● □	● □	● □	●	
2 1/4″											●	●	●		
2 1/2″									●	●	● □	● □	● □	● □	
2 3/4″									■ ☆		■ ☆	■ ☆	■	■	■
3″									■		●	● □	● □	● □	■
3 1/2″											■	●	●	●	■
4″												■	●	●	■
4 1/2″													■	■	■
5″													■	■	■
6″													■	■	■

LENGTH OF SCREW (vertical label for the rows above)

STRAIGHT SLOT   PHILLIPS SLOT

Fig. 13-70. Types of slots on standard wood screws.

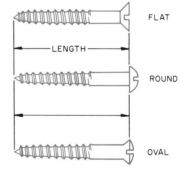

FLAT

LENGTH

ROUND

OVAL

Fig. 13-71. Length of wood screws.

Maintenance

Store screws in a dry place.

Topic 121.

Driving Wood Screws

Classification

Fastening

Procedure

1. Select the proper size, type, and quantity of

screws for the job. Keep in mind that, wherever possible, two-thirds of the length of the screw should be in the second piece. Also remember that the diameter should be large enough to withstand the probable strain. Where the head of the screw is to show, oval-head or round-head screws are usually used.

2. Whenever possible, locate the screws no closer than 1/2" from the end of the board. Arrange the screws in a straight line for appearance or stagger them for strength.

3. Drill holes in the first piece. These holes should be equal to the size of the shank (the smooth part of the screw). See Table 13-3. These holes are called **shank holes.** Countersink for flat-head and oval-head screws.

4. Drill holes in the second piece the size of the root diameter (base of thread) of the screw. See Table 13-3. These holes are called **pilot holes** or **lead holes.** To locate the position for these holes, hold the pieces in position and mark through the shank holes in the first piece with an awl, Fig. 13-73.

5. Select a screwdriver with a blade tip as wide as the diameter of the screwhead. The screwdriver tip should fit the slot snugly, Fig. 13-74.

6. Secure the pieces to be fastened and place the screw into the holes. Drive the screw by turning it in a clockwise direction until the two pieces are held firmly in place and the head is seated, Fig. 13-75. Soap or wax may be applied to the screw threads as a lubricant for easier driving.

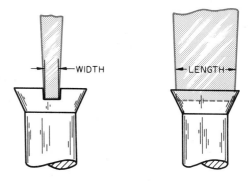

Fig. 13-74. Proper fit of screwdriver tip.

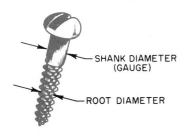

Fig. 13-72. The diameter of the screw shank and the diameter of the thread root determine the drill sizes needed for shank and pilot holes.

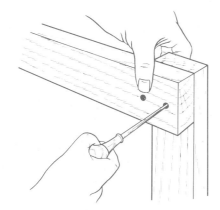

Fig. 13-73. Locating pilot holes with an awl.

Table 13-3
Screw and Screw-Hole Chart

Gauge No. Wire Size	Counterbore for Head Drill Size	Shank-Hole Drill Size	Pilot or Lead-Hole Drill Size	
			Hard Wood	Soft Wood
0	.119 ($^1/_8$)	$^1/_{16}$	$^3/_{64}$	
1	.146 ($^9/_{64}$)	$^5/_{64}$	$^1/_{16}$	
2	$^1/_4$	$^3/_{32}$	$^1/_{16}$	$^3/_{64}$
3	$^1/_4$	$^7/_{64}$	$^1/_{16}$	$^3/_{64}$
4	$^1/_4$	$^1/_8$	$^3/_{32}$	$^5/_{64}$
5	$^5/_{16}$	$^1/_8$	$^3/_{32}$	$^5/_{64}$
6	$^5/_{16}$	$^9/_{64}$	$^3/_{32}$	$^5/_{64}$
7	$^3/_8$	$^5/_{32}$	$^1/_8$	$^3/_{32}$
8	$^3/_8$	$^{11}/_{64}$	$^1/_8$	$^3/_{32}$
9	$^3/_8$	$^3/_{16}$	$^1/_8$	$^9/_{64}$
10	$^1/_2$	$^3/_{16}$	$^5/_{32}$	$^9/_{64}$
12	$^1/_2$	$^7/_{32}$	$^3/_{16}$	$^9/_{64}$
14	$^1/_2$	$^1/_4$	$^3/_{16}$	$^{11}/_{64}$
16	$^9/_{16}$	$^9/_{32}$	$^{15}/_{64}$	$^{13}/_{64}$
18	$^5/_8$	$^5/_{16}$	$^{17}/_{64}$	$^{15}/_{64}$
20	.650 ($^{11}/_{16}$)	$^{11}/_{32}$	$^{19}/_{64}$	$^{17}/_{64}$
24	.756 ($^3/_4$)	$^3/_8$	$^{21}/_{64}$	$^{19}/_{64}$

Fig. 13-75. Driving a screw.

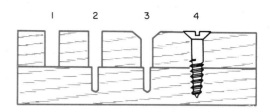

Fig. 13-76. Shank, pilot, countersink, and screw holes.

- Take care to avoid stripping out the stock or breaking the screw off in the stock.

Safety Considerations

- Be careful not to let the screwdriver slip. It could injure your hand and/or mar the workpiece.
- Don't rub your fingers over the head of the screw. Small slivers are sometimes raised on the head of the screw by the screwdriver.

Standards and Results

- The slot of the screw should not be burred.
- There should be no splitting of the materials being fastened.
- No screwdriver marks should show.

Topic 122.

Corner Irons (Braces), Flat Corner Irons, Mending Plates, T Plates

Classification

Fasteners and reinforcements

Composition or Description

Braces are stamped out of a wrought-iron, steel, or brass plate. The wrought iron is usually galvanized or plated to prevent rusting.

Properties

Braces and **plates** add stiffness and evenly distribute the stress.

Stanley Tools

Fig. 13-78. Flat corner iron.

Stanley Tools

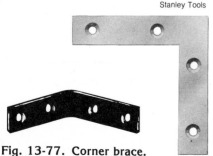

Fig. 13-77. Corner brace.

Fig. 13-79. Mending plate.

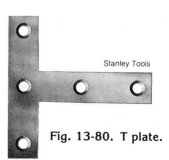

Stanley Tools

Fig. 13-80. T plate.

Uses

This type of hardware is used as a reinforcement in strengthening joints or cracks and in holding two or more pieces together or in place. The head of the screw should fill the countersunk hole and should fit flush with the surface.

Market Analysis

Sizes

See Table 13-4.

Grades

Braces are made either of brass, steel, or galvanized iron. The strength is dependent mostly upon the thickness of the metal.

Sales Units

Braces and plates may be purchased singly, in cards of three, by the dozen, or in boxes of 24.

Maintenance

Braces should be stored in a dry place, and should be straightened out when they become bent. Braces that are not rust resistant should be painted before being used in places where they will be exposed to moisture.

Table 13-4
Sizes of Fasteners and Reinforcements
(In Inches)

	Side Lengths	Lengths
Corner Braces (Fig. 13-77)	1	$1/2$
	$1 1/2$	$1/2$
	2	$5/8$
	$2 1/2$	$5/8$
	3	$3/4$
	$3 1/2$	$3/4$
Flat Corner Irons (Fig. 13-78)	$1 1/2$	$3/8$
	2	$3/8$
	$2 1/2$	$3/8$
	3	$1/2$
	$3 1/2$	$5/8$
	4	$3/4$
Mending Plates (Fig. 13-79)	2	$5/8$
	$2 1/2$	$5/8$
	3	$3/4$
	$3 1/2$	$3/4$
	4	$3/4$
T Plates (Fig. 13-80)	$2 1/2 \times 2 1/2 \times 1/2$ wide	
	$3 \times 3 \times 5/8$ wide	

| **Hinges** | **Topic 123.** |

Classification

Mechanical fasteners permitting a fixed motion

Composition or Description

Hinges are made either from iron, steel, bronze, brass, brass plate, or chromium plate. Hinges usually have two leaves and have a pin that ties them together and permits motion according to their particular design.

Properties

The hinge is a movable fastener that permits motion or change of direction. The appearance, the amount of motion, and the strength of the hinge are determined by the design of the hinge and the material from which it is made.

Uses

A hinge is used as a joint, permitting the movement of one of two members. Hinges are used to hang doors or gates, and serve as movable fasteners for table leaves, desks, or chest covers.

Market Analysis

Shapes

Butt Hinges

Butt hinges or "butts," as this type of hinge is commonly called, are made in many varieties. They may have a plain or fancy leaf, a fixed or loose pin, and a dull or bright surface. Butt hinges are probably the most difficult to apply. The leaves are fitted into a recess called a **gain.** This gain conceals the leaves. Only the knuckle is exposed when the hinge is closed. See Fig. 13-81.

1. The **swaged hinge** is a butt hinge that allows tighter joints between the separate members, Fig. 13-82.
2. The **box hinge** is a concealed hinge, used to hinge box or chest lids, Fig. 13-83.
3. The **double-action screen hinge** is used on folding screens or doors, to permit accordion-like folding of the front or back, Fig. 13-84.
4. The **table hinge** is used on table leaves, Fig. 13-85. One leaf is longer, allowing room for the molded edge when using a rule joint on a drop leaf.
5. The **narrow cabinet hinge** is used for hanging doors on cabinets, Fig. 13-86.
6. The **piano hinge** or **continuous hinge** is a long cabinet hinge used to hinge long expanses, Fig. 13-87.

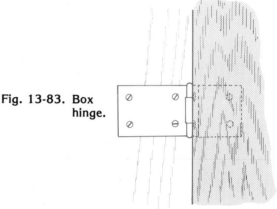

Fig. 13-83. Box hinge.

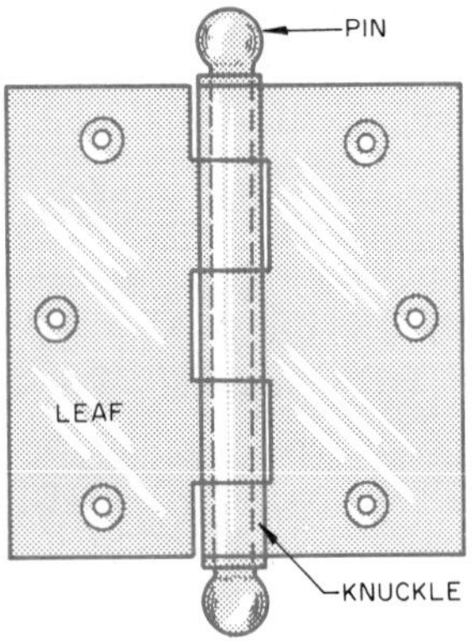

Fig. 13-81. Hinge nomenclature (butt hinge).

PIN

LEAF

KNUCKLE

Stanley Tools

Fig. 13-84. Double-action screen hinge.

Stanley Tools

Fig. 13-85. Table hinge.

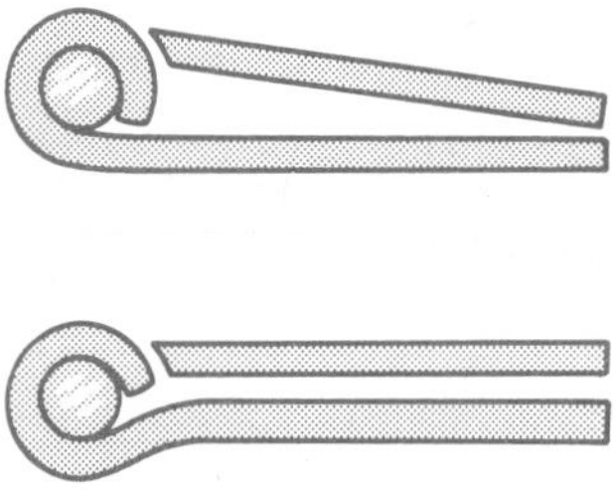

Fig. 13-82. Top view of butt hinge (top) and swage hinge (bottom).

Stanley Tools

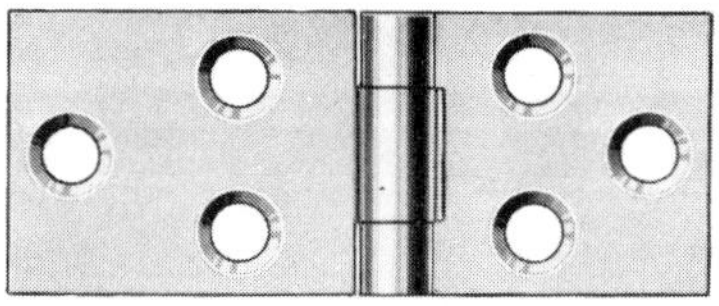

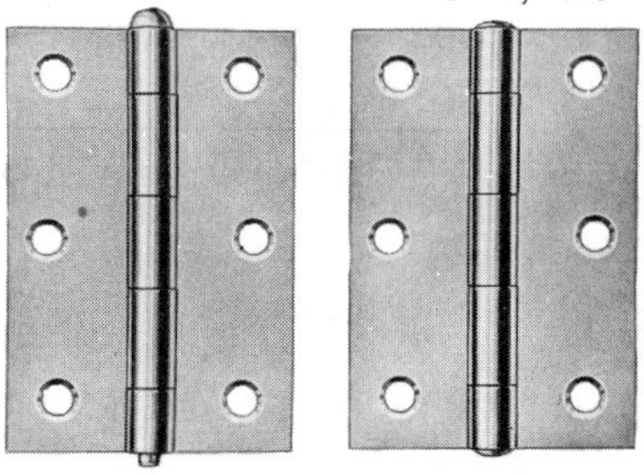

Fig. 13-86. Narrow cabinet hinges.

Fig. 13-87. Continuous (piano) hinge.

Stanley Tools

Fig. 13-88. Back flaps.

Fig. 13-89. Half-surface butt hinge.

Stanley Tools

Fig. 13-90. Hook and eye.

Stanley Tools

Fig. 13-91. Cabinet hinge.

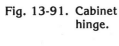

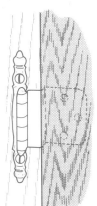

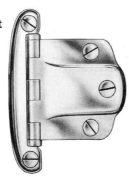

Fig. 13-92. Semi-concealed hinge.

Surface Hinges

Surface hinges are fixed-pin butts whose leaves are applied to the exposed surface of the door or frame.

1. The **hook and eye** is the simplest form of hinge, Fig. 13-90. The hook is screwed into one of the matching pieces and the eye is screwed into the other matching piece.
2. The **cabinet hinge** is used on the surface of flush cabinet doors, Fig. 13-91.
3. The **semi-concealed hinge** is used to hinge cabinet doors in cases where the door is raised or protrudes from the frame, Fig. 13-92.
4. The **T hinge** is used for heavy applications such as shed doors and fence gates, Fig. 13-93.
5. The **cabinet T hinge, H hinge,** and **HL hinge** are all decorative hinges, used to give furniture an Early Colonial appearance. See Figs. 13-94, 13-95, and 13-96.
6. The **card-table hinge** is used to fasten the leg of a folding card table to the tabletop, Fig. 13-97.

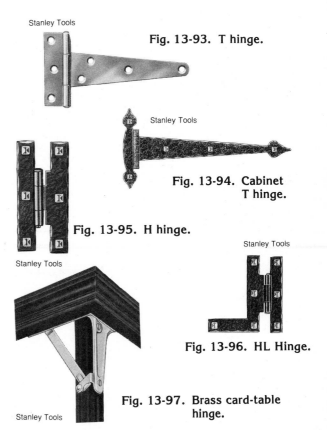

Stanley Tools

Fig. 13-93. T hinge.

Stanley Tools

Fig. 13-94. Cabinet T hinge.

Fig. 13-95. H hinge.

Stanley Tools

Fig. 13-96. HL Hinge.

Stanley Tools

Fig. 13-97. Brass card-table hinge.

7. **Back flaps** are used when the swinging member must fold flat to the joining surface, Fig. 13-88.
8. The **half-surface butt hinge** is a combination butt hinge and surface hinge. One leaf is recessed into the cabinet and the other is applied to the front surface of the cabinet door, Fig. 13-89.

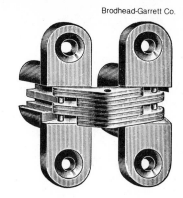

Fig. 13-98. Invisible or soss hinge.

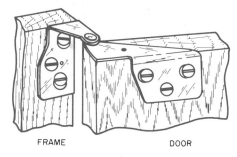

FRAME   DOOR

Fig. 13-99. Concealed hinge.

Miscellaneous Hinges

1. **Invisible pivot hinges** are fitted into the top and bottom edges of a door and frame. These hinges are easy to apply but are not very strong.
2. The **invisible hinge** or **soss hinge** is used on cabinet construction in cases where the hinge is to be completely hidden when the door is closed. See Fig. 13-98. Soss hinges are often used on reproductions of Duncan Phyfe, Empire, and Victorian furniture.
3. The **concealed hinge** is used for cabinet doors. Only the pivot point is visible when the door is closed, Fig. 13-99.

Sizes

Table 13-5
Sizes of Hinges

Name	Size of Leaf	
	Length	Width
Fixed Pin, Brass Butts	$1/2''$ to $2''$ by $1/4''$	$1/2''$ to $1\,3/8''$ by $1/8''$
Piano Hinge	$12''$ to $72''$	$1\,1/16''$ to $1\,1/2''$
Table Hinge	$1''$ to $2''$	$2\,5/8''$ to $3\,13/16''$
Strap Hinges	$4'' \times 1''$ $6'' \times 1\,3/32''$	
T-Hinge	$2'' \times 2''$ $3'' \times 2\,3/8''$ $5/8'' \times 5/8''$ $1'' \times 3/8''$ $1\,11/16'' \times 3/8''$	
Invisible or Soss	$1'' \times 3/8''$ to $4\,5/8'' \times 1''$	
Cabinet Hinges	$3/8''$ lip offset	
Concealed Hinges used on $3/4''$ flush doors		

Sales Units

Hinges are usually sold singly, in pairs, or by the dozen.

Maintenance

The flexible joint must be kept lubricated.

Topic 124.

Hanging a Cabinet Door with Fixed-Pin Butts

Classification

Joinery and assembly

Procedure

The following information is very useful as a guideline in locating fixed-pin butt hinges:

When only two hinges are used, the distance from the top of the door to the center of the top hinge should be 2" for every foot (12") of door length. This is the same as one-sixth the length of the door. For example, the center of the upper hinge on a 24" door would be 4" down from the top edge. The lower hinge should be this same distance up from the bottom.

Fitting the Door to the Opening

1. Plane the door to fit the opening. It is good practice to plane the door approximately 1/16″ smaller than the opening on all four sides. The clearance on all four edges must be about the thickness of a nickel. This will allow for both finish and expansion.
2. On the edge of the door opposite the hinged side, plane a slight bevel toward the inside. This is done to keep the door from binding as it swings open and closed.

Laying Out and Cutting Gains on the Door

1. Locate the center of the gain on the edge of the door. From this point, measure upwards a distance equal to one-half the length of the hinge. Mark this distance with a sharp knife.
2. Place the end of the leaf of the hinge on this line and mark the opposite end.
3. Set a butt gauge or marking gauge to a distance equal to the width of the leaf. (Do not include the knuckle.) See Figs. 13-100 and 13-101.
4. Mark the width of the leaf on the edge of the door.
5. With a knife and try square, square the marks indicating the end of the leaf to the line indicating the width of the leaf.
6. Set the second bar of the butt gauge (or marking gauge) to a distance equal to the thickness of the leaf. Mark a line on the face of the door.
7. With a chisel and a mallet, rough out the waste within the marked area. Best results are obtained when the bevel side of the chisel is facing down.
8. Pare the gain to the finished depth with either a chisel or a router plane.
9. Place the leaf of the butt in the gain. Locate the center of one screw hole and fasten with a screw.
10. Follow the same procedure for the other hinge(s).

Laying Out and Cutting Gains on the Case

1. Place the door in the proper position, using a piece of 1/16″ cardboard under the door and on the edge opposite the butts.
2. With a thin-bladed, sharp knife, mark the top and bottom edges of the leaves.
3. From the front of the case, square these lines to a distance equal to the width of the leaves.

Stanley Tools

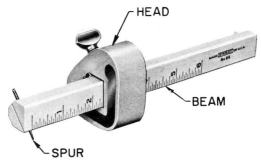

Fig. 13-100. Boxwood marking gauge.

Stanley Tools

Fig. 13-101. Butt gauge.

4. Connect the ends of these two lines, using a butt gauge or marking gauge.
5. Mark the depth of the gain on the front of the case, as described in Step 6 under the preceding heading.
6. Repeat Steps 7, 8, and 9 described under the preceding heading.
7. Follow the same procedure on the other gains.
8. Holding the door open, with the leaves in the newly cut gains, insert one screw in each leaf.
9. If the door swings properly, insert the remaining screws in the leaves. If the door tends to swing open, it may be because the leaves are set too deep. This can be remedied by padding the gains with thin cardboard, which brings the surface of the leaves flush with the surrounding area. If the door binds, either remove the leaf and cut the gain deeper or plane that portion of the door which is binding.

Standards and Results

- Leaves should fit tightly in the gains.
- Leaf surfaces should be flush with the surrounding area.
- Screwheads should be flush with the surface of the leaf.

- The door should swing freely and should stay in any position.

Safety Consideration

- Observe all safety practices pertaining to the particular tool or machine you are using.

SECTION FOURTEEN.

Veneering

Topic 125.

Veneer and Transveneer

Classification

Surface enrichment

Veneering is a process of applying very thin sheets of wood (1/28″ to 1/20″ in thickness) to a core. This is done to obtain greater strength and a more attractive surface. Flat, veneered stock consists of (a) a core, (b) crossbanding, and (c) face veneers. The **core** usually consists of yellow poplar or particleboard. **Crossbanding** is a layer of inexpensive veneer. The grain of crossbanding runs at right angles to each face of the core. The grain of the **face veneers** must run in the same direction as that of the core. See Fig. 14-1. Exposed faces are usually figured veneers. These veneers are produced by one of three methods — rotary cutting, slicing, or sawing. See Fig. 14-2.

Rotary cutting is the most widely used method of cutting veneer. In this method, the prepared log is mounted in a huge lathe and is rotated against a sharp knife. The knife cuts a long, continuous veneer as the log turns. See Fig. 14-3.

Slicing is another method of cutting veneer. See Fig. 14-4. This method is used

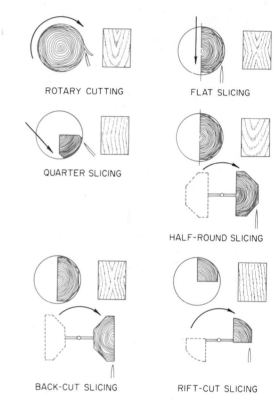

Fig. 14-2.   Methods used to cut veneers.

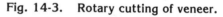
Fig. 14-3.   Rotary cutting of veneer.

American Forest Institute

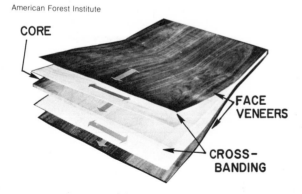

Fig. 14-1.   Veneer sheets, layered to form plywood.

Fig. 14-4.   Veneer slicer.

primarily for face veneers. There are many variations of slicing, used to produce attractive grain patterns.

Veneers can also be produced by **sawing.** This method is not widely used, however, due to the great amount of waste created by the saw cut.

Composition or Description

Veneer

There are three classes of **veneer.** These classes are as follows:

Face veneers are sometimes called fancy veneers. These veneers are cut by various methods, Fig. 14-2, and from different portions of the tree. The result is a variety of grain, figure, and color patterns, Fig. 14-5. Very rare and beautiful veneers are cut from the stump, burl, and crotch portions of the tree. Most

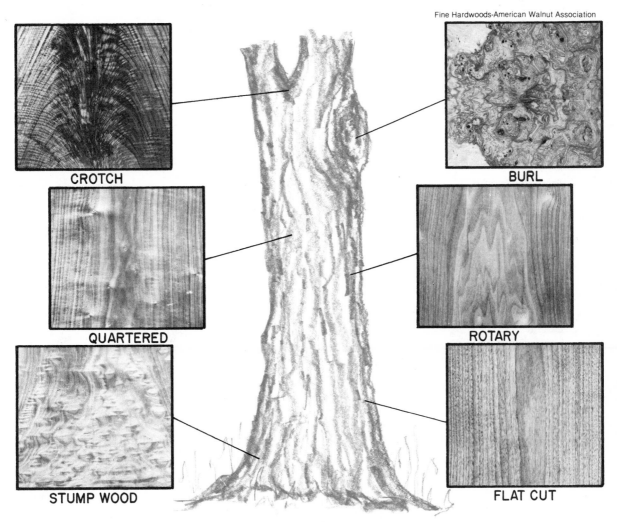

CROTCH

BURL

QUARTERED

ROTARY

STUMP WOOD

FLAT CUT

Fig. 14-5. Veneers are selected from different portions of a tree for various effects.

common face veneers, however, are cut from the trunk area.

Commercial veneers are usually made of domestic wood. They are not selected for color or grain, as this class of veneer is usually used only for crossbanding and backing.

Veneers for packaging and boxing are made of domestic wood and are selected for their hardness. Defects such as knots are permissible in this class.

Transveneer

Transveneer is a paper-thin film of lacquer on which color prints are made from photoengravings of actual wood, marble, and leather. This film is covered with a paper coating. Unlike a decal, the **film must be cemented to the surface** to be covered. The paper coating is then soaked with warm water and removed. Transveneers are used on furniture, radio and television cabinets, and automobiles.

Properties

1. Veneer strips or sheets are flexible, weak, and easily split. However, when veneer strips are applied to a core and a sheet of crossbanding is placed under the face veneer, the completed piece is stronger than solid wood of the same dimension. It also has a more even grain pattern than ordinary wood.
2. Transveneers should not be applied over open-grained woods.

Uses

1. Veneers are used in the construction of furniture, panels, casework, boats, airplanes, and in the manufacture of plywood.
2. Transveneers are used strictly in decorative applications.

Market Analysis

Shapes and Sizes

1. Veneers are available in sheets. They are made in thicknesses of 1/28", 1/24", and 1/20", in widths of 4" to 24", and in lengths of between 3' and 12'.
2. Transveneers are available in sheets 24" × 32" and 32" × 48" and 1/100" thick. They are sold by the square foot.
3. Veneer used for edge banding is sold in narrow strips.

Grades

Veneers are graded **select, standard,** or **common.**

Sales Units

Veneer sheets are sold by the square foot. A **flitch** is several sheets of veneer, cut from the same log and sold as a unit. Matched veneers are available in taped, matched patterns. Strips are sold by the lineal foot.

Maintenance

Veneers should be stored flat and in a place where they will not dry out.

Topic 126.

Veneering a Surface

Classification

Decorative banding and facing

Procedure

Preparing the Core

1. Select several pieces of stock of the proper size for the core and glue them up edge-to-edge. An alternate method is to find a sheet of plywood or particleboard slightly larger than the finished size of the piece.
2. If glued-up stock is used for a core, dress the stock, making it reasonably smooth and parallel in thickness.

Preparing the Veneer

1. Lay out the veneer for direction of grain, matching, and arrangement of figure. This may be done in various ways, as shown in Fig. 14-6.
2. With a veneer saw (Fig. 4-10) or knife, cut each piece of veneer slightly larger than the core.
3. Select two pieces of heavier stock. These pieces must have smooth faces and straight edges. Place the veneer between these pieces. The edge to be jointed should protrude 1/16" or less. Joint this edge with a jack plane. This step is performed on crossbanding as well as on face veneers, Fig. 14-7.
4. Arrange the jointed pieces of surface veneer edge-to-edge, according to the desired pattern. Tape (on the better face) with veneer tape. Veneer tape is a water-soluble, gummed tape made of paper or cloth. Tape is not necessary for holding crossbanding together, as the glue on the core and on the

underside of the face veneer will hold it in place.

Assembly and Gluing

1. Obtain two slightly oversize **cauls.** A caul is a wood, zinc, aluminum, or (less frequently) galvanized-iron mold, conforming in shape to the core. The caul serves to distribute pressure and heat. Place one caul in the veneer press. See Fig. 14-8.
2. Cover the exposed surface of the caul with newspaper to prevent glue from adhering to the caul. Take care to avoid uneven thickness or overlapping of the newspaper, as this will result in an indentation in the face veneer.
3. Place the face veneer, taped side down, on the newspaper on the caul. Coat the exposed surface of the veneer with glue. A

Fig. 14-7. **Joining edges of veneer.**

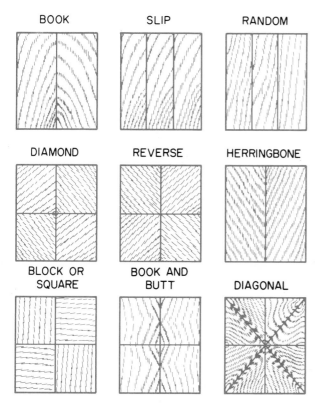

Fig. 14-6. **Common methods of matching decorative veneer.**

Fig. 14-8. **Cauls mounted in a veneer press.**

slow-setting glue (such as urea-resin glue) should be used so that there will be ample time to spread the glue on all surfaces and to apply pressure before the glue sets.

4. Coat one side of the crossbanding with glue and position it on top of the face veneer. The grain must run at right angles to the grain of the face veneer.

5. Coat both the exposed surface of the crossbanding and one surface of the core with glue. Place the core in position on top of the crossbanding. The grain must run at

right angles to the grain of the crossbanding (that is, in the same direction as the face veneer).

6. Coat the exposed surface of the core with glue. Coat one surface of the second piece of crossbanding with glue and set this piece in position on top of the core. The grain must run at right angles to the grain of the core.

7. Coat the exposed surface of the crossbanding with glue. Coat the untaped side of the back face veneer with glue and place this face veneer on top of the crossbanding. The grain must run at right angles to the grain of the crossbanding, and in the same direction as the opposite face veneer.

8. Cover the taped side of the back face veneer with newspaper, being careful to avoid uneven thickness and overlapping of the newspaper.

9. Place the second caul on top of the newspaper. Veneer pins or brads can be driven into the waste area to prevent the laminations from slipping as pressure is applied.

10. Insert 2 × 4's or heavier material under the screws of the press and apply sufficient pressure to ensure that all glued surfaces have even contact.

Note: For small surfaces, the assembly may be made on a bench top or other flat surface. A series of hand screws may be used instead of a veneer press. Apply pressure, working from the center toward the edges and being careful to distribute pressure evenly.

Chester B. Stem, Inc.

Fig. 14-9. Visual grading of veneer sheets.

J.M. Huber Corporation

Fig. 14-10. Applying glue to veneer sheets.

Squaring and Cutting to Size

1. Joint one edge on the jointer and square one end on the table saw. Cut this piece to length and width on the circular saw, and joint the other edge on the jointer.

2. Cap all ends and edges with strip veneer. This may be fastened with fast-setting glue, contact cement, or a hot-melt adhesive. See Fig. 14-11.

Sanding

Sand all surfaces with 100-grit cabinet paper. A minimum amount of sanding should be done because of the thinness of the veneer. Sand only enough to produce a smooth surface.

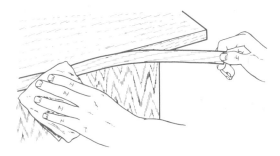

Fig. 14-11. Applying flexible veneer to a table edge.

Standards and Results

- Veneer joints should be tight and no glue line should be visible.
- There should be no air pockets under the veneer. These will cause blisters on the surface. (If a blister appears, the veneer should be slit, glue forced under the surface, and the piece reclamped.)
- The surface should be smooth and free of depressions.

Safety Considerations

- Wear safety glasses when using woodworking tools and equipment.
- Observe all safety practices pertaining to the particular tool or machine you are using.

Fig. 14-12. Veneered furniture.

Hardwood Plywood Manufacturers' Association

A. American highboy.

B. American sideboard.

Topic 127.

Inlay and Insets

Classification

Surface decoration

Composition or Description

Inlay may be made of plastic, pearl, metal, ivory, bone, or wood. Wood inlay is made up of one or more sheets of veneer, cut and glued together to form a pattern. Often, the pattern is of different colors and shapes. When this built-up unit is sawed to 1/20″ thickness, inlay strips are produced. See Fig. 14-13.

An **inset** consists of flat pictorial patterns, formed of veneer woods of a variety of colorings. The face of this veneer wood is glued to paper or cloth to hold the inset in position until application. See Fig. 14-14.

An interesting variation from inlay and inset work is **marquetry.** This is a similar form of decorative woodwork. In marquetry, the entire surface is covered with pieces of thin wood and other materials. The differences in natural color, figure, and grain pattern of these pieces form pictorial scenes or designs, Fig. 14-15.

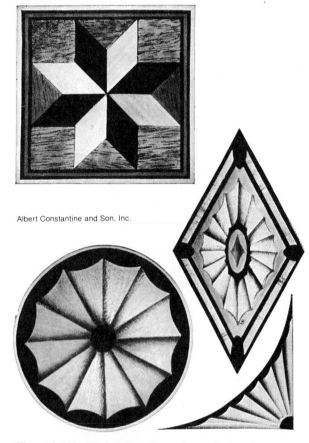

Albert Constantine and Son, Inc.

Fig. 14-14. Examples of ready-made insets.

Albert Constantine and Son, Inc.

Albert Constantine and Son, Inc.

Fig. 14-13. Examples of ready-made inlay strips.

Fig. 14-15. Marquetry.

Properties

Inlay is flexible because of the grain structure of the wood, but is brittle and weak as a result of the method of fabrication. Its function is purely decorative.

Uses

Inlay is used in furniture, paneling, and casework.

Market Analysis

Shapes and Sizes

1. Inlay line is available in 12″ and 36″ lengths and in widths from 1/16″ to 1-1/4″.
2. Insets are available in various shapes and sizes.

Sales Units

Inlay lines are sold by the running foot or yard. Insets are sold by the unit.

Maintenance

Inlay should be stored in a dry place.

> INTERESTING FACT: *Furniture made from overlaid and inlaid veneers has been found in ancient Egyptian tombs.*

Table 14-1
Woods Used for Inlay and Their Colors

Amaranth	Purple
Avodire	Light straw
Benin	Golden brown
Boxwood	Lemon yellow
Bubinga	Reddish brown
Cocobolo	Brown with red streaks
Dao	Light brown with dark streaks
Ebony	Black
Holly	White
Koa	Brown
Maple	White-tan
Narra	Brown
Primavera	Yellowish white
Rosewood	Brick red, deep purple to black
Satinwood	Light yellow
Sycamore	Cream to light tan
Teak	Tan
Tulip	Red and yellow
Vermillion	Bright red
Walnut	Chocolate brown
Zebra	Tan with dark brown stripes

Applying Inlay and Insets

Topic 128.

Classification

Applying decorative units

Procedure

Cutting Gains for Inlay (machine process)

1. Accurately locate the position of the inlay line.
2. If the line runs parallel to an edge or end, use an electric router (if one is available) to cut the gain. See Topic 56, "Using a Portable Hand Router."
3. Select a cutter that has a diameter equal to the width of the inlay. The inlay should be inserted with a press fit.
4. Set the cutter to cut a gain slightly less in depth than the thickness of the inlay. This is done so that the inlay may be sanded even with the surrounding surface after it has been inserted and glued.
5. Set the fence in such a way that the gain will be cut at the desired distance from the edge of the stock. The edge must be already finished.
6. Make a trial run on a scrap piece of stock.

7. Cut the gain. Take care not to go beyond the line at the end of each cut.
8. Corners and ends will need to be cut square. Use a marking gauge, square, and knife to lay out the cut. Remove the waste material with a router plane or a chisel.
9. Fit the line into the gains, making sure each section is of proper length and the joints are tight. (This is called a **dry run**.)
10. If the inlay line runs into a corner, the ends of each piece must be mitered. This may be done with either a knife or a chisel.
11. Remove the pieces and apply a thin coating of glue to the bottom and sides of the gain.
12. Inlay may be pressed into the gains with the bell face of a claw hammer, using a rubbing motion. If the inlay springs out of the gain, it may be held in place with veneer tape until the glue sets.
13. If several pieces are to be inlaid to form a design, glue in one piece at a time.

Cutting Gains for Inlay (hand process)

1. If an electric router is not available, the gain can be laid out with a mortise gauge or two marking gauges. Set one spur to mark one side of the gain and the other spur to mark the opposite side. Cut the lines with a sharp, thin knife blade. Then, make a V-cut on the waste side of each line. Remove the waste

Fig. 14-16. Tilt-top table with inlay around the perimeter and an inset in the center.

Fig. 14-17. Drop-leaf table with fine inlay work.

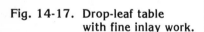

A.W. Marlow

material with either a router plane or a chisel. Proceed as in Steps 7-13 under the preceding heading.
2. If the line does not run parallel to an edge or an end, the gain may be laid out with a metal template, a French curve, or a compass. Use a sharp, hard pencil to make the line.
3. Remove stock (as described in Step 1) to a depth slightly less than the thickness of the line. This is done so that the inlay may be sanded even with the surrounding surface after it has been inserted and glued.

Applying Insets or Inlays

1. Some insets are set into a piece of veneer. This is done to protect the edges in handling. The insets may be separated with a sharp knife.
2. Using a mill file, file a slight taper away from the face side on all edges. Remember that the face side of the inlay is always covered with a cloth or paper tape.
3. Locate the position of the inlay and trace around it with a sharp, hard pencil.
4. With a sharp knife, cut straight into the surface, on the inside of the line. Then make the V-cut on the waste side of the line.
5. Using either a router plane or a chisel, remove the waste within the area marked by the knife lines.
6. The depth of the gain should be slightly less than the thickness of the inlay. This allows for sanding that will be done later. Proceed as in Steps 7-13 under the heading, "Cutting Gains for Inlay (machine process)." To hold the inlay in place until the glue has set, either clamp the inlay or place a block over it to weight it down.

Standards and Results

- All joints should be tight.
- The inlay should be slightly higher than the surface so that it can be sanded.
- The inlay should be tightly glued in the gain.
- Lines should not be wavy or irregular, but should be positioned as intended.
- No glue line should show.
- Shoulders of the gains should not be chipped.

Safety Considerations

- Wear safety glasses when using woodworking tools and machinery.
- Observe all safety practices pertaining to the particular tool or machine you are using.

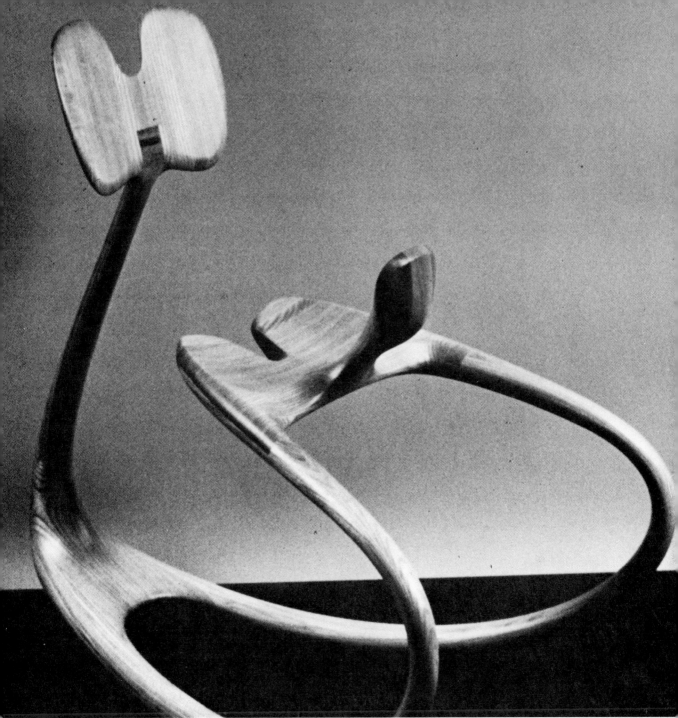

William Hammersley, Richmond, VA

SECTION FIFTEEN.

Bending, Laminating, and Molding

Topic 129.

Bending Wood to a Form

Classification

Shaping

Procedure

Wood may be bent to a shape by any of three methods — **plasticizing by steaming, laminating,** or (where strength is not an important factor) by **relief kerf cutting.** In all cases it is important that straight, clear-grained wood be used. The grain is re-formed to follow a curve, resulting in a piece that is stronger than one that has been cut to shape. For parts requiring severe bending, use stock that is cut in such a way that the annual rings are flatwise. This stock will bend with less chance of breakage than that on which the grain is edgewise to the bending form. Holes or mortises should not be cut prior to bending. The end grain of stock that has been shaped or cut to length should be painted or coated to prevent checking.

Steaming Method

When wood is bent, the fibers within the piece undergo change. Those on the inside of the curve are made shorter (compressed) and the fibers on the outer radius are stretched. Before this change can be made, the fibers within the board must be made pliable. This is done by steaming.

Fig. 15-2.   Bending a water ski.

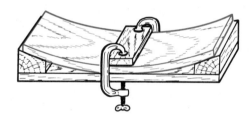

Fig. 15-3.   Bending a chair back.

Heywood-Wakefield Co.

Fig. 15-1.   Removing stock that has been processed in a steam oven prior to bending.

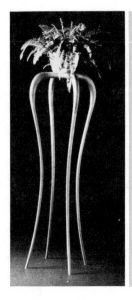

Fig. 15-4.   Bentwood plant stand.

Mark Levin

1. Stock to be bent should be dried to no less than 12% to 15% moisture content.

2. Surface finish all stock slightly larger than the final size to allow for shrinkage.

3. Tanks, boilers, and pipes may be rigged up as chambers to hold the wood for steaming.

4. Prepare the steaming equipment. Because steaming action is more effective when the wood is not immersed in water, some method of supporting the wood above the water level should be devised.

5. The volume of water should be great enough to maintain a constant supply of steam during the entire process.

6. Steaming time should be judged by the thickness of stock. One hour for each 1" thickness is a good rule. Steaming lessens the strength of wood and excessive heat should be avoided.

7. When only a portion of a piece of stock needs to be plasticized and bent, it may be more convenient to use boiling water than to steam the wood. The effectiveness of using boiling or near-boiling water is approximately equivalent to the effectiveness of steaming. Steaming is the preferred method, however, since boiling is apt to cause saturation of the cells, making bending more difficult. Boiling may also cause discoloration of the stock.

8. As soon as the wood is pliable, it is bent to shape. To allow for springback, the forming die should be slightly smaller in radius than the finished bend.

9. The method of securing the piece in the form should be adequate to hold the piece in place and to allow air to circulate for efficient drying. See Figs. 15-2 and 15-3.

10. After bending, the wood must remain in the forms until it is sufficiently dry to retain its shape. This drying time varies from a fraction of an hour (under industrial conditions) to a week or more (in a school shop).

11. If a piece is bent and dried in the form and then is placed in extremely dry air (which further dries out the wood), the bend will increase. If the piece absorbs moisture, it will tend to straighten slightly, back towards its original shape. If a part fractures on the outside of the bend, it is too dry. If it compresses too much and wrinkles on the inside, it has been steamed too much.

Bending Machines

There are four basic machines used in the furniture industry to bend steam-softened wood:

The simplest form of machine bending or forming is done on the **platen press.** This machine is used to make such parts as flat-curved chair backs. The pieces are first bent, then are dried in the press, using heat. This process takes only a short time. See Fig. 15-5.

The **ram-type bending machine** has hinged arms. These arms hold the workpiece, which is wrapped around a mandrel, producing a horseshoe-like bend. The shaped parts are clamped

Heywood-Wakefield Co.

Fig. 15-5. **Hydraulic bending press using platen.** Steamed stock (or unsteamed wood of exactly the right moisture content) is placed between cauls (metal forms). These cauls are hollow on the inside, like a radiator. Tons of pressure is hydraulically applied and the heated cauls cause the moisture in the stock to turn to steam. Thus, the stock is self-steamed. The heat sets the bends and reduces (dries) the moisture content during the hour it is between the cauls. For this reason, no further drying is necessary after the bent wood is removed from the press.

Heywood-Wakefield Co.

Fig. 15-6.   Bending with steel band and dogs.
The flexible steel band draws the steamed wood into shape around the steel ring form. Clamps are driven into position to hold the wood in shape until it has dried and set.

Fig. 15-7.   Bending with steel band and dogs.

in retainer pans. This restrains the outer surface and prevents the wood fibers from stretching as they are being compressed by the inside radius.

The third type is called a **pretzel bend.** This is done on small-diameter, round pieces. The pieces are bent over, around, and under the form, into a continuous leg shape. Both ends must be bent into the form at approximately the same rate to obtain symmetrical curves and to avoid breakage. Metal restraining straps, with clamps on each end, retain end pressure. These straps conform to the outside of each radius to secure inside compression and to help prevent outside stretching, which could result in breakage. Parts must remain clamped in the bending form, with restraining straps, until the wood is dry. The drying process usually takes 24 hours.

The fourth type of bending is made with a **pusher mechanism.** With one end restrained, the workpiece is pushed around the form on a turntable similar to that used in metal bending.

The parts must be left in the form until they have dried to 6% to 8% M.C., Figs. 15-6 and 15-7.

Laminating Method

This method involves layering and bonding wood veneers in a particular shape. Individual veneers are pliable and easily bent, but when layered and glued together, their shape becomes permanent.

1. In laminating larger surfaces, such as seat forms or chair backs, it is sometimes necessary to strengthen the piece. This is done by crossing the grain pattern in alternate layers, a process requiring an odd number of sheets.

   Narrow strips may be built up and glued. The grain of these strips must run parallel to the bend.

2. Spread the glue evenly between each layer of lamination and clamp it into the form in such a manner that the entire piece will be of even thickness and strength.

3. If a sharp radius is desired, or if the strips to be laminated are too thick to bend dry, steam bending is necessary. The bent pieces are then laminated.

4. Prepare the wood or metal form to a radius slightly less than the required curve. This allows for springback.

5. Formed pieces are clamped together by mechanical pressure, hydraulic pressure, or

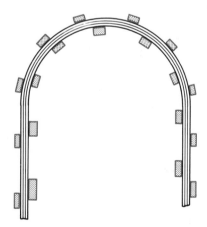

Fig. 15-8.   Laminating form with glue blocks positioned in the desired arc of the finished piece. The veneers are placed inside the blocks and clamped until the glue is dry.

Fig. 15-9. Laminated stairway.

Malleable Founders Society

Fig. 15-10. Matched form, used for laminating the top portion of a wooden medicine chest.

Fig. 15-11. Laminating press that uses an inflatable bladder to apply pressure to a one-piece mold.

Vega Industries, Inc.

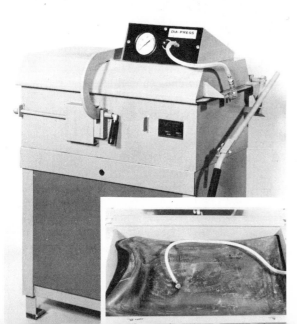

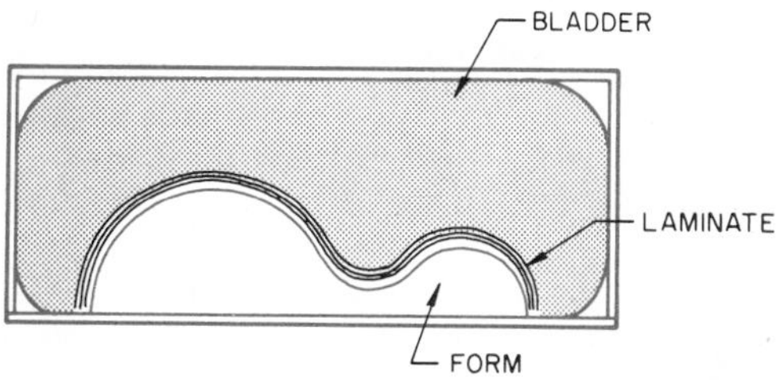

Fig. 15-12. Cross section of an air-operated lamination press. When the bladder is inflated, the lamination is forced against the form.

air pressure. One type of form is composed of two preshaped sections that fit together. See Fig. 15-10. Another type of form has a lower die of the desired shape and has an outer, flexible band. This band follows the bend and equalizes the pressure along the curve, preventing splintering.

6. Apply glue to the surfaces to be joined and place the pieces in position in the forming jig. Use enough clamps to provide evenly distributed pressure.
7. Allow these pieces to stand under pressure until the glue has set.

Laminating Method, Using an Air-Operated Press

Small laminations can be glued to shape using a bladder-type **lamination press.** This type of press uses compressed air to inflate a rubber bladder, which in turn applies pressure to the laminated stock. See Figs. 15-11 and 15-12. A major advantage of this type of press is that only a one-piece form is needed.

1. Prepare a wood form of the desired shape and size. Smooth the surface of the form and round the edges slightly. This will eliminate the danger of the bladder being cut as air pressure is applied.
2. Cut the number of pieces of veneer necessary to make the final product in the desired thickness. Veneers should be cut about 1 " longer and about 1/2 " wider than the finished dimensions. This allows for slippage and for the edge and end trimming that will be done after the glue has set.
3. Apply glue to the inside of both the top and bottom veneer and to both sides of the inner veneer.
4. Place the laminate on the form, tacking one end to hold the laminate in the proper position.

Fig. 15-13. Finished clock, made with two laminated pieces such as those shown in Fig. 15-12.

5. Cover the entire object, the form, and the laminate with polyethelene to control the squeeze out of glue.
6. Place in a diaphragm press (lamination press). This is a strong metal box with a hinged cover that can be closed and locked to resist internal pressure.
7. A large, rectangular rubber bladder is placed over the laminate and form. See Fig. 15-11. The top is then closed and locked.
8. Air is pumped into the bladder with an air compressor that applies 29 psi (pounds per square inch) to the laminate and forces it into the shape of the form. See Fig. 15-12. A valve is used to hold this pressure until the glue dries.
9. When the glue is dry, release the pressure in the bladder, open the press, and remove the laminate from the form.

Saw-Kerf Method

In cases where the ends are fixed, where only the face of the bent piece is to show, and where strength is not an important factor, a bend may be made by making saw kerfs in the back side of the piece.
1. Measure the radius of the bend.
2. Lay out this length on the board to be bent, starting the measurement at the point at which the curve is to begin.
3. At point **A,** in Fig. 15-14, make a saw cut partway through the board. Try a depth of three-fourths the thickness of the stock. The depth may vary according to the sharpness of the bend.
4. Lay the board on a flat surface, the kerf side up. Raise one end of the board, closing the saw kerf, and measure the distance **B.** See Fig. 15-14. Divide this distance into the radius of the bend in order to find the number of saw kerfs that need to be cut for a bend of 90°.

5. If a handsaw is used, use a stop to make certain that all saw kerfs are the same depth and width.
6. A miter box with a depth gauge may be used for a fine kerf, and a circular saw may be used for a larger kerf.
7. For maximum strength, saw cuts should be closed up on the inside surface after bending is completed. See Fig. 15-15. A heavy coating of glue, applied in the saw kerfs before bending, will help maintain a strong, rigid bend.

Standards and Results

- Formed stock should be of the desired curvature and dimension and should be free of twist.
- There should be no surface splinters, cracks, or flat spots.
- All laminations should be securely joined.
- All saw kerfs should be of the proper width and depth.
- There should be a minimum loss of strength at the bend.

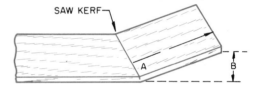

Fig. 15-14. Bending with single saw kerf.

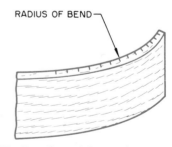

Fig. 15-15. Bending with multiple saw kerf.

Fig. 15-16. Curve formed by saw-kerf method.

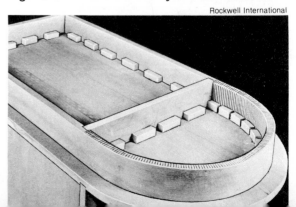

Plastic Laminates

Topic 130.

Classification

Plastic covering materials

Composition or Description

The base material of **plastic laminates** is cellulose, cotton, nylon, or fiberglass. This base material is covered with a resin binder and, after being subjected to heat and pressure, forms a hard, strong panel. Several brands are available, in a variety of patterns and colors.

Properties

Plastic laminates are tough, lightweight, and strong but are quite brittle. Because of these properties, they resist most abrasive wear, denting, and cracking. Plastic laminates may be sawed, drilled, and routed, and the edges may be planed. Because of their brittleness, however, care must be taken to prevent chipping. Normally, they may be bent to fit curved surfaces as small as 8" in radius. With heat and the proper equipment, however, they can be bent to a radius of less than 1". Plastic laminates are nonconductors of electricity. Consequently, they are good insulators. They resist heat, alcohol, water, and fruit acids.

Uses

Plastic laminates are commonly used in the home for tops of kitchen counters, kitchen-table tops, coffee-table tops, and bar tops. They are also commonly used in restaurant countertops and tabletops and in the construction of office furniture. Because of their insulating properties, plastic laminates are often used in electrical work.

Market Analysis

Shapes

Plastic laminates are available in sheets, rods, tubes, and molded shapes.

Sizes

Sheets of plastic laminates are available in thicknesses of between .010" and 6", but they are usually less than 1/16" thick. Sheets are available in the following sizes:

24" wide × 6', 8' long
30" wide × 6', 8', 10', 12' long
36" wide × 6', 8', 10', 12' long
48" wide × 8', 10' long
60" wide × 12' long

Fig. 15-17. Plastic-laminated filing cabinets are both attractive and durable.

Miller Desk, Inc.

Second-quality pieces may be purchased in smaller, random lengths and widths.

Maintenance

1. Plastic laminates are usually cleaned with a damp rag, but may be cleaned with any household soap or detergent.

2. Plastic laminates should be stored in a horizontal position to prevent buckling and curling and to prevent the surfaces from becoming chipped.

3. Surfaces covered with plastic laminates may be waxed periodically in order to preserve their luster and to minimize scratching.

Topic 131.

Contact Cement

Classification

Adhesive

Composition or Description

Contact cement is a synthetic resin, produced in either liquid or paste form. There are four types of contact cement available on the market today: **solvent-based, latex-based, neoprene-latex-based** and **acrylic-latex-based.** Acrylic-latex-based contact cement is water soluble for 20 to 40 minutes after application, depending on the humidity. Cleaning up of the hands, tools, and work area can be done by using cold water if acrylic-latex contact cement is used. Contact cements range from clear to slightly amber in color.

Properties

When two surfaces that have been coated with contact cement and allowed to dry 20 to 40 minutes are placed in contact with one another, the bond is immediate and permanent. After contact, it is practically impossible to move or separate the two parts. Contact cement will adhere to most surfaces, but once it has dried it will not adhere to another surface not coated with contact cement. Because of this property, it is possible to make a perfect alignment of two coated and dried surfaces by inserting a sheet of paper between them. When the paper is carefully withdrawn, the surfaces bond on contact. The surface should be rolled, hand-pressed or tapped with a rubber mallet to

ensure complete contact. Contact cement is not recommended for use at temperatures below 21° C (70° F).

Contact cement should be applied in a well-ventilated area, using a brush or a roller. Do not join pieces until the cement is dry to the touch. Joining should take place within two hours of application of the cement.

Uses

Contact cement is used to adhere any combination of wood, glass, leather, paper, cloth, rubber, fiberglass, metal, and plastic laminates. It is most commonly used to adhere plastic laminates to plywood, but it is often used to adhere aluminum or plywood panels to walls.

Market Analysis

Shapes

Contact cement is available in liquid or paste form.

Sizes

Contact cement is sold in pint, quart, gallon, and 5-gallon containers.

Maintenance

1. Do not store or use contact cement in extreme heat or cold.
2. Keep the lid of the container tightly closed when contact cement is not in use.

SECTION SIXTEEN.
Structures

Topic 132.

Structures

Wood has a long history as a structural material. It has long served as the basic framework or skeleton for buildings, scaffolding, bridges, trestles, piers, docks, boats, planes, wagons, freight cars, and other vehicles and conveyances. Wood-frame construction is also used in making crates, concrete forms, and stage scenery. The high strength of wood in proportion to its weight, as well as its flexibility and beauty, assures its continued popularity in the construction of structures.

Wood is the major structural material used in the construction of buildings and homes. Eight of every 10 houses built today are framed with wood. In addition to being used in the basic framework, wood is used extensively for other structural components. Some of these components are doors, window frames, floors, sheathing, shingling, planking, and siding.

Western Red Cedar Lumber Association

Columbus Home Builders Association

Fig. 16-1. Modern house design, showing the versitility of wood as a structural material.

Fig. 16-3. Wood-framing members in house construction.

Fig. 16-2. Wood is the traditional material used in boatbuilding.

Fig. 16-4. Modern wood-framed house near completion.

National Homes Corporation

House Design

Wood framing is an old tradition in the construction of homes. Basic construction principles and framing members have remained relatively unchanged, although many refinements have been made in framing and new and radically different techniques have been developed.

Outwardly, the wood-frame house of today bears little resemblance to its counterpart of the previous century. The modern house has a lighter, more graceful, and more striking appearance. Its design is also more functional. In North America, modern house design has been greatly influenced by styles such as that of the American designer, Frank Lloyd Wright, and the graceful and functional Japanese-style house.

Quality framing lumber is being used with a view toward letting the structure itself provide the decoration. Ceiling joists and studs are often left exposed. Trussed rafter construction is widely used because it eliminates the need for load-bearing walls. Post-and-beam construction carries the structural load on a few supports. Besides providing greater height, it permits more flexible planning of room layout and allows for easy expansion. On the exterior, studs are exposed as frames for picture windows. Wide overhangs make the house look larger and more attractive. They keep summer sun out and let winter sun in.

Glued wood arches and beams of much greater length than standard solid members are appearing with increased frequency. In houses and larger structures, the use of laminated lumber is becoming more widespread. Their use permits post-free interior areas of great dimension and remarkable attractiveness.

Many homes and buildings are built to utilize solar energy for heating and cooling needs, Fig. 16-5. This has had a marked effect on home design, since such buildings must be constructed in such a way as to take maximum advantage of available sunlight. There are many factors that must be considered in designing this type of structure, as much of the building's efficiency is dependent on the environmental conditions.

A-frame houses have a unique design that incorporates the roof and wall structures into one unit, Fig. 16-6. This type of construction is ideal for use in areas where there is heavy snowfall, as the steep pitch sheds the snow. Be-

Fig. 16-5. Home equipped with solar-heating panels.

Exxon Corporation
Robert Phillips, photographer

cause it is essentially a braced triangle, it is a very rigid and strong structural unit. It has the disadvantage of decreased headroom near the interior walls. Because this building design may be somewhat taller than others, it has greater resistance to wind.

Modular houses are a preassembled, factory approach to home design. In this type of construction, the materials for the home are

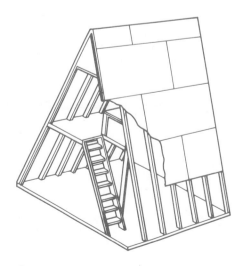

Fig. 16-6. A-frame house.

cut and assembled in a factory and are shipped to the construction site in modules or preassembled units. These modules or components are attached in various combinations to form the finished house. See Fig. 16-7.

Guerdon Industries, Inc.

Fig. 16-7. Pre-manufactured module being lowered in place in modular construction.

Topic 133.

The Carpenter

Carpentry is that branch of the woodworking industry which is concerned with the building of structures. **Structures** include the forms into which concrete is poured for foundations, bridges, and buildings; scaffolds and platforms; and, most commonly, the building of frame houses.

There are many types of carpenters. **Form makers,** for instance, construct and set concrete forms for foundations and building members, Fig. 16-8. **Framing carpenters** build the basic framework and shell of a building or home, Fig. 16-9. This work includes setting the sills, joists, and floors, erecting studs and rafters, and applying sheathing, siding, and roofing boards. It also involves many other operations, including building stairs and installing exterior doors and windows. The finish woodwork, such as the door and window trim, interior wall covering, molding, and cabinetwork, is done by **finish carpenters,** Fig. 16-10. Carpenters whose duties are even more specialized include, for example, **siders, roofers, floor layers, stair builders,** and **repair carpenters.** A **master carpenter** is one who is proficient in all the carpentry tasks needed to completely build a structure. **Carpenter's helpers** are workers who do some of the routine jobs, assist the carpenter with heavy or long pieces, or carry out specific tasks under close supervision.

A qualified carpenter must be skilled in the use of a wide variety of hand tools and portable machines. This worker must know the characteristics of many different kinds of

Fig. 16-8. Form makers constructing the concrete forms for a building foundation.

Fig. 16-9. Framing carpenters build the basic skeleton or framework of structures.

Fig. 16-10. Finish carpenter applying interior house trim.

building materials and must be familiar with the basic systems of frame construction. The carpenter must be familiar with and know how to use the tools and practices for layout and must know enough about structural design to recognize the purpose and use of each member. He or she must also be able to read plans and blueprints, and must be able to estimate the amount and cost of materials and the time necessary to complete a job.

The carpenter's work is often dependent upon weather conditions and progress of construction. Much of the carpenter's work is done in conjunction with that of other tradespeople such as masons, plasterers, plumbers, and electricians. As a consequence, the carpenter

should have a general knowledge of the work these other people will be doing.

Training in the area of carpentry may be acquired through trade and vocational schools, on-the-job training, or an apprenticeship program.

Apprenticeship programs have been established to provide consistent training for those who want to be carpenters. These programs consist of related trade instruction in addition to on-the-job training.

Since so many skills are involved in becoming a successful carpenter, carpenters are always in demand and their pay scale compares favorably with that of other skilled workers.

Leveling Tools

Topic 134.

Classification

Layout or testing devices for checking horizontal or perpendicular surfaces

Application

Principle of Operation

1. The **level** consists of a crowned glass tube containing a spirit liquid. An air bubble is

Stanley Tools

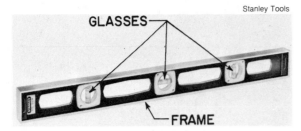

Fig. 16-11. Aluminum level.

encased within this liquid. The crown of the glass is set in the "up" position, causing the bubble to seek the highest point on center when the frame is held in a horizontal or vertical position. This position is marked by etched lines in the glass.

2. A **plumb bob,** suspended on a string from a fixed position, will locate a point directly below the point of suspension.

Kinds and Uses

Levels are commonly named according to their use. (See "Market Analysis.")

1. A **level** is used in laying out foundations, calculating grades, and setting framing members to the horizontal and vertical. Some levels have a glass set to test for 45° angles. See Fig. 16-12.
2. A **line level** is used with a long line to determine a level position at two points. The line level must be near the midpoint of the line. See Fig. 16-13.
3. A **plumb bob** is used in determining a vertical position, Fig. 16-14.

Principal Parts and Function of Each

1. **Glasses** are set in the frame. When the bubble in the glass is centered between the marks, the piece being tested is either plumb (vertical) or level (horizontal).

   Glasses are available in two types — ground and proved. **Ground glasses** are made of glass tubing, internally ground to a barrel shape so that the high point is in the center. The bubble settles slowly and is very accurate. Ground glasses are used in precision tools such as machinist's levels and surveyor's transits. **Proved glasses** are made of glass tubing, bent slightly so that the high point is exactly in the middle. The bubble settles quickly and with sufficient accuracy for carpentry work.
2. The **liquid** in the level is alcohol.
3. The **frame,** which forms a straightedge to aid in testing a surface, is made of cast iron, aluminum, cherry, or mahogany. The frame is well seasoned to ensure against warpage.
4. The **plumb bob** is made of machined brass or steel. Its design is such that the point will hang directly below the point of suspension.

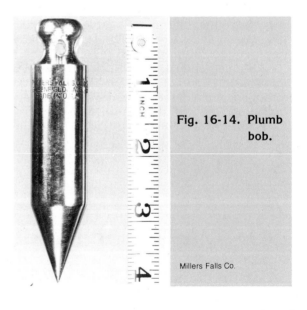

Fig. 16-14. Plumb bob.

Millers Falls Co.

Stanley Tools

Fig. 16-12. Torpedo level.

Stanley Tools

Fig. 16-13. Line level.

Stanley Tools

Fig. 16-15. Pocket level.

Maintenance

Levels should be checked periodically for accuracy. The better levels have an adjustment for the bubble position. Broken glass may be replaced.

Market Analysis

Sizes

Levels are made in various sizes and shapes according to their intended use.
1. Carpenter's levels are from 12″ to 30″ long, Fig. 16-11.
2. Mason's levels are 48″ long.
3. Torpedo levels are 9″ long and have tapered oval sides, Fig. 16-12. They are used by inspectors and mechanics.
4. Machinist's levels, made from cast iron, are from 6″ to 24″ long.
5. Line levels are round or hexagonal in shape and are made from plastic, aluminum, or bronze. They are 3-1/4″ long, Fig. 16-13.

Jason Bushness, Vernon, Vt.

Fig. 16-16. Early wooden level with dial indicator and adjustable wooden thumbscrews.

6. Pocket levels are made of brass and are 2″ to 3-1/2″ long, Fig. 16-15.
7. A substitute for a line level or transit is a plastic, transparent hose or a hose with glass tubes fitted to both ends. The level of liquid within the hose will determine a level position.

Attachments

Level sights are used in conjunction with a level to sight a line or level a wall.

Laying Out Straight Edges with a Chalk Line or String

Topic 135.

Classification

Marking and checking

Chalk lines are used extensively in construction for marking long, straight lines as guides for cutting or for alignment purposes. Manufactured chalk lines consist of a spool of string, which pivots in a housing filled with powdered chalk, Fig. 16-17. When the string is pulled from the spool, it becomes coated with chalk. This chalk is deposited in a line when the string is pulled tight and snapped over the workpiece. Chalk lines may also be made by rubbing a cake of chalk along an ordinary line or string.

Lines or strings are also used in construction as guides for positioning and checking alignment of building members. See Fig. 16-18.

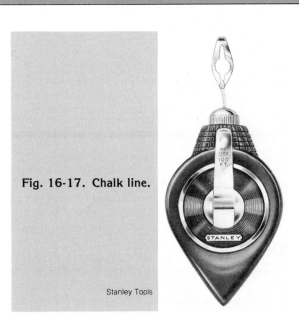

Fig. 16-17. Chalk line.

Stanley Tools

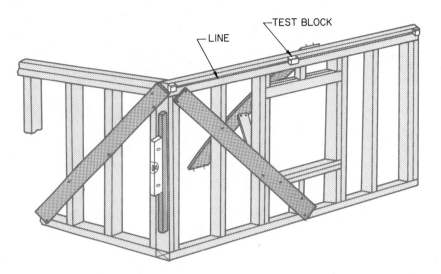

Fig. 16-18. Aligning a long expanse, using a line and test blocks.

Procedure

1. To lay out a straight edge on stock that has a crook, measure a distance in from each end of the board so when the line is stretched between these two points, it will fall just inside the crook. On each end of the board, tack a small nail at the points measured. Secure one end of the chalk line at one nail and pull the line tight to the second nail. Carefully hook the line over the second nail so as not to dislodge the chalk. Snap the line by raising it 2" to 3" above the board and then releasing. See Fig. 16-19.

2. Chalk-line marking, as described in Step 1, is used also in applying interior and exterior sheathing, in applying asphalt paper and shingles, and in marking distances on stud-framed walls. It is also used for many other operations in which long distances or many separate members must be marked quickly and accurately.

3. A chalk line or plain line may also be used to align vertical or horizontal structural members. In this application, the line is held tight between two outside members or reference points. The members between these points are then positioned so each just touches the line.

    In long layout, it is common to use test blocks in conjunction with the line. A block is placed at each end of the expanse being laid out and the line is drawn tight between them. A third block, the same size as the first two, is used to test the clearance at various points to ensure proper alignment. See Fig. 16-18.

Standards and Results

- The chalked line should be sharp and clear-cut.
- The line should be tight enough so that there is no sag in testing.
- The line being used should be clean and should have no knots.

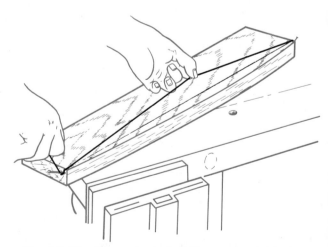

Fig. 16-19. Snap a taut chalk line square with the surface for straight lines on long boards.

Laying Out Batter Boards

Four frames, called **batter boards,** are erected in a level position, three or four feet outside of the corners of the proposed foundation. Lines are stretched from adjacent sets of batter boards, indicating the position of the footings and/or foundation. From these intersecting lines, a plumb bob may be dropped, both to determine the exact corners of the foundation and to plumb the wall. This method is most commonly used with stone or block foundations.

A large triangle, such as the one on the ground in Fig. 16-23, is made by carpenters to check the squareness of the corners. The sides of the triangle are 6', 8', and 10', respectively. This is commonly called the **6-8-10** method of layout.

When the four corners are square, diagonals from opposite corners should be equal. A transit (instrument used to measure vertical and horizontal lines) is also an accurate method of checking for squareness.

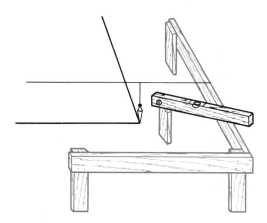

Fig. 16-20. Leveling batter boards.

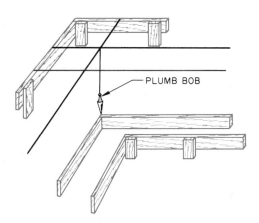

Fig. 16-21. Locating corners.

Fig. 16-22. Laying out the foundation.

Fig. 16-23. Checking squareness of corners.

Topic 137.

Foundations

Builders are well aware of the need for stability in any building they erect. A completed building represents many tons of weight. Furniture and equipment add significant weight, and snow loads increase the weight even more. **Unless proper engineering procedures are followed, the building weight will cause movement of the soil.** Uneven movement will cause uneven settling, causing distortion of the framing. This distortion affects such things as walls, windows, doors, and plaster. Examples of the need for stability can be seen in nature. For example, large animals such as elephants have broad feet to provide stability. Adopting this principle, people erect **foundations** for buildings on a broad base. These foundations are called **footings.** The importance of the quality of the soil and its reaction to structural composition are also recognized as important considerations. See Table 16-1.

Factors Determining the Size of Foundation Wall and Footings

In the construction of buildings, there are two types of loads that must be adequately supported by the foundation wall and footings. These are called dead loads and live loads.

The **dead load** is the weight of the material that forms the structural walls and roof. The **live load** is the weight of the furniture and movable items in the building, plus the wind and snow loads on the exterior.

The sum total of these weights must be supported by the footings. **Footing size will also be governed by the bearing quality of the soil.** Table 16-1 indicates the safe loading of soil types.

The **actual load** on a floor may be calculated by the weight of the material and the weight of the intended live load. However, it is common practice to use the following weights for small house construction:

Lbs./Sq. Ft.	Type of Load
10	dead load of floor
20	dead load of floor and plastered ceiling
20	live load attic storage
30	live load sleeping area
40	live load living area
20	dead load partition wall

Roof loads will vary according to climatic conditions of snow and wind loads.

Area	Lbs./Sq. Ft. Snow and Wind Load
Northern States	40
Central States	30
Southern States	20

The dead weight of a roof covered with asphalt shingles is 10 lbs./sq. ft. (pounds per square foot), but this is affected by the slope of the roof. Slopes under a pitch of 3″ in 12″ have a 20-pound dead load with asphalt shingles. Roofs with a slope greater than 3/12 are figured with a load of 15 lbs./sq. ft. Local building codes should be referred to before calculating weight loads.

The dead weight of the wall includes such elements as studs, sheathing, and plaster, and is figured as 20 lbs./sq. ft.

Table 16-1
Safe Loading of Soil Types

Type of Soil	Safe Load in Lbs./Sq. Ft.
Ledge rock	200,000
Hard pan and compact gravel	20,000
Compact sand and gravel	12,000
Firm sand and clay	8,000
Loose gravel	8,000
Coarse sand	6,000
Fine sand	4,000
Soft clay and loam	2,000

Adapted from **Architectural Graphic Standards**

Material	Lbs./Cubic Ft.
Concrete	150
Concrete blocks	80
Brick	120

Figuring the load for a single-floor building on one lineal foot of footing (Fig. 16-24) is as follows:

				Lbs./Ft.
Roof live load (Northern)	40 lbs.	× 12	=	660
Roof dead load	15 lbs.			
Attic live load	20 lbs.			
Attic floor dead load	20 lbs.	× 5 (½ span)	=	200
First floor live load	40 lbs.	× 5	=	400
First floor dead load	20 lbs.			
Partition	20 lbs.			
Concrete wall 150 × 7.5 × 8/12			=	750
Total weight on footing per foot				2010

$$\text{Weight of footing} \quad 150 \times \frac{16}{12} \times \frac{8}{12} = \frac{133}{2143}$$

$$\text{Total weight of footing per sq. ft. bearing on soil} \quad 2143 \times \frac{12}{16} = 1607$$

Referring to Table 16-1, "Safe Loading of Soil Types," it is found that this weight is well under the maximum load of each soil type. Therefore, a wall of 8″ concrete with a footing 8″ deep and 16″ wide will be adequate.

Concrete Forms

Concrete will mold to any shape, depending on the form or surface of the mold. Most form surfaces are made of plywood or sheet metal. These materials produce a relatively smooth surface. Wet concrete has tremendous weight and settling power, so forms must have rugged construction and be well braced in order to stay in alignment.

It is common building practice to rent forms for footings and/or foundations or to hire a contractor who does only this type of work. These forms are usually made of exterior plywood that has either been plastic coated or treated with oil to prevent the wood from absorbing water from the concrete. Form panels are available in the following sizes: 2′ × 4′, 4′ × 4′, 3′ × 8′, 2′ × 8′, and 4′ × 8′. These

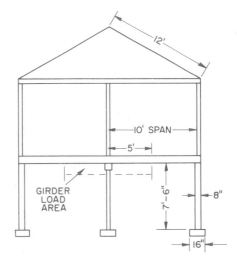

Fig. 16-24. Building structure.

sizes fit various foundation lengths and heights and are made in 1/2″ and 5/8″ thicknesses.

Footings (the base for the foundation walls) are poured first, often with a keyway on the top to provide a better joint with the foundation wall. Footings should be as thick and twice as wide as the wall thickness. See Fig. 16-25.

The wall forms are assembled over the footings. To provide for door and window openings and to allow cavities for supporting ends of the girt or for carrying timbers, these areas are blocked in. When the cement is poured, it forms and hardens around these blocked-in areas, forming the proper shape.

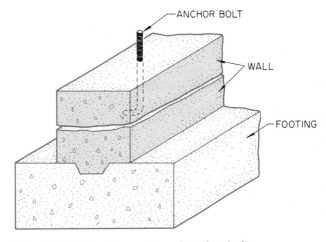

Fig. 16-25. Footing, wall, and anchor bolt.

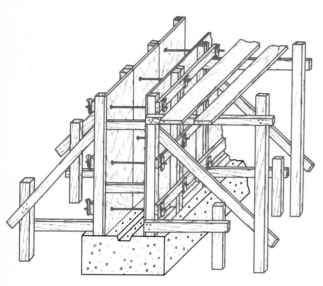

Fig. 16-26. Concrete forms.

Fig. 16-27. Forms for reinforced concrete.

Commercial ties can be used. These act as both separators and spreaders to hold the form in position. These consist of steel rods with washers or cones to hold the inside form apart and a clamp to hold the outside of the form in place. So that the excess rod can be removed, each rod has a breaking point. At this point, the rod breaks inside the concrete, leaving only a small hole, which can be plugged. See Fig. 16-26.

When commercial ties are not available, separators are tacked in place to hold the forms an equal distance apart. Because they are tacked in place, separators can be quickly removed as the concrete fills the form. The outside panels are held in position with band iron or #10 annealed wire. This wire is passed through the forms and tied around the outside studs to draw the forms tight against the spacers. To hold the forms plumb, sturdy bracing three to four feet apart is essential at both the top and bottom and at the corners. See Fig. 16-27.

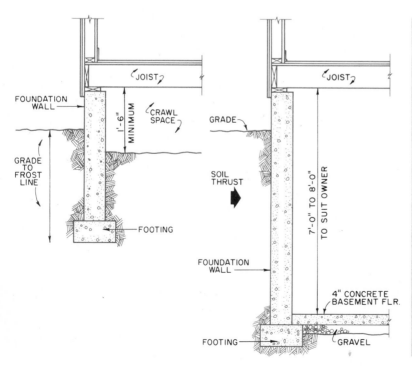

Fig. 16-28. Cross sections of foundations with a crawl space (left) and a basement (right).

The concrete should be poured in one continuous operation. To remove air pockets, the concrete should be leveled and tamped as the forms are filled. (**Tamping** works the air bubbles out of the concrete.) The forms should stay in place until the concrete is able to support its own weight. In warm weather this will take one to two days. In cold weather it may take as long as a week. The forms slow the drying process and, in so doing, aid in curing the concrete. Forms left in place allow for shrinkage and make removal easier. It is recommended that the forms be left in place for three to four days. In curing, concrete continues to increase in strength for a period of 28 days (provided it is kept damp) and continues to increase in hardness for seven years.

Anchor Bolts

The frame structure should be fastened securely to the foundation and made into one solid unit. This is accomplished by **anchoring** the sill (to which the framing members are fastened) to the foundation.

Anchor bolts are set into the concrete foundation wall before it is hard. See Fig. 16-25.

The anchor bolts are 1/2" × 12"-18" long. They are set into the concrete in such a way that the thread portion will project through the center of the sill to accommodate a washer and nut. They are placed 12" from each side of an opening and corner and at least eight feet **on centers** (**oc**).

House Framing

Topic 138.

House framing refers to the construction of the skeletal framework that will provide the house with its basic dimensions and support. There are three common framing methods currently used in the construction of homes. These are platform framing, post-and-beam construction, and balloon framing.

Platform framing is the most popular framing method used today. In this method, the wall studs are attached to the top of the floor joists and subflooring. See Fig. 16-29. This allows the floor to be constructed first, providing a safe and convenient working surface on which wall sections can be laid out and constructed. On two-story homes, the second floor is also built in this fashion. That is, the floor is constructed first and then the second-story walls are erected.

Post-and-beam construction is a fast and simple framing method using large posts and beams for structural support. See Fig. 16-30. The posts provide vertical support for the beams that support the floor and roof. Because of the high load-bearing capacity of these members, there can be more open space, free from load-bearing walls and partitions. Large, unobstructed interior areas can thus be obtained.

In **balloon** framing, the outside wall studs run continously from the sill plate to the top plate. See Fig. 16-31. The floor joists on the first floor rest on the sill, but the floor joists of the second floor rest on a ribbon board that is let into the studs. It is extremely difficult today to get studs long enough for this type of construction. This was the most widely used type of framing method in the early 1900's.

Framing Lumber and Timber Sizes

The structural lumber used in the construction of homes and buildings must meet certain standards set by the U.S. Department of Commerce. A "Simplified Practice Regulation" sets standards by which lumber is cut and sold. It includes three requirements:
1. All lumber sold "dry" must have a moisture content of no more than 19%.
2. Lumber dressed to the new standards must be milled when the moisture content is no more than 19%.
3. Rough-dressed lumber must be of sufficient oversize that its dressed use matches the standard dimensions.

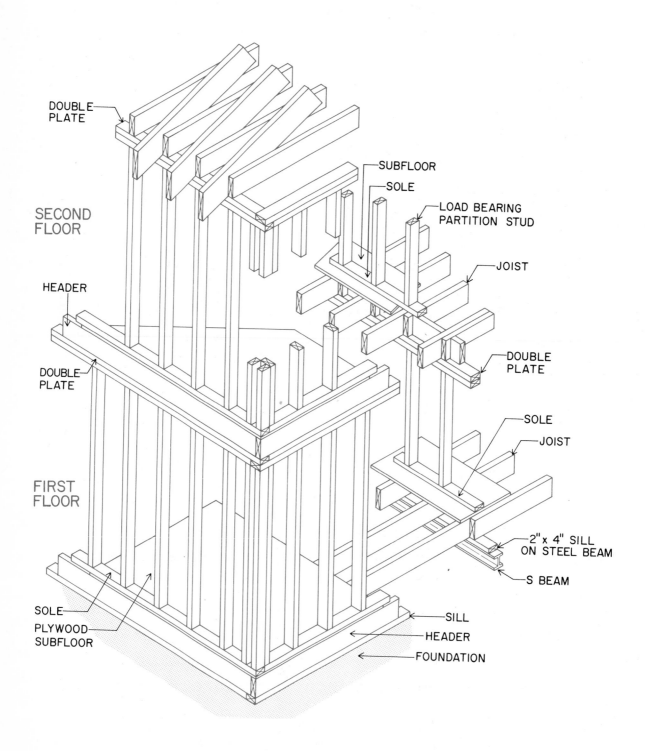

Fig. 16-29. Platform framing is the common method used for house construction.

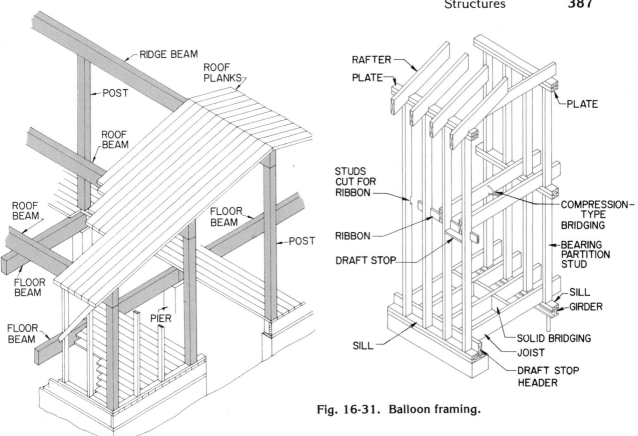

Fig. 16-31. Balloon framing.

Fig. 16-30. Post-and-beam framing.

Table 16-2
Comparison of the Most Common Structural Woods

This table shows a comparison of various properties of several structural woods. Each column shows the relative rank of each wood when compared with the others. Number 1 is the highest rank and number 6 is the lowest.

	Modulus of Rupture	Modulus of Elasticity	Compression Parallel to Grain	Compression Perpendicular to Grain	Hardness End	Hardness Side	Nail Holding
Oak (Red)	1	2	3	1	1	1	1
Redwood	3	4	1	2	2	4	3
Western Hemlock	4	3	5	5	4	3	3
Eastern Hemlock	4	5	4	3	5	5	5
Fir (Douglas)	2	1	2	3	2	2	2
Spruce (Englemann)	6	6	6	6	6	6	5

Table 16-3
Table of Minimum Lumber Sizes
(In Inches)

Normal Size	Dressed Green	Dressed Dry Moisture 19%
1	$^{15}/_{32}$	$^3/_4$
2	$1^9/_{16}$	$1^1/_2$
3	$2^9/_{16}$	$1^1/_2$
4	$3^9/_{16}$	$3^1/_2$
5	$4^5/_8$	$4^1/_2$
6	$5^5/_8$	$5^1/_2$
8	$7^1/_2$	$7^1/_4$
10	$9^1/_2$	$9^1/_4$
12	$11^1/_2$	$11^1/_4$

There will be loss of lumber size, but it is not considered great enough to change lumber strength or framing specifications.

Example of table use:

A 2″ × 4″ would be 1-9/16″ × 3-9/16″ dressed green or 1-1/2″ × 3-1/2″ dressed dry with a moisture content of no more than 19%.

Sills

Box Sill

Used in platform construction, the **box sill** is anchored to the top of the foundation wall. It is made up of a 2″ × 8″ sill and a 2″ × 8″

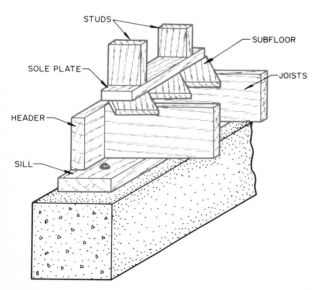

Fig. 16-32. Box sill used in platform construction.

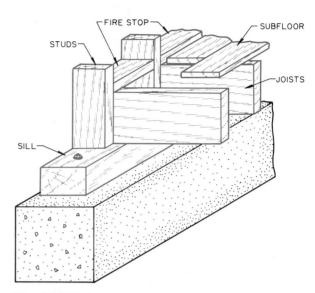

Fig. 16-33. Solid sill used in balloon-frame construction.

header. The ends of the floor joists rest on the sill and are fastened in place with nails placed through the header. The subflooring is laid on the upper edge of the floor joists. The soleplate is laid on top of the subflooring and the lower ends of the studs rest on the soleplate. This is the most common type of construction for single-story buildings because the walls can be assembled on the subfloor and then raised into position. See Fig. 16-32.

Solid Sill

Used in balloon frame construction, the **solid sill** is a 6″ × 8″ timber, anchored to the top of the foundation wall. The ends of the floor joists and the ends of the studs rest on the sill. A fire stop of 2″ × 4″ material is fastened between the studs on top of the floor joists. This slows the spread of fire from one floor to another by eliminating the "flue" or chimney effect that would otherwise be present between studs. The subfloor is laid on the top edge of the floor joists. See Fig. 16-33.

Girders and Joists

Factors in Determining the Size of Girders

Girders are required when the span of the building is too great a distance to permit the joists to extend from sill to sill. Girders may be of solid wood or may be built up by nailing or bolting several 2"-thick members together to form a single unit. Built-up girders have less bearing strength due to the smaller size of the dressed material. A solid 6 × 8 would measure 5-1/2" × 7-1/4", while a built-up girder of three 2 × 8's would measure 4-1/2" × 7-1/4" (new structural lumber sizes). Built-up girders should be joined only over bearing posts.

The size of the girder will depend on the weight to be supported and the distance the girder must span. The greater the span, the heavier the girder must be. It is common practice to use steel columns (steel pipe filled with concrete) to bear weight at even intervals. This is done to decrease the length spanned and to decrease the size of the girder. Girders are supported at intervals so that the deflection caused by the weight of the building will not be greater than 1/360 of the length of the span. This will ensure against cracking plaster and sagging floors. With the use of shorter spans, the girder size may be decreased, giving more headroom in the basement.

Table 16-4 gives the strength of the various woods used to make the girders. These strengths may be expressed in modules of elasticity or fiber stress (in pounds per square inch) working limits.

To determine the size of the girder, use the following calculations: Assume that the girder is 30' long. To find the total area supported by the girder, multiply one-half the floor load on each side of the girder by the length of the span between columns. To this total, add the weight of the attic floor and partition wall. See Fig. 16-24.

Use the following method of computation to find the total floor load:

Attic floor live load	20 lbs.	× 10'	=	400
Attic floor dead load	20 lbs.			
Partition wall	20 lbs.		=	20
First floor live load	40 lbs.	× 10'	=	600
First floor dead load	20 lbs.			
		Total weight	=	1020
Span of columns 7'	1020	× 7'	=	7140 lbs.

Next, select the type wood to be used in the girder. This will determine which of the tables you should use — the 1200 lbs./sq. in., 1400 lbs./sq. in., or the 1600 lbs./sq. in. table. Reading the table figures to the right of the stepped line will cause a bending of more than 1/360 of the span. This is to be avoided. See Tables 16-5, 16-6, and 16-7.

If a wood girder is to be of 1600 lbs./sq. in. fiber stress, a 6 × 8 would be used. For 1400 lbs./sq. in. fiber stress, use a 6 × 10 or 8 × 8. For 1200 lbs./sq. in. fiber stress, use an 8 × 8.

If a built-up girder made up of 2" milled stock is to be used, a factor number is used with the table reading to allow for loss of material. If two 2" pieces make up a 4" girder, multiply by .897. If three 2" pieces make up a 6" girder, multiply by .887. If four 2" pieces make up an 8" girder, multiply by .867. Thus, a 6" × 8" girder that has a 1600 lbs./sq. in. rating (see Table 16-7) is 7260 × .887 (three 2" stock), which is equal to a load-bearing capacity of 6938 lbs./sq. in. This load bearing is just below the 7140 lbs./sq. in. of the bearing on the girder, so it cannot be used. The next size is a 6 × 10 or an 8 × 8.

6" × 10" = 9160 × .887 = 8067
This will satisfy the load of 7140.

Table 16-4
Fiber Stress of Woods for Girders

Wood	Lbs./Sq. In. Fiber Strength
Eastern Hemlock #1 Common	1100
Western Hemlock #1 Common	1450
Douglas Fir Common Structural	1450
Southern Pine #1 Common	1450
Eastern Spruce Standard Structural	1200

Table 16-5
Span of Solid Wood Girders with 1200 Fiber Stress Lbs./Sq. In.

Size	7 ft.	8 ft.	9 ft.	10 ft.	11 ft.	12 ft.	14 ft.
2 × 6	961	837	738	660	595	541	454
2 × 8	1605	1503	1331	1191	1075	980	827
2 × 10	2020	2020	2020	1912	1730	1578	1336
2 × 12	2435	2435	2435	2435	2435	2328	1973
4 × 6	2144	1866	1647	1471	1327	1206	1012
4 × 8	3570	3340	2953	2643	2388	2175	1836
4 × 10	4500	4500	4500	4267	3864	3520	2981
6 × 6	3111	2708	2389	2134	1924	1747	1467
6 × 8	5420	5064	4481	4011	3625	3300	2786
6 × 10	6830	6830	6830	6473	5860	5341	4524
8 × 8	7390	6905	6110	5464	4941	4500	3799
8 × 10	9320	9320	9320	8827	7980	7284	6179

Table 16-6
Span of Solid Wood Girders with 1400 Fiber Stress Lbs./Sq. In.

Size	7 ft.	8 ft.	9 ft.	10 ft.	11 ft.	12 ft.	14 ft.
4 × 6	2507	2184	1930	1726	1559	1418	1194
4 × 8	4165	3904	3456	2906	2800	2552	2160
4 × 10	5265	5265	5265	4992	4520	4125	3500
6 × 6	3638	3168	2800	2504	2260	2055	1731
6 × 8	6330	5924	5244	4698	4250	3873	3277
6 × 10	7990	7990	7990	7576	6860	6261	5312
8 × 8	8630	8078	7151	6406	5793	5281	4469
8 × 10	10920	10920	10920	10330	9351	8537	7244

Table 16-7
Span of Solid Wood Girders with 1600 Fiber Stress Lbs./Sq. In.

Size	7 ft.	8 ft.	9 ft.	10 ft.	11 ft.	12 ft.	14 ft.
4 × 6	2875	2505	2213	1981	1791	1630	1375
4 × 8	4770	4470	3960	3549	3212	2930	2484
4 × 10	6035	6035	6035	5419	5177	4731	4019
6 × 6	4165	3633	3211	2873	2596	2363	1995
6 × 8	7260	6783	6008	5386	4875	4446	3768
6 × 10	9160	9160	9160	8680	7862	7179	6100
8 × 8	9880	9247	8193	7344	6646	6063	5139
8 × 10	12500	12500	12500	11835	10720	9790	8318

Table 16-8
Safe Spans of Floor Joists Carrying 40 Lbs. Live Load

Size	Spacing on Centers	Span Limit
2 × 6	12″	10′-2″
	16″	9′-3″
2 × 8	12″	13′-6″
	16″	12′-4″
2 × 10	12″	17′-0″
	16″	15′-6″
2 × 12	12″	20′-5″
	16″	18′-9″

Table 16-9
Safe Spans of Ceiling Joists Carrying 20 Lbs. Live Load

Size	Spacing on Centers	Span Limit
2 × 6	12″	11′ - 6″
	16″	10′ - 6″
2 × 8	12″	15′- 2″
	16″	13′-11″
2 × 10	12″	19′- 1″
	16″	17′- 6″

Another example, using a fiber strength of 1400 lbs./sq. in. is as follows: The reading for an 8″ × 8″ girder is 8630 × .867 = 7482, which will satisfy the load of 7140.

Steel girders may be used in place of wood girders. Sizes of steel girders may be found in tables available from steel companies or in structural handbooks.

Columns that bear the weight of the girder must have footings of adequate size. The area of the footing must be large enough to support this weight and is figured by the same method as that used for the footing for the wall.

Sizes of Floor Joists

The size of the floor joist is determined by the live load, the length of the span, and the spacing between joists.

Joists are used in 2″ thickness and in widths of 6″, 8″, 10″, and 12″. A joist should be able to support the live load with sufficient stiffness to prevent vibration that will cause wall and ceiling plaster to crack. The two tables follow-ing (Tables 16-8 and 16-9) indicate the size of joists and the spacing required for a live load of 40 pounds per square foot, which is generally adequate for house construction.

When selecting the joist to be laid in position, sight along the length of the joist and place it in position so that any crown is to the top. (The **crown** is a mild crook along the edge of the board.) The weight of the floor will tend to even out the crowns.

All joists under bearing walls should be **doubled.** If the wall is to contain heating or plumbing connections, space these joists to give an opening the size of the units. To increase the strength, use material of the same dimension to block between the joists at frequent intervals. This ties the joists together.

Figure 16-34 shows several methods of joining floor joists to girders. The strongest method is that in which the joists bear directly on the girder, but headroom in the basement is sacrificed when this construction is used. The other methods shown are compromises used to secure headroom and sufficient strength.

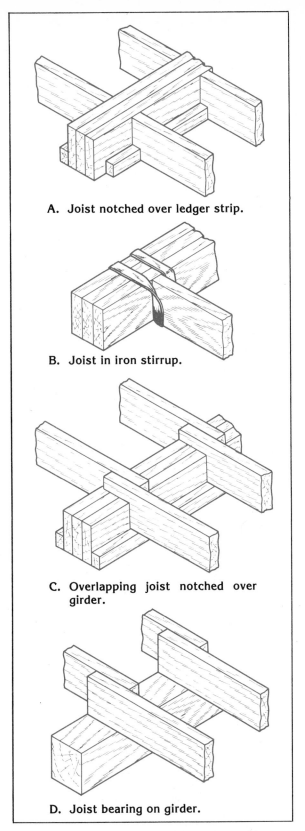

A. Joist notched over ledger strip.

B. Joist in iron stirrup.

C. Overlapping joist notched over girder.

D. Joist bearing on girder.

Fig. 16-34. Methods of joining floor joists to girders.

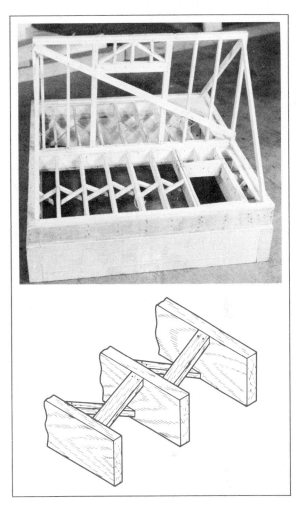

Fig. 16-35. 1 × 3 bridging. Lower ends are not nailed until flooring is laid.

Figure 16-35 shows the application of bridging between joists. Bridging helps to minimize twisting or warping of joists, serving to maintain a more level floor and to stiffen the floor framing.

The method of framing around an opening such as a stairway or chimney is shown in Fig. 16-36. The joists forming the width of the opening are secured in place. These need not be in the standard spacing of the rest of the floor joists. Along these two joists, lay out the position of the opening for the double headers. Note that the first header put in place should leave enough space so the second header added to the opening will be correctly spaced.

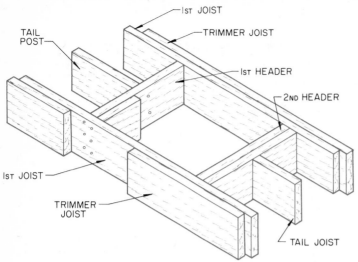

Fig. 16-36. Framing around an opening.

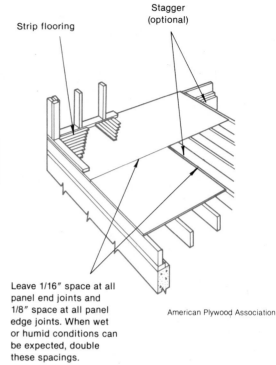

Leave 1/16″ space at all panel end joints and 1/8″ space at all panel edge joints. When wet or humid conditions can be expected, double these spacings.

American Plywood Association

The first header is secured in place at each end of the opening by fastening three 20-penny nails through the joist. In positioning these headers, use a framing square to check squareness, both horizontally and vertically, to the opening.

The tail joists are cut and put in place. Space them 16″ on center with the joist spacing pattern of the floor. Secure these tail joists by driving three 20-penny nails through the header.

When all tail joists are secured in place, nail the second header to the first header and framing joist, using 16-penny nails spaced 8″ to 12″ apart along the length of the header and through the joist.

The two trimmer joists are put in place and are secured to the first joist. This is done by inserting 16-penny nails along the upper and lower face, the length of the joist. Trimmer joists are used to carry the load of the tail joists on the headers.

Flooring

The floor joists are covered with boards or plywood to form a subfloor. Since strength and stiffness are the prime considerations, the material does not have to be of finish grade. The subflooring boards may be laid at right angles or diagonally to the floor joists. The right-angle method, shown in Fig. 16-33, is the fastest to lay because it requires a minimum of cutting. However, the boards in the finish floor must be laid at right angles to those in the sub-

Plywood Subflooring

Panel Identification Index	Plywood Thickness (inches)	Maximum Span (inches)
$^{30}/_{12}$	$^{5}/_{8}$	12*
$^{32}/_{16}$	$^{1}/_{2}$, $^{5}/_{8}$	16**
$^{36}/_{16}$	$^{3}/_{4}$	16**
$^{42}/_{20}$	$^{5}/_{8}$, $^{3}/_{4}$, $^{7}/_{8}$	20**
$^{48}/_{24}$	$^{3}/_{4}$, $^{7}/_{8}$	24
1$^{1}/_{8}$″ Groups 1 & 2	1$^{1}/_{8}$	48
1$^{1}/_{4}$″ Groups 3 & 4	1$^{1}/_{4}$	48

* May be 16″ if $^{25}/_{32}$″ wood strip flooring is installed at right angles to joists.

** May be 24″ if $^{25}/_{32}$″ wood strip flooring is installed at right angles to joists.

Fig. 16-37. Plywood subflooring.

floor. The diagonal method of subflooring, Fig. 16-32, requires much more cutting, which results in higher labor costs and increased waste. This method, however, produces a stronger, stiffer floor and permits the finish floor to be laid either parallel or perpendicular to the floor joists. Plywood subfloors, which are economical to lay, have the same advantages as diago-

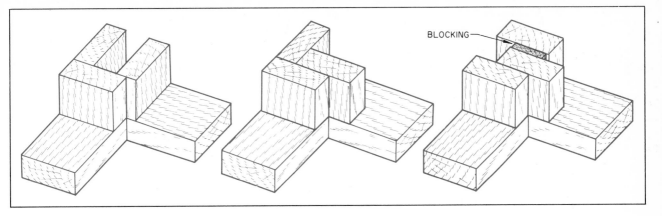

Fig. 16-38. Corner-post construction.

nal subflooring, but the cost of material is greater. See Fig. 16-37.

Corner Posts

Corner posts are the built-up members located at the outside corners of a building. These usually consist of three 2 × 4's positioned so as to provide both interior and exterior nail-ing surfaces for adjacent walls. There are several types in common usage, as shown in Fig. 16-38. If a solid corner post is used, it is customary to use a 4 × 4, with a 2 × 4 nailed to it on each adjacent inside corner. This provides for interior nailing surfaces. Occasionally, in heavy construction, a 4 × 6 is used. If this is done, only one 2 × 4 needs to be added to provide for interior nailing surface at that corner.

Framing a Wall

Topic 139.

Classification

Framing

Procedure

Ceiling heights commonly range between 7' and 8' for the first floor, and 7'-6" for the floors above. Allowance should be made in basement ceiling heights to provide adequate headroom where air conditioning or warm-air heating ducts are to be installed.

Obtain and cut the number of full-length studs needed. Recent developments in exterior wall construction recommend that 2" × 6" studs be used instead of 2" × 4", to accommodate 6" of insulation in the exterior walls. In accordance with this change in stud width, the soleplate and top plate must also be 2" × 6".

Three Common Methods

1. Frame in all full-length studs before laying out and cutting any openings.
2. Mark the openings by laying them out on the shoe or soleplate. Fasten full-length studs in place and frame in the openings.
3. Lay out a wall frame on the subfloor or ground. Fasten full-length studs in place, frame in the openings, and raise the wall to the vertical position. Plumb and fasten.

Framing Door Openings

Doors are available in the following sizes:

Exterior
  Width: 2'-8" to 3'-0"
    by 2" increments
  Length: 6'-8" to 7'-0"
    by 2" increments

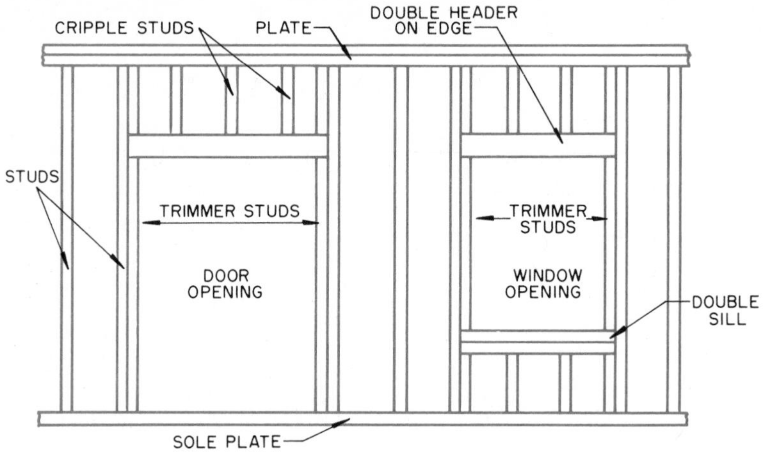

Fig. 16-39. Framing for windows and doors.

CRIPPLE STUDS　　PLATE　　DOUBLE HEADER ON EDGE

STUDS

TRIMMER STUDS

TRIMMER STUDS

DOOR OPENING

WINDOW OPENING

DOUBLE SILL

SOLE PLATE

Interior

Width: 2'-0" to 3'-0"
by 2" increments
Length: 6'-6" to 7'-0"
by 2" increments

1. Lay out and mark the position of full-length studs on the top plate and on the soleplate.

    Studs used in house construction are commonly 16" on centers. Depending upon types of structures and locality, studs are also spaced 20" and 24" on centers. See Fig. 16-39.

2. Cut and fasten full-length studs to the top plate and soleplate.

3. Cut two 2 × 4's and fasten in position for the header. To calculate the height of a header, do the following: To the height of the finished door, add 1" for the thickness of the casing, 3/4" for the thickness of the threshold, and 1" for the "horns" of the side of the casing.

    To figure the width of the door opening for framing, add 3" to the width of the door. This will allow for the thickness of the casing and for wedging between the casing and trimmer studs.

4. Cut and fasten the trimmer and cripple studs above and below the header. Cripple studs are usually 16" on center.

5. Cut and fasten the cripple studs between the plate and header.

6. Wide door openings or those that will support heavy overhead loads should be trussed. See Fig. 16-40.

7. Cut out the section of the soleplate within each door opening.

Framing Window Openings

The procedure described below is for all types of windows. See Fig. 16-39. For specific size of rough openings and installations, see manufacturer's specifications. These can be obtained from your lumber or building-supply dealer.

For a balanced outside appearance, the tops of the windows and outside doors are usually set in line.

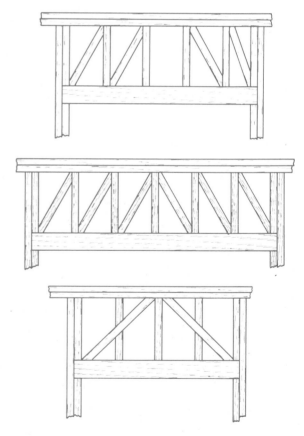

Fig. 16-40. Trusses for wide windows and door openings.

1. Lay out and mark the position of the full-length studs on the soleplate.
2. Cut and fasten full-length studs to the top plate and soleplate.
3. Cut four 2 × 4's for the double sill and header and fasten in position. To figure the height of a window opening, compute the glass height in the top and bottom sash and add 10". To figure the width of a window opening, add 10" to the width of the glass.
4. Double headers should be placed on edge for greater strength. These headers should be securely nailed together, with spacer blocks between so that their outer faces will be flush with the thickness of the studs. The Federal Housing Authority recommends the following header sizes for openings:

   Spans up to 4' in length — two 2 × 4's on edge
   Spans 4' to 5-1/2' in length — two 2 × 6's on edge
   Spans 5-1/2' to 7' in length — two 2 × 8's on edge
   Spans more than 7' in length — two 2 × 10's on edge

5. Cut and fasten trimmer studs on each side of the opening.
6. Cut and fasten cripple studs above and below the header and sill. These are usually placed 16" oc.

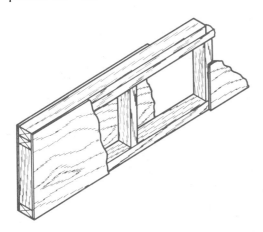

Fig. 16-41. Plywood box beam.
These hollow structural units are made from lumber and plywood. The 2" × 4" frame carries most of the bending force and the plywood skin absorbs the shear stress. This type of beam construction provides the lighter weight needed for spanning wide openings such as garage doors.

Framing Wider Openings

1. Wide openings in bearing walls that are to support heavy overhead loads (such as bathrooms and kitchens) should be trussed, Fig. 16-40.
2. Another method of spanning wide openings is to use a plywood box beam, Fig. 16-41.

Standards and Results

- Openings should be the correct height and width and in the specified location.
- Studs should be plumb (vertical) and headers and sills should be level (horizontal).
- Each stud should be secured with the specified size nails.

Safety Considerations

- Observe all safety precautions pertaining to the particular tool or machine you are using.
- Avoid dangerous working positions.
- Be careful in lifting and carrying lumber.

Fig. 16-42. Wall frames are usually laid out and constructed on the subfloor. When the wall is complete, it is raised and fastened in a vertical position.

Fig. 16-43. Fireproof framing using steel studs, rafters, and ridgepole. This framing is used as a skeletal structure for brick veneer and drywall construction.

Topic 140.

Plumbing a Wall or Corner

Classification

Aligning and squaring

Procedure

Plumbing a Corner

1. Set a straightedge with spacer blocks and a level, as shown (#1 in Fig. 16-44). Move the corner and hold it at the point where both the upper and lower bubbles read between the hairlines. In this position, the corner post must be plumb.
2. Temporarily nail a corner brace in place to hold the corner plumb (#2A, Fig. 16-44).
3. Repeat Step 1 on the adjacent side of the corner post and nail the corner brace (#2B, Fig. 16-44).

Aligning the Plate and Wall

1. Use a line and three blocks equal in thickness.
2. Tack two of the blocks at opposite ends of the plate, and draw a line taut over these blocks.

3. To test the position of the plate, place a third block under the string at spaced intervals along the length of the plate (#3, Fig. 16-44).
4. To move the plate (and wall) in or out for alignment, tack a board to the floor and plate.
5. Driving the board toward the wall will move the plate out (#4, Fig. 16-44).
6. To move the plate in, place a short brace under the board in order to make a bow in it, thus drawing the wall in (#5, Fig. 16-44).
7. These braces may be left in place until the ceiling joists and sheathing have been nailed in position.

Standards and Results

• Walls should be plumb and straight.
• Studs should be vertical.

Safety Consideration

• Observe all safety precautions pertaining to the particular tool you are using.

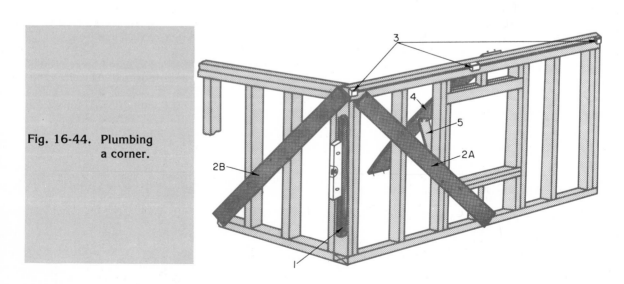

Fig. 16-44. Plumbing a corner.

Roofs

Topic 141.

The primary function of any roof is protection from the elements. Therefore, the type of the roof is determined by climatic conditions and architectural style. In some regions, roofs must be designed to shed and bear the weight of snow and ice. Such roofs usually have pronounced pitch or curvature.

Roof overhangs are designed to serve several purposes. They may add to the appearance of a building and serve to protect the upper walls from moisture. On ranch-style buildings, overhangs may provide shelter and shade for outdoor walks. When the house is properly oriented and the roof pitch and overhang are correctly figured with respect to the height of the sun in each of the seasons, the sun's heat will be properly controlled. The winter sun will provide warmth to the rooms, yet the direct rays of the summer sun will be deflected. See Fig. 16-45.

The **shed roof** is the simplest form of roof construction. It has one slope, usually to the rear of the building, and a greater overhang at the front. Shed roofs have added simplicity and attractiveness to modern architectural styles.

A recent trend in roof construction is the **butterfly** style. This is actually two shed roofs, sloping to the center of the building, with the low point in the center. This roof may be designed with an extensive overhang on the front and back to provide both protection and benefit from the sun.

The **gable roof** is probably the most common type of roof. It is so popular because it serves several practical purposes and is easily constructed. The gable roof has two surfaces, sloping away from the ridge. The slope can vary from nearly flat to a steep pitch.

The **hip roof** has four surfaces, slanting from a peak or ridge. The visual effect of this style of roof is a shortening of the building's length. The hip roof is widely used in modern ranch houses.

The **gambrel roof** has two surfaces, each of which slopes on two separate planes. The upper slope forms about a 30° angle and the lower angle is approximately 60°. This type of roof is common in Dutch Colonial houses and in barn construction. It provides greater headroom in the loft or uppermost story.

The **mansard roof** is another form of double-sloped construction. The upper section has only a slight slope, about 15°. It is more or less flat. The lower slope approaches the vertical. This type of roof makes it possible to have attic rooms.

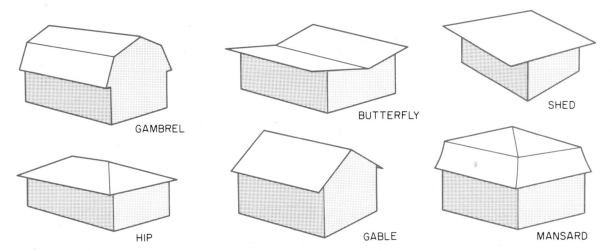

GAMBREL   BUTTERFLY   SHED

HIP   GABLE   MANSARD

Fig. 16-45. Types of roofs.

Topic 142.

Reading a Rafter Table to Figure the Length of a Common Rafter

Classification

Computing, laying, out, and testing

Procedure

A **common rafter** is one that extends from the plate (**1** in Fig. 16-46) to the ridgeboard (**2**). The length is figured along the center line that runs from the outside edge of the plate to the center line on the width of the ridgeboard.

1. To find the pitch of a roof, divide the rise (**4** in Fig. 16-46) by the span (**3**). The pitch of the roof in Fig. 16-46 is 3/8, since the rise is 8', the span is 21', and 8 ÷ 21 = .381 or 3/8.

2. To find the rise-per-foot run, multiply the rise (**4**) by 12 (to convert feet to inches) and divide by the run (**5**).

$$\frac{8 \times 12}{10.5} \approx 9''$$

The rise-per-foot run is always the same for any given pitch and, for ordinary pitches, can be easily remembered: A 1/2 pitch has a 12" rise-per-foot run. A 1/3 pitch has an 8" rise-per-foot run. A 1/4 pitch has a 6" rise-per-foot run, and a 1/6 pitch has a 4" rise-per-foot run.

3. The rafter table is found on the body of a framing square. See Fig. 16-47. The length of common rafters is found on the first line, indicated as "Length of common (main) rafters per foot run." There are 17 of these tables, beginning at 2" and continuing to 18".

Example: Find the length of a common rafter where the rise is 9" per foot run or 3/8 pitch and the building is 21' wide:

First, find the inch line on the top edge of the body which is equal to the rise per foot. In this case, this would be 9".

On the first line below the figure 9 is the number 15. This number (15) is determined in the following manner: The figure 9 on the body of the square is the rise or altitude of a right triangle. The figure 12 on the tongue is the base, or one foot of run. The shortest distance between these two points, the hypotenuse, actually measures (in this case) 15", which is interpreted as 15"-per-foot run.

Multiply this by the run of the rafter, that is, 15" × 10.5 = 157.5" or 13' 1-1/2". The above is the length of a common rafter of 3/8 pitch with a 10' 6" run, as shown in Fig. 16-46.

4. To lay out the bottom cuts (bird's-mouths) of a common rafter, use the 12" mark on the body of the square and the rise per foot on the tongue of the square. With the square in the position shown in Fig. 16-48, lay out the cut for the plate by drawing a line along the body of the square for the horizontal cut. The length of the bird's-mouth should be at least the width of

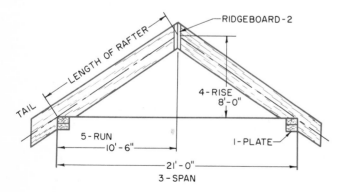

Fig. 16-46. Roof framing nomenclature.

Fig. 16-47. Rafter or framing table.

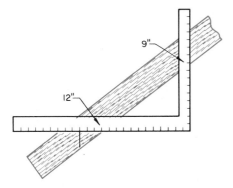

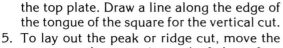

Fig. 16-48. Layout of bird's-mouth cut for top plate.

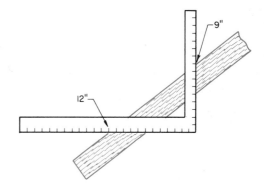

Fig. 16-49. Vertical cut on common rafter at ridge.

the top plate. Draw a line along the edge of the tongue of the square for the vertical cut.

5. To lay out the peak or ridge cut, move the square to the opposite end of the rafter, keeping the square in the same relative position. Draw a line along the edge of the tongue of the square for the vertical cut, Fig. 16-49.

6. Remember that the length of the rafter as figured from the tables is to the center line of the ridgeboard. Therefore, the thickness of one-half the ridgeboard must be subtracted from the total length. This is done by measuring at right angles to the plumb cut. See Fig. 16-49. The heel cut of the bird's-mouth starts from the length of the common rafter on the center line, Fig. 16-48. The amount of overhang desired,

called the **tail** or **eave,** should be added to the total length of the common rafter.

7. Lay out one rafter using this procedure and use this rafter as a pattern to mark out the number of rafters required.

Standards and Results

- All figuring should be accurate.
- Lines should be sharp.
- Check all figures and lines before making any cuts.

Safety Consideration

- Observe all safety practices pertaining to the particular tool you are using.

Reading a Rafter Table to Lay Out the Length of Hip and Valley Rafters

Topic 143.

Classification

Computing, laying out, and testing

Procedure

A **hip rafter** extends diagonally from plate to the ridge at the outside corner of a building. See Fig. 16-50.

A **valley rafter** extends diagonally from the plate to the ridge at the inside corner of a building. See Fig. 16-50.

1. The lengths of hip and valley rafters are found on the second line of the rafter table on the body of a framing square, just under the line labeled, "Length of common rafters per foot run." See Fig. 16-51.

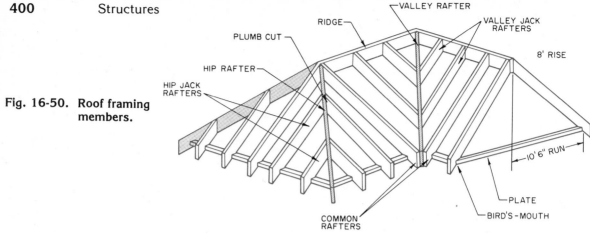

Fig. 16-50.   Roof framing members.

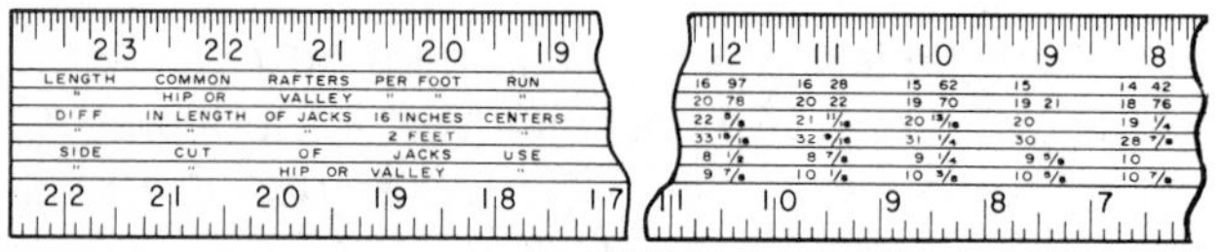

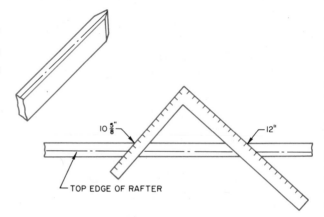

Fig. 16-51.   Rafter or framing table.

2. If there is a 10′ 6″ run and an 8′ rise, the rise-per-foot run will be $\frac{8 \times 12}{10.5} \approx 9″$.

3. **Example:** On the framing square, find the length of a hip or valley rafter when the rise per foot is 9″ and the building is 21′ wide. Look on the second line below the 9″ mark and you will find 19.21, which is the length of a hip or valley rafter-per-foot run of 9″ rise. Since the run is 10′ 6″ or 10.5, multiply this by 19.21. The length of the hip and valley rafter is 201.705″, or 16.8′, or 16′ 10″.

4. The length of all hip and valley rafters is figured along the center of the top edge. To this dimension, the length of tail or eave must be added and one-half the thickness of the ridgeboard must be subtracted. This measurement is made at right angles to the plumb mark.

Fig. 16-53.   Top and bottom side cuts on hip or valley rafter.

5. To lay out the top and bottom cuts, use the 17″ mark on the body of the framing square. Since all hip and valley rafters are in effect the diagonal of a cube, the ratio between the diagonal of a 12″ cube (17″) and the rise per foot of run establishes the angle of the cut. The 17″ mark on the body of the square will give the seat cut (or bird's-mouth) and the 9″ mark on the tongue in the given problem will give the ridge or top cut. See Fig. 16-52.

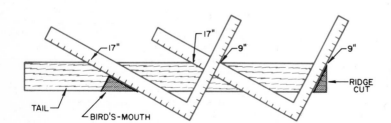

Fig. 16-52.   Seat and ridge cut on hip or valley rafter.

6. Hip and valley rafters require side cuts as well as top and bottom cuts. The table for these side cuts is found on the bottom line of the rafter table. On the body, locate the rise-per-foot run (in this case 9"). Directly below this figure, on the line marked, "Side cut of hip or valley," find the number 10-5/8". Lay the square on the top edge of the rafter so that 10-5/8" on the body and 12" on the tongue are even with the ridge mark, Fig. 16-53. Mark the side cut along the tongue. Turn the square over and repeat this layout from the opposite side. This is the layout for the side cuts at the ridge for hip and valley rafters. The finished layout will resemble a point.

Standards and Results

- All computations should be accurate.
- Cutting lines should be sharp.
- Check all figures and lines before making any cuts.

Safety Consideration

- Observe all safety practices pertaining to the particular tool you are using.

Reading a Rafter Table to Lay Out the Length of Jack Rafters

Topic 144.

Classification

Computing, laying out, and testing

Procedure

A **jack rafter** is one that runs from the plate to a hip or from the ridge to a valley. Jack rafters lie in the same plane as common rafters. Hence, they have the same rise-per-foot run as common rafters. See Fig. 16-54.

1. The lengths for jack rafters are located on the third and fourth lines of the rafter table found on the body of a steel square. The third line reads, "Difference in length of jacks 16 inches on centers." The fourth line reads, "Difference in length of jacks 2 feet on centers." See Fig. 16-51.

2. The figures in the table indicate the length of the first or shortest jack. This figure is also the difference in length between the first and second jack, the second and third jack, and so on.

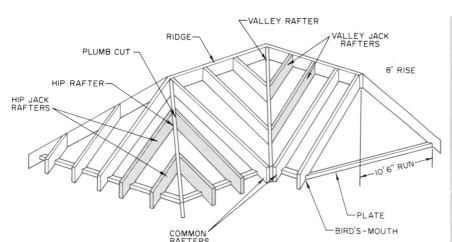

Fig. 16-54. Roof framing members.

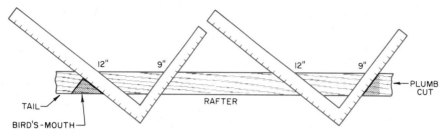

TAIL

BIRD'S-MOUTH

12"   9"

RAFTER

12"   9"

PLUMB CUT

Fig. 16-55. Bird's-mouth and plumb cut for jack rafters.

3. Jacks are numbered in order, the shortest being #1, the next #2, next #3, and so on. To find the length of a jack rafter, multiply the figure in the table by the number of the position of the jack. Then, subtract one-half the thickness of the hip or valley rafter. This measurement must be made 90° to the plumb cut.

4. If there is a 10' 6" run and an 8' rise, the rise-per-foot run will be $\frac{8 \times 12}{10.5} \approx 9''$.

   If the rafters are 16" on centers, look on the third line under the 9" mark and locate the number 20. If it is the first jack, it will be 20" long; if it is second, it will be 2 × 20" or 40" long; the third, 3 × 20" or 60" long, and so on.

   If the jacks are spaced 24" on center, look on the fourth line under the 9" mark and locate the figure 30, which is the length in inches of the first jack. The second jack would be 2 × 30" or 5' long.

5. To lay out the top and bottom cuts of jack rafters, use 12" on the body and the rise-per-foot run on the tongue, as in cutting common rafters. The body will indicate the seat or bird's-mouth cut, and the tongue will give the plumb cut, Fig. 16-55.

6. Jack rafters also require side cuts. Hip jacks require side cuts on the plumb cut and valley jacks require these cuts on the seat cut. Find the figure under the 9" mark on the fifth line labeled, "Side cut of jacks." In this case this figure would be 9-5/8. With this figure on the body and 12" on the tongue, lay out the side cuts as in Fig. 16-56. Subtract one-half the thickness of the hip or valley rafter. This measurement should be made at right angles to the plumb cut.

Standards and Results

• All figuring should be accurate.

• All cutting lines should be sharp.
• Check all figures and lines before cutting.

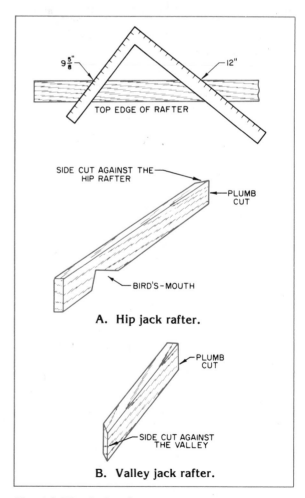

9 5/8"

12"

TOP EDGE OF RAFTER

SIDE CUT AGAINST THE HIP RAFTER

PLUMB CUT

BIRD'S-MOUTH

A. Hip jack rafter.

PLUMB CUT

SIDE CUT AGAINST THE VALLEY

B. Valley jack rafter.

Fig. 16-56. Jack rafters.

<table>
<tr><td>

Trusses and Their Use

</td><td>

Topic 145.

</td></tr>
</table>

When a long span, bridge, or roof is not supported by intermediate columns or partitions, a built-up frame, known as a **truss,** is usually used rather than a solid beam or girder. Trusses are used to distribute load, to stiffen the structure, and to build up strength. In designing a structural truss, any one or a combination of the basic truss patterns may be used. In actual practice, engineers determine the bearing load that must be supported and design a truss suitable for carrying such a load. See Fig. 16-57.

A truss is put together in a series of triangles. Since a triangle cannot change shape with-

out changing the length of at least one side, the truss is strong and rigid. The use of roof trusses in construction provides for preassembly and provides flexibility of the enclosed span. Roof trusses also provide strength and rigidity. Many of the arrangements used to divide a span into different-shaped trusses can be compared to the bridge truss.

In trussing over an opening such as a door or window, the load of the thrust is distributed along the direction of the brace from top to bottom, Fig. 16-40. This principle is also used in the straightening of sagging doors and gates and in the use of draw bolts to straighten and

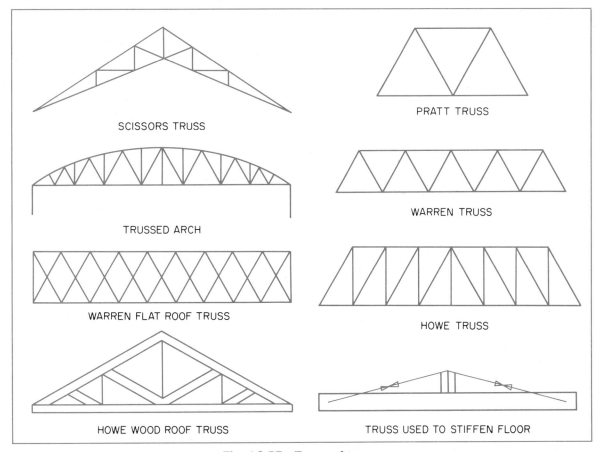

SCISSORS TRUSS

TRUSSED ARCH

WARREN FLAT ROOF TRUSS

HOWE WOOD ROOF TRUSS

PRATT TRUSS

WARREN TRUSS

HOWE TRUSS

TRUSS USED TO STIFFEN FLOOR

Fig. 16-57. Types of trusses.

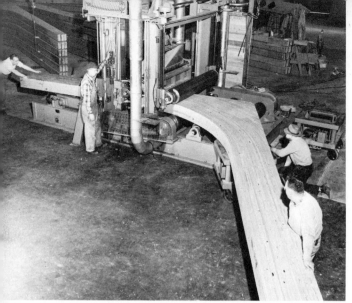

Fig. 16-58. Laminating an arch.

Timber Structures, Inc.

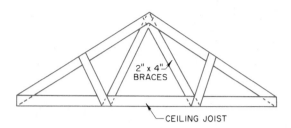

Fig. 16-59. Wood trussed rafter.

2" x 4" BRACES

CEILING JOIST

align beams and carrying timbers. Bridging, properly inserted between floor joists, forms a truss with the subflooring. This serves to stiffen and align the floor joist and distribute the load, Fig. 16-35. Collar ties between pairs of rafters of a hip roof act in the same manner. Ceiling joists (if tied in at the heel end of a rafter) and the bracing on concrete forms are additional applications of the truss.

In the truss, connectors are used to tie in the bearing area of joining members. The high compressive strength of short lengths of lumber aids in distributing the load evenly over the entire length of the truss.

Fig. 16-60. Model showing use of cables and turnbuckles to strengthen assembly of sill, studs, and rafters.

Exterior Sheathing, Roofing, and Siding

Topic 146.

Sheathing

Sheathing is the covering of the structural members of a frame with tongue-and-grooved, square-edged stock or manufactured board. This is done for the purpose of adding strength and insulation, but is not necessarily done to improve the appearance. Sheathing is applied to the roof and walls of a building.

There are three methods of applying wood sheathing. The first and most common is to **place the boards horizontally** on the studs or rafters. The second method is **diagonal boarding,** where the boards are nailed to the studs at an angle of 45°. This construction is much stronger and eliminates the need for corner bracing; however, it is more expensive because there is greater waste and it takes longer to apply.

The third method, called **hurricane construction,** is a combination of the two preceding methods. Sheathing from the outside corners is run diagonally through the first four studs and the center section is covered horizontally.

Another type of sheathing involves nailing sheets or panels of plywood or other manufactured board to the studs or rafters. See Fig. 16-64. This type of sheathing is stronger than boards, is faster to apply, has greater nail-holding power, and results in a more tightly constructed building.

In applying plywood or manufactured board, the alternate rows should be laid out so that the joints are staggered on the studs or rafters. This strengthens the framing members and tends to align the studs or rafters.

Roofing

The pitch or slope of the roof is generally the determining factor in selecting the roofing material to be used. Low-pitch roofs (those with a rise of less than 5-1/2"-to-the-foot run) require a rolled type of roofing material. Roofs with a rise of over 5-1/2"-to-the-foot run can be covered with shingles.

Rolled Roofing

Rolled roofing requires less labor in application but does not have the same ap-

pearance value as shingles. Rolled roofing is a felt-base material treated with asphalt, which provides a waterproof, weatherproof, and adhesive backing. The face is coated with a mineral that gives it both color and a durable surface. Rolls are made in 18" and 36" widths, and in weights of 45 to 125 pounds per roll or square. Most rolls cover one **square** or 100 square feet.

Before roll roofing is applied, felt paper should be laid directly over the roof sheathing. This seals the roof and smooths out surface imperfections. The roll roofing should then be applied with the sheets overlapping one another. The amount of overlap at each sheet will depend on the roof pitch. The overlap may be as great as 18" for a 36"-wide roll on a flat pitch, or not less than 2" on a steep slope. All laps at the joining of sheets and between courses should be coated with an even layer of asphalt cement.

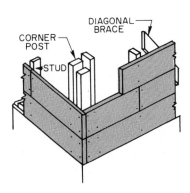

Fig. 16-62. Horizontal sheathing.

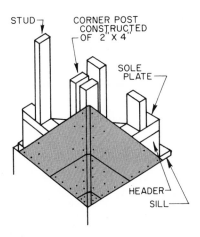

Fig. 16-63. Diagonal sheathing.

Fig. 16-61. Applying plywood sheathing to framing members.

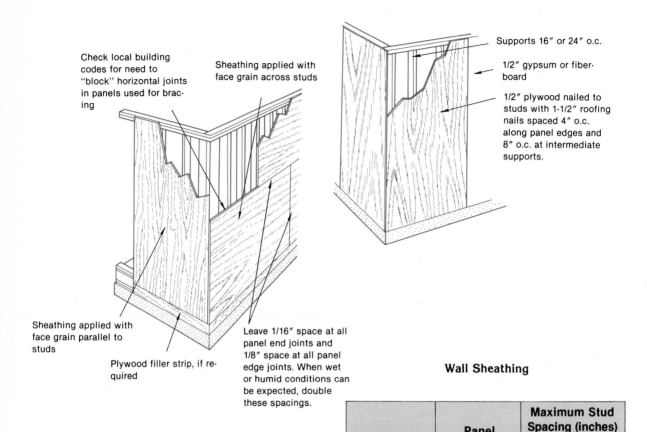

Check local building codes for need to "block" horizontal joints in panels used for bracing

Sheathing applied with face grain across studs

Supports 16″ or 24″ o.c.

1/2″ gypsum or fiber-board

1/2″ plywood nailed to studs with 1-1/2″ roofing nails spaced 4″ o.c. along panel edges and 8″ o.c. at intermediate supports.

Sheathing applied with face grain parallel to studs

Plywood filler strip, if required

Leave 1/16″ space at all panel end joints and 1/8″ space at all panel edge joints. When wet or humid conditions can be expected, double these spacings.

American Plywood Association

Fig. 16-64. Wall sheathing.

Wall Sheathing

Panel Identification Index	Panel Thickness (inch) and Construction	Maximum Stud Spacing (inches) Exterior Cover-Nailed to:	
		Stud	Sheathing
$^{12}/_0$, $^{16}/_0$, $^{20}/_0$	$^5/_{16}$	16	16*
$^{16}/_0$, $^{20}/_0$, $^{24}/_0$, $^{32}/_{16}$	$^3/_8$ and $^1/_2$ 3-ply	24	16
			24*
$^{24}/_0$, $^{32}/_{16}$	$^1/_2$ (4 & 5 ply)	24	24

* Apply plywood sheathing with face grain across studs.

In laying the roll, start nailing at the center and work toward the ends to allow the sheet to stretch. A large-headed aluminum or galvanized coated roofing nail is used to secure the material in place. Some workers prefer to use the nails only on the top edge of the sheet and to depend on the cement to hold the sheet secure to the roof on the exposed lower edge. When this method is used, no nails are exposed.

Shingles

The most common type of roofing shingles is **asphalt shingles.** These are manufactured in many patterns, using asphalt-base felt. Asphalt shingles average 12″ in width and 36″ in length. They are classed by weight to the square, ranging from 210 to 310 pounds. (One square covers 100 square feet.) Unlike rolled roofing, shingles are available in a great range of colors (including black and white). Colors will vary according to the type of covering material used.

Applying Asphalt Shingles

To calculate the number of squares of shingles needed to cover a gable roof (Fig. 16-65), do the following:

Multiply the length of the ridge (34') by the length of the slope (14')	34 × 14 =	476 sq. ft.
Multiply by 2 for each side of the roof	2 × 476 =	952 total sq. ft.
Add one sq. ft. for each foot on the ridge for the ridge cap		34 sq. ft.
Add 1/2 sq. ft. for the length of the eaves for the double cornice	$\dfrac{34 \times 2}{2}$ =	34 sq. ft.

Total sq. ft. = 1020

Since one square of shingles covers 100 square feet, divide the total number of square feet of the roof by 100 to get the number of squares.

$$\frac{1020}{100} = 10.2 \text{ squares of shingles}$$

To apply the shingles, first lay out the metal strips for the edge and eave. These strips support the overhang of the shingles. A 15- to 45-pound felt paper is laid directly over the sheathing. This seals the roof and smooths out the surface imperfections. See Fig. 16-66.

To assure that the shingle pattern will be even at both ends of the roof, determine what portion of a full shingle will have to be cut to fill out a course. Each shingle strip is 36" long, so divide 3' into 34' (the length of the roof). $\dfrac{34}{3}$ = 11-1/3. This indicates that 1/3 of a shingle will be cut (12" length), to finish the course. If this figure were to come to a number that did not equal the sections on one strip of shingle, one-half the odd length would be started at the edge to make the row balance.

The first course of shingles will be a double layer to cover over the cut tabs. The underneath layer is laid with the tabs or pattern facing up. This row is then covered with shingles laid in the correct manner. Be sure to half lap the second layers so that the slots will not be exposed. Large-head galvanized coated shingle nails are used above the slot to secure the shingle. The length of the nail should not penetrate the sheathing, as condensation will collect on the exposed tips. The nails are spaced directly above the slots and 1" in from the edges. Nail the shingles from the center out to allow for stretching of the shingle.

Asphalt shingles are spaced with 4-1/2" to 5" exposed to the weather. The second course of shingles will start with a cut strip so that the slots will be half over the lower slot.

Asphalt shingles are self-aligning, but it is best to snap a chalk line every few courses to keep the weather laps even. Always nail from the center of the strip shingle to the ends to keep the strip from buckling.

When both sides of the roof have been shingled, the ridge is covered. This is done by cutting the strip shingle at the two slots, making three pieces. These pieces are laid over the ridge with an even lap to both slots, Fig. 16-67. Nails are placed at the inside corner so that the

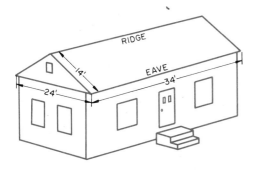

Fig. 16-65. Measurements needed for calculating the total square feet of a roof.

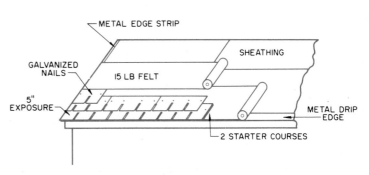

Fig. 16-66. Materials used for a shingle roof.

Fig. 16-67. Covering the ridge with shingles.

Fig. 16-68. Shake shingles are often used on roofs instead of common asphalt shingles. Shake shingles are durable and very attractive. They are, however, more expensive and much harder to apply than asphalt shingles.

National Park Service

Fig. 16-69. Hand method of cutting shake shingles with a froe and mallet. Modern shake shingles are cut by machine.

second piece of shingle will cover the nails. It is good practice to start the shingles on the ridge so that the exposed surface edges of the lap will be pointed in the direction of the prevailing wind. It is recommended that shingles or roll roofing be applied when temperatures are moderate. If the temperature is too low, the material will be brittle and may crack or break. If the temperature is too high, the shingles will be very soft and will be apt to scuff or mar easily.

Siding

Siding is the finished covering applied over sheathing. It is used primarily for the purposes of waterproofing, insulation, and giving an attractive appearance to the exterior.

The two most common types of wood siding are **clapboards** and **shingles.** In laying out a wall to be covered with either of these types of siding, it is common to divide the height into three sections — **below** the windows, **beside** the windows, and **above** the windows. If it has been decided to expose a certain amount of siding to the weather (4″ for example), divide the distance from the base of the wall (usually slightly below the sheathing) to the bottom of the window by four. The nearest whole number equals the number of courses. Next, divide this whole number into the distance from the base to the bottom of the window casing. This gives the exact amount each course is to be exposed to the weather.

Example: The distance from the base of the wall to the bottom of the window is 41″. Thus, 41 ÷ 4 ≈ 10; 41 ÷ 10 = 4-5/64. If 10 courses were used, each course would expose 4-5/64″ or 4-1/8″ to the weather. If nine courses were used, the exposure on each course would be 4-1/2″, and if 11 courses were used, 3-11/16″ would be exposed on each course.

It is considered good design to have a full course showing at both the top and bottom of

A. Lap siding.

Masonite Corporation;
Boise Cascade Building Products

B. Rough-sawed shingle siding.

C. Patterned lap siding.

Fig. 16-70. Exterior siding used in modern home construction.

windows. This procedure also requires less cutting.

To make the layout of the entire wall, it is more efficient to use a **story pole.** This is a piece of wood 1″ × 1″ or 2″ of any convenient length (up to 10′), having markings on the edge indicating the amount that each course of siding is to be exposed to the weather. Pencil marks are transferred from the story pole to the wall near each end of the building. A chalk line is run between these marks and then snapped.

Applying Siding

In applying clapboards, the worker should proceed from top to bottom. By doing this, the entire side of a building may be laid off at one time. Starting at the corner board, the first course of clapboards is cut, fitted, and then nailed **at the top.** For the remaining courses, nails should be driven about 1/2″ up from the butt edge so that the nail will hold the butt edge of one clapboard and the thin edge of the next one. Nails should not be driven all the way in until the undercourse has been laid. Starting again at the corner board, the courses are begun by slipping a clapboard under the butt of the clapboard above it. Move the lower clapboard until the second butt coincides with the chalk line. The first course is then nailed at the bottom, securing the lower clapboard in place. The entire side of the building is done in this manner. It is a good practice to stagger the joints in clapboards by at least 4″ to minimize the possibility of leaks. See Fig. 16-71.

The application of wood shingles, shakes, and composition shingles is very similar to the application of clapboards. However, shingles are applied from the bottom up and a chalk line must be snapped after each course is laid. To shed water at the base of a wall, a double course of shingles is laid. Narrow-course shingles are not usually nailed at the butt, but instead are nailed slightly above the weather line. Wide-course shingles are nailed above the butt to prevent curling. To speed the application of shingles, a straightedge is often tacked along the chalk line, and the butts of the shingles are rested on the edge. This assures that the shingles are held in the proper place until nailing. To ensure a watertight wall, stagger the joints.

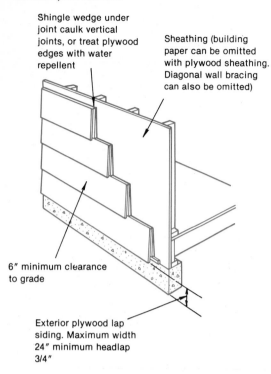

Shingle wedge under joint caulk vertical joints, or treat plywood edges with water repellent

Sheathing (building paper can be omitted with plywood sheathing. Diagonal wall bracing can also be omitted)

6″ minimum clearance to grade

Exterior plywood lap siding. Maximum width 24″ minimum headlap 3/4″

Fig. 16-71. Application of exterior siding.

Exterior Plywood Lap Siding Over Nailable Plywood or Lumber Sheathing*
(For plywood siding over other types of sheathing, see Sturd-I-Wall recommendations.)

Lap Siding Description (all species groups)	Nominal Thickness (inch)	Max. Stud Spacing (in.) of Vertical Rows of Nails — Face Grain Horizontal
MDO EXT-APA	$^{11}/_{32}$, $^3/_8$	24
	$^1/_2$ and thicker	24
303-16 o.c. Siding EXT-APA	$^5/_{16}$, $^{11}/_{32}$, $^3/_8$	24
303-16 o.c. Siding EXT-APA 303-24 o.c. Siding EXT-APA	$^7/_{16}$	24

Nail Size (Use non-staining box, siding or casing nails)	Nail Spacing (in.)	
	Panel Edges	**Intermediate**
6d for siding $^3/_8$″ thick or less; 8d for thicker siding	4″ @ vertical butt joints; 6″ along bottom edge	8″ (if siding wider than 12″)

NOTE:
Nailable plywood or lumber sheathing includes:
1. Nominal 1″ boards with studs 16″ or 24″ o.c.
2. 1/2″ 4 or 5 ply plywood face grain parallel or perpendicular to studs 16″ or 24″ o.c.
3. 3/8″* or 1/2″ 3 ply plywood, face grain perpendicular to studs 16″ or 24″ o.c.; and with face grain parallel or perpendicular to studs 16″ o.c.
4. 5/16″* plywood, face grain perpendicular to studs 16″ o.c.

*Check local building code.

Fig. 16-72. Applying siding over exterior sheathing.

To give a wider shadow line, a double layer of shingles is often laid. The butt of the top layer is spaced 1/2″ below the layer directly under it.

Some types of siding can be applied directly over the studs, eliminating the need for sheathing. Novelty siding is usually used on unheated buildings. It is molded for decoration and is usually tongue-and-grooved. Novelty siding acts both as a sheathing and a siding. It is applied horizontally over the studs.

Many types of textured plywood patterns are also available. These act as both sheathing and siding. Tests show that this type of construction is stronger than and insulates as well as inch boards.

Other types of siding are prefinished hardboard, aluminum, and vinyl siding. All three have become quite popular.

| Laying Out Straight-Run Stairjacks | Topic 147. |

Classification

Computing and laying out

Procedure

If stairs are to run from an uncovered concrete slab to the first floor, all risers will be of equal height except the bottom and top risers. To determine the height of the bottom riser, subtract the thickness of the tread from the height of the other risers. To determine the height of the top riser, deduct the thickness of the tread from the combined thicknesses of the subfloor and finish floor, then deduct this amount from the height of the regular riser.

For example, assume that the thickness of the tread used is 1", the height of the regular riser is 7", the subfloor is 5/8" thick, and the finish floor is 25/32" thick. Calculations for the bottom and top risers would be as follows:

Bottom riser: 7" – 1"   = 6" height
Top riser: 5/8" + 25/32" = 45/32" or
              1-13/32" – 1" = 13/32"
              7" – 13/32"   = 6-19/32" height

The following procedure is a good general guide for figuring stair risers:

1. Determine the perpendicular distance from the surface of the first floor to the top surface of the second floor.
2. The number of risers needed may be found by dividing the total height (in inches) from floor to floor by the desired height of the riser. (The riser is usually 6-1/2" to 7" high.) Dividing the required number of risers into the total height in inches will give the exact height of the individual risers. See Fig. 16-73.

Example:
Total height equals 8' (96")
        Desired height of riser is 7"
    96 ÷ 7 = 13-5/7. 13 or 14 risers will be needed.
    96 ÷ 13 = 7.384" or 7-3/8", which may be too high.
    96 ÷ 14 = 6.857" or 6-7/8", which may be more desirable.

3. The run of the stairs may be limited to a fixed distance. If so, the tread must be figured by the same method as was used to determine the height of the riser. The length of each tread is as near to 10" as possible. The total of the tread plus the riser is equal to 17" or 18". It must also be remembered that there will be one less tread than the number of risers because the top floor forms a tread.

Example:
Total run equals 11' (132")
12 equals one less tread than risers

$$\frac{132}{12} = 11" \text{ length of tread}$$
    or, if 14 risers are preferred:

$$\frac{132}{13} = 10.154" \text{ or } 10\text{-}1/8" \text{ length of tread}$$

4. If the riser is 7-3/8" and the tread is 11", lay the framing square so that the 7-3/8" mark on the body and the 11" mark on the tongue fall on the edge of the jack, as shown in Fig. 16-74. Start the layout a sufficient distance from the edge to form the bottom riser. The bottom riser will be 6-3/8" high (allowing for the thickness of the tread).

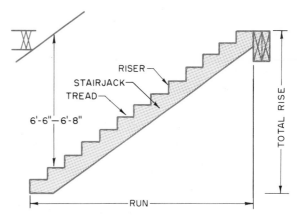

Fig. 16-73.   Stair nomenclature.

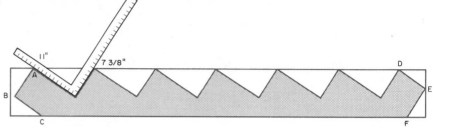

Fig. 16-74. Laying out stairjacks with a framing square.

5. Draw lines along the outside edges of the square to indicate the tread and the riser.
6. Reverse the square to draw lines AB and BC, Fig. 16-74. AB = 6-3/8″.
7. Mark out the required number of treads and risers as in Step 5.
8. The top riser should be modified according to the materials used in flooring. EF should be square with DE, Fig. 16-74.

Standards and Results

• All risers should be of equal length, except the bottom riser, which is 1″ shorter to allow for the thickness of the tread.
• All treads should be of equal length.
• All treads should be level and risers perpendicular, except on outside stairs, where the tread will have a slight forward pitch.

Safety Consideration

• Observe all safety practices pertaining to the particular tool you are using.

Topic 148.

Figuring Board Measure by Using the Essex Scale

Classification

Computing

Procedure

On most framing squares, the **Essex board-measure table** is on the body and faces the user when the tongue is down and to the left. See Fig. 16-75. As the name indicates, the table gives the number of board feet in any piece of lumber from 2″ to 24″ wide and from 8′ to 30′ long.

1. Each number on the outer edge of the body represents the width of lumber in inches (2″-24″). Since 12″ is the unit of width in figuring board measure, the number 12 on the outside edge of the body is the focal point in using the table. Each number in the column of figures under the number 12 represents a given board length (in feet). Since the width of boards under this column is 12″, the figures also represent the **board feet** of each particular length of board.

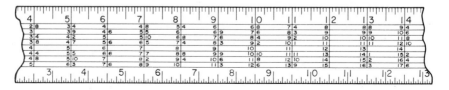

Fig. 16-75. Essex board-measure table.

2. To determine the board feet of stock that has a width other than 12", find the number under 12 that corresponds to the board length. Then, move to the left or right to find the correct width.

   For example, if you wish to find the number of board feet in a piece of stock 10" wide and 14' long, find 14 in the column under 12. Then, follow this line to the left until you are directly under 10. You will find the number 11 on the left and the number 8 on the right of the vertical line.

This is read as 11-8/12 or 11-2/3 board feet.

3. The figures given in the board-measure table are for 1" stock. To find the board measure for other stock, multiply the figure found on the table by the standard rough-stock dimensions of that particular thickness.

Standards and Results

• The student should be able to figure board feet by using the Essex table.

Interior Sheathing

Topic 149.

The interior surfaces of structures are usually covered with some type of **sheathing** to provide a smooth surface. This sheathing stengthens the walls and gives additional structural support. Sheathing also provides decorative surfaces, soundproofing, and insulation.

There are several types of material used to cover walls and ceilings. These include plaster, gypsum board, fiberboard, solid wood paneling, and sheet paneling.

Plaster is made from combinations of sand and water mixed with lime. Plaster is used in conjunction with a base material such as expanded metal, wood, or fiberboard **lath.** The lath is attached directly to the framing members and provides a surface to which the plaster is applied. Perforated steel corners are used on the inside and outside corners to give added strength and to provide resistance to cracking. Wood strips called **plaster grounds** are used to provide thickness guides for the plaster around the window and door openings and at the base of the walls. See Fig. 16-77. When the final coat of plaster is dry, it is sanded and then painted or covered with wallpaper.

Gypsum board is made with gypsum core, covered on each surface with a cardboard facing. It is made as a plasterboard that is

Fig. 16-77. Applying plaster with a trowel. Notice the plaster grounds on the outside edge.

Fig. 16-76. Plaster is applied in layers. The first layer is put directly over the lath. It is applied rough so that a second coat will bind to its surface. A finish coat is then applied for smoothness.

Plastering Industries

Fig. 16-79. Drywall is cut by scoring the surface paper with a utility knife and applying pressure to the opposite side. After the drywall has broken along the line, the backing paper is cut to separate the pieces.

Fig. 16-78. Drywaller fills joints between drywall sheets with joint compound and tape. Drywallers may use stilts to reach high areas.

Fig. 16-80. Gypsum board is applied directly to the studs.

3/8″ × 16″ × 4′ and as drywall available in 3/8″ and 1/2″ thicknesses, 4′ wide, and in 8′, 10′, 12′, 14′, and 16′ lengths.

Gypsum board is generally applied directly to the framing members, using nails, screws, or adhesives. In drywall construction, gypsum board is usually applied in a single thickness. However, for extra strength, soundproofing, and leveling, 3/8″ drywall may be applied in double thickness. Strength is also increased by staggering the joints of adjacent sheets.

The gypsum walls are made ready for painting by filling the joints between sheets and inside corners with a joint compound and special tape. See Fig. 16-78. The nails or screws that hold the gypsum board to the wall or ceiling should be sunk below the surface. The depressions should be filled with joint compound. Outside wall corners are protected with a perforated steel cap, which must also be covered with joint compound. When the joint compound is dry, these areas are lightly sanded to produce a smooth surface.

Fiberboard generally has a rough-textured factory finish. It is used for ceilings and has high acoustical properties. See Fig. 16-81.

Fig. 16-81. Installing acoustical fiberboard to furring strips attached to the ceiling.

Fiberboard is available in 12″ and 16″ squares and 12″ × 24″ sheets. To apply this type of ceiling, furring strips must first be attached at right angles to the ceiling joists. The center-to-center spacing of the furring strips must equal the width of the fiberboard squares or sheets.

Western Wood Products Association

Fig. 16-82. Applying solid wood paneling to horizontal wood strips attached to framing studs.

The strips provide the surface to which the fiberboard is attached.

Solid wood paneling is available in various wood types, in widths of 4″ to 12″. It is applied directly over the studs, using finish nails concealed in the tongue portion of tongue-and-groove joints. When the paneling is to be applied vertically, horizontal wood strips should be attached to the regular studs to provide a fastening surface. See Fig. 16-82.

Sheet paneling is made of thin (usually 3/16″ or 1/4″) core material over which is applied a decorative wood face veneer. The paneling comes in 4′ × 8′ sheets. It is available with either a plain surface or with pattern grooves cut into the face veneer to simulate solid-wood paneling. Sheet paneling has many advantages over other types of wall coverings because of its attractive appearance, its high strength, its puncture resistance, and its easy maintenance and application. It may be applied directly to studs or over previously applied wall coverings.

A less expensive alternative to actual veneered paneling is **printed paneling.** This type of paneling is made with an inexpensive core, covered with paper that has been printed to simulate the grain pattern and color of an attractive veneer. The paper is vinyl-coated, resulting in a smooth, attractive, hard, and easy-to-clean surface.

Applying Wall Paneling

Topic 150.

Classification

Cutting, fitting, and fastening

Procedure

1. Starting in one corner of the room, place a sheet of paneling against the wall.
2. Plumb the sheet of paneling and, using a pencil compass, scribe along the edge of the paneling, using the corner as the guide. This is done by setting the compass equal to the greatest gap between the corner of the room and the edge of the sheet and scribing a line the total length of the sheet. See Fig. 16-83. (This step may not be necessary if the walls are plumb and the corners are square.)

Fig. 16-83. Using pencil compass to scribe an irregular shape on a wall panel.

Table 16-10
Panel Adhesives

Type	Solvent	Color	Health and Fire Hazard	Setting Time	Use
Elastomeric Polymer	Mineral Spirits	Light tan	No	30-45 Min.	A, B, C, G
Elastomeric Polymer and Resin	Manufacturer's Solvent	Tan	Yes	30-45 Min.	A, B, C, D, E
Neoprene Emulsion	Water Tolvene	Cream to light tan	No	60 Min.	B, C, E
Neoprene Solvent (Contact Cement)	Water	Clear	No	15 Min.	C, D, F, H, I, J
Synthetic Resin Polymer	Water	Buff	No	10-20 Min.	B, C, E, K, L
Synthetic Elastomer	Tolvene Lacquer Thinner	Beige	No	20-30 Min.	D, F, M
Neoprene Elastomer	Manufacturer's Solvent	Light yellow	No	15 Min.	N

KEY

A Plywood
B Gypsum Board
C Plastic Laminate
D Hardboard
E Polystyrene

F Particleboard
G Tile
H Leather
I Steel
J Ceramics

K Upsom Board
L Wood
M Metal
N Plastics (except polystyrene)

Panel adhesives are available in liquid and paste form. They have a shelf life of one year, require contact pressure at room temperature and have high strength. The paste type has gap-filling properties. All types should be kept tightly covered. Some are not harmed by freezing, but it is recommended that they be kept at a temperature above 10° C (50° F). Sales units range from quarts to 55-gallon drums and tube cartridges.

3. Using a plane or saw, cut to the scribed line.
4. If the floor or ceiling is not level, it may be necessary to scribe to the floor or baseboard. If the panel is larger than the ceiling height, measure and mark the panel length on each edge and in the middle. Connect the points with a line and cut.
5. If panel adhesives are used, the panel may be glued in position. See Table 16-10, "Panel Adhesives." Follow the manufacturer's specifications. If specially coated nails are used, the panel should be nailed in position. The nails should be located where they will be driven into solid wood (studs).
6. If brads are used, they should be set slightly below the surface and the indentation should be filled with a filler that matches the color of the panel. This may be done by tinting putty with oil tinting color or by using a color stick made for this purpose.
7. Continue to panel the wall, scribing and

Fig. 16-84. Applying paneling to furring strips on a basement wall.

cutting the panels where necessary to fit into corners, and around windows, doors, and electrical outlets. Joints should be tight and plumb.

8. If paneling is applied to a masonry wall, furring strips must be fastened to the wall with masonry nails or adhesive. The paneling is then applied to the furring strips as in Steps 1 through 7, preceding. See Fig. 16-84.

Standards and Results

• All joints in the corners of the room, between the panels, and at the floor and ceiling should be tight.

• Sheets should be securely fastened to the walls over the entire surface of the panel.

• If brads are used to secure the paneling, they should be set below the surface and the holes should be filled with material that matches the color of the paneling.

Safety Consideration

• Observe all safety practices pertaining to the particular tool or machine you are using.

Fitting and Hanging a Door

Topic 151.

Classification

Joinery and assembly

Procedure

Before the door is hung, it should be properly fitted. There should be a minimum allowance of 1/8″ clearance at the top and at each side, and enough clearance at the bottom to clear the finished floor, carpeting, and threshold when the door is open. After the door has been properly fitted, the edge opposite the hinged side and away from the swing of the door should be planed on a 2° to 3° bevel.

The following is a good general rule for locating hinges. For built-up or flush doors, the top of the upper butt is located 6″ down from the top of the door. The bottom of the lower butt is located 8″ to 10″ from the bottom of the door. On panel doors, the top hinge is usually placed just below the upper rail and the lower hinge is usually attached just above the lower rail. Because of the mortise-and-tenon joint, the hinges should not be opposite a rail. Heavy doors should have three hinges. The third hinge is usually centered between the upper and lower hinges.

On cabinetwork, the top and bottom hinges are spaced an equal distance from the opposite ends of the door. The distance from the end of the door to the center of the butt is usually about one-sixth the length of the door. For example, the centers of the top and bottom hinges on a 2′ door would be 4″ from the respective ends of the door.

Setting a Butt Hinge

1. Locate the position of the top edges of the hinges on the frame and mark with a sharp knife.
2. Place the door in position, keeping it tight against the top and the hinge side. This may be done with shingles or other wedge-shaped pieces.
3. Project the position of the hinges on the door and mark with a sharp knife.
4. Remove the door. With a knife and a square, extend the marks made on the face onto the edge of the door. Still using the knife and square, mark short lines on the frame to indicate the length of the butt.
5. Set a butt gauge or a marking gauge a distance equal to the width of the leaf, not including the knuckle. The knuckle should project beyond the frame of the door to allow it to swing freely. Mark the width of the leaf on both the door and the frame.

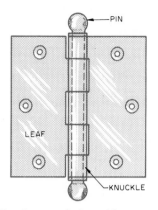

Fig. 16-85.   **Loose-pin butt hinge nomenclature.**

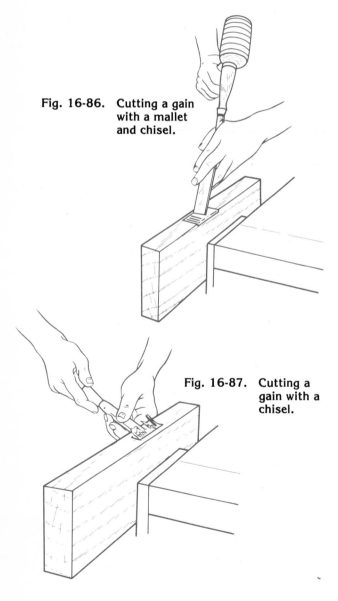

Fig. 16-86. Cutting a gain with a mallet and chisel.

Fig. 16-87. Cutting a gain with a chisel.

6. With a knife and square, extend the mark indicating the length of the butt to the line indicating the width of the butt.

7. Set the other spur of the butt gauge (or another marking gauge) to the thickness of the leaf. Mark this thickness on the face of the door and the edge of the frame. Be careful not to mark beyond the lines marking the length of the butt.

8. On the lines indicating the ends of the butt, score the ends of the gains with a chisel and mallet. Keep the bevel side of the chisel toward the waste side of the work.

9. Cut the gain by making a series of feather cuts with the chisel, bevel side down, as shown in Fig. 16-86.

10. Remove the surplus by paring toward the gauge line as shown in Fig. 16-87.

11. Repeat Steps 9 and 10 for all gains on the door and the frame.

Note: Gains for hinges may also be cut with the router and template. (See Topic 56, "Using a Portable Hand Router.")

12. Place the hinges in position on the door and mark the position of the screws. Using an awl, mark back slightly from the center of the holes. This will draw the leaf tight against the back of the grain.

13. Repeat the above operation on each of the gains on the frame.

14. If installing loose-pin butts, remove the pin and separate the leaves. Drill the hole nearest the center of each leaf on both the door and the frame. Fasten each leaf with one screw, in such a way that the pin opening is up. If tight-pin butts are used, fasten the butts to the door. Hold the door up to the frame in the opened position and, starting at the top, fasten the leaves to the frame.

15. Check to see that the door opens and closes properly. A properly hung door should stay in any position. If it has a tendency to swing open, it may be **hingebound.** That is, the gains may be too deep. This may be remedied by padding the gains with cardboard or with a thin piece of wood. When all adjustments have been made, drive in the remaining screws.

Standards and Results

- Leaves should fit snugly in the gains.
- Leaves should fit flush with the surrounding surface.
- Screws should be flush with the surface of the leaf.
- Gains should have no chipped edges.

- The door should swing freely.
- The pins should be parallel to the face of the door.

Safety Consideration

- Observe all safety practices pertaining to the particular tool or machine you are using.

Fitting Preassembled Door Units

Topic 152.

Classification

Leveling, plumbing, and fastening

Procedure

Exterior and interior door units are available as a preassembled unit. See Fig. 16-88. The doors are fitted to a jamb that can be adjusted for use with any wall thickness. Exterior doors are 6' 8" high and 32"-36" wide. Interior doors are either 6' 6" or 6' 8" high and are available in common widths of 24", 28", 30", and 32".

Exterior doors usually open into the room, so they must be made to swing either to the right or left. Interior doors also swing either right or left. Interior doors must be set in such a way that they will be out of the traffic when open. The procedure is similar for fitting either type of door.

1. Apply a strip of 15-pound felt paper to the subflooring and to the exterior sheathing at the perimeter of the rough door opening.
2. Set the door unit on the subflooring. The exterior trim should be outside and flush with the papered sheathing. The hinge side of the door should be against the studs.
3. Adjust the expandable jamb until it is flush with the inside wall.
4. Plumb the hinge side of the trim, using wood-shingle wedges between the stud and the jamb if necessary. (A long straight-edge used with a level will make it easier

to keep the door straight and plumb.) Level the door sill on the subfloor. With the assembly set in this position, temporarily tack this side of the unit by driving 10-penny finish nails through the exterior trim, into the framing stud.

5. Check the top corners of the jamb with a framing square to make sure the assembly is square.
6. Plumb the opposite jamb and fill in the spaces between the jamb and stud with shingle wedges. Temporarily tack in position.

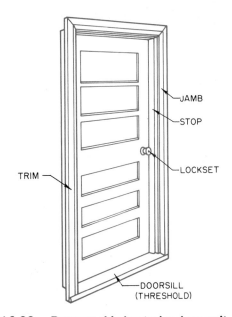

Fig. 16-88.   Preassembled exterior door unit.

7. Test the swing of the door for binding and spacing between the door and the jamb. An 1/8″ clearance is desirable. When open, the door should stay in one position. If it does not, the hinge side of the jamb is not plumb.

8. When the door is properly set, secure the jamb by nailing through the exterior trim with 10-penny finish nails. Space the finish nails 14″ to 18″ apart.

9. Level the top jamb. Wedge and nail the jamb in position. The wedges are secured in place by nailing through the jamb, through the wedge, and into the stud.

10. Trim off excess wedge length. The wedges should be flush to the inside of the jamb.

11. Set all nailheads below the trim surface.

Standards and Results

- The door should swing freely and should stay in any position when open.
- The door should fit flush against the lip of the jamb.
- The door should not rub or bind against any portion of the jamb or sill.
- The adjustable jamb should be flush with the inside wall.

Safety Consideration

- Observe all safety practices pertaining to the particular tool or machine you are using.

Topic 153.

Installing a Cylindrical Lockset in a Door

Classification

Cutting, boring, and fitting

Procedure

Some **locksets** do not have a deadlocking plunger, and locksets for inside doors have no locking function in the knobs. Most manufacturers provide a template with the lock, indicating the size and position of all bored holes, mortises, and gains for the latch plate and strike plate. See Fig. 16-89.

Locating Center

1. Place the template on the face of the door and locate the hole for the cylindrical case. The distance from the floor to the center of the knob is usually between 34″ and 36″, and the distance in from the edge of the door is 2-3/4″.

2. Select the proper size bit, as indicated in the manufacturer's instructions, and bore through the face of the door. Care must be taken not to split out the stock on the inside face of the door.

3. Using the template, locate the center of the hole on the edge of the door.

4. Select a bit of the size recommended by the manufacturer and bore a hole from the edge of the door. This hole will house the latch unit. The latch-unit hole is bored to meet the hole that has been bored in the face of the door. (See Step 2.)

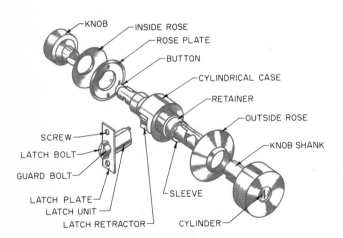

Fig. 16-89. Parts of a cylindrical lockset.

5. Insert the latch unit in the hole just bored.

6. With a sharp knife, mark around the latch plate for the size of the gain.

7. Using a mallet and chisel, remove the waste material from within the marked area. Chisel only to a depth equal to the thickness of the latch plate.

8. Insert the latch into the hole and attach it with screws.

Locating and Installing Strike Plate

1. From the front edge of the jamb, measure back a distance equal to one-half the thickness of the door. This is the center line for the layout of the strike plate.

2. Place the strike plate over the latch and close the door until it comes to the jamb. Mark the top and bottom edges of the gain for the strike plate.

3. Place the strike plate in the proper position and mark around the plate with a sharp, thin-bladed knife.

4. Remove the stock from within the lines to a depth equal to the thickness of the plate. This may be done with a chisel and mallet.

5. Some strike plates have a cutout. Others have a built-in receptacle to receive the latch. The slope in the receptacle should be opposite the swing of the door.

6. In either type, a deeper cavity must be cut to receive the full depth of the latch.

7. Fasten the strike plate in position with screws.

Inserting Lockset in Door

1. Remove the inside knob, the rose, and the retainer sleeve from the lockset.

2. See manufacturer's specifications for the distance between the outside rose and the cylinder case. This distance will vary with the thickness of the door.

3. From the outside of the door, insert the lockset and knob into the large hole on the face of the door. Make sure that the edges of the opening in the cylindrical case properly engage the prongs on the latch. Also see that the latch unit is properly interlocked with the reactor. Test the action by turning the knob.

4. Attach the inside knob by sliding it onto the spindle.

5. Fasten the two parts together.

6. Turning either knob and releasing it should move the latch in and out.

Standards and Results

- The hole for the lockset and latch case should be of the proper size and in the correct location. There should be no chipping around the hole.
- The hole for the latch unit should be of the proper size and in the correct location.
- The strike plate should be in the proper position and should be flush with the surface of the door jamb so that the latch will engage easily.
- Turning either knob should unlatch the door.
- The key should turn easily to lock or unlock the door.

Safety Consideration

- Observe all safety practices pertaining to the particular tool or machine you are using.

Fitting Preassembled Window Units

Topic 154.

Classification

Plumbing, leveling, and fastening

Procedure

Preassembled window units are made in many styles. The common ones are **double-**

hung, casement, sliding, bay, and **bow and awning.** The window frames are made for the minimal 3/8″ drywall thickness, with additional add-on strips to accommodate wall thicknesses of 1/2″ and 5/8″ drywall and 3/8″ plasterboard and plaster. The window unit is sized according to glass size. (See manufacturers' charts for available sizes.)

1. Apply strips of 15-pound felt paper to the exterior sheathing, at the perimeter of the rough window opening.
2. Set the preassembled unit on the rough sill and level with wedges if necessary.
3. Plumb the sides of the exterior trim, Fig. 16-91, and check the top with a level.
4. Secure the window unit by driving 10-penny finish nails through the trim and into the stud framing. Window frames are not nailed through the jamb (as in the door units) because of the sash mechanism.
5. When the interior trim is applied, the window jambs are secure in position. Any detailed instructions supplied by the manufacturer should be carefully followed.

Standards and Results

- The window sash should move freely.
- The window sash should fit square against the jamb.

Safety Consideration

- Observe all safety practices pertaining to the particular tool or machine you are using.

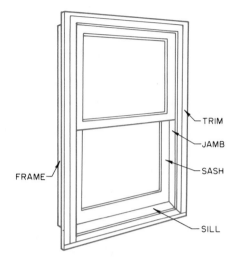

Fig. 16-90.   Preassembled window unit.

Fig. 16-91.   Plumbing the sides of a window unit.

Glossary of Structural Terms

Abutment — that part of a pier or wall from which an arch is suspended. The support at either end of an arch, beam, or bridge is also called an abutment.

Anchor bolt — the bolt that anchors the sill to the foundation. See Fig. 16-25.

Apron — the inside trim below a window stool.

Baluster — small vertical pillars that frame the opening beneath the handrail, usually used in stair and porch construction.

Baseboard or **skirting** — a finish trim at the base of a wall.

Batten — a narrow strip of wood used as a reinforcement or for covering for a joint.

Batter board — a temporary framework from which the level lines are run in establishing guides for the positioning, layout, and erection of a foundation. See Figs. 16-20, 16-21, 16-22.

Beam — a horizontal timber used to support bearing loads.

Bearing walls — the walls that serve as partitions and that support the roof and upper stories.

Bracing — the ties and rods used for strengthening and reinforcing the framework of a buiding.

Bracket — a triangular brace used as a support for a shelf or projection.

Bridging — furring or strips of metal banding, crossed in pairs between floor joists, forming a truss. Bridging helps prevent distortion, distributes the load, and stiffens the floor.

Canopy — a roof-like structure projecting from a wall and supported on pillars.

Cantilever — a bracket-like projection unsupported at one end.

Casement — a type of hinged or pivoted window that swings open along its entire length.

Casing — the trim around a door or window.

Clapboard — a standard siding, shingle-shaped in cross section.

Cleat — a strip of wood used both for fastening and as a support.

Collar beam — a horizontal member that serves to tie together and stiffen two opposite common rafters.

Corner post — a member that provides for exterior and interior nailing at corners. See Figs. 16-38, 16-44.

Cripple stud — a stud above or below a window opening, running from either the soleplate to the sill or from the header to the top plate.

Cupola — a small structure built on top of a roof for ornamentation, ventilation, or observation.

Cornice — that portion of a roof (rafters) which extends beyond the exterior walls. The crowning members at the top of interior or exterior walls are referred to as the cornice molding.

Door frame — the finished frame that forms a door opening.

Dormer — an upwards and outwards projection on a section of a roof, providing light, ventilation, style, and interior headroom.

Ell — an extension of a building at right angles to the main structure.

Fascia — the horizontal, flat member of a cornice.

Fire stop — a horizontal obstruction of wood or masonry, filling the opening between studs at floor level. The fire stop prevents the spread of fire by draft.

Flashing — sheet metal used around openings and valleys in roof and wall construction to prevent seepage of moisture.

Footing — an enlarged course of either concrete or stone, placed under foundations or columns to provide a larger weight-bearing surface. See Fig. 16-25.

Framing — the skeleton framework of a building, including walls, floor, and roof. See Figs. 16-29, 16-30 and 16-31.

Furring strips — 2"-3" strips of wood, nailed to the rough framing to build up an even surface and to provide a nailing surface at desired intervals.

Gable — a roof projection that terminates in a triangular vertical wall above the eaves. See Fig. 16-45.

Gambrel roof — a symmetrical roof with two different pitches on each side, the lower of which is often 60° and the upper of which is 30°. See Fig. 16-45.

Girder — the main carrying timber used to support the interior ends of the floor joists. See Fig. 16-34.

Girt — a horizontal strip set in the studs to support floor joists. Girts are most commonly used in balloon framing.

Grounds — strips of wood 3/4" in thickness, fastened around openings and at the base of surfaces to be plastered. Grounds serve as the surface to which plaster is leveled and finished and to which trim is nailed.

Gusset — a thin piece of material such as a wood or metal plate, which is fastened to the face of two or more structural members to secure or reinforce a joint.

Hanger — a U-shaped, stirrup-like bracket used to support the end of a beam or joist at a masonry wall or girder. See Fig. 16-34.

Header — a horizontal framing member, used to support the load over an opening. The header is attached to full-length studs and is supported by a trimmer. See Fig. 16-39.

Heel — that part of any structural roofing member which rests on the top plate.

Hip — the ridge formed at the point of intersection of two inclined roof surfaces at an exterior corner.

Jamb — the finish trim on a door or window opening.

Joist — one of a series of parallel, horizontal structural pieces, laid on edge and used to support the floor or ceiling. See Fig. 16-34.

Knee — an angular reinforcement between two or more structural members.

Lally column — a vertical member, usually made of tubular steel filled with concrete, used to support a girder or beam.

Lath — a strip of wood, expanded metal, or composition material, fastened to the frame of a building as a foundation for plaster.

Ledger strip — a bearing strip nailed along the side of the main carrying girder, forming a seat to support the joists.

Lintel — a supporting horizontal structural member, spanning window and door openings.

Louver — a slatted device, fitted into an opening to provide ventilation and to keep out rain or snow.

Mansard, French, or curb roof — a roof with a double slope on each of the four sides. The lower slope is very steep and the upper slope is relatively flat. See Fig. 16-45.

Mullion — a pier separating pairs of windows.

Muntin — a slender divider between panes of glass in a window.

Newel — the center post about which a circular staircase is built. The main supporting posts at the extreme ends of a handrail are also referred to as newels.

Parting strip — a dividing retaining strip, set into the window frame of a double-hung sash.

Pilaster — a built-in projecting column, used to reinforce a straight wall.

Pile — a heavy timber, driven into the earth as a supporting foundation.

Pitch — the angle or degree of the slope of a roof, usually expressed as a ratio between the rise and the span, Fig. 16-46.

Plancher — a horizontal piece of trim that forms a part of the cornice closing in the lower protruding ends of the rafters.

Plate — the uppermost horizontal member of a framed wall, Fig. 16-46.

Plinth block — a rectangular block at the base of a casing or column, to which the baseboard is butted. This block is usually somewhat thicker than either the casing or baseboard.

Purlin — a horizontal supporting timber, running from truss to truss and forming a bearing surface for the rafters.

Rafters — the members that form the skeletal, rib-like framework of a roof, Fig. 16-46.

Ridgepole, ridgeboard, or saddle board — the uppermost horizontal member of the roof framework. This piece ties the rafters into a unit on gable and gambrel roofs, Fig. 16-46.

Rise — in roof construction, the vertical distance from the top of the plate to the peak of the roof. In stair construction, the rise is the vertical distance from one floor to the next. See Figs. 16-46 and 16-73.

Run — in roof construction, the horizontal distance spanned by the rafters. In stair construction, the run is the horizontal distance spanned by the jacks. See Figs. 16-46 and 16-73.

Sash — the window framework in which the glass is bedded.

Scaffold or staging — a temporary platform used in construction.

Sheathing — the material used to close in the skeletal framework.

Sill — the lowest supporting member of a structural framework, as in a building or bridge or in window openings, Fig. 16-39.

Sleeper — wood strips placed in or on concrete or on dirt as a base for nailing the floor joist, subflooring, or finished flooring.

Shiplap — a type of siding having a molded edge that forms a tight, water-shedding joint.

Shoring — timbers used for bracing to prevent sagging or bowing.

Soffit — the underside of a large cornice or arch.

Span — the distance between vertical exterior points of structural supports. See Fig. 16-46.

Structure — a unified construction of interrelated parts.

Story pole — a rod used in measuring heights such as ceilings and in laying out window and door openings, courses of shingles or siding, and stairjacks.

Stringer — a term sometimes applied to joists and stairjacks and other horizontal structural timbers, Fig. 16-73.

Stud — a supporting frame member, running from the soleplate to the top plate.

Subfloor — rough flooring made of boards, matched lumber, or plywood and laid on joists to serve as a base for the finished floor.

Transom — the hinged window over a door.

Tread — the step portion or horizontal part of a stair, Fig. 16-73.

Trim — decorated finish applied in corners and around openings. Examples of trim are baseboards, chair rails, and moldings.

Trimmer — a beam, such as a stud, joist, or rafter, used in framing an opening. Trimmers add strength to the sides of the opening and secure the header.

Truss — a triangular arrangement of members used in supporting and dispersing bearing loads. See Fig. 16-57.

Valley — the angle formed where two roof slopes meet at an interior corner. See Fig. 16-50.

Wainscoting — the interior trim paneling applied to the lower portion of a wall, usually to chair-rail height.

SECTION SEVENTEEN.

Patternmaking

Topic 155.

Patternmaking

In wood **patternmaking,** a model, built up of one or more parts, is made to specifications. This model or pattern is used as the form around which a mold is made. Metal, plastics, or other materials reducible to a molten or liquid state, may then be cast in the mold. When the material has solidified, it becomes a counterpart of the pattern. Many objects are made first as wood patterns and serve as the model from which castings are produced, either singly or in quantity. Patterns vary in size and complexity from those used for casting such small objects as handles to those used for casting large machine bases or engine blocks.

Some patterns are solid wooden models of the castings that are to be made from them. Other patterns are made in sections, which makes it easier to remove the pattern from the mold. Patterns made in sections are also used for castings that are to have internal cavities. There are three basic types of patterns — solid, one-piece patterns, sectional patterns, and patterns containing cores or core prints.

One-Piece Pattern

The **one-piece pattern,** Fig. 17-1, is almost an exact model of the object intended for casting. The pattern is made larger to provide for the following factors: (a) **draft,** which eases removal from the mold, (b) **shrinkage** of the material to be cast, and (c) **finishing.**

Split Pattern

The **split pattern** is one that is made in halves. The split between the halves falls at the largest dimension of the pattern. The two sections are fitted very closely together and are held in this position either with regular dowels or with dowel pins (male and female) made especially for this purpose. See Fig. 17-2.

Patterns with Cores

In cases where the casting is to contain an internal cavity, the patternmaker must make

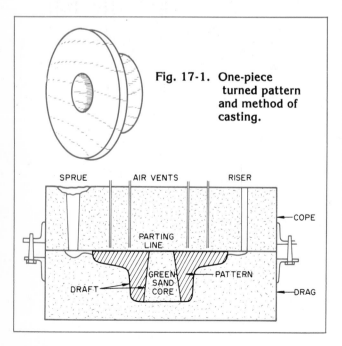

Fig. 17-1. One-piece turned pattern and method of casting.

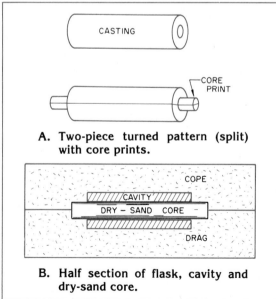

A. Two-piece turned pattern (split) with core prints.

B. Half section of flask, cavity and dry-sand core.

Fig. 17-2. Two-piece turned pattern and method of casting.

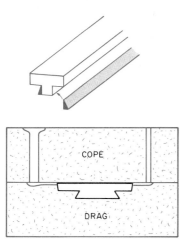
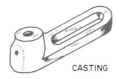
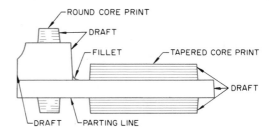

Fig. 17-3. Patterns having angles or shapes that would make removal from the mold difficult may be made with loose pieces. This makes it possible to remove the pattern in steps, leaving the mold undisturbed.

Fig. 17-4. Built-up pattern with core prints.

provision for the hollow or recess. This is done by making either a projection on the pattern or a recess or hole in the pattern. This process is called **coring.** In sand molds, the core is a body of sand projecting into the cavity of the mold and forming the opening in the casting. Some openings are such that the pattern may be constructed to leave its own core in the mold. This part of the pattern usually has a greater degree of taper, which makes it easier to remove the pattern from the mold. See Fig. 17-4.

Shallow recesses, exposed cavities, and shallow holes are cored out wherever possible by means of a **greensand core.** In such applications, the cavity or hole will be made in the pattern. When the greensand is rammed into the mold, it forms the core. See Fig. 17-1.

If the recesses and cavities are too deep or if they are too narrow to mold, they are generally cored out, in the same manner as interiors of castings, by means of a **dry-sand core.** A dry-sand core is a body of sand that has been mixed with core oil and formed in a specially prepared box called a **core box,** made to specified shape and dimension. This formed mixture is baked into a hardened dry-sand core. When the casting is poured, the dry-sand core will provide the recess or cavity specified for the casting. See Fig. 17-2.

Woods Used in Patternmaking

Common pattern woods are reasonably close-grained and are easily worked. They stay in place well and do not expand or contract to any notable degree. Clear white pine is used for patterns that are to be used only a few times. Mahogany is used for patterns to be used a greater number of times. Cherry is used for production work.

Considerations for Laying Out a Pattern

Topic 156.

Classification

Providing allowance through measuring and laying out

Procedure

To the finished dimension of the object to be cast, allowances must be added for draft, shrinkage, and finish.

Draft Allowance

1. **Draft** is the name given to the slight taper on all vertical surfaces. This slope or taper extends from the parting line at the widest point to the section that will lie deepest in the mold. Draft makes it easier to withdraw the pattern from the mold, Fig. 17-4.
2. Draft is actually a dimension that is added to the finished size. An outsized dimension of 1/8″ to 3/8″ taper per foot is added at the parting line and tapers off to the finish dimension at the base of the pattern.

Shrinkage Allowance

1. All metals expand when they change from a solid to a liquid state. They shrink when they change back to a solid state. Each metal expands and contracts differently. The cavity in the mold, therefore, must be larger than the finished casting will be. This oversize allowance is made by using a shrink rule with the appropriate calibrations for the particular metal to be cast.
2. Iron shrinks 1/8″ to the foot. Therefore, in laying out patterns to be cast of iron, the actual measurements on the pattern stock would be made with the 1/8″ shrink rule. The same casting made of brass or bronze would be laid out with the 3/16″ shrink rule.

For aluminum, the 1/4″ shrink rule would be used. See Topic 11, "Rules."

Finish Allowance

Since the casting will be rough as it comes from the mold, allowance must be made for finishing. Finishing is done by removing stock by filing or machining.

1. The allowance for machine finish is usually a minimum of 1/8″, although greater allowance may be made.

   Machine finish is indicated on the drawing by the letter "f."
2. The allowance for finish by filing is usually 1/32″. File finish is indicated on the drawing by an "ff" or a "v."

Standards and Results

- All measurements and layout should be accurate.
- All vertical surfaces should have the proper amount of draft.
- Proper allowance should be made for the types of finish to be obtained.
- Proper allowance should be made for shrinkage. This allowance is determined according to the kind of metal to be used in casting.

Topic 157.

Making a Simple Pattern

Classification

Measuring, laying out, and shaping

Procedure

A **simple pattern** is a one-piece pattern that is to be molded in the drag section of a flask. See Fig. 17-1.

1. Determine the type of metal to be used in the casting and select the proper shrink rule.
2. Obtain a piece of stock of the appropriate

kind. (See Topic 155, "Patternmaking," and the discussion of woods used in patternmaking.) This stock should be an inch or so greater in length and width and slightly thicker than needed for the finished pattern.
3. Plane or joint one face true and smooth and square one edge with the face.
4. On this prepared surface, lay out the length, width, and shape of the pattern. If any surface of the casting is to have a machined or filed finish, proper allowance must be made. This allowance is 1/8″ for a

Stanley Tools

Fig. 17-5. Cornering tool, used for breaking arrises.

machined finish and 1/32" for a filed finish. Draft of between 1/8" per foot and 3/8" per foot must also be added to the dimensions of all vertical surfaces.

5. Surface the opposite face to the specified thickness.
6. Cut the pattern to shape. Both edges and ends of the pattern should form an 88° to 89° angle with the layout face. This will form the draft. This taper may be cut with hand tools or by tilting the saw table or blade of the circular saw, band saw, or jigsaw, or by tilting the fence on a jointer or the table on a disk sander.
7. Smooth all rough edges with a plane or file and sand with sandpaper.
8. If the pattern is to consist of two or more pieces, such as ribs to strengthen the casting, these pieces must also have draft.
9. Attach the ribs and bosses with glue and brads. Brad heads should be set below the surface.
10. All arrises (sharp corners), except those on the parting surface, should be rounded by sanding.
11. Seal all surfaces with a coat of shellac.
12. Apply fillets to the inside corners and fill all nail holes. (See Topics 160 and 161.)
13. Apply necessary coats of finish, complying with patternmakers' practice. (See "color code," Glossary of Patternmaking Terms.)

Standards and Results

- The pattern should be of the proper shape and dimension.
- The pattern should have draft on all vertical surfaces.
- Surfaces to be machined should have proper allowance.
- All fillets should be smooth.
- All nail holes and blemishes should be filled with wax or wood filler.
- The patternmakers' color code should be followed.

Safety Considerations

- Wear safety glasses when using tools or machines.
- Observe all precautions pertaining to the use of hand and machine tools and heating devices.

Laying Out and Shaping a Cylindrical Split Pattern

Topic 158.

Classification

Measuring, laying out, and shaping

Procedure

Some patterns would be impossible to withdraw from the mold unless they were made of two or more pieces. Cylindrical patterns are usually made in two pieces. One half of the pattern will be in the **drag** section of the flask and the other half will be in the **cope** section, Fig. 17-2.

1. Select two clear pieces of stock of the appropriate kind. (See Topic 155, "Patternmaking," and the discussion of woods used in patternmaking.) These pieces should be about 2" longer and at least 1/8" wider than the required pattern, and should be at least 1/16" thicker than one-half the finished pattern.
2. Joint one face of each piece so that these surfaces match.

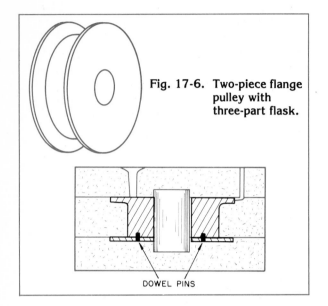

Fig. 17-6. Two-piece flange pulley with three-part flask.

DOWEL PINS

3. Determine the type of metal to be cast and select the proper shrink rule to lay out the full-size pattern.

4. Locate matching dowel holes near each end, at points that will be of sufficient thickness after turning. (See Topic 92, "Reinforcing Joints with Dowels.")

5. If wooden dowels are used, one end of the dowels should be shaped like a blunt-nose bullet. Dowels should be cut to length so that they will protrude from the cope section of the pattern no more than 1/4". They should be fitted in such a way that they keep the parts in register but do not bind when parts are separated, Fig. 17-6.

6. Glue the square ends of the dowels in the holes of the cope section. Metal dowels are screwed in with a special wrench.

7. Fasten the two pieces of stock together. If the pieces are under 1' in length, this may be done by using screws on each end. If the pieces are longer, they should be spot glued. Place a piece of paper between the pieces of stock during this process. Fasten the pieces with screws at each end.

8. Turn the pattern to shape on the lathe. (See Topic 81, "Spindle or Between-Center Turning.") Do not cut into the screws.

9. Remove the pattern from the lathe and cut off the extra stock.

10. Separate the cope half of the pattern from the drag half. If the glued-paper method was used, hold one end of the pattern upright and place a chisel along the glue line on the end grain. Force the two pieces apart.

11. Cut the proper draft allowance on all vertical surfaces by filing or sanding.

12. Apply the coats of shellac necessary to seal all surfaces.

Standards and Results

• The turning should be of the proper shape and dimension.
• Dowels should keep both halves in register.
• Halves should separate easily.

Safety Considerations

• Wear safety glasses when using tools or machines.
• Observe all safety practices pertaining to the particular tool or machine you are using.

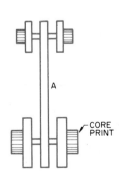

Fig. 17-7. Method of building up a pattern.

CORE PRINT

Laying Out and Constructing a Simple Cylindrical Core Box

Topic 159.

Classification

Measuring, laying out, and cutting

Procedure

If the two sides of a core are identical in shape and size, it will be necessary to construct only half of the core box. Make two half cores and cement their faces together with core oil.

1. Select a piece of surfaced stock of the appropriate kind, approximately 3/8″ larger in width, thickness, and length than the finished dimensions. (See Topic 155, "Patternmaking", and the discussion of woods used in patternmaking.)
2. Select the better face and draw a center line the full length of the piece.
3. Set compass or divider to the radius of the core and, with the centers located on the center line, scribe or lay out a semicircle on each end of the stock.
4. Draw parallel lines along the face of the stock, connecting the ends of the two half circles. The material within these lines must be removed.
5. This material may be removed in one of three ways: (1) by making a series of depth cuts with a circular saw and removing the waste with a gouge; (2) by using a round molding plane the same size and shape as the core; (3) by using a core-box plane. (See Topic 39, "Special-Purpose Planes.")
6. Remove any rough imperfections by smoothing the surface with sandpaper held over a block that is of a slightly smaller radius than the core.
7. To provide proper draft for the removal of the core, saw one end at an angle of 87° or 88° from the parting line.

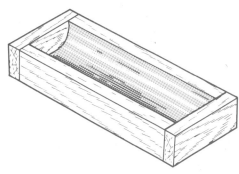

Fig. 17-8. Cylindrical core box.

8. Lay out the length of the core print and cut the opposite end in a similar manner.
9. Select two pieces of stock, surfaced to 3/8″ thickness and large enough to cover each end of the box. Glue in place and secure with brads. The top edges should be positioned flush with the parting line.
10. Apply coats of shellac as necessary to seal the surfaces.

Standards and Results

- The core cavity should be of the proper size and shape.
- The core cavity should be smooth.

Safety Considerations

- Wear safety glasses when using tools or machines.
- Observe all safety practices pertaining to the particular tool or machine you are using.

Topic 160.

Fillets

Classification

Filler material used in patternmaking

Composition or Description

Sharp corners in a mold tend to crumble and wash away with the flow of molten metal. Rounding the inside corners with **fillets** permits the metal to flow more smoothly and actually adds strength to the casting. Eliminating sharp corners also reduces the occurrence of cracks and craters at the corners of castings. Such faults are caused by the metal shrinking away from the sharp edges.

Fillets are made from beeswax, paper, leather, or plastic. They are cove-shaped. See Fig. 17-9.

Properties

Fillets are pliable and relatively easy to form. They retain their shape and are readily attached to wood.

Uses

Fillets are relatively narrow moldings of pliable material, used for filling out the interior section of a corner. See Fig. 17-4.

Fig. 17-9. Filleting tool and shapes of fillets.

Market Analysis

1. Fillets are commonly available in cove shape, in radii of 1/8" to 1" (by eighths).
2. Standard lengths are 24" and 36".

Maintenance

Store fillets flat and in a cool place.

Topic 161.

Applying Fillets

Classification

Filling by rounding inside corners on a pattern

Procedure

Applying Wax Fillets

1. Apply a coat of shellac to the entire pattern.

2. Select the size of fillet to be used and the size of filleting tool to fit that fillet.
3. Secure an alcohol lamp or other suitable heating unit to provide low, constant heat.
4. Measure and cut a length of fillet material and fit it into a corner of the pattern.
5. Heat the ball end of the filleting tool so that it will be warm enough to smooth out the fillet but not melt the wax. Slowly move the filleting tool over the fillet, pressing and shaping the fillet into the corner. See Fig. 17-9.
6. Work the warm filleting tool back and forth, making sure that the thin edges of the fillet adhere to the pattern and that the radius is uniform throughout.
7. Repeat the preceding steps and continue to fill all inside corners of the pattern. Remove excess wax from the surrounding surface by scraping.
8. Apply a second coat of shellac to seal both the fillet and the entire pattern.

Applying Paper, Leather, and Plastic Fillets

Leather fillets should be softened in water so that they will be more flexible.
1. These fillets are usually bonded to a pattern with hot glue or shellac. If hot glue is used, the pattern should not be given a coat of shellac until all fillets are applied.

2. Apply a thin film of fast-setting glue to the corner and quickly place the fillet in position.
3. Heat the ball end of the filleting tool so that it will be warm enough to smooth out the fillet and keep the glue soft and tacky. Slowly move the filleting tool over the fillet, pressing the fillet into the corner.
4. Continue to fill all corners of the pattern. Work the warm filleting tool back and forth, making sure that the thin edges of the fillet adhere to the pattern and that the radius is uniform throughout.
5. Apply at least two finish coats of shellac to seal the pattern.

Standards and Results

- All fillets should be smooth.
- The edges of fillets should be bonded to the pattern.
- Fillets should be of the proper size for the pattern. Except in special cases, large patterns require large fillets.

Safety Considerations

- Exercise care in the use of heating equipment.
- The filleting tool should not be overheated.

The Patternmaker

Topic 162.

Patternmaking is the shaping of materials and construction of models from which molds are made. These molds are then used to cast metal or plastic parts. A **patternmaker,** in addition to making new patterns, is often required to repair and redesign stock patterns that have been previously used and stored.

Patternmaking requires technical knowledge of the shaping of wood and metal. A patternmaker uses all common woodworking machines as well as some special types developed particularly for the trade. In addition to shrink rules, core-box planes, and filleting tools, the patternmaker uses all the common woodworking hand tools.

The patternmaker must be able to interpret ideas sketched by a designer. To do this, the patternmaker must be able to visualize the finished work from the very beginning. This is necessary because the design of the pattern is determined by (a) the shape of the object to be cast, (b) the method by which the pattern will be molded, and (c) the method by which the casting will be machined. A background in mechanical drawing is necessary for this work, as the patternmaker must be able to make accurate layouts.

Patternmaking is one of the highest-paid skilled trades. A five-year apprenticeship is required to learn the trade. Although the number of patternmakers in modern industry is relatively small, almost every industry has need for workers having this skill. Patternmaking is essential for development work in the construction of new models.

Glossary of Patternmaking Terms

Boss — a built-up section of a pattern, providing a raised section in the casting to add strength where machining is to be done.

Chaplet — a specially designed shape of the same metal as that to be cast, arranged in the mold so as to support the core wherever the core seating is inadequate.

Color code —
  a. Black — surfaces that are to be left unfinished.
  b. Red — surfaces that are to be machined.
  c. Red stripes on yellow background — seats of loose pieces.
  d. Yellow — core prints and seats for loose core prints.
  e. Diagonal black stripes on a yellow base — stop-offs (ribs that strengthen the pattern but that are not cast).

Cope — the upper section of the flask. The top half of a split pattern that contains the dowel pins is also referred to as the cope. See Fig. 17-1.

Core — a body of sand that projects into the cavity of the mold, forming an opening in the casting. See Fig. 17-2. There are two types of cores — **greensand cores** and **dry-sand cores.** A greensand core is a projection formed in the mold by the pattern itself. A dry-sand core is a body of hardened sand that will become the recess or cavity in the casting. Core sand is coarse sand, free of clay, that has a large percentage of silica. The silica is mixed with water and core oil and the sand and silica mixture is baked. The core oil may either be a commercial brand or may be made of linseed oil. A good substitute for core oil in the school shop is a mixture of one part polyvinyl-acetate glue to five parts water.

Core box — a specially prepared box, Fig. 17-8, into which sand is pressed to shape and dimension to form a core.

Core print — a projection on a pattern, forming a recess in the mold so as to seat and support a dry-sand core. See Fig. 17-4.

Draft — a slight bevel or taper, ranging from 1/8″ to 3/8″ per foot on all vertical parts of the patterns, which serves to ease the removal of these patterns from the molded sand. The lesser amount of draft is used for those surfaces that are to be finished. See Fig. 17-4.

Drag — the lower section of the flask. The lower half of a split pattern containing the dowel holes is also referred to as the drag. See Fig. 17-1.

Fillet — a filler material (one-quarter concave shape) of a radius 1/8″ or greater, added to the inside corners of patterns. The fillet is used to minimize the danger of craters, cracks, and washing of sand; to improve the flow of molten metal; and to provide added strength to the casting. See Fig. 17-9.

Finish — an increase in the size of a pattern, allowing for working of the casting to dimension. The usual allowance is 1/8″ for machine finish and 1/32″ for file finish.

Flask — an open rectangular or circular frame in which sand molds are made for casting. Flasks are made either of wood or pressed metal. They consist of two fitted sections — the lower section, called the **drag** or **nowel,** and the upper section, called the **cope.**

Match plate — an assembly of small patterns, mounted on a reinforced, flat board. The drag section is attached to one face. If there is a cope section, it is attached to the opposite face of the board, with corresponding parts in alignment. The match plate is essentially a split pattern with a board between the sections.

A group of small patterns (a **gang**) may be attached to a board of this type by using **gates** to connect the patterns. Gates are channels in the mold, which form a path for the flow of metal.

Parting line — the point at which the cope and drag separate. The parting line intersects the pattern at its widest dimension.

Pattern — a wood, metal, plastic, or plaster model made in one or more parts, from which a sand mold is made for casting the part in molten metal.

Ribs — thin strips of wood, attached to a pattern. Ribs strengthen the casting.

Shrink rules — patternmaker's rules made with graduations scaled larger than those of a standard rule, in accordance with the rate of shrinkage of specified metals. See Topic 11, "Rules" and Topic 156, "Considerations for Laying Out a Pattern."

Tail print — a core print extended to the parting line of the pattern so as to permit withdrawal from the mold.

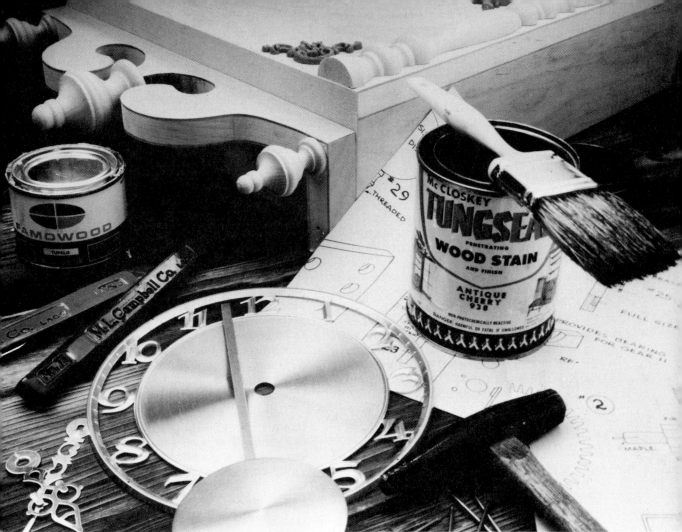

The Woodworker's Store

SECTION EIGHTEEN.

Finishing

Topic 163.

Finishing

Wood finishing is the application of selected materials to wood. These materials include stains, fillers, varnishes, lacquers, paints, enamels, oils, waxes, and transfers. They may be applied by brushing, spraying, dipping, wiping, rolling, or rubbing.

There are numerous reasons for finishing. Wood is a porous, absorbent material. Unfinished, it tends to absorb moisture, fumes, and oils, which cause the wood to shrink, swell, check, warp, and discolor. Wood is also subject to fungi and insects and it burns readily under normal conditions.

Selected finishes can retard or offset these tendencies. Finishes provide a protective coating, which helps to stabilize the condition of wood at the time of its finishing. Thus, the occurrence of radical change in moisture content is reduced. Some finishes serve as preservatives because they deter germs, fungi, and insects. Finishes improve sanitary conditions, and make cleaning of wood easier. Some finishes are fire and chemical resistant. Particular colors are used to suggest in varying degrees the presence and absence of space, weight, mass, heat, and light. Finishes enable artists and woodworkers to create desirable effects, match different kinds of wood, enhance the natural beauty of wood, or conceal its blemishes.

Stains provide transparent coloring that can change or emphasize the natural color of wood.

Sealers are used before paste filling open-grained woods, in order to prevent oils in the filler from soaking into the wood. Sealers are also used after paste filling, to prevent oils from bleeding through the finish. In finishing close-grained woods (softwoods and small-pored hardwoods), sealers are used as a liquid filler.

Paste fillers are used to fill the pores of open-grained woods after sealing.

Varnish gives wood a relatively hard but reasonably elastic finish, depending on the kind and grade. Varnish may be classified as either natural or synthetic. **Natural** gums are derived from plants, insects, and vegetable matter, some of which have been buried for centuries and have fossilized. Practically all modern varnishes, however, contain **synthetic resins.** The name **synthetic varnish** has come to mean a quick-drying, hard, tough material, which produces a film with high resistance to weathering, chemicals, and mechanical wear. Polyurethane is the best-known synthetic-resin varnish.

Shellac, a spirit varnish, is one of the few totally natural finishes in use today. It is derived from the secretions of the lac bug found in India. This finish has good penetration, is easy to apply, and produces a smooth, hard surface. It has poor resistance to water and heat, which limits its use.

Lacquer is a synthetic, transparent, water-resistant finish. It dries very rapidly by evaporation. It is a very popular production finish because of its fast drying time; its resistance to heat, alcohol, and water; and its attractive appearance.

Oil finishes are penetrating finishes that are actually absorbed into the wood. This type of finish gives wood a natural appearance. This finish will not crack, check, or peel, but it has poor moisture resistance.

Waxes are an easily applied surface coating. They are used as a type of rubbed finish on bare wood, as a protection for gum finish, and for providing and maintaining shine.

Paint is an opaque finish, used as a protective coating against the climate and against such things as insects, germs, fungi, water, acids, fire, dirt, and oil. The general properties of a good paint are color consistency, color retention, brushability, durability, package stability, drying speed, gloss retention, covering and leveling ability, and resistance to running, flooding, and sagging. There are also many special-purpose paints, including metallic, crackle- or wrinkle-finish, luminous, plastic, waterproofing, and many others. This group of finishing materials is rapidly changing and improving through industrial research.

Enamel is varnish paint. It is a mixture of varnish and paint pigment. It may be flat, medium-gloss, or high-gloss. Enamels have poor covering qualities and require undercoating. They have most of the other properties of paint and provide a hard, long-wearing surface. They are generally more brittle than paint.

Super finishes are relatively new finishes. These finishes cure by chemical reaction. They are long-lasting, stain resistant, and highly resistant to wear and abrasion.

Most finishing materials are liquid in form and are sold by volume. In the United States, paints and finishes are sold in pints, quarts, and gallons. At present, however, a transition is being made that will involve changing from U.S. Customary measurement to the metric system. This conversion will involve a change in sales units. Thus, what is now sold by the pint (.47 liters) will be sold by the half liter (1.06 pints). Quantities now sold by the quart (.95 liter) will be sold by the liter (1.06 quarts). An amount now sold by the gallon (3.78 liters) will be sold in 5-liter units (1.32 gallons). For more information on metric measure, see Topic 10.

Preparing the Surface for Finishing

Topic 164.

Classification

Leveling, smoothing, and cleaning

Procedure

1. Carefully examine the article to be finished, noting and correcting any defects.
2. If the surface is dented, raise the grain in the following manner: (a) Apply a drop of water to the dent. (b) Place a small cotton pad or absorbent paper soaked in warm water on the dent and allow it to remain until the grain is raised. (c) Touch the pad with a hot soldering copper. This changes the water to steam and causes the wood to swell quickly. See Fig. 18-1.
3. When the dent has been raised as much as possible, or when it is raised above the surface of the wood, sand the surface until it is flat.
4. If there are shallow defects, scrape the surface with a hand scraper until all such defects are removed or are feathered out until they blend with the surface.
5. Remove grease and oil by sponging with naphtha, benzene, or lacquer thinner.

6. Scrape or sand to remove all traces of glue from the surfaces to be finished.
7. Stains that are not removed by sanding may be bleached with oxalic acid or commercial bleaches.
8. Nail holes, checks, open joints, and large defects should be filled with patching material such as stick shellac, plastic wood, glue and sawdust, cabinetmaker's cement,

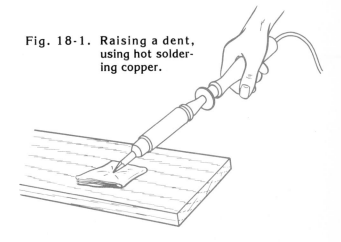

Fig. 18-1. Raising a dent, using hot soldering copper.

or putty. Since patching materials will not accept wood stain, they should match the finished color of the wood. If the defect is large, patch it with an insert of wood.

9. Sand all surfaces, using 120-grit sandpaper and a sandpaper block. Sand with the grain, removing all pencil marks and small scratches.

10. Remove dust from the surfaces and from the pores of the wood by brushing surfaces thoroughly with a medium-stiff brush. Excess dust may be removed with a vacuum or a tack rag. A tack rag may be made by applying turpentine to a damp rag and sprinkling this rag with varnish until it is somewhat sticky.

Standards and Results

- The article to be finished should be free of all previously mentioned defects.
- Patching materials should match the finished color of the wood.
- All pores should be free of dust.
- The surfaces should be smooth but should not have a glazed appearance. Such an appearance is caused by using worn or too fine a grade of sandpaper, and will prevent stain from properly penetrating the surface.

Safety Considerations

- Wear safety glasses when applying finishing materials.

Fig. 18-2. Used rags should be placed in a safety container to minimize potential fire hazard. The cover of the container keeps air out and the legs keep the bottom off the floor so that fire will not spread.

- Naphtha, benzene, and lacquer thinner should be applied in a well-ventilated room, as fumes have a toxic effect. These materials should be stored in a fireproof cabinet.
- Wear rubber gloves when applying oxalic acid and commercial bleaches. Bleach may burn your skin or your clothing, so be very careful to avoid splatters.
- Approved fire extinguishers must be provided in the finishing area.
- Use safety containers for cloths and rags. See Fig. 18-2.

Topic 165.

Bleaches

Classification

Color removers

Composition or Description

Bleaches are acid or alkali solutions. Household bleaches and ammonia work well where a mild solution is needed.

Properties

Bleaches are toxic oxidizing agents that break down the lignin (binding substance between cell walls) on the surface of wood, causing it to become white. Bleaches may be mixed in various proportions to either remove or lighten the color tone of wood. Some experimentation with different types of bleaches may be necessary to achieve satisfactory results.

Uses

Bleach is most often used in preparing an article for a blond finish, where the color tone of the wood is to be made light and even. It is also used to minimize the contrast between heartwood and sapwood and to remove dark stains or blemishes. Bleach is also used in refinishing, to remove or lighten previously applied stains.

Apply bleach by brushing, swabbing, or dripping it on the area where color is to be removed. The solution is flowed onto the surface and left to stand until the desired penetration has occurred. More than one application may be necessary to remove the desired amount of color. If an alkali-type bleach is used, it must be neutralized with an acid solution before it is thoroughly dry. Acid bleaches must be washed off with water. Strong acid bleaches may be neutralized by one ounce of borax, dissolved in a quart of water. See Table 18-1, "Bleach Solutions." Bleaches must always be handled with extreme caution. Wear goggles, rubber gloves, and a rubber apron at all times when you are using bleaches.

Oil or grease on the surface should be removed with acetone, benzine, or alcohol before bleaching.

Table 18-1
Bleach Solutions

Formula	Application	Neutralization	Notes
4 lb. sodium hydroxide in 10 gal. water with 28%-35% hydrogen peroxide	Brush on sodium hydroxide solution, dry 30 min., then coat evenly with hydrogen peroxide, let dry	Wash with cold water, spray with 1 lb. oxalic acid or 1 lb. acetic acid dissolved in 10 gal. water. Let set 15 min., rinse with water, dry. Sand to remove raised grain	Can be mixed as one solution but has a short life. Two-solution application is most effective
One volume 20 oz. flake sodium hydroxide in 7 parts water & 9 oz. Epsom salts in 1 pt. water. Two volumes 28% hydrogen peroxide	Apply as in above. Caution: Epsom salts must be added to the caustic solution very carefully	Same as above	Epsom salts help stabilize peroxide in wood with high mineral content
4 – 32 oz. oxalic acid in 1 gal. hot water or 1 gal. denatured alcohol	Apply desired concentration until bleached effect is obtained	Wash with hot water. Neutralize with borax (3 oz. in 1 gal. water) Rinse with hot water, dry and sand	Alcohol mixture has stronger bleaching effect than water mixture
4 lb. oxalic acid and 4 lb. sodium hypophosphite in 1 gal. hot water	Apply even coat until desired bleaching is obtained	Neutralize with borax (4 oz. to 1 gal. water) rinse with hot water, dry and sand	Used for removal of mineral streaks, dark spots, and iron stains in oak
6 oz. sodium bisulfite in 1 gal. water 8 oz. oxalic acid in 1 gal. water	Brush on sodium bisulfite solution. Dry, then coat evenly with oxalic acid solution, let dry	Wash with hot water Neutralize acid with borax (3 oz. in 1 gal. water). Rinse with hot water	Bleach for walnut, not as powerful as first formula
5% sodium hypochlorite diluted (1/2 pt. in 1 gal. water)	Apply evenly until desired bleaching is obtained	Wash surface with water, dry and sand	Bleach for light blue stain discoloration. Not for use on oak or yellow poplar
1 oz. potassium permanganate in 1 gal. water, 3 oz. sodium bisulfite in 1 gal. water	Apply potassium permanganate. While still wet, apply bisulfite solution	Apply light water rinse, dry and sand	Bleach for French Hugenot walnut finish

Woodworking and Furniture Digest

The bleaching solutions and the wash coats of water will raise the grain. Sanding must be done in preparation for the finish coats. This sanding is done only after the surface has dried for at least 48 hours. (Since sanding dust may be toxic, a mask should be worn.)

Market Analysis

1. Acid powder or crystals are sold by the ounce or pound.
2. Commercial bleaches are available in two-part containers, in either liquid or powder form.
3. Household bleaches are sold by the quart, half gallon, and gallon.

Maintenance

Storing

Any bleach neutralizer must be mixed in a glass container. Before storage, such a container must be labelled, "POISON."

Safety Considerations

- Wear goggles, a rubber apron, and rubber gloves when using bleaches.
- If bleaching solutions come in contact with the skin, the affected area(s) should be treated immediately with a corresponding neutralizer. See Table 18-1, "Bleach Solutions."

Topic 166.

Paintbrushes

Classification

Bristle applicators for finishing materials

Application

Principle of Operation

The bristles of the **paintbrush** hold the finishing material, using the principles of adhesion and cohesion. The finishing material is transferred to the surface being finished by brushing with a back-and-forth motion.

Kinds and Uses

1. **Flat brushes** are used for general-purpose finishing. The common flat brush is available in sizes ranging from 1/2" to 4". **Sizes given for flat and oval brushes refer to width of the bristle area.** Some special-purpose brushes do not fall within these limits. (For example, artists' brushes may be smaller than 1/2", while calamine brushes may be as wide as 8".) Some flat brushes are manufactured by arranging the bristles to form a chisel-shaped end. These are used for enameling and varnishing. Another type of flat brush is made with the bristles arranged in a slanting ferrule so that one edge appears longer than the other. This brush, called a **sash tool,** is commonly used for painting window sash. Sash tools range in size from 1" to 2-5/8".

2. **Oval brushes** are used for applying paint and varnish on sash or trim. The shape permits more bristles to come in contact with the surface at any given time. This gives better spreading and a longer flow of the finishing material. Oval sash brushes range in size from 7/16" to 2", and oval trim brushes and varnish brushes range in size from 1-7/8" to 2-3/4".

3. **Round brushes** have characteristics similar to those of oval brushes. They range in diameter from 11/16" to 1-1/16". Round trim brushes range in diameter from 1-7/8" to 2-5/8".

A polyurethane sponge, shaped like a paintbrush and attached to a handle, is a good substitute for a paintbrush in painting trim or sash or in applying stain.

Principal Parts and Function of Each

1. **Bristles** are set in rubber, glue, or cement. They hold the finishing material and permit smooth application.

    A good paintbrush will have tapered bristles that have flagged (split) ends. The flagged ends give the bristles greater paint-holding capacity and provide a soft edge for smooth paint application. The taper of the bristles allows for easy flexing at the brush tip while providing adequate support at the heel. A brush that is too stiff will not easily smooth out the finishing material and will leave brush marks on the surface.

    Bristles may be made of natural hair, nylon, or polyester.

    a. **Natural bristles** are best suited for oil-base paints, alkyds, varnish, and shellac. These bristles are made from hogshair, horsehair, or the hair of other animals such as skunks, badgers, minks, genets, Siberian squirrels, and camels.
    b. **Nylon bristles** are best suited for water-base finishes, vinyl, acrylic, and latex paints. Natural bristles tend to go limp in these types of finishes.
    c. **Polyester bristles** are more flexible than nylon bristles and may be used with either oil- or water-base finishes. Both polyester and nylon bristles are much more durable and long-lasting than natural bristles.

2. **Handles** are usually made of plastic, birch, or maple, but in larger brushes, plastic or softwood is used to reduce weight. Wooden handles are usually coated with a hard finish to prevent damage from finishing materials and solvents.

3. Metal or leather **ferrules** fasten the bristles securely to the handle. Together with the handle, the ferrule helps to determine the shape of the brush.

4. The **filler strip** is made of wood or hard rubber. It is used to separate the bristles, leaving a hollow space in the center of the brush. This center space makes the brush able to hold more paint and gives greater flexibility to the bristles. On large brushes, more than one filler strip may be used.

Maintenance

Breaking In New Brushes

A new paintbrush should be soaked in linseed oil for approximately 12 hours to prepare

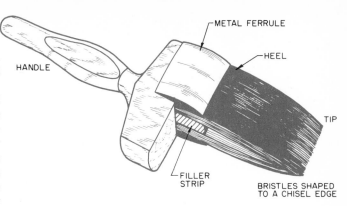

Fig. 18-3. Cutaway view of a paintbrush.

the bristles for use. Paint pigments cling to bristles that have not been treated in this way, making cleaning more difficult.

Cleaning

1. Clean paintbrushes by washing them in the solvent of the finishing material used. Use turpentine or mineral spirits (or even kerosene) to clean brushes used in oil paint, oil stain, and varnish. Use alcohol to clean

Fig. 18-4. Wrapping a clean brush for storage.

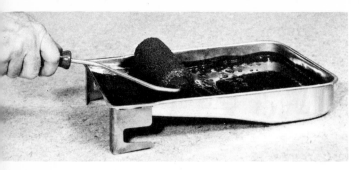

Fig. 18-5. Paint rollers are used instead of brushes for large, flat surfaces.

brushes that were used to apply shellac. Use lacquer thinner to clean brushes that were used to apply lacquer, and use water to clean brushes that were used to apply water stains, latex-based paints, and other water-soluble materials.

2. Some finishers complete the cleaning process by washing all brushes with soap and warm water.

3. Commercial brush cleaners may be used to clean brushes.

Storing

Brushes should be wrapped in folds of absorbent paper after cleaning. This preserves the shape of the bristles and prevents the entrance of foreign materials, Fig. 18-4. Brushes should be laid flat for storage. They may be stored for short periods of time in a brush keeper or may be wrapped in folds of waxed paper to prevent the solvent from evaporating.

Topic 167.

Paint

Classification

Protective opaque coloring agent

Composition or Description

Paints are made of four major ingredients — pigments, vehicles, thinners, and driers. **Pigments** provide paint with its opaque and color characteristics. **Vehicles** provide the suspension fluid for the pigments and act to bind the pigments to the surface being painted. **Thinners** are used to regulate the viscosity (flow quality) and penetration of the paint. **Driers** increase the paint's drying speed.

Paint is classified as either **oil-base** or **latex** (water-base). The major difference between oil and latex paints is the vehicle used. Oil-base paints use oil as the vehicle, while latex paints use a latex vehicle. Latex consists of water mixed with small particles of resin.

There are two types of latex paint — **polyvinyl acetate** and **acrylic**. Both types are film-forming and pigment-binding. Water is the vehicle of both types of latex paint.

Properties

Oil paints produce an opaque, colored finish ranging from flat to glossy. The surface of oil paints may be anywhere from hard and brittle to tough and elastic. Because oil paints are less porous than latex paints, they are water resistant. As a result, they give greater protection against moisture entering the wood than do latex paints. Equipment used for applying oil paints must be cleaned with brush cleaner or solvent, then washed with warm water and soap.

Latex paints have excellent color retention and a tough, durable finish that resists alkali and water. They have no odor, are fast-drying, and mildew resistant, and can be easily applied with a brush or roller or by spraying. Latex paints do not, however, have good adhesion to smooth surfaces, such as those previously painted with gloss paints. Equipment may be cleaned in cold water. This must be done immediately after use or every four hours, whichever is first.

In a fire, **acrylic-latex fire-retardant paint** will form a foam, which acts as insulation to the combustible surface underneath. This type of paint has excellent covering properties. It may be applied by either brush, roller, or spray. Thinning is not normally required, as this paint is applied while of the consistency of heavy cream. It may be thinned with water, if necessary. This paint dries in 30 minutes and may be recoated in two to three hours. It may be used at temperatures as low as 10° C (50° F).

Acrylic-latex primer helps prevent the cracking and checking that occurs as a result of weathering and moisture on plywood or solid stock. This primer is a semitransparent yellow that cannot be tinted. It may be topcoated with either oil or latex paints, and may be applied either by brush or roller or may be sprayed at temperatures of 10° C (50° F) or above. It dries in 20 minutes and may be painted over in two hours. Equipment may be cleaned with soap and warm water.

Uses

Paints are used to decorate, preserve, and protect wood, metal, and other materials. Paints may be applied for cleanliness, to make objects match or harmonize with their surroundings, and to make the material more durable. Oil paints and latex paints may be used on either interior or exterior surfaces, depending on the composition of the paint. Generally speaking, oil-base paints are more durable and weather resistant than latex paints.

Interior paint may be used on plaster, woodwork, wallpaper, wallboard, drywall, brick, and plywood. It may be applied over flat or semigloss paints.

Exterior paint may be used on shingles, clapboard, exterior wood surfaces, masonry, stucco, concrete, brick, asbestos, galvanized iron, and aluminum. It may be applied with either a brush, spray, or roller.

Market Analysis

Oil paints may be purchased in the following finish types: flat, semigloss or eggshell, and high-gloss. Oil paints are also available in luminous colors and in metallic colors such as aluminum and bronze.

Latex paints are available in flat, semigloss, and gloss finishes.

Sales Units

These paints are available in pint, quart, gallon, 5-gallon, and 55-gallon containers.

Maintenance

Storing

Paints should be stored in airtight metal containers. Extremes in temperature should be avoided. Containers that have been opened should be tightly sealed. After the container has been sealed, it may either be shaken or stored upside down to help prevent a "skin" from forming on the surface. Store paints in containers of the approximate size for the quantity and label the container.

Preserving

To preserve oil paint, pour a thin film of linseed or tung oil over the surface. For latex paint, follow the same procedure, using water instead of oil. Another method of preserving paint is to seal the top of the container with melted wax.

Reconditioning

If paint has oxidized in the can and a film has formed, this skin should be removed from the paint. Paint that contains undissolved particles is termed "lousy" in the trade and should be strained through nylon or cheesecloth. Paint colors may be changed by adding universal tinting colors.

Enamel

Topic 168.

Classification

Opaque coloring agent

Composition or Description

There are four types of **enamel:** varnish enamel, lacquer enamel, epoxy enamel, and alkyd enamel.

Varnish and lacquer enamels are clear finishes to which universal tinting colors have been added in order to make the finish opaque.

Epoxy two-component enamels consist of one-third catalyst and two-thirds pigment base. This type of enamel is mixed by stirring and is allowed to stand one hour before use. It must be used within 12 hours of mixing. Epoxy ready-to-use enamels do not require a catalyst. They are available in a great variety of colors and may be applied by either brush or spray. These enamels should be applied over a primer.

Alkyd enamels are made of universal tinting colors suspended in alkyd resin and thinned with mineral spirits. A drier is added to speed oxidation.

Properties

Enamels range in finish from flat to high-gloss. They are generally more durable than paint and have good adhesion qualities. Enamels are also resistant to abrasion, acids, alkalies, alcohol, detergents, water, waxes, and corrosion. All types of enamel are heat resistant up to 121° C (250° F).

Varnish enamels dry in eight to 12 hours. Lacquer and epoxy enamels dry in two hours. Epoxy two-component enamels may be recoated in six hours. Regular epoxy enamels require 18 hours between coats. Alkyd enamels dry to the touch in two to three hours and dry hard in eight hours.

All enamels should be applied in a well-ventilated area maintained at a temperature between 21° and 27° C (70° to 80° F). Enamel should be flowed onto the surface and should not show brush marks, laps, or sags. Enamel should be of sufficient body to hide the base coat or material.

Uses

Enamel may be used on walls, woodwork, wallboard, brick, plaster, masonry, steel, aluminum, and galvanized iron. On wood it covers more efficiently if applied over a primer. Alkyd enamels may be used on lawn furniture, playground equipment, and boats.

Market Analysis

Enamels are available in semigloss or high-gloss finish.

Sales Units

Enamels are available in pint, quart, gallon, 5-gallon, and 55 gallon containers. Two-component epoxies must be purchased in two packages.

Maintenance

Storing

Enamel should be stored in an airtight metal container at a temperature of about 21° C (70° F).

Topic 169.

Oil Stain

Classification

Transparent coloring agent

Composition or Description

Pigment stains are made with color ground in raw linseed oil, a solvent, and japan drier. Solvents used include turpentine, linseed oil, benzene, and mineral spirits.

Preservative stains are made of pigments (chrome green, red and brown iron oxides) and creosote. Linseed oil, turpentine, benzene, and japan drier are often added.

Penetrating oil stains, or volatile oil stains, are made from oil-soluble coal-tar colors and a solvent (turpentine, naphtha, benzene, or benzol).

Properties

Oil stain is the easiest type of stain to apply. It does not raise the grain of the wood and, if properly wiped, does not show laps and streaks.

Oil stains are especially recommended for staining to be done by beginners.

Oil stain is a slow-drying coloring agent with limited penetrating qualities (particularly when used on hard woods). Oil stain possesses the following general properties:

a. Its coloring varies somewhat, depending on the consistency of the stain. It also varies according to the number of applications and the ability of the stain to penetrate the wood.

b. Its color changes in drying but is restored when finish is applied. Penetrating oil stains are easy to apply using a rag or brush, but they do not provide permanent color (they fade in the sun).

c. It must have a sealer coat to prevent bleeding.

Uses

Oil stains preserve the wood and bring out its beauty without raising the grain. They produce a uniform tone or color.

1. Pigment oil stains are used on furniture to blend colors and to give highlight effects. These stains have a tendency to mask the beauty of the grain.

2. Penetrating oil stains work better on soft woods than on hard woods because they can penetrate deeper into the wood. They are also used to color paste wood fillers.

3. Preservative oil stains are used to protect exterior wood surfaces such as siding, porch floors, fencing, and any wood surface in contact with the ground.

Market Analysis

Sales Units

Oil stain may be purchased ready-mixed or the ingredients may be purchased and mixed as required. It is available in half pints, pints, quarts, half gallons, and gallons.

Maintenance

Storing

1. Containers must be airtight. Waxed paper, spread over the top of the can before the cover is pressed into place, will prevent air from getting into the can and will make the top easier to remove when the can of oil stain is next used.

2. Oil stains should not be stored in strong light.

Applying Oil Stain

Topic 170.

Classification

Staining

Procedure

1. The surface to be stained should be clean, smooth, dry, and free of oil, wax, and glue.

2. Select a suitable brush. Almost any clean brush may be used but one with moderately soft bristles is preferred, especially when using penetrating oil stains. A piece of lint-free rag may also be used.

3. Dip about one-fourth to one-half the length of the bristles into the stain.

4. Brush the stain on the wood. Start at the bottom of a vertical surface and work up to prevent runs. Work from the least conspicuous to the most conspicuous part. Oil stain may be applied in any direction because the wood will absorb only limited amounts of the colored oil and the excess that remains on the surface may be wiped off without leaving laps or streaks.

5. Allow the stain to set from a few minutes to 20 minutes (follow the manufacturer's recommendations for the brand used). Using a soft, lint-free, absorbent material, wipe off the stain in the direction of the

grain. This removes the excess stain before it dries on the surface, muddying or hiding the grain of the wood.

6. The manufacturers of some penetrating oil stains (blond and modern finishes) recommend that these stains be applied evenly and lightly and that they be permitted to dry on the surface, partially obscuring the grain of the wood to give uniformity of color.

7. Normally, successive applications of oil stain will cause no noticeable change in color. This is not true, however, if the preceding coat has been washed with naphtha or carbon tetrachloride to permit penetration of the next coat of stain.

8. Oil stains should be permitted to dry at about 21° C (70° F) for at least 18 hours before other finishes are applied.

9. It is advisable to apply a sealer coat of shellac prior to varnishing a surface that

has been oil stained. This prevents the color from lifting or bleeding through.

10. Oil stains may also be applied by spraying or dipping.

Standards and Results

- Oil stain should be rubbed off evenly to prevent streaks.
- Stained surfaces should have a clear color tone. They should not have a muddy appearance.

Safety Considerations

- Wear safety glasses when applying stain.
- Rags used to wipe off excess stain are highly flammable. Always deposit them in a self-closing safety can for disposal as soon as possible after use.

Topic 171.

Water Stain

Classification

Transparent dye

Composition or Description

Water stain consists mainly of aniline (or coal-tar powder) dissolved in water.

Properties

Water stain is a fast-drying coloring agent with excellent penetrating qualities. Its color does not fade appreciably in strong light and it will not bleed through lacquer or varnish. Water stain raises the grain on wood that has

not been sponged, sized, and sanded prior to the application of stain.

Uses

Water stain is used to bring out the beauty of wood grain, to secure more uniform tone or color, and to color wood to harmonize with other finishes for the purposes of matching, contrast, or imitation.

Market Analysis

1. Colors can be purchased in tablet or powder form. Powdered water stain is sold by the ounce or by the pound.

2. Water stain is the cheapest stain for school shop use.

Maintenance

Cleaning

After mixing powdered color with hot water, filter or strain the solution to remove undissolved powder and impurities.

Storing

1. Powders should be stored in a moisture-proof container.
2. Solutions should be stored in covered glass or earthenware containers. This is necessary both to prevent evaporation and to prevent the chemical reaction that would occur if stain were placed in a metal container.

Reconditioning

1. The color may be changed by adding water-soluble powder of the same type as the stain.
2. A shade may be changed by adding water-soluble powder of another color or by adding more water. If powder is added, it must be of the same type as the stain.

Applying Water Stain — Brush Method

Topic 172.

Classification

Staining

Procedure

Water stain is best applied by spraying, but good results may be obtained by brushing or by dipping. Water stain is difficult to apply because of its thin consistency. It tends to drip and run, producing dark streaks.

Preparation

1. The surface to be finished should be clean, smooth, dry, and free of oil and wax.
2. When water stain is applied to wood, it tends to raise the grain, producing a fuzzy surface. This condition may be minimized by one of the following methods:
   a. Apply glue size to the surface to be stained. This raises the grain and stiffens the raised fibers so they may be cut smooth by light sanding. This sanding is done after the surface has dried thoroughly. A glue size may be mixed by blending a tablespoon of animal glue in a quart of warm water.
   b. Sponge the surface to be stained with water and allow to dry. This raises the grain. Apply a wash coat of shellac (seven parts alcohol to one part 4-pound-cut shellac) and allow to dry. This stiffens the fibers so they may be cut smooth by sanding. Either of these operations decreases penetration and makes a smoother surface for staining.
3. Sand lightly with 120-grit sandpaper to smooth the stiffened, raised fibers.
4. Dissolve aniline or coal-tar powder in warm water. Determine the approximate amount of water needed. Slowly add small portions of the selected powder or powders until the desired shade is obtained. Several light coats of water stain are better than one heavy coat because successive coats color the wood more uniformly and laps and streaks are less noticeable. Vinegar may be added to secure deeper penetration in hard woods. Ammonia may be used for this same purpose on woods that do not contain tannic acid. Test for color on a scrap piece of the same type of wood as that used in the project.
5. Select a brush with moderately stiff, clean bristles. It is difficult to apply water stain evenly with a soft brush, particularly on open-grained woods.

Applying the Stain

In staining, hidden areas and inaccessible parts are stained first and the most conspicuous parts are stained last. This will make handling easier and will make it easier to check results.

1. Dip about half to two-thirds the length of the bristles into the stain. Apply the stain to the **least conspicuous** part of the article first. (For example, bottom, back, and underneath portions are stained first. The top or front is stained last, depending on which will be seen most.) To prevent runs, start from the base of a vertical surface.

2. End grain absorbs more stain than surfaces and edges. This results in a darker shade on the end grain, a condition that frequently occurs in staining sapwood. Therefore, in order to secure an even tone, it is necessary to do one of the following:
   a. Sponge sapwood or end grain with water and then apply water stain while the wood is still moist.
   b. Glue size sapwood or end grain before applying water stain.
   c. Dilute the stain used on sapwood or end grain.

3. Apply water stain in the direction of the wood grain, working quickly so that the edge or end of one stroke does not dry before the next stroke is applied. Tipping the working surface of the object slightly permits the stain to flow to the lower edge of the brush stroke, thus keeping the working edge wet until the next stroke is applied. It is advisable to brush from the bottom upward to prevent runs and streaks.

4. Take care not to let the stain run over edges or onto the surfaces, as streaks will be seen in the stained surface. Care should also be taken to prevent the stain from dripping from the brush onto the work.

Standards and Results

• The article being stained should be uniform in color. There should be no noticeable difference in the color of ends, heartwood, and sapwood unless highlights are desired.
• There should be no holidays (unfinished areas), brush marks, or laps in the stained surface.
• The stained surface should be reasonably smooth.

Table 18-2
Selection of Wood Stain

Stain	Advantages	Disadvantages	Application
Pigment Oil Stain	Colorfast Used to imitate maple, mahogany, & walnut Non grain-raising	Tends to hide grain pattern May affect drying quality and adhesiveness of succeeding coats	Brushing Spraying Dipping
Penetrating Oil Stain	Non grain-raising Good color tone and permanence Dries quickly	Tendency to bleed into top coat if not well sealed Retards drying of finish coat	Brushing Spraying Dipping
Preservative Oil Stain	Resists decay Some types water repellant	Strong odor Dries slowly Not used on furniture	Brushing Spraying Dipping
Water Stain	Uniform, rich color Excellent color retention Non-bleeding	Raises grain Requires sponging, sizing, and sanding before staining Requires sanding and sealing after staining	Brushing Spraying
Spirit Stain	Bright colors Quick-drying	Color has tendency to fade with exposure to light Slight grain-raising Tendency to bleed	Brushing Spraying

Sealer

Topic 173.

Classification

Transparent gum finish

Composition or Description

A **sealer** is a penetrating finish that preserves the natural beauty of the wood, helps to control grain raising, increases moisture resistance, and prevents fillers and stains from bleeding into the finish coat. One coat completely soaks into the wood, leaving little or no surface film.

Sealers can be lacquer, varnish, or shellac type, and can be thinned up to 50%.

Properties

Sealers dry quickly (in two hours), do not darken wood, do not attract dust, and do not make surfaces slippery. They make an excellent base for all types of varnish, including polyurethane. When sanded, they do not gum up or load the sandpaper. Sealers are heat resistant up to 60° C (140° F). They minimize unsightly color streaks on the grain of fir plywood, and reduce the tendency of grain to show through paint or enamel. Most sealers can be tinted with universal tinting colors. One of the features of sealers is that they can be sanded easily.

Uses

Sealers may be used as a base for other types of gum finishes, on all types of interior finish, such as woodwork, floors, furniture, and paneling. They may also be used as a clear gum finish if several coats are applied. They are also used on metal to prevent oxidation and on concrete to seal the surface.

While there is some flexibility in the use of sealers, all sealers cannot be used under all top coats. It is important that the sealer be compatible with the finish coat. It is advisable to follow the manufacturer's recommendations for the type of sealer to go under a given finish.

Sanding sealers seal the surface of woods, permitting greater and smoother buildup of finish.

Market Analysis

Sizes

Sealers are available in quart, gallon, and 5-gallon containers.

Kinds

The three basic kinds of sealers are lacquer sealers, varnish sealers, and shellac sealers.

Maintenance

Sealers should be stored in airtight metal containers and should be kept at approximately 21° C (70° F).

Paste Wood Filler

Topic 174.

Classification

Paste for filling pores of open-grained wood

Composition or Description

Oil-base paste wood filler is made of silex, linseed oil, japan drier, and turpentine. Color is sometimes added for various shades. It is easy to rub off because of its lubricating qualities. Synthetic-resin base filler is quick-drying, but is hard to rub off the surface.

Properties

Deposits of filler material dry in the pores of open-grained woods, filling them and producing a smooth surface for shellac, varnish, or lacquer.

Uses

Wood filler is used to fill the pores of oak, ash, chestnut, hickory, mahogany, walnut, and other open-grained woods. This is done to produce a smooth surface for finishing. A two-toned effect may be obtained by using a filler contrasting in color to the final finish.

Market Analysis

Grades

Paste wood fillers are graded according to (a) their degree of fineness, (b) whether they are colored or natural, and (c) whether they are fast- or slow-drying.

Sales Units

Ready-mixed wood filler is available in half pints, pints, quarts, and gallons.

Formula for Oil-Base Filler

- 2 qts. linseed oil (boiled linseed oil is recommended)
- 1 qt. japan drier
- 1/2 pt. turpentine
- Enough silex to produce a thick paste

Dilute this mixture with turpentine until it is a creamy consistency.

Note: Silex should be suspended in oil several weeks in advance of use.

Paste filler can be colored by adding colors that have been ground in oil or by using universal tinting colors. Use the following colors to obtain walnut and mahogany shades:

Walnut —Vandyke brown or burnt umber
Mahogany —burnt sienna, rose-pink, or Venetian red

Maintenance

1. Store in airtight glass or metal containers.
2. Containers that have been opened should be tightly covered.
3. Homemade fillers should be made well in advance of actual use and should be stored until the ingredients have properly mixed.
4. Filler may be softened or thinned by adding turpentine or linseed oil to oil-base filler and a synthetic-resin vehicle to the alkyd type.

Topic 175.

Applying Paste Wood Filler

Classification

Filling of pores

Procedure

Applying Oil-Vehicle Paste Wood Filler

1. Make sure the surface is smooth.
2. Clean the wood with a stiff brush, a vacuum, or a tack rag.
3. If the paste filler is too thick, it should be thinned with turpentine to a creamy consistency. (See Topic 174, "Paste Wood Filler.")

4. Apply paste filler by brushing evenly with or across the grain.
5. When filler becomes dull-looking (indicating that it has begun to set), rub it with a piece of burlap or similar material. This rubbing is done across the grain to prevent filler from being lifted out of the wood pores, Fig. 18-6. Some finishers follow this step by rubbing with the heel of the hand to compact the filler in the pores.
6. Do final rubbing with a clean, soft cloth to remove all surplus oil and filler.
7. Clean out all corners with a pointed hardwood stick.

8. Allow filler to dry for at least 12 hours. (Some fillers, particularly colored fillers, may take as long as 48 hours to dry.)

9. If the pores are not completely filled, a second coat of filler may be applied. This second coat may be thinned if the pores are small or need little additional buildup.

10. When the filler is dry, the surface should be sanded lightly with 120-grit sandpaper, if necessary.

Fig. 18-6. Filler should be rubbed across the grain.

Standards and Results

- Pores should be completely filled, and the surface should be smooth and even.
- Colored fillers accent the natural grain of the wood.
- Unless they have been stained darker color, oak, limba (Korina®), and ash are filled with a natural paste filler.
- The surface should be clear.
- All corners should be clean.

Safety Considerations

- Wear safety glasses when applying finishing materials.
- Liquids used in paste filler are flammable and should be kept away from open flame.
- Material used to wipe off excess filler should be placed in a safety can after use and should be disposed of as soon as possible.
- Apply fillers in a well-ventilated room.

Table 18-3
Selection of Finish

Finish	Use	Advantages & Disadvantages
Shellac	Sealer for knots and pitch pockets. Finish for paneling and furniture other than tabletops, chair seats and backs	Good sealer, dries quickly Not waterproof
Oleoresinous Varnish Short Oil (Cabinet Rubbing)	Furniture, musical instruments	Dries quickly, rubs or polishes well Poor water resistance
Medium Oil (Floor Varnish)	General purpose, floors	Dries quickly, wears well
Long Oil (Spar Varnish)	Boats, exterior use	Tough, waterproof; Slow-drying
Polyurethane Varnish	Furniture, paneling, boats, floors	Tough, waterproof, wear resistant, fast-drying Hard to touch up
Acrylic Varnish	Furniture, paneling	Non yellowing, odorless, good abrasion resistance; Difficult to spray
Catalyzed Synthetic Varnish	Furniture, floors, paneling	Water, alcohol, & detergent proof Must be used within 8 hrs of mixing
Lacquer	Furniture, paneling, metal	Fast-drying; rubs well; water, heat, alcohol resistant; Toxic fumes; doesn't have much body, needs many coats
Catalyzed Synthetic Lacquer	Furniture, paneling	Wear resistant; water, alcohol & detergent proof; Toxic fumes
Epoxy Clear Finish	Furniture, floors, metal, concrete, brick	Fast-drying, waterproof, hard
Epoxy Enamels	Wood, metal, concrete, brick	Quick-drying, waterproof, hard
Latex Emulsion Paint	Interior walls, woodwork, brick, plaster, plywood	Odorless, quick-drying, elastic, easy to clean up brushes
Oil Paints and Enamels	Interior and exterior walls, toys, floors, and furniture	Covers well, wide range of hardness and gloss, durable; Slow-drying
Epoxy Paint	Wood, metal, concrete, and brick	Wear-resistant finish
Rubbed Oil Finish Linseed Oil & Tung Oil	Tabletops, gunstocks	Not affected by water, alcohol, or heat; easily applied and easily restored

Table 18-4
Finishes and Solvents

Finish	Solvent
Oil paint and enamel	Turpentine or mineral spirits
Latex paint	Water
Epoxy	None
Oil stain	Turpentine or mineral spirits
Water stain	Water
Spirit stain	Denatured alcohol
Paste filler	Turpentine or mineral spirits
Shellac	Alcohol
Oleoresinous varnish	Turpentine or mineral spirits
Polyurethane varnish	Mineral spirits
Water reducible varnish	Water
Lacquer	Lacquer thinner
Catalyzed synthetic lacquer	None
Catalyzed synthetic varnish	None

Topic 176.

Shellac

Classification

Spirit varnish

Composition or Description

Shellac is composed of denatured alcohol and gum shellac.

Properties

Shellac dries dust-free in a few minutes and hardens to a pleasing luster. It can be rubbed to a fine finish, does not scratch white, and, if damaged, can be easily repaired. Moisture causes it to turn white and heat softens it. Orange shellac is more elastic and longer wearing than white shellac. Some finishers maintain that orange shellac has a special quality of bringing out the tone of dark woods such as walnut and mahogany. White shellac darkens when exposed to strong light, air, or unlined metal containers. Shellac prevents oils and sap from bleeding through finish.

Uses

Shellac is used as a finish on furniture, floors, and interior work. It is used as a sealer to prevent oils, stains, and sap from bleeding through other types of finish. It is also used as a liquid filler. Shellac is used in the manufacture of playing cards, sealing wax, pencils, shoe polish, and numerous other articles. It is used in straw, felt, and wool hats. **Stick shellac** is used as a patching material.

Market Analysis

Shapes

Shellac is sold in flake, powder, liquid, and stick form.

Grades

Shellac is classified according to the amount of shellac gum dissolved in one gallon of alcohol. Four pounds of shellac gum dissolved in one gallon of alcohol is known as **4-pound cut.** Four-pound cut is the most common shellac sold.

Kinds

1. **Orange shellac** is partially refined shellac, dissolved in alcohol. It is used where color is desired or not objectionable.
2. **White shellac** is bleached shellac gum, dissolved in alcohol. The result is a very light-colored shellac.
3. **Colored shellac** contains colors soluble in alcohol, added to the shellac to produce the required color.
4. **De-waxed shellac** is shellac with the wax removed. This process produces a shellac that is perfectly clear.
5. **Stick shellac** is a hard stick of shellac. It is available in various shades for filling defects in wood. The shellac is softened with an alcohol torch and smoothed with a knife.

Sales Units

Liquid shellac can be bought in 2-, 3-, 4-, 5- and 6-pound cut. Shellac can also be bought by the pound and in sticks. Liquid shellac is available in half pints, pints, quarts, gallons, and in 5-gallon drums.

Maintenance

1. It is recommended that shellac be stored in an airtight wood container, a lead-lined can, or a glass container. Shellac should be protected from light.
2. Poor drying will result when white shellac is kept longer than one year and orange shellac is kept more than two years.
3. Do not pour used shellac back into the new mixture.

Varnish

Topic 177.

Classification

Transparent gum finishing material

Composition or Description

There are four types of varnish: oil varnish, polyurethane varnish, acrylic varnish, and spirit varnish.

Oil varnishes are manufactured by dissolving fossil gums or resins in oil, turpentine or mineral spirits, and driers. The percentage of oil in varnish has a marked effect on its properties. Varnish that has a high percentage of oil, such as spar varnish, is classed as **long-oil varnish.** Long-oil varnish is highly resistant to water and alcohol and forms a fairly elastic film. Varnish that has a small amount of oil, such as cabinet rubbing varnish, is classed as a **short-oil varnish.** Short-oil varnish rubs well but is quite brittle. **Medium-oil varnish,** such as floor varnish, is an all-purpose varnish. It is reasonably tough and elastic.

Polyurethane varnish is a synthetic varnish, made from polymers and resins thinned with mineral spirits. It is moisture curing and is oil-free.

Acrylic varnish is water-white (colorless). It contains acrylic-resin glycols, mineral spirits, and water.

Spirit varnishes are made of gums or resins, dissolved in volatile (quick-evaporating) solvents such as alcohol or turpentine. They dry quickly through evaporation of the solvent and provide an attractive but less-than-durable finish. Shellac is the most common spirit varnish and is discussed in detail in Topic 176, "Shellac."

Properties

1. Oil varnish has good durability and hardness. It is transparent, heat resistant, and moisture resistant. Its drying time varies from 45 minutes to 48 hours although four-hour varnish is most commonly used. Oil varnish may be applied either with a brush or by spraying.
2. Polyurethane varnish is a very tough, hard, flexible finish. It has superior resistance to

chipping and abrasion. It also resists solvents, detergents, acids, alcohol, and water. It dries to the touch in 20 minutes, is hard in four to five hours, and requires no sealer. It is the only transparent sealer or finish that can be used over polyethylene glycol 1000, a wood stabilizer. To cure properly, it must be used when the relative humidity is between 30% and 90%. Used in another humidity range, the finish may bubble.

3. Acrylic varnish is a non-yellowing, clear finish that dries in two hours, has little odor, and has good abrasion resistance. It must be used at a temperature above 10° C (50° F) and should not be used in drafty areas. It can be thinned by adding a small quantity of water (a half cup per gallon) and may be tinted by adding up to 1.6 ounces of universal tinting color per gallon.

   Tools and equipment may be cleaned with warm soapy water immediately after use. Although acrylic varnish is water resistant, it should not be used where it will be subject to long periods of contact with water or detergents.

   Both the flow and the leveling ability of acrylic varnish are excellent providing the film is not overbrushed. A full coat of this varnish should be flowed on and quickly leveled. Brush the freshly applied varnish into the coated areas and always maintain a wet edge.

Uses

1. Oil varnish is used as a finish on furniture, floors, woodwork, boats, and musical instruments; as an insulator for electrical conductors; and as a vehicle for artists' oil colors.
2. Polyurethane varnish is used on furniture, woodwork, boats, and floors.
3. Acrylic varnish is used as a primer and finish on all interior finishes except floors. It may be applied over stains, fillers, and other gum finishes.

Market Analysis

Grades and Kinds

1. Oil varnish — rubbing, spar, floor, mixing, flat, and spraying
2. Polyurethane varnish — clear gloss and semigloss
3. Acrylic varnish — gloss and satin

Sales Units

All types of varnish are available in half pints, pints, quarts, gallons, and 5-gallon and 55-gallon drums.

Maintenance

Storing

Containers must be airtight and should be stored in a warm place. For use, small portions of varnish should be poured into a small container. Leftover varnish should not be poured back into the supply. To prevent air bubbles, varnish containers should not be shaken and care should be taken in pouring. When varnish is in use, keep it away from open flame.

Reconditioning

Varnish that is not clean (called "lousy" in the trade) should be strained through lint-free cheesecloth or nylon. To make these fabrics lint-free, dip them in a very thin solution of shellac or glue and allow the cloth to dry before straining the varnish.

Topic 178.

Applying Varnish — Brush Method

Classification

Flowing and spreading to cover a surface

Procedure

Preparation

1. The varnish, the surface to be finished, and the work room should all be at a temperature of approximately 21° C (70° F).

2. The room should be reasonably dust-free. If it is not, the dust should be settled by sprinkling the floor with water. The room should be well-ventilated. Polyurethane varnishes require 30% to 90% relative humidity for proper curing.

3. Good light should shine on the surface from the side opposite your work position.

4. The working surface should be cleaned with a **tack rag,** made by applying turpentine to a damp rag and sprinkling the rag freely with varnish until it is somewhat sticky.

5. A small quantity of varnish (roughly the amount needed for the job) should be poured into a clean container. This varnish should be thinned with about 25% turpentine for the first coat. Succeeding coats need not be thinned. Leftover varnish should not be returned to the can.

Applying Oil or Polyurethane Varnish

1. Select a well-made, clean, chisel-type brush with fine bristles. Dip one-third to one-half the length of the bristles in the varnish. Remove surplus varnish by tapping the brush briefly inside the rim of the can.

2. Flow the varnish onto the clean, dry surface, in the direction of the grain; then brush it out across the grain. Finish with long, even strokes, in direction of the grain, using the tip ends of the bristles to smooth out the varnish. See Fig. 18-7.

3. Dust specks, loose bristles, and other imperfections may be removed from the wet, varnished surface with the tip of the brush.

4. When the finish is dry to the touch, it may be lightly sanded to remove imperfections and then recoated. Always sand in the direction of the grain and remove all dust before applying successive coats.

Applying Acrylic Varnish

1. Using a nylon brush, generously apply the acrylic varnish and level it quickly. Final brush strokes should be made in the direction of the grain.

2. When the finish is dry to the touch, sand lightly and recoat.

3. Acrylic varnish rarely needs thinning, but if it does, it may be thinned with water. Soap and water are used for cleanup.

Applying Spirit Varnish (Shellac)

1. Wipe the surface dust-free before applying finish.

2. Pour a small quantity of spirit varnish (usually shellac) into a glass or porcelain container and thin it with the proper solvent. For the first coat, 4-pound-cut shellac is thinned to half strength; that is, one part shellac to one part alcohol. For the second coat, the shellac is thinned to a formula of two parts shellac to one part alcohol. For successive coats, the shellac is used without thinning.

3. Flow a light film of spirit varnish onto the surface, in the direction of the grain, always keeping the working edge wet. Work quickly, because spirit varnishes dry quickly and will not permit repeated brushing.

4. Sand lightly between coats to remove imperfections.

Standards and Results

- The coating should be smooth and even and should be free of imperfections (such as dust, loose bristles, lint, brush marks, sags, laps, crawls, pits, holidays, and fat edges).

- A sufficient number of coats should be applied to build up good body.

Fig. 18-7. Final strokes should be with the grain and toward the edge of the surface.

Safety Considerations

- Wear safety glasses when applying finish.
- Some solvents can be harmful and should be handled with care. Keep solvents away from your mouth and from open cuts.
- Carefully dispose of tack rags.
- Because of the toxic effect of the fumes produced by many varnishes, the room should be well-ventilated.
- Most solvents are flammable and should be kept away from open flame.

Topic 179.

Lacquer

Classification

Synthetic transparent or opaque gum finishing material

Composition or Description

Clear Lacquer

Clear **lacquer** consists of the following:
1. **Nitrocellulose** (cotton treated with nitric and sulphuric acids).
2. A **solvent** (such as acetone) that will dissolve nitrocellulose.
3. **Varnish resins.**
4. A **diluent** (diluting agent) that will dissolve the varnish resins. (Toluene is considered the best, but benzene and other diluents are also used.)
5. **Plasticizers** or **softeners** (derivatives of phosphoric and phthalic acids), which produce a more elastic finish.

Tinted Lacquer

Tinted or opaque lacquers are made of the same ingredients as clear lacquer, but a pigment is added. (Color ground in oil is not suitable.)

Properties

Lacquer produces a hard, celluloid-like finish that dries very quickly. Most lacquer may be brushed or sprayed on either wood or metal, although spraying is the preferred method of application. Other types of lacquer may be applied by dipping or padding. See Topic 180, "Applying Lacquer."

Lacquer should not be applied over oil stain, spirit stain, paste wood filler, paint, enamel, or varnished surfaces. The reason for this is that the ingredients of lacquer are similar to those found in paint remover and varnish remover and will lift these finishes. In industry, the viscosity (thickness) is often lowered by heating the lacquer. This method is not recommended for the school shop, however, because lacquer is highly flammable.

Lacquer dries rapidly to a hard finish. Once it has dried, all chemical action ceases. It produces a finish that is durable, moisture resistant, and alcohol resistant. This finish is not noticeably affected by ordinary temperature changes or by a reasonable amount of heat. Lacquer does not change color in drying.

Dust specks in the finished surface of lacquer are minimized by rapid drying. The quick-drying properties of lacquer shorten the time necessary to completely finish an article. Thinners made by one company are not recommended for lacquer made by another company because of the wide variety of chemical formulas used. To be reasonably sure of good results, it is best to purchase colored or tinted lacquers rather than trying to color or tint clear lacquer.

Uses

Lacquer is used as a finish on such things as furniture, toys, jewelry, hardware, models, novelties, electric light fixtures, automobiles, and sports equipment. Clear metal lacquer is the recommended finish for articles of copper and brass, as it prevents tarnishing (oxidation). Lacquer sticks are used to patch defects.

Market Analysis

Kinds

1. Clear gloss lacquer
2. Clear flat lacquer
3. Water-white lacquer
4. Bronzing lacquer
5. Brushing lacquer
6. Dipping lacquer
7. Shading lacquer
8. Novelty lacquer
9. Bar-top lacquer
10. Shellac-mixing lacquer
11. Tinted lacquer
12. Padding lacquer
13. Lacquer sealer
14. Lacquer-based primer
15. Dope (model-making lacquer)

Sales Units

Available in 27-cc, 70-cc, 113-cc, quarter-pint, half-pint, pint, quart, and gallon containers, and in 55-gallon drums. Also available in half-pint aerosol cans (self-contained spray). For patching, colored lacquer sticks are also available.

Maintenance

1. Lacquer should be stored in airtight metal containers in a room temperature of approximately 21° C (70° F).
2. Lacquer may be thinned either by adding a thinner recommended by the manufacturer or by heating.

> INTERESTING FACT: Oriental lacquer, the earliest known lacquer finish, was not the same as what we call lacquer today. It was made from the sap of certain trees. It dried by means of oxidation, rather than evaporation, the drying method of modern lacquers.

Applying Lacquer

Topic 180.

Classification

Flowing and spreading to cover a surface

Procedure

Lacquer is best applied by spraying, but it may also be applied by brushing, dipping, or padding.

Preparations

The surface to be finished should be clean, smooth, dry, and free of oil and wax. It may have an undercoat of shellac or lacquer sealer. Lacquer should not be applied directly over paint, enamel, paste filler, oil stain, or oil finish because the ingredients of lacquer are similar to those of paint remover and will lift these finishes.

Applying by Spraying

1. If sprayed at room temperature, lacquer should be thinned with the particular thinner specified by the manufacturer. Proportions of two parts lacquer to three parts thinner will produce a good consistency for spraying.
2. A much thinner consistency of lacquer may be produced by heating the lacquer to a temperature ranging from 27° to 71° C (80° to 160° F). Special facilities will be needed.
3. The spray-gun pressure should be between 35 and 70 psi (pounds per square inch).
4. Adjust the nozzle of the spray gun until the desired spray is obtained.
5. Squeeze and hold the trigger of the spray gun and, with a slow, sweeping motion, apply the spray along the entire length of the

article being sprayed. Swing past the end of the surface and release the trigger at the end of each stroke.

6. The nozzle should be held from 6″ to 12″ away from the surface to be finished. When the most effective distance has been determined, the nozzle should be kept at this distance for the entire length of each stroke. Your body should move with the motion of the spray gun. Each stroke should be lapped sufficiently to blend in with the previous coat.

7. Successive coats may be applied without sanding the preceding coat, but sufficient time should be allowed between coats for lacquer to dry thoroughly.

8. Lacquer is available in pressurized spray containers for use in shops that do not have spray equipment.

Applying by Brushing

1. Apply brushing lacquer with a good-quality, soft-bristle brush. The lacquer should be reasonably thin.

2. Because lacquer is quick-drying, it is necessary to work fast, keeping the working edge wet.

3. To prevent lapping and to avoid lifting previous coats, a minimum amount of brushing should be done.

Applying by Dipping

This is an industrial method. It does not lend itself to the school shop unless the object is extremely small, in which case the object may be dipped into a jar or can containing a small amount of lacquer. Suspend the object to dry.

Applying by Padding

The use of padding lacquer is almost entirely restricted to patching defects in lacquer surfaces.

1. Padding lacquer is applied to a lint-free pad, which is rubbed on the surface to be finished. Rubbing may be done with a straight or circular motion. Use light pressure and squeeze the pad to keep the surface wet.

2. In applying successive coats, be careful not to rub too long or with too much pressure. Either action might lift previously applied coats.

Standards and Results

- The coating should be smooth and even and should be free of imperfections. (This includes such things as bubbles, pinholes, blisters, runs or sags, orange peel, fat edges, bridging, granular effects, dust, loose bristles, brush marks, laps, and holidays.)
- A sufficient number of coats should be applied to build up good body.

Safety Considerations

- Wear safety glasses when applying finish.
- Fumes are toxic. To prevent inhalation of these fumes, always wear a mask while spraying lacquer.
- Wipe the mask with medicinal alcohol prior to use, so as to prevent transmission of germs from one wearer to another.
- Because fumes are toxic, lacquer should be applied in a well-ventilated room.
- Lacquer must be kept away from open flame. Special equipment should be used to apply heated lacquer.

Topic 181.   Super Finishes

Classification

Protective opaque or transparent finishes

Super finishes are synthetic coatings that cure by a chemical reaction. There are three types of super finishes: catalyzed synthetic lacquer, catalyzed synthetic varnish, and epoxy finish.

Composition or Description

A super finish is a two-component finish, composed of a resin and a catalyst. Before application, the catalyst must be mixed with the resin to activate the finish. The finish will then harden, by chemical reaction, within a specified time period.

Properties

Catalyzed synthetic lacquer is highly resistant to wear, marring, water, alcohol, and detergent. It can be pigmented (colored) like any conventional finish and is available in gloss types ranging from low-luster to high-gloss. It rubs well. After the catalyst is added, the pot life is 14 days. This finish must be applied by spraying.

Catalyzed synthetic varnish is a two-coat clear finish. It rubs well and has excellent resistance to marring, abrasion, water, alcohol, detergent, and other household cleaners. It is more difficult to spray than conventional finish, and a special undercoat is required. The pot life varies according to the catalyst used. Some catalyzed synthetic varnishes will air-dry at room temperature, while others need heat. This heat should be a temperature of 49° to 60° C (120° to 140° F), applied for 20 to 30 minutes.

Epoxy clear finish is a hard, high-gloss finish with good chemical and abrasion resistance. It dries in two hours and reaches maximum hardness in seven days. It is non-yellowing and is heat resistant.

All three of these finishes are unharmed by foods, fruit juices, ammonia, cleaning fluids, bleach, nail polish, and nail-polish remover.

Uses

Super finishes are used on household and institutional furniture, kitchen cabinets, and wall paneling. Because of the equipment required for application and drying, super finishes are not normally used in school shops.

Table 18-5
Common Finishing Problems

Problem	Symptoms	Causes	Solution
Air Bubbles	Air pockets form as finish dries	Too-heavy coating Insufficient brushing Inadequately filled pores Too-quick drying	Proper surface preparation Apply thin coat, well brushed out Adequate ventilation and temp.
Alligatoring Checking Crazing Hairlining	Irregular lines or cracks in finish	Application of a finish over another finish with a different base. Result is in unequal expansion and contraction, with the least-elastic coat rupturing Too-heavy application of top coat, whose surface dries first	Select compatible finishes Use same finish throughout at room temperature on well-dried wood
Bleeding	Color of stain or resin penetrates finish	Finish does not seal stain or resin	Seal oil stains, knots, and pitch pockets with shellac (Aluminum paint may be used if an opaque finish) Use nonbleeding stains
Blistering Pinholes	Blisters form and lift off finish	Excessive heat (such as sun) or excessive cold Uneven drying Surface too smooth	Temperature of room, piece to be finished, and finishing material between 10°-27° C (50°-80° F)
Crawling	Finish contracts and separates, leaving heavy patches	Surface too smooth, oily, waxy, or wet Applied in cold temperature	Clean and sand surface so it is not glazed Apply at room temperature
Crinkling	Finish shrinks and shrivels up	Too-heavy coating Surface temperature cold	Even application on clean surface at room temperature
Orange Peel	Pebbled, uneven surface, dimpled like peel of orange	Too-rapid drying Incorrect spray-nozzle adjustment Incorrect thinner	Proper temperature Proper application Use correct thinner

Market Analysis

Sales Units

Most super finishes are packaged in large units for industrial use, but two-component epoxy clear finish may be purchased in two pint-sized units that are mixed for home or school use.

Maintenance

Storing

Super finishes should be stored in separately packaged, airtight metal containers, and should be kept at a temperature of 21° C (70° F) or above.

Topic 182.

Spray Gun

Classification

Controlled-pressure atomizer for applying finishing materials

Application

Principle of Operation

Spray guns operate by means of a stream of compressed air or a pressure pump, either of which atomizes the liquid being sprayed, applying a controlled, uniform coating of finishing material to the surface.

The material to be sprayed must be thin to allow even application through the atomizer. This liquid must set quickly enough to prevent sagging. Solvents used for thinning must be compatible with the base material so the cohesiveness of the finish will not be altered. An ideal solvent will blend in with the base but will evaporate before most of the paint particles reach the surface. The remaining solvent keeps the paint wet enough to form a nonsagging film.

Overthinning or using too much solvent can change the chemical and physical characteristics of the finishing material. This may result in a film that is too thin, which may cause such problems as orange peel, solvent bubbles, or dry spray.

Temperature and humidity affect the evaporation or drying of the paint particles. Cold and humidity decrease evaporation, increasing the drying time.

Kinds and Uses

Spray guns are used to spray paints, lacquers, stains, liquid fillers, sealers, varnishes, and other liquids.

Different nozzle types produce various shapes of spray — round, oval, and fan, for example. Nozzles angled at 45° for overhead spraying are also available in the above shapes.

There are several types of spray guns. Each type has a different system of forcing material to the nozzle, of mixing, and of controlling the flow of air or finishing material.

Feed Systems

1. **Suction type.** Compressed air passes through the fluid tip, causing a low-pressure area. This low pressure at the tip allows atmopheric pressure to push the fluid from the cup up to the nozzle. This type of feed system is designed for light-bodied finishing fluid.
2. **Pressure type.** The material to be sprayed is forced to the nozzle by air pressure within the container. This type of feed system is used for heavy-bodied fluids and for volume spraying. See Fig. 18-9.

Mixing Systems
(See Fig. 18-10)

1. **Internal-mix type.** The material to be sprayed is mixed with compressed air inside the nozzle. This type of system is used for slow-drying fluids and for low-pressure spraying.

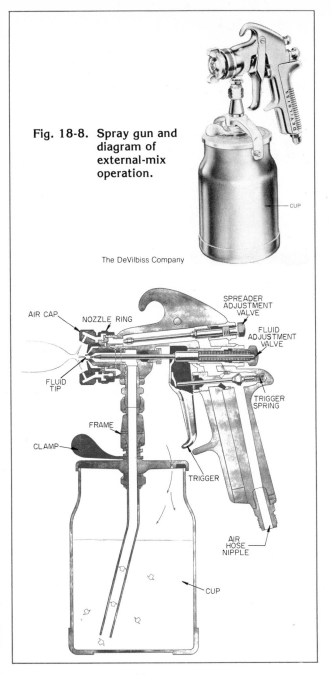

Fig. 18-8. Spray gun and diagram of external-mix operation.

The DeVilbiss Company

SPREADER ADJUSTMENT VALVE

FLUID ADJUSTMENT VALVE

AIR CAP

NOZZLE RING

FLUID TIP

TRIGGER SPRING

FRAME

CLAMP

TRIGGER

AIR HOSE NIPPLE

CUP

CUP

Fig. 18-9. Pressure-feed spray-gun setup.

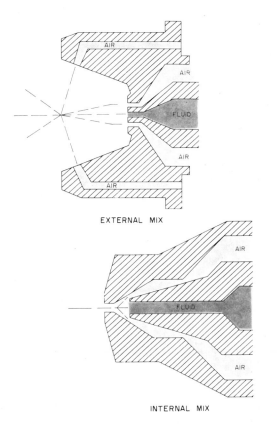

AIR

AIR

FLUID

AIR

AIR

EXTERNAL MIX

AIR

FLUID

AIR

INTERNAL MIX

Fig. 18-10. External and internal mixing systems used in spray guns.

2. **External-mix type.** The material to be sprayed is mixed with air outside the nozzle. This mixing system is designed for light, fast-drying finishing materials.

Air-Flow Control Systems

1. **Bleeder type.** Compressed air flows continuously through the nozzle. Only the material being sprayed is controlled by the trigger.

2. **Non-bleeder type.** The trigger controls the flow of both the compressed air and the material being sprayed.

Fig. 18-11. An air brush is used for very small, detailed work.

The suction-feed, external-mix, non-bleeder type gun is the gun most widely used for spraying wood finishes.

Principal Parts and Function of Each

1. The **cup** or **container,** made from an aluminum alloy, holds the spraying liquids.
2. The **cap** has a **tube** attached to it. The liquid flows to the nozzle through this tube.
3. The **frame** contains passages for air flow.
4. The **trigger** and **fluid-adjustment valve** regulate the flow of air and/or finishing material. The liquid flows through the hardened-steel **fluid tip** when the needle is drawn back.
5. The **spreader-adjustment valve** regulates the size of the spray pattern.
6. The **spring** closes the needle valve and holds the trigger forward.
7. The **nozzle** determines whether air and liquid will mix internally or externally. Air and liquid are projected from the gun through this nozzle.
8. The **nozzle lock ring** holds the nozzle in fixed position.
9. A **clamp** secures the cup to the gun assembly.
10. The **air-pressure hose** is connected to an **air-hose nipple.**

OSHA Regulations

Spray Booths and Equipment

1. Spraying shall not be conducted outside of predetermined spraying areas.
2. All spraying areas shall be kept as free from the accumulation of deposits of combustible residues as practical.

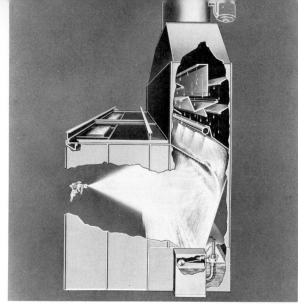

Fig. 18-12. Cutaway of a spray booth.

3. A clear space of not less than 3' on all sides of the spraying booth shall be kept free of storage and combustible construction material.
4. Each spray booth shall be separated from other operations by not less than 3'.
5. All metal parts of spray booths, exhaust ducts, and piping systems shall be properly electrically grounded.
6. Portable electric lamps shall not be used in any spraying area during spraying operations.
7. Approved metal waste cans shall be provided wherever rags or waste matter have been saturated in finishing material. All such rags or waste must be deposited in these waste cans immediately after use.

Market Analysis

Capacity

Spray guns used in schools and home workshops usually have a one-pint container. However, quart, half-gallon, and gallon sizes are also available. Industrial spray guns spray directly from large drums.

Maintenance

Cleaning

1. Remove the cap from the container and pour out the liquid.

2. Partially fill the container with the solvent of the material that has just been sprayed. Replace the cap.
3. Spray the solvent, first using a steady flow and then using intermittent spurts to clean the nozzle.
4. With a lint-free cloth that has been satu-

rated in solvent, wipe off the nozzle and the other parts.
5. Remove the cap and pour out the remaining solvent.

Lubrication

Periodically, lubricate the trigger assembly.

Using the Spray Gun

Topic 183.

Classification

Applying finishing material with a controlled-pressure atomizer

Procedure

The surface to be finished should be clean, dry, and free of oil and wax. Each type of material to be sprayed requires different spraying adjustments to produce satisfactory results.

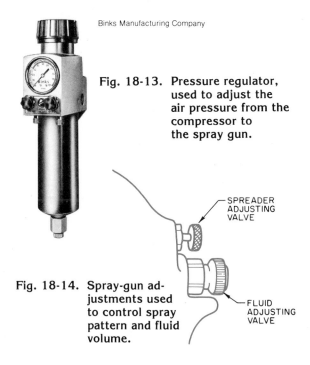

Binks Manufacturing Company

Fig. 18-13. Pressure regulator, used to adjust the air pressure from the compressor to the spray gun.

Fig. 18-14. Spray-gun adjustments used to control spray pattern and fluid volume.

SPREADER ADJUSTING VALVE

FLUID ADJUSTING VALVE

The nozzle type, the spray pattern, and the gun pressure should be determined by spraying on a scrap piece of wood.

If the material being sprayed is at room temperature, it should be thinned with the thinner specified by the manufacturer. If lacquer is being sprayed, it may be heated to 27° to 71° C (80° to 160° F) and applied full-strength. This will require special equipment.

1. Adjust the spray-gun pressure. It should be between 35 and 70 psi. Normally, the pressure should be held at a minimum. This is done to allow for proper atomization with a minimum of kickback and a minimum of bounce of spray particles. See Fig. 18-13.
2. Adjust the spray pattern of the gun by turning the spreader-adjustment valve. See Fig. 18-14. Adjusting the valve clockwise will produce a small, cone-shaped spray pattern. Adjusting the valve counterclockwise will produce a larger, fan-shaped pattern. Use a large spray pattern for large work and a small pattern for small work. Some common spray-pattern problems are shown in Fig. 18-15.
3. The fluid-adjustment valve should be adjusted in conjunction with the spreader valve in order to regulate the volume of the fluid flow from the gun nozzle. See Fig. 18-14.

A greater volume of finishing material will be required for a large spray pattern than for a small pattern. Too great a flow of fluid for the size of the pattern can produce a heavy, sagging finish. Too low a fluid adjustment may cause a dry, rough finish.

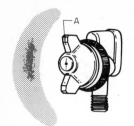

CAUSE — Dried material in side port **A** restricts passage of air through port on one side. Results in full pressure of air from clean side of port in a fan pattern in direction of clogged side.

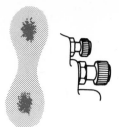

CAUSE — A split spray pattern (heavy on each end of a fan pattern and weak in the middle) is usually caused by: (1) atomizing air pressure too high, (2) attempting to get too wide a spray with thin material, (3) not enough material available.

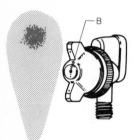

CAUSE — Dried material around the outside of the fluid nozzle tip at position **B** restricts the passage of atomizing air at one point through the center ring opening of the air nozzle. This faulty pattern can also be caused by a loose air nozzle or a bent fluid nozzle or needle tip.

CAUSE — A fan spray pattern that is heavy in the middle, or a pattern that has an unatomized "salt-and-pepper" effect indicates that the atomizing air pressure is not sufficiently high, or there is too much material being fed to the gun.

JERKY OR FLUTTERING PATTERN — check for:
• Air leaking into fluid line or passageway.
• Lack of paint.
• Loose or cracked fluid siphon tube.
• Loose fluid nozzle.
• Loose fluid packing nut or worn packing.

Fig. 18-15. Faulty spray patterns and their causes.

4. Squeeze and hold the trigger of the spray gun. With a slow, sweeping motion, apply the material along the entire length of the article being sprayed. Swing past the end of the surface and release the trigger at the end of each stroke. Your body should move with the motion of the spray gun. Each successive stroke should be lapped sufficiently to blend in with the previous stroke. Be careful to keep the nozzle of the spray gun an even distance from the workpiece, as any arc in the spray pattern may cause uneven coverage or dry areas. See Fig. 18-16.
5. Successive coats may be applied without sanding the preceding coats, but sufficient time should be allowed between coats for the material to dry thoroughly. In spraying large pieces with lacquer, a second coat is recommended. Apply this coat while the first coat is still somewhat wet, thereby allowing greater flow.

Standards and Results

• The coating should be smooth and even and should be free of imperfections (such as

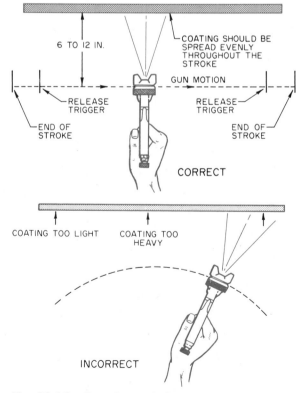

Fig. 18-16. Spraying technique.

APPEARANCE	CAUSE	REMEDY	PREVENTION
CHALKING Loss of gloss Powdery surface	Weathering of paint films Insufficient paint agitation Use of poorly balanced thinning solvents	Remove powdery film with a mild paste abrasive Sand and refinish a chronic failing condition	Agitate paint thoroughly Use only balanced thinning solvents
CHECKING, CRAZING, CRACKING Crowfoot separation (check) Irregular line separation (alligator check) Formation like dried mud (cracking)	Insufficient drying of films prior to recoating Extreme temperature changes Coats too heavy (checking) Ingredients not thoroughly mixed Adding improper materials (incompatibility) Recoating checked finish Thinner softening acrylic (crazing)	Remove finish down through the checked paint film and re-finish Use solvent recommended by the paint manufacturer	Allow sufficient drying time before recoating Avoid extreme temperature changes Avoid heavy coats of lacquer Mix paint thoroughly before applying Avoid incompatible additives
BLISTERING Broken edge craters Small, swelled areas like a water blister on human skin	Rust, oil, or grease under surface Moisture in spray line Trapped solvents Exposure of film to constant or repeated high humidity	Sand and refinish damaged areas	Thoroughly clean and treat Drain water from air lines often Thin products properly Allow sufficient drying time between coats
PEELING Separation of top coat from previous surface	Improper surface cleaning Improper undercoats Unbalanced thinning solvents	Sand and refinish damaged areas	Thoroughly clean old surface Use recommended primers Follow recommended practices
FISHEYES, POOR WETTING Separation of the wet film Previous finish can be seen in spots	Improper cleaning of old surface Spraying over finishes that contain silicone	Wash off paint while still wet	Clean surface properly Use fisheye preventer in paint sprayed over old film containing silicone
DIRT IN FINISH Foreign particles dried in the paint film	Lack of proper cleaning, blowing off, tack-ragging Defective air-regulator cleaning filter Dirty working area Defective or dirty air inlet filters Dirty spray gun	Rub out finish with a polishing compound Sand and refinish	Clean surface thoroughly Blow out cracks, body joints Clean equipment thoroughly Clean up spray area Replace inlet air filters Strain out foreign matter Keep all containers closed
LIFTING Rising and swelling of wet film Peeling when surface is dry	Improper drying of previous coating Sandwiching enamel between two lacquers or acrylics Recoating improperly cured enamel Spraying over dirty surface	Remove lifted surfaces and refinish	Clean old surfaces thoroughly Allow sufficient drying time for all subcoats Seal old finishes
BLUSHING Finish turns milky	Fast thinners in high humidity Unbalanced thinners Condensation on old surface	Add retarder to thinner and respray Sand and refinish	Keep paint and surface at room temperature Use good-quality thinner Use a retarder or reflow solvent when spraying in high humidity, warm temperature
RUNS Running of wet paint film in rivulets	Over reduction Extra slow thinning solvents Cold surface being painted Improperly cleaned surface	Wash off, or sand and re-finish	Clean surface thoroughly Do not paint over old surface Reduce as recommended, using specified solvents
SAGS Partial slipping of paint Heavy thickness in the form of curtains	Insufficient thinner Insufficient drying time between coats Low air pressure, causing insufficient atomization Gun too close to work Gun out of adjustment	Sand, or wash off and refinish	Reduce viscosity as recommended Use proper thinning solvent Adjust the air pressure and gun for correct atomization Keep gun at correct distance from work
ORANGE PEEL Ball peen hammer dents in surface Resembles the skin of an orange	Lack of proper flow Insufficient reduction Improper thinning solvent Surface drying too fast Improper air pressure	Enamel — Rub surface with mild polishing compound Lacquer — Sand or use rubbing compound Sand and refinish	Correct air pressure Adjust gun properly Correct thinning solvents

Fig. 18-17. Respirator used to prevent the inhalation of toxic fumes during spraying operations.

bubbles, pinholes, blisters, runs or sags, orange peel, granular effects, or dust). See Table 18-6, "Spray Finishing Problems."

- A sufficient number of coats should be applied to build up good body.

Safety Considerations

- Because fumes may be toxic, a mask or respirator should be worn during spraying to prevent inhalation of these fumes, Fig. 18-17.
- The mask should be wiped with medicinal alcohol prior to use, in order to prevent transmission of germs from one wearer to another.
- Because of the toxic effect of the fumes, spraying should be done in a well-ventilated booth.
- There should be no open flame or non-explosion-proof electrical outlets within 20' of a spray booth.

Topic 184.

Abrasive Flours — Pumice and Rottenstone

Classification

Fine powdered abrasive

Composition or Description

Pumice is a light, porous substance obtained from volcanic lava. The word "pumice" means **foam,** an indication that pumice is produced by the expansion of water vapor in an underwater lava eruption. This solidified foam is ground into a very fine abrasive powder. This powder is grayish white in color. **Rottenstone** is a very soft, greenish-gray abrasive powder, made from ground decomposed limestone. Rottenstone is finer than pumice.

Properties

1. Pumice is a sharp cutting agent that smooths and polishes by abrasion. It leaves fine, hairlike scratches.

2. Rottenstone is a sharp cutting agent, finer than pumice. Like pumice, it smooths and polishes by abrasion, but the scratches it leaves are very fine (practically invisible).

Uses

1. Pumice is used with water, paraffin oil, or various rubbing oils. It produces a very smooth, polished surface on finished objects. The degree of luster is determined by the lubricant and the fineness of the abrasive flour.
2. Rottenstone is used with water, paraffin oil, or various rubbing oils. It is used, after the finished object has been rubbed with pumice, to produce an extremely smooth surface with a polished or lustrous appearance.

A smooth, dull finish is produced using either of the above abrasive flours in combination with water as a lubricant. When the lubricant is soap and water, a semigloss finish is produced. A glossy finish results when paraffin oil is used as the lubricant. A high-gloss finish is produced when lemon oil is used as the lubricant.

The abrasive is applied with a felt pad, dipped first in the lubricant and then in the abrasive flour. The abrasive is then rubbed on the finished surface, in a straight-line motion. Rubbing is done in the direction of the grain.

Market Analysis

1. Both pumice and rottenstone are available in powder form.
2. Pumice is available in F (floated), FF

(double-floated) and FFF (triple-floated). The higher the F grade, the finer the pumice.
3. Rottenstone is available in only one grade.
4. Both pumice and rottenstone are sold by the pound or multiples of a pound.

Maintenance

1. Both pumice and rottenstone are often kept in shakers. This is done for ease of application and to prevent foreign substances from getting into the flour.
2. Abrasive flours should be stored in a dry place.

Waxes

Topic 185.

Classification

Protective and polishing film

Composition or Description

Waxes are vegetable, animal, or mineral fat-like substances, which are harder and not as greasy as fats.

Vegetable Waxes

1. **Carnauba wax** is a cream-colored wax, obtained from the leaves of the carnauba palm of Brazil.
2. **Candelilla wax** is obtained from a Mexican plant.
3. **Japan wax** is obtained from the berries of Japanese and Chinese sumac trees.

Animal Waxes

1. **Beeswax** is the amber-colored wax secreted by the honeybee. Bees use this wax to form honeycomb.
2. **Shellac wax** is produced by the lac bug.

3. **Chinese wax** or **insect wax** is secreted by insects found on certain evergreen trees in China.
4. **Spermaceti** is obtained from the oil of the sperm whale and the dolphin.

Mineral Waxes

1. **Paraffin wax** is an opaque white wax distilled from petroleum.
2. **Montan wax** is obtained from peat and lignites (coal).
3. **Ozocerite** is a colorless or white mineral wax.

Synthetic Waxes

Ceresin (or ceresine) wax is a hard wax used as a substitute for beeswax.

Properties

Waxes are dissolved either in turpentine, mineral spirits, gasoline, or kerosene. They are only partially soluble in alcohol and are insoluble in water. Some waxes will turn white when they come in contact with water, and most waxes can be removed from a surface by applying hot water. They may be colored by adding pigments to the natural wax. Carnauba wax and ceresin wax are the hardest of the waxes and have good polishing qualities. Because of these properties, most commercial waxes contain some carnauba wax mixed with other kinds of wax.

Uses

Wax is used to produce a hard, tough film on a surface. This film of wax protects the surface, making it water repellent and abrasion resistant. It is widely used on furniture, floors, automobiles, and plastic products. It is used in etching to prevent acid from coming in contact with surfaces that are not to be etched. Wax fillets are used in patternmaking, and melted beeswax is sometimes used to flatten the gloss of varnishes and enamels. Waxes are used to reduce friction on sliding surfaces such as drawer slides and skis. Wax is also used on tool and machine parts, both as a lubricant and to prevent rust. Vegetable waxes are the most common type used in finishing and polishing furniture.

Note: Wax can not be used interchangeably with the oil lubricants used for bearings.

Market Analysis

Shapes

Wax is available in paste, liquid, cake, fillet, flake, or powdered form.

Sizes

Fillets can be 1/8", 3/16", 1/4", 5/16", 3/8", or 1/2" in radius.

Sales Units

1. Paste wax is sold by the pound (and in fractions and multiples of a pound).
2. Liquid wax is sold in pint, quart, half-gallon, gallon, and 5-gallon containers and 55-gallon drums.
3. Cake wax is sold in 1-pound cakes.
4. Wax fillets are sold in boxes containing a number of 2' lengths. The number of lengths varies according to the radius of the fillet.
5. Flaked and powdered waxes are sold by the pound.

Maintenance

To soften waxes, heat them in hot water.

Topic 186.

Preparing and Applying a Wipe-On Gum Finish

Classification

Building up a gum finish by wiping on successive coats of film

Procedure

A suitable wiping finish can be made by mixing 25% **boiled** linseed oil and 75% 4-pound-cut white shellac or by mixing 25% **boiled** linseed oil, 25% mixing lacquer, and 50% 4-pound-cut shellac. Either mixture should be shaken well before application. The second mixture is more water resistant.

1. Cut a piece of lint-free cotton cloth about 8" square. Make a wad of cotton waste about 2" in diameter and place it in the center of the cotton cloth.
2. Saturate the ball of cotton waste in the solution. Wrap the saturated ball in the piece of cotton in such a way that the loose ends are gathered at the top.
3. Rub the mixture on the wood surface in a back-and-forth motion, following the direction of the grain. Keep enough mixture on the rag to evenly coat the entire surface.
4. After coating the entire surface three or four times, let the finish dry for 24 hours. Repeat this process until satisfactory body is built up. Sanding between coats is not

usually necessary, although light sanding may be done if irregularities appear.

5. If a high luster is desired, the object may be waxed after the final coat is dry.

Standards and Results

- The coatings should be smooth, even, and free from laps and streaks.

Safety Considerations

- Wear safety glasses when applying finishing materials.
- Finish should be applied in a well-ventilated room.
- Saturated rags should be disposed of or kept in an airtight safety container.

Preparing and Applying an Oil Finish

Topic 187.

Classification

Wipe-on, oil-based finish, which penetrates the surface of wood

Procedure

Oil finishes are durable and very easy to apply. The finish penetrates the surface pores of the wood, sealing and toughening the wood fibers.

An oil finish may be prepared by mixing 75% either raw or boiled linseed oil with 25% turpentine. To one pint of this mixture, add one tablespoonful of cider vinegar. Boiled oil will oxidize more quickly than raw oil. The acetic acid (vinegar) prevents the oil from becoming tacky after oxidation.

Many ready-made oil finishes are also available. These generally have a linseed- or tung-oil base and are applied in essentially the same way as the mixture mentioned above. Some manufactured oil finishes such as Danish Oil® are produced in several shades so that the finished appearance of the wood can be controlled.

To apply an oil finish, follow this procedure:

1. Pour a sufficient amount of oil finish on the wood.
2. Work the oil finish into the wood with either a clean, lint-free piece of cotton cloth or with your hand. The friction caused by vigorous rubbing generates heat, permitting greater penetration.

3. Let the oil soak into the wood for 20 to 30 minutes, then wipe off the excess with a clean, dry, lint-free cloth.
4. After eight hours drying time, apply a second coat. Continue this procedure until four or five coats have been applied. At this point, wait two days between additional coats. Continue this process until sufficient buildup has been obtained.

Oil finish has many advantages. It is heat proof, alcohol proof, and waterproof. If it is stained, scratched, or loses its luster, it can be restored to its original condition simply by applying another coat. There are, however, some disadvantages to oil finish. It does not prevent atmospheric moisture from entering and leaving the wood. As a result, greater expansion and contraction takes place and the oil finish may get tacky in hot, humid weather.

Standards and Results

- The surface should be smooth, even, and free of oil.
- The surface should not be tacky.

Safety Considerations

- Wear safety glasses when using finishes.
- Dispose of oily rags or keep them in a tightly sealed metal can.
- Finish should be applied in a well-ventilated room.

Topic 188.

Finish Schedules for Close- and Open-Grain Woods

Finish Schedule for Close-Grain Woods

1. Surface preparation is very important on close-grain woods. Make sure all sanding scratches have been worked out using fine-grit abrasive paper. (See Topic 164, "Preparing the Surface for Finishing.")
2. On softwood it is recommended that a non grain-raising stain, such as an oil stain, be used. On hardwoods, such as maple or birch, use a water stain. This will give better tone quality.
3. Oil stains may be applied to the surface without other preparation. Water stain will raise the grain, so the surface must be either sponged or glue-sized prior to staining. (See Topics 170 and 172.)
4. If the surface is to have a natural finish, Steps 2 and 3 are omitted.
5. Apply a sealer coat. (See Topic 173.) Dry according to specifications. A thinned coat of lacquer or varnish may be used as a sealer coat if succeeding coats are of the same material. Sand lightly, using 220-grit paper.
6. Apply the finish. Be sure the finish and sealer coat are compatible. Allow to dry 24 hours. Sand lightly with 220-grit paper to produce a level surface.
7. Apply a second coat of finish. Let this coat dry 24 hours.
8. Inspect the surface to be sure buildup of finish is adequate. Several more coats may be necessary to produce leveling. Proceed with each coat as in Step 7. Sand lightly between coats.
9. Apply the final coat.
10. Rub the final coat with 400-grit wet or dry abrasive paper, using water as a lubricant. A stearate paper may be used dry. Remove any lumps or irregularities from the surface.

11. To produce a high-gloss finish, rub the surface with pumice stone and oil, then with rottenstone and oil. (See Topic 184.)

Note: Some finishers use steel wool to smooth the surface between coats. This is not recommended. Small particles of the steel remain in the surface to rust and cause imperfections.

12. A coat of paste wax applied over the finished surface will protect the wood and make cleaning easier.

Finish Schedule for Open-Grain Woods

1. Surface preparation is very important for any finish. (See Topic 164.)
2. Select a water stain to match the desired shade or the color tone of the wood.
3. Apply a glue size or a shellac wash coat to stabilize the wood fibers. Lightly sand smooth with worn 120-grit paper. (See Topic 172.)
4. Apply the stain to the least-noticeable surfaces first. Allow to dry 12 hours.
5. Apply a wash coat of shellac to seal in the stain. Let this dry 30 minutes to one hour.
6. Apply paste filler, colored to match the desired tone. (See Topics 174 and 175.) Allow to dry 24 hours.
7. Apply a sanding sealer. (See Topics 173.) Let this dry according to specifications. Sand lightly with 220-grit paper, being careful not to remove any stain.
8. Apply a coat of finish. Be sure that the finish and sealer are compatible. Allow finish to dry 24 hours. Sand with 220-grit paper to level the surface.
9. Apply a second coat of finish, and allow to dry 24 hours.

10. Inspect the surface to be sure buildup of finish is adequate. Several more coats may be necessary to produce leveling. Proceed with each coat as in Step 9. Sand lightly between coats.
11. Rub the final coat with 400-grit wet or dry abrasive paper, using water as a lubricant. A stearate paper may also be used dry. Remove all lumps or irregularities on the surface.
12. To produce a high-gloss finish, rub the surface with pumice stone and oil, followed by rottenstone and oil. (See Topic 184.) See "Note" under Step 11 of "Finish Schedule for Close-Grain Woods."
13. A coat of paste wax applied over the finished surface will protect the wood and make cleaning easier.

Glossary of Finishing Terms

Abrasive — a graded grit in the form of flour, compound, or coating on paper or cloth. Abrasives are used in cutting and smoothing.

Acrylic resins — a polymer resin, soluble in acetone.

Adhesion — the mechanical or molecular affinity of one material to another (as in paints).

Air bubbles — a defect in finishes, caused by air vapors or gasses being trapped in the surface, and resulting in bubbling, pitting, and blistering.

Alligatoring — a pattern of cracks in a finished surface, caused by uneven expansion and contraction of separate coats of finish.

Aniline dyes — soluble colors, made from aniline oils or coal-tar derivatives and used in the manufacture of fast-color dyes and stains.

Banana oil — a common name for amyl acetate, a colorless liquid used as a solvent and vehicle for lacquers and bronze powders.

Bite — the characteristic of a finishing material that tends to soften or partially dissolve the preceding coat.

Bleach — a chemical solution used to blanch or permanently lighten the coloring of the wood.

Bleeding — the seeping of colors through a finish.

Blending — the uniform mixing of liquids and colors.

Blushing — a milky, cloudy effect in clear finishes, caused by excessive humidity or improper solvent balance.

Body — the weight or thickness of a film or the viscosity of a finishing material.

Boxing — the intermixing or blending of the ingredients of finishing materials, achieved by pouring the mixture back and forth from one container to another.

Burning in — the process of patching by melting stick shellac into a surface defect or scratch.

Checking — small pattern of cracks, caused by uneven surface drying or film failure.

Cohesion — the molecular attraction of molecules of the same material.

Crawling — the formation of patches of finishing-material globules, caused either by excessive surface tension of the material or by lack of bite with the undersurface.

Crinkling — a shriveling of thick edges of finishing materials, caused by a coating that is too heavy or by improper bonding.

Cut — the term used to designate the number of pounds of shellac resin per gallon of solvent, as 4-pound-cut shellac.

Drier — a liquid with high oxidizing properties, added to finishing materials to accelerate drying and hardening.

Earth pigments — dry, finely ground, colored mineral matter, used as coloring in paints.

Eggshell — a term used to denote a low-gloss, hard finish.

Elasticity — a property of flexible film finishes that permits bending and contracting of materials without damage to the finish.

Enamel — an opaque, relatively glossy, pigmented varnish-paint mixture, used to color and coat a surface.

Extender — a filler substance used to increase coverage in paint or enamel.

Fat edges — built-up finish on an edge due to overlapping.

Filler — a finishing material used to fill open grain or minor defects to obtain a level, compact wood surface.

Flow — that property of a liquid which enables it to spread or level to an even film.

French polish — a high-gloss finish, obtained by using a pad to apply a solution of shellac and alcohol and then adding a few drops of linseed oil for lubrication.

Glue size — a thin glue solution, applied to a wood surface to raise and stiffen the fibers prior to finish sanding. Glue size is also used to partially seal end grain.

Grain raising — the swelling and lifting of the short surface wood fibers.

Gum finish — a gum material, dissolved and suspended in an oxidizing or evaporating liquid.

Holiday — a trade expression describing a section of the finish surface that was missed by the finisher.

Lacquer — a finishing material with a nitrocellulose base. Lacquer dries as a result of evaporation of the solvents.

Lap — to extend or overlay one coat of paint or finishing material over the edge of another coat.

Leveling — the ability of a material to flow evenly, free of brush marks, runs, sags, or fat edges.

Linseed oil — a prepared vegetable oil, raw or boiled, used as a vehicle and a binder in paint and other finishes. Linseed oil dries by oxidation.

Lousy — a condition of small foreign particles in the paint materials or brush.

Mineral spirits — a by-product of the distillation of petroleum, used as a solvent or thinner.

Oil rubbing — the process of smoothing and leveling by rubbing with abrasives (fine sandpaper, fine pumice, and rottenstone) and one of the mineral oils, in order to produce a smooth finish.

Opacity — the ability of a pigment to cover or hide a surface.

Orange peel — a pebbled surface condition caused by rapid drying or improper application.

Paint remover — a compound used to dissolve or destroy finish.

Pigment — coloring matter used in the preparation of finishing materials.

Pumice — a porous volcanic lava that has been finely pulverized into a graded abrasive flour. Pumice is used in smoothing, polishing, and cleaning.

Resin — natural or synthetic gum having properties specially suited to the preparation of varnishes and enamels.

Retarder — a solvent used to slow the drying or hardening rate of a finish.

Rottenstone — soft, greenish-gray limestone clay, pulverized into very fine abrasive flour and used for smoothing and polishing. Rottenstone is finer than the finest grade of pumice.

Rubbed finish — a smooth, flat, built-up, uniform body of gum, produced by the application, leveling, and rubbing of successive coatings.

Rubbing oil — any one of several kinds of mineral oil, used as a lubricant with fine abrasives in rubbing down a finish.

Sheen — the luster of a rubbed surface.

Shellac — a natural resin that is dissolved in alcohol to form a sealer or gum finish.

Silex — graded, powdered quartz, used as a base for paste filler.

Silicate — a finely ground (floured) powder of quartz.

Solvent — a thinner used to dissolve a finish, in order to assist in oxidizing and to give good brushing and flowing quality.

Stain — a coloring substance or dyestuff with a water, oil, or spirit-base, used to color or define the natural grain pattern of wood.

Substrate — the unfinished base material to which finish is applied.

Thinner — a liquid used in finishes to extend the vehicle or gum.

Vehicle — the liquid in which the base material is suspended.

Wash coat — a thin solution of shellac, lacquer, or other gum finishing material.

SECTION NINETEEN.

Sharpening

Topic 189.

Sharpening

Sharpening is a technique of forming a sharp edge on a tool or knife by filing or grinding or by grinding and whetting. Saw blades, auger bits, and spade bits are sharpened by filing. Twist drills are sharpened by grinding. Plane irons, knives, chisels, gouges, router bits, and carving tools are sharpened by first grinding and then whetting to a keen edge.

All woodcutting tools, regardless of their type, have a wedge-shaped cutter or series of cutters. The wedge or wedges pare the wood fibers, and the incline of the force of the wedge causes the fibers to curl or separate, producing shavings, chips, or dust. These wedges must be sharpened to the proper cutting angle, lip clearance, and rake angle. See Figs. 19-1 and 19-2.

The **cutting angle** is simply the bevel or edge that does the actual cutting. The **lip clearance** is the relief given the cutting edge so it may enter the material being cut. The **rake angle** is the angle at which the face of the cutting edge actually enters the work.

Tools need sharpening when they are nicked or distorted from abuse or when they are simply dull from use. Some woods, such as fir, have a high grit content, which tends to dull tools more quickly. Hardened glue on wood joints also dulls the edges of tools.

In most cases, when keen-edge tools become dull they only need whetting to bring them back to a sharp edge. This is done on a medium then fine oilstone. This procedure may be followed by stropping the edge on a piece of leather to produce an extra-sharp edge. After continuous whetting and strapping, the proper cutting angle should be restored by **regrinding.**

Chisels, gouges, and plane irons should have a blade angle of about 30° to 35°. An angle of more than 35° will hold an edge longer (because there is more metal behind the edge), but will not be as sharp. An angle of less than 30° will not hold its edge as long but can be whetted to produce a sharper edge.

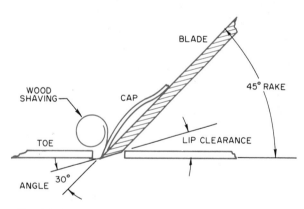

Fig. 19-1.   Cutting action of plane blade.

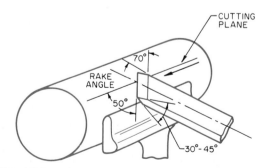

Fig. 19-2.   Cutting action of skew chisel.

Fig. 19-3.   The knife grinding attachment used on a jointer allows the knives to be sharpened while they are still in the cutterhead.

Rockwell International

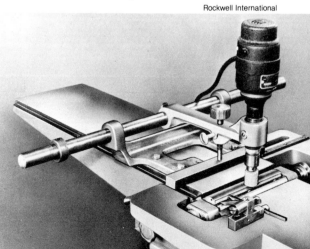

Rockwell International

Fig. 19-4. Grinding surfacer knives with a knife-grinding attachment.

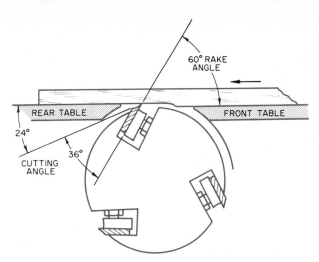

Fig. 19-5. Cutting action of a jointer.

Large woodcutting machines, like surface planers and jointers, often have grinding and honing attachments that sharpen the cutter knives while they are still in the machine. See Figs. 19-3 and 19-4. Each blade is ground to protrude the same distance from the cutterhead, and then is honed to a fine edge.

On machines that are not equipped with grinding attachments, the blades must be removed from the cutterhead and sent to a company that specializes in sharpening. The knives are ground, balanced, and honed. The blades must then be reset in the cutterhead to the correct height. So that jointer knives will remain sharp between grindings, they may be honed or jointed. This is done while the knives are still mounted in the cutterhead. This operation is described in Topic 46, "Jointer."

There are many services specializing in sharpening a wide range of woodworking tools. Most woodworking tools, however, can be easily sharpened (with some practice) in the shop or laboratory. A minimum amount of equipment is required.

Grinder — Bench, Floor Models

Topic 190.

Classification

Power-driven abrading tool for shaping metal

Application

Principle of Operation

The **grinder** works on the principle of a series of cutting wedges. A large number of cutting wedges revolve at a speed of between 400 and 3600 rpm, Fig. 19-6.

Kinds and Uses

Grinders are used for shaping the cutting edges of tools. The type most often found in

Fig. 19-6. Bench grinder.

Rockwell International

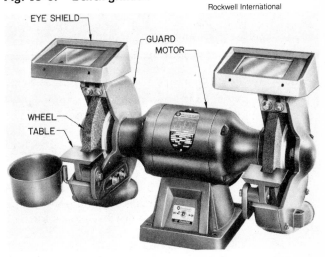

school shops is called a **dry grinder,** but there are also **wet grinders** and **vapor grinders.** Standard wheel shapes that may be attached to bench and floor models are **straight, straight-tapered, cylindrical, cup, flaring cup, dish,** and **saucer.**

Principal Parts and Function of Each

1. The **abrasive wheels,** which do the cutting, are made of silicon carbide and aluminum oxide. They are graded alphabetically according to size of grain. For sharpening woodworking tools, the recommended hardness is **N,** and the recommended coarseness is 46 to 60 grit.
2. The 1/3- to 1-HP **motor** provides the power.
3. The tool-steel **spindle** or **arbor** drives the wheel.
4. The cast-iron **table** or **tool rest** provides an adjustable bearing surface for materials or tools to be ground.
5. The cast-iron or pressed-steel **guards** protect the operator from injury.
6. The plastic or safety-glass **eye shields** protect the operator's eyes from the particles that are torn loose from the abrasive wheel or stock.
7. The **stand** (on floor models) supports the grinder.
8. Some grinders have a **reservoir** to hold water, which is used to cool the work being ground.

OSHA Regulations

Grinding Machines

1. Maximum exposure of the grinding wheel periphery and sides shall not exceed 180°. This exposure shall begin at a point not more than 65° above the horizontal plane of the wheel spindle. The remaining portion of the wheel shall be guarded.
2. Work rests shall be kept adjusted close to the wheel and shall have a maximum opening of 1/8", so as to prevent the work from being jammed between the wheel and the rest. Adjustments shall not be made while the wheel is in motion.
3. Immediately before mounting, all wheels shall be closely inspected and sounded (given the Ring Test) by the operator, to make sure they have not been damaged in

transit, in storage, or by some other means. The spindle speed of the machine shall be checked before the wheel is mounted. This is done to assure that this speed does not exceed the maximum operating speed marked on the wheel. To ascertain whether a wheel can be used, tap it gently with a light, nonmetallic implement. For light wheels, use an implement such as the handle of a screwdriver. For heavier wheels, an instrument such as a wooden mallet should be used. If the wheels sound cracked ("dead"), they shall not be used. An undamaged wheel will give a clear, metallic tone. This is known as the **Ring Test.** Wheels must be dry and free from sawdust when the Ring Test is performed. Otherwise, the sound will be deadened. It should also be noted that organic bonded wheels do not emit the same clear, metallic ring as do vitrified and silicate wheels.

Maintenance

1. Grinding wheels should be kept **dressed.** Dressing is a process of removing the dull or clogged grit from the surface of the wheel by using a grinding-wheel dresser. See Figs. 19-7 and 19-8.
2. Unless they are sealed, grinder bearings should be periodically lubricated.

Market Analysis

Capacity

The capacity is determined by the size and kind of the largest grinding wheel that may be installed and the throat clearance between the tool rest and the arbor support.

Fig. 19-7.   Grinding-wheel dresser.

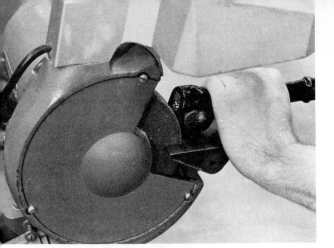

Fig. 19-8.   Dressing a grinding wheel.

Rockwell International

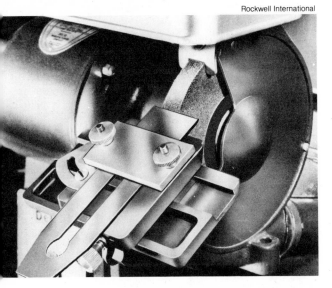

Fig. 19-9.   A grinding attachment may be used to grind the proper angle on a plane iron or other similar edge tools.

Attachments

1. **Drill-grinding attachment.** This attachment is used to sharpen twist drills. See Fig. 19-43.
2. **Edge-tool grinding attachment.** This is used

**Table 19-1
Standard Grinding-Wheel Markings**

Standard grinding-wheel markings accepted by the Grinding Wheel Manufacturers Association are in six parts, designated by letter and number. Example: — **B60M5VE**					
B	**60**	**M**	**5**	**V**	**E**
Type of Abrasive	Grain Size	Grade	Structure	Bond	Manufacturer's Number
Abrasive letters — A Aluminum oxide, regular B Aluminum oxide, refined AB Combination of above C Silicon carbide, regular CD Silicon carbide, refined D Corundum E Emery F Garnet					
Grain Size — number of mesh openings in the grading screen per inch. #8 coarse to #500 very fine.					
Grade — Letters A-Z, soft to hard.					
Structure — 1-15, most dense to most open.					
Bond — V — Vitrified S — Silicate E — Shellac or elastic R — Rubber B — Resinoid O — Oxychloride					
Manufacturer's number — used as a reference for sales purposes.					

to hold edge tools at the desired angle for grinding, Fig. 19-9.
3. **Wire brush.** The wire brush is used for removing foreign material (such as rust and paint) from metal.
4. **Dust collector.** The dust collector is a separate unit attached to the grinder to collect the dust produced in grinding.
5. **Lights.** Lights provide concentrated light on the grinding operation.
6. **Buffing and polishing wheels.** These are used in finishing processes.

Grinding Edge Tools

Topic 191.

Classification

Shaping by abrasion

Procedure

Grinding is a process of reshaping the cutting edge of a tool. An abrasive wheel or stone is used to give the proper wedge-shaped edge, while an oilstone is used to hone to a keen edge. A medium-grain abrasive wheel is used for rough shaping and a fine-grain wheel is used for dressing the tool.

1. Chisels, plane irons, gouges, spokeshaves, and drawknives have a single-bevel, wedge-shaped cutting edge, the angle of which is between 20° and 30°, depending on the hardness of the material to be cut. A 20° bevel will produce a fine cutting edge for soft materials, but the tool will not hold this edge when used on harder woods.

2. Adjust the tool rest slightly below the center of the wheel for straight-on grinding and above the center for bevel grinding.

3. Dress the cutting edge square with the sides of the tool by feeding the tool straight onto the grinding wheel, Figs. 19-10 and 19-11. This is also done to remove nicks. With a light pressure, work the tool across the face of the wheel, producing a fine cut.

4. Adjust the tool rest so that the angle of contact of the wheel and tool is about 30°, Figs. 19-12 and 19-13. To grind the bevel, work the tool across the face of the wheel. Keep the edge being sharpened square with the side of the tool. Apply only enough pressure to make a light cutting action. Too much pressure causes overheating. Frequently dip the tip of the tool in water to cool it. Face grinding produces a slightly hollow bevel, which may be honed several times before regrinding is necessary.

5. Router bits may be reshaped by grinding the flat faces on the bit. This is done by mounting the bit in a special attachment that fastens to the base of the router. A special abrasive wheel is then inserted in the router collet and, with the router running, each flat of the bit is gently brought into contact with the wheel. See Fig. 19-14. The bit should then be lightly honed with a slipstone.

Standards and Results

- The cutting edge should be square.
- The hollow bevel should be ground to a fine edge at an angle of about 30°.

Stanley Tools

Fig. 19-14. Grinding attachment for router bits.

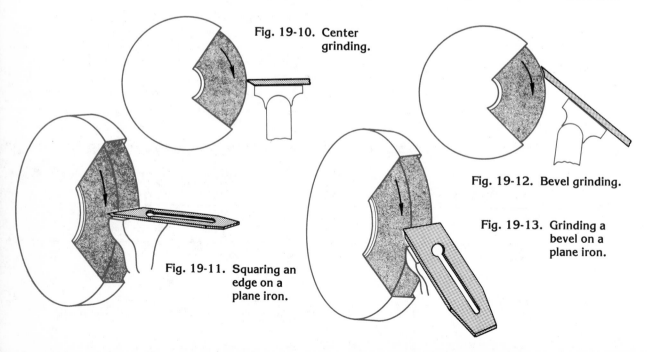

Fig. 19-10. Center grinding.

Fig. 19-11. Squaring an edge on a plane iron.

Fig. 19-12. Bevel grinding.

Fig. 19-13. Grinding a bevel on a plane iron.

- Sides of the bevel should be of equal length.
- The tool should show no evidence of over-heating.

Safety Considerations

- Eye shields must be in proper position and goggles should be worn.
- Tool rests should be no more than 1/8" away from the wheel.

- The tool being ground should be held firmly.
- Clogged and out-of-true wheels should be dressed. See Fig. 19-8.
- Badly worn wheels should be replaced.
- Avoid jamming the tool.
- Always grind on the face of the wheel.
- Replacement wheels should be those recommended for use at the speed of the machine.
- Stand to one side of the wheel's rotation when starting the grinder.

Oilstone

Topic 192.

Classification

Abrasive material graded and formed to a shape for sharpening or dressing

Application

Principle of Operation

The hard crystal edges on the face of the **oilstone** act as wedges or teeth, shearing off the rough or high spots of a carbon-steel surface to produce a smooth finish, Fig. 19-15.

Kinds and Uses

Oilstones are used to produce a fine cutting edge. They are usually rectangular, but are also available in single-bevel, double-bevel, conical, and wedge shapes. Stones of cylindrical shape are used for machine-knife sharpening.
1. There are three major **natural stones:**

The Arkansas stone is quarried in Arkansas River areas. It is white in color, has a close texture, and produces a fine sharpened edge. It is often used in sharpening surgical instruments.

Behr-Manning Co.

Behr-Manning Co.

Fig. 19-15. Crystolon combination oilstone.

Fig. 19-16. India stones, used for honing edges with complex shapes.

Washita stone is a whitish gray color. It varies in degree of hardness, and is not as fine as Arkansas stone.

Turkey stone is bluish brown, sometimes streaked with white. The quality of this stone varies, and a poor one will wear unevenly.

2. **Artificial stones** are usually made with one fine face and one coarser face.

India stone is a light brown, flat, durable cutting stone, made of aluminum oxide. See Fig. 19-16. The **auger-bit stone** is a type of India stone used for sharpening auger bits.

Crystolon and **carborundum** are fast-cutting stones made of silicon carbide.

Carborundum files are used for general work — for touch-up after a steel file has been used or to take the place of a steel file on case-hardened stock.

3. **Slipstones** can either be natural or artificial. They are used for honing or deburring convex, concave, and/or irregularly shaped tools. See Figs. 19-17, 19-18, and 19-19.

Principal Parts and Function of Each

Artificial stones are usually made with one **fine face** and one **coarse face.** The coarse face removes material reasonably quickly, but it does not give a keen edge. The fine face is used to produce a keen cutting edge.

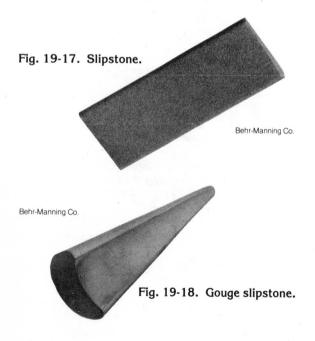

Fig. 19-17. Slipstone.

Behr-Manning Co.

Behr-Manning Co.

Fig. 19-18. Gouge slipstone.

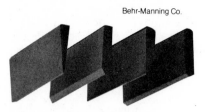

Behr-Manning Co.

Fig. 19-19. Carving-tool slipstones.

Maintenance

1. For protection against breakage and for ease in handling, a hardwood or metal frame should be used.
2. A stone may become worn from constant use. The surface may be renewed or trued by rubbing the face on a flat piece of steel or granite. Coat the surface of this material with ground emery and kerosene or with sand and water. A hard, coarse abrasive or a rust-pitted steel plate may also be used.
3. A glazed stone may be reconditioned by heating in a medium-warm (121° C/250° F) oven. The stone should not come in direct contact with flame.

Market Analysis

Sizes

The stone size varies with the type of stone and the type of work to be done.

1. Oilstones or sharpening stones are made in various rectangular sizes, ranging from 4″ × 1-3/4″ × 5/8″ to 8″ × 2″ × 1″.
2. Slipstones are made in 4″ to 4-1/2″ lengths, 7/16″ to 1/2″ back-edge widths, and 1/16″ to 3/16″ front-edge widths. See Figs. 19-17, 19-18, and 19-19.
3. Machine-knife stones are round in shape and are between 2″ and 4″ in diameter. The combination coarse- and fine-grit type can be as thick as 1-1/2″.
4. Carborundum files are shaped like a steel file. They have a fixed handle and are 14″ long. See Fig. 19-20.
5. Auger-bit stones are triangular in shape. One end of the auger-bit stone is larger than the other. Auger-bit stones are usually only available in one size: 4″ in length × 5/16″-1/2″ in width × 1/16″-1/4″ in thickness.

Fig. 19-20. Carborundum file.

Behr-Manning Co.

Attachments

The oilstone can be stored and protected in a specially designed **hardwood box.** This box is also used to secure the stone during whetting.

Whetting or Honing a Cutting Tool

Topic 193.

Classification

Sharpening by abrasion

Behr-Manning Co.

Fig. 19-21. Section of cutting edge (magnified 20 times). Top: Dull. Center: Sharpened on coarse stone. Bottom: After final stoning on hard, fine stone.

Procedure

Sharpening Wedge-Shaped Tools

Whetting is the process of sharpening to a fine edge. It is done to remove the wire edge after grinding or to restore a sharp edge. See Fig. 19-21. A **combination oilstone** is usually used for this process. This type of oilstone includes a coarse face for rough, rapid cutting and a fine face for dressing a sharp edge.

1. Select a coarse or fine stone, depending upon the condition of the tool edge. Coarse stones cut rapidly but do not produce a fine edge. Fine stones produce a keen edge but should be used only after the tool has been sharpened on a medium stone. A good general-purpose stone is the medium grade.

   Note: When changing to a fine-grade stone, wipe the tool with cotton waste to remove coarse grit particles that might scratch the finer stone.

2. Secure the oilstone in a level position on the bench. Apply a few drops of thin machine oil to the surface. The purpose of this oil is to float away the particles of metal being cut from the tool, preventing them from becoming embedded in the surface of the oilstone.

3. Hold the tool diagonally across the face width of the stone. The bevel of the tool should form an angle of between 30° and 35°, Fig. 19-22. The harder the material on which the tool is to be used, the greater the required bevel angle.

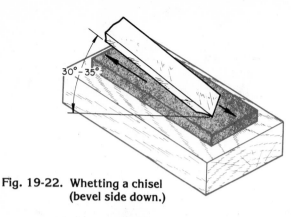

Fig. 19-22. Whetting a chisel (bevel side down.)

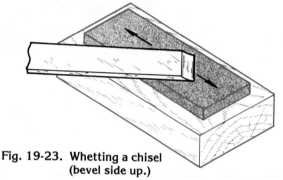

Fig. 19-23. Whetting a chisel (bevel side up.)

Fig. 19-24. Special attachment for honing a plane iron at the proper angle.

Stanley Tools

4. Move the tool back and forth along the stone. Take long, straight strokes, holding the tool at a constant angle. Avoid rocking the tool, as this action produces a rounded edge. For double-beveled tools, whet each bevel equally.

5. Use the entire face of the stone and occasionally turn it end-for-end to ensure even wear. The face of the stone should be kept perfectly flat.

6. After the bright edge on single-edge tools has disappeared, place the tool against the oilstone. The surface opposite the bevel should be flat against the stone. Remove the burr with several sidewise strokes, Fig. 19-23.

7. Some workers test for sharpness by drawing the edge lightly across the back of the thumbnail. If it catches or scores a mark on the thumbnail, the edge is sharp.

8. Using a leather strap after whetting will produce a keener edge. A piece of leather secured to the cover of the oilstone holder will serve this purpose. Hold the cutting edge flat on the strap and draw the tool away from you. Several strokes will remove any fine wire edge.

Special Techniques

1. The **drawknife** is sharpened by holding the tool securely in a convenient position. The edge is then whetted by holding the oilstone at the proper angle and rubbing it back and forth over the entire length of the blade. See Fig. 19-25.

2. The **turning gouge** and **outside-bevel gouge** are sharpened by following the established curve of the tool. Hold the tool at the proper angle, as before, but instead of the back-and-forth movement, produce a rocking motion by rolling the tool from side to side as you are moving it over the stone, Fig. 19-26. To remove the wire edge, use a slipstone that fits the contour of the tool. See Fig. 19-27. Care must be taken not to produce a bevel on the inside of the tool.

3. To sharpen **sloyd or pocket knives,** use a medium or fine stone. Hold the blade diagonally to the width of the stone. With the back of the blade raised very slightly, rub the blade back and forth with long, even strokes and even pressure. A straight stroke cuts better than a rolling, circular motion. Turn the blade over to sharpen the edge on both sides. See Figs. 19-28, 19-29, and 19-30.

4. **Router bits** may be sharpened by honing the inside flats of the bit on a fine stone. Take care that the cutting face does not become beveled or change shape.

Note: Wipe all oil from the stone when whetting is completed.

Standards and Results

• There should be no nicks or burrs on the blade.

Fig. 19-25. Sharpening a drawknife.

Fig. 19-28. Blade movement in sharpening a pocket knife.

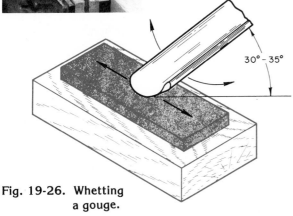

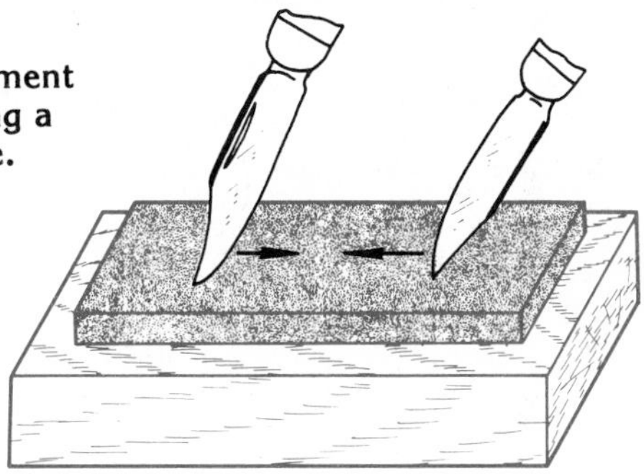

Fig. 19-26. Whetting a gouge.

Fig. 19-27. Using a slipstone to sharpen a gouge.

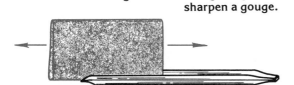

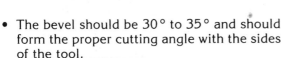

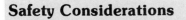

- The bevel should be 30° to 35° and should form the proper cutting angle with the sides of the tool.
- On single-edge tools, the surface opposite the bevel should be flat.

Safety Considerations

- Wear safety glasses.
- Keep both hands on the tool.
- Be careful not to cut yourself while testing the sharpness of the cutting edge.
- Make sure the stone is secured to the bench.
- Be careful not to cut yourself when using a slipstone to hone a sharp edge.

Behr-Manning Co.

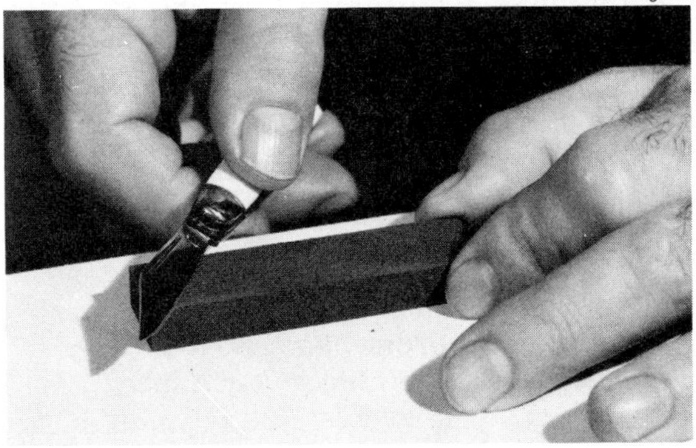

Fig. 19-29. Beginning to sharpen a knife.

Behr-Manning Co.

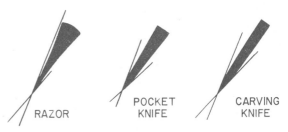

Fig. 19-30. Sharpening the second side.

Fig. 19-31. Comparison of sharpening angles of razor, pocket knife, and carving knife.

Topic 194.

Sharpening Hand Scrapers and Cabinet Scrapers

Classification

Forming a cutting wedge by shaping, whetting, and burnishing

Procedure

Hand Scraper

1. File off the remaining burr by holding the scraper flat with one hand and making a few strokes with a mill file on each face.
2. Place the blade in a vertical position in the vise and drawfile the edge straight. Hold the file horizontally and at a right angle to the side of the blade, Fig. 19-32.
3. Whet the edge and the two adjoining faces of the blade on the medium oilstone, taking full-length strokes, Fig. 19-33. Hold the blade at a right angle to the stone and then hold each face flat against the stone.
4. Place the blade back in the vise and turn each edge with a burnisher. Start by holding the burnisher in a horizontal position. With a downward pressure, move the burnisher along the edge, rolling the edge on both sides of the blade. Tilt the burnisher slightly until the last stroke is 5° to the horizontal. See Figs. 19-34 and 19-35.

Fig. 19-32. Drawfiling the edge of a hand scraper.

Fig. 19-33. Whetting the edge of a hand scraper. The two adjoining faces are whetted in a similar fashion.

Fig. 19-34. Burnishing a hand scraper.

Fig. 19-35. Burnishing a scraper.

Stanley Tools

Fig. 19-36. Burnisher.

Cabinet Scraper

1. Remove the blade from the frame.
2. Using a mill file, file off the old burr.
3. Place the blade in a vise and drawfile a new edge at an angle of about 45°.
4. Remove the cabinet scraper from the vise and whet the blade, using a medium oilstone, Fig. 19-37. Remove any new burr formed in filing and whetting.
5. Place the blade back in the vise and, with a burnisher, turn the edge to an angle of about 75°. (**Note:** Check the procedure for sharpening a hand scraper.) See Fig. 19-38.
6. Place the blade in the frame, the bevel toward the front, and slide it in from the base. Place the blade and frame on a flat surface and tighten the clamp thumbscrews.
7. Adjust for depth of cut by turning the adjustment thumbscrew. If the scraper does

Fig. 19-37. Whetting a cabinet scraper. Bevel should be at approximately 45°.

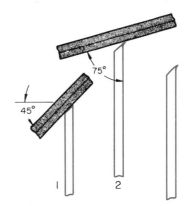

Fig. 19-38. Burnishing a cabinet scraper.

not cut a shaving, the burr may have been turned too much. This may be corrected by turning the burr back slightly. Do this by drawing the point of the burnisher directly under the edge of the burr. A dull blade may be touched up in this way.

8. The cutting edge of the blade should form a slight arc to prevent the corners from scoring the surface.

Hook Scraper

Hook scrapers are sharpened by drawfiling the cutting edge to an angle of 35°.

Standards and Results

- Scrapers should cut a shaving rather than scrape dust.
- Blades should not leave scratches or ridges caused by chatter.
- Scraper blades should take an even cut.

Safety Considerations

- Wear safety glasses.
- Observe all safety practices pertaining to the particular tool or machine you are using.
- In filing or burnishing, be careful not to cut your hands.

Topic 195.

Sharpening Drilling and Boring Tools

Classification

Shaping by abrasion

Procedure

Twist Drill

In sharpening a twist drill, three factors must be considered. These factors are: (1) lip angle, (2) clearance angle, and (3) lip length. See Fig. 19-39.

The **lip angle** may vary from 60° to 90° for wood and other soft materials to 118° for metal. A sharp lip angle weakens the drill point but reduces the tendency of the drill to wander off center while being used to start a hole. The lip angle must be the same on each lip. This angle is measured with a drill gauge, Fig. 19-40.

The **lip clearance** is the clearance between the lip and the heel of the drill tip. See Fig. 19-41. On most twist drills this clearance is between 12° and 15°. If there were no clearance between the lip and the heel, the drill could not cut.

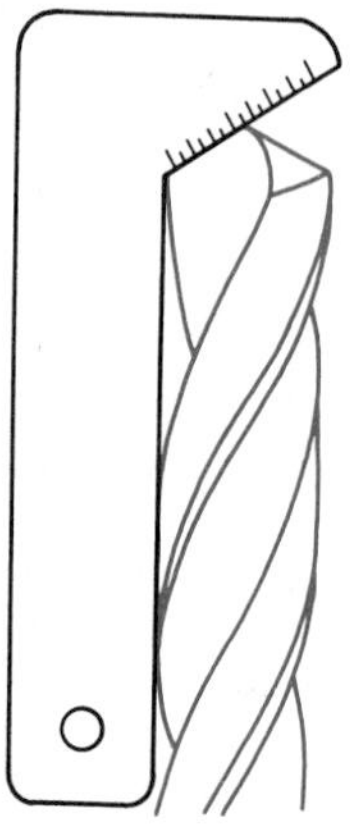

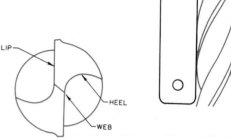

Fig. 19-40. Drill gauge — 118° for metal, 60°-90° for wood.

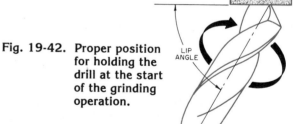

Fig. 19-41. Drill-tip nomenclature.

Fig. 19-42. Proper position for holding the drill at the start of the grinding operation.

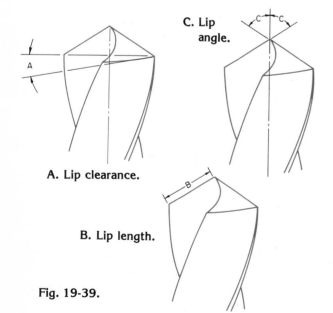

C. Lip angle.

A. Lip clearance.

B. Lip length.

Fig. 19-39.

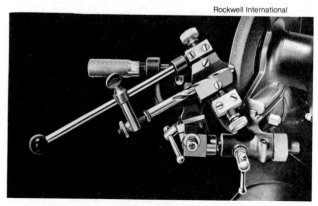

Rockwell International

Fig. 19-43. Drills may be sharpened quickly and accurately on the grinder using a drill-grinding attachment.

Lip length is simply the comparative length of each lip. The lips on the drill tip must be of equal length. If they are different lengths or if the lip angles are different, the drill will not center properly and will cut an oversized hole.

The twist drill is sharpened on a bench grinder:

1. Select a medium-coarse abrasive wheel and dress the face until it is flat.
2. Hold the drill so that the point extends between the thumb and forefinger of the right hand.
3. Rest the back of the forefinger on the tool rest of the grinder. The drill shank should slope slightly downward and should point to the left at the proper lip angle, Fig. 19-42.
4. With the left hand, steady the shank of the drill and move one of the lips of the drill into contact with the face of the wheel. The edge of the lip should be in a horizontal position as it contacts the wheel.

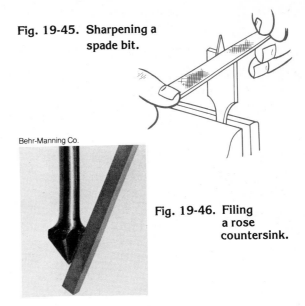

Fig. 19-45. Sharpening a spade bit.

Behr-Manning Co.

Fig. 19-46. Filing a rose countersink.

5. When the lip contacts the grinding wheel, lower and twist the drill shank to continue the grind to the heel. By lowering the drill, more material is removed near the heel, and the lip clearance is maintained. Be careful not to let the drill tip overheat, as this will remove its hardness.
6. Grinding should be done first on one lip and then the other. The drill tip should constantly be checked with a drill gauge for lip angle and length, Fig. 19-40.

Auger Bit

Auger bits are sharpened on the inside of the spurs so that the diameter will remain the same. The shape of the cutting angle is filed on the top of the lips with a special auger-bit file. This file fits into the opening between the lips and the spurs. A 4″ mill warding file may also be used. See Fig. 19-44.

Forstner Bit

Forstner bits are sharpened with a metal scraper and a file. The scraper is used to make a sharp edge on the circular steel ring. It is used on the inside of the ring and is held to form an angle of 75°. A warding file is used to file the top surface of the lips.

Spade Bit

Spade bits can be sharpened by dressing the cutters and the point with a file held at the same angle as the original cutting surface. See

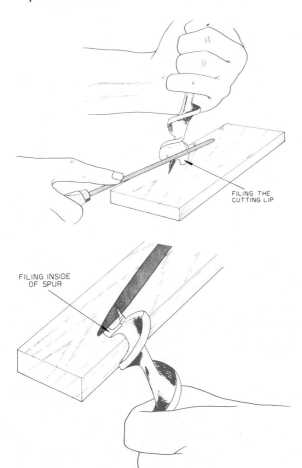

FILING THE CUTTING LIP

FILING INSIDE OF SPUR

Fig. 19-44. Filling an auger bit.

Fig. 19-45. When filing the cutters, be careful not to undercut and thus weaken the point.

Standards and Results

- Each lip of the twist drill should be ground to the proper angle, clearance, and length.
- All bits should be sharpened to maintain the cutting edges. That is, the correct angle must be filed on each type of bit and no filing done should change the outside diameter of the bit being sharpened.

Safety Considerations

- Wear safety glasses when sharpening tools.
- Observe all safety practices pertaining to the particular tool or machine you are using.

Topic 196.

Sharpening Saw Blades

Classification

Reshaping cutting wedges by jointing, setting, and filing

Procedure

The process of sharpening a saw blade is time-consuming and must be carried out with extreme precision for good results. For these reasons, dull saws are often sent to a sharpening service for reshaping. In these establishments, the saws are sharpened by machine. See Fig. 19-47.

The sharpening of any saw requires three basic procedures — jointing, setting, and filing. **Jointing** assures that the saw teeth are all the same height. **Setting** provides the clearance necessary for the saw to cut a kerf wider than the thickness of the blade. **Filing** produces the sharp cutting wedges.

Sharpening Handsaws

1. Place the saw in a saw clamp. Joint the saw by running a mill file, at right angles to the blade, over the top edges of the saw teeth. Using a forward motion, move the file over the ends of the teeth until they are all the same height, Fig. 19-48. A special tool may be used to assure perpendicular filing.
2. With a saw set, bend the saw teeth alternately to the left and right along the entire length of the saw, Fig. 19-49. Set every other tooth on one side of the blade, then set the remaining teeth on the other side. The saw set should be adjusted to bend each tooth a distance of about half the tooth thickness. Bend only the top half of each tooth. Setting the saw produces the needed clearance between the saw kerf and the blade thickness.

Fig. 19-47. Handsaw being sharpened with an automatic filing machine.

Foley Manufacturing Company

Fig. 19-48. Jointing a saw.

Nicholson-The Cooper Group

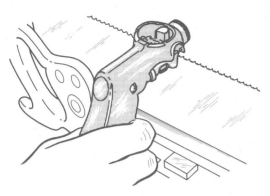

Fig. 19-49. Alternate saw teeth are set with a saw set.

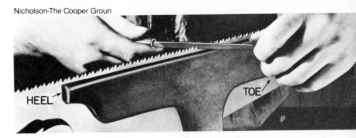

Nicholson-The Cooper Groun

HEEL   TOE

Fig. 19-51. Crosscut teeth are filed at 60°.

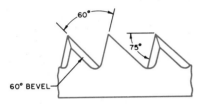

60°

75°

60° BEVEL

Fig. 19-50. Crosscut teeth.

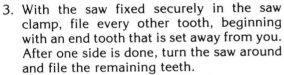

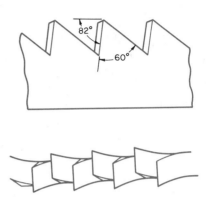

82°

60°

Fig. 19-52. Ripsaw teeth.

3. With the saw fixed securely in the saw clamp, file every other tooth, beginning with an end tooth that is set away from you. After one side is done, turn the saw around and file the remaining teeth.

4. Crosscut saws are filed with a three-square, slim-taper mill file. The file should fit into the saw gullet and, when held at a 60° angle, should file both the back edge of one tooth and the front edge of the adjacent tooth. See Figs. 19-50 and 19-51.

5. Ripsaws are filed in the same manner as crosscut saws, except that the file is held at a right angle to the saw blade. See Fig. 19-52.

   The teeth of the saw should be filed until the flats (produced by jointing) are removed.

Sharpening Circular-Saw Blades

Jointing

1. While the blade is still mounted in the saw, lower the arbor so the teeth of the blade barely protrude above the surface of the saw table.

2. Obtain an old, worn 6″ or 8″ grinding wheel or a medium oilstone. Place the flat side on the saw table (**not above** the saw blade). A piece of paper should be placed underneath the stone to avoid scratching the saw table.

3. Start the saw and move the stone over the revolving blade, being careful not to place your hands in the path of the revolving saw blade.

4. Stop the saw and examine the tips of the teeth. When the tip of each tooth is slightly flattened, the saw is perfectly round. If some tips are not flattened it may be necessary to raise the saw slightly and repeat the jointing process.

Setting

1. Disconnect the machine from the power source and remove the saw blade from the arbor.

2. Set the teeth with a trip-hammer saw set. Position the hammer in such a way that it bends the outer one-third to one-half of the saw tooth. See Fig. 19-53. Set alternate teeth around the saw blade, then turn the blade over and set the remaining teeth in the opposite direction.

Fig. 19-53. Using a trip-hammer saw set to set circular-saw teeth.

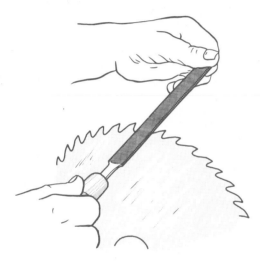

Fig. 19-54. The backs of ripsaw teeth are filed flat with a flat mill file.

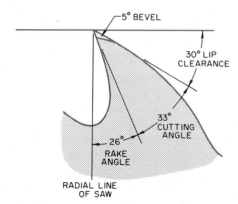

Fig. 19-55. Cutting angles of combination circular-saw blade.

Filing

1. Place the saw blade in the saw clamp.
2. File the teeth set (bent) away from you. Rip teeth are filed at right angles to the blade and crosscut teeth are filed at a 60° angle. A three-square slim-taper mill file is used for sharpening crosscut teeth. A flat mill file is used for sharpening rip teeth. See Fig. 19-54. File the back of the teeth until all of the grinding marks caused by jointing are removed. Take one or two strokes on the top of each tooth to produce a 5° bevel. See Fig. 19-55.
3. Turn the blade around and repeat the preceding steps on the teeth that are now set away from you.

Side Jointing or Dressing

A smoother cut will be made if the sides of the teeth are jointed. This will remove burrs left from filing and will ensure that each tooth is bent exactly the same amount. This is done by using a medium oilstone to rub in the direction of the teeth while the saw is resting flat on a bench or table. The saw is then turned over and the stone is rubbed in the direction of the teeth on the other side.

Gumming

After saw blades have been sharpened six to eight times, the slots between the teeth (called **gullets**) become very shallow. **Gumming out** (increasing the depth of the gullets) is done with a special jig on the grinder that has a dish wheel. When gumming is necessary, it should be done prior to setting.

Note: Carbide-tipped saws should be sent out to be sharpened by machine. It takes a special diamond wheel to do the job on the sides, front, and top of the tooth.

Standards and Results

- Sharpened saws should cut a straight, even kerf. The finished cut should be smooth and flat.

Safety Considerations

- Wear safety glasses when sharpening saw blades.
- Observe all safety practices pertaining to the particular tool or machine you are using.

Index